Feudal Empires
Norman and Plantagenet

John Le Patourel

THE HAMBLEDON
PRESS

The Hambledon Press 1984
35 Gloucester Avenue, London NW1 7AX

History Series 18

ISBN 0 907628 22 2

British Library Cataloguing in Publication Data

Le Patourel, John
    Feudal Empires.
    1. Great Britain — History — Medieval period,
    1066-1485
    I. Title
    942.02 DA175

This book contains 410 pages.

CONTENTS

ACKNOWLEDGEMENTS

The articles collected here, with the exception of Chapters IX and XVIII which are new, appeared originally in the following places and are reprinted by the kind permission of the original publishers.

I	*Société Guernesiaise Report and Transactions*, xii (2)(1935).
II	*Solicitor Quarterly*, 1 (1962).
III	*English Historical Review*, lvi (1941).
IV	*SGRT*, (1975).
V	*E.H.R.*, lxi (1946).
VI	Historical Association Pamphlet 4 in 1066 Commemoration Series. First published by Hastings and Bexhill Branch of The Historical Association (1966); reprinted by The Historical Association (1971).
VII	Stenton Lecture, University of Reading (1970).
VIII	*History*, 1 (1965).
X	*Mémoires de la Société d'Histoire et d'Archéologie de Bretagne*, lviii (1981); *Annales de Normandie*, xxix (1979), 376-7, and xxx (1980), 321-2.
XI	*The Hundred Years War*, ed. Kenneth Fowler (Macmillans, London, 1971).
XII	*History*, xliii (1958).
XIII	*Transactions of the Royal Historical Society*, 5th Series, 10 (1960).
XIV	*Revue du Nord*, xxxiii (1951).
XV	*Europe in the Late Middle Ages*, ed. by J.R. Hale, J.R.L. Highfield and B. Smalley (Faber, London, 1965).
XVI	*Thoresby Society Miscellany*, 13, Part I (1959).
XVII	*Northern History*, xii (1976).

FOREWORD

This collection of selected papers by John Le Patourel is largely based on a list which he drew up in July 1981 shortly before his death. The general ideas behind his choice were 'to pick out the papers I thought best worth including, while avoiding overlapping as much as possible; that the Channel Islands should not be over-represented; and that the category I have labelled 'The Fourteenth Century' should be represented pretty well in full'. In making a final selection these criteria have been respected as far as possible but since his sequel to *The Norman Empire* (1976), provisionally entitled *The Plantagenet Realm*, on which he was working at the time of his death, remains unfinished and in a form too incomplete for publication, it has seemed appropriate to include more preparatory essays on this theme than the author had originally intended to represent his latest views. Among such essays is a previously unpublished one on 'Angevin Successions and the Angevin Empire' delivered as a lecture in Cambridge in May 1980. In part this complements an earlier important article on 'The Norman Succession, 966-1135' (*English Historical Review*, lxxxvi(1971), 225-50) which is not reproduced here. Another paper, previously unpublished, 'France and England in the Middle Ages' was delivered as the Clapton Lecture at Leeds in 1977. It gives 'preliminary expression to the general ideas I have been forming over a lifetime'. Indeed it will be apparent that one of the most striking features of this anthology is the unity, modification and development of Professor Le Patourel's thought from his earliest to the latest essays included in this volume.

Born and brought up in Guernsey, one surviving territorial link between the English Crown and the former Duchy of Normandy, he was uniquely conscious among modern scholars of the fact that in the period which most interested him 'the effective political units from 1066 until some time in the fourteenth century were not England and France as we ordinarily think of them, but a Norman empire and an Angevin empire and a kingdom of France (the 'Capetian empire'), overlapping and interpenetrating'. From early days he sensed that a comparative approach to many issues, whether seen in a local or wider context, would yield new insights and understanding. Remarks à propos the underdeveloped form of urban institutions in the Channel Islands, Normandy and Brittany made in

'The Early History of St. Peter Port' (1935), for example, are already as perceptive as any made in much more recent work on the same topic. Whilst the latest essay on the Channel Islands included here, 'Guernsey, Jersey and their environment in the Middle Ages' (1975) is a splendid example of Le Patourel's ability to examine parallels in an illuminating fashion, setting local issues in a general context, revealing the development of his own ideas, many in this instance first expressed in *The Medieval Administration of the Channel Islands 1199-1399* (1937) and refined by further research and reflection. The Norman dimension of Channel Islands history is well brought out in 'The Origins of the Channel Islands Legal System' (1962) and 'The Authorship of the Grand Coutumier de Normandie' (1941), whilst the impact of the Normans on England is examined from different angles in the short but incisive article on the knotty problem of 'The Date of the Trial on Penenden Heath' (1946), a contribution to the celebrations at Hastings in 1966 ('Norman Barons') and the very rewarding Stenton Lecture 'Normandy and England, 1066-1144' (1971), pieces which either anticipate or usefully supplement the argument of *The Norman Empire*.

As a prolific lecturer and contributor over many years to conferences in both England and France, this side of Le Patourel's career is well represented by the lectures on 'The Plantagenet Dominions' delivered to the Fifty-Ninth Historical Association Conference (1964), 'Angevin Successions' (1980) and 'Henri II Plantagenêt et la Bretagne' (1981). To the latter there have been appended the summaries of two papers in French on Angevin seneschals, which provide further evidence, were it needed, of Le Patourel's interest in the individual, of the value of a prosopographical approach to some of those aspects of administrative and institutional history which intrigued him, to demonstrate how the modern categories of 'England' and 'France' break down when the careers of some administrators are examined in detail and the range of their experiences and interests is seen to have been gathered by service in many parts of the Plantagenet 'realm'.

Le Patourel's ability to take well-known and much-discussed themes and to treat them in a new and challenging way is perhaps best seen in some of the pieces on the Hundred Years War in its fourteenth century phase. His interest in this area, already apparent in *Medieval Administration*, was stirred again, perhaps by experiences of a different occupation during the Second World War, by the problems of English administration of captured or subject territories in Valois France. An early contribution was on 'L'occupation anglaise de Calais au XIVe siècle

(1952). This was followed by important work on Brittany and Normandy during Edward III's reign. Much of this was presented to conferences in France during the 1950s and only brief summaries have ever been published, although it proved to be the basis for some of his own most provocative later arguments advanced in 'Edward III and the Kingdom of France' (1958) and 'The Treaty of Brétigny, 1360' (1960) and in the valuable synthesis 'The King and the Princes in Fourteenth-Century France' (1965). 'The Origins of the War' (1971) usefully sets it in that longer perspective of which he was so fond and links up with the earlier work on the Norman and Angevin 'empires'. It is fair to say that some of the views advanced in these papers — on Edward III's general intentions and strategy, on technical matters relating to what was at stake during the series of negotiations after the battle of Poitiers between Edward III and his representatives and King John of France and his advisers, whether some of these agreements were 'peace treaties' or merely 'ransom treaties' — have given rise to critical debate and have not been universally accepted. But in part this was, of course, his intention, in his deceptively mild and unassuming fashion, to stimulate discussion and further research. It was a characteristic which made him not only a gifted expositor and advocate of his own, often original, views but also a very effective and productive director of his pupils' research. He had the ability to spot good topics for investigation and it is no surprise that many of these were in periods or areas where he himself had only briefly ventured but in which he had glimpsed the possibilities and comprehended the need for further work.

The final section in the volume contains a miscellaneous haul. One from a series of Presidential addresses given to the Thoresby Society on 'The Medieval Borough of Leeds' (1954) foreshadows the more substantial edition of *Documents relating to the Manor and Borough of Leeds, 1066-1400* (1957) and must represent here both Le Patourel's long association with that city and university and his inability, as he himself put it, 'to keep my fingers out of the history of the place in which I happen to be living or working'. Some of the pieces on Yorkshire history which have had to be omitted here with regret show how productive these forays could be and they also reveal his abiding interest in matters archaeological and architectural, his sense of place, which is perhaps not so well represented in the collection as it should be. Nevertheless though he claimed that he had 'never done more than dabble in one or two very localized bits of northern history', the lecture 'Is Northern History a subject?' (1976) not only reveals his characteristic understanding but is important for material which 'is the nearest I am likely to get to an expression of my working philosophy of history'. It also seems appropriate to conclude with 'France and England in the Middle Ages' (1977), a conscious if briefer imitation of T. F. Tout's famous essay in comparative history, which fittingly sums up the major theme which so fruitfully dominated Le Patourel's working life.

In preparing these papers for re-publication the editor and publisher are grateful to Mrs Jean Le Patourel and her family for constant help and cooperation, especially to Mrs Nicolette Christie, the author's daughter, for compiling the Index. Prof. J. C. Holt gave advice and assistance with the preparation of the previously unpublished papers. Apart from correcting a number of minor errors in the text of these and the published papers, all the articles have been reprinted without change, although for this volume the two maps illustrating 'The Early History of St. Peter Port' have been redrawn by Mr. Keith Bowler of the Department of Geography, University of Nottingham. In a few cases it has also proved possible to add a short note on work subsequently published which has advanced discussion from the point at which it was left by John Le Patourel's contribution.

Michael Jones

SELECT BIBLIOGRAPHY OF JOHN LE PATOUREL

Select bibliography of the books and articles of John Le Patourel (a more complete list for the period 1935-1975 is provided in *Northern History*, x (1975), 188-195).

1935

The Early History of St. Peter Port, *La Société Guernesiaise Report and Transactions*, xii (2), 171-208. See below I.

1936

The Medieval Administration of Sark, *ibid*., xii (3), 310-36.

1937

The Medieval Administration of the Channel Islands, 1199-1399, Oxford.

1939

Un premier exemple de contrat sous le sceau de la baillie de Jersey, *Travaux de la semaine d'histoire du droit normand tenue à Guernsey 1938*, Caen, pp. 401-7.

1941

The Authorship of the Grand Coutumier de Normandie, *English Historical Review*, lvi, 292-300. See below III.

1943

Channel Island Institutions – Past and Future, *History*, xxvii, 171-81.

1944

The Political Development of the Channel Islands, *Nos Iles-A Symposium on the Channel Islands*, pp. 11-20 (republished in *Soc. Guernesiaise Rep. Trans.*, xiv (1), 27-34).
Geoffrey of Montbray, bishop of Coutances, *EHR*, lix, 129-61.

1945

Earlier invasions of the Channel Islands (published by the Channel Islands Study Group).

1946

The Charters and Privileges, Laws and Customs of the Island of Guernsey, *Bulletin of the Guernsey Society*, ii (1), 3-8.
The Date of the Trial on Penenden Heath, *EHR*, lxi, 378-88. See below V.

1948

The Reports of the Trial on Penenden Heath, in *Studies in Mediaeval History presented to Frederick Maurice Powicke*, ed. R. W. Hunt, W. A. Pantin and R. W. Southern, Oxford, pp. 15-26.

1949

The First Castle Cornet, *Quarterly Review of the Guernsey Society*, v, 3-7.

1950

The Capture of Sark by a Flemish Corsair in 1553, *Soc. Guernesiaise Rep. Trans.*, xiv (4), 358-60.

1951

The murder on Lihou Island, *Quarterly Rev. Guernsey Soc.*, vii, 3-6.

1952

L'Occupation anglaise de Calais au XIVe siècle, *Revue du Nord*, xxxiii, 228-41. See below XIV.
The Account of Hugh of Saint-Philibert, 1226, *Annual Bulletin, Société Jersiaise*, xv, 465-73.

1953

(With H. E. Jean Le Patourel) Lihou Priory: Excavations 1952, *Soc. Guernesiaise Rep. Trans.*, xv, 180-5.

1954

A 14th-century List of Guernsey Ships and Shipmasters, *Quarterly Rev. Guernsey Soc*, ix, 4-7.
L'Administration ducale dans la Bretagne montfortiste 1345-1362, *Revue historique du droit français et étranger*, 4e sér. xxxii, 144-7.

1955

(With H. E. Jean Le Patourel) Castle Cornet: Excavations, 1953, *Soc. Guernesiaise Rep. Trans.*, xv, 350-61.

1957

Documents relating to the Manor and Borough of Leeds, 1066-1400, Publications of the Thoresby Society, xlv for 1956.

1958

The Building of Castle Cornet, Guernsey: I, Documents relating to the Tudor Reconstruction, Manchester U.P. for the Royal Court of Guernsey.
Edward III and the Kingdom of France, *History*, xliii, 173-89. See below XII.

1959

Medieval Leeds: Kirkstall Abbey — The Parish Church — The Medieval Borough, Pubs. of the Thoresby Society, xlvi (*Miscellany*, xiii, I, 1-21). See below XVI for The Medieval Borough.

1960

The Treaty of Brétigny, 1360, *Transactions of the Royal Historical Society*, 5th series, x, 19-39. See below XIII.

1961

Jersey's Political Status in the Middle Ages, *Bulletin of the Jersey Society in London*, 4-10.

Le rôle de la Ville de Caen dans l'histoire de l'Angleterre, *Annales de Normandie*, xi, 171-7.

1962

The Origins of the Channel Islands Legal System, *The Solicitor Quarterly*, i. 198-210. See below II.

1963

Ilkley Parish Church. The British Publishing Company (2nd edition, 1968).

1965

The Plantagenet Dominions, *History*, 1, 289-308. See below VIII.

The King and the Princes in Fourteenth-Century France, in *Europe in the Late Middle Ages*, ed. J. R. Hale, J. R. L. Highfield and B. Smalley, pp. 155-83. See below XV.

1966

Norman Barons, Hastings and Bexhill Branch of the Historical Association (Reprinted by the Historical Association, 1971). See below VI.

Guernsey and the Norman Conquest, *Quarterly Rev. Guernsey Soc.*, xxii, 26-32.

1967

L'empire normand, *Revue de l'Avranchin et du pays de Granville*, xliii, 65-75.

1968

The Parish Church and Kirkstall Abbey, *University of Leeds Review*, xi, 135-51.

1969

The Norman Colonization of Britain, in *I Normanni e loro espansione in Europa nell'alto medioevo*, Centro italiano di studi sull'Alto Medioevo, Spoleto, *Settimane di Studio*, xvi, 409-38.

(With D.H. Giffard and R.H. Videlo). *List of the Records in the Greffe, Guernsey*, I, List and Index Society, Special Series, ii.

1971

The Norman Succession, 996-1135, *EHR*, lxxxvi, 225-50.
The Origins of the War, in *The Hundred Years War*, ed. K. Fowler, pp. 28-50. See below XI.
The Norman Conquest of Yorkshire, *Northern History*, vi, 1-21.
Normandy and England 1066-1144. The Stenton Lecture, 1970, University of Reading. See below VII.

1973

What did not happen in Stephen's Reign, *History*, lviii, 1-17.
Feudal Empires: Norman and Plantagenet, in *Les Grands Empires, Recueil de la Société Jean Bodin*, xxxi, 281-307.

1975

Guernsey, Jersey and their environment in the Middle Ages, *Soc. Guernesiaise Rep. Trans.*, xix (4), 435-61. See below IV.

1976

The Norman Empire, Clarendon Press, Oxford.
Norman Kings or Norman 'King-Dukes'?, in *Droit privé et institutions régionales. Etudes historiques offertes à Jean Yver*, Rouen, pp. 469-79.
Is Northern History a Subject?, *Northern History*, xi (1976), pp. 1-15. See below XVII.

1979

The Norman Conquest, 1066, 1106, 1154?, *Proceedings of the Battle Conference 1978*, ed. R. Allen Brown, pp. 103-20, 216-20.
Medieval France in Modern Yorkshire, *University of Leeds Review*, xxii, 100-118.

1981

Henri II Plantagenêt et la Bretagne, *Mémoires de la société d'histoire et d'archéologie de Bretagne*, lviii, 99-116. See below X.

1982

Le gouvernement de Henri II Plantagenêt et la mer de la Manche, in *Recueil d'études offert en hommage au doyen Michel de Boüard, Annales de Normandie*, numéro spécial, Caen, pp. 323-33.
Le monachisme normand dans les Iles de la Manche pendant le Moyen Age, *Aspects du monachisme en Normandie (IVe-XVIIIe siècles)*, ed. L. Musset, for La Bibliothèque de la Société d'histoire ecclésiastique de la France, Paris, pp. 109-14.

THE EARLY HISTORY OF ST. PETER PORT

1.—INTRODUCTION

The Channel Islands lie in the Gulf of St. Malo, some ten to twenty miles west of the Cotentin Peninsula. Of these islands the westernmost is Guernsey, which therefore lies farthest out into the English Channel, and more directly on the track of ships using the Channel as a highway.

The shape of Guernsey is roughly that of a right-angled triangle, of which the hypoteneuse forms the north-west coast, about nine miles in length ; the other two sides form the eastern and southern coasts, of about six and seven miles in length respectively. The town of St. Peter Port has grown up at the mid-point of the eastern coast. Here there was a firm and sheltered beach, on which boats might be drawn up, and a good anchorage protected by the king's Castle Cornet.

As the site of St. Peter Port has so greatly influenced its development, it is necessary to describe it briefly. Unfortunately no useful evidence of the medieval topography of the town has come to my knowledge ; my only guide, therefore is an impression formed from the present appearance of the town, and from its appearance in ancient representations.[1] It seems to have centred about the church (" ecclesia Sancti Petri de Portu " in 1048)[2] which was built almost on the sea-shore, at the point where a small valley with its stream reaches the sea. On either side, that is to the north and to the south of the church, there is high ground forming low cliffs at the coast. The medieval town seems to have spread westwards up the valley and northwards along what is now the High Street, the houses on the eastern side of which were built actually on the cliff ; but there seems to have been no considerable extension towards the south. Some evidence in support of this theory may be found in the fact that the entrances to the church are on the north and west sides. The chief entrance is on the north side, an unusual position in a parish church only found where the village lay on that side of the church, as at Witney in Oxfordshire.

Near the church, and for some little distance to the north and south of it, there was firm beach, protected by reefs of rocks running out to sea on either side. Rather less than half a mile from the coast, and directly opposite the church, lay a rocky islet which could be reached dryshod only at low spring tides. On this islet, during the thirteenth century, was built Castle Cornet, the king's castle in Guernsey. The roadstead off St. Peter Port was protected, therefore, from the prevailing westerly and southwesterly winds by Guernsey itself ; from a southerly wind, to some extent, by this islet. Easterly winds of any severity are comparatively rare ; and as the small islands of Herm and Jethou lie less than three miles to the east of Guernsey, a wind from this direction cannot stir up much sea near St. Peter Port. The only winds, in fact, which do produce a heavy sea there come from the south and south-east. Considerable protection from such weather might be found in what is now called Havelet Bay ; but during the thirteenth century a jetty was built " between the castle and the vill of St. Peter Port," and must have been designed as a protection from this very wind. A most important consideration for ships using this anchorage was that they could rely on Castle Cornet to protect them from the king's enemies and from pirates.

St. Peter Port could therefore offer advantages as a port of call far superior to those of any other haven in the archipelago. The two " ports " in Jersey, St. Helier and St. Aubin, were both open to all southerly winds ; they were subjected to the enormous tides of the Bay of Avranches, and their approaches were strewn with rocks and shallows. Besides being nearer to a coast which was frequently hostile, they enjoyed no military protection, for Gorey Castle was four or five miles away on another coast, and was in any case not adapted to the protection of shipping. Of the lesser islands, Alderney and Sark were both small and difficult of access ; the others were too small to be of any account. St. Peter Port, on the other hand, has a perfectly clear approach from the south. To this day many ships coming from England approach St. Peter Port from this direction, having practically circumnavigated the island to do so. The mailboats come between the north end of Guernsey and the island of Herm, a difficult channel known as the Little Russel ; but large ships and strangers to local waters generally use the southern approach, either by way of the Great Russel between Herm and Sark, or by the western and southern coasts of Guernsey. These were in all probability the medieval routes.

St. Peter Port has not at present, and apparently never has had, any separate municipal administration. For administrative purposes the island is divided into ten civil parishes coinciding with the ten ecclesiastical parishes. Each has its parish council, or " douzaine." One of these parishes, St. Peter Port, includes the town, but there is no administrative distinction between the town and the parish. In consideration of the fact, however, that so large a proportion of the population of the island lives in this parish, the parochial administration of St. Peter Port is in some ways exceptional. It retains its douzaine, now called " the Central Douzaine," which transacts all important parochial business ; but in order to increase the representation of this parish in the States, it has been divided into four cantons, each of which elects one representative in addition to the two elected by the central douzaine. On a map these cantons are subdivisions of the parish, but their boundaries are so drawn that each includes a portion of the " built-up " area, as though the men who devised this scheme were at pains to show that they were dividing up the parish and were not distinguishing between town and parish. Guernseymen speak of the " Town Parish," indicating thereby that though it is a town, yet it is still, from the administrative point of view, only a parish.

St. Peter Port to-day is a market, a port, the seat of the island's government and the point from which the important roads of the island radiate. Its parish church is usually called the " Town Church," and it derives some dignity from its position ; but the dean of the island, though frequently rector of the Town Church, may be, and indeed often has been, rector of one of the other parish churches. St. Peter Port is the " business quarter " of the island and the centre of its communal life. There is no question of divergent interests between the town and the island ; and a little reflection makes this easily understandable. The island is much too small for an " independent " town to grow up upon it. On the other hand, any community, however agricultural in character, requires a market and a centre for its communal life. It will be my endeavour to show that St. Peter Port was this, and much more besides, in the Middle Ages.

It is necessary, I think, to insist upon this peculiarity of St. Peter Port, that it should have no municipal government or status, and to insist that this situation is known to have existed at least since the beginning of the sixteenth century, when the regular series of insular records begin. Bearing this in mind, we should not be surprised to find that in the Middle Ages, St. Peter Port, if indeed it was a town, was not a town of the type that has been made familiar to us by the works of Luchaire and Pirenne, that is a highly self-conscious community, markedly distinct in many respects from the surrounding countryside.

Only in one respect has the town of St. Peter Port ever been legally distinct from the rest of the Island, and this exception is not such that it would seriously affect the above generalisations. Before proceeding to a division of property at the death of the holder, the sons, by the custom of the island, took out a " vingtième," or twentieth part of the whole. This was divided among them. In addition, the eldest son took his " préciput," which consisted of the house and its appurtenances. This " préciput " might be regarded as the nucleus, or the " caput " of the estate. After these shares had been taken, the property was divided among the children according to the rules which governed such a division. But the provision respecting the " vingtième " and the " préciput " did not apply within the " barrières de la ville," that is, an arbitrary boundary, which has once been altered, and which marked the " built-up " area of the town ; for, to give the eldest son a " préciput " in an urban area would amount to giving him the whole, or almost the whole property.[3]

This rule can be traced back to the sixteenth century ; but while it is most probable that it grew up during the later Middle Ages, no definite evidence of this seems to be forthcoming. There are indeed several examples in the assize rolls of the early fourteenth century of the " vingtième " being taken in the parish of St. Peter Port, but none that can be definitely located in the town itself.[4] The question must therefore remain open ; but in any case, such a custom, like the modern parochial administration of the parish of St. Peter Port, proceeds from the fact that an urban area has come into existence, and it does not imply any special municipal law or administration.

The medieval development of St. Peter Port has received little attention from historians. The " standard histories " of the Channel Islands, and even those of Guernsey alone, barely mention it, though a reference in Dupont's " Histoire du Cotentin et de ses Isles "[5] to the connection between the port and the Gascony trade evidently did much to inspire Mr. Trevor Williams's dissertation on "The Importance of the Channel Islands in British relation with the Continent during the Thirteenth and Fourteenth Centuries".[6] This work first demonstrated the economic importance of Guernsey; but unfortunately Mr. Williams elected to illustrate his thesis by attempting to connect this economic development with the supposed "communal" character of Channel Island institutions in the Middle Ages. On closer examination, however, the Channel Island jurats (strictly speaking they should be "jurés") can be shown to bear little significant resemblance to a Gascon "jurade", and by that analogy the "communal" character of Channel Island institutions must stand or fall.[7] It is the thesis of this paper, on the other hand, that this economic development is better illustrated by the growth of St. Peter Port; though the extent of my debt, which I gratefully acknowledge, to Mr. Williams's work will appear in what follows.

The early history of St. Peter Port has, however, been the subject of one monograph,—Mr. C. Cox, "St. Peter Port in Bygone Times",[8]— but this work was written at a time when much less information was accessible than at present, and new facts often necessitate the revision of old opinions. I feel, moreover, that Mr. Cox assumed his "town of St. Peter Port" too easily. In reference to Edward I's injunction to build a quay in 1275 he says, "in the year 1275 St. Peter Port is, for the first time, honoured with the name of a town"—*i.e.* "villa nostra Sancti Petri de Portu".[9] In the belief that something more than this is required, I have prepared the argument which this paper endeavours to express; recognising, however, that if this argument succeeds it will only bring me, through much dust and heat no doubt, to the same conclusion as Mr. Cox reached so easily more than forty years ago.

2.—CONDITIONS PRECEDENT.

(a) LIBERTIES.

As it seems to be generally agreed that urban conditions cannot develop in a community unless the members of that community are to some extent delivered from the bonds of serfdom, it is necessary to show that the inhabitants of St. Peter Port enjoyed sufficient liberties to enable them, if they so desired, to indulge in trade and industry—or at least to take part in some non-agricultural pursuit. But it has been shown that there is no reason to suspect that the condition of the inhabitants of St. Peter Port differed in any important respect from that of the inhabitants of the countryside around them. We must therefore begin with an examination of the customs and liberties of the Island of Guernsey.

Some of the main characteristics of the administration of the Channel Islands in the Middle Ages have been made familiar to us by the works of Charles le Quesne, Dupont, Havet and, more recently of Mr. Trevor Williams.[10] Nevertheless it will not be out of place to give a brief account of the administration of Guernsey, especially as the argument of this paper depends upon our interpretation of familiar facts.[11]

At least until the middle of the fourteenth century, which is our present *terminus ad quem*, the islands were for general purposes regarded as a single administrative unit under the care of a warden (*custos*), appointed by, responsible to and representing the king or, to be strictly accurate, the duke. Both in Guernsey and in Jersey the warden appointed a bailiff who presided over the king's court in the island, and therein represented the warden and exercised his judicial functions. The bailiff, however, was not a judge ; judgment was rendered and amercements were " affeered " by a body of twelve jurats, whose functions seem to have been much the same as those of the Frankish *scabini* or their descendants the territorial *échevins* in Flanders. These jurats were appointed for life ; they were chosen by the king's ministers in the island and by the more important landholders. In Guernsey the executive officer of the court was the prévôt, who was chosen by the community.

The civil administration was under the direction of the warden, and was carried out by subordinate officers whom he appointed. These were the receiver, the granger and the collector of customs, whose duties were such as are implied by their titles. Military matters were either directed by the warden in person or, if he were unable to do this, by a constable whom he appointed to keep the king's castle in each island.

The administration, therefore, as a whole, was in the hands of the king's ministers, in the appointment of whom the islanders had no voice. There was never a suggestion that the islanders should manage their own financial affairs, that, as a community, they should farm the king's revenue in the island, or that they should erect communal courts of their own over against the king's court. There was, that is, no suggestion as yet of self-government. Administration was still royal and feudal ; it still concerned primarily only the royal domain—" Fief-le-Roy".

The inhabitants were not, however, left unprotected. There had grown up a considerable body of local custom, which most officers in the island were bound by the terms of their appointment to respect ; and these customs might go a long way towards restraining the predatory instincts of administrative officers, by laying down definite rules of procedure and by defining the king's rights on the one hand and the islanders' rights on the other. Such customs were variously called " franchises", " liberties " or simply " laws and customs "—" leges et consuetudines insulæ " ; and in the fourteenth century, as in the sixteenth, they were considered to be a series of local divergences from, or modifications of the law of Normandy. When called upon to do so, the islanders were usually ready to state what these customs were ; thus our knowledge of them is derived from a series of inquisitions, extents and the records of pleas " de quo waranto " held before the king's justices in eyre. They await, and they would amply repay the patient investigator who would collect and study them, and who would tell us what precisely is their relation to the customary law of Normandy and to other local customs both in Normandy and elsewhere.

Let us take one or two significant examples. A document dating apparently from Edward I's reign begins thus : " These are franchises of the people of Guernsey : Firstly, in respect of 70 li. of aid which our lord the king takes from the whole island of Guernsey, they should be quit of " ost " and " chevauché " and of tallage, save in case the body of our lord the king should be held in prison—from which God defend him.

And they should have justice or peace (" droit ou pais ") by the judgment of twelve " jurés " without going out of the island (" pais "), unless it should be to give gage or pledge that they had made a false judgment."[12]

It is convenient to take the points in the reverse order. Other statements of the custom tell us that these jurats were to be chosen from among the islanders themselves, and we may infer that they were to be men of substance. No session of the king's court might be held in the Island, even though it be presided over by the king's justices, save in the presence of at least seven, or in certain cases two of them. They must render every judgment and " affeer " every fine or amercement. We know further that they took an oath to conserve and maintain the rights of the king and of all others in the Island, to render lawful judgments in cases pleaded in the king's court, having no respect of persons and taking no bribes. We may therefore describe them as the standing guarantee of the islanders' liberties ; they must render the judgment because they knew the local custom ; they must assess the fine because they were islanders themselves, and because the bailiff, or even the king's justices, could not be presumed to have interests in common with the islanders.

In the extents, " aid-le-roy " (" Firma seu auxilium regis "), mentioned above as the consideration for which the islanders were to be quit of ost, chevauché, tallage etc., is found to be paid by a class of men called in most documents " the king's tenants," in some others " the king's 'hospites' ". That these two terms apply to the same people,[13] and that these people were living on the royal domain, seem to be beyond doubt. Each of these " tenants " with his parceners held, in the great majority of instances, one bouvée (i.e. 5 acres), and for this he paid certain dues and rendered certain services. At first sight these dues appear to be heavy :— for each bouvée 2 sols tournois per annum of " aid-le-roy", 2 deniers tournois of " brassage", 1 bushel 2 denerels of wheat of " mêlage " ; panage at the rate of 2 deniers tournois for each pig over a year old ; " poulage "— *i.e.* 2 fowls for each inhabited house ; " champart "—*i.e.* the twelfth sheaf of corn and the twelfth bundle of flax, together with a number of other miscellaneous, sometimes incomprehensible, but generally unimportant dues. There were some slight services in connection with the upkeep of the king's mills. His tenants were bound to do suit at his mills and to carry his champart to his grange. But the really significant point is that all these obligations were fixed and precisely regulated by custom, and were, generally speaking, uniform. The regulations for the cartage of the king's champart to his Grange, for example, are most minute. There is no question of service on the domain, of week-work, of tallage or other arbitrary exactions, many of which seem to have been commuted by the " aid-le-roy". In short, since most of the dues to which they were still liable bore on the land, any of the king's tenants or " hospites " in Guernsey who desired to live in an urban area and make his living by trade would find no serious feudal obstacles to his doing so. He might sell his land, subject to a seignorial congé which would cost him " the thirteenth penny " of the sale price, and subject to " retraite lignager " and perhaps " retraite féodale " as well. There was, however, no question of free devise. It is important finally to note that these tenants formed the characteristic class of peasantry in Guernsey and that there was no inferior form of tenure on the royal domain ; therefore, *a fortiori*, those who held by nobler tenures were even more free, if they so desired to embark on commercial ventures.

Most of the parish of St. Peter Port was on the royal domain, the only possible exception being a tenement, which was held by the abbot of Marmoutier.[14] We have no indication of the manner in which the abbot's tenants held of him, but we do know something of the conditions of tenure on another ecclesiastical fief in Guernsey, from the record of a case in which the villeins of the prior of the Vale took action against him for exacting new and unaccustomed services. Certain remarks in this record enable us to generalise the conclusions to be drawn from it.   It appears that the condition of these " villeins " differed in no important respect from that of the king's " hospites". They paid, it is true, the sixth sheaf instead of the twelfth for champart, but in other respects their services correspond.[15] Here again, the significant point is that these obligations were fixed by custom, and that there is no mention of work on the domain.

I have chosen what seem to me to be the most important points in the customs of Guernsey for our present purpose. There are many others, but they all amount to this : that lordship has been subjected to regulation, and thus its arbitrary character has been removed. Knowledge of our obligations is the beginning of liberty ; strict limitation of those obligations takes us far toward the goal. Only where the lord preserves his arbitrary rights over his serfs, rights of main-morte, tallage, chevage and formarriage, are commercial and industrial undertakings unthinkable.

There was therefore in Guernsey a privileged community ; a community not so far advanced that it might claim any rights of self-government, but yet enjoying certain guarantees that the administration that was imposed upon it should not be oppressive—should be such, in fact, that it left room for development. I have been impressed by the resemblance which this privileged community bears to a very numerous class of " free villages " to be found in England and Germany but chiefly in France during the Middle Ages.[16] In England they seem to have had no generic name, but many of them might ultimately establish themselves as " boroughs " ; in France they were known as " villes neuves", " sauvetés " or " bastides ". For the most part they were artificial, and might even be laid out in rectangular blocks. The lots were generally uniform in size, and settlers were attracted by the promise of privileged conditions of tenure. Normally a village or small town of this sort would not be given rights of self-government. The lord would reserve his administration, though the inhabitants would be given specific guarantees against exploitation. The condition of their inhabitants may be compared in detail with that of the king's tenants in Guernsey. They were frequently called " hospites", sometimes " burgesses". As in Guernsey, they held uniform tenements, and though they still owed many rents and services, these had been strictly regulated by grant or custom. Duties of military service were abolished or drastically reduced in such " villes neuves", just as the " hospites " of Guernsey were quit of " ost " and " chevauchée " in respect of the " aid-le-roy " which they paid. In short, these men were personally free, and their obligations were such as need not interfere with mercantile pursuits. Their liberties were secured by making them answerable only to the court of the village, where their own custom would be administered, and by limiting amercements to fixed maxima—just as in Guernsey the islanders could not be summoned to a secular court outside the island, and were protected from arbitrary amercements by customary provision and by the rights of the jurats.

Now it may be generally observed on the Continent that such a village, should it be endowed with a market, and should it happen to stand on a trade route in such a position as to attract merchants, might very well develop into a town of some importance.[17] Such liberties, though not ambitious, were sufficient to set it going ; and from this I conclude that though the tenure of the Guernsey " hospites " was not burgage tenure, and though they had no rights of self-government or even a court of their own, they were sufficiently delivered from the bondage of the " régime domaniale " to permit urban development to take place in the island without the addition of further liberties ; that is to say, the inhabitants of St. Peter Port, even without the more favourable conditions which they may have enjoyed, might, as members of the community of Guernsey, freely engage in commercial ventures. What need, therefore, had St. Peter Port to cut itself off from the rest of the Island and demand separate administration after the manner of the conventional medieval town?

(B) TRADE AND INDUSTRY

Mr. Williams in his dissertation " The Importance of the Channel Islands in British relation with the Continent during the Thirteenth and Fourteenth Centuries " first showed the connection between the Channel Islands, especially Guernsey, with the sea-borne trade which exchanged the corn, cloth and salted fish of north-west Europe for the wine and spices of the south.[18] Bearing in mind that any ship whose course is set clear to Ushant and Cap de la Hague must pass within sight of Guernsey, and that medieval ships, if they could avoid doing so, rarely passed out of sight of land, we should expect Guernsey, if the island could provide an adequate roadstead, to develop into an important port of call. It has already been shown that such a roadstead existed at St. Peter Port, and it therefore remains only to see how far these expectations were fulfilled.

The importation of wine from Bordeaux into England, Normandy and Flanders, seems to have assumed some importance in the twelfth century, and it developed phenomenally in the thirteenth and fourteenth centuries. Most of it came by sea ; for the return journey the ships were laden with wool (later with cloth as well) from England, cloth from Flanders, grain from England, Normandy and Brittany, metals from the west of England for the manufacture of arms in Bordeaux, and salted fish caught and prepared on the coasts of Normandy, Brittany, Devon and Cornwall, though much of it came from Scandinavia in Hanseatic ships to Yarmouth and London to be re-exported thence to Gascony. Bordeaux itself took little interest in shipping. The carrying trade thus fell into the hands of the men of Bayonne and the Flemings, though the English and Normans took their share, a share that tended to grow. In the Middle Ages, therefore, there must have been a continuous stream of ships passing, perhaps, within sight of Guernsey, northbound laden with wine, spices and salt, southbound with cloth and grain and salted fish. What indications have we that this island took an active part in this trade ?

First of all we know definitely that Guernsey was an important land-mark in the Middle Ages. On a ship coming from La Rochelle and bound for England or Normandy, the pilots taken after the Ile de Batz had been passed were to be regarded as coasting pilots, to be paid by the merchants, and those employed after the ship had passed Guernsey must be English or Norman.[19] Ships bringing skins from Ireland to Normandy must, after they had passed the " point of Guernsey " unload their wares at Rouen and nowhere else.[20] From these rules I conclude that Guernsey was regarded as the westernmost point of Normandy, and as the natural landfall for ships approaching the Channel from the south and west. Mr. Williams has also shown that the islands were so used not only by mer-chants, but by military expeditions proceeding from England to France. Among the examples he cites is the poet Guillaume Guiart's descrip-tion of Edward I directing his fleet, in 1292,

> " Vers les illes de Guernesi
> Que mer parfonde açaint et lie
> En l'un coste de Normandie."[21]

Such a conclusion is supported by evidence of the number of wrecks which occured in these parts, particularly on the west coast of Guernsey. The assize rolls of the early fourteenth century supply examples. In the rolls of the Eyre of 1309 alone there is mention of a Spanish ship wrecked near Saints, a ship of Rouen wrecked on Matthew de Sausmarez' lands, a Flemish ship stranded at Cobo, and other ships from Winchelsea, Cherbourg, Spain, Normandy and Gascony which had met with disaster on the coast of Guernsey.[22] They also tell us of an arrangement by which the king, the abbot of Mont Saint Michel and the seigneur of Fief le Comte agreed to share the profits of wreck, in the proportion 2 : 1 : 1 on all coasts of the island except on the domain lands of Matthew de Saus-marez and the abbot of Blanchelande. The rule according to Norman law, which was followed in Jersey, was that seigneurs enjoying this right took the profits of wrecks occurring on their fiefs, the king elsewhere. But since the profitable west coast of Guernsey lay almost entirely in the Fiefs St. Michel and le Comte, the king's ministers had made this arrange-ment, which must have been greatly to the king's profit ; while the fact that it was made at all is a testimony to the value of this right in Guern-sey, and so to the volume of shipping in these waters.[23]

Likewise, in the early fourteenth century, complaints of piracy off Guernsey became serious, though Channel Islanders were not as yet the culprits. For example, it was alleged in 1323 that merchants of the Cinque Ports had plundered off Guernsey certain Spanish vessels which were going from Abbeville to Spain, and, in the same year, that men of Kent had despoiled a ship of St Omer near the Island as she was journeying from La Rochelle to Calais.[24] Similar complaints are common from this time onward. Just about a century before, the king had had to restore wines to the Countess of Flanders, wines which had been taken from her merchants by royal officials in the islands without, apparently, any warrant.

Sailors may, however, have used Guernsey as a landmark and been wrecked or robbed there for their pains, but we require evidence that they actually used the port. The assize rolls are of considerable help in this matter, for they have much to tell us about the nefarious doings of foreign sailors in the island. " Unknown malefactors from Bayonne slew an unknown man in a Spanish ship in St. Peter Port harbour and fled immediately after the deed " ;[26] " Peter de Bayonne slew an Englishman in St. Peter Port " ;[27] other malefactors from Bayonne sacked the Vale Priory, " and took Reginald Pastey, then prior of that Priory, led him to their ships, and imprisoned him therein ; then they tied him up in a sack and dangled him in the water near their ships, until he made a fine with them for 200 li., of which he paid them 40 li. tournois for the redemption of his body and to save his life " ;[28] John de Hospital of Bayonne robbed the prior of Blanchelande and the parson of St. Martin's church.[29] But the malefactors did not always come from Bayonne ; English and Spanish sailors seem to have been almost equally violent in their habits.[30] All this seems to show that the population of Guernsey must often have seemed unpleasantly, if not dangerously cosmopolitan in the early fourteenth century.

Further evidence of the use of St. Peter Port by foreign shipping as a port of call may be obtained from orders addressed to the warden to arrest ships in time of war, or to release them at the conclusion of hostilities. Thus in 1225 Geoffrey de Lucy was ordered to liberate a ship from Poitou which had been arrested at Guernsey ; in the same year to deliver a ship belonging to a Rouen merchant similarly arrested ; to deliver wine belonging to merchants of Caen and Pont Audemer.   In the next year Richard de Grey was ordered to deliver a French ship laden with salt, and a ship from La Rochelle, both arrested at Guernsey.[31]   In 1294 the bailiffs of the islands were ordered to arrest certain ships of Bayonne which were known to have entered the harbours of the islands, and similarly to arrest all ships and goods belonging to Norman merchants which they might find there.[32]

The most impressive evidence, however, of the volume of foreign shipping calling at St. Peter Port in the early fourteenth century is afforded by the accounts of the Great Custom levied during the years 1328-1330. These show that, from Michaelmas 1328 to Michaelmas 1329, 245 foreign ships called at Guernsey (according to the Extent of 1331, these figures do not include ships coming from or bound for a port within the king's realm) ; while during the eleven months from Michaelmas 1329 to August 29, 1330, custom was levied on no less than 487 foreign ships.   During these two periods the custom realised 275 li. 11s. 6d. and 450 li. 8s. 4d. tournois (" strong money ") respectively.   In Jersey it was farmed, together with the Little Custom, at 20 li. tournois (" strong money ") per annum.[33]   The extents of 1331 give the estimated annual yield for Guernsey as 160 li.,[34] and for Jersey 9 li. ;[35] but an extent must needs give a conservative estimate, for the yield might well be drastically reduced during a war period.   Such figures alone would be sufficient to demonstrate the importance of Guernsey as a port of call.

But our case is not yet complete, for it is quite conceivable that the mere use of St. Peter Port roadstead, even to this phenomenal extent, should not affect the character of the community in any important respect. To show that this trade gives rise to a reasonable presumption of urban development in Guernsey, we must adduce evidence that Guernseymen took part in it, and that the island produced goods for export to pay for imported luxuries.

Unfortunately the nature of our evidence is such that we only hear of Guernsey merchants when they are in trouble. Thus, William " le Engleis " of Guernsey had had his wine arrested in his own island in 1227 ;[36] in 1299, Robert le Picard and three other Guernsey merchants admitted to the king's justices that they had sent a shipload of herring and mackerel to Abbeville contrary to the king's orders ;[37] in 1328 a ship belonging to Channel Island merchants, and laden with salt from Poitou was captured by men of Normandy ;[38] a ship called " La Nôtre Dame " of Guernsey had been freighted with wine at Bordeaux in 1336, and was plundered at sea by men of Weymouth and Melcombe ;[39] in 1343, the ship " La Katerine " of Guernsey had met with a similar fate at the hands of the men of the bishop of St. Malo while sailing near the island of Oléron.[40]

When a national system of " customs " was developed in England, the islanders endeavoured to show that they, not being " aliens", should not be required to pay these duties. In 1309, and again in 1311, the collectors of the " New Custom " at Southampton, Weymouth, Dartmouth and Lyme Regis were ordered not to distrain on them to pay customs on goods imported or exported at those ports, as the king regarded the islanders as men of his realm and not aliens.[41] This order seems, however, to have become ineffective ; for in July 1335, following a petition of the islanders, the collectors of customs at Southampton, Chichester, Exeter, Winchelsea and Melcombe were ordered to cease exacting customs from them until Easter, so that the king might meanwhile inquire into the truth of their assertions.[42] Possibly in consequence of an enquiry the islanders were exempted in April 1337 from payment of the " New Custom " for two years, not as a matter of right, but " in consideration of their constant fidelity and their burdens in defence of the islands."[43] As their " constant fidelity " was to be put to a severe strain during the next year or two, this was perhaps a wise concession on the king's part. But in the next decade the islanders seem to have found lucrative employment in evading the customs ;[44] while the establishment of the staple at Calais only revealed new possibilities in the business of smuggling.[45]

These exemptions and concessions may have seemed very desirable in the fourteenth century, but the modern historian must regret that they deprive him of a most useful source of information on the activities of Channel Island merchants in the customs accounts. Systematic search did not seem worth while, although, exemptions notwithstanding, one or two instances of Channel Islanders paying the customs appear in the specimen accounts printed by Mr. Gras. In 1309 James de Gernesey brought a shipload of conger and haddock to Southampton, presumably from his island, and paid the custom ; in 1322 Nicholas L'Evêque, master of the ship " La Nicholas de Gerneseye", paid custom on the wool that he was exporting from Bristol.[46]

The most interesting indication, however, of Guernsey's participation in mercantile ventures comes from a lawsuit pleaded before the justices in eyre in 1299. From the record of the proceedings it appears that certain Guernsey merchants had combined together (they called themselves " socii mercatores ") for the sale of fish in Rouen and Dieppe, since the dispute concerns the disposition of certain common property in those towns.[47] Now this implies a regular trading connection ; and such a conclusion is supported by evidence from Rouen itself. From a clause in " Les droitures, coustumes et apartenances de la vicomté de l'eaue de

Rouen", which dates from the thirteenth century, it appears that preferential treatment was given to ships coming from Dieppe and Guernsey.[48] The island is also mentioned in M. de Fréville's book as a regular source of salted conger for the city.[49] Such evidence seems to show that Guernsey's part in the coasting trade of Western Europe was not merely passive.

Agricultural produce seems to have been fairly regularly exported from these islands to England ; and though precise evidence is not forthcoming, we may well suppose that the wine ships took back corn as well as fish on the return journey to Gascony. The Norman monasteries which held land in the islands were also responsible for the export of considerable quantities of victuals to the mainland, since few of the insular priories were conventual.[50]   As early as 1234 the bailiffs of Guernsey were ordered to see to it that English merchants coming to the Island to buy corn suffered no hindrance ;[51] while in the fourteenth century there is quite a series of " protections " for such merchants ; *e.g.* for Hugh Madefrey, a merchant of the city of London, buying victuals in the islands in 1316 ; for William Aubyn and Robert " de Barflete", burgesses of Southampton in 1317 ; for Nicholas Edrich and others of Southampton in the same year (these were going to buy 400 quarters of wheat and barley in the islands) ;[52] for Richard Bagg, a burgess of the same town, in 1325 ; for John le Flemyng and others, also of Southampton, in 1326.[53]

A custom was payable in the islands on all goods imported from or exported to a place outside the " realm " ; though all goods produced by the exporter himself, or destined for the importer's own sustenance, were exempt. This was called the " Little Custom", of which a tariff has survived. The custom can be traced back to John's reign, and was instituted, doubtless, to restrain the islanders' export of victuals to their friends and relations in Normandy and Brittany who, after 1204, had to be considered their enemies.[54]

The conclusion I draw from this evidence is that agriculture in the islands had developed to the point where its products more than sufficed for the needs of the inhabitants. When this point is reached it may be regarded as an industry, and an element in economic development. The really important Channel Island industry at this time was, however, fishing ; and the history of their fisheries shows more clearly than anything else the place of the islands in the " Bordeaux wine trade". We have shown Guernsey as a port of call, we have seen Guernseymen participating in this trade ; we have now to discover how Guernsey produce helped to feed the toilers in the Gascon vineyards.

The few indications that we have go to show that Guernsey was the centre of the medieval fishing industry in the islands.[55] The industry was strictly regulated ; and though there is no trace of gild organisation, yet Edward I issued his regulations in the form of a charter " to the community of Guernsey fishermen." These regulations concerned seasons and fishing grounds, but mostly, as we should expect, the disposal of the catch and the dues to be paid.[56] " The custom of mackerel " was a due of two deniers on every hundred mackerel caught between Easter and Michaelmas ; the " custom of fish " was a due of two sols levied on every boat-load of fish, 20 deniers on every thousand mackerel and 20 sols on every hundred conger sent to Normandy or elsewhere out of the king's realm.

The most interesting institution, however, was the " éperquerie " of conger. Originally this seems to have been the name given to a drying-place established by a lord having the right to do so, and to which he forced his men to do suit. The king had his éperqueries for his men, and, in Guernsey, the abbot of Mont Saint Michel, the seigneur of Sausmarez and the abbot of Blanchelande had their éperqueries for their men. Later it developed into a right of pre-emption on the catch so that, in John de Roches' accounts (1329), it could be defined as " a custom by which certain tenants of the king and certain other fishers of conger are bound to sell (their fish) to merchants of the lord king appointed for the purpose, that is between Easter and Michaelmas of each year, if they can agree upon the price. If they cannot so agree, the fish is to be valued by men chosen from either party, and then the merchants have the option of taking or leaving it. (If they do not take it,) then the fishermen may sell it to whomsoever they will. But the fishermen are not bound to sell to the merchants any conger so small that it can be grasped about the middle by the hand ; and the fishermen may also take from among the small conger as much as they need for their own sustenance, and to give one or two to their friends." [57]

The king, thus, usually farmed out his rights over the island fisheries, and it is significant that the farmers were usually Gascon merchants. Indeed the earliest mention of the éperqueries of Guernsey, *eo nomine*, that we have is the account of the 25 li. for which Vital de Biele of Bayonne farmed them in 1195, by virtue of a grant from Richard I.[58] In 1248 the king's fisheries of the islands were granted to Peter Arnaud de Saint-Jean and his fellows for five years at an annual farm of 12 li. 10s.[59] At the expiry of this term, the lease was renewed for six years, but at the enhanced rent of 74 li. per annum.[60] When Otto de Grandison became lord of the islands, he obtained the King's licence to farm out the fisheries in the islands to " Amatus de Saubanihay " in 1278, and later to William de Saint-Remy, bailiff of Guernsey.[61] Likewise the abbot of Mont Saint Michel farmed out his éperqueries in the islands in 1270 to Arnaud Jean, a merchant of Bayonne and in the next year bailiff of the islands, in 1296 to Peter d'Arcis, who was probably at that time bailiff of Jersey, and in 1319 to Michael de Gallart and Peter de Garis, Gascon merchants.[62] In 1329 the farm of the king's fisheries in the islands amounted to 226 li. 13s. 4d. tournois.[63] When we observe further that merchants of Bayonne obtained the monopoly of the whale fishery " from Mont Saint Michel to Dartmouth " and the monopoly of " buying, salting and drying " conger and haddock in Cornwall,[64] and that they possessed important drying places at St. Mathieu in Brittany, in Ushant and along the coast of Léon,[65] it becomes apparent that the Channel Islands belonged economically to a region comprising Western Normandy, Brittany and the West of England, the chief products of which were fish and corn, and that the Gascons had come to regard this region as an important source of their food supply. As their own district had devoted itself so exclusively to the production of wine that it had to depend very largely on imported foodstuffs, they found it necessary to acquire important concessions in this region in order to make sure of a constant supply of these necessities.

The connection between the Channel Islands and Gascony was very close in the thirteenth and fourteenth centuries. Of the wardens of the islands in the thirteenth century, seven were at one time or another (sometimes simultaneously) seneschals of Gascony—Henry de Trubleville, Nicholas " de Molis", William " de Boell", Drew de Barentin, Richard de Grey, John de Grey and Otto de Grandison. Arnaud Jean, who was bailiff of the islands under the Lord Edward (1271-1275) was a citizen of Bayonne, and so, apparently, were Peter Bernard de Pynsoles and Laurence du Gaillars, joint-wardens in 1330-1331.[66] Moreover these Gascons were acquiring land in the islands ; Peter de Gariz, " marchant de Gascoigne," bailiff of Guernsey 1324-1326, acquired considerable property in the Câtel parish, Guernsey ;[67] the jury of St. Andrew's parish presented in 1309 that Gérard de Cassade of Gascony had purchased certain lands in the island ;[68] while in 1290, Otto de Grandison granted a house called " Cornilot," in the vill of St. Peter Port to Peter d'Arcis " his merchant " at a yearly rent of 40s.[69]   Evidently their business connection with the island was of such importance to these Gascon merchants that they thought it worth their while to acquire land and establish themselves there.

The significance of this evidence seems to be that it puts the Channel Islands in their " economic milieu " ; and it shows that if they were of any importance to England as a military outpost in the Middle Ages, they were of equal importance to Gascony as a port of call, an entrepôt, and as a source of the necessities of life.

To conclude this chapter there should be mentioned one further manifestation of the economic development of Guernsey which seems to clinch my argument ; that is the appearance of a mercantile jurisdiction in the island.   The king's court is, in fact, found to be hearing mercantile cases, and to be hearing them " according to the law of merchants".   The extent of 1331 speaks of a " cour des étrangers " which, if necessary, might sit from day to day,[70] and there are one or two examples in the assize rolls of its activities.   Perhaps the best of these is to be found in the record of the Eyre of 1331.[71]   It was alleged that Thomas and Nicholas Galyen, of the vill of St. Peter Port, had loaded a ship which put in at the port of Caen on Sunday, January 1, 1325, where, so Thomas and Nicholas said, their ship and its contents were seized by the men of that town. On the Sunday following, therefore, when a ship laden with salt belonging to certain merchants of Caen was found in St. Peter Port harbour, Thomas and Nicholas obtained a judgment from the jurats " according to the law of mariners " empowering them to distrain on this cargo to the value of their ship and its contents.   Such was their story, and it is a familiar one. The jurats, in the presence of the king's justices, denied that they had given such a judgment ; but that such a judgment was in their power to give was never questioned. This incident, taken with one or two others of which record has been found, if we bear in mind that we have no records that would naturally record the work of this court unless its judgments required revision, proves the existence of a form of the king's court acting as a merchant court in Guernsey. No clearer indication of the existence of a strong mercantile element in the population of the Island could be desired.

3.—THE TOWN OF ST. PETER PORT IN THE EARLY FOURTEENTH CENTURY.

(A) ST. PETER PORT AS A MILITARY AND ADMINISTRATIVE CENTRE.

I have endeavoured to show in .the previous section, firstly, that the inhabitants of Guernsey had attained sufficient tenurial and personal freedom to enable them to engage in mercantile ventures if the opportunity came to them, and, secondly, that in point of fact there is considerable evidence that the island was not only of great importance to merchants of Gascony, England and Normandy, both as a port of call and as a source of the supply of victuals, but that it was already taking an active part in the trade with which it found itself concerned. If I have made out my case in these respects, then we are justified in looking for urban development in Guernsey ; and it only remains, therefore, to show that this development took place in St. Peter Port, which thus became the focus of this privileged community and the centre of its trade and industry.

Let us first consider some non-economic reasons for the pre-eminence of St. Peter Port. Of these the most important must surely be the proximity of the king's castle. The origin of this castle is most probably to be sought, like that of Gorey Castle in Jersey, in the reign of John. This seems a likely time for the king to be fortifying the islands, and there is no historical evidence whatever of the existence of any castles in the islands before John's reign. The earliest known reference to Gorey Castle is dated 1212, and we have to wait until 1226 for a specific mention of Castle Cornet. From this date onwards, however, the records concerning both castles are very full indeed, and show that these strongholds had more than a local significance.[72]

Something in the nature of a small town almost invariably springs up beside an important castle. The garrison must be fed, labour is required for building and repairs, and military equipment of all kinds must be supplied. It is therefore interesting to note that Castle Cornet is frequently referred to in the fourteenth century as " the castle of the vill of St. Peter Port".[73] The garrison moreover was considerable. The earliest figures we have refer to the period from June 12 until Michaelmas, 1328, when there was a constable, a porter, a watchman, three men-at-arms and fifty foot-soldiers in the castle.[74] This may have been above the average, but it could not be reckoned as full war-time strength.

Castle Cornet was certainly the Warden's headquarters in the bailiwick of Guernsey, and there are not wanting indications that it might be regarded as his general headquarters in the archipelago. It seems the most likely place to be the centre of his administration.[75] If this were so it would add greatly to the importance of St. Peter Port, making it the political as well as the commercial centre of the Channel Islands. In any case, by the beginning of the fourteenth century the internal administration of Guernsey seems to have been settling down in St. Peter Port. At a time when the king's court in Jersey was very uncertain of its habitat, his court in Guernsey showed a decided preference for St. Peter Port. In fact, unless the indeterminate date " in Guernsey " be taken as doubtful, I have not yet found an instance before 1350 which showed the king's court in Guernsey in regular session anywhere else.[76] The general eyres from 1299 onwards invariably conducted their proceedings in St. Peter Port.[77]

" In St. Peter Port", says the extent of 1331, " the King has a manor called ' the Grange'. From the buildings he derives no profit, save that the corn and the champart of the island are placed and stored there." Here we may suppose the granger, an officer chosen by the community, performed his official duties and compiled his accounts; here rents in kind were stored until they were sold.[78] A very important part, that is to say, of the internal administration of the island had its " head office " in St. Peter Port.

In Guernsey, therefore, the king's castle, the king's court, and the king's grange, which together represent the king's administration, were centralised, and centralised in St. Peter Port. There is no evidence of any such centralisation of the administration in Jersey. These considerations alone would do much to explain why St. Peter Port developed so much sooner than St. Helier.[79]

(B) URBAN DEVELOPMENT.

Probably the oldest thing in St. Peter Port is the port. When, about 1048, Duke William gave six Guernsey churches to the Abbey of Marmoutier, he included among them " The Church of St. Peter Port "— " Ecclesia Sancti Petri de Portu ".[80] From the earliest times, therefore, the chief landing place in the island must have been just where the town subsequently grew up.

In 1275 the king, hearing that many wrecks might be avoided if a wall were built " between our castle there and our vill of St. Peter Port," granted a custom of 12 deniers tournois to be levied on every ship and six deniers on every small boat calling at the port for three years, the proceeds of which were to defray the cost of building the wall.[81] The position indicated for this wall shows that protection was required against the south-easterly gales which alone could produce a dangerous sea in St. Peter Port roadstead. After the disastrous French raid of 1295, however, Richard Rose, John le Barber, Peter Benart " et touz les autres bone gentz de la vile de Seint Pere-port en l'isle de Gernere " petitioned the king to renew the quayage of 1275; for, they said, " l'avaunt dite ville " had been burned and destroyed on two occasions, many of the inhabitants slain and the quay broken down, and they were unable to repair the damage without assistance.[82] In 1305, therefore, the quayage was re-granted to them for five years; and the grant was made to " the burgesses of the vill of St. Peter Port "—" burgensibus ville de Sancto Petro Portu in insula de Gernes'."[83]

Whatever this quay may have been as a building, the " port " was something very definite; for, in the fourteenth century the collector of customs was paid twice as much for collecting the Great Custom from ships " outside the port and the place called ' Bancum ' wherever they may be within the bounds of the Island " as from those " within the port."[84] A useful indication of the amount of shipping that might be congregated in the port at one time is to be found in a letter of William de Saint-Remy, Denis de Tilbury (attorneys of Otto de Grandison in the islands) and the jurats of Guernsey, inquiring how they should deal with ship-masters who refused to pay the custom of ships. The case in point concerned " Gilbert Mayn, master of a ship called ' La Benedicite ' of Yarmouth and a merchant of Toulouse", who, being in the king's port of the island with merchandise, and having been asked to pay the custom due, had refused to pay and had raised their standards and banners and made off with violence. William Bernere master of the ship " Le Covyn " of Yarmouth, Roger Martin, master of the ship " La Blythe " of Ipswich, Thomas Perot, master of the ship " Saint Mary " of Lyme, William Germain, master of " La Mazeline " of Seaford, William Salekyn, master of " La Plente " of Sandwich, " and many others " who were in the harbour at the same time followed Gilbert Mayn's example.[85] The king's officials were evidently quite unable to cope with so large a fleet.

An important fish market may have been held in St. Peter Port from early times, for the Inquest of 1248 states that in the reign of John " it was ordained and provided for the sustenance and convenience of the lord king's castles and garrison and of all the people of the island that all fishermen should come together three days a week to sell their fish, that is on Tuesdays, Thursdays and Saturdays " ; and a letter of May 1308 ordered Otto de Grandison to proclaim " in the market towns and else-where in the said islands the king's prohibition that anyone should impede the fish called mackerel from being taken to the vill of St. Peter Port between Easter and Midsummer."[86]   But the general market of the island had been held from of old in the Câtel Parish, though as early as 1243 there had evidently been an agitation in favour of moving it, for the warden was then ordered to prevent any such change from taking place.[87] There is no evidence that the question was raised again until the early fourteenth century, when the leader of the agitation seems to have been a certain John du Vivier.   If I read his difficult petition aright, he had obtained a writ directing that inquiry should be made concerning the market which had been held from September to March at " Nostre Dame de Chastel " and from March to September at " une plache ke est appellez Les Laundes " in the same parish.   The inquest, apparently, reported in favour of removal, but a later writ forbad this to be carried out.[88]

The whole question was reopened before the king's justices in 1309. When it was found that eight of the ten parishes supported John du Vivier, it was agreed that two men should be chosen from each of the larger parishes and one from each of the lesser parishes, and that these men should take counsel with the justices and make some definite decision.   When this had been done the following statement was issued : " Having found that the lord king's vill of St. Peter Port is a sort of borough ("quasi-burgum "), and that all the other parishes are country vills with houses which are not contiguous but dispersed in the fields ; and also that both among their countrymen and among strangers there is a far greater concourse of men at St. Peter Port than in any other parish of the aforesaid island ; and that the market had previously been held far from the vill of St. Peter Port, although on Saturday*.............. bringing many other goods for sale, they came to the aforesaid vill of St. Peter Port on Sunday, and there, during service, they used to hold a market to the great scandal of Christianity etc., it was unanimously agreed that the market should be held in the future exclusively in the vill of St. Peter Port*.............. the market being opened every Thursday at day-break ; and that the day should be changed*....(only by ?).... the assent of all "....   There follow some more or less legible regulations for holding the market.[89]

* MS. defective.

In 1305 the king's chancery thought that there were burgesses in St. Peter Port. In 1309 the clerk who wrote up the eyre roll of that year decided that " villa " was inadequate to describe St. Peter Port, and he rendered whatever word the " committee " may actually have used by the curious phrase " quasi-burgum "—" a sort of borough." We seem to be very near a " town " of St. Peter Port, for its inhabitants— its burgesses—can levy a quayage for a public utility, it has a port and a market, while the king's castle, his court and his grange are closely associated with it.

There are, moreover, indications in the extent of the island made in 1331, which, if I only knew how to interpret them with confidence, might give us a more definite idea of the development of the " town ".[90] In each parish in Guernsey the royal domain, on which the " hospites " had been settled, was divided into " bordages". Each " bordage " was administered by a bordier, who usually farmed the king's rents and dues within his bordage, saw to it that services due to the king were performed, levied distraints and performed other duties of a like nature. In return for this he held a tenement which might also be called " the bordage".

The royal domain in the parish of St. Peter Port was divided into six such bordages—the Bordages Durant, Cornet, Rongefer, Trousse, Landry and Lésant. Now we may obtain some rough idea of the density of population in each bordage (although it must be observed that we are not justified in assuming that they were of equal, or even approximately equal area) by comparing the number of " poulages " paid in each. The bordages in St. Peter Port paid, in the order they were mentioned above, 32, 47, 42, 18, 120, and 86 poulages. For comparison, the two bordages in the Forest parish paid together 92 poulages, the two bordages in St. Martin's parish paid 100, the three bordages in St. Sampson's parish paid 74. Evidently 30-40 inhabited houses was the average number in a bordage ; therefore the Bordage Landry with its 120 and the Bordage Lésant with 86 must be studied further.

Unfortunately there are no clear indications of the location of these bordages, though there are reasons, other than the number of poulages due from each, for thinking that the Bordages Landry and Lésant included the site of the town. In both these bordages, and in these bordages only, there were tenants paying " bancage " a due levied on houses built on " La Banque " near the sea. In both these bordages, and in the Bordage Cornet, there were tenants paying " costillage "—a due paid for " certain pieces of pasture near the sea-shore which cannot be ploughed". It is evident then that these three bordages all touched the coast, and must therefore have included the site of the town. A memory of the Bordage Cornet seems to linger in Cornet Street to the south of the church ; and so, until the situation of these bordages can be definitely established by other evidence, I suggest that the Bordage Landry included a stretch of coast immediately to the north of the church, and that the Bordage Lésant lay against its northern boundary.

If this theory be accepted then the information contained in the extent offers possibilities of the highest interest. But there is a difficulty. In both these bordages the men who compiled the extent had two classes of tenants to deal with ; and, judging by the fragment of the original document preserved in the Public Record Office, they dealt with this difficulty by writing the names of the tenants in one column, their common services in the other, and connecting tenants with their services by means of brackets. Unfortunately this fragment does not include the account of the bordages in which we are interested, and, which is still more unfortunate, the copies and translations of the document which have survived have abandoned this arrangement. The result is confusion, for now we have no certain means of deciding which services were rendered by which tenants. The recent edition of the extent does nothing to help us, for the editor gives no evidence that he collated the copy he printed with the many copies of the French translation which still exist, or with the original fragment in the Record Office. The problem of the original arrangement of the document is therefore not discussed in his work, nor has he shown why the copy he prints has greater validity than other copies.

The first class of tenants accounted for in these bordages creates no difficulties. Most of them held with their parceners one bouvée, and they may be identified at once with the " king's tenants " or " hospites " to be found throughout the royal domain in the island. Their status and services have already been studied in this paper. But there is a second group of tenants the extent of whose tenements is not stated. Instead, a sum of money, usually 12 deniers or a simple fraction of that sum, is written against their names. In the enumeration of services which follows, it will be noticed that two items are duplicated, that is, there are two totals of " aid-le-roy " and two totals of melage in the account of each bordage. In the account of the Bordage Lésant we are told definitely that the second group of tenants pays " aid-le-roy " at twice the usual rate, that is, at four sols per bouvée. Thus the tenants who also pay " aid-le-roy " at this enhanced rate in the Bordage Landry are identified. Now in St. Sampson's parish, the tenants of the three bordages paid " aid-le-roy " at the rate of three sols, four sols, and five sols per bouvée, but this is stated to be " for all rents and other services." I suspect therefore that these tenants in the Bordages Landry and Lésant paid " aid-le-roy " at this enhanced rate for the same reason ; and therefore that in the account of these bordages the extra render of " aid-le-roy " and melage was due from them, and that the other services mentioned were performed by the ordinary " hospites " and did not concern these tenants. This indeed is the natural interpretation to put on the accounts of these bordages ; but we cannot be quite certain, because we only have copies of the extent, and copies which do not seem to have preserved the original arrangement. It is easy to see that these things could be expressed quite clearly by the arrangement which I suggest was originally adopted throughout by this document, and also how easily they might be confused by the abandonment of this arrangement.

What then did the sum of money placed against the names of these tenants represent ? Let us first note what these sums were. In the Bordage Landry they were, in the order in which they are set down in the extent, 12, 10½, 22, 12, 12, 18, 6, 6, 6, 6, 12, 12, 4, 20, 2, 4, 10½, deniers tournois ; and in the Bordage Lésant similarly, 12, 2, 18, 6, 6, 6, 12, 6, 6, 5, deniers tournois. Now there is something obviously artificial about these figures, for the great majority of them are either six, twelve, or eighteen deniers, or a simple fraction of these figures. When we remember that twelve deniers was the normal rate of burgage rent in Normandy, and that these tenants were probably paying " aid-le-Roy " at a high rate " for all rents and services", that is, they had commuted their

" feudal " obligations to a fixed rent, is it too much to suggest that this additional rent was a kind of burgage rent, and that they had risen to the status of being " almost burgesses", just as the vill in which they lived was a " sort of borough " ?   The English chancery had, indeed, already called them burgesses without qualification.

The number of poulages paid in the Bordages Landry and Lésant is suggestive of a growing population. . There are other indications of the same thing.   In 1309 it was found that whereas the tenement of the Bordier Landry used to contain seven vergées of land, one of these vergées had been alienated, and that fourteen cottages had been built on it.[91] In the same year it was stated that the tenement of one " hospes," apparently in St. Peter Port, which Duke William had granted to the Abbey of Marmoutier in 1048 " had been divided into many parts, where the abbot's tenants live."[92]   Both these instances show a concentration of buildings far greater than would have been possible save in a definitely urban area.

There are one or two scraps of evidence which tend to support these conclusions.   In 1309, a certain Peter le Corner was deriving revenue from the lease (locagium) of houses in St. Peter Port.[93]   In 1323 it was reported by the jury of St. Peter Port that " the shops which are opposite the house which used to belong to Master William de Saint Remy towards the south are situated on the royal way..........These shops belong to Thomas de Estfeld and his wife."[94]   Evidently some encroachment had been going on here.   In 1331 the astounding number of 41 wine-sellers, 12 beer-sellers and 70 bakers had broken respectively the assizes of wine, beer and bread ; while 22 people were convicted of using false measures in St. Peter Port.[95]

Attached to the eyre roll of the year 1323 is a set of ordinances issued by the king's justices.[96]   At the head it is stated that they were promulgated for the " utility of the island of Jersey " ; but this is either a mistake for Guernsey, or these ordinances were intended to have a more general application, as is shown by the reference to St. Peter Port in the body of the document.   Many of these ordinances bear almost a municipal character—the public ways are to be cleaned and kept clean ; taverners who mix bad wine with good are to be punished, and so with fraudulent bakers.   Two of these provisions are of special interest here : " Item that the office of wine-porters (bermanni) and porters (portitores) be committed to good men who can be answerable to the king and to the people if they should be the cause of any loss that may occur ; and that satisfaction should be made for their labour at the estimation of six good men of the vill of St. Peter Port chosen for the purpose by the bailiff and jurats, taking into consideration the amount of the labour, the distance and other circumstances which in equity should be considered.   Item that no one should exercise the office of broker (corretarius) unless he be admitted to the office by the bailiff with the counsel of the jurats ; and he shall take an oath that he will do nothing nor cause anything to be done that would prejudice or damage the king, the people of the island or other business-men.   Further, no one shall be admitted as a partner in merchandise brought to the accustomed warehouses in the time of mackerel, or at other times, unless he have sufficient substance to pay for the merchandise.   If anyone contravene this ordinance, let him be punished at the discretion of the bailiff and jurats."

These strange words " bermanni " and " corretarii " give the affairs of Guernsey a very business-like appearance. It is to be observed, moreover, that the " good men of St. Peter Port " were intimately concerned in these affairs, and that the bailiff and jurats were being told, though they may not have needed the telling, that they must regulate local trade. This greatly strengthens the theory that the king's court might in the fourteenth century or even earlier constitute itself a merchant court to administer the law merchant, and shows that this development was connected with the growth of St. Peter Port as a town of merchants.

One more point concludes my argument. In 1350 the king, hearing that Jerbourg Castle had fallen into hopeless disrepair and that the people of Guernsey had therefore no place of refuge in time of war, ordered that the " vill of St. Peter Port " should be enclosed by a good and strong wall, since his " vill of St. Peter Port. . . . is a place suitable to provide a refuge and defence in these warlike times." To pay for this he ordered " the good men of St. Peter Port " to levy, for one year, four deniers in the pound tournois upon all merchandise bought or sold within the island, half to be paid by the vendor, and half by the buyer. This first order was dated February 18, 1350.[97] On August 4 following, a second letter was issued which recited the first order and expressed official astonishment that it had not been obeyed. The excuse which had been put forward was that this levy was in the nature of a tallage, from which the Islanders were exempt by reason of the " aid-le-roy " which they paid. The letter reminded them, however, of the disaster which might fall upon them by reason of their neglect ; and also that although they might be privileged in the matter of tallage, they must give attention to their defence, especially as the proposed levy could not justly be regarded as a tallage since they, not the king, were to profit by it. This letter concluded by ordering the warden, John Mautravers, to see that the levy was collected by certain good men of St. Peter Port who should render account ; and it gave him power to imprison all who disobeyed.[98]

It matters not, for my argument, whether this wall was built or not— and I have still to be convinced that it was. It is sufficient that these letters show St. Peter Port to have been in 1350 so definite an entity, so much a " town", that the king should order the islanders to build a wall around it.

4. CONCLUSION

In this paper I have endeavoured to show what reasons there are for thinking that a town was growing up in St. Peter Port in the later Middle Ages. We found that the inhabitants enjoyed a very considerable degree of personal and tenurial freedom, together with certain guarantees against seignorial exploitation ; and that trade and industry were developed to a surprising extent in early fourteenth century Guernsey. These we considered to be conditions essential to urban development, in the absence of which it would have been useless to look for a " town " of St. Peter Port. In this we were, so I believe, following the orthodox doctrine of to-day, which is that municipal origins in medieval Europe can only be explained by reference to economic factors. Secure in this belief we sought and found traces of the town, a " sort of borough", which was coming to life in St. Peter Port. We found that it had become a centre of administration, that it had a port of some repute and a market, that there was considerable evidence of the concentration of population there, with possible traces of burgage tenure, and that the king had ordered the islanders to build a wall round it.

I submit that these are definitely urban characteristics, that taken together they justify our description of St. Peter Port as a " town " in the later Middle Ages.   But where are the municipal institutions which are characteristic of the fully developed medieval town—the court, the council, the self-administration, the community (by this time almost the " corporation ") of burgesses, the gild-merchant ?   There are no traces of them in medieval St. Peter Port.   Even the wall is doubtful.   " La ville du Moyen Age," concludes Professor Pirenne, " telle qu'elle apparaît dès le xii⁰ siècle, est une commune vivant, à l'abri d'une enceinte fortifiée, du commerce et de l'industrie et jouissant d'un droit, d'une administration et d'une jurisprudence d'exception qui font d'elle une personalité collective privilégiée."[99]   Medieval St. Peter Port could never pass that test.

Modern writers on municipal origins in the Middle Ages concentrate their attention upon the growth of urban institutions.   The first expression of Professor Pirenne's doctrines, for example, was entitled " L'origine des constitutions urbaines au moyen âge".[100]   In their final form the title became " Les villes du moyen âge " ; but the subject-matter remains the same in substance.   It has, of course, long been recognised that a town's size and prosperity bore no constant relation to the dignity and importance of its institutions ; and yet institutions have been the criteria by which towns have been selected for study and have subsequently been classified.   The reason for this is clear ; institutions leave records, and you cannot write history with no evidence at all.   Here in Guernsey, however, we seem to have the paradox of a town which achieved a considerable degree of size and importance without evolving any municipal institutions.

We may attempt to resolve this paradox by two lines of argument. The first has already received some attention in this paper.   It is this : that St. Peter Port found its municipal institutions in the institutions of the island, which, throughout the Middle Ages, were ever becoming more municipal in character.   St. Peter Port therefore had no need to evolve separate institutions for itself, especially as its interests were so closely identified with those of the island.   The second line of argument I cannot fully work out here for lack of knowledge.   Some day it may run something like this : Guernsey found herself economically associated with Normandy and Brittany as a predominantly agricultural and sea-faring community.   In Normandy no towns received spectacular privileges. Many of the communes that did come into being were the ephemeral creations of King John's constant need of money, and even the great city of Rouen only possessed powers of self-administration which were modest in comparison with those of much smaller towns in other districts.[101] In Brittany there were, indeed, very few towns of any consequence, but none of these developed any true municipal institutions during the Middle Ages.[102]   St. Malo, however, grew into a very flourishing port contemporaneously with St. Peter Port, in much the same way and for very similar reasons.   It may be simply a coincidence, but one worthy of remark, that the nearest approach to the formation of a " commune " that took place in Brittany during the Middle Ages occurred in St. Malo in 1308, that is at the same time as men were agitating for the removal of the Guernsey market into St. Peter Port's "sort of borough".[101] The conclusion of this argument then would be that St. Peter Port lay in a district where towns did not evolve important urban institutions, and seem to have got on very well without them. It was not always to a town's advantage, in the long run, to manage its own affairs ; and it would appear that neither St. Peter Port nor her immediate neighbours thought it worth while to try.

5.—SELECT DOCUMENTS.

RULES OBSERVED IN TRANSCRIPTION.

Whenever possible abbreviations have been extended. When it was found to be impossible to extend a suspension, the medieval mark of suspension has been indicated by an apostrophe, thus " Rotherhith'."

Whenever the manuscript was defective, but words not now legible could be supplied with reasonable certainty from the context or from other evidence, such words, or parts of words, are printed in italics. When there was no clue whatever to the missing words, I have endeavoured to indicate the length of the omission as nearly as possible.

All words or phrases added to the text as originally set down, whether they were clearly a later interpolation or whether they were inserted over a caret in the same hand and ink and probably at the same time as the rest of the document, have been printed in brackets, thus (   ).

All words or phrases cancelled in the manuscript, either by striking them through or by partial obliteration, are printed in square brackets, thus [   ].

No attempt has been made to reproduce medieval punctuation or use of capitals.

The principle on which these rules are based is that the manuscript should be reproduced as meticulously as is consistent with making a modern printed text readable.

---

(1) Second grant of quayage (1305), Patent Rolls, 33 Edward I, part II, m. 6. Cf. *Calendar of Patent Rolls*, 1301-1307, p. 392. For the petition to which this patent is the answer, see *Rotuli Parliamentorum*, I, 465. For the text of the first grant, see Berry, *History of Guernsey*, p. 162. Cf. *Calendar of Patent Rolls* 1272-1281, p. 82.

PRO BURGENSIBUS VILLE DE SANCTO PETROPORTU IN INSULA DE GERNES'.

Rex dilecto et fideli suo Ottoni de Grandisono custodi Insularum de Gereseye et Gerneseye vel ejus locum tenenti salutem. Monstraverunt nobis Ricardus Rose et ceteri burgenses nostri ville de Sancto Petroportu in dicta insula de Gerneseye quod, cum villa predicta per quosdam homines de potestate Regis Francie nuper inimicos et rebelles nostros combusta et destructa fuisset, et eciam quedam kaya, que juxta costeram maris ibidem pro salvacione ejusdem ville facta fuit, per eosdem inimicos dirruta sit

et confracta, ad nocumentum et grave dampnum ville predicte et bur-
gensium predictorum ceterorumque mercatorum cum navibus suis ap-
plicancium ad portum ville supradicte; et quia villa predicta de novo
construi aut eadem kaya absque magno auxilio reparari non potest, concedimus eisdem burgensibus de gracia nostra speciali quod de qualibet
nave de potestate predicta infra predictum portum applicante per quin-
quennium percipiant duodecim denarios parvorum turon*ensium*, et de
quolibet parvo vase maritimo ibidem similiter applicante per eundem
terminum percipiant sex denarios turon*ensium* predictorum, pro villa sua
predicta secundum ordinacionem vestram de novo construenda, et pro
predicta kaya reparanda et sustentanda ut predictum est.   In cujus
etc.   Teste rege apud West*monasterium*, primo die Novembris.   Per
peticionem de consilio.

---

(2)   The petition of John du Vivier, Ancient Petitions, No. 5691.
I am indebted to Mr. H. C. Johnson of the Public Record Office for the
text of this document, which was beyond my powers to transcribe.   Cf.
Société Jersiaise, *Ancient Petitions*, Jersey 1902, pp. 14-15.

A vous seignors justices nostre seignor le rey en lyle de Gernerrie
mostre Joh' du *Vivier* ke come il eust estee artorney de faire le suete de
un bref en la cort le rey por aucuns denonciacions contenus en iceu bref,
en quel bref estoet contenu ke lon enquisist de une plache ki fut establie
por le commun pueple a tenir le marche des la Nostre Dame en Setembre
juskes a la meitei de meis de mars ki siet a Nostre Dame de Chastel et
lautre meitei de lan a une plache ke est apellee Les Landes en chelle meismes
paroesse, le quel bref fut mis a execucion et par enqueste et par jugement
si comme le bref le voleit ensi selon la loi et la costume de la dite yle et
fu mis le dit Joh' tant comme artorney selon lenqueste en possecion, et
pues de volentei par aucuns de artorneis Sire Otes en fu mis hors, et tous
ceus ki i estoient asembles par cri fait par Guill' Tus serjant le rey sus
peinne de C livres et de enprisonement par plusors feis, et sus ceu lavant
dit Joh' tant comme artorney vint a la cort le rey en jugement et requist
par plusors feis ad atorneis sire Otes estre maintenu en la gaegne ke il
avoet faite et de la quelle il aveit estei pessiblement en possecion juskes a
tant ke par le cri en fut mis hors ou ke eus enquisissent par quelle reson
eus le avoent deseissi contre la ley et la costume, distrent qe par le bref
le rey avoet este fait le cri, et le dit Joh' dist ke il le vouleit veer en jugement ; le quel bref i fut aportei et leu et i *avoet* contenu ke le rey i estoet
decheu et ke ce estoet aperte deseritanche de luy, de la quelle chose le
rey avoet estei decheu par ceus ki enpetrirent le bref si comme il apart,
ker le dit Joh' se voliet . . .er de ce bref et requist comme artorney non
pas en renonchant a la gengne qe il avoet faite ke le bref fust mis a execucion et qe il fust enquis par bonnes gens dignes de foy se le rey i estoet
de reins decheu ne desente ke le marche fust des la meitie du meis de
*Setemb*re juskes a la meitei du meis de mars a Nostre Dame du Chastel
por la marche de h*iver* (?) et la remenant de lan en une plache ki est apelle
Les Landes en la dite paro*esse ke tout* (?) par mei lan es landes, et de ceu
enquist sire Joh' de Dittune en la presence des jures le rey par xii leaus
prodhommes de chescune paroesse par sei et puis *cia* (?) par les viii paroisses

ke ce estoet plus le prou le rey ke il fut le terrage de la meitie de lan a Nostre Dame du Chastel, si comme est avant dit, ke tout par mei lan es Landes, por la quelle chose le dit Joh' comme attornei requit a vos seignors justices estre maintenu en la gaengne ke il a faite et si comme le prou le rey i est trove par les meismes *dit* (?) viii paroesses quer a la gregner et a la plus sein*eure* partie est ac*cord*e (?) et si comme *primerment* (?) fut resgardei.

---

(3) Extract from Assize Roll No. 1161 (2 Edward II) m. 4 d. (Cf. Société Jersiaise, *Rolls of the Assizes* . . . . 1309, pp. 103-106, and also Société Jersiaise, *Lettres Closes*, partie Ire , p. 81, *Calendar of Close Rolls*, 1307-1313, p. 34).

ADHUC DE COMMUNIBUS PLACITIS

*De p*eticione Johannis de Vivariis monstrantis se secutum fuisse quoddam breve de sugges*tione di*rectum custodi insularum hic, quod, inquisita veritate de mercato hujus insule, illud *teneret* in locis et forma ab antiquo debitis et consuetis, videlicet a medio mense Septembris *usque ad* medium mensem Marcii apud Sanctam Mariam de Castro, et exinde per totum annum *apud Les* Laundes. Et viso similiter alio brevi quod dominus rex nunc misit hic in hec *verba* : *E*dwardus dei gracia Rex Anglie, Dominus Hibernie et Dux Aquitanie dilecto et fideli suo Ottoni de *Grandi*sono custodi suo insule de Jerneseye salutem. Quia intelleximus quod quoddam *mercatum* quod in feod*q* nostro in quodam loco qui vocatur Les Laundes in insula predicta *teneri c*onsuevit ab eodem loco per quosdam de eadem insula est subtractum et ad feodum *alterius* quam nostri translatum in nostri prejudicium et exhereditacionis periculum manifestum; vobis mandamus *quod, si* ita est, tunc mercatum illud in dicto loco de Les Laundes tenendum publice proclamari *faciatis* prout ibidem teneri debet et teneri consuevit, non permittentes mercatum illud alibi teneri *quam in* dicto loco de Les Laundes, si hoc ad comodum nostrum fore videritis faciendum. Teste me *ipso* apud West*mo*nasterium, v die Maii, anno regni nostri primo. Intellectoque quod octo parochiate hujus insule *sunt* totaliter de parte predicti Johannis, et due parochiate residue ex adversa parte ; perpensoque quod unus . . . . primi brevis est de feodo abbatis de Monte Sancti Michaelis totaliter ; et habitis et auditis quampluribus *r*acionibus inter eos : tamdem concordatum est utrimque per omnes etc., quod de qualibet parochia eli*gantur d*uo homines, vel saltim unus de minoribus parochiis, qui cum justiciariis hic ordinent de . . . . o prout viderint pro domino Rege et populo hujus Insule competencius et melius *expedire*, et quod ordinacio illa firma sit et stabilis imperpetuum. Et sic electis de parochia Sancti Petri *Portus*, Guillelmo Gros, Ricardo Gosce ; de parochia de Bellosa, Jordano Choffin et Jordano Discart ; *de parochia* de Foresta, Guillelmo le Jeovene et Guillelmo Roger ; de parochia Sancti Petri de Bosco, ... ; de parochia de Torteval, Petro Chivin*; de parochia Sancti Salvatoris, Michaele Lestur,

---

* It is quite impossible to determine what this name should be. This interpretation of the six minims is purely conjectural.

.... Blaunche ; de parochia de Castro, Petro Nicole, Ricardo Harphat ; de parochia de *Valo*, Ricardo de la Mare ; de parochia Sancti Sampsonis, Guillelmo de la Rivere, Baudewyn Davy ; *de* parochia Sancti Andree, Roberto Renald, Ricardo le Cok' ; et auditis racionibus singulorum ; comperto*que quod* villa domini regis de Sancti Petri Portu est quasi burggum, et omnes alie parochie sunt ville cam*pe*stres non mansionate contigue sed separatim in campis ; et eciam tam de forinsecis quam *intr*insecis major accessus hominum multipliciter est apud Sancti Petri Portum quam in omnibus aliis *parochiis* insule *predicte* ; *et quod* mercatum prius fuerat longe a villa Sancti Petri Portus licet per diem Sabbati................ *et plura* alia venalia venerunt ad predictam villam Sancti Petri die dominica, et ibi durante serv*icio consueverunt ten*ere mercatum, in magnum scandalum Christianitatis etc ; concordatum est sine c*ontradiccione quac*unque quod mercatum integre teneatur de cetero ad predictam villam Sancti Petri Port*us.*............... Jovis, incipiente mercato singulis diebus Jovis ad ortum solis, et mutatur dies *solummodo per* assensum omnium ; et ....ius conceditur ne mercatum domini regis de Jereseye, quod est .... Et preceptum est ballivo et vicecomiti quod ista pupplice et sollempniter proclamari *faciant* die Sabbati in vigilia Sancti Bartholomei in pleno mercato, et s*imiliter* .... Bartholomei ad singulas ecclesias. Et tam ad ecclesias quam in predicto .... singulis et injungi, quod cum bladis, bestiis et aliis rebus suis v............... .... predictis diebus Jovis in posterum ad predictam villam Sancti Petri, ea non alibi .... portantes sub forisfactura bonorum eorumdem. Quod si quis facere presumpserit .... statim bona illa capiant ad opus domini regis totaliter forisfacta. Et exinde .... in assisis, scilicet tam de bonis sic forisfactis que ceperunt, quam de illis que per necgligenciam suam dimiserint non percepta. Faciant eciam sollempniter inhiberi sub consimili forisfactura quod mercatum de cetero non teneatur per diem dominicum nisi tantummodo de pane, carne, pisce, vino vel cervisia, sed durante magna missa in ecclesia nichil vendatur sub gravi forisfactura versus dominum regem, unde transgressores de quindena in quindenam ad curiam coram ballivo graviter puniantur. Et ballivus coram justiciariis graviter puniatur si in premissis necgligens fuerit vel remissus. Preceptum est eciam predicto ballivo quod per nullum breve qualitercumque per quempiam impetratum de suggestione qualicumque de predicto mercato nichil mutet vel minuat de predictis ordinacione et preceptis nisi breve illud de predictis concessione, concordia et ordinacione expressam fecerit mencionem. Et assignatur ad predictum mercatum talis locus, videlicet quedam placea continens ii virgatas terre et dimidiam a diu jacens ut pastura inculta, cujus unum capud versus Aquilon' abbutat super fontem qui vocatur La Fontaine Cache Vassal', et aliud capud abbutat super Le Vaal Wydecok', et fere quasi in medio transit via regalis. Et fuit illa placea divisa inter plures ; ita quod Robertus Floires, Thomas de Bello Campo habuerunt inde circiter i virgatam et quartam partem unius virgate terre, Nicholaus de Bosco duas partes unius virgate terre, Willelmus le Esmitet terciam partem unius virgate terre et Galfridus des Maners quartam partem unius virgate terre. Et ipsi omnes terram illam concedunt domino regi pro precio racionabili inde reddendo sibi et heredibus (suis) imperpetuum, **juxta** taxacionem fide dignorum etc. Et appreciatur ad v bussellos frumenti per annum, videlicet quelibet virgata ad ii bussellos frumenti et redditus ille eis assignatur solvendus de cetero etc., scilicet post istum annum.

---

(4) First order to enclose the town. Patent Rolls, 24 Edward III, part I, m. 28 r. Cf. *Calendar of Patent Rolls*, 1348-1350, p. 478.

DE VILLA DE PORTU SANCTI PETRI IN INSULA DE GERNESEYE INCLUDENDA

Rex dilectis et fidelibus suis probis hominibus de Portu Sancti Petri in insula de Gerneseye, salutem. Attendentes Castrum de Chirburgh' in insula predicta in quo populus ejusdem insule tempore guerre habere solebant suum refugium et succursum fore dirrutum nec posse ad nostrum commodum reparari prout plenius informamur : ac volentes proinde salvacioni ipsius populi nostri ac bonorum et catallorum suorum cum guerrina tempora imineant providere, de assensu consilii nostri ut dictam villam nostram de Portu Sancti Petri bono muro et forti includere et murum illum kernellare valeatis licenciam duximus concedendam, et in auxilium sumptuum vestrorum in hac parte apponendorum quandam custumam per unum annum duraturam, dicto anno primo die Aprilis proximo futuro incipiente, percipiendam per manus illorum quos ad hoc deputaveritis concedimus per presentes ; videlicet de qualibet librata mercandisarum infra dictam insulam venditarum et emptarum in moneta turon*ensi*, quatuor turon*enses* et de qualibet dimidia librata hujusmodi mercandisarum emptarum et venditarum duos turonen*ses*, de quibuslibet eciam centum* solidatis mercandisarum in forma predicta venditarum unum turonens*em*, cujusquidem custume unam medietatem venditor et aliam emptor solvat. Et ideo vobis mandamus quod a predicto primo die usque ad finem anni proximo sequentis custumam predictam in forma predicta percipiatis et in muragio et kernellagio ville predicte apponatis ex causa antedicta. Completo autem anno predicto custuma predicta penitus cesset nec ulterius capiatur. In cujus etc. Teste rege apud Westm*onasterium*, xviii die Februarii. Per ipsum regem et consilium.

---

(5) Second order to enclose the town. Patent Rolls, 24 Edward III, part II, m. 14 r. Cf. *Calendar of Patent Rolls*, 1348-1350, p. 559.

DE CUSTUMA IN INSULA DE GERNESEYE COLLIGENDA PRO CLAUSURA VILLE SANCTI PETRI.

Rex dilecto et fideli suo Johanni Mautravers custodi insularum suarum de Gereseye, Gernereye, Serk' et Aureneye, salutem. Cum nuper attendentes Castrum de Chirburgh' in dicta insula de Gernereye in quo populus ejusdem Insule tempore guerre suum refugium et succursum habere solebant fuisse dirutum, de assensu consilii nostri ordinaverimus

---

* Sic. Compare the second writ (no. 5).

quod villa nostra de Portu Sancti Petri, que est locus aptus dicto populo nostro pro hujusmodi refugio habendo pro defensione ejusdem populi et salvacione bonorum suorum hiis guerrarum temporibus, muro forti includeretur ; et concesserimus probis hominibus dicte ville de Portu Sancti Petri in auxilium sumptuum circa clausuram ejusdem ville apponendorum quandam custumam per unum annum duraturam percipiendam, videlicet de qualibet librata mercandisarum infra dictam insulam venditarum et emptarum in moneta turon*ensi,* quatuor denarios turon*ensium,* de qualibet dimidia librata hujusmodi mercandisarum emptarum et venditarum duos denarios turon*ensium,* et de quibuslibet quinque solidatis mercandisarum ipsarum unum denarium turon*ensium,* cujus quidem custume unam medietatem venditor et alteram medietatem emptor solvat ; et jam intelleximus quod quidam de dicta insula nobis et mandatis nostris rebelles ordinacionem et concessionem (nostras) predictas enervare machinantes, asserentesque dictam custumam esse quoddam tallagium super ipsos assessum, et ipsos et alios homines ejusdem insule de hujusmodi custumis et omnibus aliis tallagiis pro una certa pecunie summa vocata auxilio regis quam ipsi annuatim solvant quietos esse debere, ad dictam custumam solvendam assentire omnino denegant et eam penitus solvere recusant : Nos, advertentes gravia pericula que per rebellionem hujusmodi subditorum nostrorum tam nobis quam dictis insulis ac fidelibus nostris in eisdem commorantibus, pro quorum tuicione et defensione contra hostium nostrorum invasiones viis et modis quibus poterimus providere et disponere tenemur, possent iminere, et quod dicti homines pro defensione et salvacione sua propria se et sua maxime hiis guerrerum temporibus, licet in forma predicta privilegiati essent de quo nobis non constat exponere, teneantur, ac volentes custumam predictam, que tallagium dici non potest ex quo aliquid inde ad usum nostrum non percipitur, pro clausura ville predicte, que necessariam salvacionem et defensionem fidelium nostrorum dicte insule de Gernerey conceruit, colligi et levari juxta formam ordinacionis et concessionis nostrarum predictarum, quibuscumque privilegiis seu immunitatibus per hujusmodi rebelles pretensis non obstantibus, vobis committimus et mandavimus in fide et ligeancia quibus nobis tenemini firmiter injungentes quod dictam custumam de omnibus et singulis hujusmodi mercandisas in dicta insula vendentibus et ementibus, nulli in hac parte parcendo, a festo Sancti Bartholomei proximo futuro per unum annum proximo sequentem plenarie completum per aliquos probos homines ville predicte, quos ad compotum de exitibus custume predicte reddendum teneri voluimus, colligi et levari et in clausura ville predicte cum omni celeritate apponi, et omnes illos quos levacionem et colleccionem custume predicte impedientes seu contradicentes vel alias in hac parte rebelles inveneritis sine dilacione capi et in prisona castri predicti salvo et secure custodiri faciatis, quousque de eorum punicione aliter duxerimus ordinandum. Et hoc sicut de vobis confidimus et sub incumbenti periculo nullatenus omittatis. In cujus etc. Teste rege apud Rotherhith', quarto die Augusti. Per ipsum regem et consilium.

6.—NOTES.

1. An especially interesting picture, showing the Town and the Roadstead in the late seventeenth century has recently been reproduced by La Société Guernesiaise, *Transactions*, XI, p. 277.

2. Société Jersiaise, *Cartulaire des Iles Normandes*, Jersey 1924, p. 379-380. Round, *Calendar of Documents preserved in France*, H.M. Stationery Office, 1899, no. 1165.

3. *Approbation des Lois, Coutumes, et Usages de L'Ile de Guernesey*, Guernsey 1897, p. 14-15. Warburton, *Treatise on the History, Laws and Customs of the Island of Guernsey*, Guernsey 1822, p. 88. This mysterious work is held in high repute by Guernsey lawyers.

4. E.g. Assize Roll, 17 Edw. II (no. 1165), m. 11 r., m. 14 r. All documents in manuscript to which reference is made in this paper are to be found in the Public Record Office, London, unless the contrary is explicitly stated.

5. Caen, 1870-1885, 4 vols.

6. Société Jersiaise, *Bulletin*, XI, pp. 1-91. (1928.)

7. The distinction between a board of judgment-finders, which would be an apt description of the Channel Island jurats in the Middle Ages, and a town council is concisely expressed in C. Stephenson, *Borough and Town*, Mediaeval Academy of America, Cambridge, Mass., 1933, pp. 36-37.

8. Guernsey Society of Natural Science and Local Research, *Transactions*, V, pp. 333 ff.

9. In this instance " villa " very probably does mean " town ", or else has no very precise significance. My point is that there is no justification for assuming such a definite meaning in view of the difficulties which the word presents. Cf. L. Delisle, *Etudes sur . . . la Classe Agricole . . . en Normandie au Moyen Age*, Evreux 1851, p. 148.—" Le mot ' villa ' est bien embarrassant à traduire. Il désigne évidemment que la même territoire que la paroisse, mais il s'applique aux rapports civils et féodaux par opposition aux rapports religieux." In another work, he says : " Dans la langue du moyen âge surtout quand on s'arrête au douzième siècle, le mot ' ville ' réveille une idée différente de celle que nous lui attachons aujourd'hui : il était alors l'équivalent de manoir ou village. Ce que nous appelons ' ville ' était connu sous le nom de ' cité ' ou de ' château ', suivant que c'était ou non la résidence d'un évêque." — *Des Revenues publics en Normandie au douzième siècle*, Bibliothèque de L'Ecole des Chartes, III, i, p. 403. Cf. R. Génestal, *La Tenure en Bourgage*, Paris 1900, p. 210. — " Quant au mot ' villa ', de son acceptation romaine de domaine rural, qu'il conserve encore parfois au xiiie siècle, il en est arrivé à désigner généralement un village, une agglomération d'habitants qui se livrent à la culture de la terre environnante. C'est là son sens normal. Quelquefois cependant il peut se traduire par le mot français qui en est tiré : ' ville '." Examples of the use of this word in all these senses may be found in contemporary documents relating to the Channel Islands : e.g. " In parochia Sancti Petri de Bosco, per manus prepositi domini Regis in eadem villa " : Société Jersiaise, *Rolls of the Assizes . . .* 1309. Jersey, 1903, p. 41. " Ipse (sc. Rector hujus ville) et omnes parochiani qui cum eo fuerunt . . ." — Ibid., p. 277. " In parrochia Sancti Michaelis de Wallia in Insula de Gernerre in villa Baudu inter domum Jaqueline ex parte una et rivum maresci de Wallia ex altera." — Société Jersiaise, *Cartulaire*, p. 238.

10. C. Le Quesne, *A Constitutional History of Jersey*, London 1856. J. Havet, *Les Cours Royales des Iles Normandes*, Paris 1878, reprinted from Bibliothèque de L'Ecole des Chartes, tomes XXXVIII, XXXIX ; and *Série Chronologique des Gardiens et Seigneurs des Iles Normandes*, Paris 1876, reprinted from Bibliothèque de L'Ecole des Chartes, XXXVII.

11. The following account of the administration and customs of Guernsey is based upon a large number of documents in addition to the works cited above. Of these documents, the most important are :
(i) The Inquest of 1248, Chancery Inquisitions Miscellaneous, File 2, 22. This has been printed in *The Second Report of the Commissioners appointed to enquire into the state of the Criminal Law in the Channel Islands, Guernsey*, Parliamentary Papers, 1848, pp. 291-293 ; in the *Calendar of Inquisitions Miscellaneous*, H.M. Stationery Office, 1916, I, pp. 15-18. It has been re-printed from these two printed texts by Sir Havilland de Sausmarez, *The Extentes of Guernsey*, Guernsey 1934, pp. 23-28. Compare the similar inquest taken in the previous year, which is printed in *Close Rolls*, H.M. Stationery Office, 1902, 1242-1247, pp. 546-547, and in Société Jersiaise, *Lettres Closes*, Jersey 1891, partie Ire, pp. 44-45.
(ii) The Extent of 1331. Only a fragment of what may have been the original of this document is known to exist, Various Accounts, Exchequer, bundle 89, no. 14. There are, however, several copies extant of a translation into French which was made towards the end of the fifteenth century. A Latin copy has been printed by Sir Havilland de Sausmarez, op. cit., pp. 47-126. This edition, however, gives no evidence of any attempt to ascertain the relation between this copy, the fragment of the "original", and the French texts.
(iii) "Les Franchises" (Temp. Edward I). Printed in Dupont, op. cit., II, pp. 213-215; in Havet, *Les Cours Royales*, pp. 183-186; in Société Jersiaise, *Cartulaire*, pp. 224-226; and in Sir Havilland de Sausmarez, op. cit., pp. 38-40.
(iv) Statements made by the Islanders in answer to pleas *de quo warranto*, viz., (1) Assize Roll, 2 Edw. II (no. 1160), m. 4 r., printed in Société Jersiaise, *Rolls of the Assizes* . . . 1309. pp. 29-34; (2) Assize Roll, 13 Edw. 11 (no 1163), m. 2; (3) Assize Roll, 17 Edw. II (no. 1165), mm. 7, 8, which is printed in the *Second Report*, pp. 295-299; (4) Assize Roll, 5 Edw. III (no. 1167), m. 8 d.
(v) The petition of 1333, Coram Rege Roll, 5 Edw. III, Michaelmas, m. 183, and the "Articles" appended to this petition, ibid. ; both printed in Havet, *Les Cours Royales*, pp. 228-233.
(vi) The Particulars of the Account of John de Roches, 3 Edward III, Various Accounts, Exchequer, bundle 89, no. 11, and the enrolled accounts of the same warden, Pipe Roll, 4 Edward III, mm. 47, 48.

12. "Les Franchises"; see preceding note.

13. The clearest proof of this is contained in a document which appears to be the original return of the jury of presentment of St. Martin's parish, Guernsey, in 1309 : "Respondent quod dominus rex habet campartum bladorum, melagia, avenam, brosagium, firmas denariorum, poulagia, gallinar' de hospitibus regis; pasnagium porcorum de hospitibus regis, pro quolibet porco I denarium."—Chancery Miscellanea, bundle 10, no. 4. These obligations correspond in detail to those of "the king's tenants" in the Extents, etc.

14. Société Jersiaise, *Cartulaire*, pp. 379-380, *Rolls of the Assizes* . . . 1309, pp. 111-114.

15. Assize Roll 17 Edw. II (no. 1165), m. 4 r.

16. I have made use of the following works in preparing this comparison : (1) General works : Flach, *Les origines de l'ancienne France*, Paris 1886-, II ; Paul Viollet, *Les communes françaises au Moyen Age*, Académie des Inscriptions et Belles Lettres, Mémoires de l'Institut, XXXVI, ii, pp. 365-366; M. Bloch, *Les Caractères originaux de l'histoire rurale française*, Oslo 1931, pp. 5-17; Stephenson, *Borough and Town*, pp. 29-34. (2) Special works : M. Prou, *Les coutumes de Lorris et leur propagation aux xiie et xiie siècles*, Nouvelle Revue historique de droit français et étranger, VIII ; E. Bonvalot, *Le tiers état d'après la charte de Beaumont*, Paris 1884 ; M. Bateson, *The Laws of Breteuil*, English Historical Review, XV, XVI. (3) On the "hospites"; H. Sée, *Les classes rurales et le régime domanial en France au Moyen Age*,

Paris 1901, pp. 212-238; C. Stephenson, *The Origin and Nature of the Taille*, Revue Belge de philologie et d'histoire, V, pp. 831 ff. (4) A somewhat different type of enfranchised village seems to have been common in Normandy. Such villages have been described by L. Delisle, *Etudes sur . . . la classe agricole*, pp. 121-171.

17. A very apt example is Etampes as described by M. Prou, *Une ville-marché au xiie siècle, Mélanges . . . Pirenne*, Brussels 1926, pp. 379-389.

18. To obtain a general idea of the nature and mechanism of the " Gascon wine trade ", I have made use of the following works : F. Sargent, *The Wine Trade with Gascony*, in *Finance and trade under Edward III*, edited by G. Unwin, Manchester 1918 ; F. Michel, *Histoire du commerce et de la navigation à Bordeaux* Bordeaux 1867-70 ; T. Malvezin, *Histoire du commerce de Bordeaux*, Bordeaux 1892 ; C. Jullian, *Histoire de Bordeaux*, Bordeaux 1895 ; J. Balasque et E. Dulaurens, *Etudes historiques sur la ville de Bayonne*, Bayonne 1862-75. Details concerning shipping tracks and the size and equipment of ships engaged in this trade have been worked out by Williams, op. cit.

19. Williams, op. cit., pp. 53-54.

20. Giry, *Etablissements de Rouen*, Paris 1885, II, pp. vii, 61.

21. Williams, op. cit., pp. 54-55.

22. Société Jersiaise, Rolls of the Assizes . . . 1309, pp. 49-53, 146, 190.

23. V^r. L. de Gruchy, *L'Ancienne Coutume de Normandie*, Jersey 1881, pp. 49-51 ; Société Jersiaise, *Rolls of the Assizes . . .* 1309, pp. 22-23 and passim ; Various Accounts, Exchequer, bundle 89, no. 11.

24. *Calendar of Patent Rolls*, H.M. Stationery Office 1893 -, 1321-1324, pp. 310, 371.

25. *Close Rolls*, 1234-1237, p. 513 (December 1236).

26. Assize Roll, 5 Edw. III (no. 1166), m. 7 r.

27. Ibidem.

28. Ibid., m. 6 r. There are many other examples in this roll.

29. Assize Roll, 17 Edw. II (no. 1165), m. 20 d.

30. Assize Roll, 5 Edw. III (no. 1166), mm. 3 r., 4 r., 6 r., 7 r ; Assize Roll, 32 Edw. I (no. 1159), m. 2 d.

31. *Rotuli Litterarum Clausarum*, Record Commission 1833-1834, II, pp. 48 129, 163.

32. F. Michel and C. Bémont, *Rôles Gascons*, Paris 1885-1906, III, nos. 3424, 3440.

33. Various Accounts, Exchequer, bundle 89, no. 11 ; Pipe Roll, 4 Edw. III, mm. 47, 48. 4 livres tournois " strong money " =1 pound sterling. 8 livres tournois " weak money " =1 pound sterling.

34. Sir Havilland de Sausmarez, *The Extentes of Guernsey*, pp. 69-70.

35. Société Jersiaise, *Extente de l'Ile de Jersey . . .* 1331, Jersey 1876, p. 16.

36. *Rotuli Litterarum Clausarum*, II, p. 184.

37. Assize Roll, 27 Edw. I (no. 1157), m. I d.

38. *Calendar of Close Rolls* H.M. Stationery Office 1892-, 1327-1330, p. 318,

39. *Calendar of Patent Rolls*, 1334-1338, pp. 358-9.

40. *Calendar of Close Rolls*, 1343-1346, p. 116.

41. *Calendar of Close Rolls*, 1307-1313, pp. 112, 342. Cf. a letter printed in C. L. Kingsford, *Sir Otho de Grandison*, Transactions of the Royal Historical Society, 3rd series, III, p. 192.

42. *Calendar of Close Rolls*, 1333-1337, p. 513.

43. *Calendar of Patent Rolls*, 1334-1338, p. 416.

44. Ibid., 1343-1345, p. 180.

45. *Rotuli Parliamentorum*, Record Commission 1832, 1V, p. 53.

46. N.S.B. Gras., *The Early English Customs System*, Cambridge (Mass.) 1918, pp. 248, 362.

47. Assize Roll, 27 Edw. I (no. 1157), m. 7 r.

48. E. de Fréville, *Mémoire sur le commerce maritime de Rouen*, Rouen 1857, II, pp. 25-79 (c. xvi).

49. Ibid., pp. 294, 305.

50. E.g. *Calendar of Patent Rolls*, 1232-1247, pp. 217, 359.

51 *Close Rolls*, 1231-1234, p. 394.

52. *Calendar of Patent Rolls*, 1313-1317, pp. 459, 622, 624.

53. Ibid., 1324-1327, pp. 108, 318.

54. Sir Havilland de Sausmarez, *The Extentes of Guernsey*, pp. 28, 70. Other versions of the tariff are given in Assize Roll, 5 Edw. III (no. 1166), m. I d , m. 6 r., and in Various Accounts, Exchequer, bundle 89, no. 11.

55. E.g. The éperqueries of the Channel Islands were always farmed together, and the farm is accounted for in the Guernsey accounts. Edward I's regulations for the fisheries were issued in the form of a charter " to the community of Guernsey fishermen "—Assize Roll, 13 Edw. II (no. 1163), m. 7 r., Ancient Deeds, Series D, no. 389. There is a full description of the éperqueries in the Guernsey Extent of 1331 (Sir Havilland de Sausmarez, op. cit., p. 69) but they are not mentioned in the corresponding Jersey extent, Société Jersiaise, *Extente de l'Ile de Jersey*. It seems clear that the account in the Guernsey extent was intended to cover the archipelago.

56. Cf. preceding note.

57. There is abundant material concerning the éperqueries and other institutions connected with the fisheries. The most important documents are : Various Accounts, Exchequer, bundle 89, no. 11; the charter of the community of Guernsey fishermen noted above; references in the Extent of 1331 (Sir Havilland de Sausmarez, op. cit., p. 69), and in the Inquest of 1248 (ibid., pp. 24-28, etc.). On the seignorial éperqueries in general, the most interesting reference is to be found in a petition of certain Jersey seigneurs, c. 1310 — Chancery Miscellanea, bundle 10, no. 7. References to the éperqueries of Fief St. Michel in Guernsey will be found in Société Jersiaise, *Rolls of the Assizes* . . . 1309, pp. 39 ff., *Cartulaire*, pp. 190, 192-3, 222, 234, 426-7; to those of the Abbot of Blanchelande in the same Island, in Société Jersiaise, *Rolls of the Assizes* . . . 1309, p. 14-15, *Cartulaire*, pp. 364-372; to those of the Seigneur of Sauzmarez, in Société Jersiaise, *Rolls of the Assizes* . . . 1309, pp. 34-8, Ancient Correspondence, LV, 4.

58   T. Stapleton, *Magni Rotuli Scaccarii Normanniae*, London 1840-1844, I, p. 225, II, p. 390. Cf *Rotuli Chartarum*, Record Commission 1837, p. 17; J. Balasque et E. Dulaurens, *Etudes historiques sur la ville de Bayonne*, I, pp. 450-451.

59. *Calendar of Patent Rolls*, 1247-1258, p. 27.

60. Ibid, p. 245. F. Michel et C. Bémont, *Rôles Gascons*, I, no. 2113.

61. *Calendar of Patent Rolls*, 1272-1281, p. 283, 1281-1292, pp. 393, 486.

62. Société Jersiaise, *Cartulaire*, pp. 190, 234, 426.

63. Pipe Roll, 4 Edw. III, m. 47.

64. *Rotuli de oblatis et finibus*, Record Commission 1835, p. 191.

65. J. Balasque et E. Dulaurens, *Etudes historiques sur la ville de Bayonne*, II, p. 447. H. Bourde de la Rogerie, *Les fondations de villes et de bourgs en Bretagne du xie au xiiie siècles*, Mémoires de la Société d'histoire et d'archéologie de Bretagne, IX, p. 100. (1928.)

66. J. Havet, *Série Chronologique des gardiens et seigneurs*, passim; H. Marett Godfray, *Notes et Additions a ' la Série chronologique des gardiens et seigneurs '*, Société Jersiaise, Bulletin, II, pp. 30 ff. F. Michel & C. Bémont, *Roles Gascons*, I, supplément, intro., III, intro.

67. Assize Roll, 5 Edw. III (no. 1166), mm. 3 r., 3 d., 7 r.; Assize Roll, 2 Edw. II (no. 1161), m. 2 d. (Cf. Société Jersiaise, *Rolls of the Assizes . . . 1309*, pp. 100-101); Société Jersiaise, *Cartulaire*, pp. 237, 414-415.

68. Société Jersiaise, *Rolls of the Assizes . . . 1309*, p. 158.

69. *Calendar of Patent Rolls*, 1281-1292, p. 362.

70. Sir Havilland de Sausmarez, *The Extentes of Guernsey*, p. 74 (cf. p. 132). Cf. C. Gross, Select Cases in the Law Merchant, Seldon Society, London 1908, especially p. xx.

71. Assize Roll, 5 Edw. III (no. 1167), m. 2 d. Another example is to be found in a writ directing the warden of the Islands to take certain action with respect to arrested ships " prout de jure et secundum legem mercatorum ", Ancient Correspondence, XXXIV, 67.

72. On Castle Cornet see T. W. M. de Guérin, *The Early History and First Siege of Castle Cornet*, Guernsey Society of Natural Science and Local Research, Transactions, IV, pp. 337 ff., and the same writer's *The English Garrison of Guernsey from Early Times*, Ibid., V, pp. 66 ff. Copious references to build ings, repairs, etc., will be found in the Close and Patent Rolls passim, the *Calendar of Liberate Rolls*, H.M. Stationery Office, 1917-, I, p. 7 (this is the earliest known reference to the king's castle in Guernsey), II, pp. 36, 104, 189, 238-9; in the Pipe Rolls of 10 Henry III, m. 3 d.; 26 Henry III (Ed. H. L. Cannon, *The Great Roll of the Pipe*, 26 *Henry III*, New Haven 1918, pp. 60-61); 34 Henry III, m. 6 r.; 4 Edward III, mm. 47, 48; 5 Edward III, m. 50; 15 Edward III, m. 44; 20 Edward III, mm. 52, 55; 21 Edward III, m. 44. There are also several isolated documents. On the whole, the medieval history of the king's castles in Guernsey and Jersey must be almost as well documented as any.
     That Castle Cornet was begun in John's reign seems to be shown by (1) the negative evidence that no reference to any castles in the islands in the twelfth century has survived, (2) the positive statement of the jurors in 1248, " sed tempore illo castella non fuerunt in insulis " apparently in reference to the " time " before John's reign, and (3) the copious references to " castle works " in progress during the thirteenth century.

73. E.g. Assize Roll, 13 Edw. II (no. 1163), m. 3 r., " Walterus le Clerk' constabularius castri de villa Sancti Petri in Portu ".

74. Pipe Roll, 4 Edw. III, m. 47.

75. Although, after reading a number of thirteenth and early fourteenth century documents, it is hard to resist the impression that this was so, it is equally difficult to adduce any evidence which would definitely prove it. I can only suggest, that, since (1) the justices itinerant came to Guernsey first, (2) in the wardens' accounts any item which concerns all the islands is always entered under the Guernsey heading, (3) the expenses of the warden's journeys from one island to another are always entered in the Guernsey account, and give the impression that the warden and his staff were " going " to Jersey, etc., or " coming back " to Guernsey (e.g. Various Accounts, Exchequer, bundle 89, no. 11), and finally (4) Castle Cornet was clearly the better fitted geographically and strategically to be the warden's headquarters, and in fact usually had a larger garrison than Gorey Castle, there is a presumption in favour of my statement, on which, however, I do not propose to insist, that Castle Cornet was probably the centre of the administration of the Channel Islands in the Middle Ages.

76. E.g. Société Jersiaise, *Cartulaire*, p. 27. Assize Roll, 5 Edw. III (no. 1167), m. 4 d., m. 15 r. In Jersey an Assize was held at La Hougue in 1269 (*Cartulaire*, pp. 130-131), an inquisition was held in Gorey Castle in 1330 (Various Accounts, Exchequer, bundle 89, no. 16), the Assizes of 1331 were held at Longueville (Assize Rolls, 5 Edw. III, nos. 1166, 1167).

77. In 1299, " apud Portum Sancti Petri " (Assize Roll, 27 Edw. I, no. 1157, m. I r.); in 1304 ' apud Gerner ' " (Assize Roll, 32 Edw. I, no. 1159, m. I r.); in 1309, " in Grangia domini regis in villa Sancti Petri " (Société Jersiaise, *Rolls of the Assizes* . . . 1309, p. 95); in 1320, " apud villam Sancti Petri in Portu " (Assize Roll, 13 Edw. 11, no. 1163, m. 8 r.); in 1323, " in manerio domini Regis in Portu Sancti Petri " (Assize Roll, 17 Edw. 11, no. 1165, m. 3 r.); in 1331, " in villa Sancti Petri de Portu " (Assize Roll, 5 Edw. III, no. 1167, m. 2 r.).

78. Sir Havilland de Sausmarez, *The Extentes of Guernsey*, p. 74. Cf. Various Accounts, Exchequer, bundle 89, no. 11.

79. Cf. E. T. Nicolle : *The Town of St. Helier*, Jersey N.D. (1931), p. 18.

80. Société Jersiaise, *Cartulaire*, p. 379. Round, *Calendar of documents preserved in France*, no. 1165.

81. *Calendar of Patent Rolls*, 1272-1281, p. 82. The text of this writ is printed in W. Berry, *History of Guernsey*, London 1815, p. 162.

82. *Rotuli Parliamentorum*, 1, 465.

83. *Calendar of Patent Rolls*, 1301-1307, p. 392. Cf. section 5 of this paper. There is an interesting direction, reported in the Eyre Roll of 1309, that the proceeds of a deodand should be devoted to the repair of this quay; Société Jersiaise, *Rolls of the Assizes* . . . 1309, p. 167 : " Judicium infortunium. Precii porci . . . et dantur in elemosinam ad parandam cayam super mare. '

84. Various Accounts, Exchequer, bundle 89, no. 11.

85. Ancient Correspondence, XX, 97.

86. Sir Havilland de Sausmarez, *The Extentes of Guernsey*, p. 28. Calendar of Close Rolls, 1307–1313, pp. 34-5. Cf. Société Jersiaise, *Lettres Closes*, partie 1re, p. 81.

87. *Close Rolls*, 1242-1247, p. 36. F. Michel et C. Bémont, *Rôles Gascons*, I, no. 1468.

88. See section 5, no. 2; *Calendar of Close Rolls*, 1307-1313, p. 34.

89. See section 5, no. 3.

90. For what follows, see Sir Havilland de Sausmarez, *The Extentes of Guernsey*, pp. 57 ff. In one or two instances I have also used two French copies in the Guernsey Greffe, the "Official Copy" dated 1818 and another copy dated 1579, where they seemed to present fewer difficulties than the printed text. I have made no attempt to produce a critical text; the following notions of "burgage tenure" in St. Peter Port must therefore be regarded purely as a hypothesis. The reference number of the "Original fragment" is Various Accounts, Exchequer, bundle 89, no. 14.

91. Assize Roll, 2 Edw. II (no. 1161), m. 11 d. Cf. Société Jersiaise, *Rolls of the Assizes . . . 1309*, pp. 121-2.

92. Cf. note 14.

93. Société Jersiaise, *Rolls of the Assizes . . . 1309*, p. 185.

94. Assize Roll, 17 Edw. II (no. 1165), m. 16 d. Thomas de Estfeld was bailiff of Guernsey in 1331. Cf. also Assize Roll, 5 Edw. III (no. 1166), m. 7 d.— "Item presentant quod heredes Willelmi Cheroun occupaverunt quandam viam regiam juxta ecclesiam ejusdem parochie (St. Peter Port) per con struccionem ejusdem domus ad nocumentum tocius patrie."

95. Assize Roll, 5 Edw. III (no. 1166), m. 7 d.

96. Printed in *Second Report*, pp. 299-300.

97. See section 5, no. 4.

98. See section 5, no. 5.

99. H. Pirenne, *Les villes du Moyen Age*, Brussels 1927, p. 185.

100. Revue historique, LIII, pp. 52 ff., LVII, pp. 57 ff, 293 ff.

101. L. Delisle, *Cartulaire Normand*, Caen 1852, pp. xv-xviii. S. Packard, *The Norman Communes under Richard and John, 1189-1204*, in *Anniversary Essays in Mediaeval History by Students of Charles Homer Haskins*, edited by C. H. Taylor, New York 1929.

102. H. Sée, *Note sur les origines de l'organisation municipale en Bretagne*, Annales de Bretagne, XXXV, pp. 388 ff. (1921-3.) H. Bourde de la Rogerie, *Les fondations de villes et de bourgs en Bretagne du xie au xiiie siècle*, Mémoires de la Société d'histoire et d'archéologie de Bretagne, IX, pp. 69 106. (1928.)

103. H. Sée, op. cit., pp. 390-1.

This map is intended to demonstrate the position of Guernsey in relation to mercantile traffic in the English Channel. With the exception of the northern part of Guernsey (see map 2.) it has been assumed that the coast line and the submarine contours were the same in the Middle Ages as they are now. This cannot be proved, but it is unlikely that any significant change has taken place.

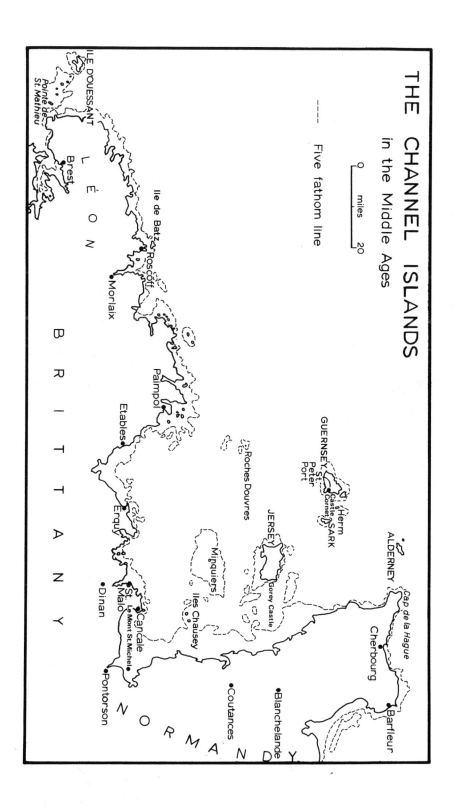

THE CHANNEL ISLANDS
in the Middle Ages

- - - - Five fathom line

0   miles   20

ILE D'OUESSANT
Pointe de St. Mathieu

Brest

L É O N

Ile de Batz
Roscoff
Morlaix

B R I T T A N Y

Paimpol

Etables

Erquy

Dinan
St. Malo
Le Mont St. Michel
Cancale

Pontorson

NORMANDY

Roches Douvres

GUERNSEY
St. Peter Port
Castle Cornet
Herm
SARK

JERSEY
Gorey Castle

Minquiers

Iles Chausey

Coutances

Blanchelande

ALDERNEY

Cap de la Hague

Cherbourg

Barfleur

The object of this map is to show the lie of the land about St. Peter Port and, in particular, to show the relative positions of the town, the roadstead and the Castle. With the exception of the northern part of the Island, the coastline has been taken from Admiralty Chart No. 3,400. The tidal channel dividing the " Clos du Val " from the rest of the Island, reclaimed in 1808, has been sketched in from " An Accurate Survey and Measurement of the Island of Guernsey Surveyed by Order of His Grace the Duke of Richmond, etc., Master General of the Ordnance, by William Gardner, 1787."

I have tentatively identified the " Locus qui vocatur Bancum " of the accounts of the Great Custom of Ships with what is now known as the " Great Bank." As there is never less than three fathoms of water over it, it cannot have formed a serious obstacle to mediaeval ships.

On shore, the contours have been sketched in at intervals of fifty feet. Modern parish boundaries have been inserted; but though there is no evidence to show that they are ancient in detail, there is no reason to believe that there have been extensive changes. Parishes have been indicated thus : A=Vale, B=St. Sampson, C=St. Peter Port, D=St. Martin, E=St. Andrew. St. Peter Port Church is indicated thus ⊕ On the assumption that the fourteenth century quay underlies the Elizabethan structure and the modern Albert Pier, its position has been indicated on the map.

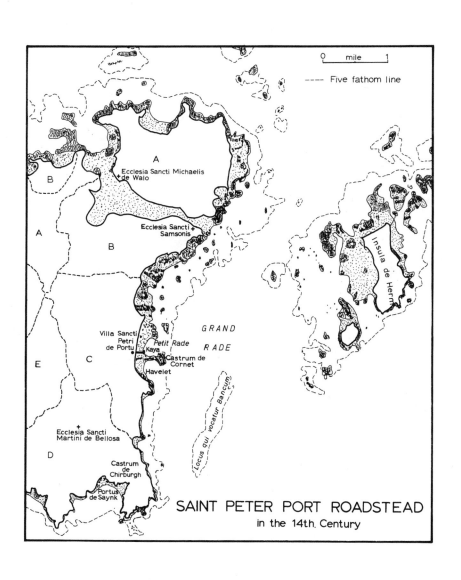

0   mile   1

---- Five fathom line

A

Ecclesia Sancti Michaelis
+de Walo

B

Ecclesia Sancti +
Samsonis

A

B

Insula de Herm

GRAND

RADE

Villa Sancti
Petri
de Portu   Petit Rade

E   C   Kaya

Castrum de
Cornet

Havelet

Locus qui vocatur Bancum

+
Ecclesia Sancti
Martini de Bellosa

D

Castrum
de
Chirburgh

Portus
de Saynk

SAINT PETER PORT ROADSTEAD
in the 14th. Century

II

THE ORIGINS OF THE CHANNEL ISLANDS
LEGAL SYSTEM

THE legal systems of the Channel Islands are of considerable antiquity. They can claim perhaps a thousand years of continuous development, with no revolutionary change at any time. Their origin as autonomous systems lies in the circumstance that, having once been included in the legal administration of Normandy, they were subsequently separated politically from the duchy. For various reasons, although included among the dominions of the king of England, they were not incorporated into the kingdom; and their fidelity to their Norman law and to their own local customs meant that they must be given, or allowed to develop for themselves, a legal administration of their own. There was indeed a moment, early in the fourteenth century, when it looked as though they might be brought into the English system by sending justices in eyre across the Channel. But nothing came of this; partly, perhaps chiefly, because of insular resistance. Thereafter Jersey and Guernsey were left to develop each its own law and legal administration, autonomous save only for correction by way of petition to the sovereign and his council. These points are now to be demonstrated.

1. Before the conquest of Normandy by the king of France in 1204, the Channel Islands formed an integral part of the duchy. Most of the estates in the islands formed part of larger baronial estates on the Norman mainland (Guernsey was at one time divided between the hereditary vicomtes of the Bessin and of the Cotentin); all the parish churches were held by French abbeys (all Norman except Marmoutier, which had close connections with Normandy); while, in addition, the Norman abbeys of Mont-Saint-Michel, Cherbourg, Blanchelande, Saint-Sauveur-le-Vicomte and others held considerable lands there, as indeed did the duke himself. The islands were included in the Norman diocese of Coutances.

There is no direct evidence to show how this situation had come about. The islands may well have been inhabited by Breton communities during the period of Breton expansion in the ninth century, if not before. These were probably brought under the rule of the Norman dukes when William Longsword acquired the Cotentin and the Avranchin in 933. But the Cotentin was separately colonised by Norman settlers later in the tenth century, and the islands may owe their "Normanization" to them. The organization of the ducal domain and government, together with ecclesiastical administration, was almost certainly the work of the first half of the eleventh century, as it was in western Normandy generally. While these matters are to some extent speculative, it is quite clear that, by the twelfth century, the ducal revenues in the islands were being collected by the duke's officers (for revenue purposes Guernsey seems to have formed one unit, Jersey three), and these officers were rendering their accounts at the Norman exchequer. The duke also had his courts in the islands, and his itinerant justices from Normandy seem to have visited them as regularly as other parts of the duchy. Since, therefore, the Channel Islands were then, from a governmental point of view, as much a part of Normandy as if they had been attached to the mainland, we may take it that their law was the law of Normandy—which indeed, in the absence of any direct statement to this effect, is what may be gathered from contemporary charters as well as from later evidence.

2. The law of Normandy seems to have taken shape as a coherent and distinctive system of customary law during the course of the eleventh century. Made up of the same elements as other customary systems in the north of France (for the Scandinavian element in it is surprisingly small, almost negligible), it seems that it was political conditions, the exceptionally strong rule of the dukes, that made it into a distinct system; for the boundaries of the region in which it was effective correspond very closely with the political boundaries of the duchy, and its very strongly feudal character suggests, in this case, that the duke's courts had had a powerful hand in its making. Certainly it was sufficiently formed to resist influences from England, Anjou and the Ile de France in the twelfth century, when they might have been expected to affect it; and even Roman law, though it was known and studied in the duchy at the same time, had relatively little influence. By the time that the first treatise included in the compilation known as the *Très Ancien Coutumier* was composed, that is, in the first years of the thirteenth century, it was compact and well-developed.

3. In Normandy, the catastrophe of King John's reign had shattering effects politically, though it made remarkably little difference to the development of Norman law. Normandy was added to the domain of the king of France and the lands of those seigneurs who remained loyal to the king of England were confiscated; there was no longer a duke; the office of seneschal was abolished; the exchequer as a high court survived, but it was no longer sovereign, for appeals could be taken to the king's court in Paris; the exchequer as an accounting department also survived, but it was staffed with royal officials who accounted to Paris; and local government was reorganised on the

French model. On the French side everything was done that could be done to break the links which, for 150 years, had held Normandy and England together. Yet Norman law survived in Normandy substantially unaffected by these profound changes; and the great medieval treatise upon it, the *Grand Coutumier de Normandie*, written some forty or fifty years after the break with England, shows its strength and its individuality.

This survival of Norman law had important results. When, towards the end of the thirteenth century, the Normans had occasion to complain of royal efforts to tax them, and when, also, Norman seigneurs resisted the centralising policy of royal officers who sought to circumscribe their rights of jurisdiction, all complained that their laws and customs, the laws and customs of Normandy, were being disregarded. They clearly saw, among other things, that appeals from the Norman exchequer to the king's court at Paris would weaken the individuality of their law, on which their own status and privileges were founded. Thus the struggle against royal centralization and royal taxation which developed towards the end of the thirteenth century, took the form of a demand that their laws and customs should be respected, and that these should be recognised as a distinct system, not to be modified from the outside. In this struggle they were largely successful; for by the *Charte aux Normands* of 1315 the king guaranteed that no Normans should be judged outside Normandy and that no appeal could be made from the Norman exchequer. Therefore, in spite of the French conquest of Normandy in 1204, and in spite of the centralizing policy pursued by the French monarchy thereafter, the sovereignty of Norman law in Normandy was recognised; the Normans became a privileged community within the kingdom of France; Norman law continued to develop according to its own logic

4. Precisely what happened to the Channel Islands during King John's critical reign, when the fate of Normandy and much else was decided, is something which no one can yet say. It is possible that they changed hands more than once, and that their destiny was not finally settled until after John's death; but early in the reign of King Henry III, and thereafter, the king of England was in possession. This created a very anomalous situation. The islanders were as Norman as the citizens of Rouen; linguistically, economically and socially they belonged to the Cotentin; their bishop was the bishop of Coutances, and, although King John was later stated to have tried to transfer them to Exeter or Salisbury, he remained their bishop. Yet their ruler, who had hitherto been duke of Normandy and king of England, and who had governed the islands as part of his duchy of Normandy, was no longer duke. Neither John nor Henry III, it is true, despaired of recovering the duchy, nor did they give up the title, until 1259; thus, for fifty

years and more, relations between England and France were in a state of war or, at best, of truce. The situation of the Channel Islands was, therefore, provisional. In those circumstances the policy of the king of England would naturally be to maintain their law and institutions as fully as possible; and several surviving mandates, addressed to the men he put in charge of them, show that this was indeed his policy. In 1218 the keeper of the islands was informed that it was the king's will that the "assizes which were observed in the time of Henry II, Richard and John" should be observed there now; in the next year, that he should take *fouage* in the Islands according to the use and custom of Normandy at times when *fouage* is taken in Normandy; in 1236, an order on a judicial matter begins with the words "Whereas the law and custom of Normandy is . . . we command you"; while important inquiries were ordered to be made in 1230, 1233, 1247, and 1248 to discover what the customs of the islands were and what they had been before the loss of Normandy.

During this half-century of war and truce, therefore, when the situation of the Channel Islands, as between England and France, was anomalous, their Norman law was preserved to them. The Treaty of Paris in 1259, which was an attempt at a general settlement, altered this situation, for, although it is not as explicit on the point as we could wish, it seems to provide a legal basis for the position in which the islands found themselves: By this treaty the king of England renounced all rights which he might have in the duchy and the land of Normandy, and in the islands, if any, which were at that time in the possession of the king of France; and he undertook to do liege homage in the future, not only for those lands in Gascony which he had succeeded in defending, but also for those lands in Aquitaine which the king of France undertook to convey to him, "and for all the land which he holds on this side (i.e. the French side) of the sea of England, and for the islands if there are any which the king of England holds which are of the kingdom of France." The islands off the French coast which the king of England held in 1259 were the Channel Islands and the Ile d'Oléron. In the text of the treaty, therefore, "the islands . . . . . . which the king of England holds which are of the kingdom of France" must include the Channel Islands. It follows, then, that they were in law a part of the kingdom of France, like Aquitaine, held by the king of England of the king of France by liege homage. The full implications of this feudal relationship need not be discussed here, for, in contrast with Aquitaine, they do not appear to have affected the islands very deeply; but it is significant that when the French kings' court pronounced the confiscation of Aquitaine and Ponthieu (as in 1294) the islands were at once attacked by French forces, and in the interminable legal arguments that followed the treaty of 1259, the fact that they were in law a parcel of the realm of France seems to have been accepted by both sides.

For some time after this treaty, therefore, the position of the islands seems clear; but when the Hundred Years War broke out, following the confiscation of Aquitaine and Ponthieu by the Court of France in 1337, Edward III continued to hold the Channel Islands, together with what he retained or acquired from time to time on the mainland of France, *de facto* only, by force of arms. When he assumed the title and style of "king of France" in 1340, he made provision for exercising sovereign jurisdiction in those parts of France which, from time to time, were in his possession; and he did this in a way which shows that, if he had ever made his title a reality, the two kingdoms would have remained distinct, though united in his person. So far, however, no evidence has been found to show that Edward would have included the islands in the administration of "his kingdom of France." Their final separation from France, *de facto* at first and perhaps never formally recognised by the French, dates therefore, from the early years of the Hundred Years War.

And so, just as the king of England had an interest in maintaining the Norman law of the Channel Islands during the first fifty years after the loss of Normandy, as tending to strengthen his claims to Normandy itself; likewise, after his renunciation of all claims to the duchy, his duty, as liege vassal of the king of France until 1337, would be the same. All the evidence of the late thirteenth and the fourteenth centuries is in accord, that the law of the Channel Islands was the law of Normandy. But this does not mean that Norman law in the islands was frozen, as it were, at the point of development reached when the islands and continental Normandy were politically separated. Lawyers in the islands were clearly in contact with legal authorities in Normandy and kept themselves, and were kept, up to date with developments there. When, for instance, Edward I instituted a seal for the islands in 1279, the ancestor of the present bailiwick seals, it was to be used, *inter alia*, for sealing contracts between individuals. In making this provision, long after the separation from Normandy, the king was making it possible for the islanders to use a form of procedure that was only then coming into use in Normandy and elsewhere in France. Perhaps the most interesting incident that shows the continuing relations between the legal authorities in the islands and those of Normandy occurred in 1328. The keeper, John de Roches, was ordered to report to the king on the law of Jersey concerning the rights of a priest's illegitimate children. In his report, two things stand out clearly: first that there was a copy of the Latin text of the *Grand Coutumier de Normandie* in Jersey at that time, and that it did not merely repose there but was used in the court; and second, that in a case of difficulty the keeper had no hesitation in referring, for a ruling, to the bailli of the Cotentin and his legal experts. This particular contact may have an even greater significance, for the *Grand Coutumier* is thought to have been composed in the Cotentin and to represent, particularly, the custom of that part of Normandy; and since there are several other references to it in Channel Island records of the early fourteenth century, it may be that the law of the islands was as near to the central tradition of Norman law as it could well be.

5. Basically, then, the medieval law of the Channel Islands was the customary law of Normandy, which found its fullest expression in the *Grand Coutumier* of the mid-thirteenth century. The origin of their legal systems has therefore to be sought in this general context, for the fact that they were ruled by the king of England who respected their Norman law was in itself a sufficient reason for giving them a very independent judicial administration. But, like many other more or less isolated or otherwise distinct communities in Europe during the Middle Ages, the islands had a body of custom which was all their own. There are many surviving statements of these customs, mostly, by the luck of survival, relating primarily to Guernsey, though enough remain from Jersey to show that the difference between the two larger islands were differences of detail only.

The general position is put most clearly in the initial phrases of a statement made on behalf of the islanders before the court of King's Bench in 1333—

> To our lord the King and to his Council show his liege people the community of the islands of Guernsey and Jersey, that whereas the Islands are, from of old, a parcel of the duchy of Normandy, and in such manner hold of our lord the king as duke, and in the said islands they hold and use and have always used the custom of Normandy which is called the *Summa* of Maukael, together with certain other customs used in the islands time out of mind. . . .

The *Summa* of Maukael has been identified with the *Grand Coutumier* in its original Latin form, and there is no room for doubt about the identification; the "other customs" are those with which we are now concerned.

The various statements of these customs that were made in the thirteenth and fourteenth centuries are reasonably consistent, and it would be possible to draw up a general custumal from them. The earliest put the customs relating to the tenants on the royal domain ("fief-le-roi") in the forefront, their conditions of tenure, their rents in money, their rents in kind, their services, and the *banalités* to which they were subject. What is important is that these rents and services were fixed, that the services were light, almost vestigial. The peasantry on the royal domain, that is to say, were substantially free economically as well as personally, and there is nothing to show that the condition of tenants on other fiefs differed materially. But, whether they indicated a free or servile peasantry, customs of this sort might be found on almost any manor.

An important group of customs relate to the administration of justice. All courts held in the king's name in the islands, whether they were presided over by his visiting justices or by his resident bailiff, must be attended by the appropriate quota of jurats, who gave judgment on all pleas whatsoever arising in the islands (save in cases of treason and assault upon a royal officer in the exercise of his duty), assessed all fines and amercements, bore record with justices or bailiff and advised the justices on the custom of the island. They should be natives of their island, elected by the king's officers and the "optimates" of the island, and take oath to maintain the rights both of the king and of the islanders, to render lawful judgments in the king's court, having no respect of persons and taking no gifts to maintain the cause of any party in court. No plea initiated in the islands should be adjourned elsewhere. These customs gave to the jurats, who themselves were islanders, that exclusive jurisdiction which is a characteristic of communities with customs of their own, and which indeed was necessary to the maintenance of those customs.

Other customs relating to the administration of justice are more miscellaneous. No one need answer for his free tenement without a writ: no resident should be called upon to answer for a stranger's debt unless he were a surety: those convicted of felony outside the islands should not forfeit their *héritages* within the islands. There were rules for the *clameur de haro* and restrictions on royal and seigneurial rights of distraint or imprisonment. In addition, there were customs relating to weights and measures, the islanders' rights in fisheries, wreck and the taking of rabbits, together with regulations for the collection of the custom which the king levied on all foreign shipping calling at the islands. Some were political in their implications. The islanders claimed to make all payments to the king in the money current in Normandy at the time, for which, they said, they paid *monnéage* or *fouage*. They claimed that they were not bound to do homage unless the king came to Normandy, or sent his officer specifically commissioned to take their homages; and finally, though this was usually put first, they claimed that, for the fixed annual rent which they paid to the king, they should be free from all forms of military service, unless it were to release the king if he were held in prison by his enemies (or, in another version, to go with the duke of Normandy in person to recover England if it should be necessary), and free from all arbitrary tax.

In very general terms these are the sort of customs that might be found among small communities in many parts of contemporary Europe. No one has yet studied the customs of the Channel Islands comparatively, but it is likely that analogies would be found in other islands and coastal communities along the French coast, particularly perhaps in the north east, in Picardy and Flanders. When they have been put into their context geographically, as it were, we shall know a great deal more about them and their origin than we know at present. But their general character is plain enough. Fundamentally they concern the relations between the islanders and their lord the king, and they constituted a barrier against seigneurial exploitation. They are not concerned with private law which, in the Islands, was the law of Normandy. They made the islands into privileged communities, and the courts of privileged communities must have exclusive jurisdiction, otherwise privileges could not be maintained.

However, the matter goes a little further than that. The jurats were already claiming that they declared the custom, that, as with other judgment-finders and doomsmen, what they said was the law. Their judgments were thus making law, and this must be the source, in large measure, of the differences in detail between the laws of Jersey and Guernsey, differences that were already apparent in the fourteenth century. Similar conditions had produced a single general pattern of law and institutions in the four larger Channel Islands: the character of their courts and the role of the jurats, made it certain that they would diverge in detail.

6. The essential feature of the king's courts in the Channel Islands was, then, the benches of jurats—benches of twelve in Jersey, twelve in Guernsey, seven in Alderney and six in Sark. The presiding officers were the king's bailiffs in Jersey and Guernsey, his prévots in Alderney and Sark; and there was the usual complement of ushers, executive officers and clerks in each. According to the records, as they have survived, these courts do not appear as fully organized until the reign of Edward I; and the enormous work of reorganisation which Edward carried out in Aquitaine suggests that this may not be an accident, and that he may have done something similar in the Islands. But in some form or other, these courts go back much further.

The origin of the jurats is a problem to which, at present, there is no clear solution. In 1248, that is not more than forty years after the event, twenty-three Guernsey jurors said on oath that King John had "instituted twelve sworn coroners to keep the pleas and rights pertaining to the crown. He ordained, also, and granted, for the security of the islands, that the *bailli* could, in future, hold pleas of *novel disseisin* (within the year), of *mort d'ancestor* (within the year), of dower similarly, of *fief et de gaige* at any time and of *mariage encombré*, all without writ, by view (*per visum*) of these said coroners." These "twelve sworn coroners" have generally been identified with the jurats, and it is difficult to see what else they could be; but the terms used in this inquest are not altogether appropriate to the character and functions of the jurats as they appear when evidence is more plentiful. In later times they do, it is true, perform the functions of a coroner, in company with the bailiff, but they did much besides; and in their other functions, those of doomsmen or judgment-finders, they represent an institution that was already ancient in King John's time, so that these functions are not likely to have been added subsequently. It may, however, be significant that the one surviving record we have of a royal court, *curia regis*, in the Channel Islands before 1200—it was held in Guernsey in 1179 and it was held by an officer described as "vicomte"— has no mention of jurats, though it records an act which, somewhat later, would certainly have been witnessed by jurats, specified as such. It is still possible that King John, if he did not "institute" the benches of jurats, adapted an older institution; or that the jurors of 1248 were emphasising one particular function in a particular context; but this is speculation.

If the origin of the jurats—the guarantee of the islanders'customs— is still obscure, there are some hints of the origin of the customs themselves. The phrase used in the inquest of 1248: "that the islanders should be free from all military services and tallages, oppressions and other exactions, save only that they will go with the duke of Normandy in person to recover England if it should be necessary," could have no meaning after 1204. But it might have been very much to the point between 1150 and 1153, when young Henry Plantagenet had already been made duke of Normandy by his father but had not yet induced King Stephen of England to recognise him as his heir. The earlier date might possibly be pushed back to 1144, when Henry's father, Geoffrey Plantagenet had conquered Normandy from Stephen, for we know that he regarded England and Normandy as inseparable.

However, the ultimate origins of the customs could be a hundred years earlier still. In many documents of the thirteenth and fourteenth centuries, the peasantry living on the royal domain in the islands are called *hospites*. The term is not used exclusively but it is used quite frequently. Now, during the eleventh and twelfth centuries, *hospites* in Normandy, as in France generally, were colonists. They were people attracted to a place which a seigneur wished to develop by the offer of favourable terms of tenure—a strict limitation of the rights which the seigneur normally exercised over his tenants, the sort of limitation of seigneurial rights which was in fact enjoyed by the tenants on the royal domain in the islands. There may well have been a time, after the Viking destructions, when the duke wished to attract colonists to the islands; and the most likely time for this is the middle years of William the Conqueror's rule in Normandy, and perhaps in the time of his father and grandfather, when, as we know, a good deal was done to open up the western extremity of the duchy. It is significant, therefore, that a *hospes* is mentioned in the charter, to be dated c. 1048, by which Duke William gave the church of St. Peter Port, and other churches in Guernsey, to the abbey of Marmoutier; for that *hospes* is not likely to have been the only one of his kind in the island, and if *hospites* were already in the islands before the middle of the eleventh century, we must suppose that they were already in enjoyment of their customs.

7. The origin of the legal institutions of the Channel Islands, as autonomous systems, then, lies in the circumstance that, from 1204, although ruled by the king of England, their law was the law of Normandy, and that this law of Normandy as administered in the islands was not cut off and atrophied but constantly enlivened by contact with legal authorities on the Norman mainland. As long as this situation was respected by the English government, as it has been and still is, it required, in itself, that the islands should have a largely autonomous legal administration. But this requirement was strengthened by the fact that the islands were privileged communities, having customs of their own, supplementing the law of Normandy and going back, in some form, to the early part of the eleventh century at least; and one of the essential features of such customs was an exclusive jurisdiction over all matters concerning them

Yet this need not exclude an overriding royal jurisdiction. In many English boroughs the jurisdiction of the borough court stopped short at the "pleas of the crown," and none could resist the jurisdiction of the justices in eyre. There is clear evidence that the islands had been visited by itinerant justices from Normandy in the twelfth century; and during the thirteenth century there seems to have been a distinction between the powers of the King's courts in their ordinary form and when sitting to "hear the assizes." Since justices could no longer come from Normandy to take the assizes, the practice through most of this century was to give the keeper, in association sometimes with one or two local men, a mandate to "take" the assizes according to the Norman rule that they should be "taken" every three years. In this phase when, it will be remembered, the "international" position of the islands was anomalous, their judical administration seems to have been completely self-contained, for the assizes as well as the ordinary courts were organised locally.

During the reign of Edward I, however, the commissions of assize changed their character. Commissions of oyer and terminer to deal with complaints (*querele*) against the administration were interspersed with them; commissions of assize were issued for each specific occasion, generally to three or four of the king's officers in the islands; more important, their commission was enlarged into a commission *ad omnia placita*. In 1299 these various commissions were amalgamated, and

3

pleas *de quo warranto* appear in the records of this visitation. Early in the fourteenth century the old triennial rule is forgotten, judges from England head the commissions, and their sessions in the islands take on all the terror and majesty of the English general eyre.

The eyres of 1299, 1304, 1309, 1320, 1323 and 1331 have left an abundance of records and an abiding memory in the islands. In the end they stirred up a furious resistance, chiefly because the *quo warranto* proceedings called in question not only the privileges of local seigneurs and the customs, in the narrow sense, of the island communities, but treated their fundamental Norman law as one of the customs for which a title must be shown. These proceedings, adjourned eventually to the Court of King's Bench (contrary to the custom), were inconclusive; but the eyre of 1331 was the last. It was almost the last to be held anywhere, for the institution was in full decline; and whether for that reason, or because King Edward III thought it politic to humour the islanders in view of the outbreak of war with France, the episode was closed with a royal charter guaranteeing, in general terms, "all their privileges, liberties and customs" (1341).

What then took the place of the justices itinerant? Apart from occasional, *ad hoc* commissions of inquiry or of oyer and terminer, there can be no doubt that it was the royal courts of Jersey and Guernsey, which, most likely, were amply ready to do this. The position was regularised, from 1348, by giving the Keeper of the Islands, full judicial powers, for these powers could only have been exercised by the courts.

The final step in the process came twenty years later. In 1368 an attempt was made to bring an action of trespass, committed in Jersey, before the Court of King's Bench, and it was defeated. The record runs thus—

> And since the matter aforesaid cannot be determined in this Court, because the Jurats of the said Island cannot come here (to appear) before the Justices, nor are they bound to do so by law, nor may any matter arising in the said Island be determined otherwise than by the custom of the said Island, therefore let the whole record of this matter be sent to the Lord King's Chancery, so that his commission may be addressed to such persons as he pleases, to hear and determine the matter aforesaid in the said Island according to the custom of the said Island.

All the holes had been stopped up. Apart from petition to the sovereign as a matter of grace, the exclusive jurisdiction of the jurats was established. Therein lies the origin of the legal systems of the Channel Islands.

BIBLIOGRAPHICAL NOTE

1. THE CUSTOM OF NORMANDY

(*a*) R. Besnier, *La Coutume de Normandie: histoire externe* (Paris, 1935).

A. Coville, *Les États de Normandie* (Paris, 1894).

R. Génestal, "La Formation et le Développment de la Coutume de Normandie," *Travaux de la Semaine d'histoire du Droit Normand. . . . Guernesey. . . . 1927* (Caen, 1928), pp. 37–55.

J. Yver, "Les caractères originaux de la Coutume de Normandie," *Mémoires de l'Académie des Sciences, Arts et Belles-Lettres de Caen,* N.S. XII (1952), pp. 307–56.

J. Yver, "Les caractères originaux du groupe de coutumes de l'ouest de la France," *Revue historique de droit français et étranger,* 4e série, XXX (1952), pp. 18–79.

(*b*) E. J. Tardif (ed.), *Coutumiers de Normandie.* I, i, *Le Très Ancien Coutumier de Normandie, Texte latin* (1881).

I, ii, *Le Très Ancien Coutumier de Normandie, Textes français et normand* (1903).

II, *La Summa de legibus Normannie* (1896).
Société de l'histoire de Normandie (Rouen) (all published).

W. L. de Gruchy (ed.), *L'Ancienne Coutume de Normandie* (Jersey, 1881).

2. The Medieval Law and Custom of the Channel Islands

(*a*) J. Havet, *Les Cours Royales des Iles Normandes* (Paris, 1878).

J. H. Le Patourel, *The Medieval Administration of the Channel Islands,* 1199-1399 (London, 1937). [Detailed references to documents quoted in this paper will be found here].

J. Yver, "Les Caractères originaux de la Coutume normande dans les Îles de la Manche," *Travaux de la Semaine d'histoire du Droit Normand . . . Guernesey . . . 1938* (Caen, 1939), pp. 481–503.

J. H. Le Patourel, "Un premier exemple de Contrat sous le Sceau de la Baillie de Jersey," *ibid.,* pp. 401–7.

J. H. Le Patourel, "The Authorship of the Grand Coutumier de Normandie," *English Historical Review,* LVI (1941), pp. 292–300.

G. F. B. de Gruchy, *Medieval Land Tenures in Jersey* (Jersey, 1957).

(*b*) *First Report of the Commissioners appointed to inquire into the State of the Criminal Law in the Channel Islands: Jersey* (1847).

Second Report . . . . : Guernsey (1848).

Report of the Commissioners appointed to inquire into the Civil, Municipal and Ecclesiastical Laws of the Island of Jersey . . . . (1861).

The Attorney-General's Memorandum in the Printed Papers prepared in connection with the Jersey Prison Board Case, heard before the Privy Council (1894). These papers were not published, but copies may be found in the British Museum, The Bodleian Library, the London Library and in the public libraries of Guernsey and Jersey.

(*c*) The following are the more important early documents concerning the law and custom of the Islands:—

(1) The Inquest of 1248. Printed in *Second Report*, pp. 291–3; *Calender of Inquisitions Miscellaneous*, I, pp. 15–18; Sir Havilland de Sausmarez, *The Extentes of Guernesy* (Société Guernesiaise, 1934), pp. 24–28.

(2) "Copie des franchises que le roi d'Engleterre a en Guernerie & que les hommes de Guernerie ont" (temp. Edward I.) Printed in G. Dupont, *Histoire du Cotentin et de ses îles* (Caen, 1870–85), ii, pp. 213–5; Havet, *Cours Royales*, pp. 183–6; *Cartulaire des îles Normandes* (Société Jersiaise, 1924), pp. 224–6; *Extentes of Guernsey*, pp. 38–40.

(3) Statements made in *quo warranto* proceedings:
    1309—*Rolls of the Assizes held in the Channel Islands . . . 1309* (Société Jersiaise, 1903), pp. 29–34, 69–74.
    1320—Assize Roll no. 1163, mm. 2 (*Second Report*, pp. 296–8), 10 Havet, *Cours Royales*, pp. 214–7) and 11.
    1323—Assize Roll no. 1165, mm. 7, 8r (*Second Report*, pp. 295–9).
    1331—Assize Roll no. 1167, mm. 8d (*Second Report*, pp. 300–1), 17r.

(4) Extents of 1331 (see *Med. Admin. C.I.*, pp. 13–14)—Jersey: *Extente de l'Ile de Jersey*, 1331 (Société Jersiaise, 1876). Guernsey: *Extentes of Guernsey*, pp. 57–126.

(5) Proceedings in the Court of King's Bench, 1331–3: printed in Havet, *Cours Royales*, pp. 224–33.

(6) Edward III's charter of 1341 is printed in Rymer, *Foedera*, (Rec. Comm. ed.), II, ii, 1167.

III

THE AUTHORSHIP OF THE
GRAND COUTUMIER DE NORMANDIE

Le Grand Coutumier de Normandie, one of the greatest legal treatises of the middle ages, is an obstinately anonymous document. The problem of its authorship has provoked a good deal of speculation. It has been attributed by different commentators to many improbable persons, such as Philip de Beaumanoir, Peter de Fontaines, King Philip Augustus, and even Edward the Confessor ; but when E. J. Tardif made the first attempt to tackle the problem seriously and scientifically he came to a very much less definite conclusion though with better reasoning. In 1885 he published a preliminary article entitled ' Les auteurs présumés du Grand Coutumier de Normandie ' ; [3] and this he reprinted, with one or two important modifications, in the introduction to his great edition of the Latin text of the custumal, the title of which, he decided, should be *Summa de legibus Normannie in curia laicali*.[4]

---

[2] This note is a revised version of a paper read during the ' Semaine de Droit Normand ', held at the University of Caen in June 1939.

[3] *Nouvelle revue historique du droit français et étranger*, ix. 155–205 ; *tirage à part*, Paris, 1885. References are given to the *tirage à part* in this note.

[4] *Coutumiers de Normandie :* Textes critiques publiés par E. J. Tardif ; tome ii, *La Summa de Legibus Normannie in curia laicali ;* Rouen and Paris, 1896.

Tardif's argument, in the first article, ran somewhat as follows. The internal evidence of the custumal itself gave no indication of the identity of its author, though it did suggest that western Normandy, probably the Cotentin, was the district in which it was composed. This was deduced from the fact that the manuscript which, in Tardif's opinion, best preserved the original form of the treatise, was copied in the Cotentin, and that many of the earlier existing manuscripts come from western Normandy. Greater precision, he thought, might be possible. When place-names were required in the forms of writs quoted in the custumal, many manuscripts used the names of real places rather than ' in tali villa ' ; and from a study of these Tardif came to the conclusion that Valognes enjoyed a preference such as might be given to it by a writer living in or near that town. For more positive indications of authorship, however, he found it necessary to look beyond the custumal itself ; and such indications were discovered among the records of the justices itinerant who visited the Channel Islands on several occasions in the early years of the fourteenth century.[1]

In the eyre of 1309, for example, the community of the island of Jersey was summoned to state what law it recognized, the law of England, the law of Normandy, or special customs granted by the king. The community's spokesmen replied that they were ruled by the law of Normandy, save that there were certain customs, peculiar to the island and dating back from time immemorial, which had been set forth in a schedule. The king's advocate, William Dumaresq, himself a Jerseyman, objected to this, saying that the islanders were not in fact observing their ancient customs ; for since it could not be denied that the inhabitants of all the islands spoke the same language and that the islands had once formed a part of the duchy of Normandy, for these and other reasons the islands ought all to have the same body of customs ; yet he could quote many instances in which the customs of the islands differed one from another, whence it was clear that they had departed from their ancient custom. Furthermore, the community of Jersey had lately adopted a legal treatise which had been written by a certain Norman called Maucael long after the Normans had transferred their allegiance to the king of France. Wherefore he sought, on behalf of the king, that the ancient custom should be restored, and that all the islands should observe the same law. The spokesmen of the community answered that they and their ancestors had always observed the customs which they now claimed, and said that

---

[1] Tardif ; *Les Auteurs présumés*, 22–42 ; cf. Le Patourel : *The Medieval Administration of the Channel Islands*, Oxford, 1937, pp. 52–60, 105 ff.

they set great store by this ' Summa de Maukael ' because they found the law of Normandy well written therein.[1]

In 1332 similar statements were made in a joint petition addressed to the king in council by the communities of Guernsey and Jersey :—

> Come les Isles soient de auncienete parcele de la Duche de Normendie et en tiel manere tiegnent de nostre seignur le Roi come de Duc, et es dites Isles tiegnent et usent et eient touz jours usez la coustume de Normendie qest appele la summe Mankael, ovesqes aucunes certeignes coustumes usees es dites Isles del temps dont memorie ne court. . . .[2]

These passages made it perfectly clear that there was a treatise on Norman law in Jersey early in the fourteenth century, and that it was in some sense official. The title it bore, ' Summa de Maukael ', seemed to indicate the name of its author. Several analogies could be quoted, for example, *Summa Azonis* or *Summa Henrici de Bracton*. It remained only to identify with certainty this ' Summa de Maukael ' with the *Grand Coutumier*. Such an identification was probable on general grounds ; it is consistent with William Dumaresq's statement that this treatise had been written by a Norman long after the Normans had transferred their allegiance to the king of France, for the generally accepted date of the *Grand Coutumier*, at least in its original form, is 1254–8 ; learned tradition in the islands has always taken the identification for granted ; and since there is no consistency in the title given to the treatise by different manuscripts of the Latin text, there is no reason why ' Summa de Maukael ' should not refer to the same work as ' Summa de legibus '.

Tardif was unable to take the argument very much further. He found, it is true, a family called Maucael living at Valognes in the thirteenth century, and he pointed out that as the assizes of the *bailliage* of the Cotentin were very frequently held at Valognes, anyone living there would have opportunities for that practical experience of the working of the courts which is so evident in the *Grand Coutumier*, and would presumably have access to the library of the abbey of Nôtre Dame du Voeu at Cherbourg. Furthermore, if it should seem strange that so much of the evidence on which this argument is based comes from the Channel Islands which, in the fourteenth century, were politically separated from Normandy, then it must be emphasized that the relations between the Islands and the Cotentin were very close even at this time ; indeed, the monastery of L'Islet, near St. Helier,

---

[1] Société Jersiaise, *Rolls of the Assizes held in the Channel Islands . . . in 1309*, Jersey, 1903, pp. 69–74.

[2] J. Havet, *Les Cours royales des Iles Normandes*, Paris, 1878, pp. 228–9. Tardif showed that the name should be ' Maukael ' or ' Maucael '. It is usually impossible to distinguish between *n* and *u* in the court-hand of this period.

in Jersey, was a priory of the abbey of Cherbourg.[1] All this circumstantial evidence fitted in very well with the evidence of the manuscripts, but with it all we have learnt little of Maucael save his name.

In the long introduction to his edition of the Latin text of the *Grand Coutumier*,[2] Tardif examined the question afresh, and introduced one or two complications. Firstly, it was his opinion that the *Grand Coutumier*, as it has come down to us, includes a number of additions to the original work, notably chapters cxiii–cxxv. He then noticed that most passages in which the name Valognes occurs are to be found in just those chapters. Hence he was led to conclude that Maucael was a continuator rather than the author of the *Grand Coutumier*. This conclusion seemed to be confirmed by the use of the term 'Summa de Maukael' in Jersey; for Tardif had been led to believe that the title of the original treatise was 'Registrum de judiciis Normannie' (the title borne by the earliest surviving manuscript), while the later, enlarged form of the work was entitled 'Summa de legibus Normannie', the title he chose for his edition of the Latin text of the custumal.

Tardif's treatment of this problem was subjected to exhaustive analysis by Paul Viollet in 1906, and, in general, approved: 'cette Somme de Maukael est évidemment nôtre Grand Coutumier'.[3] But Viollet was not convinced that chapters cxiii–cxxv were in fact a later addition, and he pointed out that the name Valognes was used in a form of writ cited in chapter ci, a chapter which Tardif had accepted as part of the treatise in its original form. He was therefore inclined to regard it as being, in general, a homogeneous work, and Maucael, whoever he may have been, as its author. In a very recent book, however, M. Robert Besnier has reverted to Tardif's opinion that chapters cxiii–cxxv and others are additions to the original treatise, though he does not comment upon the bearing of this opinion on the problem of its authorship.[4]

The learning on this subject up to the present, then, amounts to this: the *Grand Coutumier de Normandie* itself tells us practically nothing about its author, though it provides some indications that it was composed in western Normandy, possibly in the Cotentin: early in the fourteenth century there existed in Jersey a treatise on the law of Normandy which was regarded as authoritative and which was called 'Summa de Maukael': it is probable that this 'Summa de Maucael' was in fact the Latin text of the

---

[1] Le Patourel, *op. cit.* pp. 32–5.   [2] Tardif, *La Summa de Legibus*, pp. i–ccxxxv.
[3] *Histoire littéraire de la France*, xxxiii. (Paris, 1906), 41–190: 'Les Coutumiers de Normandie'.
[4] R. Besnier, *La Coutume de Normandie, histoire externe*, Paris 1925, pp. 106–10.

Grand Coutumier, and that Maucael therefore was the name of its author, or one of its authors. Moreover, it has been found that Maucael was the name of a family living in the neighbourhood of Valognes in the thirteenth century. From all this it may be concluded that the *Grand Coutumier* was written (or perhaps only edited) in the Cotentin by a man of whom nothing is known but his name Maucael.

The problem is perhaps a small matter, but it has an intriguing quality which endows any new scrap of evidence with some interest. One such scrap has lately turned up among the Channel Island documents in the Public Record Office and is here presented for what it may be worth. This document comes at the end of a curious little story which must first be told.

Not long before the year 1328, a Jersey priest called John de Calais devised a scheme whereby he hoped to make provision for his illegitimate children, three boys and four girls. The difficulty he had to face was the law which prevented a bastard from succeeding to lands by way of inheritance, and prevented anyone but the bastard's own children from inheriting from him. John de Calais proceeded in this way : ' in the hearing of the parish ' [1] he handed over to the children and their mother a sum of money with which they were to acquire lands and tenements *en heritage*, to be held jointly among them in such manner that when any of the children died the survivors were to add his share to theirs until, eventually, the sole survivor should accumulate the whole ; and John made a formal statement at the time that he had given them the money for no other purpose. The children and their mother carried out his instructions. They acquired lands and rents in different parts of Jersey, lands that were all held directly of the king.

In course of time one of the boys died, and the king's officers, evidently in some doubt as to the precise legal position, seized all the property into the king's hands. As this was in any case an injustice, John de Calais, who was still living, appealed to the king in council. The king, therefore, by a writ dated 2 June 1328, ordered the warden of the Channel Islands to send him a report on the facts of the case and on the custom of the Islands in such matters. The warden, John de Roches, reported as follows :—

Ego Iohannes de Roches custos insularum de Gerner', Gers' etc., inueni per inquisicionem fidedignorum plurimorum quod Iohannes de Qualais cappellanus in audiencia parrochiarum de Gers' etc. diuersas pecuniarum summas dedit Iohanni, Philippo, Guillelmo, filiis suis, Iohanne, Guillemote, Raoline, et Symonete, filiabus suis, ac Reginalde eorumdem puerorum matri, ad terras et tenementa sibi hereditarie

---

[1] ' In audiencia parochie '—cf. Le Patourel, *op. cit.* pp. 100–1.

possidèndas, emendas; ita tamen quod ille qui superuixerit eorumdem, easdem terras et tenementa integraliter possideret, protestando se alias dictarum pecuniarùm sommas non dedisse. Item et quod iidem pueri et mater forma qua supra acquisierunt in diuersis parrochiis in insula de Gers' xij virgatas terre vel circa valoris annis communibus iiij quarteriorum frumenti. Item et acquisierunt vt supra vj quarteria frumenti annui redditus. Qui quidem pueri et eorum mater racione dicte acquisicionis de predictis tenementis coniunctim saysiti fuerunt. Item et quod racione mortis Guillelmi vnius dictorum puerorum bastardorum, omnia dicta terra et tenementa saisita fuerunt in manu domini Regis etc.; et non alia de causa. Item et quod dicta terra et tenementa et redditus tenentur de domino Rege etc. per seruicia communia. Item et quod in consimili casu est consuetudo patrie talis quod cum aliquis bastardus coniunctim feofatus fuerit de aliquo tenemento, et diem clausit extremum, illa porcio que sibi de iure contingeret, in manu domini Regis siue aliorum dominorum capitalium de quibus tenerentur dicta tenementa, tamquam eschaeta sua sibi remaneret, condicione aliqua inter ipsos bastardos facta non obstante.

Endorsement : ' pro pueris '.[1]

On receipt of this report, the king ordered, in October 1328, that restitution of the lands should be made except for that portion which was deemed to have belonged to the deceased child.[2] What happened as the result of this royal command is not clear, for a month later the king sent another writ to the warden of the Islands. This recites the substance of the two earlier writs together with the warden's report, and then goes on to state that on account of certain difficulties in this report the king required further information; in particular, supposing a foreigner (*extraneus*) had acted in the same manner as John de Calais, what then would be the law of Jersey on the point ?[3]

The reply made by the warden to this second inquiry is the document with which this note is principally concerned. This document as it stands is either a very careless copy (though contemporary with its exemplar) or a very careless draft. It is here transcribed with all its mistakes, for in most instances emendations could only be made by guesswork :—

Significo Regie Magestati me plenius informari et diligenter inquisisse per sacramentum Philippi de Sancto Martino, Petri Hugun, Radulfi Tourgis, Guillelmi le Petit, Matthaei le Loreour, Thome Hughe, iuratorum vestrorum,[4] necnon Colini Hastayn, Cliui Tourgis, Roberti le Bas, Thome Estur, Colini de Ponte, Iohannis Saugreys, Ricardi dicti Cock Larchier, et Ricardi de Carpendoit super quo ad articulum in breui contentum vbi dicit si in casu vbi extraneus huiusmodi dona-

---

[1] Writ and Return, Public Record Office, Chancery Miscellanea, bundle 10, no. 9 (11).

[2] *Calendar of Close Rolls, 1327–1330*, p. 333 (Writ dated 20 October 1328).

[3] P.R.O., Ancient Correspondence, xxxvii. 140

[4] I.e. jurats of the king's court in Jersey.

cionem condicionem etc. Qui quidem iurati et alii mihi pretulerunt per sua iuramenta, quod per consuetudinem in Geresoye vsitati [1] etc., extraneus veraciter bastardus potest facere condicionem et donacionem terrarum et tenementorum etc., que quidem condicio post mortem vnius bastardorum dictorum iuxta formam condicionis tenebit et habebit in se roboris firmitatem. Item requisiti [2] dictos iuratos et alios de inquesta, eo maxime quod consuetudines dicte patrie iuraueram obseruare ; qui quidem mihi dixerunt per sua iuramenta quod vtuntur et vti tenentur consuetudinibus antiquis per bone memorie illustris domini Regis Anglie ac ducis Normannie ibidem [3] quod registram [4] dictarum consutudinum feci legi ; videlicet in capitulo de impedimento hereditagii,[5] vbi dicit in quadam casula : [6] bastardus autem nemini debet succedere hereditarie,[7] casualiter autem potest vt per empcionem seu condicionem aliquam. Bastardo autem nemo potest succedere nisi ex ipso et vxore propria originem duxerit coniugalem ; et licet bastardus in hereditate [8] succedere non debeat, hereditatem [9] potest acquirere quam potest dare, vendere uel vadiare sicut legitimi quibus voluerit,[10] exceptis tamen illis qui in bastardia ex ipso fuerint procreati. Item quod super contentis in predicto breui maiestatem regiam plenius sertificare cupio tenorem ac totalem substanciam huius breuis balliuo Constantini et eius sapientibus qui in consuetudinibus ac legibus Normann' sunt experti demandaui, quarum quidem consuetudinem [11] insulani Gersoye tenentur vsitari vt prefertur ; qui quidem balliuus, per suas literas mihi partem [12] predicti Iohannis de Calays, super huius rei casu mihi rescripserit in hec verba : En cas ou la acquisicion des bastards seroit tant soulement au temps ou a vie la condicion mise et acordee entre eux, ou par celuy q' acquiroit en noun de eux, tendroit ; cest assau' q' le plus viuant auroit tout. E par consequent si lun de ceux morreit le seignour neaueroit pas la successcion de celuy. Mes en cas ou la dite acqisicion seroit fait a heritage, la condisscion ne tendroit ne ne lieroit pas le droit du seignour, mes apres la mort de lun aueroit la succession en tant come apartener peust au d . . .[13] de la chose ainsi acquise.[14]

Unfortunately the documents stop at this point and we do not know the end of the story. In any case the legal point at issue is not immediately relevant ; what is now of interest is the information that this document can give on the history of the *Grand Coutumier de Normandie.*

In the first place, the quotation from the ' registrum ', being in fact a quotation from the Latin text of the *Grand Coutumier,*

---

[1] *Sic.* [2] Requisivi ?

[3] Part of this sentence is evidently missing. [4] *Sic.*

[5] Tardif, *La Summa de Legibus,* 87, c. xxv, ' De impedimentis successionis '. No manuscript quoted by Tardif gives the title in the form ' De impedimento hereditagii '.

[6] *Ibid.* p. 90, c. xxv, paragraphs 6 and 7.

[7] Tardif's text—' hereditarie succedere '.

[8] Tardif's text—' hereditatem '. [9] Tardif's text inserts ' tamen '.

[10] Tardif's text—' vendere vel invadiare quibus voluerit, sicut legitimi '.

[11] *Sic.* [12] In parte ?

[13] One word illegible. [14] P.R.O., Ancient Correspondence, xxi. 141.

shows quite conclusively that there was a copy of this text of the custumal in Jersey in or about the year 1328; and the document as a whole suggests that this copy was in official use in the royal court of that Island. When it is remembered that the two references in Jersey to the ' Summa de Maukael ' occur, the one (in 1309) before, and the other (in 1332) just after 1328, then the identification of this ' Summa de Maukael ' with the Latin text of the *Grand Coutumier* is substantially confirmed. As far as can be ascertained from Tardif's edition, however, the quotation from the *Grand Coutumier* given in this document tallies with no known manuscript of the custumal. Perhaps, then, we have here a trace of the official copy of the custumal in use in the royal court of Jersey in the fourteenth century, a copy which has otherwise completely disappeared.

It will be remembered also, from Tardif's argument, that in his opinion the original title of the custumal was ' Registrum de judiciis Normannie ', while it was the later, enlarged version that bore the title ' Summa de legibus Normannie '; therefore, he argued, when the men of Jersey spoke of a ' Summa de Maukael ' they must have been referring to a copy of the later version; consequently Maucael may have been only an editor not the author of the treatise. But in the document just quoted the warden of the Islands speaks of the custumal as ' Registrum dictarum consuetudinum ',[1] and he presumably had before him the very same text as the Jerseymen had in mind when they spoke of the ' Summa de Maukael '. In view of this evidence, it is hard to maintain Tardif's distinction between manuscripts entitled ' Registrum . . .' and manuscripts entitled ' Summa . . .'; and thus, with Viollet, we may the more confidently salute this enigmatic Maucael as the author of the *Grand Coutumier de Normandie*.

The warden's appeal to the *bailli* of the Cotentin also calls for some comment. It would be interesting to know whether he chose this particular official because he happened to be nearest, or whether he was applying to an acknowledged authority. The *Grand Coutumier* seems to have been composed in the Cotentin; Maucael may have lived in or near the town of Valognes; the assizes of the *bailliage* of the Cotentin met very frequently in that town; it was the *bailli's* chief duty to hold the assizes. Is there any connexion between these facts and possibilities ? Was there a tradition of high legal wisdom in the officials of the *bailliage* ? Some suggestion of this is contained in the warden's phrase : ' ballivo Constantini et eius sapientibus qui in consuetudinibus ac legibus Normannie sunt experti '.

---

[1] Cf. ' librum seu registrum dictarum consuetudinum seu statutorum Normannie ' in an act of Philip IV, dated 1302 ; and ' Registrum Consuetudinis Normannie ' in the ' Charte aux Normands ', both quoted by Viollet, *op. cit.* pp. 70–2.

The argument has already become purely speculative and it is time to point the moral of this note. Both the authoritative position of the *Grand Coutumier de Normandie* in Jersey early in the fourteenth century, and the correspondence between the warden of the Islands and the *bailli* of the Cotentin prove, if proof were necessary, that the law of the Channel Islands in the fourteenth century, as in later times, notwithstanding the break with Normandy in 1204, was Norman law. The ' customs used in the Islands of Guernsey and Jersey which differ from the custom of Normandy ' were no more than local usages such as grew up in all parts of Normandy save in the Cotentin. These local usages were set down in writing by the Islanders on several occasions during the early part of the fourteenth century, and most of these statements have survived.[1] We can thus be fully informed concerning them, and so, discounting them, we can apply existing knowledge of medieval Norman law to the solving of problems of Channel Island history.

There is a more important deduction to be made from this equation. Records of the jurisprudence of local courts in medieval Normandy are conspicuously deficient, for, although rolls were kept, hardly any have survived. On the other hand, the existing *corpus* of documents relating to the administration of law in the Channel Islands during the middle ages is very large ; [2] and, since this law has been shown to be Norman law, these Channel Island documents have clearly more than a local importance. They are preserved in the Public Record Office and are therefore readily accessible in normal times ; but they have not yet caught the eye of a specialist in the history of Norman law and are still, for the most part, unprinted. If they, and our interest in such matters, survive present troubles, then, if they fall into capable hands, they will show that the Channel Islands have more to contribute to the history of Norman law than a couple of references to a possible author of the *Grand Coutumier* who is otherwise but an empty name.

---

1   Le Patourel, *op. cit.*, pp. 105ff. A list of the more important statements of Channel Island custom made during the thirteenth and fourteenth centuries is given *ibid.*, p. 106, n. 2.

2   A preliminary attempt to list these documents is made *ibid.*., pp. 12-13.

GUERNSEY, JERSEY AND THEIR
ENVIRONMENT IN THE MIDDLE AGES

In the way that historians usually speak, the history of Guernsey and Jersey is local history. It is a term which is still sometimes used in a rather patronizing way, partly because local history has often been written in a narrow and antiquarian spirit, but more perhaps because it has been felt that local history is a somewhat lower form of historical writing than national history or the history of great movements of continental or of even wider scope. Prejudice apart, however, one clear characteristic of local history is that it cannot be understood except in the context of the history of the larger communities or groups of which any local entity forms a part. The history of Weymouth, say, has to be seen in the context of the history of Dorset, and the history of Dorset in the context of the history of Wessex or of England and ultimately of Britain; equally, the history of Weymouth would have to be seen in the context of the development of English towns and then of Western European towns, of English ports and watering-places. The implications of this example, however, soon lead to the conclusion that all 'units of study' in historical investigation, whether they are as particular or as local as may be, or as national or supra-national, have to be seen as relative to something more general, something analogous or even something profoundly different in order to be intelligible, and the distinctions between local and national history come to have very little significance. Historians, in any case, frequently have to deal with times when nations, in the modern sense, did not exist or were still in process of formation.

Since they are islands, separated by quite a few miles of turbulent sea from one another and from their mainland, Guernsey and Jersey are both well-defined units, and the communities they have supported have been given a certain autonomy simply by their 'insulation'. Yet physical insularity works both ways. In one way it tends to separate, to throw the population of an island in upon itself and to provide the means of keeping strangers out. But the sea has always been as much of a highway as a barrier; new people, influences, ideas do in fact reach islands, often because they happen to be passing that way. Yet an island community, through its own natural

* The substance of this paper was originally expressed in the form of three lectures delivered in Jersey under the auspices of the 'Don Balleine' Trust in April 1964. Shorter versions were subsequently read to La Société Guernesiaise in 1969 and to the Guernsey Society (in London) in 1973. I am grateful to the 'Don Balleine' Trustees for the invitation which provided the initial impetus and to the Council of La Société Guernesiaise for encouraging me to prepare the thing for publication.

cohesion and its relative insulation, has the capacity to absorb such novelties: they will modify it but they will not change it out of all recognition, or only over a long period of time.

Apply these general notions to Guernsey and Jersey and it will be seen that their history, like the history of other communities large and small, can only be made intelligible in relation to some larger unit, political, cultural, economic or whatever it may be. Their immediate environment is the sea, with the particular balance of isolation and accessibility which the sea imposes; but beyond the sea are the political and cultural structures formed on the continent of Europe and in the British Isles. The Islands could not but be profoundly affected by the great movements of peoples that took place in these lands during the first millenium of this era, or by the social, political and economic order that historians call feudalism as it was formed in the eleventh and twelfth centuries, or by the great upheavals of the Reformation and the various political, industrial and technological revolutions of more recent times. These cannot be taken for granted in any history of the Channel Islands, precisely because the extent to which they may have been modified in the Islands by their insularity and adapted into a particular insular variety is the very stuff of that history.

Moreover, this is not just a historical technicality such as professional historians might discuss only with one another. It is a matter of practical importance to all who consider the past of the Islands in any capacity, as archaeologists or historians, as students of legal, political or economic problems. Where do such scholars look for analogies? What is the general form to which specific examples from the Islands must be related? Which of the insular characteristics have been formed within them, which have been derived from some source outside them, and in what proportion and with what adaptations? Such problems abound in their history, from the identification of a carved roundel found at Cobo in 1968 to such questions as the origin of the jurats or the long survival of English political allegiance combined with French language and culture. On most of the really important matters in the history of Guernsey and Jersey, what was going on beyond their shores was at least as important and as relevant as anything happening on their small land-surfaces.

Since the history of Guernsey and Jersey has not generally been looked at in this way but has been regarded more as a series of events taking place on the islands themselves, this essay attempts to redress the balance somewhat by concentrating, disproportionately by intention, on their historical environment. During the Middle Ages this environment has a special interest because it was constantly changing. Almost from one century to another the Channel Islands found themselves in one political or cultural environment and then in another, partly because they were forcibly taken into one after another, partly because the political and cultural units around them were themselves developing and changing rapidly. At one time they were included in an autonomous Brittany, then in an autonomous Normandy, then in a Norman empire, then in an Angevin one and finally, so far as this survey goes, among the appendages to the kingdom of England that were politically within the kingdom of France. Put like this there is perhaps little to distinguish them from other borderlands which have found themselves now in one country and now in another according to the fortunes of politics and war; but they are differentiated in this respect from a city such as Strasbourg, for example, by their insularity, which has assisted them to take advantage of their relationship to this changing environment in order to secure a privileged autonomy. The nearest analogy is perhaps the independent and quasi-independent communities that have developed in scarcely accessible mountain valleys.

The immediate geographical environment of the Channel Islands is a region that may be described as 'the Western English Channel', a region comprising the south-west peninsula of England to the north, Brittany and the western part of Normandy to the south, and the sea between them. This is a region of ancient rocks, thrown up originally by the great Hercynian mountain-building convulsion, worn down, raised and worn down again into the moors of Devon and Cornwall and the hills of Brittany and western Normandy, with lower hill-tops appearing out of the sea between them as islands. (1) Geographically, the Channel Islands are no more than such off-shore islands, very closely associated with the immediate mainland; and from the time when the rising sea finally separated them from that mainland until the time when the political authority of Rome began to falter they were no more than off-shore islands in every sense, as Belle-Ile or the Isle of Wight still are. In all this time such people as lived in Guernsey and Jersey cannot have differed in any material respect from those of the adjacent mainlands on either side of the sea, or these from one another; and whether new peoples, new fashions and new techniques came to this Western Channel region overland from the east or by sea along the 'western seaways', whether the coastlands of north-western Gaul ('Armorica') and south-western Britain were remote from political and cultural centres or in the mainstream of civilization, whether political authority there was in the hands of Gaulish and British chieftains, whose relations even across a hundred miles or so of sea were always close, or was exercised by a vast organization centred ultimately on a Roman emperor, the region was homogeneous.

Though the purely geographical homogeneity naturally remained, this homogeneity in its human dimension began to break up with the great movement of peoples which heralded and partly caused the disintegration of the Roman Empire. Before this the Romans, or Romanized Gauls, had certainly known the Channel Islands and may have introduced some dilute elements of Roman civilization into them; but in those times the Islands shared in the remoteness of Armorica, which had some of the characteristics of the 'Highland Zone' in Britain, (2) and Romanization can have been little more than a veneer. (3) When they came, beginning in the third century A.D., the movements which most affected the Western Channel region were those of the Saxons from North Germany and Denmark, coming by sea, Britons from southern Britain, also moving by sea, and the Franks expanding overland from the Rhineland.   The Saxons settled in eastern and south-eastern England and gradually pushed westward, though they did not colonize Devon effectively until the seventh century or Cornwall until the tenth, and then only partly. There was a Saxon settlement in what was later Normandy, though not, so far as it is known, in the immediate vicinity of the Channel Islands. The Islands may, however, have been involved in the Roman scheme of defence against them, for the Nunnery on Alderney could have been a small late-Roman fort or signal station in its original form, though this has still to be proved. (4) The Britons, whatever it was

1.   P. Vidal de la Blache, *Tableau de la géographie de la France (Histoire de France*, general editor E. Lavisse, i. 1, 1911), pp. 11-13, 323-38.

2.   C. Fox, *The Personality of Britain* (4th ed. 1943), pp. 28-50. L. Pape in *Histoire de la Bretagne* (ed. J. Delumeau, 1969), pp. 89-115, argues, however, that the remoteness of Brittany in Gallo-Roman times should not be exaggerated.

3.   *The Archaeology of the Channel Islands;* i., T. D. Kendrick, *The Bailiwick of Guernsey* (1928), pp. 13-14; ii., J. Hawkes, *The Bailiwick of Jersey* (1937), p. 18.

4.   Kendrick, *Bailiwick of Guernsey*, pp. 13, 254-9. On the problem of the Nunnery, D. E. Johnston, 'Archaeology study of the Nunnery', *Alderney Society and Museum Quarterly Bulletin*, Oct.-Dec. 1971, pp. 15-16. There are maps showing the late Roman coastal defences in Britain and Gaul with a discussion of some of the problems in D. A. White, *Litus Saxonicum* (1961). I am indebted to Professor Mattingly and Dr Hind of the University of Leeds for this last reference.

that impelled them to move from their original homes, settled in the territory of the modern departments of Finistère,, Côtes-du-Nord and the northern part of Ille-et-Vilaine, spreading later into Morbihan. (5) The geographical position of the Islands, lying directly in the line of any movement from south-western Britain to north-western Gaul, together with memories of St. Samson and other 'Celtic saints' (6) suggests that they too were colonized. They were certainly said to be inhabited by 'Bretons' at the turn of the eighth and ninth centuries.(7) The Franks took possession of the lands which later became Normandy and eastern and southern Brittany late in the fifth century. Save perhaps to the north of the Seine, they seem to have formed no more than a landed aristocracy in these countries, and much of the Romano-Gaulish population, with the ecclesiastical organization in particular, survived to form a large element in Frankish civilization and political organization. Whether any people who could be called Franks settled in the Channel Islands at this time is doubtful, for Frankish colonization in the west of the future Normandy was very much slighter than in the east. (8).

By the seventh and eighth centuries of our era, then, the environment of the Channel Islands had broken up in terms of people and political structures — Saxons to the north, Franks to the east and Bretons to the south, with a substantial substratum, however, of more or less 'de-Romanized' Britons or Gauls in most parts. The destiny of the Islands lay in the interrelations of these peoples and their respective political development. It was first involved in the attempts of the Frankish kings and emperors to contain the Bretons and to prevent their expansion, if possible to subdue them, and the Breton reaction to these attempts. Charlemagne, in particular, made a great effort to bring the Bretons effectively into his realm, partly by military conquest, partly by making local chieftains his officers there, the second a device that was also being used in Aquitaine and elsewhere. But these chieftains were soon seeking a real independence from Charlemagne's weaker and quarrelsome successors. In the early part of the ninth century they conquered the Frankish territories of the modern departments of Morbihan, Loire Atlantique and Ille-et-Vilaine, and by adding them to the northern and western lands colonized earlier formed the historic Brittany, for ever to be half-Breton, half-Frankish. (9) In 867 Charles the Bald, king of West Francia, agreed to the annexation of the Cotentin (apart from his rights over the bishopric of Coutances) by Salomon, now king of this Brittany, (10) in return for a promise of fidelity. The Avranchin was not

5.   On the problems of the Breton migration, e.g. P. Riche in *Histoire de la Bretagne* (ed. J. Delumeau), pp. 117-21; K. Jackson, *Language and History in Early Britain* (1953), pp. 11-30; N. K. Chadwick, 'The Colonization of Brittany from Celtic Britain', *Proceedings of the British Academy*, li (1965), 235-99.
6.   R. Fawtier, *La Vie de Saint Samson* (Bibliothèque de l'Ecole des Hautes Etudes, fasc. 197, 1912), pp. 64-71, 72, 153, 169-70; T. Taylor, *The Life of St. Samson of Dol* (1925), pp. 57-8, 75. Whatever doubts there may be concerning the historicity of the Life, the fact remains that there is a church dedicated to St. Samson in Guernsey, that the dedication can be traced back to the eleventh century, and is most unlikely to have been made by people of Scandinavian descent.
7.   According to the 'Miracles of St. Wandrille', Geroaldus, abbot of Saint-Wandrille (789-807) was sent by Charlemagne'to an island called Augia, which is inhabited by Bretons and Iles near the Cotentin, at that time ruled by a leader called Anowarith' (Bouquet, *Recueil des historiens de la France*, ed. L. Delisle, v., 1869, 455). 'Anowarith' seems to be a good contemporary Breton name *(Cartulaire de l'Abbaye de Redon en Bretagne*, ed. A. de Courson, 1863, pp. 45, 54, 62, 69). Cf. the Life of St. Magloire, *Acta Sanctorum*, October, x, 782-91. I am indebted to Professor L. Musset for helping me to identify these references. See also his footnote in 'Les domaines de l'époque franque . . .', *Bulletin de la Société des Antiquaires de Normandie*, xlix (1946 for 1942-5), p. 73.
8.   C. Verlinden, 'Frankish Colonization, a New Approach', *Trans. Royal Historical Society*, 5th series, iv (1954), 13-17; L. Musset in *Histoire de la Normandie* (ed. M. de Bouard, 1970), pp. 77-88; P. Riche in *Histoire de la Bretagne* (ed. J. Delumeau), pp. 121-8.
9.   *Ibid.*, pp. 128-36.
10.   The royal title had been assumed by his cousin and predecessor, Erispoé.

mentioned, no doubt because it was already in Breton hands; nor is there any mention of the Channel Islands in the report we have of the treaty; but it is inconceivable that they should not have been included with the adjacent coast in this enlarged Breton realm; (11) and the Bretons or people of Breton descent living in the Islands were probably reinforced at this time, for Breton settlements seem to have been made in the Cotentin, mostly by the coast, though extending as far east as Caen and even beyond. (12)

At all events it is clear that from 867 until the early years of the tenth century the Channel Islands were part of a large and apparently well-organized Breton kingdom, extending into the western Normandy, Maine and Anjou of later times and independent in fact, for the obedience promised in 867 could not be enforced by King Charles the Bald or his successors. It is not difficult to imagine conditions in which this situation might have endured; and if it had done so it would have been easy to explain at least in geographical terms, for the territory ruled by the Breton kings of the second half of the ninth century corresponded very closely with the region of the Western Channel on the southern side of the sea, a region identified by geology, climate and natural resources. The later duchy of Normandy which united the lower Seine valley with the Cotentin, the Avranchin and the Islands was, in these terms, 'against nature'.

::   ::   ::   ::

The Breton kingdom and the Frankish kingdom to the east of it were, however, violently disrupted by the raids of the Northmen (Vikings) in the ninth century and by their settlements early in the tenth. These Northmen came from two countries and by two routes. Those who came ultimately from Denmark came through the Straits of Dover, though often more immediately from early settlements in England, north eastern France and the Low Countries; those who came from Norway had mostly rounded the northern coasts and islands of Scotland, though they or their recent ancestors likewise often came immediately from settlements in the Western Isles, Ireland and western Britain. It was those who came ultimately from Denmark, chiefly, who operated in France, using the rivers as a means of penetration into the interior, the Seine and the Loire being those used most extensively. This was happening at the same time as the Breton leaders were building up their kingdom; indeed the Bretons found their opportunity in the confusion caused by the Northmen, for the successors of Charlemagne seemed unable to find any defence against their raiding and plundering until King Charles the Simple (898-929), adapting the device which his predecessors had used in their attempt to control the Bretons, seized the occasion of a somewhat isolated military victory to make an agreement with the leader of a band of Northmen operating chiefly in the Seine valley. This leader is known to history as Rollo, and by the agreement he and his followers were permitted

11. '(King) Charles (the Bald), after hostages had been given, received Pascuithen, (King) Salomon's ambassador, at Compiègne on 1 August (867), and granted to him as Salomon's agent *(uicario)* the county *(comitatum)* of the Cotientin; with all the royal lands and estates *(fiscis et uillis regis)* and the abbeys in that county, and all things pertaining to it, except the bishopric *(episcopatu).* and confirmed this grant with an oath of the magnates. For this he obtained from Salomon, through his agent aforesaid, an oath promising fidelity and peace and assistance against his enemies.' *Annales de Saint-Bertin,* edd. F. Grat, J. Vieillard and S. Clémencet (Société de l'histoire de France, 1964), p. 137. On the Avranchin, A. Le Moyne de la Borderie, *Histoire de Bretagne,* ii (1906), 89-90, note 3.

12. H. Prentout, *Etude critique sur Dudon de Saint-Quentin* (Mémoires de l'Academie nationale . . . de Caen, 1915), pp. 285-7; H. Chanteux, 'Le toponyme "Bretteville" en Normandie et son origine', *Recueil de travaux offert à M. Clovis Brunel* (1955), pp. 248-54; G. Souillet, 'Les Brette et Bretteville de Normandie: sont-ils des établissements bretons?', *Annales de Bretagne* lxii (1955), 408-12.

to settle in and around the city of Rouen on condition of accepting Christianity and some form of political subordination to the Frankish king, a subordination which it is impossible to define now and was in all probability less than precise then. By giving them lands of their own to defend, the king might hope that they would not only block the Seine valley against other raiders and so protect his kingdom from dangers in that direction, but that, through their acceptance of Christianity and their association with surviving Frankish people in the territory assigned to them, they would ultimately be absorbed into the Frankish social and political order. The agreement is generally known as the treaty of Saint-Clair-sur-Epte, and it was made in or about the year 911. (13) Very soon after it was made, a similar device was tried in order to subdue the Northmen who were operating in the Loire valley. Their devastations throughout the length and breadth of Brittany had been such that there seems to have been a general exodus of the chief leaders of the people there after the death of Alan the Great (the last Breton ruler to take the royal title) in 907, as well as of the monks with their relics and treasures, most towards the interior of France, some to England. In 921, according to the well-informed chronicler Flodoard, Robert, count of the Breton March, (14) who, though as powerful in fact as King Charles the Simple and soon to be in open rebellion against him, must have been acting at least formally with his authority, granted 'Brittany which they had devastated' to them, 'together with the county of Nantes', also on condition of accepting Christianity. (15)

The destiny of the Channel Islands then hung on the fortunes of these two Viking settlements and on the question whether they would coalesce (the Northmen of the Seine were making raids in all directions and secured a further grant of territory, in 924, to the west of their original acquisition around Rouen) or, if they remained separate and distinct, where the boundary between them would be drawn. The Bretons themselves had a hand in the issue, for those who had remained in their own country began to recover themselves about the year 930 and, with the help of returning exiles, were able to dispose of the Northmen of the Loire. While this operation was still in its early stages, King Rudolf intervened, in 933, by assigning a

13.   The treaty between King Charles and Rollo survives only in the description of it by Dudo de Saint-Quentin, written about 100 years later and embellished with a great deal of legendary matter *(De Moribus et actis primorum Normanniae Ducum,* ed. J. Lair, (Mém. de la Soc. des Antiquaires de Normandie, 1865), pp. 166-71; cf. Prentout, *Etude critique sur Dudon de Saint-Quentin, passim,* and D. C. Douglas, 'Rollo of Normandy', *English Historical Review,* lvii, 1942, 417-36). It is, however, alluded to in a more matter-of-fact way by Flodoard in his 'History of the Church of Reims': '(The archbishop of Reims) laboured hard to convert the Northmen and to mitigate (their savagery) until at length, after the battle which Count Robert fought against them at Chartres, they began to adopt the faith of Christ, having been granted certain maritime *pagi,* with the city of Rouen which they had almost destroyed, and other *pagi* dependent on it' (edd. J. Heller and G. Waitz, *Monumenta Germaniae Historica,* Scriptores xiii, 1881, 577). This is supplemented by a short passage in a diploma of King Charles the Simple, dated 918, recording the grant of the abbey of La Croix-Saint-Leufroi to Saint-German-des-Prés: 'We have given . . . that abbey . . . except the part (of its lands) which we have granted to the Northmen of the Seine, that is to Rollo and his companions, to safeguard the kingdom' *(Recueil des actes de Charles III le Simple,* ed. P. Lauer; Chartes et diplômes relatifs à l'histoire de France, 7bis, i., 1940, no. xcii, p. 211). It should be noted that this initial grant of territory to the Northmen of the Seine was limited to lands around Rouen, undefined except that they are described as an unspecified number of *pagi* and except for the one point in Charles's diploma. The *pagi,* or 'counties', were units of local administration in the Carolingian realm, comparable with the English shires. When, however, there is occasion to refer to these units as they were in the eleventh or later centuries, the French word *comté* will be used in this paper; for by then there was little in common between them and the English shires or counties.
14.   The 'Breton March' was a large military district organized by the Carolingian kings to contain the Bretons.
15.   'For five months Count Robert besieged the Northmen who occupied the River Loire, then, after taking hostages, granted to them Brittany which they had devastated, with the *pagus* of Nantes, and they began to adopt the faith of Christ': Flodoard, *Annales,* ed. P. Lauer, Collection de Textes pour servir à l'étude et à l'enseignement de l'histoire, 1906), p. 6. The close parallel between the phrases used by Flodoard in this passage and in his description of King Charles's agreement with the Northmen of the Seine can hardly be missed.

territory described by Flodoard as 'the land of the Bretons by the sea coast' (16) to William Longsword, Rollo's son and successor as ruler of the Northmen of the Seine. It has generally been thought that Flodoard used this phrase to mean the Cotentin and the Avranchin, with the Channel Islands, that is, the land that had been ceded to the Bretons in 867, and that this marks the third and final stage in the territorial formation of the duchy of Normandy; but whereas Flodoard normally uses precise terms in describing such cessions of territory, he is here quite vague. (17) It may be regarded as certain that the Northmen of the Seine, then and later, were doing their best to occupy the Cotentin peninsula, the country around Dol and lands even further into Brittany; (18) and it may well be that King Rudolf was trying to assist the Bretons by assigning to the Northmen of the Seine what had already been given to the Northmen of the Loire, thus setting one lot of Vikings against the other. The outcome in any case was the recovery of what was to be the historic land of Brittany by the Bretons themselves under the leadership of Alan Barbetorte (who and whose successors were styled duke or count rather than king), crowning their achievements in 939 with a great victory over the Northmen at Trans not far from Pontorson. (19) It is reasonable to suppose that the defeated were primarily Northmen of the Seine, and that it was this battle which decided that the little river Couesnon nearby should ultimately be the boundary between Brittany and their territory, which we can now call Normandy, when the two principalities had organised themselves sufficiently to need a precise frontier. It also no doubt decided that the Channel Islands would be at the western extremity of Normandy rather than a north-eastern outpost of Brittany; for the defeat of the Normans at Trans did little to reduce the pressure which they kept up against the country around Dol and there was little chance that the Bretons would recover the Cotentin. For the Islands it was certainly a momentous decision.

Nevertheless, if it was decided by the middle of the tenth century that the Channel Islands should not be Breton, it was some time before it could be said with any real meaning that they were Norman, for the duchy of Normandy was not made in a day. (20) There was much to be done before the Viking settlement in and around Rouen could mature into the principality that William the Conqueror ruled. Rollo and his descendants had to dispose of rival Viking leaders, maintain their authority over their followers and extend it over later Viking settlers who were arriving independently in Normandy at intervals throughout the tenth century (one of these, of Norse origin, which settled in the Cotentin, must have affected the Islands) (21) and over the survivors of the Frankish population, achieve a state of equilibrium in relation to neighbouring principalities and construct an administration for the

16.   'William, prince of the Normans, commends himself to the king, who gives him the land of the Bretons by the sea-coast *(terram Brittonum in ora maritima sitam)*': Flodoard, *Annales,* p. 55.
17.   Generally he describes the territories granted in terms of *pagi,* which were still clearly defined areas; though he does not always specify which *pagi* he is referring to.
18.   Flodoard, *Annales.* p. 94; *Chronique de Nantes,* ed. R. Merlet (Collection de textes pour servir à l'étude et à l'enseignement de l'histoire, 1896), pp. 111-12; D. C. Douglas, 'The Rise of Normandy', *Proceedings of the British Academy.* xxxiii (1947), pp. 106-10.
19.   The battle is alluded to by Flodoard in *Annales.* p. 74 and in the *Chronique de Nantes,* p. 91.
20.   The argument for what follows on the early history of Normandy, and on Norman expansion in France and in Britain, is set out with references in my forthcoming book, *The Norman Empire.* It owes a great deal to L. Musset, 'Naissance de la Normandie (Ve-XIe siècles)' in *Histoire de la Normandie,* ed. M. de Bouard, pp. 75-130; J. Yver, 'Les premières institutions du duché de Normandie', *I Normanni e la loro espansione in Europa nell'alto medioevo* (Centro italiano di studi sull'alto medioevo, Settimana di studi xvi, 1968; Spoleto, 1969), pp. 299-366; and D. C. Douglas, 'The Rise of Normandy' and *William the Conqueror. The Norman Impact upon England* (1964).
21.   L. Musset, 'Aperçus sur la colonisation scandinave dans le nord du Cotentin', *Annuaire des Cinq Départments de la Normandie.* cxi, Année 121, 1953), 34-7 (title only on off-print).

exploitation of the lands they dominated. It was a long and complex process lasting well over a century from the settlement of 911; and the final stabilizing of the frontier depended as much on governmental effectiveness and military conquest as upon royal concessions.

The phenomenal success which Rollo's descendants achieved was due to a fortunate succession of able rulers, the solidarity of their family and the enormous wealth they derived from their raiding and trading, as well as from the lands taken from the Frankish Church, Frankish landowners and the royal estates in Normandy; for the greater part of all this seems to have fallen into their hands. They used this wealth to build up a military aristocracy, devoted to their service and often bound to them by family ties, and to re-establish and re-endow the Church in Normandy which would consecrate their power and, to a very large extent, their ambitions and aggressions. They were able, in ways that are now quite mysterious though the result cannot be denied, to construct a government on the basis of Frankish institutions and Frankish law which they must have found not entirely ruined in the lands that became Normandy.

In all this the Channel Islands had their part, though not perhaps in the earliest stages. The activity of the dukes (22) in the tenth century and even in the earlier years of the eleventh, was very largely confined to the eastern part of their duchy. In the Cotentin there had been Breton and independent Scandinavian settlements, and the condition of that country was such that the bishops of Coutances who had taken up their residence in Rouen at the time of the main Viking invasions, did not return to their diocese until about 1025 (an attempt by the duke to re-establish them there in or about 990 failed); apart from Mont-Saint-Michel, which is exceptional in many ways, no monastery was founded in either of the two western dioceses before Lessay (c. 1060); and the revolt of 1047, in which the *vicomtes* of the Cotentin and the Bessin were among the chief leaders, may well have been a last gesture of a hitherto virtually independent west, at least in part.

The earliest Norman document of which the text survives and which concerns the Channel Islands is to be dated to some year between 1022 and 1026; though it has to be said that there are not many documents surviving from any part of Normandy of a date earlier than this.(23) We have in fact about seventeen documents in some form that record transactions in or relating to the Islands and entered into before 1066.(24) They show that in the time of Duke Robert I (1027-

22. The terms 'duke' and 'duchy' will be used for convenience, though the style 'duke of the Normans' was not stabilized or in any sense 'official' until after the middle of the twelfth century.

23. In M. Fauroux, *Recueil des actes des ducs de Normandie, 911-1066* (Mém. de la Soc. des Antiquaires de Normandie, xxxvi, 1961) the text is given of 6 acts of Duke Richard I (942-96), 50 of Richard II (996-1026), 33 of Richard III and Robert I (1026-35) and 114 of William the Conqueror up to 1066. In fact, as was pointed out by a reviewer, this is a very respectable number for any part of contemporary France, though it is small by comparison with the surviving acts of the kings of England during the same period of time. 'Private' charters have certainly survived from pre-1066 Normandy (e.g., L. Delisle, *Histoire du château et des sires de Saint-Sauveur-le-Vicomte*, 1867, pieces justificatives), but they have not been collected together.

24. These documents are printed or noticed in *Cartulaire des Iles Normandes: Recueil de Documents concernant l'histoire de ces Iles* (Société Jersiaise, Jersey, 1924), Fauroux, *Recueil* (as above), Delisle, *Histoire du château . . . de Saint-Sauveur-le-Vicomte*, and elsewhere. As these are the earliest formal documents known in the history of the Channel Islands, it is worth giving the references, in approximately chronological order: (1) *Cartulaire* no. 3 — *Recueil* no. 49; (2) *Cartulaire* no. 114 — *Recueil* no. 73; (3) *Cartulaire* nos. 148 (?), 149; (4) *Cartulaire* no. 150 (?), cf. Delisle, p. 21 note 3; (5) *Cartulaire* no. 291 (ii) — *Recueil* no. 99; (6) *Cartulaire* no. 151 — *Recueil* no. 110; (7) *Cartulaire* no. 115 = *Recueil* no. 111; (8) *Cartulaire* nos. 298, 299 — Delisle, pièces justificatives, nos. 20, 21; (9) *Cartulaire* no. 116 — *Recueil* no. 133; (10) *Cartulaire* no. 300 — Delisle, pièces justificatives, no. 31 (the original of this charter is now in the Greffe, Guernsey); (11) *Cartulaire* no. 297 — *Recueil* no. 141; (12) *Cartulaire* no. 326 — *Recueil* no. 198; (13) *Recueil* no. 214; (14) *Cartulaire* no. 316 — *Recueil* no. 224; (15) *Cartulaire* no. 319 — *Recueil* no. 231. Those marked with a query may not have been composed before 1066, but it is very likely that they were.

35), and probably before that, the duke had been in direct possession of the whole of Guernsey and the smaller islands, with a part of Jersey (probably a large part though its extent cannot now be certainly known), and of extensive rights over the churches in all the islands. It is an example in detail of the great wealth of the early dukes and of the use they made of it. At one point half of Guernsey had been given to Nigel de Saint-Sauveur,*vicomte* of the Cotentin, and the other half to Ranulf fitzAnquetil, *vicomte* of the Bessin, two members of that partly military partly ministerial aristocracy that the dukes were building up in Normandy; while the knight Adelelmus, who held a moderate estate in the Avranchin and a small one in Jersey directly of the duke is an example of the lower ranks of the same aristocracy. They show also that, as the first reaction of the laity in the eleventh and twelfth centuries to the reforming movement in the Western Church which attacked among other things the lay ownership of churches was to give their churches to monasteries, so churches as well as property in land in the Channel Islands were being given by the duke and his barons to monasteries on the Norman mainland. The chief beneficiaries at this time were Mont-Saint-Michel, Cerisy, Montivilliers, the college of canons (later monastery) at Saint-Sauveur-le-Vicomte and a great religious house which was not in Normandy though much favoured by the Norman dukes, Marmoutier near Tours. By the time of the Norman conquest of England, therefore, though there is indeed evidence of small estates contained within one island or the other, the larger estates there were generally relatively small appendages to much greater estates held by barons or religious communities on the Norman mainland, a feature which characterized the Islands until the thirteenth century.

Although there is no indication of a ducal administration in the Channel Islands at this time, the duke, his barons and the monasteries must have made some provision for the exploitation of their properties there as well as for the service of the churches. It was in this way that the Islands were being integrated into the western part of Normandy which at that very time was itself being developed and integrated with the remainder of the duchy by the dukes. They were doing this by building castles (Falaise, Cherbourg, Brix, Saint-James-de-Beuvron), encouraging urban growth (Caen, Cherbourg, Saint-Lô, Coutances) and assisting in the re-establishment of the Church. The last was accomplished within the diocese of Coutances during the episcopate of Bishop Geoffrey de Montbrai (1049-93). It was he who finally re-settled the bishops of Coutances in their ancient cathedral city; re-constituted the cathedral staff and diocesan organization; recovered the property of the see and obtained lands in the Channel Islands from Duke William; took some part in the foundation of the first three or four monasteries to rise in his diocese since the invasions, and was responsible for the greater part of the building, certainly the completion, of the great Romanesque cathedral church of which some vestiges still remain. There is clear evidence that the churches and parishes of Guernsey and Jersey existed in some form before he was made bishop, so that he cannot be responsible for their foundation; but we may reasonably infer from an apparently contemporary account of his episcopate that he brought them fully into the organization of the diocese and that by the time of his death the Islands were integrated into the ecclesiastical as they were into the secular structure of the duchy — so far as these can be distinguished at this time. (25)

---

25. On Bishop Geoffrey, Le Patourel, 'Geoffrey of Montbray, Bishop of Coutances (1049-1093)', *English Historical Review*. lix (1944), 129-61. The growth of Caen as a symptom of the ducal development of the west is described by M. de Bouard in *Guillaume le Conquérant* (Coll. Que Sais-Je ?, 1958), pp. 58-60. The early testimony to the existence of the parish churches in the Islands is something of a problem, given their remoteness and the condition of the diocese of Coutances in the early eleventh century. Nevertheless, the existence of the churches as parish churches in the first half of the century seems clear (e.g. *Cartulaire*, pp. 230-31, 374-5, 379-80).

This integration not only involved the Channel Islands in the development of Norman society and government — somewhat remotely, perhaps, for they lay on the very extremity of the duchy—but also in the great enlargement of Norman interests that took place during the eleventh century. Normandy itself had been founded at least as much upon violence as upon the lawful cession of territories and transmission of authority by the king to the Viking leaders. Throughout the tenth century contemporaries referred to the Normans, those settled in Normandy, as 'pirates', for their wealth still derived in large part from activities in which raiding and trading were not always clearly distinguished. At the turn of the century, however, a great change was coming over Normandy. Its connections with Scandinavia and the Scandinavian settlements in Britain were breaking and it was turning more to France. The military aristocracy which the dukes were creating, partly to enable them to hold their own against neighbouring princes, partly as an essential element in the structure of their duchy, was coming to be organized, like neighbouring nobilities, more and more on the basis of a system of personal and tenurial relationships that historians call 'feudal'. The fact that the loyalty and service of able and ambitious men could only be maintained by grants of land from time to time meant that the duke must look for new sources as the lands at his disposal were exhausted. Up to a point he could rob the Church, confiscate the lands of rebels and still distribute and redistribute the lands of his vassals with some freedom until a little after the middle of the century; but sooner or later he would have to look beyond his duchy as neighbouring rulers were looking beyond their principalities for the same purpose. A developing feudal state was by its nature expansionist and aggressive, as modern industrial organization must continually expand in order to survive on its present basis.

The need to expand became explosive under William the Conqueror. His father had already established some form of superiority over the duke of Brittany and perhaps over the small but strategically important territory of the Vexin Français between the Seine, the Epte and the Oise, and the Normans already had interests in England; but there are some indications that under Duke Robert the ducal resources in land were running dangerously low. As they can hardly have improved during William's troubled minority, he had to be a conqueror or go under. Already before 1066 he had conquered the neighbouring *comté* of Maine from which he annexed Domfront and the surrounding district of the Passais to Normandy, imposed his suzerainty on the count of Pontieu, probably on the count of Boulogne as well, and, although it is not easy to see what part William himself had in the process, Norman interests in England were growing in a way that almost seems like a conscious preparation for the conquest of 1066-72. This conquest, when it came, was a good deal more than a simple military operation. It involved the detailed taking possession of the whole of English land by William, his Norman aristocracy and churchmen who, since they retained their lands and interests in Normandy, built up huge cross-Channel estates. Thus, among those who had or came to have interests in the Channel Islands, Ranulf 'le Meschin', *vicomte* of the Bessin, eventually acquired the vast earldom of Chester in 1120 and the dignity from which his Guernsey estate, 'Fief-le-Comte', took its name; (26) the de Carteret family from the Cotentin, whenever precisely they obtained their lands in Jersey, secured estates in the West

26. G.E.C., *Complete Peerage.* iii (1913), 166; T. W. M. de Guérin, 'Feudalism in Guernsey', *Transactions of the Guernsey Society of Natural Science and Local Research.* vi (1913 for 1909-12), 58-9.

Country soon after 1066; (27) and most of the Norman abbeys which had interests in the Islands also obtained lands or other profitable rights in England. (28) Furthermore, William, his barons and their immediate descendants went on from this to conquer and colonize a large part of Wales and to establish a suzerainty over the surviving Welsh princes, to establish a similar suzerainty over the kings of Scots and an important interest in their kingdom and to intensify their suzerainty over their neighbours in France.

All this affected the Channel Islands not simply because they were a part, if a remote part, of a rapidly expanding principality, nor because they must have been brought into some indirect contact with England through those who administered the lands of Norman monasteries and landholders, but because they were included in the integrated political structure which the Norman kings built upon their conquests. These rulers made the relationship between Normandy and England, and between those countries and the outlying overlordships, a great deal more than union in their persons alone. They and their family came to treat the whole of their property and their governmental prerogatives as a single, indivisible inheritance, and in this they were supported by their barons and churchmen who had similar interests. (29) Though they were never given the title 'king of the Normans' their power and authority in the duchy was effectively as royal as it was in England (30) (which fundamentally is why we speak of a Royal Court rather than a ducal court in Guernsey and Jersey to this day); (31) and they worked out a practical system of government for their lands and overlordships as a whole, based on an itinerant king, household and court, common to Normandy and England, with delegated and interrelated institutions for financial and political administration in each. It was a comprehensive and coherent scheme, if still in an early stage of development, designed to ensure the perpetuation of the union of Normandy and England and their progressive integration, so far as institutions could do this. It was the basic element in the relationship between Guernsey and Jersey on the one hand and the kingdom of England on the other, for it was preserved in its essentials even after the Islands had been separated from the rest of Normandy.

This Norman empire — there is much to justify the use of the term though it was not employed at the time — broke up early in the reign of King Stephen as the result of a disputed succession, in the way that so many great empires have broken up. In the late 1140's, with Stephen firmly in possession of the greater part of England and

27.   Domesday Book, i. fos. 91 b 2-92 b 2; *Exon Domesday,* p. 258 fo. 278; *Victoria County History, Somerset,* i (1906), 412, 473-82; L. C. Loyd, *The Origins of Some Anglo-Norman Families* (Publications of the Harleian Soc., ciii, 1951), p. 25; *Cartulaire.* pp. 56-7 — but there is no specific evidence that any member of the family actually took part in the battle of Hastings, however probable it may be.

28.   D. Matthew, *The Norman Abbeys and their English Possessions* (1962), esp. ch. 2; *Cartulaire, passim.*

29.   Le Patourel, 'The Norman Succession, 996-1135', *English Historical Review.* XXXVI (1971), 225-50.

30.   Le Patourel, 'Norman Kings or Norman "King-Dukes"?' *Etudes historiques offertes au Professeur Jean Yver* (forthcoming).

31.   It is true that a Guernseyman, early in the fourteenth century, declared that 'the lord king of England has nothing in this island save the status of duke' and that the term 'curia ducis' was coming to be used in Normandy towards the end of the twelfth century. The relationship between Normandy and England was indeed modified by the Angevin kings (see below), yet a good deal of the integration between the two countries, characteristic of the reign of Henry Beauclerc, survived; and the Guernsey declaration quoted above continues 'and whoever should be lord of this island having the status of duke has power to grant liberties in the same manner as the lord king has in England': Le Patourel, *The Medieval Administration of the Channel Islands* (1937), p. 37.

Geoffrey Plantegenet, count of Anjou, as firmly in possession of the whole of Normandy, it looked as though the two countries would go their separate ways; for Stephen and Geoffrey belonged to different families which had been rivals for many generations and each had a son to succeed him. There can be no doubt that Geoffrey had taken possession of the Channel Islands in the course of his conquest of Normandy, probably in 1142; and they would therefore follow the fortunes of the Norman mainland. If neither Geoffrey nor his son Henry could make good his claim to England the Islands would never be more than Norman-French off-shore islands.

As it turned out, Geoffrey's eldest son Henry (the 'Henry II' of English historians) was able to secure recognition as Stephen's heir and successor-designate in England in 1153, but only after more than a show of force and only when he had received Normandy from his father (1150), succeeded to the little empire his ancestors had been building up in the Loire valley (Anjou, Maine and Touraine, 1151), had married the duchess in her own right of the vast duchy of Aquitaine (1152) and had thus made himself by far the most powerful ruler in France. When he did succeed to England in 1154 he was able to extend this huge complex still further and to revive and to realize the latent claims of earlier rulers of his lands. He re-established the old overlordships of the Norman kings in Scotland and Wales, took over a conquest of Ireland begun by vassals of his from South Wales, converted the Norman suzerainty over Brittany into what was to all intents and purposes direct rule, re-established Norman interests in Boulogne and Flanders and extended them, secured a recognition of his overlordship from the count of the vast *comté* of Toulouse, and besides several 'frontier rectifications' to his advantage was extending his influence into Spain and Italy. (31a)

This vast assemblage of kingdoms, principalities and overlordships, which historians have generally agreed to call the 'Angevin Empire', should be regarded as an entirely new political edifice, even though it embodied older structures in its composition. As a tiny part of this new empire, the Channel Islands found themselves much less remote than they had been in the empire of the Norman kings, for they were now very near to the main lines of traffic. The Norman kings, it is true, had depended upon easy communication across the English Channel; but their routes lay between the Barfleur-Southampton crossing to the west and the Wissant-Dover crossing to the east. (32) No one can say how intense the traffic had been in the western Channel during their time, between Brittany on the one hand and Devon and Cornwall on the other, though there must have been a good deal in order to maintain the unity of the Breton and Cornish languages for so long; (33) but however intense it can only have been of local significance. The important people and the trades that were becoming important took the shorter sea routes further east. An empire that encompassed England, Ireland, Brittany and Aquitaine as well as Normandy and the Loire counties, however, must depend in part at least on the ancient 'western seaways' by the Western Approaches and across the Bay. Yet the full potential of this new situation would not be realized, so far as Guernsey and Jersey were concerned, until something like a hundred years had passed, for it was not until the thirteenth

---

31a. On the early development of the Angevin empire, Le Patourel, 'The Plantagenet Dominions', *History*, L (1965), 290-96, and references there given; but since that was written the subject has been transformed so far as the earliest phases are concerned by O. Guillot, *Le comte d'Anjou et son entourage au XI siècle* (1972). See below VIII.

32. Guernsey was clearly regarded as marking the western extremity of Normandy. The privileges of Rouen specified that a ship coming from Ireland, after it had passed the *capud de Guernes'*, must proceed to that city (A. Giry, *Les Établissements de Rouen*, Bibliothèque de l'Ecole des Hautes Etudes, fasc. 55, 59, 1883-5; ii., 60-61).

33. Jackson, *Language and History in Early Britain*, pp. 11-12, 24-8.

century was well advanced that the sea-borne trade in wine from Gascony really developed or the Italians began transporting goods to and from north-western Europe regularly by sea. (34)

The place of the Channel Islands in this empire, and what their inclusion in it may have meant to them, can be indicated by one or two examples. When St Helier's Abbey was founded on the islet opposite the church of St Helier in Jersey about 1155, it was given land in Jersey, naturally, but it was also given properties in Herm, in Normandy, in England and even in Scotland. (35) William fitzHamon, the founder, had been in Henry II's entourage even before Henry became duke of Normandy; and later, after Henry had made himself king, took a leading part in the conquest of Brittany and subsequently held office as seneschal of Brittany. (36) Robert of Torigny, the chronicler, who was abbot of Mont-Saint-Michel and who paid a visit to Jersey and Guernsey in 1156, (37) tells us that St Helier's Abbey was founded with the counsel and support of King Henry himself; and Henry's interest is attested by his charters making or confirming grants. (38) In its early days the abbey whose founder was so near to the king must have felt almost at the centre of things; and the distribution of its possessions, if inconvenient for exploitation, shows how a small monastery could benefit by the very extent of Henry's empire.

The implications of King John's well-known charter to Peter des Préaux in 1200 are similar, for in one and the same document the king recorded that he had granted to Peter the lordship of the islands of Jersey, Guernsey and Alderney, a rent in England drawn on property in Alton (Hampshire), and a rent of 100 pounds in Angevin money to be drawn from the market stalls and other revenues in Rouen. (39) Besides showing how the Islands could be caught up in a great estate extending into England and Normandy, though this had already happened while John himself was count of Mortain, lord of the Islands and of vast lands in England and Ireland, (40) it is also a reminder that when Count Geoffrey of Anjou, Henry II's father, conquered Normandy, he had suppressed the ancient though long decadent money of Rouen and had extended the currency of the money of Angers to Normandy, (41) and so into the Islands. Any number of examples in the charters show that Angevin money was current there as in Normandy during the second half of the twelfth century; (42) just as later, when the king of France had conquered Normandy in 1204, he replaced the Angevin currency with the money of Tours, which he had just taken over, the *tournois* which has been known in the Islands ever since — notwithstanding the fact that it was introduced into Normandy by the king of France at the time when they were being separated from the duchy. A glimpse of even wider horizons for them is afforded by the fact that as early as 1195 a citizen of Bayonne,

34.   On the wine trade, see below; and on the Genoese and Venetian fleets, A. Ruddock, *Italian Merchants and Shipping in Southampton* (Southampton Record Series, 1951), pp. 19 ff.
35.   *Cartulaire des Iles Normandes*. pp. 307-23; L. Delisle and E. Berger, *Recueil des actes de Henri II*. (Chartes et Diplômes relatifs à l'histoire de France, 1909-27), i. no. cccxii (pp. 460-61), ii. nos. cccclxxxv (pp. 35-6), dclii (pp. 267-8).
36.   Delisle and Berger, *Recueil des actes de Henri II*. Introduction. pp. 220, 479; W. L. Warren, *Henry II* (1973), p. 309; *Regesta Regum Anglo-Normannorum*. iii (edd. H. A. Cronne and R. H. C. Davis, 1968), p. xxxv and index s.v. fitzHamon, William.
37.   He was clearly carrying out a visitation of the monastery's properties at the beginning of his abbacy. In the following year he went to England and, returning to Normandy by Southampton, came to the king at Mortain and obtained privileges for his abbey. *The Chronicle of Robert of Torigni*. ed. R. Howlett *(Chronicles of the reigns of Stephen, Henry II and Richard I*. iv, Rolls Series, 1889), pp. 335-7.
38.   *Chronicle of Robert of Torigni*. p. 313 and above, note 35.
39.   *Rotuli Chartarum* (ed. T. D. Hardy, Record Commission, 1837), p. 33b.
40.   Le Patourel, *Medieval Administration of the Channel Islands*. p. 121.
41.   A. Blanchet and A. Dieudonné, *Manuel de numismatique française* (1912-36), iv., 305-6; J. Boussard, *Le gouvernement d'Henri II Plantegenêt* (1956), pp. 302-4.
42.   *Cartulaire des Iles Normandes*. index, s.v. 'Monnaie'.

Vital de Biele, was farming the éperqueries by grant of King Richard I. (43) This is the earliest suggestion of that interest in the Channel Islands (chiefly Guernsey, for reasons which will become apparent) which Gascon merchants were to take later on when the Anglo-Gascon wine trade really developed and the Islands found their place in it.

The governmental structure of this vast empire was in most respects a development of that of the Norman kings, though employed now by a different dynasty and extended to very much wider dominions. As before, the 'central' government, consisting of the king himself, his household (which included the chancery and the chamber, forming respectively the secretariat and the central financial departments) and the king's court in its highest form, was itinerant, dividing its time as seemed appropriate between the various lands under the rule of Henry and his sons. But since this central organization had so much further to travel, so many more countries to visit, so many more affairs to deal with, it was forced to delegate more; and the institutions of delegated government, which were only beginning under the Norman kings, grew prodigiously. By the end of the century the king had a complete administrative organization in England, a vice-regal justiciar with an exchequer which was both a high court and an auditing body, a system of treasuries in castles about the country and of itinerant justices regularly taking the king's justice to all parts of it. A very similar administrative structure was being extended to Ireland and another had grown up beside it in Normandy with only minor differences (the chief officer was coming to be called seneschal rather than justiciar and local institutions retained much of their traditional form). The other lands were less developed though the principle was the same. There was a vice-regal seneschal in Anjou, who held the 'king-count's' court and managed the collection and routine spending of his revenues; and likewise in Brittany and also in Poitou and Gascony, for in the administration of Aquitaine the duchies and counties of which it was made up were often treated as separate units. Beyond all this were the client states, the kingdom of the Scots, Welsh and Irish kings and princes, and *comtes* and *vicomtes* on the periphery of Aquitaine whose degree of independence was not always easy to distinguish from the degree of independence enjoyed by those within the traditional bounds of the duchy. (44) This vast and complex structure thus appears as a three-tiered organization. On top was the king, his household and court, constantly on the move; in the middle, a complex of delegated institutions which, though ideas and personnel moved to some extent from one country to another, were nevertheless growing into administrative unities; and, at the bottom, traditional institutions of local government which varied from one land to another and within each land but which were also in process of renewal and standardization.

Though this structure appears as a development of the government of the Norman kings there were important differences, and these do much to explain the later history of the Channel Islands. The king's authority in his continental lands, for

---

43. *Magni Rotuli Scaccarii Normanniae.* ed. T. Stapleton (1840-44), i., 225; ii., 390. Since Vital, in 1199, exchanged the farm for a rent of 50 pounds of Angevin money on two whales in the port of Biarritz, it is likely that relations between Gascony and the Islands were still not sufficiently organized to make collection of the revenues from the éperqueries profitable *(Rotuli Chartarum.* p. 17b; Le Patourel, 'The Early History of St Peter Port', La Société Guernesiaise, *Report and Transactions,* xii (1933-6), 183; B. Bolton, 'Esperkeria Congrorum', *Ibid.,* xviii (1966-70), 288-96. See above I.

44. On this interpretation of the governmental structure of the Angevin empire, Le Patourel, 'The Plantagenet Dominions', *History.* L, 294-8, and references there given. General treatment in C. H. Haskins, *Norman Institutions* (1918), esp. ch. v; J. Boussard, *Le gouvernement d'Henri II Plantegenêt;* H. G. Richardson and G. O. Sayles, *The Governance of Medieval England from the Conquest to Magna Carta* (1963); W. L. Warren, *Henry II.* See below VIII.

instance, was much more clearly conceived of as ducal or comital than it had been in Henry I's time, even if this made little difference to his actual exercise of power there. Between 1066 and 1144 no man who was king of England had done homage to the king of France for his lands in France; Henry II, Richard and John performed it regularly, specifically as liege homage and specifically for the continental lands, and important political doctrines were being deduced from this. In 1066 neither the law of Normandy nor the law of England had been clearly formed as a consistent territorial system, and it was possible for the courts and the justices of the Norman kings to bring about a considerable degree of assimilation between them; but when Geoffrey of Anjou conquered Normandy in the 1140's the respective *coutumes* of Anjou and Normandy were so far 'crystallized' and territorialized that there was virtually no assimilation between them; and Geoffrey and his successors, the Angevin kings, ruled on the principle that each of their lands must be governed according to its own native laws and customs. Thus, with the establishment of this principle and the more developed institutions of delegated judicial and financial administration, the law of England and the *coutume de Normandie*, for all that they owed to their early formation in common under the Norman kings, were coming to be regarded as two distinct territorial systems. By the end of the twelfth century the term *curia ducis* is sometimes used in Normandy, though the courts both there and in England were held under the authority of the same king. Yet the relationship between Normandy and England remained closer than that between any other of the elements that made up the Angevin empire. There were still many important families with properties in both countries; and in all the Angevin partitions, actual or projected, England and Normandy went together. (45).

For the first time, in the later twelfth century, the position of the Channel Islands in the larger political structure of which they formed a part is tolerably well defined. The evidence comes chiefly from the rolls of the Norman exchequer, now a fragmentary series which has preserved only one complete and two almost certainly incomplete entries for the Islands (for the years 1180, 1195 and 1198). (46). These show that for financial purposes the Islands were divided into four units, of which Guernsey formed one and Jersey three. The king seems to have been deriving no revenue from Alderney or Sark at this time. Accounts were rendered at the exchequer at Caen and the balance of the revenue collected, after certain deductions and local payments had been made, was paid into the treasury, presumably there also. These accounts also show that the Islands were being visited by itinerant justices from Normandy. As to the local courts in the Islands, there is only one indication at this time, a charter dated 1179 which records an action 'in the court of the lord king in Guernsey before Gilbert de la Hougue then *vicomte*.' None of the witnesses is described as a jurat (if the office had existed at that time it is almost certain that it would have appeared in this context); and since Gilbert de la Hougue is not specifically described as *vicomte* of Guernsey, and as he appears as the farmer of the king's revenues in Guernsey and in one of the financial units in Jersey where the

45.   As the detailed and technical comparison between English and Norman law and institutions in the twelfth century, such as would be needed to support these generalizations, still has to be made, they are offered as hypotheses only. The problem is briefly stated in Le Patourel, *Normandy and England, 1066-1144* (University of Reading, Stenton Lecture 1970, 1971), pp. 21-2. J. Yver in his masterly article, 'Le bref anglo-normand', *Revue d'histoire du droit,* xxix (1961), 313-30, shows what could be done. See below VII.
46.   *Magni Rotuli Scaccarii Normanniae,* i., 25-7, 225-6; ii., 385, 390, 393; G. F. B. de Gruchy, 'The Entries relating to Jersey in the Great Rolls of the Exchequer of Normandy of A. D. 1180', Société Jersiaise, *Bulletin Annuel,* ix (1922), 18-44; T. W. M. de Guérin, 'Notes on the Early Constitutional History of the Channel Islands', Guernsey Society of Natural Science and Local Research, *Report and Transactions,* viii (1918-20 for 1917-19), 174-91.

office of *vicomte* continued, it seems likely that for judicial purposes, and perhaps for all non-financial purposes, the archipelago then formed one *vicomte*. (47)

The Channel Islands were thus completely integrated into the delegated administration of Normandy. The visitations of the justices would ensure that their law would differ only in detail from the *coutume* of Normandy; the collection and expenditure of the king's revenues in the Islands was part of the financial system of the duchy. The money current in the Islands was the same as that current in Normandy. They were also included in the Norman ecclesiastical organization. Although not fully documented before the middle of the thirteenth century, this organization so far as they were concerned was almost certainly complete before the end of the twelfth. The ten parishes of Guernsey, together with the three of the smaller islands, formed one rural deanery and the twelve parishes of Jersey another, both in the archdeaconry of the Bauptois in the diocese of Coutances. The patronage of all the island churches was in the hands of continental patrons (the Norman abbeys, the archdeacon of the Val de Vire, the bishop and the chapter of Coutances). (48) The property of the Norman monasteries in the Islands was still growing: Marmoutier had assigned its interests in Guernsey to its priory of Héauville in the Cotentin; (49) even later foundations in Normandy such as Longues (1168) (50) and Bellosanne (1198), (51) received lands or rents there. Many Channel Island estates still formed a part of larger estates centred on the Norman mainland. (52) It is true that the toing and froing implied by the fact that several monasteries and some laymen had lands in England (53) as well was also increasing and that Gascon merchants had begun to take an interest in the Island fisheries; but, as an anxious warden observed some 130 years after their political separation from the Norman mainland, by far the greater number of the Islanders were 'de sang, d'alliance et d'affinité à les gens de Normandie', (54) and the chief effect of the increasingly sophisticated administrative structure made necessary by the sheer extent of the Angevin empire was to make the Islands still more effectively a part of Normandy. This integration, together with the Angevin principle now established that each land should be ruled by its own native laws and customs, did much to ensure that if the Channel Islands should be torn from continental Normandy and still ruled by the heirs of King Henry II, as they were early in the thirteenth century, they would preserve their Norman law and institutions and would not be absorbed into the kingdom of England. It was the foundation of that degree of autonomy that they have enjoyed ever since.

47.   *Cartulaire des Iles Normandes*. pp. 220-21; Le Patourel, *Medieval Administration of the Channel Islands*, pp. 27-8.
48.   Register of the patrons of churches in the diocese of Coutances, c. 1251-1316: Bouquet, *Recueil des Historiens de la France*. edd. de Wailly, Delisle and Jourdain, xxiii (1894), 517-9, where the section relating to the Channel Islands can be read in context. This section is reprinted in *Cartulaire des Iles Normandes*, pp. 429-32. The church of Alderney is omitted. It was held by the chapter of Coutances *(ibid.*. pp. 393-9). The churches and their parishes were certainly in existence long before 1200; a dean of Jersey is mentioned before that date *(Magni Rotuli Scaccarii Normanniae, i. 26; Cartulaire, p.* 356); a document surviving only in a late translation records the collation of a priest to the church of St. Mary in Jersey by the bishop on the presentation of the abbot and monks of Cerisey, c. 1185 *(Cartulaire*, pp. 375-6).
49.   *Cartulaire*. pp. 360-62, 386-7.
50.   *Cartulaire*. pp. 392-3.
51.   *Cartulaire*. pp. 417-9.
52.   G. F. B. de Gruchy, *Medieval Land Tenures in Jersey* (1957), *passim;* further studied by Dr. Wendy Stevenson in her unpublished doctoral thesis, England and Normandy, 1204-1259 (University of Leeds, 1974). I am grateful to Dr. Stevenson for permission to refer to her thesis.
53.   Such a relationship did not cease, for example, when Fief-le-Comte in Guernsey passed from the earls of Chester to the Wake family, for the latter were lords of Négreville in the Cotentin as well as of Bourne in England *(Cartulaire des Iles Normandes*. pp. 202-3; E. King, 'The Origins of the Wake Family: The Early History of the Barony of Bourne', *Northamptonshire Past and Present*. v (part 3, 1975), 3-9. The family chose the English allegiance in 1204 and lost their Norman lands. The Guernsey fief eventually passed to the de Cheney family, though the abbey of Mont-Saint-Michel retained an interest until at least the end of the thirteenth century.
54.   Société Jersiaise, *Bulletin Annuel*. iii (1891-6), 289.

This Angevin empire passed through a great crisis in the early years of the thirteenth century. (55) It survived that crisis in the sense that it did not fall apart as the Norman empire had done in the 1140's; but it emerged transformed. The most obvious change was territorial. The Angevin kings lost Normandy, Brittany, Anjou (the home of their dynasty), Maine, Touraine, the northern part of Aquitaine (Poitou) and much of its periphery, including suzerainty over the counts of Toulouse. Yet institutional continuity was preserved. There never was a moment when all their continental possessions were lost; in addition to those retained some were recovered later in the century, and as though by compensation for what they had lost across the Channel the kings, particularly Edward I, strove to increase their hold over Scotland, Ireland and Wales, with some temporary success in Ireland and a more lasting success in Wales. This increasing concern with the lands in the British Isles beyond England did not imply any neglect of remaining or recovered interests on the Continent: the heirs of the Angevin kings continued to be much more than kings of England.

The effect of these territorial changes, however, was to alter the whole political balance of their lands. In the time of Henry II, it could be said that the weight of his interests and responsibilities lay on the French side of the Channel, and the political centre of gravity in his empire nearer to the Loire than to the Thames. After the changes, the balance tipped decisively to the English side. Moreover, Henry II's and Richard I's lands had been continuous apart from the narrow English Channel. The king could journey from Dieppe or Barfleur to Bordeaux or Bayonne overland and over his own territory. After the loss of Normandy and the Loire *comtés*, he must go from England to Gascony by sea, a very different matter. During the twelfth century the king had ruled his empire directly by itineration, giving proportionate time and attention to each of his lands; and although he made increasing use of institutions of delegated jurisdiction and administration in each as the problems of government grew more complex, he still kept everything under his direct control and supervision by frequent visitation. During the course of the thirteenth century this manner of governing gradually ceased; the king was coming to spend his time more in England, and by the end of the century exclusively so, apart from very occasional military expeditions. The administration of his overseas dominions would have to be reorganized to cope with his permanent absence. If he was more than a king of England still, he was becoming primarily a king of England.

The fundamental cause of these changes was the enormous growth in the power and authority of the king of France. In the eleventh century he had been unable to prevent the conquest of England by William the Conqueror who was then, according to the forms of the time, his vassal; nor, after William had made himself king, was he able to obtain homage from him or his son Henry. Neither was he able to prevent the future Henry II from gathering up his huge assemblage of lands in France and across the Channel in the middle of the twelfth century; but already the relationship was changing. Henry II was prepared to do homage, and liege homage, for his continental lands. (56) The implications of this were worked out in the reign of his son John, when, on a charge that he had failed in his duty as a vassal, King Philip Augustus obtained a judgment in his court (1202) condemning John to the loss of all the lands he held in the kingdom of France. (57) Such a judgment could only be enforced by

55. For what follows, Le Patourel, 'The Plantagenet Dominions', *History*, L., 298-301. See below VIII.
56. J.-F. Lemarignier, *Recherches sur l'hommage en marche et les frontières féodales* (1945), ch. iii.
57. Sir Maurice Powicke, *The Loss of Normandy, 1189-1204* (2nd ed. 1961), ch. vi.

war; and a state of war, or at best of truce, lasted for over fifty years. During this time, naturally, there was no legal relationship between the king of England, in any capacity, and the king of France; although both John and Henry III continued to use the style 'duke of Normandy and Aquitaine and count of Anjou' until peace was made in 1259.

By that time the French king and his advisers had come to understand that the relationship created by liege homage could be exploited very much to the king's advantage, and the fact that King Philip Augustus had been so successful in enforcing the judgment of his court against John, by far the greatest of his vassals, gave him the power. Consequently, when the time came to make peace between the kings of England and France, by the Treaty of Paris of 1259, Louis IX was prepared to make what was regarded as a generous territorial settlement in return for liege homage, and the treaty did not come into force until Henry III had performed the act in Paris. Henry had renounced his rights to the duchy of Normandy, to the *comtés* of Anjou, Maine and Touraine and the *comté* of Poitou, all of which were now beyond any hope of recovery; and indeed to many contemporaries the military situation did not seem to require the king of France to make any territorial concessions at all. (58) However, provisions were included in the treaty which made it possible for Henry III and his successor Edward I to reconstruct the ancient duchy of Aquitaine to a considerable extent, to preserve the title 'duke of Aquitaine' and even, later on, to acquire the *comté* of Pontieu in the north, but only on condition of recognizing in the most unambiguous terms that all which they held in the kingdom of France was as much a parcel of that kingdom, as it was then thought of, as any other part of it. That is what liege homage had come to mean. (59)

The obligations which liege homage imposed do indeed provide a ready explanation for the importance which the king of France laid upon it. The king of England must journey to France at his accession, and whenever there was a new French king, to renew his homage; and the French insisted that this must be done in person at whatever cost to English royal dignity or convenience. The king of France would claim the right to legislate for the lands of the king of England in France, as for other parts of his kingdom held by liege homage; the courts held in the name of the king of England in those lands would not be sovereign in the contemporary sense, that is an appeal could be made as of right from their judgments to the court of the king of France and, as a result, the administration of those lands could be brought under his supervision; and finally, since a vassal must be loyal to his lord and not oppose his interests or policies, the king of France was given in effect a considerable control over the external relations of the king of England—for however cleverly the king of England could be distinguished from the duke of Aquitaine in theory, they were ultimately one and the same man. The recognized penalty for any breach of these obligations was confiscation, a sanction that had to be taken seriously for the lands which the king of England held in France were militarily very vulnerable.

It seems that Henry III in the last years of his reign, and Edward I until 1294, saw nothing impossible in this relationship and tried honestly to make it work, but that after it had broken down badly in that year Edward and his lawyers tried to change it, to argue that the lands in France were not in fact held as fiefs of the French

58. *Histoire de Saint Louis par Jean, Sire de Joinville*, ed. Natalis de Wailly (Société de l'histoire de France, 1868), pp. 244-5.
59. The text of the treaty is best read in *Treaty Rolls*, i (ed. P. Chaplais, 1955), 37-40. See also, P. Chaplais, 'The Making of the Treaty of Paris (1259) and the Royal Style', *English Historical Review*, lxvii (1952), 235-53 and M. Gavrilovitch, *Etude sur le Traité de Paris de 1259* (Bibliothèque de l'Ecole des Hautes Etudes, fasc. 125, 1899).

king but unconditionally. This was naturally not accepted by the French, and the dispute eventually became the fundamental cause of what we call the Hundred Years War. Edward III took the English argument to its logical conclusion when, having failed to make the French accept his view of their relation, he declared himself 'king of France' so that, as 'king of France' he could determine the relationship between himself, the duchy of Aquitaine, the Channel Islands and his other lands in France. A war between two 'kings of France', one of whom was also king of England, might begin as a French civil war but would end as a national war; and in that struggle through the fourteenth and fifteenth centuries, English and French nationalities were formed, certainly in relation to one another, changing the environment of the Channel Islands among many other things once again.

From the time of the judgment delivered against King John in 1202 until well into the fourteenth century, that environment was determined by the conditions of the war from 1202 until 1259 and then by the political conditions created by the Treaty of Paris. Before the treaty the position of the Channel Islands was precisely that of the other remnants of the Angevin lands in France still unconquered by the French or recovered from them. It seems that the Islands were taken, with the rest of Normandy, during the French campaigns of 1202-4 but that they were recovered for the king of England very soon after.[60] That he and his advisers soon saw what their value could be to him, a foothold in Normandy to support a legal claim to the whole or to provide a base for recovery by military means, a secure point on the sea-route from England to Gascony, is strongly suggested by the immediate steps that were taken to fortify them — taken in conjunction with the efforts that were made to secure a friendly Brittany. The fact that a clause was inserted into the Treaty of Lambeth of 1217 stipulating that the Channel Islands, which had been seized again for the French, should be returned to King Henry III,[61] shows that already, within a dozen years or so of the loss of continental Normandy, a special effort was being made to hold the Islands for the king of England.

During the long period of war and truce from 1202 until 1259, further attacks were feared though none seems to have materialized.[61a] Although they are not mentioned by name in the Treaty of Paris, it clearly provided for them, for it included among the lands in France for which King Henry III was to do liege homage 'the islands if there are any which he holds and which are of the kingdom of France'.[62] The Channel Islands were certainly held by the king of England at the time that the treaty was made, not indeed by Henry III directly, but by his son and heir Edward under him,[63] and, as part of Normandy, they had certainly been 'of the

60. How and why this happened has been explained, perhaps as fully as it is ever likely to be, by Dr. Wendy Stevenson in her thesis (above, note 52). It is very much to be hoped that she will publish this shortly.

61. This was the treaty which secured the withdrawal of Prince Louis of France and his armies from England. The text is printed in T. Rymer, *Foedera* (Record Commission edition, 1816-69), i(1), 148.

61a. Le Patourel, 'The Account of Hugh of Saint-Philibert, 1226', Société Jersiaise, *Bulletin Annuel*, xv (1949-52), 470-71.

62. 'Et de ce que li rois de france donra al roi de Angletere . . . li rois de Angletere et si hoirs feront homage lige au roi de France et a ses hoirs rois de france et ausi de Bordiaus et de Baione et de Gascoigne et de tote la tere que il tient deca la mer de Angletere (i.e. in France) en fiez et eh demaines et des isles saucune en i a que lis rois de Angletere tiegne qui soient del roiaume de france' *(Treaty Rolls*, i. 38).

63. An appanage was created for 'the Lord Edward' in 1254. It consisted of Gascony, Oleron, the Channel Islands and lands in England, Wales and Ireland. It has been most fully studied by J. R. Studd in his unpublished doctoral thesis, A Catalogue of the Acts of the Lord Edward, 1254-1272 (University of Leeds, 1971). Until this is published some of the facts can be obtained from Sir Maurice Powicke, *The Thirteenth Century* (Oxford History of England, iv., 1953), pp. 118-19, 318, 401; Le Patourel, *Medieval Administration of the Channel Islands*, pp. 38-40, 123. For Edward's possession of the Islands in the very year 1259, *Cartulaire des Iles Normandes*, no. 16bis (pp. 28-30). The original is stated to have been in the Archives de la Manche at Saint-Lô before 1944; but the text is on Gascon Roll, 44 Henry III and is summarized from an *inspeximus* in *Calendar of Patent Rolls, 1272-81*, p. 435. The date should be 2 November 1259 as noted by Dr. Studd. I am grateful for his permission to quote his thesis.

kingdom of France' before the war started. Although there may have been reserves on the English side (represented possibly by the fact that the Channel Islands were not named in the treaty) there can be no doubt at all that the French regarded them as a parcel of their kingdom, held by the king of England in his capacity as duke of Aquitaine and peer of France, under the same conditions of loyalty and service as his other lands in France. This is shown by the fact that they were included in the sanctions imposed by the king of France from time to time, when the king of England renounced his homage or was judged to have forfeited his French lands for some feudal offence. They were attacked in 1294, when Aquitaine was declared forfeit and was invaded and occupied; at the time of the 'War of Saint-Sardos' (1324-5), when again Aquitaine was overrun, an attack was feared though it did not materialize; and when the feudal issue led once more to an attack on Aquitaine and precipitated the 'Hundred Years War', the Islands were not only attacked, Jersey twice, but Guernsey and the smaller islands were held by the French for two years (1338-40) and Castle Cornet for seven. (64)

The English government, however, had introduced a complication of its own. When Henry III constituted an appanage for his son the Lord Edward (the future Edward I) in 1254, he assigned to him among other things, Gascony, (65) the Isle of Oleron and the Channel Islands 'in such manner that the said lands . . . may never be separated from the Crown, and that no one by reason of this grant made to the same Edward may be able to put forward any right or claim to the said lands . . . but that they should remain to the kings of England in their entirety for ever.' (66) In a sense this was an internal matter. It gave the Plantagenet (67) lands a constitution at least for English lawyers; for whereas they had hitherto been regarded as partible, those which were still held in France at that date were to 'remain to the kings of England in their entirety for ever', so that whoever was the lawful king of England was by that fact alone the lawful duke of Aquitaine and lord of the Channel Islands. But this was done at a time when the relationship between the kings of England and France was only one of truce, and the annexation of Gascony and the Channel Islands to the crown of England would not have been accepted by French lawyers as in any way affecting their relationship, in normal times, with the kingdom of France.

When an attempt was made in 1311 to settle the differences created by this declaration and by the English argument that the French lands were not in fact held by liege homage, on the one hand, and the French insistence upon their feudal subjection on the other, among other differences between the two kings and their peoples, the French proctor argued that whereas the Channel Islands had always been a part of Normandy and, up to the time of the war of 1294, had lain within the jurisdiction of the *bailli* of the Cotentin and, on appeal, of the exchequer of Rouen,

64.   Le Patourel, *Earlier Invasions of the Channel Islands* (Channel Islands Study Group, Teddington, 1945) and references there given (reprinted in *Bulletin of the Jersey Society in London*. 13 Jan. 1956, pp. 7-12). For the anxieties of 1324, *Calendar of Patent Rolls. 1324-7*, pp. 14, 21, 302.
65.   The terms 'Gascony' and 'Aquitaine' can be very confusing in the later Middle Ages. The earlier duchies of Aquitaine (centred on Poitou) and Gascony had been united in the eleventh century; and when Henry II took the title 'Duke of the people of Aquitaine' he used it to include both. This remained the title of his successors; but in the early thirteenth century most of the original Aquitaine was lost to the French and was only partly recovered after 1259. Consequently, though the king was styled 'Duke of Aquitaine', he normally held only Gascony and often only a part of that. Both terms were used, even officially. The chief representative of the 'duke of Aquitaine' was the 'seneschal of Gascony'.
66.   Le Patourel, 'Plantagenet Dominions', *History*, L., 301-2. The text is in Rymer, *Foedera*, i (1), 297. See below VIII.
67.   Perhaps the term 'Plantagenet' is preferable to 'Angevin' when referring to a time when the family had lost Anjou. 'Plantagenet' was one of the sobriquets given to the father of Henry II, Count Geoffrey of Anjou; but it was not applied to his descendants until late in the fifteenth century. Historians have generally used it retrospectively of the family which ruled England and other lands from 1154 to 1485 *(Dictionary of National Biography*, s.v. 'Plantagenet').

the king of England had, since the end of the war (1303), forced the Islanders to take their appeals to his court in England, thus denying the sovereignty of the king of France. (68) It is difficult to know just what basis he had for the first part of his charge, apart naturally from the indisputable statement that the Islands had once formed a part of Normandy; (69) but it may well be that the visitations of the itinerant justices (the 'justices of assize') from 1299 onward provided him with the facts for the second. He was confusing English and French procedure (for there was no system of appeals in England like that in France), and the English reply is not known; but the proceedings of the king's justices in the Islands often resulted in adjournments to the court of King's Bench, and the Islanders were sending petitions to the king's Council and Parliament. (70) To the French this could be nothing but an exercise of English sovereignty over the Islands, detaching them completely, at least in intention, from the kingdom of France. (70a)

It is possible that this detachment was never formally recognized in France, though this is a matter that needs further investigation; but the English had no doubt on the matter. When Edward III proclaimed himself 'king of France' he and his advisers envisaged no more than a personal union between the two kingdoms; (71) and neither, apparently, did they intend that the Channel Islands should be a part of Edward's kingdom of France if that had ever become a reality.(72) The lands which Edward had inherited on the mainland of France or which he conquered in pursuit of this kingdom were eventually re-conquered by the French and incorporated into their kingdom; but although Edward and his successors defended the Channel Islands successfully, they did not incorporate them into the kingdom of England. There never was a formal treaty which concluded the Hundred Years War, and the effective result of the long struggle so far as they were concerned was that they were thenceforward included in neither kingdom.

As long as they were among the lands held in France by the king of England, however, the Channel Islands shared their conditions as well as their fortunes. The fact that their Norman law with their own local customs was preserved in the Islands after their political separation from Normandy(73) is only one example of a general rule. The same thing happened in Aquitaine; in fact throughout the thirteenth and fourteenth centuries lands in France changed their allegiance from one king to the other and back again with hardly any disturbance of the administrative routine.(74) It was applying the Angevin rule, which had become much more

---

68.   Le Patourel, 'Jersey's Political Status during the Middle Ages', *Bulletin of the Jersey Society in London*, 13 January 1961, pp. 8-10. Cf. P. Chaplais, 'Le Duché-pairie de Guyenne', *Annales du Midi*, lxix (1957), 32; Gavrilovitch, *Etude sur le Traité de Paris de 1259*, p. 141.
69.   But cf. the curious Guernsey document, 'Le Precepte d'Assize', *The Extentes of Guernsey*, ed. Sir Havilland de Sausmarez (Société Guernesiaise, 1934), pp. 135, 147-8. So far the records on the French side have not shown an appeal from the Channel Islands in due form; though the 'Assize Rolls' of the Islands contain a number of charges that Channel Island cases which ought to have come before the king's courts there were being heard in courts on the Norman mainland.
70.   Le Patourel, *Medieval Administration of the Channel Islands*, pp. 15-16, 18-19.
70a.   Provisions made by Edward I and his successors for hearing appeals from Gascony and for receiving petitions in Council and in Parliament had the same implication; but not all Gascons could be restrained from taking their appeals to the Court of France.
71.   Letter of Edward III to the people of England, printed in *Oeuvres de Froissart*, ed. Kervyn de Lettenhove (1867-77), xviii., 129-30. Cf. his declarations to the people of France and of Gascony, Rymer, *Foedera*, ii(2), 1111, 1127.
72.   Suggested by the fact that after Edward III had taken the title 'King of France', he empowered his officers in occupied territories to hear appeals 'according to the procedure of our court of France', that is the court of France which theoretically functioned in his name; e.g. Rymer, *Foedera*, iii(1), 201. I have found no such provision in any order relating to the Islands.
73.   Le Patourel, 'The Origin of the Channel Islands Legal System', Above II, 198-210 (esp. p. 201).
74.   E.g., review of *Comptes Royaux (1314-1328)* in *English Historical Review*, lxxix (1964), 789-92 and Edward III's letter to the people of Gascony in 1340, Rymer, *Foedera*, ii(2), 1127.

general, that communities should be ruled according to their own laws and customs, whoever was their ruler.(75) This did not simply mean that laws and customs should be preserved in the state they were when the community or territory changed ruler, but that they should continue to develop in their own native tradition. Thus the king of England ruled the Channel Islands as though he had continued to be the duke of Normandy. The bailiwick seals, for example, which originate in Edward I's grant of 1279, though in their present form they date from c. 1304, served as seals of contracts, connected with a form of procedure which originated in France well after the French conquest of Normandy and which had no close analogy in England;(76) the classic treatise on the *coutume*, the *Grand Coutumier*, though composed in Normandy between 1235 and 1258, was taken as authoritative in the Islands, and there is clear evidence that there was a copy in Jersey in 1328, perhaps an 'official' copy.(77)

In Aquitaine and the surrounding lands not only law but political authority had been fragmented to a high degree. Thus when King Louis IX ceded 'what he held' in the three dioceses of Limoges, Cahors and Perigueux to King Henry III by the Treaty of Paris, not only did he have to use ecclesiastical units to define what he was ceding, but it turned out, after the transfer, that he had in fact very few rights in those dioceses to transfer, apart from his ultimate sovereignty which he did not give up. Henry had to deal with a number of towns and seigneurs who often had very extensive privileges; and just as the king of France and other lords might have rights here and there in the lands which he held, so he might have isolated rights and possessions in lands which were generally theirs. There were no clear frontiers in the modern sense, whatever the impression given by our historical atlases, and it is hardly surprising that what largely took the place of international politics in the thirteenth and fourteenth centuries were the problems of overlapping jurisdictions and the administration of laws and customs which differed from place to place, often over very short distances.(78)

These conditions applied as much to the Channel Islands as to any place on the mainland of France at this time, in spite of their being islands. Although, after 1204, they were separated politically from mainland Normandy, they remained in the Norman diocese of Coutances, fully subject to the ecclesiastical authority of the bishop. Whether or not he himself ever visited them in person, there were certainly archidiaconal visitations from the mainland;(79) the patrons of the parish churches were still monasteries and other ecclesiastical authorities in Normandy which also held a good deal of property in the Islands; and a considerable proportion of their clergy must have been of Norman birth or education.(80) To be politically attached to one country and ecclesiastically to another was bound to give rise to problems, particularly in war-time, though it was by no means an exceptional situation at the

75.   There is a partial exception to this in Edward I's treatment of Wales and Scotland, but in both he preserved more than he changed.
76.   Le Patourel, 'Un premier exemple de contrat sous le sceau de la Baillie de Jersey', *Travaux de la Semaine d'Histoire du droit normand tenue à Guernesey . . . 1938* (Caen, 1939), pp. 401-7, and below.
77.   Le Patourel, 'The Authorship of the Grand Coutumier de Normandie', *English Historical Review*, lvi (1941), 292-300. See above III.
78.   In general, Le Patourel, 'The Origins of the War', in *The Hundred Years War*, ed. K. Fowler. See below XI.
79.   E.g. *Cartulaire des Iles Normandes*, pp. 67-8. For other documents illustrating ecclesiastical administration, *ibid.*, pp. 62, 63-5, 151-2, 173, 222 (223), 268, 277-8, 280-81, 282-3, 298-9, 300-301, 301-2, 343-4.
80.   This can only be an impression until *fasti* of the rectors of the Island churches have been compiled. Ecclesiastical as other 'Norman' property in the Islands was taken into the king's hand in war-time; which simply meant that whatever rents or dues were normally paid to the Norman holders would be paid to the king for the duration.

time. The fact that some of the bishop's jurisdiction was delegated to the deans of Jersey and Guernsey(81) may have been due as much to the geographical isolation of the Islands as to war-time difficulties; and although it may be that King John had tried to get them transferred to the diocese of Exeter,(82) the only transfer that took effect during the Middle Ages was to Nantes, temporarily during the Great Schism.(83)

At the time of the French conquest of Normandy King John had imposed certain limitations on trade, particularly in foodstuffs, between the Islands and the Norman mainland(84) — as much, perhaps, to ensure supplies for the garrisons he was placing in them as for any other reason; but he could not prevent constant communication between the Islands and Normandy except to some extent in war-time. It was said that one could cross the sea between the Islands and the Norman coast twice in the day; (85) in 1299 it was ordered in the court of the justices itinerant in Jersey that a debt should be repaid by annual instalments at the Montmartin fair (near Coutances),(86) implying that Jersey folk regularly attended the fair; in his account for 1328-30 the warden of the Islands refers to his changing an amount of sterling into *tournois*, the money current in the Islands, at the exchange at Coutances,(87) an operation which he and all royal officers in the Islands who received money from the exchequer in England must have had to perform frequently; an association of Guernsey merchants regularly sold fish in Dieppe and Rouen, holding property jointly in those towns, and Rouen even gave preferential treatment to ships coming from Guernsey and Dieppe. (88)

Others besides these Guernsey merchants still managed to hold property in Normandy, the events of the early thirteenth century notwithstanding. When war broke out they had to choose. Thus in 1337 William de Saint-Helier decided to remain in France and consequently lost his land in Jersey; but the *bailli* of the Cotentin gave him, by way of compensation, the land which Reginald de Carteret had lost in Normandy by making the contrary choice.(89) This sort of thing was happening on an enormous scale in the lands in dispute, or potentially in dispute, between the kings of England and France, and was so much a matter of course that when, in 1384, land in Normandy was conveyed to a John de Saint-Martin for a rent payable in Jersey, provision was made in the contract for the times when it might not be possible to make payments on account of war;(90) and just as the king of England maintained proctors in the court of the king of France to watch over his interests there, and the (English) seneschal of Aquitaine likewise in the courts of the (French) seneschals of Périgord and Toulouse, so Philip de Carteret — and possibly the 'community of the island of Jersey' — maintained a legal representative in Normandy for similar reasons.(91)

81.   Le Patourel, *Medieval Administration of the Channel Islands*. pp. 33-4.
82.   *Ibid.*, p. 28.
83.   *Ibid.*, p. 34; E. Perroy, *L'Angleterre et le grand schisme d'Occident* (1933), pp. 106-9.
84.   *The Extentes of Guernsey* (ed. Sir Havilland de Sausmarez), p. 28.
85.   *Ancient Petitions of the Chancery and the Exchequer* (Société Jersiaise, 1902), p. 48.
86.   Public Record Office, Assize Roll (J.I. 1) 1158, membrane 3r.
87.   Public Record Office, Pipe Roll, 4 Edward III, rot. 48.
88.   Le Patourel, 'The Early History of St. Peter Port', Société Guernesiaise, *Report and Transactions*, xii. 181-2.   See above I.
89.   Société Jersiaise, *Bulletin Annuel*, xi (1928-31), 381.
90.   Société Jersiaise, *Bulletin Annuel*, i (1875-84), 190-93.
91.   *Rolls of the Assizes held in the Channel Islands . . . 1309* (Société Jersiaise, 1903), p. 218. The word translated as 'legal representative' is *narrator*.

The normal procedure when war broke out was for the king of England to cause a proclamation to be made in the Islands that all who had property there from which they were absent should 'come into his peace' by a certain date. Those who failed to do so had their property confiscated for the duration, no more. One Guernseyman defended his absence with the plea that he had stayed in Normandy to gain a living and for no other purpose; and this plea was accepted. There must have been many such.(92) When it was alleged for the king that people of the Islands were being cited not only by the bishop's court at Coutances but to a court at La Haye-du-Puits, and on matters which should have come before the king's courts in the Islands, it could only be because of the property they held, or at least their very frequent presence, on the Norman mainland.(93) They were after all 'de sang, d'alliance et d'affinité à les gens de Normandie', they could cross the intervening sea twice in the day, they could see the spires of Coutances Cathedral from the cliffs by Mont Orgueil Castle, as we still may, and the Cotentinois could then as now watch the bonfires on Jersey from Cap de Carteret.

The same general principle applies to institutional development. It was some time before the full implications of the loss of the northern lands in France, and the consequent difficulty of getting the king with his court and his armies to Bordeaux, were understood. There was indeed some institutional development in Gascony through the middle of the thirteenth century to take account of the king's lengthening absences, but it was not until Edward I's time, by measures gradually introduced and codified in a great ordinance promulgated at the end of his long visit to the duchy in the years 1286 to 1289,(94) that an administration was set up there which could function in his absence for an indefinite length of time. In fact no king of England set foot in Gascony as duke of Aquitaine after this last visit of Edward's. The administration he set up was a direct development of existing institutions; the seneschal's office, being by this time, far beyond the capacity of any man to carry out personally, was 'departmentalized'. The seneschal was given an official council to form policy; a constable of Bordeaux and his office took over the finances; an elaborate system of courts under judges who were in principle the seneschal's lieutenants, exercised most of his judicial powers; though he still retained direct responsibility for defence, when a royal lieutenant was not appointed over him, and appointed the castellans of royal castles. However much expanded and developed, however, this administration was entirely in the native tradition; and though many of the higher officers were sent out from England its analogies were with other parts of France, not with England. It would not have developed so far or so fast if its ruler had been a resident duke with no other possessions, but it would have moved in the same direction.(95)

It is likewise difficult to form a clear and coherent picture of the administration of the Channel Islands before the reign of Edward I, though it can be seen to be

---

92.   There are a number of cases establishing these points in the Channel Island Assize Rolls for 1299 (Public Record Office, J.I.1, 1157, 1158), referring to the period of hostilities between 1294 and 1297. Cf., for example, *Calendar of Close Rolls. 1327-1330*. p. 317; *1341-1343*, p. 375. It was clearly possible, equally, for 'Normans' to possess lands etc. in the Islands; *Rolls of the Assizes . . . 1309*. pp. 282-3.

93.   Renunciation of possible rights in the patronage of Grouville Church in Jersey was made both in the court of the *bailli* of the Cotentin at Valognes and in the Royal Court at St. Helier held by the bailiff of Jersey (1315-16; *Cartulaire des Iles Normandes*. pp. 345-50).

94.   *Gascon Register A*. edd. G. P. Cuttino and J. P. Trabut-Cussac (British Academy, 1975), i, pp. 206-17.

95.   Le Patourel. 'The King and the Princes in Fourteenth Century France', in *Europe in the Late Middle Ages*. edd. J. R. Hale, J. R. L. Highfield and B. Smalley (1965), pp. 159-63. Since that was written the important but tragically unfinished and posthumous work of J. P. Trabut-Cussac, *L'Administration anglaise en Gascogne sous Henry III et Edouard I de 1254 à 1307* (1972) has appeared, greatly amplifying and partly correcting it. See below XV.

substantially complete in its medieval form before his death. If there was ever a great codifying ordinance for the Islands, no trace of it seems to have survived; but the principles are the same as in Gascony. With all allowances for the vast difference in scale, the warden's office was very similar to that of the seneschal (in the middle of the thirteenth century the two offices were sometimes held by one man, occasionally even concurrently),(96) and an administration was constructed by 'departmentalizing' it. Bailiffs of Jersey and Guernsey and *prévôts* of Alderney and Sark held the royal courts; receivers in Jersey and Guernsey took over the management of the king's revenue and expenditure in those islands; and, as in Gascony, the warden retained responsibility for defence though there were constables under his immediate command in each of the royal castles. The bailiwick seals combined the functions of the seal of the court of Gascony (or 'seal of the seneschal' as it later came to be called) and the contract seals of the duchy, and they were almost identical physically.(97) These seals are indeed an excellent symbol of the analogy. In some respects the Channel Islands resembled the 'duchy of Aquitaine' as a whole, for they had a direct relationship with the royal government and a complete administrative structure; in other respects, as in their special customs and in their jurats, they resembled more closely, perhaps, a small privileged community within the duchy.

Beyond analogy, and common political circumstances which the Islands shared with the king's other lands in France during the thirteenth and fourteenth centuries, a very close economic relationship with Gascony grew up which opened new possibilities to them. Before 1204 England had imported most of its wine from the parts of France which could export through Rouen or the ports of the Loire. After the loss of Normandy and the northern lands it looked for a while as though La Rochelle would become the chief port for trade and communications with England, but that city was lost as well in 1224. After that it was Bordeaux; and the great wine-producing industry of the south-west of France grew up on the geographical and administrative advantages that Bordeaux was found to possess for exporting its produce. The chronology of the growth of this industry is not at all well known. It hardly appears in the twelfth century and had certainly not developed fully by the middle of the thirteenth; yet it reached its peak immediately after the war of 1294-1303.(98) The wine was taken, of necessity by sea, to England, to the Low Countries, to north Germany and beyond; and the route taken by the ships closely followed a very dangerous coast. Hence the interest which the kings of England (to whom the taxation of the wine as it passed through Bordeaux was of very great importance) took in Brittany as long as the trade lasted; hence the elaborate system of pilotage, convoying and insurance which the dukes of Brittany developed, very much to their own profit;(99) hence the place of the Channel Islands in this enormously important trade route.

Guernsey was chiefly involved, indeed almost solely, for the island lay on the shipping lane (testified by the number of wrecks about its coasts, even in the

---

96. Le Patourel, *Medieval Administration of the Channel Islands*, pp. 30, 122-3.
97. *Ibid., passim.* On the seals, cf. P. Chaplais, 'Le sceau de la cour de Gascogne ou sceau de l'office de sénéchal de Guyenne', *Annales du Midi*, lxvii (1955), 19-29; *idem*, 'The Chancery of Guyenne, 1289-1453' in *Studies presented to Sir Hilary Jenkinson* (ed. J. Conway Davies, 1957), pp. 61-96 (note esp. pp. 63, 78); Trabut-Cussac, *ubi supra*, pp. 388-95.
98. Y. Renouard, 'Le grand commerce des vins de Gascogne au moyen age', *Revue historique*, ccxi (1959), 261-304; *Bordeaux sous les rois d'Angleterre* (ed. Y. Renouard, 1965), pp. 53-68, 233-292; M. K. James, *Studies in the Medieval Wine Trade* (1971).
99. Le Patourel, 'The King and the Princes', pp. 163-5. The detailed study by H. Touchard, *Le commerce maritime breton à la fin du moyen âge* (1967) is concerned with a somewhat later period and with the trade of Brittany itself.
See below XV 163-5.

fourteenth century) and possessed in St Peter Port roadstead, protected by Castle Cornet, one of the few safe anchorages between Ushant and Barfleur along the coast of France. The extent of this involvement is indicated by an account of the 'great custom' which was collected from 245 ships calling at Guernsey from Michaelmas 1328 to Michaelmas 1329 and from no less than 487 during the following eleven months. According to the regulations this custom was not collected from ships belonging to the realm of England unless loaded abroad, nor from any ships bound for England. But the involvement of the Islands was active as well as passive, Gascony had invested so heavily in viticulture that the country had to import food. The wine ships returned with corn and fish from the West of England, the Channel Islands and Brittany ('the Western Channel region' reappears as an economic unit) as well as other things. We hear of this because Gascon merchants, to ensure supplies, leased or owned drying and salting places or fishing monopolies in these countries — the éperqueries in the Channel Islands. They also found positions in the Channel Island administration and some even settled permanently in the Islands. Moreover ships of Channel Island ownership (chiefly Guernsey) and most likely of Channel Island construction took part in the trade. In 1370 ten Guernsey ships were found large enough to be impressed for service in the transporting of an army from England to France. Ships from the Islands are found in Bordeaux and in Bristol, as well as in the chief ports of the south coast of England; and in Abbeville and Caen as well as in Dieppe and Rouen.(100)

The position of the Channel Islands in the early fourteenth century is well illustrated by some statements made by John de Roches (warden, 1328-30) when he was charged with unnecessary expenditure on works in Castle Cornet and on the garrisons he had maintained there during his period of office. It was a time of tension though not of general war: as he had wearily observed on another occasion, 'we do not know whether it is peace or war, but at sea we find nothing but war'.(101) 'The king of France', he said, 'ordered his galleys which were in Poitou to proceed towards Normandy. After the winter these galleys came past the duchy of Brittany, and on the way seized all they could find in the two islands of Groix and Sein and killed many men there. Afterwards one of them came to Guernsey with evil intent, stood by for two days and nights and attacked the island; but the warden and his men drove them off, with God's help, and killed many of their men. The survivors withdrew to Harfleur ('Harflete'), complaining of the loss of their men in the Islands; and then, with other Normans, threatened to burn and slay in the Islands, making preparations for this throughout the summer. This was reported to the warden by friends of his who heard about it'. On another occasion, 'the lord de Sully, to whom the Lord Edward, father of the present lord king, had granted the reversion of the Islands upon the death of Otto de Grandison, and Robert Bertram, who is one of the greater men in all Normandy and son-in-law of de Sully, were hunting with others in the Forest of Bricquebec and were talking about the Islands, saying among themselves that they would get them by one means or another. Word of this spread throughout

100. Le Patourel, 'The Early History of St. Peter Port', La Société Guernesiaise, *Report and Transactions*, xii., esp. pp. 179-184; 'A 14th Century List of Guernsey Ships and Shipmasters', *Quarterly Review of the Guernsey Society*, ix (Winter 1953-4), 4-7. The rules for levying the Great Custom are defined in the Guernsey extent of 1331 *(The Extentes of Guernsey*. ed. Sir Havilland de Sausmarez, pp. 69-70). See above I.
101. Société Jersiaise, *Bulletin Annuel*. iii (1891-6), 291.

the Cotentin and was conveyed to the warden by his friends, who advised him to take care . . . Moreover, about Easter time(8 April 1330) several magnates from England arrived there making a great to-do about the death of the earl of Kent (19 March) and of others; and this gave rise to serious fears of war, as did also the fact that the king's castle of Saintes had been captured and destroyed by the French'.(102)

The implication of these statements, which were confirmed by jurors, that a warden of the Channel Islands at that time had his intelligence service not only on the Norman mainland, where relatives and friends of the people under his charge were living, but in the coastal lands all down the Bay, is revealing. It shows how far the fortunes of the Islands were bound up with all the lands facing the sea from Bayonne to Bristol, their fourteenth-century environment.

Others must explore later phases in the changing environment of the Channel Islands — the emergence of England and France as national monarchies; the effects of the final conquest of Gascony by the French; the Reformation, the wars of Religion and the Islands' privilege of neutrality in the sixteenth and seventeenth centuries; the opening of the Atlantic and trade with the Americas; the Revolutionary wars on the Continent and the industrial revolution in England, and so on. But enough has been said to show that the history of Guernsey and Jersey, Alderney or Sark, or all together, does not consist simply of events that occurred or conditions that obtained in the Islands themselves, but is concerned as much, and sometimes more, with what was going on around them. That was made brutally apparent in 1940; but it was always so.

---

102. These quotations are taken from the Assize Roll (Guernsey) for 1331 (Public Record Office, J.I.1 no. 1166), membrane 13r.

V

THE DATE OF THE
TRIAL ON PENENDEN HEATH

THE date of the ' famous ' trial on Penenden Heath is one of those
minor historical problems which, though it has received a good
deal of attention in the past, is still worth discussing ; partly because it raises an interesting question of principle in the treatment
of historical evidence ; partly because, if it were possible to establish
another date in William the Conqueror's reign, that would be
worth doing for its own sake ; and partly because it has provoked
so large a measure of disagreement among English historians.
At present it is possible to quote at least one modern historian—
no writer is mentioned here who published his statement before
1860—in support of each year from 1070 to 1077 inclusive. Thus
W. de Gray Birch suggested in one work that the trial took place
' about the year 1070 ' ; [2] in another, though this appears to be
a mistake, he stated that it was held in 1074.[3] Bigelow conjectured
' about 1071 ; ' [4] Benjamin Thorpe, in the chronological index to
his edition of the *Anglo-Saxon Chronicle*, ascribed the trial to the
year 1073 ; [5] while Hamilton [6] and Stubbs,[7] without giving any
reasons, both assigned it to 1076. Freeman,[8] Round [9] and
Plummer [10] were in agreement on 1072, a date which was strongly
supported by a document published by W. Levison in this REVIEW[11]
and accepted as conclusive by Adams,[12] Mr. Macdonald,[13] Professor

[1] As the name is variously spelled, the spelling here adopted is that of the Ordnance
Survey, Popular Edition, 1-inch to the mile, sheet 116, 3G.

[2] *Domesday Studies*, ed. P. E. Dove (London, 1888–91), ii. 496.

[3] W. de Gray Birch, *Domesday Book : a popular Account* (London 1887), pp. 291–2.
This must be a mistake as Birch quotes Thorpe's edition of the *Anglo-Saxon Chronicle*,
where the date is given as 1073.

[4] M. M. Bigelow, *Placita Anglo-Normannica* (London, 1879), pp. 4 ff.

[5] B. Thorpe (ed.), *The Anglo-Saxon Chronicle* (R.S. 1861), ii. 298.

[6] N. E. S. A. Hamilton (ed.), *W. Malmesbiriensis . . . de gestis pontificum*, etc.
(R.S. 1870), p. 70.

[7] W. Stubbs (ed.), *Memorials of Saint Dunstan* (R.S. 1874), p. 144.

[8] E. A. Freeman, *The Norman Conquest*, iv. (2nd edn.), 363.

[9] *Encyclopœdia Britannica*, 11th edn., art. ' Geoffrey de Montbray '.

[10] C. Plummer (ed.), *Two of the Saxon Chronicles Parallel* (Oxford, 1892–9), ii. 314.

[11] W. Levison, ' A Report on the Penenden Trial ', *ante*, xxvii, 717–720.

[12] G. B. Adams, *Council and Courts in Anglo-Norman England* (New Haven, 1926),
pp. 79 ff.

[13] A. J. Macdonald, *Lanfranc* (Oxford, 1926), pp. 126 ff.

Douglas,[1] and others. This date, indeed, was regarded as established until Professor Stenton lately, in his *Anglo-Saxon England,* gave it as his opinion that the trial must have taken place 'in 1075 or 1076',[2] because Arnost, bishop of Rochester, whose appointment and death both fall in the sixth year of Archbishop Lanfranc's pontificate, is stated in one document to have been present at the assembly. More recently still Professor Douglas, revising his earlier conclusion, has placed the trial 'between August 1076 and August 1077'.[3] No less remarkable than this divergence of opinion is the fact that nearly all these statements must have been based upon the same body of evidence; for although the text of the document published by Dr. Levison did not appear until 1912, it had already been noticed by Sheppard in his report on the manuscripts of the dean and chapter of Canterbury for the Historical Manuscripts Commission as far back as 1876.[4] The other documents in the case have long been accessible to scholars.

The argument of this short paper is that the date of the trial on Penenden Heath cannot be determined on the evidence available, and is unlikely ever to be determined. This is so, not only because the evidence is in conflict, but because in this instance the conflict cannot be resolved and seems unlikely to be resolved in the future. To maintain this somewhat bold thesis, it is necessary first to examine this evidence. There are three important documents.

1. The fullest account of the trial is that which is printed in Wharton's *Anglia Sacra,*[5] Wilkins' *Concilia,*[6] Bigelow's *Placita Anglo-Normannica,*[7] and elsewhere. Professor Douglas has shown that, among the printed editions, there are two versions of this account, a shorter and a longer; and he has identified these, respectively, with the copy included in the *Textus Roffensis* and that in a thirteenth century manuscript in the British Museum,

---

[1] D. C. Douglas, ' Odo, Lanfranc and the Domesday Survey ', in *Historical Essays in Honour of James Tait* (ed. Edwards, Galbraith and Jacob; Manchester, 1933), pp. 47 ff.

[2] F. M. Stenton, *Anglo-Saxon England* (Oxford, 1943), p. 641. The present writer adopted the date 1072 in an article on Geoffrey, bishop of Coutances (*ante*, lix. 144), which was written and set up before this work was published. The following note arises out of the *post mortem* which he felt bound to make on his own conclusions after reading Prof. Stenton's opinion.

[3] D. C. Douglas, *The Domesday Monachorum of Christ Church, Canterbury* (Royal Historical Society, London, 1944), p. 30. The revision of Prof. Douglas's opinion seems, however, to have been somewhat reluctant, for he writes, ' Two years after Lanfranc's accession to the primacy, that long dispute (i.e. between Odo and Lanfranc) reached a climax in the trial on Pennenden Heath, between August 1076 and August 1077 . . . ', and on the next page he again refers to the trial as having taken place in 1072. I cannot see by what argument or calculation he arrives at the date 1076–7.

[4] *Fifth Report of the Royal Commission on Historical Manuscripts* (1876), p. 462.

[5] H. Wharton, *Anglia Sacra* (London, 1691), i. 334–6.

[6] Wilkins, *Concilia* (1737), i. 323–4.   [7] Bigelow, *op. cit.* pp. 5 ff.

Cotton MS. Vespasian A. xxii.[1] The differences between these two versions are immaterial to the present discussion, as the chronological data afforded by this document are common to both. In this paper, therefore, it will only be necessary to refer to one of these ; and for convenience the shorter version, that which is found in the *Textus Roffensis*, and which appears to be the older and in general the better, will be used.

The evidence which these chronological data provide is, at best, indirect. The account of the trial is given in the form of a narrative, which opens with a few sentences giving what we may describe as the historical setting. The purport of these sentences is as follows : since Odo, bishop of Bayeux, came to Kent some time before Lanfranc, he was able to enrich himself at the expense of the church of Canterbury ; but when Lanfranc had been archbishop for some time (*aliquandiu*), and had been able to acquaint himself with the dilapidated condition of the property of his see, he approached the king as quickly as he could (*quam citius potuit*), and the king commanded that the county should meet without delay. For what it may be worth as evidence, this story implies that the trial took place within a few years of Lanfranc's consecration (29 August 1070).

The only other indications of the date of the trial to be found in this document are such as may be argued from our knowledge of the persons stated to have been present, to wit, Archbishop Lanfranc, Bishop Odo, Bishop Geoffrey of Coutances, Arnost, bishop of Rochester, Aethelric, ' bishop of Chichester ', and certain laymen of whom we hardly know sufficient to help in this matter. The trial cannot in any case have taken place before Lanfranc's consecration, and it is unlikely to have occurred before the settlement of the primacy dispute in the early summer of 1072, for in addition to that distraction, Lanfranc must have found much of the year 1071 taken up with his journey to Rome. As far as Lanfranc is concerned, therefore, Whitsun 1072 is a likely *terminus post quem*. After this, the archbishop seems to have resided in England continuously until the autumn of 1077, when he paid a short visit to Normandy in order to take part in the consecrations at Caen and Bec.[2] Of Odo's movements we know that he was in England at the time of the settlement of the primacy dispute and that he paid a visit to Normandy in the same year. He was in Normandy again in the autumn of 1074, in England to take part in the suppression of the revolt of 1075, and in Normandy once more for the consecration of his own cathedral church and for other festivities in 1077.[3] Geoffrey of Coutances, on the other

---

[1] Douglas, ' Odo, Lanfranc . . . ', in *Historical Essays in Honour of James Tait*, pp. 48–51.

[2] Macdonald, *Lanfranc*, pp. 182–6.   [3] G.E.C., *Complete Peerage*, vii. 127.

hand, seems to have resided in England continuously from 1068 until 1078, and was then abroad until late in 1080.[1] As the trial is most unlikely, on general grounds, to have been held later than 1080, these dates suggest 1078, or perhaps 1077, as the *terminus ante quem*, though they do not enable us to compress the range of possible years more closely. Nor does the appearance of Aethelric afford much evidence on this point. Strictly speaking he had never been ' bishop of Chichester '. He was deprived of his bishopric of Selsey in 1070, though his deposition was not finally confirmed until 1076, and documents of the late eleventh and early twelfth centuries refer both to Aethelric and to his successor Stigand as ' bishop of Selsey ' and ' bishop of Chichester ' almost indiscriminately.[2] Thus neither the title given to Aethelric in this document nor the transference of the see from Selsey to Chichester provide any sure indication of the date of the trial on Penenden Heath.

The reported presence of Arnost, bishop of Rochester, on the other hand, provides the material for a more precise argument. According to the *Acta Lanfranci*, Arnost was consecrated in the sixth year of Lanfranc's pontificate, i.e. between 29 August 1075 and 28 August 1076, and died in the same year.[3] The Vita Gundulfi adds that he held the bishopric for ' scarcely half a year ',[4] and Wharton quotes a Canterbury obit roll for the statement that he died on 15 July.[5] On this evidence his brief episcopate can have lasted only through the first six months of 1076 ; and it follows from this, that any assembly which he attended while he was bishop of Rochester can only have been held at some time during those months.

To summarize : the document copied into the *Textus Roffensis* begins with an ' historical introduction ' which implies that the trial took place in the early years of Lanfranc's pontificate ; it mentions a number of persons as present at the trial, and from what we know of them it can be argued that 1072 and 1077 are probably the outside limits of date ; finally the reported presence of Arnost, bishop of Rochester, seems to indicate that the trial must have been held in the first half of the year 1076. All this is perfectly consistent.

2. In 1912 Dr. Levison printed in this REVIEW a fragmentary account of the trial which had been found on a thirteenth-century roll in the library of the dean and chapter of Canterbury.[6] So far

[1] *E.H.R.*, lix (1944), 143-5.

[2] Hamilton Hall, ' Stigand, Bishop of Chichester ', *Sussex Archaeological Collections*, xliii, 88–104. The chief documents are to be found in Wilkins, *Concilia*, i, 323, 325, 326, 363, 364, 367.

[3] Plummer, *Two Saxon Chronicles Parallel*, i. 289.

[4] Wharton, *Anglia Sacra*, ii. 279.   [5] *Ibid.*

[6] *E.H.R.*, xxvii (1912), 717-20.

as it goes, this fragment agrees so closely with the document in the *Textus Roffensis* that it should probably be regarded simply as another version of it.   There is, however, one important difference between them.   In place of the historical introduction at the beginning of the *Textus Roffensis* account, this document opens with a very precise dating clause :

> ' Anno ab incarnacione domini nostri Iesu Christi MLXXII, pontificatus domini Alexandri pape undecimo, regni vero Guillelmi regis sexto, presidente Lanfranco archiepiscopo ecclesie Cantuariensi pontificatus sui anno secundo. . . .'

All these expressions are consistent with one another, and if it is legitimate to deduce a more precise date by taking their highest common factor, then the trial, according to this evidence, must have taken place between 25 March and 28 August 1072.[1]   This fragment breaks off, however, before it reaches the point where, if it had followed the *Textus Roffensis* account closely throughout, it would have enumerated the important persons present at the trial.   Thus the statement in the dating clause cannot be checked by comparing it with any statements concerning the persons composing the court such as might have been found in a complete text of this document, if one ever existed, nor can the document as a whole be compared with the account in the *Textus Roffensis*.

3. The third document which provides direct evidence for the date of the trial on Penenden Heath is an appendix to the Parker MS. of the Anglo-Saxon Chronicle known as the *Acta Lanfranci* or ' The Latin Acts of Lanfranc '.   Its statement on the matter is quite unequivocal :

> ' Tercio anno (*sc.* Lanfranci) . . . habitum est magnum placitum in loco qui dicitur Pinenden, in quo Lanfrancus diratiocinavit se suamque aecclesiam omnes terras et consuetudines suas ita liberas terra marique habere, sicut rex habet suas. . . .' [2]

The third year of Lanfranc extended from 29 August 1072 to 28 August 1073.

Besides these three documents, which provide the only specific evidence for the date of the trial, there are one or two more or less vague references to it in the chronicles of the time.   The account of the trial given by Eadmer reads like a brief summary of the *Textus Roffensis* document (Query: is there any connexion between them ?), and contains no chronological data save that

---

[1] ' A.D. 1072 ', i.e. 25 December 1071 to 24 December 1072, or, 25 March 1072 to 24 March 1073 ; ' the eleventh year of Pope Alexander (II) ', i.e. 1 October 1071 to 30 September 1072 ; ' the sixth year of King William ', i.e. 25 December 1071 to 24 December 1072 (or, just possibly, 14 October 1071 to 13 October 1072) ; ' the second year of Lanfranc's pontificate ', i.e. 29 August 1071 to 28 August 1072.   All are consistent with a date between 25 March 1072 (or possibly 25 December 1071) and 28 August 1072.

[2] Plummer, *Two Saxon Chronicles Parallel*, i. 289.

it reproduces in substance the story of Odo's depredations before Lanfranc's arrival in this country.[1]   The account given by Gervase of Canterbury,[2] and a passage in William of Malmesbury's *Gesta Pontificum* [3] in which the trial is not specifically mentioned though a reference to it is probably intended, provide no chronological information. Nor does the story told by Osbern in his *Miracula Sancti Dunstani*,[4] though its context might be regarded as connecting the trial chronologically with the laying of the foundations for Lanfranc's new cathedral at Canterbury, an event which has usually been assigned, with circumstantial though not with specific evidence, to the very earliest years of his pontificate.[5]   These references afford no more than a general, though consistent indication that the trial took place early in Lanfranc's pontificate, and are therefore of no great help in this argument.

The statements of the three documents affording specific evidence of the date of the trial may now be summed up as follows : the first, a narrative copied into the *Textus Roffensis*, gives information from which it may be argued that the trial took place in the early months of 1076 ; the document published by Dr. Levison, which seems to be another version of the *Textus Roffensis* document, opens with a formal statement which can be interpreted as affirming that the trial was held at some date between 25 March and 28 August 1072, in Lanfranc's second year ; the *Acta Lanfranci* states precisely that it took place in Lanfranc's third year, i.e. between 29 August 1072 and 28 August 1073. Superficially, there is no means of reconciling these three witnesses ; the only way in which the conflict could be resolved is by rejecting the testimony of two of them. To see if this may justly be done, the credentials of all three must be tested.

It might seem at first sight that the evidence of the *Acta Lanfranci* would be the easiest to discredit, for it is contained not in a document purporting to be a record of the litigation but in what may best be described, perhaps, as a short private memoir of Lanfranc's pontificate. Therefore, its evidence, in theory at least, is less direct (some might say less compelling) than that of the other two documents. But it can by no means be dismissed on that account. The writer is anonymous, but he is well-informed ; Dom Knowles thinks he may have been one of the monks whom Lanfranc established in St. Augustine's Abbey [6] ;

---

[1] *Historia Novorum* (ed. M. Rule, R.S. 1884), pp. 16–17.

[2] W. Stubbs (ed.), *Historical Works of Gervase of Canterbury* (R.S. 1879–80), ii. 369.

[3] Ed. N. E. S. A. Hamilton, p. 70.   [4] *Memorials of St. Dunstan*, p. 143–4.

[5] The documentary evidence relating to the building of Lanfranc's cathedral has been collected together in R. Willis, *Architectural History of Canterbury Cathedral* (London, 1845); pp. 13–15 ; cf. A. W. Clapham, *English Romanesque Architecture after the Conquest* (Oxford, 1934), p. 21.

[6] Dom David Knowles, *The Monastic Order in England* (Cambridge, 1940), p. 116, n. 1.

and wherever his dates can be checked, as they can in most instances, they are shown to be accurate.[1] Moreover, although this work has survived in one manuscript only, so far as is known, that manuscript, on palaeographical grounds, could have been written by a man who had known Lanfranc and therefore, not impossibly, by the author himself.[2]   In short, there is nothing in what we know of the history or nature of the *Acta Lanfranci* which would cast any doubt upon the statement contained therein that the trial on Penenden Heath took place in the third year of Lanfranc's pontificate.   The evidence of this memoir on other matters has been generally accepted ; in particular, though the date of Arnost's short episcopate might have been deduced from other evidence,[3] the direct statement that he was consecrated in the year 1075-6 and died in the same year comes from the *Acta Lanfranci*.[4]

The attack may now be directed against Dr. Levison's document.   Against its testimony it may be urged that it is fragmentary and that this prevents us from comparing it fully with the account copied into the *Textus Roffensis* and so from assessing fully the relative merits of the two as evidence.   It is, further, preserved only in one late copy, so far as is known, and apart from the fact that it comes from Canterbury and is found in association with other Canterbury documents, nothing is known of its origin. But this criticism is not really very destructive.   Taking the document as we find it, *prima facie* there is nothing wrong with it as far as it goes.   Dr. Levison observes that ' there are very few similar reports of that age, and it would be difficult to write a diplomatic dissertation on such documents '; nevertheless, there is a precise analogy for the important opening clause, which supplies a date for the trial, in the document which embodies the primacy agreement of 1072.[5]   It would be difficult, therefore, to find any cogent reason for rejecting Levison's cautious suggestion that ' we have here a kind of official Canterbury record of the litigation ', however impressive the evidence of other documents may seem.

[1] The writer has checked as many as he could.

[2] The manuscript has recently been printed in facsimile, R. Flower and H. Smith (edd.), *The Parker Chronicle and Laws . . . A Facsimile* (Early English Text Society, London, 1941), fo. 32*a*, 32*b*.   Plummer gave it as his opinion that the *Acta Lanfranci* was written in a hand of the late eleventh century or early twelfth century (*op. cit.* ii. p. xxvi), and quoted E. M. Thompson and Warner for the view that it is rather of the late eleventh century (*ibid.* p. xxxvi) ; cf. Stenton, *Anglo-Saxon England*, p. 657, *n.* 2.   I am indebted to Professor Galbraith for examining the facsimile in response to my request for his opinion on the matter.   He is in favour of the early twelfth century.

[3] His predecessor Siward died in 1075 (Freemen, *Norman Conquest*, iv. 365–6), his successor Gundulf was consecrated 19 March 1077 (R. A. L. Smith, ' The place of Gundulf in the Anglo-Norman Church ', *ante*, lviii. 260). *E.H.R.*, lviii (1943), 260).

[4] Plummer, *Two Saxon Chronicles Parallel*, i. 289.   [5] *E.H.R.*, xxvii (1912),

Oddly enough, it is the best known account of the trial, the document copied into the *Textus Roffensis*, which seems to be the most vulnerable. If it is compared with the Levison document, it will be seen at once that the two must have a common exemplar, though at how many removes it is impossible to say. Further comparison will leave a strong impression that, of the two, the Levison document is probably the nearer to a hypothetical 'original report'; for, though it is possible to imagine a copyist or an editor embellishing his version with a historical introduction in place of a formal dating clause, it is not so easy to think of him inventing such a dating clause when he had a narrative before him. On the other hand, the fact that a document should seem to have been edited or embellished is not in itself a sufficient reason for rejecting its testimony. On the chronological point, the *Textus Roffensis* document is consistent throughout; and in any case we cannot tell how far the supposed embellishments may have extended. Were they confined to the opening sentences, or must we suppose that the list of important persons present at the trial is also (wholly or in part) a piece of decoration? Since Levison's document breaks off so early in the narrative, no answer to this question is possible. Moreover, the section of the *Textus Roffensis* in which the document is contained is thought to have been compiled early in the twelfth century from documents borrowed for the purpose from Canterbury.[1] This account of the trial, therefore, in its present form, is a good hundred years older than Levison's document, its associations are good, it is not *prima facie* untrustworthy and it has in fact been generally accepted by historians.

All three documents thus survive the ordinary tests, and the conflict in their testimony is not resolved by criticism. Nothing is plainer than this : if only one of these documents had come down to us, no doubt would have arisen on the date of the trial on Penenden Heath. But as things are, there is (in a sense) too much evidence. Many generally accepted dates in William's reign rest ultimately upon the testimony of one document ; it is a little discouraging, though it may be salutary, to find that when we have three or more our knowledge seems less secure than when we have one. It would seem that when evidence conflicts in this manner the only way to reach a clear and positive conclusion is by selecting one's evidence in accordance with a 'hunch' or a general sense of probability. Thus, by ignoring Levison's document altogether, by accepting the statements of the *Acta Lanfranci* relating to Arnost's consecration and death while rejecting its statement on the trial itself,[2] and by accepting the

---

[1] F. Liebermann, *Die Gesetze der Angelsachsen* (Halle, 1903–16), i, pp. xxvi–xxviii.

[2] The form and nature of the *Acta Lanfranci* seem to preclude the possibility that there has been a simple mistake in the numerals, a ' vi ' wrongly transcribed as a ' iii ', for example.

unsupported word of the *Textus Roffensis* account that Arnost *as bishop of Rochester*, was present at the trial, it is possible to conclude that the trial took place in 1075 or 1076. On the other hand, should one's fancy or convenience light on 1072, a rather better argument could be constructed in favour of it somewhat as follows : the references in the chronicles all suggest an early date ; the Levison document appears to be a close copy of something like an ' original report ', and it has a formal dating clause which states that the trial took place in 1072 ; the *Acta Lanfranci* mentions both the trial and bishop Arnost, but does not connect the two ; the first sentences of the *Textus Roffensis* account look very like an elaboration of a formal dating clause such as is found in the Levison document, and in any case are not inconsistent with an early date ; as for the mention of Arnost, he may very well have been in Lanfranc's entourage some time before he became a bishop,[1] and, if he had attended the trial as one of Lanfranc's assistants, there would be nothing unusual, in a document written fifty years after the event, in giving him the title by which he was remembered in Rochester even though he did not actually enjoy it at the time of the trial—the reference to Aethelric shows that the writer of this account was no pedant over titles. Such an argument might be held to justify the conclusion, for what it may be worth, that the weight of evidence is in favour of 1072 ; but this conclusion could only be reached by explaining away Bishop Arnost's title with a hypothesis, and by ignoring the discrepancy between Levison's document and the *Acta Lanfranci*, a discrepancy which, however small, is still a discrepancy, for, though both refer to a part of the year 1072, the first includes only that part of the year which comes before the anniversary of Lanfranc's consecration, the second that part which comes after the anniversary ; there is no overlap.

[1] Nothing seems to be known of Arnost's career save that he had been a monk at Bec (e.g. ' Vita Herluini ', printed in J. Armitage Robinson, *Gilbert Crispin Abbot of Westminster*, Cambridge, 1911, p. 103 ; Eadmer, *Historia Novorum*, ed. Rule, pp. 1–2, 15), and that he was consecrated and invested with ring and staff by Lanfranc in the chapter house at Canterbury (Eadmer, p. 2. The author of the *Acta Lanfranci* states that Lanfranc ' gave the church of Rochester to Arnost ' in the chapter house at Canterbury and consecrated him in London, though the next paragraph suggests that London might be a mistake for Canterbury—Plummer, *Two Saxon Chronicles Parallel*, i. 289 ; cf. Gervase, ii. 367). Eadmer also states that Arnost and his successor Gundulf were the only exceptions to the rule that all bishops and abbots appointed in William's reign were invested by the king. Now it seems that when Lanfranc was made archbishop of Canterbury, he brought Gundulf (also a product of Bec) with him to act as an assistant ; and Lanfranc, according to a recent writer, was setting out to make Rochester ' an *eigenkirche* of Canterbury and its bishop . . . a *chorepiscopus* ' (R. A. L. Smith, *loc. cit.*, pp. 259–62). It rather looks as though Arnost had been intended originally by the archbishop for the part later played by Gundulf, and the little we know of his training and the manner of his appointment supports this. It is by no means impossible, therefore, that, like Gundulf, he spent some time at Canterbury as Lanfranc's assistant before he was made bishop of Rochester ; and he may quite conceivably have attended the trial in the former capacity rather than the latter.

Thus it would seem that there is little hope here of adding a well-established date to the still sketchy chronology of William's reign ; at least, before any attempt is made to do so there is a question of principle to be discussed. What conclusion should a historian draw from such evidence ? There are, it appears, three possible courses for his argument. He may decide in favour of one of the three dates for which there is some specific evidence, 1072, 1073 or 1076 ; if so, however clever his argument, he will know that his conclusion is based ultimately upon a 'sense of probability' rather than clear evidence ; for, whichever date he chooses, the evidence for the other two remains strong enough at least to throw doubt upon the date of his choice. Or he may say that no clear conclusion is possible in view of the conflict of evidence, but that there is something to be said for each of 1072, 1073 and 1076, and therefore the trial must have taken place on one of those dates. Such a conclusion reduces the range of speculation, it is true ;. but, unless it is advanced specifically *ad interim*, it is unsatisfactory ; for since the claims of each date deny the claims of the other two, it is in effect no conclusion. Or, finally, he may argue that, because the quality of the evidence is such, and because it is in conflict, no positive conclusion whatever is possible, at least as the matter stands at present. Any authority, however good, may make a mistake over a date ; when there are three 'authorities', with little to choose between their merits as witnesses, and all saying something different, there is no telling which may be right. All may be wrong.

This last argument, which is the thesis of this paper, may be made into a protest against the doctrine that a positive conclusion, however vague, however diminished by qualifications, however equivocal, is better than no conclusion. For one thing, the consideration that evidence, hitherto unknown, might at any time come to light reminds us that we can have no idea what relation the evidence we possess bears to all the evidence that may once have existed, and that the survival or destruction of historical evidence seems to be a matter of chance. When the evidence that we have points fairly consistently in one direction, or when the apparent conflict between witnesses can be satisfactorily explained, we can feel some confidence in the conclusions we draw from it ; but when it is at variance, as it is in the case in point, and it does not seem possible to explain away the conflict, then the 'lost evidence' cannot be left wholly out of account. It is as though ten people witnessed an event, and, of these ten, seven subsequently disappeared and could not be traced. If the remaining three agree substantially on a point of detail we should normally accept their statement as true. But if they disagree wholly on such a point and if their reliability as witnesses is about equal, then, it seems, we have no basis whatever for knowledge of the matter. The seven lost witnesses, could they be produced, might support one or the other, or they might be unanimous on yet a fourth different story, or they might disagree among themselves. In a historical argument such as this paper has pursued, we cannot tell how large this unknown element may be, what are its proportions and qualities relative to the evidence we possess, or even if there is any such thing ; and this makes it very difficult, save as a matter of conjecture, to arrange the conflicting accounts we have in any order of merit. Thus, even if one seemed better than the other two, its evidence on a single point of fact could not be regarded as conclusive unless it could be shown that its evidence was not merely in competition with theirs, but actually discredited it in some way. In the case in point this condition is not fulfilled ; and therefore, unless new evidence comes to light which is not only inherently sound but discredits such of the existing documents as are at variance with it (an unlikely contingency, it is suggested), the date of the trial on Penenden Heath is likely to remain a matter for guesswork or open agnosticism.

Note

The literature on this subject was further enriched by John Le Patourel's discussion of 'The Reports on the Trial on Penenden Heath' in *Studies in Medieval History presented to Frederick Maurice Powicke*, ed. R. W. Hunt, W. A. Pantin and R. W. Southern, Oxford 1948, pp. 15-26. Both these contributions have been recognized as fundamental to an understanding of the land plea, though the discovery of three additional reports to the four known in 1948 has recently led D. R. Bates to undertake a major re-assessment of the whole subject: 'The Land Pleas of William I's Reign: Penenden Heath Revisited', *Bulletin of the Institute of Historical Research*, li (1978), 1-19. Among other matters, he argues that the original process began in 1072 and that the differing reports represent various stages in the long-lasting attempt by the archbishopric of Canterbury and the bishopric of Rochester to recover and reorganize their lost property.

VI

NORMAN BARONS

WHEN you honoured me with an invitation to take part in your Commemorative Lectures, it was suggested that I should devote my lecture to one of the great barons, to correspond with Professor Southern's lecture on one of the great churchmen. It seemed then, and it still seems, much better to deal with the barons of the Conquest period collectively; for while it might be possible to make a lecture out of a William fitzOsbern, a Hugh of Avranches or a Robert of Bellême, such a lecture would of necessity have to deal with many technical details of evidence and would hardly provide a ready vehicle for the discussion of those questions about Norman barons which seem to be interesting historians at the present time. Besides, even a brief acquaintance with these barons shows the importance of the family unit. It may be that many of those who made fortunes in the conquest of England were of ancestry so obscure that we can find out little or nothing about it; but, as soon as the tendency towards the hereditary tenure of land develops, the greatest barons were usually the product of one or two generations, each adding to its predecessors' accumulation of land and wealth; and a man's influence and power might already consist as much in his connections as in his possessions and reputation. For the family often functioned as a unit; and lands and wealth divided among its members in one generation might be reunited into one pair of hands in the next. What I have done, therefore, is to choose three or four important families, with one or two individuals. I shall try to describe their fortunes briefly to you, pick out what appear to be common characteristics and generalize them—not as conclusions, but as suggestions. I do not pretend that my choice is in any way a properly controlled sample; the only principle of selection has been a negative one—to omit the families which made a name for themselves in Spain or in Italy or on the Crusade. Clearly, this cuts out a great part and a most interesting part of the Norman achievement; but families like Hauteville and Grandmesnil have been excluded partly because their inclusion would make the subject uncontrollably large, and partly because, since it is the Norman Conquest of England that we are commemorating in this year 1966, the links which the Norman barons created between Northern France and Britain seem more relevant.

At the outset, there are two points in the history of the ducal and royal family which should be kept in mind, for they are very material to the argument of this lecture. First, the ducal consorts are important, since it was through them and their families that many

DUKES OF NORMANDY — KINGS OF ENGLAND

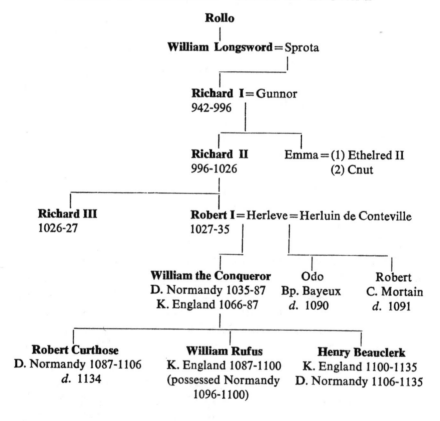

of the Conquest barons could claim kinship with the duke[1]; and that, as we shall see, is often a significant element in their rise to pre-eminence. To avoid cluttering the genealogy, only those directly concerned with the families I have chosen have been included. Second, whatever his original intentions may have been, William the

Conqueror in the end divided his wealth and his lands among his sons—but none of them accepted the division as permanent. Within a year of the Conqueror's death there was a movement to put Robert Curthose on the throne of England; and when Rufus had frustrated that, he forced Curthose virtually to share the government of Normandy with him. Such an arrangement could not last long. When it broke down, Rufus set about the conquest of Normandy; and this, in effect, he achieved when Curthose gave him possession of the duchy in return for the 10,000 marks of silver that Rufus lent him for the crusade. A very similar sequence of events followed Henry's seizure of England after Rufus's death and before Curthose's return from the East. As soon as Curthose reached Normandy, he mounted an invasion of England. Once again the brothers came to an agreement; but Henry was soon preparing the conquest of Normandy which he accomplished at Tinchebrai in 1106. For the rest of his life, Normandy and England were united under his rule. These events are in themselves a very good illustration of the point that has already been made—that while there might still be an instinct in parents to divide their wealth and possessions among their children, the children, for their part, retained an interest in each other's shares and would reunite them if they could. But they also form the political background against which we shall have to try to judge the actions of some of our barons.

Let us begin[2] with the family of William the Conqueror's great friend and counsellor, William fitzOsbern.[3]

Its origins seem to lie in a family of Scandinavian antecedents which can be traced back to the tenth century. One member of this family, Gunnor became the duchess of Duke Richard I; a brother of hers, Arfast, eventually became a monk at Saint-Père-de-Chartres, to which monastery he gave such lands as he possessed. But before he became a monk he had a son, Osbern, who became the steward or seneschal of Duke Robert I, and was one of the guardians of the young duke William after Robert's death. Since his father had given his lands to the monastery to which he had retired, Osbern had to find his own fortune; and this he did by his marriage to a daughter of Rudolf, count of Ivry, a half-brother of Duke Richard I. The lands he acquired, so far as they can be traced, are so intermingled with ducal lands, that it is almost certain that they had been carved out of the ducal domain, presumably as an endowment for Count Rudolf. The principal units were Paci, on the Eure, and the honour of Breteuil.

THE FAMILY OF WILLIAM FITZOSBERN

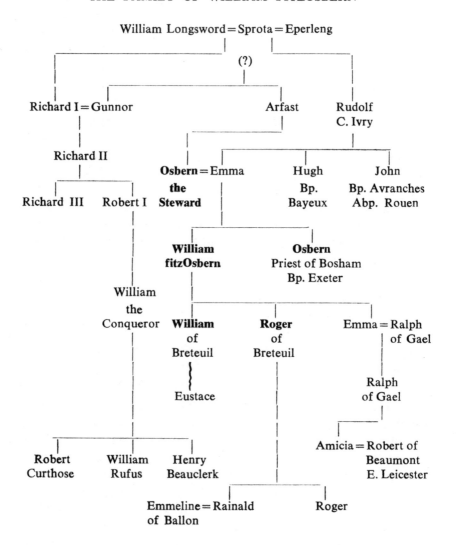

Osbern met his death in the disorders of Duke William's minority, apparently as he was defending the person of the young duke. He had two sons, William, who became a knight, and Osbern, who became a clerk. The young Osbern seems to have been one of the chaplains whom Edward the Confessor brought to England, for he held the immensely valuable church of Bosham on Chichester Harbour before the Conquest. William, his brother, had evidently grown up in the household of Duke William, and first comes into the news as one of the leading young warriors, with Roger of Montgomery, in the campaign during which Duke William captured Domfront and Alençon; and a little later he received the custody of the duke's castle of Breteuil, built to counter the French castle at Tillières. He inherited Paci and the honour of Breteuil from his father, and strengthened his position by marrying a daughter of Roger of Tosny. Some time before the conquest of England, he was wealthy enough to found two monasteries in Normandy, Cormeilles and Lyre. He must always have been close to Duke William, becoming, like his father, the duke's seneschal. Tradition has it that he took the lead among those who advised Duke William to invade England; and, if his brother was in Edward the Confessor's household and possessed of the church of Bosham—the port from which Harold sailed in 1064, if the Bayeux Tapestry is to be believed—then William fitzOsbern's intelligence was probably very good and great weight would be given to his opinion.

He followed this up by taking a very prominent part in the Hastings campaign and in later operations. Before King William left England in March 1067 to enjoy his triumph in Normandy, he put fitzOsbern in command of the western part of the country already conquered, with possession of the Isle of Wight and with his chief base in the old West Saxon capital at Winchester.[4] At the same time, it appears, King William gave him the earldom of Hereford, already partly organized as a frontier district against the Welsh by Ralph 'the Timid', King Edward's nephew, who had died in 1057. If this grant was indeed made in 1067, it can only have been as 'land to be conquered'; but somehow, in the very short time he had in which to do it, fitzOsbern began the organization of Herefordshire, Gloucestershire and perhaps Worcestershire as a military region on the Norman model, where he held enough land to settle his tenants around him in a compact group, and to begin the building of castles and the establishment of castleries.[5] The purpose of this was quickly shown when he attacked the Welsh princes of Deheubarth and Morgannwg, captured the whole region of Gwent, planted castles at Monmouth and Chepstow, and finally took the prince of Deheubarth into his homage by granting him manors in England.[6]

How he managed to do all this with his other responsibilities it is very hard to say. While King William was in Normandy from March to December 1067, fitzOsbern no doubt continued the process of conquest and consolidation in southern England. Florence of Worcester says that the king ordered him to build castles in suitable places[7]; the Anglo-Saxon Chronicle that he carried out the order thoroughly[8]; while Orderic speaks of the way in which he oppressed the English and made himself enormously rich in the process.[9] He may well have been with the king on the expedition to the South West early in 1068, though he spent much of that year in Normandy. In 1069 he was put in charge of the second castle at York; and in the next year he was sent across the Channel to assist Queen Matilda in the government and the defence of Normandy.

While he was in Normandy, an appeal was received from the widow of Count Baldwin VI of Flanders, King William's sister-in-law. She had two young sons to protect from the designs of their uncle, Robert le Frison; and to obtain help she offered herself in marriage to fitzOsbern who, according to some accounts, actually married her. The possibilities opened by this marriage were enormous; for here was a man with vast estates in Normandy, England and Wales, who was offered the chance of making himself, effectively, count of Flanders, already the richest principality in France. He hastily fitted out an expedition, only to be killed at the Battle of Cassel in February 1071. His body was carried home to his monastery of Cormeilles in Normandy; his (first) wife had been buried at his other foundation of Lyre; both monasteries had been liberally endowed from his acquisitions in England.

FitzOsbern was succeeded in his Norman lands by his elder son William of Breteuil, and in his English and Welsh lands by his younger son Roger of Breteuil. William, with some lapses, was a loyal vassal of Duke Robert Curthose. The most interesting incident in his career came in 1100 when, being in the hunting party in the New Forest when Rufus was killed, he rode to Winchester and urged the claims of his absent lord, Duke Robert, against those of Henry. He died in 1102, leaving only an illegitimate son Eustace. Roger is better known, for he was involved in the tragic conspiracy of 1075, in spite of Lanfranc's fatherly advice. His punishment was imprisonment for life. His estates were confiscated and ceased to exist as an entity.

This is not quite the end of the story. Roger of Breteuil had two sons, Rainald and Roger, who apparently served King Henry I well though without the reward they expected. Rainald, however, married into the Ballon family; and as a result he and his successors recovered at least an interest in the Welsh March. His sister Emma married Ralph, lord of Gael in Brittany and earl of Norfolk. Though Ralph lost his earldom, also in the revolt of 1075, he continued to hold his Breton lordship, and even added to it; and when Eustace, the son of William of Breteuil, forfeited the honour of Breteuil in 1119, King Henry allowed Ralph's son, another Ralph, to have it. From him it passed, with his daughter Amicia, to her husband Robert earl of Leicester, who, in 1153, obtained Paci as well. Thus the whole Norman inheritance of William fitzOsbern passed to the earl of Leicester and with it, naturally, a claim to the earldom of Hereford and the stewardship. Thus, in some measure, the great cross-Channel estate, built up by William fitzOsbern and divided in 1071, had been re-created by the earl of Leicester.

The history of William fitzOsbern and his family is one of ambition and failure, of great might-have-beens. By comparison, the history of the Warenne family,[10] though with one flash of great ambition, seems to represent more solid progress and is, perhaps, more characteristic. It took its name from Varenne, a hamlet on the little River Varenne, not far from Dieppe. The first member of the family that we can trace is a Rudolf who was living in the 1030's and survived into the 1070's. He was a substantial landowner (his lands were mostly on the Seine above Rouen and in the Pays de Caux); he had married, so it seems, a niece of the Duchess Gunnor; and he is described as a knight.

He had two sons, Rudolf and William. Rudolf, the elder, evidently inherited his father's estates, leaving William, the younger, to make his own fortune. He began, like William fitzOsbern, by attaching himself as a young warrior to Duke William. As far as our information goes, he first distinguished himself in the Mortemer campaign of 1054; and as a result Duke William gave him the castle of Mortemer, forfeited by his kinsman Roger of Mortemer, and other lands in the neighbourhood, including Bellencombre which became the centre and head of the Warenne estate in Normandy. He was thus established: a new man, with a new estate, firmly attached to his duke and leader.

William of Warenne took a leading part in the anxious meetings in Normandy that preceded the invasion of England; he is one of the few men of whom we can be sure that he took a personal part in the Hastings campaign[11]; and he was also one of the small band left to consolidate and continue the conquest of southern England under William fitzOsbern and Bishop Odo, while King William was celebrating his triumph in Normandy in 1067. Among the vast lands

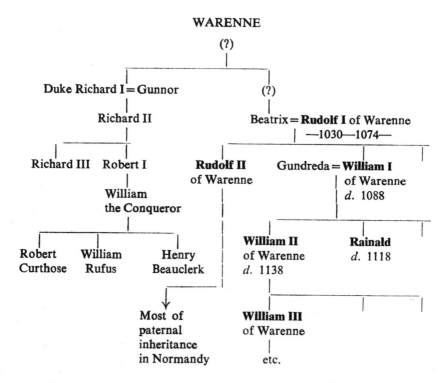

WARENNE

he ultimately received in England was the rape of Lewes, a block of territory upon which he could settle his tenants in a compact group, and this he could well have obtained within a year or so of Hastings; and having thus established himself in England he settled down to that life of movement which seems to have been the lot of Norman barons after 1066. Thus he was in Rouen for a family gathering with his father and his elder brother in 1074; in the next year he took a very prominent part in the suppression of the revolt of the earls in England; and in the early 1080's he was fighting in Maine where he was wounded at the siege of Sainte-Suzanne. In the troubles that followed King William's death he supported Rufus—possibly he had been bought by the creation of an earldom, later known as the earldom of Surrey, in his favour; for he clearly had to be offered some compensation for the lands in Normandy which he might well lose by his loyalty to Rufus. And it was at the siege of Pevensey, in 1088, that he received the wound from which he died.

Before his death he had amassed a huge estate in England, third in value after those of members of the royal family. In 1086 it streched over 13 counties; but the chief blocks were in Sussex (most of the rape of Lewes), Yorkshire (the vast compact estate of Conisburgh, probably a fairly late acquisition), and in Norfolk. The Norfolk lands centred on Castle Acre; part of them had been given to him in exchange for a portion of the rape of Lewes, part he had inherited from his brother-in-law Frederick, killed by the followers of Hereward the Wake in 1070. He had married Gundreda, a Flemish lady, sister of Frederick and of that Gerbod who was briefly earl of Chester—you may still see her memorial in Southover Church by Lewes. Together they founded the great monastery of St. Pancras near William's castle at Lewes (this they gave to the great Burgundian monastery of Cluny, though the reasons for the gift are now less clear than they once seemed to be), and the priory of Castle Acre within his castle there, dependent directly upon Lewes and therefore indirectly upon Cluny again.

Like his father, William de Warenne left two sons: William, the elder (whom we may call William II), and Rainald the younger. The immediate descent of his lands is not certain; but it looks as though Rainald got whatever Gundreda may have held in Flanders and possibly some of the Norman lands; while William inherited the English estates and eventually, if not immediately, his father's lands in Normandy as well. Rainald's career is obscure. He supported Rufus against Robert in 1090, but he was fighting for Robert against Henry in 1105, on both occasions in Normandy. William II of Warenne was a different kettle of fish. He was enormously ambitious. In the 1090's he was trying to marry Edith-Matilda, a daughter of the king of Scots who eventually became King Henry's queen; later, it seems, King Henry was prepared to give him one of his own illegitimate daughters until Archbishop Anselm objected on grounds of consanguinity (an important piece of evidence that the Warennes were ultimately connected with the family of the Norman dukes). Finally he married the earl of Leicester's widow Isobel, who was a granddaughter of King Henry I of France. So he won a royal bride in the end, if not one who could have influenced his career in quite the way that the other possibilities might have done. All the same, he added to his father's accumulation of estates both in England and Normandy—in England with the vast manor of Wakefield, adjacent to his honour of Conisburgh in Yorkshire; in Normandy with the castle of Saint-Saens.

From charter evidence, something that almost amounts to an itinerary of his life from about 1100 can be compiled.[12] It shows him as one of King Henry's counsellors, judges and generals (he commanded a division both at Tinchebrai in 1106 and at Brémule in 1119), almost ceaselessly journeying between England and Normandy; and we may be sure that he was looking after his own interests in the two countries as well as the business of the king-duke. There was a moment, in 1101-3, when he flirted with Robert Curthose; and Henry promptly confiscated his English estates. But this did not last long. He was one of these who were present at Henry's deathbed in 1135 at Lyons-la-Forêt, and also one of those who promptly accepted Stephen, whatever undertakings he may have given to Henry. For this he was put in charge of Rouen and the Pays de Caux (where the chief of his Norman lands lay) during the critical year when Stephen was establishing himself; but he was back in England again in 1136. He died probably in May 1138, and was buried with his father and mother in the family monastery at Lewes—to which he himself had been generous. His pious gifts had been well distributed: to the Norman monasteries at Saint-Evroul, Saint-Amand-de-Rouen, Longueville and Bellencombre; to the English house at Lewes, Castle Acre and the new foundation at Luffield in Northamptonshire.

Another family that acquired great power and influence by the steady accumulation of lands and offices, and by contriving to be on the right side in the political troubles or at least to accommodate themselves to both sides, was that of the Beaumonts[13]—that, at any rate, is what we may call them for convenience, whatever they called themselves. The furthest ancestor we can trace is Thorold of Pontaudemer who, it seems, married Aveline, a sister of the Duchess Gunnor. His son was Humphrey of Vieilles, who inherited his father's lands and added to them Vieilles, Beaumont and Beau-montel, all in the valley of the Risle, and much of them taken from the original endowment of the abbey of Bernay. Humphrey was a follower of Duke Robert I; and it was the duke, no doubt, who persuaded the abbey to give up those lands. Humphrey's son Roger built a castle at Beaumont (still called Beaumont-le-Roger after him), established himself and, about 1088, founded a collegiate church there. He took no part in the conquest of England, being one of those left by William to watch over the security of the duchy; though by the time of Domesday he had possessions—not of any

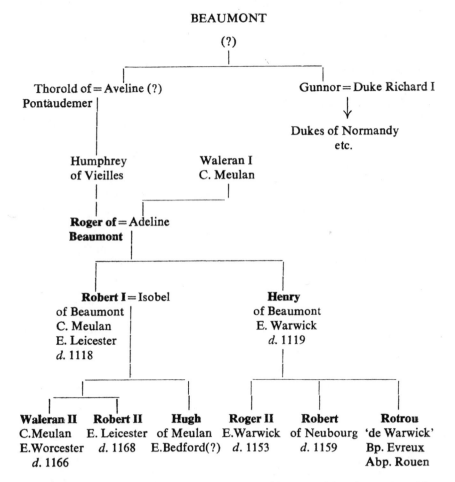

BEAUMONT

great extent—in Dorset and Gloucestershire. Besides fastening his control upon the valley of the Risle, his great contribution to the family's fortunes was his marriage to Adeline, daughter and heiress of the count of Meulan. Since Meulan was in the Vexin Français—a district then in dispute between the duke of Normandy and the king of France, though the king was winning—this marriage soon gave him an interest outside Normandy towards Paris; and his father-in-law is said to have had some connection with the ducal family of Normandy. It was thus, in all respects, a most profitable match.

Roger of Beaumont had two sons, Robert and Henry. Robert, the elder, fought in the Hastings campaign and acquired thereby, possibly in 1068 or soon after, extensive lands in Leicestershire, Northamptonshire and Wiltshire. From about 1081, when his grandfather died, he had been count of Meulan; and about 1090, when his father became a monk in the family monastery at Préaux near Pontaudemer, he inherited the bulk of the family estates in Normandy. By the end of the Conqueror's life, he had thus become a very rich and powerful person who, in the disputes that followed, put his money first on Rufus and then on Henry. He was active on Rufus's behalf before 1096; and when Rufus, then in control of Normandy, tried to recover the Vexin Français in 1097, he received and aided the royal troops in his county of Meulan. Likewise, in the early years of Henry I's reign, as well as acting as one of Henry's chief advisers in England, he was working on his behalf in Normandy and served in his army at Tinchebrai. After that, until he died in 1118, he enjoyed a position of great eminence. He had married Isobel (whom we have met before), a daughter of the count of Vermandois and granddaughter of the king of France. He could make a raid on Paris in retaliation for a French attack on his castle at Meulan. His interests, clearly, were almost as much in France as in Normandy or England. In 1102 he found a means, characteristic if rather unpleasant, of adding to his lands and influence in England. A fellow baron, Ivo de Grandmesnil, being in disgrace, appealed to him for help and pledged his lands in return for a loan that enabled him to go on crusade. When Ivo failed to return, Robert annexed the lands, in Leicestershire and the neighbouring counties; and as a result he probably became earl of Leicester.

His younger brother Henry may also have been at Hastings, though there is no direct evidence in his case. At some date (Orderic implies that it was in 1068)[14] he was made constable of Warwick Castle; but he can be shown to have been in Normandy and Maine on many occasions during the later part of William's reign. Like his brother he supported Rufus against Robert Curthose, and, as inducement or reward, was given the earldom of Warwick with extensive lands in the county (this was in 1088, and the lands included the extensive estate of an Anglo-Saxon landowner, Turchil of Arden, who had not yet been dispossessed). When his father died in 1094, he inherited the Norman barony of Annebecq; so that he, like his brother, now had important lands on both sides of the Channel. He was present at Winchester in 1100, and took a leading part in securing the succession to England for Henry. This service, and his continuing loyalty, earned for him the Gower peninsula, including Swansea where he built a castle, which Henry assumed the right to give him and which thus extended the Beaumont interests into Wales.

I must be brief with the next generation, though it is instructive to see how a family's interests grow. Isobel, Robert of Beaumont's wife, gave birth to twins in 1104—Waleran, deemed to be the elder, and Robert. While they were still very young it was settled that Waleran should have his father's continental lands, with his grandfather's estates in Dorset and Gloucestershire, and Robert the English lands though with some interest in Normandy. The twins were brought up by Henry Beauclerk and in due course each succeeded to his inheritance, Waleran to the county of Meulan, Robert to the earldom of Leicester. Both were active on Stephen's behalf, mostly in Normandy, until 1141; then both went over to the Angevin cause, but not so actively, it seems, that it cost them their English lands. Waleran, indeed, had been given the city and earldom of Worcester by Stephen, though he is not likely to have been in England much at all, after 1142; Robert, through his marriage to Amicia, daughter and heiress of the Breton lord of Gael and Montfort, eventually secured the fitzOsbern inheritance in Normandy— the honour of Breteuil and Paci—and with it a claim, which Henry fitzEmpress recognized, to the 'stewardship of England and Normandy'. Thus, although the original partition gave lands mostly in France to Waleran and lands mostly in England to Robert, each twin acquired extensive interests in the other country. Hugh de Meulan, their younger brother, may not have been born when the settlement was made, and no provision was ever made for him by the family. The kindly Stephen, as Professor Barlow would have it, did his best to make him earl of Bedford; but after the Battle of Lincoln this failed, and Hugh sank back into the obscurity from which he had only briefly emerged.

On the Warwick side, the eldest son of Henry of Beaumont, Roger, was under age when his father died, but obtained the earldom in 1123. Like his cousins he supported Stephen until 1141, and returned to him after only a brief flirtation with the Angevins. Indeed, he allowed Warwick Castle to be garrisoned by Stephen's troops; and he was so upset when the castle surrendered to Henry that he died, though it had been no fault of his. Of his brothers, Robert of Neubourg seems to have spent most of his life in Normandy, where he had succeeded to his father's lands and where he became a justiciar, eventually the seneschal-justiciar; Rotrau,[15] the youngest, inevitably a priest, became successively bishop of Evreux and archbishop of Rouen. He is known to French historians, somewhat oddly, as 'Rotrou de Warwick'. While he in turn was the seneschal-justiciar of Henry fitzEmpress in Normandy, his cousin, Robert earl of Leicester, was his justiciar in England.

The influence of such a family must have been enormous. In addition to the offices they held, Waleran II of Meulan had estates from Gournay-sur-Marne, to the east of Paris, with property in Paris itself (for all of which he was, of course, the vassal of the king of France), through to Worcestershire on the borderland of Wales. He had been on pilgrimage to Compostella, and he joined the crusade of 1147 when things were rather difficult in England and Normandy. Robert of Leicester had property in England, Normandy and Brittany; Roger of Warwick, though mainly concerned with his Midland earldom, had for brothers an important baron and officer in Normandy and a bishop of Evreux destined to much higher things. The outlook of such people cannot have been confined to England or to Normandy.

The Bellême-Montgomery family, the last to be described in this way, is better known than most, for the chronicler Orderic Vitalis knew it well and wrote a good deal about its picturesque and often very violent members. It had a double origin as I have indicated by the hyphenated name.

The Bellême root[16] may have originated in the Beauvaisis, that is in France, and its earliest possessions around Bellême were certainly held of the king of France. Though most of his lands may already have been held by his father, the real founder of the family's greatness seems to have been William of Bellême, who constructed a huge lordship on the axis Bellême-Alençon-Domfront, with castles in all three places, partly in France, partly in Normandy and partly in Maine. It lay mostly in the almost inaccessible highlands to the south of Normandy, and controlled many of the important routes between Normandy and Anjou. It thus had great strategic potential; and, as a frontier lordship in such a situation, with divided allegiance it could almost aspire to independence. The power and

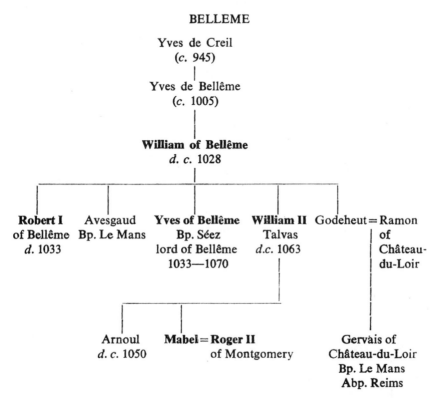

BELLEME

Yves de Creil
(*c.* 945)

Yves de Bellême
(*c.* 1005)

William of Bellême
d. c. 1028

Robert I of Bellême *d.* 1033	Avesgaud Bp. Le Mans	**Yves of Bellême** Bp. Séez lord of Bellême 1033—1070	**William II** Talvas *d.c.* 1063	Godeheut = Ramon of Château-du-Loir
	Arnoul *d. c.* 1050	Mabel = **Roger II** of Montgomery		Gervàis of Château-du-Loir Bp. Le Mans Abp. Reims

influence of the family in the eleventh century is well shown by the hold it seemed to have upon the bishoprics of Séez and Le Mans. All this descended, in 1070, to the infamous Mabel who, nearly twenty years earlier, had married Roger II of Montgomery.

The Montgomery family,[17] thoroughly Norman—'Norman of the Normans', as Roger himself boasted—cannot be traced further than his father, Roger I; but it is significant that the first Roger seems to have married a niece of the Duchess Gunnor, and that many of the early possessions of the family had once formed part of the endowment of the ducal monasteries of Bernay, Jumièges and Fécamp. Roger I was lord of Montgomery and vicomte of the Hiésmois, and his son succeeded him in his properties and honours. Roger II, like

William of Warenne, attached himself as a young warrior to Duke William and enjoyed the duke's friendship. He was already wealthy enough, in the 1050's, to found the monasteries of Saint-Martin-de-Troarn and Saint-Martin-de-Séez, and to restore Almenèches as a convent of nuns. Though intimately involved in the preparations for the invasion of England in 1066, he did not himself sail with

MONTGOMERY — BELLEME

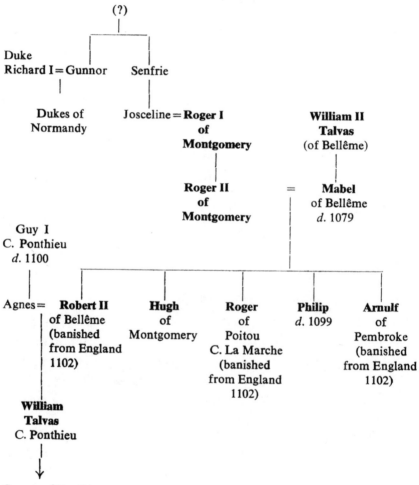

his duke, but was one of those who were detailed to assist the Duchess Matilda in the government of Normandy. However, he came to England with William in December 1067 and was

immediately given the compact lordship which became the rapes of
Arundel and Chichester; later, in 1074 or before, he received the
earldom of Shrewsbury. In both cases the significance of the grant,
as also with William of Warenne's rape of Lewes, William
fitzOsbern's earldom of Hereford or Hugh of Avranches' earldom
of Chester, or the northern honours of Richmond, Pontefract or
Holderness, lay not in the status it may have conveyed, but in the
opportunity which a compact lordship, laboriously put together
from a number of Anglo-Saxon estates and often including what
had been royal domain, gave to a lord to settle his followers, many
of whom had been his tenants in Normandy, in a compact group
immediately around his chief castle. Such a group, bound by the
ties of vassalage to their lord, anxious to prove themselves and to
make a fortune, was admirably fitted for the defence of a vital stretch
of frontier, as on the South Coast, or to consolidate the Norman hold
on imperfectly-conquered country, as in the North, or for attacking
lands to be acquired beyond the frontier, as on the Welsh borderland.
By the time of Earl Roger's death in 1094, the Shrewsbury group
had not merely annexed Welsh districts to the north and the north-
west, and founded a new stronghold to which Roger gave his name,
but had advanced through the centre of Wales into Ceredigion
and was establishing itself in Pembroke. Thus Roger's interests
stretched from farthest Wales, across England and Normandy, to
Bellême, which might still be regarded as under the suzerainty of
the king of France.

Roger and Mabel had a large family. The eldest of the sons,
Robert of Bellême, had succeeded to his mother's lands, the Bellême
inheritance, after she had been murdered in 1079, and to his father's
lands in Normandy when he died in 1094. The English lands and at
least some of the conquests in Wales, as sometimes happened at this
time, were destined for the second son Hugh, who nevertheless
seems to have spent most of his time, until he entered into his
inheritance, in Normandy. He is best known for his co-operation
with Earl Hugh of Chester in the great expedition of 1098, which
was intended to recover the hold that his father, with the earl of
Chester and his men, had once fastened on North Wales and which
had been seriously threatened by the Welsh. King William Rufus,
in two expeditions, had failed to restore the position. In their conflict
with the Welsh, the two earls were successful; but they happened
upon King Magnus Barefoot of Norway, who was doing some
raiding on his own account; and in the battle that followed Earl

Hugh was killed. This was, as it turned out, a major setback for the Normans in North Wales.

Besides this, the death of Earl Hugh had another result. Though he had younger brothers, it was his elder brother, Robert of Bellême, already lord of the huge Bellême and Montgomery inheritance in Normandy, who now succeeded to Arundel, Shrewsbury and the other English and Welsh lands of his father; to which he added the great honour of Blyth in Nottinghamshire and South Yorkshire and, through his marriage with Agnes of Ponthieu, the county of Ponthieu after the death of his father-in-law in 1100. This made him an enormously powerful baron, from the estuary of the Somme, where he could be virtually independent, through southern and central Normandy, southern and western England, to North Wales; and if we treat the family as a unit, as potentially it always was, we must take into account the possessions of his younger brothers as well. Of these Roger[18] held what is now Lancashire, together with enormous estates in the West Riding, in Suffolk, Lincolnshire and Nottinghamshire. He had married the heiress of the count of La Marche, in far-away Poitou (hence he is known to history as Roger of Poitou, or le Poitevin), and in 1091 he actually suceeded to the county. Yet when he founded Lancaster Priory he made it a cell of the family monastery of Saint-Martin-de-Séez in Normandy. The youngest brother, Arnulf, was lord of his father's conquests in Pembroke and of Holderness in Yorkshire; he, likewise, gave the priory he founded in Pembroke Castle to Saint-Martin-de-Séez. The second youngest, Philip, was that rare bird in the eleventh century, a literate knight, who joined Duke Robert Curthose and represented the family in the First Crusade. After fighting valiantly, he died in Jerusalem.

Indeed, it was their loyalty to Duke Robert, not quite uninterrupted though whole-hearted in the end, that brought the Montgomery family to ruin. Roger II of Montgomery himself seems to have managed, yet successfully, to sit on the fence in 1088; but Robert of Bellême (whose interests at that time lay wholly in Normandy and who seems to have supported Robert already in his revolts against his father King William)[19] and Roger of Poitou sided definitely with Robert Curthose. In 1101, Robert of Bellême was among those who were foremost in urging Curthose to invade England. He himself took part in the invasion and his brothers joined him. All this not unnaturally brought King Henry to the conclusion that the family must be crushed, or at least driven out of England and Wales. A little war followed and Robert of Bellême was forced to retire to Normandy where, after one unsuccessful attempt to come to terms with Henry, he threw himself energetically into the defence of Normandy on Curthose's behalf and fought for him at Tinchebrai. When Curthose had been taken prisoner, Robert made his peace with Henry so far as his Norman possessions were concerned, though he recovered nothing in England; but as soon as the claims of Curthose's son William Clito were taken up by the king of France and the count of Anjou he returned to his old allegiance. In 1112 the king of France sent him on an embassy to Henry, who treacherously arrested him and kept him in close confinement for the rest of his life. His brothers had, perhaps, been more fortunate. Roger had retired to his county of La Marche after 1102, where he and his heirs continued to hold that county for half-a-century or so; and Arnulf very nearly got himself a kingdom in Ireland.[20] Indeed, the family of Montgomery-Bellême, was not quite finished; for the son of Robert of Bellême, William Talvas, and his descendants, continued as counts of Ponthieu and lords of Alençon in Normandy. But the enormous potential of the year 1100 was gone.

These brief family sketches seem to show something that almost amounts to a consistent pattern—though they have been chosen, not quite at random it is true, but with no special axe to grind. Even from what has already been said, however, you must be drawing certain conclusions for yourselves; but I shall now venture on one or two generalizations, as suggestions rather than conclusions, for my conclusion would simply be that what has been attempted superficially in this lecture could profitably be extended and deepened.

One quality of these Norman barons must have impressed itself upon you very clearly—what one might call their 'empire-building' proclivities, their ambition and their insatiable lust for possession. Now this is characteristic of a new social group that has risen very quickly; and there is good evidence that the Norman aristocracy which supported William in his great venture, and did so well out of it, was indeed a 'new' aristocracy.[21] You will have noticed in the family histories that we can rarely, if ever, trace the ancestors of the barons of 1066 further than two or three generations. By itself, though it may be suggestive, this proves little, for Norman documents of a date earlier than the year 1000 are rare indeed. But there is a considerable amount of positive evidence as well. Many of these families could claim some family relationship with Duke William. This is true of William fitzOsbern's family, of the Warennes, the Beaumonts and the Montgomerys. The highest rank in the Norman nobility, the counts, were almost all closely related to the duke.[22] You may have noticed, also, that many of the lands possessed by the ancestors of these barons had in all probability formed part of the ducal lands originally (fitzOsbern again); and it is difficult to imagine that they had been acquired otherwise than by deliberate ducal gift. Some, also, had belonged to monasteries under ducal patronage (Beaumont, Montgomery); and again one must suppose that it was ducal pressure that induced the monasteries to part with their lands. Another element in the rise of a Norman family was personal service to the duke (Warenne, Beaumont, Montgomery); and this might take the form of a young man training himself to arms by joining the ducal troop. Such service might be directly rewarded with a gift of property, as it clearly was in the case of William of Warenne—indeed, you could say that the foundations of his fortune were laid by his service in the Mortemer campaign of 1054. And you will remember, too, that all this is happening just at the time when castles were becoming an instrument of military and political power. One of William fitzOsbern's earliest responsibilities was to keep the ducal castle of Breteuil; and while it was his son, not he, who converted it into a private castle, the custody of a ducal castle in itself offered possibilities of advancement, and in times of difficulty the distinction between custody and possession might not have much practical significance.

Now all this suggests that these families really were new, in their wealth and eminence, in 1066. It also suggests, though we must be careful how we use the word, that aristocratic society in early eleventh-century Normandy was becoming feudal; it even suggests that the duke himself was deliberately building up this feudal society as an instrument to establish and to maintain his power within his duchy and to hold his own with neighbouring rulers who were doing the same thing; and one of the principal characteristics of such early feudalism is precisely this aggressiveness and acquisitiveness; for vassals had to be rewarded in order that they might be held, and lords, to hold their position in the world, were competing for vassals. Indeed, this competition for vassals, and for the land and wealth with which to hold them, is, if you like, the sociological explanation of the Norman conquest of England. These conclusions are further reinforced by the evidence that many of the families that were coming to the top in Normandy had been brought in from outside the duchy, from France (e.g. Bellême), from Brittany (e.g. Giroy),[23] even from Germany (e.g. Baldric the German).[24] A successful leader whom, as Orderic put it, 'the divine hand protected,'[25] could attract adherents from far afield; for men on the make were looking for lords who could lead them to wealth and fortune.

This acquisitive society did, in the end, acquire England very completely. It is customary to quote W. J. Corbett's calculations from Domesday,[26] which show that by 1086 not more than 5% or 6% of English land, by value, was still in the hands of English laymen as independent holders—and it must be remembered that Norman clerks and Norman monks were taking over English bishoprics and abbeys as completely as the Norman barons were taking over English estates. But Domesday shows a process that was still not complete. The honour of Pontefract, it seems, did not begin to be formed until the 1080's (its chief castle is not mentioned in Domesday Book though it was certainly in existence a year or two later), and the English tenants on it, shown as surviving in 1086, may not have lasted much longer. Henry of Beaumont obtained the lands of Turchil of Arden in 1088; William II of Warenne did not receive the vast manor of Wakefield, hitherto royal land, until about 1107. There were fortunes still to be made in England during the time of King Henry I. Orderic has a well-known passage describing the men whom Henry had 'raised from the dust',[27] and his picture of Richard Basset returning to his home in Normandy 'bursting with the wealth of England', is famous.[28] But there is at least one interesting man whom Orderic does not mention in this connection, though he too owed his fortune to Henry I. This was Ranulf le Meschin,[29] who fits very nicely into the pattern. The origin of his family goes back to an Anschitil whose son, Ranulf I de Briquessart, married a daughter of Duke Richard III, was vicomte of Bayeux and one of the principal leaders in the great revolt against Duke William in 1047. He was certainly pardoned; but his son, Ranulf II, though he may conceivably have taken part in the conquest of England, certainly got nothing out of it. However, he married Maud, the sister of Hugh of Avranches, earl of Chester and vicomte of Avranches; and their son, Ranulf le Meschin, was taken up by Henry and put in charge of the Normans whom William Rufus had established in and around Carlisle. When young Richard, who had inherited the earldom of Chester and the vicomté of Avranches from his father Earl Hugh, was lost in the White Ship disaster of 1120, leaving no heir, his cousin Ranulf le Meschin was allowed to succeed to Chester and Avranches, and though he gave up Carlisle

THE ANCESTRY OF RANULF LE MESCHIN

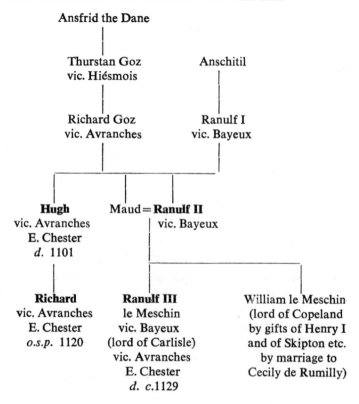

he kept Bayeux; and he thus formed, at this late date, yet another of those great cross-Channel estates that are so characteristic of the time, and one that survived intact until the French conquest of Normandy in 1204.

But if there were Normans who found their fortunes late in England, there were others who apparently had no share whatever in this vast new source of wealth. The vicomtes of the Cotentin,[30] who can be traced back to a Roger living in the time of Duke Richard I, belonged to an illustrious family second to none, on the evidence, in their service to the dukes at least until about 1040. But Nigel II took a lead, with Ranulf I of Bayeux, in the rebellion of 1047, although, like Ranulf, he was certainly pardoned and his lands were eventually restored to him. Yet it is almost certain that neither he nor his family took any part in the campaigns in England, nor did they get anything out of the Conquest. It does not seem that this was due to his rebellion twenty years before Hastings, for there were others, for instance Roger of Mortemer, who had rebelled at some time and obtained pardon and whose sons or grandsons profited from the Conquest; even Eustace of Boulogne, who attempted an invasion of England on his own account in 1067, subsequently obtained an enormous estate in a desirable part of England. Yet the vicomtes of the Cotentin got nothing. Why?

To complete the spectrum, I must quote the case of Gilbert d'Auffay.[31] Orderic tells us that Gilbert was a kinsman of Duke William, and fought by his side in all the major engagements of the 'English War' 'with his men around him'—a useful literary indication, incidentally, of the social and military units that settled down in the great compact fiefs on the frontiers of England. He had, therefore, at least two of the essential qualifications for substanial advancement. Yet, when William offered him ample estates in England he refused, saying that he would not share in the fruits of brigandage. He would be content with his own lands in Normandy; and to them he returned. That, at least, is Orderic's story, and there seems to be a moral in it.

Another point which seems to stand out from the family histories is that these Norman barons were not simply men of Norman origin who came and settled in England. There were, of course, Bretons, Manceaux, Picards, Flemings and others among them; but that is not the point. All the more important of them, at any rate, were men who retained interests in Normandy (or France), and were clearly concerned to maintain those interests, as well as to acquire new interests in England or beyond. Even when there had been a family partition, with the Norman lands going to one branch and the English lands to another, the division was not always exactly on the line of the Channel (the Beaumonts provide a good example of this) and, in any case, each branch retained an interest in the other's share, an interest which often led to reunion—as in the case of the ducal family itself, or as in the Montgomery family. Therefore family possessions were always potentially a unit, even if they might be, at any given moment, divided among relations. But one may go further and say that, for at least two or three generations, Normandy remained the homeland, and that acquisitions abroad were simply additions to the family estates in Normandy. One indication of this lies in the fact that a good deal of baronial piety was expressed, to begin with at any rate, not so much in new foundations in England (and, remember, these were men who had become suddenly and enormously rich), as in gifts of lands and churches to the family monasteries in Normandy or in nearby France[32] (such as William fitzOsbern's gifts to Cormeilles and Lyre, the Montgomery's patronage of Saint-Martin-de-Séez; even William of Warenne, in founding Lewes, gave it to the great French monastery of Cluny). It never seems to have worked the other way. English foundations did not acquire lands in Normandy. Henry of Troubleville, whose family had been settled in Dorset for some time, arranged to have his heart buried in Normandy more than 30 years after the French conquest of 1204.[33] These were Norman barons, really Norman—Norman-French if you like, but not (at least not for some time) Anglo-Norman.

If further indications of this were needed—and it is understood that I am dealing in indications, not statistical analysis—it would be provided by the Lacys.[34] Two brothers had come to England, very probably in 1066, Ilbert, the elder, in the train of his lord, Bishop Odo of Bayeux, while the younger, Walter, attached himself to William fitzOsbern. Ilbert was given lands in the Midlands by Bishop Odo, and so held them as the bishop's tenant; Walter received holdings from William fitzOsbern in the region of his earldom. When fitzOsbern's son Roger rebelled in 1075, Walter remained loyal to King William, and consequently found himself upgraded to the position of tenant-in-chief. Ilbert, a little later, was given the enormous compact fief of Pontefract in Yorkshire, also to hold in chief. The two branches became, therefore, very important barons in the West and the North respectively, and both survived, with some vicissitudes, through the twelfth century. Yet they never forgot the small estates in Normandy from which they had come. These were nursed and sustained almost to the French conquest of 1204. It would have been so easy to exchange them in order to round off some corner of their English estates; but they were kept and tended. They were the family's stake in the home country.

This brings me to a last general point. Historians sometimes write as though they were thinking in terms of an English baronage and a Norman baronage, say in the reign of Henry I. If there is anything

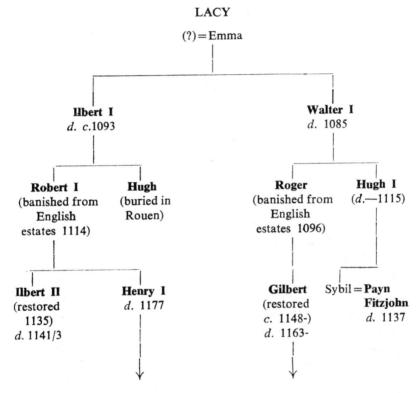

LACY

(?) = Emma

Ilbert I
*d. c.*1093

Walter I
d. 1085

Robert I
(banished from English estates 1114)

Hugh
(buried in Rouen)

Roger
(banished from English estates 1096)

Hugh I
(*d.*—1115)

Ilbert II
(restored 1135)
d. 1141/3

Henry I
d. 1177

Gilbert
(restored *c.* 1148-)
d. 1163-

Sybil = **Payn Fitzjohn**
d. 1137

in the argument of this lecture, there can have been no such division. On the contrary, there was one, homogeneous, Norman-French baronial society, whose interests extended through the length and breadth of the Norman 'empire', into England, into Wales and ultimately into Scotland, into Brittany, Maine, the Vexin, Ponthieu, Boulogne and Flanders—not each individual into every one, of course, but all the more important into more than one and in such a way that it is impossible to draw lines between them. This is why the Conqueror's division of his dominions in 1087 created so much difficulty; and the politics of 1087 to 1106 can only be understood against the background of a divided royal family and this 'one baronial society'. Orderic puts into the mouths of certain barons a most illuminating discussion of the dilemma of 1088.[35] Under William the Conqueror, they said, they had crossed the sea, subdued the English and seized their lands and wealth. But now William had been succeeded by two youths, and the government of Normandy and England was divided. How could they serve two masters? If they adhered to Robert they would lose their great possessions in England which they had won with their blood; if they kept faith with Rufus they would lose their patrimonial estates in Normandy. The only solution was to depose Rufus and to make Robert ruler of both England and Normandy, since he was the elder, the more easily led, and they had sworn fealty to him while his father was living. Hence the rising against Rufus. Some barons, faced with this problem, supported the brother in whose dominions the greater part of their estates lay; some may have acted on personal considerations or momentary calculation of interest; but one must not assume that a man like Robert of Bellême, for example, evil as he may have been, supported Robert Curthose out of sheer perversity, or that there was something inherently reprehensible in choosing Robert rather than Rufus or Henry. Both before and after the conquest of England, William had called upon his barons to do homage and swear fealty to Robert Curthose, apparently as heir to all his dominions[36]; and men might reasonably feel that they should not go back upon their oath simply because William had changed his mind. There is even a suggestion of principle behind the actions of Robert of Bellême; for the one occasion on which he served Rufus actively was in the campaigns the king led into the Vexin and into Maine. This was between 1097 and 1099, when Rufus was in lawful possession of Normandy and bound to defend the duchy and its interests. Otherwise Robert of Bellême and his family supported Robert Curthose quite consistently, save in so far as they tried, as any man would do, to be on good terms with both brothers, whether Rufus and Curthose or Henry and Curthose.

My conclusion is rather presumptuous. If what I have been trying to do in this lecture in an elementary way (and those of you who have studied the Norman Conquest will know that I have not had to dig very deep for the matter I have put before you) could be done in a big way, that is a comparative, almost a sociological study of the Norman families, and above all done in the context, not simply of England, but of the whole Norman 'empire', I am sure we should find that there is a good deal still to be learnt about the Norman conquest and colonization of this country. Take the simple questions raised in this lecture: Why did some families do so well out of the Conquest while others only profited later or not at all? What precisely were the conditions that governed the rise and fall of families? Can we get any nearer to a chronology of the Norman colonization of England—and if we could, should we see anything of the conditions under which it was carried out, whether King William was always completely in control or whether he had to respond to pressure from below? All this is the very stuff of eleventh century politics. The work has already been begun by Professor Douglas in this country and by Monsieur Musset in Normandy; Dr. Wightman and others are showing the way; and all the vast distinterested labour of the great English genealogists—Sir Charles Clay, Mr. G. H. White, Lewis Loyd, William Farrer, J. H. Round and many others—is waiting to be used, and is there for anyone to use. We have studied the constitutional and the political, the administrative, military, economic and ecclesiastical effects of the Norman Conquest upon England; but the subject still awaits its Namier.[37]

REFERENCES

1. See, in particular, G. H. White, 'The Sisters and Nieces of Gunnor, Duchess of Normandy', *Genealogist*, N.S., XXXVII (1920), pp. 57-65, 128-132.

2. At the outset, a general reference must be given to D. C. Douglas, *William the Conqueror* (1964), particularly chapters 4 and 11, which are the foundation of much of this lecture. Specific references will not be given here save exceptionally. The biographies in the *Dictionary of National Biography*, though they have to be treated with care, are often useful, as are the introductions to the 'Domesday' sections in the relevant volumes of the *Victoria County History*. These, too, will be taken for granted. For all matters relating to the origin of the Norman families, L. C. Loyd, *The Origins of some Anglo-Norman Families* (1951) has to be used constantly. Roger of Montgomery and William of Warenne also figure in Mr Mason's earlier lecture in this series, 'William the First and the Sussex Rapes'.

3. On the family of William fitzOsbern, G. E. C., *Complete Peerage*, art. 'Hereford', 'Leicester'; D. C. Douglas, 'The Ancestors of William fitz-Osbern', *English Historical Review*, LIX (1944), pp. 62-79; J. H. Round, 'The Family of Ballon', in *Studies in Peerage and Family History* (1901), pp. 181 ff.; W. E. Wightman, 'The Palatine Earldom of William fitz-Osbern in Gloucestershire and Worcestershire (1066-1071)', *Eng. Hist. Rev.*, LXXVII (1962), pp. 6-17; on William of Breteuil there is much useful material in C. W. David, *Robert Curthose, Duke of Normandy* (1920).

4. Not Norwich, as Freeman and others have thought. See Professor Barlow's note in *Antiquaries Journal*, XLIV (1964), pp. 217-9.

5. On castleries, see F. M. Stenton, *The First Century of English Feudalism* (1932), pp. 192-4.

6. On William fitzOsbern in Wales, see also J. E. Lloyd, *History of Wales* (3rd ed. 1939), II, pp. 374-6.

7. Florence of Worcester, *Chronicon ex Chronicis* (ed. B. Thorpe, 1848-9), II, p. 1.

8. Ms. D, *sub anno* 1066 (*The Anglo-Saxon Chronicle*, ed. and trans. D. Whitelock et al., 1961, p. 145).

9. Orderic Vitalis, *Historia Ecclesiastica*, (edd. Le Prévost and Delisle), II, pp. 171-2.

10. *Complete Peerage*, art 'Surrey'; L. C. Loyd, 'The Origin of the Family of Warenne', *Yorks. Arch. Journal*, XXXI (1934), pp. 97-113; C. T. Clay, *The Honour of Warenne* (Yorks. Arch. Soc., Record Series, Extra Series, 'Early Yorkshire Charters', VIII, 1949), pp. 1 ff.

11. On the evidence for the participation of individuals in the Hastings campaign and the literature of the subject, D. C. Douglas, 'Companions of the Conqueror', *History*, XXVIII (1943), pp. 129-147; J. F. A. Mason, 'The Companions of the Conqueror: an Additional Name', *Eng. Hist. Rev.*, LXXI (1956), pp. 61-69.

12. *Regesta Regum Anglo-Normannorum*, II (edd. Cronne and Johnson, 1956) *passim*.

13. Douglas, *William the Conqueror*, pp. 86-7, etc.; *Complete Peerage*, art. 'Leicester', 'Worcester', 'Bedford', 'Warwick'; E. Houth, 'Galeran II, Comte de Meulan', *Bull. Phil. et Hist.*, (1961), pp. 627-682; G. H. White, 'King Stephen's Earldoms', *Trans. Royal Historical Society*, 4th ser. XIII (1930), pp. 51-82 and 'The Career of Waleran, Count of Meulan and Earl of Worcester (1104-66)', *ibid.*, XVII (1934), pp. 19-48.

14. Orderic, II, p. 184.

15. There are brief notes on Robert and Rotrou in L. Delisle, *Recueil des Actes de Henri II, Introduction* (1909), pp. 445-47, 454-56.

16. G. H. White, 'The First House of Bellême', *Trans. Royal Hist. Soc.*, 4th ser., XXII (1940), pp. 67-99; J. Boussard, 'La seigneurie de Bellême aux Xe et XIe siècles', *Mélanges . . . Louis Halphen* (1951), pp. 43-54.

17. Douglas, *William the Conqueror*, p. 91 etc., J. F. A. Mason, "Roger de Montgomery and his Sons (1067-1102)", *Trans. Royal Hist. Soc.*, 5th ser. XIII (1963) pp. 1-28; *Dict. Nat. Biog.* àrt "Bellême, Robert of" and "Roger de Montgomery". For the Montgomery activity in Wales, Lloyd, *History of Wales*, II, pp. 388-390, 400-414.

18. On Roger of Poitou, see also J. Tait, *Medieval Manchester and the Beginnings of Lancashire* (1904), pp. 155 ff.

19. E.g. David, *Robert Curthose*, p. 22.

20. E. Curtis, *History of Medieval Ireland* (2nd ed. 1938), pp. 10-11.

21. On this 'new aristocracy', see D. C. Douglas, 'The Rise of Normandy', *Proc. British Academy*, XXXIII (1947), pp. 101-131; *William the Conqueror*, ch. 4; and cf. 'The Norman Episcopate before the Norman Conquest', *Cambridge Historical Journal*, XIII (1957), pp. 101-115; L. Musset, 'Aux origines de la féodalité normande . . . ', *Rev. hist. de droit français et étranger*, 4e sér. XXIX (1951), p. 150; 'Observations sur la classe aristocratique normande au XIe siècle, *ibid.*, XXXVI (1958), pp. 142-3.

22. D. C. Douglas, 'The Earliest Norman Counts', *Eng. Hist. Rev.*, LXI (1946), pp. 129-156.

23. Orderic, II, pp. 22-23.

24. *Ibid.*, pp. 75-6.

25. *Ibid.*, pp. 103-4.

26. *Cambridge Medieval History*, V, pp. 506-513.

27. Orderic, IV, pp. 163-7.

28. *Ibid.*, V, pp. 68-9.

29. Douglas, *William the Conqueror*, p. 93; *Complete Peerage*, art. 'Chester'; on Ranulf's position in Cumbria, G. W. S. Barrow, in *Northern History*, 1 (1966), pp. 25-6.

30. L. Delisle, *Histoire du château et des sires de Saint-Sauveur-le-Vicomte* (1867), pp. 1 ff. (esp. pp. 20-21).

31. Orderic, III, p. 44; cf. D. C. Douglas, 'Companions of the Conqueror', *History*, N.S., XXVIII (1943), pp. 139-140.

32. D. Matthew, *The Norman Monasteries and their English Possessions* (1962), ch. II (esp. p. 28).

33. *Close Rolls, 1237-1242*, p. 165; *Dictionary of National Biography*, art. 'Turberville . . . Henry de'.

34. W. E. Wightman, *The Lacy Family in England and Normandy, 1066-1194* (1966).

35. Orderic, III, pp. 268-9.

36. Cf. David, *Robert Curthose*, pp. 12-15.

37. The writer has taken some of the ideas in this pamphlet a little further, with fuller references, in 'The Norman Colonization of Britain', *I Normanni e la loro espansione in Europa nell'alto medioevo* (Settimane di studio del Centro Italiano di Studi sull'alto medioevo, xvi, 1968; Spoleto, 1969), pp. 409-438.

The following abbreviations have been used in the footnotes :

A.S.C.   *The Anglo-Saxon Chronicle,* ed. and trans. D. Whitelock and others (1961).
C.P.   G.E.C., *The Complete Peerage,* 1910-59.
D.N.B.   *Dictionary of National Biography.*
E.H.R.   *English Historical Review.*
E.Y.C.   Early Yorkshire Charters, Yorkshire Archaeological Society, Record Series, Extra Series.
Haskins, *N.I.*   C. H. Haskins, *Norman Institutions* (1918).
Orderic   Ordericus Vitalis, *Historia Ecclesiastica,* edd. A. Le Prévost and L. Delisle, Société de l'Histoire de France, 5 vols., 1838-55.
R.A.D.N.   M. Fauroux, *Recueil des actes des ducs de Normandie* (Mémoires de la Société des Antiquaires de Normandie, tome xxxvi, 1961).
R.S.   The Chronicles and Memorials of Great Britain and Ireland during the Middle Ages (Rolls Series).
Regesta, i, ii, iii   *Regesta Regum Anglo-Normannorum,* i, edd. H. W. C. Davis and R. J. Whitwell (1913); ii, edd. C. Johnson and H. A. Cronne (1956); iii, edd. H. A. Cronne and R. H. Davis (1968).
T.R.H.S., 4, 5   *Transactions of the Royal Historical Society,* 4th Series, 5th Series.

VII

NORMANDY AND ENGLAND 1066-1144

I am taking your invitation to deliver this fourth Stenton Lecture[1] as a great compliment, and I thank you for it. But in proportion as it is a great compliment it is also an intimidating one; for I cannot do other than speak on the subject that is at present uppermost in my mind; and that brings me, on this occasion and in this place, very near to Sir Frank and Lady Stenton's own field. Much of what I think I know about the Normans in the eleventh and twelfth centuries I have learnt from them; and it is always a little difficult to judge how one's teachers would take an essay that makes considerable use of their writings and yet attempts a personal interpretation. But I hope that you will be tolerant; for, basic competence apart, you would not expect a man whose roots lie in the French 'Danelaw' to approach these Normans from quite the same angle as one like Sir Frank whose roots lay deep, as Lady Stenton has shown us, in the English Danelaw. Sir Frank Stenton was a great English historian; but however English we Channel Islanders may feel when we are in France, none of us who were born and brought up in the Islands before the radio and the aeroplanes came to plague us can ever feel wholly English in England. Yet we are perhaps more deeply involved, historically, in the relationship between Normandy and England that was created as a result of Duke William's conquest than either the English or the French. It is therefore something on which I have to make up my mind, both as a Channel Islander and as a historian; and in trying to do so I have also tried to see how the thing could have worked, to look at it functionally, that is to say, rather than constitutionally, genealogically, or what you will. Of necessity I am doing this far more on the basis of my understanding of what historians have written over the last hundred years or so than of any deep personal knowledge of the evidence itself; and I am very well aware that I may often be rushing in where scholars fear to tread. Yet there is no way of deciding whether a question is sensible and worth asking before it has been asked; certainly no way of answering it – and if, in the end, I do no more than put about the idea that there are still important questions to be asked about Norman government in England and in Normandy, I should be very content.

This relationship between Normandy and England has not often been discussed, at least not in the way that I want to speak of it now; and

---

[1] In preparing this lecture for printing I have preserved the form and the language in which it was delivered. Apart from minor corrections, the only change I have made is to restore one or two of the smaller cuts which had to be made in the original draft to ensure reasonable time-keeping. Professor C. R. Cheney kindly and very helpfully read this first draft for me; but he has no responsibility for the final version.

for that reason it may be well to begin by making a *prima facie* case for thinking that there was indeed a relationship that is worth discussing. Let me put it this way. William the Conqueror did not cease to be duke of Normandy after he had made himself king of England. In fact, between Christmas 1066 and his death in September 1087, he gave at least as much of his time and attention to Normandy and its affairs as he gave to England. William Rufus, though he was never formally duke of Normandy, always had an interest in the duchy and was effectively its ruler from the autumn of 1096 until his death in 1100. Henry, likewise, had had an interest in Normandy for some time before he made himself king of England, and was actually duke as well as king from the autumn of 1106 until his death in December 1135; while Stephen was king and duke until he was gradually dispossessed of the duchy by Geoffrey Plantegenêt in the early 1140's. Altogether, out of the 77 years from William the Conqueror's coronation in Westminster Abbey to the moment in 1144 when Stephen's authority in Normandy was finally extinguished, England and Normandy were ruled by one man for all but fifteen; and even during those fifteen years the two rulers were brothers. Such a long dynastic connection, you would think, must have created a relationship of some kind between the two countries. But what kind of a relationship was it?

I

The natural starting point for any attempt to answer this question is the attitude of the ruling family itself.[2] Here, I think, we have been misled by what happened in 1087. As he lay dying in a suburb of Rouen, William the Conqueror allowed his eldest son Robert Curthose to have Normandy and Maine, he gave England to his second surviving son William Rufus; to Henry, the youngest, he gave a large sum of money with which he could be expected to buy or win for himself lands appropriate to his rank, as in due course he did. This certainly looks as though William could see no relationship between England and Normandy beyond the fact that he himself had possessed them both; and this is the interpretation of his action that historians on both sides of the Channel have generally been content to accept, at least by implication. But it is an interpretation that is worth reconsidering.

In the first place, William's partition was unusual for its time. Contemporary rulers did not, as a rule, partition their lands; they did not even distinguish between what they had inherited and what they had acquired, a distinction that has often been put forward as a part-explan-

---

[2] What follows on the attitude of the royal-ducal family to the succession and to the unity of its lands has been argued in some detail with a discussion of the evidence in an article on 'The Norman Succession, 996-1135', *E.H.R.*, lxxxvi (1971), pp. 225-250.

ation of William's action. On the contrary, they were contriving by one means or another to pass on their lands and rights undivided; and that is how kingdoms were growing – how a kingdom of the English had come into being and how a kingdom of France was being stabilized and would grow in the future. The partition was also contrary to the tradition of William's own family in which, so far back as we can see things at all clearly, each successive duke designated one of his sons, generally the eldest and generally in an assembly of the magnates, to succeed to all his lands and interests; and however it may be characterized in other respects, the rule in England at least from the early tenth century was likewise one of non-partition. Moreover, when you look closely at such accounts as we have of William's testament, it appears that the partition was not what he himself intended. Taking what seems to be the most realistic and the most nearly contemporary version[3] of the dispositions on his deathbed, with such other evidence as we have,[4] it appears that William had designated his eldest son Robert Curthose to be his successor in all his lands, Normandy, Maine and England, and that this designation held until well after 1080 when it became clear that Robert was an unrepentant rebel who was unlikely to return to filial allegiance. William then transferred the designation wholly to the faithful William Rufus. It was only when the archbishop of Rouen and others who were beside the dying king's bedside intervened on Robert's behalf, and William was evidently too weak to resist, that he accepted a kind of compromise, allowing Robert to have Normandy and Maine, giving England to Rufus and the money to Henry. The partition was as much against William's real intentions as it was out of character with the tradition of his family and the practice of contemporary rulers.

If William had never intended a partition, neither did his family accept the partition he made; for the nineteen years from 1087 to 1106 were occupied by his sons in their attempts to reunite his inheritance, each for himself. Almost as soon as Rufus had established himself in England, there was a powerful movement to make Robert king as well as duke. Then Rufus invaded Normandy. For a while the two brothers set up a kind of condominium over all their father's lands, and to that extent these were briefly reunited. But this arrangement did not satisfy Rufus, who was well on his way towards a complete conquest of Normandy when Robert gave him possession of the duchy as security for the loan that enabled him to join the First Crusade. In practice, therefore, Rufus had reunited his father's inheritance into his own hands. A very

---

[3] 'De Obitu Willelmi . . .' in Guillaume de Jumièges, *Gesta Normannorum Ducum*, ed. J. Marx (Soc. de l'Hist. de Normandie, 1914), pp. 145-9; cf. *English Historical Documents*, ii. edd. D. C. Douglas and G. W. Greenaway (1953), pp. 279-80.

[4] E.g., C. W. David, *Robert Curthose, Duke of Normandy* (1920), pp. 9-12; William of Malmesbury, *Gesta Regum*, ed. W. Stubbs (R.S., 1887-9), ii. 337; Eadmer, *Historia Novorum*, ed. M. Rule (R.S. 1884), p. 25.

similar course of events followed when Henry took possession of England in 1100. Robert invaded England and Henry invaded Normandy; but the battle of Tinchebrai was decisive.[5] Thereafter Henry was as much king of England, duke of Normandy and lord of Maine as ever his father had been; for Robert was kept securely in prison for the remainder of his long life.

Having laboriously reconstructed his father's dominions, and having constantly to defend his reconstruction, Henry was naturally much preoccupied with the succession. First he made elaborate arrangements for his only legitimate son, William Ætheling, to be count of Maine[6] and to succeed him as king of England[7] and duke of Normandy.[8] All this had just been completed and settled when William was drowned in the wreck of the White Ship. Henry, whose queen had died two years earlier, married again at once; but his second marriage did not replace the lost heir. It was only in 1125, when his daughter Matilda was widowed, that he felt he could see a possible solution. He persuaded his barons to recognize Matilda as his successor in England and Normandy. When he married her to Geoffrey Plantegenêt, then the heir to the county of Anjou and its annexes, he did so not only because she had to have a husband if she were to have any real chance of succeeding, but because the marriage with Geoffrey would break the alliance between the count of Anjou and the king of France which had been one of his principal preoccupations on the Continent, and would also resolve the old rivalry between Normandy and Anjou, particularly over Maine – that is to say, he was creating the conditions that would make the succession of Matilda and her heirs to all his lands and rights, whole and undivided, at least feasible. When a ruling family has come to regard its lands as an impartible inheritance a long step towards the political unity of those lands has been taken; and the proof that this step had been taken by 1135 seems to me to lie in the circumstances of Stephen's accession; for there can be no doubt that, whatever the merits of his claim, his acceptance in England carried Normandy with it.

As far as the royal family was concerned, therefore, Normandy and England would be held together in principle for ever, along with the county of Maine and any other lands and overlordships that they might be able to acquire. This in itself could have been the beginning of integral union, as the union first of Mercia and then of Northumbria with the kingdom of the West Saxons paved the way for the formation of a kingdom of England.

But the royal family was not the only one to think in this way. The

---

[5] For these events, e.g. David, *Robert Curthose*, pp. 42-92, 120-76.

[6] J. Chartrou, *L'Anjou de 1109 à 1151* (1928), pp. 6-7, 13.

[7] J. H. Round, *Geoffrey de Mandeville* (1892), p. 30.

[8] *Regesta*, ii. no. 1074; *A.S.C.*, p. 184; J.-F. Lemarignier, *Recherches sur l'hommage en marche et les frontières féodales* (1945), pp. 91-2.

military conquest of England had been accompanied by a drastic Norman colonization of the country.[9] By the end of the century the landowning aristocracy of Anglo-Scandinavian England had been destroyed. In its place the royal-ducal family, a Norman-French baronage and a Norm-annized Church held the land of England. The few Anglo-Scandinavian landowners or their descendants who survived generally held only a fraction of their former estates and then as sub-tenants of some Norman lord. But, like the ruling family, the Norman-French barons who ob-tained estates in England did not give up their continental lands, though their English acquisitions were often far more extensive. Why should they? The first effect of this great revolution in England was therefore the creation of a number of 'cross-Channel' estates. It is true that in some families of the Conquest generation estates were partitioned in such a way that the Norman lands went to one son and the English lands to another;[10] but where there was only one son to succeed there would clearly be no partition, and there seems in any case to have been no pol-icy that would separate the English from the Norman estates as a matter of principle.[11] There was nothing to prevent lands divided in one generation from coming together again;[12] nothing to prevent a family

[9] D. C. Douglas, *William the Conqueror* (1964), ch. xi; Le Patourel, 'The Norman Colonization of Britain', *I Normanni e la loro espansione in Europa nell'alto medioevo* (Centro Italiano di studi sull'alto medioevo, Spoleto, 1969), pp. 409-38.

[10] The greater Norman families may already have been distinguishing between *propres* and *acquêts*, as in classical Norman custom. In the Conquest generation this would normally give the Norman inheritance to the eldest surviving son and the English acquisitions to a younger son if there was a partition – cf. Douglas, *William the Conqueror*, p. 361; R. Genestal, 'La Formation du droit d'aînesse dans la cout-ume de Normandie', *Normannia,* i (1928), pp. 168, 172. It is difficult to be sure how general the practice was at this time, for it is not always easy to be sure of the facts and there seem to have been exceptions, as in the case of Henry, first earl of War-wick (*C.P.*, xii. 2 pp. 359-60 and Appendix A). I am grateful to Professor Holt for discussing this point with me, though I do not wish to implicate him in my con-clusions.

[11] E.g when Hugh de Montgomery, earl of Shrewsbury, was killed in 1098 he was succeeded not by one of his younger brothers but by the eldest of the Montgomery brothers, Robert de Bellême, who already had his father's vast Norman lands (*C.P.*, xi. 691-2); and the family settlement which gave to Waleran, the elder of the 'Beaumont' twins, his father Robert's continental lands also gave him his grandfather's lands in England (*C.P.*, vii. 526, 522). A number of cross-Channel estates, though perhaps fluctuating in extent or suffering temporary divisions, retained their identity through the twelfth century (e.g. that of the earls of Chester, *C.P.*, iii. 165-7). There would have been fewer problems after the French conquest of Normandy in 1204 if this had not been so - cf. F. M. Powicke, *The Loss of Norm-andy* (1961), pp. 328-58.

[12] E.g. the Montgomery lands (see preceding note) and the pertinacious efforts of Earl Robert of Leicester to reconstruct the fitzOsbern lands and rights (*C.P.*, vii. 528-30). The royal-ducal family itself is a case in point.

based in one country from acquiring lands in the other[13] – and in fact new cross-Channel estates, including some huge ones, were being created throughout the reign of Henry Beauclerk.[14]

This meant that characteristically, if not universally, the great magnates, and not only they, had interests both in Normandy and in England; and it would clearly be a matter of some importance to them that the two countries should be in the hands of one ruler. Orderic makes this very clear in relation to the succession of Robert Curthose and William Rufus in 1087, and again in relation to the accession of Stephen in 1135.[15] And if you try to enumerate the barons who fought for Rufus or for Henry against Robert, or for Robert against his brothers, you will not find it easy to team them up into an 'English' baronage on the one hand and a 'Norman' baronage on the other. In fact, the warfare from 1087 to 1106 was never in any sense a war between England and Normandy: it was a war of succession between brothers, each fighting for the whole of their father's inheritance; and the barons might support one or the other on principle, according to personal or even quite transient interest or what you will, but certainly not from any feeling of 'Englishness' or 'Normanness'; for there could not be an 'English baronage' and a 'Norman baronage' at this time; only one ambitious, acquisitive and often ruthless Norman-French baronial society established in both countries.

It was also in the interest of the Church, broadly speaking, that England and Normandy should remain under one ruler, certainly of all those cathedrals and monasteries in Normandy that had lands or possessions in England, and that means practically all of them.[16] It was to the advantage, likewise, of ambitious churchmen of the conquering race; for the vast majority of appointments to English bishoprics and

[13] The document published by J. H. Round in *E.H.R.*, xiv (1899), 425-6 is generally quoted for its bearing on the early history of the Norman exchequer; but R. W. Southern has pointed out that it also shows an English family recovering land in Normandy by an action in that court – *Medieval Humanism* (1970), pp. 225-7.

[14] E.g. the estates of Stephen of Blois and Robert of Gloucester. Other examples in the article cited in note 2, p. 248, note 6.

[15] Orderic, iii. 268-9; v. 54-6.

[16] All the Norman cathedral chapters ultimately acquired property in England: D. J. A. Matthew, *The Norman Monasteries and their English Possessions* (1962), pp. 13, 24-5, 31, 43, 72, 74. There is a list of French monasteries holding English lands etc. at the time of the Domesday Survey in D. Knowles, *The Monastic Order in England* (1940), p. 703; but to these should be added those which acquired property in England subsequently, e.g. Aumale and Saint-Georges-de-Boscherville, D. Knowles and R. N. Hadcock, *Medieval Religious Houses; England and Wales* (1953), pp. 83-4 etc.

important abbeys went to men of Norman or French origin,[17] and both they and their patrons would want to keep this way of advancement open. The interests of the French merchant colonies established in the English towns and countryside could not be very different;[18] for they had come to lay their hands on what they could of English trade, as the barons and churchmen had taken English land and, one might say, English spiritual endowment.

What it amounted to was this. The Norman Conquest had not been simply a military conquest; and in England its consequences were not just a change of dynasty and a number of debatable changes in institutions and government. It involved a colonization of the country by a relatively small number of masterful men, led by the royal-ducal family, men who did not cut their roots in their homelands. It was a formidable vested interest.

II

Given this vested interest, given the will of king and barons to hold on to the lands they had inherited or acquired on the Continent as well as those they had obtained across the Channel, the relationship between Normandy and England that was thereby created would clearly give rise to problems of government.

The most obvious problem was one of geography – the division of the Norman lands by the English Channel and the sheer distance between their extremities, from Carlisle and Newcastle in the north to Alençon and Le Mans in the south. Yet the seriousness of this problem should not be exaggerated. A Channel crossing might be delayed by contrary or boisterous winds; but under normal conditions it would be easier to transport men and material in bulk across a relatively straightforward stretch of sea than to move them a comparable distance by land, easier that is to say to convey the king-duke, his household and his gear – and his troops if he had an army with him – from Rouen or Caen to Winchester or London than from London, say, to York or Chester. The Channel was more of a highway than a barrier in the late eleventh and in the twelfth centuries.

---

[17] This is a point which it would be worth while to work out in more detail. Until it is done, see Knowles, *Monastic Order,* ch. vi and p. 704 for the monasteries. The bishops are listed in *Handbook of British Chronology,* edd. F. M. Powicke and E. B. Fryde (Royal Historical Society, 1961) and the origins of at least the more important of them may be found in the *D.N.B. Cf.* Le Patourel, 'Norman Colonization', p. 414. Eadmer certainly thought that Englishmen had very little chance of promotion to high ecclesiastical office in Henry's time – *Historia Novorum,* p. 224.

[18] Le Patourel, *ubi supra,* p. 415.

This is particularly important because government was still generally itinerant at this time. Even before 1066 the duke of Normandy, though he might have favoured residences, could not rule his duchy from a fixed seat of government. To keep order, to demonstrate his authority and power, to provide for his household, to take his part in great ecclesiastical occasions, he and his household were constantly on the move.[19] The conquest first of Maine and then of England simply extended his itinerary. In addition to moving up and down Normandy, the king-duke now had to take in Maine and England as well, and occasionally Wales, Scotland or Brittany.[20] This meant that many places would see less of the king-duke than they had seen of king or duke hitherto; but though he had to build castles and to take other measures to make his authority effective throughout his lands, these conquests did not immediately cause him to change his method of government in any fundamental way. Generally speaking, the king-duke simply had to travel further and work harder than his predecessors in kingdom or duchy had done previously, but in much the same old way.

This was so because the greater part of what we might think of as the 'central government' of the Norman kings itinerated with them. The king-duke himself was no mere figure-head but the very mainspring of government, whose personal character was much the most important political fact in all his lands – as may be seen at once from the relative effectiveness of a Henry Beauclerk or a Robert Curthose. And with the king-duke there itinerated his household. It is true that much of what was called the household was purely domestic and, as will appear in a moment, that men drawn from the household, or at least bearing the titles of household offices, were beginning to form the elements of departments – or perhaps one should say 'administrative groups' – that were localized in England or in Normandy; yet the king-duke had but one seal, which authenticated his mandates and grants wherever they were issued and whichever of his lands they concerned; one chancellor, one writing-office, one chamber and, it seems, one treasurer.[21] The household was, and long remained, a very important element in the government; yet it was still so personal to the ruler – it was William's household or Robert's or Henry's – that there could not be a Norman household and an English household as long as one member of the royal-ducal family ruled over both countries. We cannot imagine William the

---

[19] It would be impossible to reconstruct the itinerary of a Norman duke before 1066, even in outline; but the charters now collected and edited in *R.A.D.N.* give some idea of his movement even though relatively few state the place at which they were given. On ducal movemnts generally, *ibid.,* p. 65, and L. Musset, 'Gouvernés et Gouvernants dans le monde scandinave et dans le monde normand', *Gouvernés et Gouvernants,* Société Jean Bodin, xxiii (1968), p. 463.

[20] *Regesta,* i. pp. xxi-xxii; ii. pp. xxix-xxxi.

[21] On the unity of the royal-ducal household, G. H. White, 'The Household of the Norman Kings', *T.R.H.S.,* 4, xxx (1948), pp. 127-55.

Conqueror dismissing his Norman household and appointing a new one, or providing himself with two, on the morrow of Hastings, and there is no evidence that he did either.[22] Certainly he employed such Englishmen as he found useful, but they always seem to have been in a minority. Both William Rufus and Robert Curthose took over some members of their father's household;[23] Henry had probably formed his own before he became king, though he subsequently added elements from the households of both his brothers.[24] The household existed to serve the king-duke, not England or Normandy; and it had to be where he was.[25]

In a real sense, too, there was but one royal-ducal court, though its unity was preserved not so much by itineration as by what we might

[22] This point is made in general terms by White, *ubi supra*, pp. 127-8; and a sufficient number of men, who served in William's household both before and after 1066, can be found to substantiate it. William fitzOsbern, a seneschal, is one good example (Haskins, *N.I.*, p. 58 note 289; *Regesta*, i. p. xxiii); Hugh de Montfort, a constable, is another if we can take Orderic's word for it that he was already constable at the time of Hastings (Orderic, ii. 148; G. H. White, 'Constables under the Norman Kings', *The Genealogist*, N.S., xxxviii, 1922, p. 113) and most probably Ralph de Tancarville, a chamberlain (*C.P.*, x. Appendix F., pp. 49-50). 'Hugo Pincerna' or 'Botillarius' attests charters both before and after 1066 (*R.A.D.N.*, nos. 116, 137, 138, 156, 188, 230, 233; *Regesta*, i. nos. 48; 55; 56; 150). Some at least of these attestations must have been made by Hugh d'Ivry; and his brother Roger attested as butler both in England and in Normandy after 1066 (*Regesta*, i. nos. 23, 128, 150, 207, 270, 308). Herfast, according to William of Malmesbury (*Gesta Pontificum*, ed. N. E. S. A. Hamilton, R.S., 1870, p. 150), had been one of William's chaplains for some time before he was made chancellor (*cf. R.A.D.N.*, p. 41; *Regesta*, i. p. xvi).

[23] E.g. Gerard, who was made chancellor by William the Conqueror, remained in office under William Rufus (*British Chronology*, p. 81); William de Tancarville, a chamberlain, and Roger d'Ivry, butler, joined Robert Curthose (*C.P.*, x. Appendix F. pp. 51-2; *Regesta*, i. nos. 308, 324).

[24] E.g. Roger of Salisbury and others (Appendix); William Giffard, who had been made chancellor by William Rufus, was not immediately replaced (*British Chronology*, p. 81); while William de Tancarville, who had served both William the Conqueror and Robert as chamberlain, joined Henry after Tinchebrai and served him in both countries until 1129 (Appendix).

[25] The idea that there was a Norman and an English household seems to slip out almost inadvertently in some historians' writings (e.g. H. W. C. Davis, in *Regesta*, i. pp. xxv, xxvii; Haskins, *N.I.*, p. 114). It is made curiously and inconsistently explicit by G. H. White in *C.P.*, x. Appendix F., and it is implied by all who treat England as a self-contained political unit at this time. The first suggestion of a household officer whose title, and so presumably his functions, was limited to one of the two countries comes in Henry's grant of 'magistram camerariam meam totius Anglie' to Aubrey de Vere in 1133 (*Regesta*, ii. no. 1777). But while it may be more difficult to maintain Tout's suspicions of this charter (T. F. Tout, *Chapters in the Administrative History of Medieval England*, 1920-33, i. 90) since the publication of a seventeenth-century 'facsimile' (*Sir Christopher Hatton's Book of Seals*, edd. L. C. Loyd and D. M. Stenton, 1950, plate I), such a title is nevertheless isolated at that date and, if the charter is indeed genuine, is more probably to be explained as marking the point at which the 'master-chamberlainship' became more honorific than effective than as the beginning of an 'English' and a 'Norman'

describe as its very flexible constitution.[26] Its nucleus was the king and some of the chief officers and clerks of his household, to which might be added some of the bishops and barons of the region in which the king found himself or who interested themselves particularly in its work, with others from further afield on important occasions. There could also be a king's court without the king, sitting by his commission; and while there were some justices who, as individuals, appear to have acted only in Normandy and others who acted only in England,[27] it is certainly impossible to draw any distinction between the 'English' and the 'Norman' barons present on any particular occasion, and bishops of English or Norman sees might attend in either country.[28] All forms of the court primarily served the king-duke, and its sessions were described as *curia regis* whether it met in Normandy or in England,[29] whether the king were present or represented by a justice or a group of justices acting in his name. There could hardly be an English *curia regis* and a Norman *curia regis* any more than there could be an English household and a Norman household.

However there were difficulties in trying to govern and to exploit

household. White quotes no convincing evidence to show that this grant made Rabel de Tancarville 'chamberlain' or 'master-chamberlain' of Normandy and Aubrey de Vere certainly attended Henry on his last visit to Normandy, that is after the grant of the 'master-chamberlainship of all England' (Appendix, s.v. 'Aubrey de Vere' and 'William de Tancarville').

[26] William's *curia*, after 1066, must have been a continuation of his *curia* in Normandy before the Conquest, as his household was (in general, Douglas, *William the Conqueror*, pp. 284-8). Important Englishmen attended meetings held in England during the few years that they survived; but while this may imply an element of continuity between the Norman *curia* when it met in England and the English witan, the composition of the court, so far as it can be deduced from the attestations to charters, shows a more direct continuity between William's pre-Conquest *curia* in Normandy and his post-Conquest *curia* which met in both countries, even though its contact with the traditions of the witan may have reinforced the aristocratic and episcopal element in its composition (Musset, 'Gouvernés et Gouvernants', pp. 461 ff.). An analysis of the attestations of pre-Conquest ducal charters is given in the Introduction to *R.A.D.N.* (pp. 58-63); and F. M. Stenton provides a very clear description of the meetings in England of William's post-Conquest *curia* in *William the Conqueror* (1908), pp. 407-20.

[27] Below, note 56.

[28] Assuming, again, that attestations to charters give the names of those attending the *curia* at the time when the charter was 'given', examples of all its forms may be found in *Regesta*, i, ii, and iii. As specific examples of occasions when the bishops of English sees attended the *curia* in Normandy and bishops of Norman sees attended in England, see *Regesta*, ii. nos. 790, 1740, 1741, 1895, 1900, 1902 etc.; Round, *Geoffrey de Mandeville*, pp. 262-6.

[29] In Normandy, e.g. *Regesta*, i. nos. 92, 132; L. Delisle, *Histoire du château et des sires de Saint-Sauveur-le-Vicomte*, pièces justificatives, nos. 36 ('in regali curia'), 42 ('judicio curiae regis Anglorum').

such extended territories by itineration alone. In an age when the king's peace died with him and government was direct and personal, itineration though necessary was insufficient; for though the king-duke had to be everywhere he clearly could not be everywhere at once, and without some delegation of authority the continuity of government would be hard to maintain in either country. It is therefore a little surprising, perhaps, that no very firmly established institution of regency or vice-royalty had evolved by the end of Henry's reign. When the king-duke moved from one country to the other, a member of the royal family was often left in charge, supported by a group of bishops or barons who no doubt did most of the work. Sometimes these men had to act without a royal personage; and a few of them, such as Archbishop Lanfranc, Odo of Bayeux, Ranulf Flambard, Roger of Salisbury or John of Lisieux had some at least of the powers and responsibilities of the later justiciars and seneschals of the Angevin kings. But it does not seem to be possible to draw up a complete schedule of those who were responsible in England and in Normandy during the king-duke's absences from either country between 1066 and 1144, or to be sure of any stability or of any consistent development in the functions of those who acted in this way.[30]

The need for something more than a purely itinerant government in territories as extensive as Normandy and England taken together did, however, give rise to important developments in finance and justice; for, whatever else may be said of them, the Norman kings were efficient by the standards of their day. The primitive financial 'department', for example, both in the kingdom and in the duchy, had been the chamber, which in England at any rate seems originally to have been no more than the king's bedchamber.[31] The ruler's treasure in all its forms had been kept there and his chamberlains had administered it for him;[32] but if William had indeed been able to keep his treasure in his itinerant chamber before 1066, this became impossible after he had taken posses-

[30] Any discussion of the origin of the justiciar in England and of the 'justiciar-seneschal' in Normandy must take account of the needs and conditions of both countries. For this reason if no other the confident assertations of H. G. Richardson and G. O. Sayles in *The Governance of Medieval England* (1963), pp. 157 ff. can hardly be accepted. These writers are aware that it was the problem of governing England and Normandy together that created the need for such an office, but if they mention the situation in Normandy they do not discuss it. Other writers are more cautious, but do not keep both countries always in mind. For England, F. J. West, *The Justiciarship in England, 1066-1232* (1966), pp. 1-30; For Normandy, David, *Robert Curthose*, pp. 12-13 (and Orderic, ii. 234), Haskins, *N.I.*, pp. 87-8; 99, 127-8.

[31] Tout, *Chapters*, i. 72-3.

[32] For England, *ibid.*, and *cf.* S. B. Chrimes, *An Introduction to the Administrative History of Medieval England* (1952), pp. 8-10; for Normandy, Haskins, *N.I.*, pp. 39-41.

sion of the revenues of England,[33] not to mention the booty from the process of the Conquest itself.[34] In fact it seems probable that Edward the Confessor had already found it necessary to have a fixed treasury in England in addition to his chamber.[35] Consequently the king-dukes established storehouses or treasuries, or maintained treasuries already established, at Winchester, Rouen, Falaise and elsewhere,[36] and then detached members of the chamber-staff to look after them[37] under the overall authority of the treasurer, a new officer who seems to have had all the king-duke's treasuries under his control and who was therefore, at this time, half in the household and half out of it.[38] A part of the chamber organization, naturally, remained in the household, itinerating with the king-duke, continuing its domestic functions but also, or so it

---

[33] *Cf.* below, notes 76-7.

[34] Le Patourel, 'Norman Colonization', pp. 429-30.

[35] J. E. A. Jolliffe, *Constitutional History of Medieval England* (1937), pp. 129-30. L. M. Larson, in *The King's Household in England before the Norman Conquest* (1904), pp. 130-3, suggests that the development in the eleventh century may have been not so much that from a royal treasure always carried about with the king to a royal treasury partly located in a fixed place, as from royal treasures deposited partly in monasteries and other ecclesiastical foundations to a royal treasure kept in greater proportion in one or more royal castles. This, certainly, is what seems to have happened in Gascony in the thirteenth century where ducal records and cash were deposited in monasteries (e.g. *Calendar of Patent Rolls, 1216-1225,* p. 356, *1232-1247,* pp. 49, 406) before the constable of Bordeaux Castle became the chief financial officer and keeper of the records.

[36] E.g., Tout, *Chapters,* i. 74 *ff.*; Haskins, *N.I.,* pp. 105, 107. At Portchester there seems to have been a kind of transit store for treasure that was being shipped to or from Normandy in the time of Henry II, and this may have existed already in the early part of the twelfth century (J. H. Round in *Victoria County History, Hampshire,* i. 432).

[37] For the chamberlains of the treasury in England, see G. H. White, 'Financial Administration under Henry I', *T.R.H.S.* 4, viii (1925), 56-78; 'The Household of the Norman Kings', 130-1. This development is not so clear in Normandy, for those in charge of the Norman treasuries at this time seem to have been called 'treasurers' (Haskins, *N.I.,* pp. 106-10); but 'treasurer' and 'chamberlain' often seem to mean much the same thing (e.g. White, 'Financial Administration', pp. 68-9).

[38] For the treasurer, White, 'Financial Administration', pp. 64-72. Haskins thought that there was a treasurer for England and a treasurer for Normandy (*N.I.,* pp. 108-10), and others have accepted this explicitly or by implication (e.g. Tout, *Chapters,* i. 81; Richardson and Sayles, *Governance,* pp. 223-4); but White has argued that there was but one chief treasurer whose functions extended over both countries (*Notes and Queries,* cl (1926), 59-60). This is certainly what one would expect if the king-duke's household was unitary (as argued in this lecture) and the treasurer (according to the passage in the 'Constitutio Domus Regis' which has given rise to so much discussion – *Dialogus de Scaccario,* ed. C. Johnson, 1950, p. 133) was still a member of the household, however semi-detached. There seems to be no reason why men staffing the fixed treasuries should not also be called 'treasurers'.

would seem, serving as his central department of finance as well as being his 'privy purse.[39]

When such localized treasuries were established, it would be natural to require the English sheriffs and others who owed money to the king to pay the balance of their farms and other monies into a treasury in England, and the Norman *vicomtes* and *prévôts* to pay theirs into a Norman treasury;[40] and since you could not have the English sheriffs and other accountants pursuing an itinerant court into Normandy in order to render their accounts or the Norman *vicomtes* and *prévôts* chasing it up and down England for the same purpose, or either waiting up to three or four years for it to return to their country, the next step was to detail members of the court (including some who held household offices) to audit the accounts of the sheriffs and others in England and of the *vicomtes* and *prévôts* in Normandy. Then, because the auditors used the chequer-board as a means of computation, they could be described as 'barons of the exchequer', and later their meetings and their place of meeting would also be described as 'the exchequer'; but far more important than the method of computation was the fact that these accounting sessions were held regularly in both countries, twice a year, at Easter and Michaelmas, whether the king could be present or not; so that his local officers and others acting in his name knew that they must render their accounts at fixed times and predetermined places, and that these accounts would be regularly scrutinized.[41] This made it

---

[39]   Richardson and Sayles (*Governance,* pp. 227-8 and ch. xii) make this point, certainly for the later twelfth century; and, if the significance which they attach to the battle of Tinchebrai is ignored, as it should be, it is again what one would expect; *cf.* Tout, *Chapters,* i. 100 ff. White, however, speaks of the *Camera Curie,* after the treasury organization had hived off, as dealing with 'what we may call the Privy Purse expenses and those of the household' ('Financial Administration', p. 57). Since the king was more than a 'privy person', his purse must have been something more than a 'privy purse'.

[40] Before 1066 the English sheriffs had already come to farm most of the royal revenue for the collection of which they were responsible, and they made local disbursements on the king's order. It appears that they accounted with the chamberlains; though whether they did this regularly or only when required is not clear; nor is it clear by what means any balances of their farms, after legitimate expenditure had been deducted, actually reached the king – Jolliffe, *Constitutional History,* pp. 127-31; W. A. Morris, *The Medieval English Sheriff* (1927), pp. 30-31. In Normandy, a distinction was apparently made between extraordinary and occasional revenue which was paid directly into the chamber (how?) and ordinary domain revenue which was probably farmed by the *vicomtes* and *prévôts.* These officers, like the sheriffs in England, also made local payments on the duke's order and there was no doubt some system of accounting; but again it is not clear how any balances reached the duke (Haskins, *N.I.,* pp. 39-45).

[41] Liebermann, in his famous review of Poole's *Exchequer in the Twelfth Century* (*E.H.R.,* xxviii, 1913, 153), made the point that the 'essence' of the exchequer as an institution was a 'permanent board of royal officers commissioned with a function reaching far beyond that of a mere treasurer ... viz., with the duty of examining that

possible to achieve a degree of financial efficiency which no ruler who still relied upon an itinerant chamber for the administration of his revenue and expenditure could hope to attain.[42]

There was an analogous development in the administration of justice. Even before 1066 the dukes in Normandy, and perhaps the kings in England, had been accustomed occasionally to delegate the hearing of specific cases to special commissioners.[43] After the Conquest the king-dukes naturally continued and extended this practice,[44] for their dominions were now so much more extensive and the litigation arising out of the Norman colonization of England alone, quite apart from anything else, was enormous. The delegation of royal justice did indeed develop to such a degree that by the later part of Henry's reign a recognizable

all the sources of royal finance should really flow into the treasury and of judicially determining what was due to the king'.

The direct evidence for the holding of these audit sessions in Henry's reign on broadly the same lines as the comparatively well-known procedure of his grandson's time lies principally in the one surviving English pipe roll of the reign – *The Pipe Roll of 31 Henry I* (Rec. Comm. 1833, reprint, 1929) – and, for Normandy, in the document which Round discovered ('Bernard, the King's Scribe', *E.H.R.*, xiv, 1899; 425-6) and which shows that there were 'barons of the exchequer' in the duchy at the same time, together with the indications that Haskins found of details of procedure in the Norman exchequer of the later twelfth century that can be traced back to Henry's time and even to the time of William the Conqueror (*N.I.*, pp. 41-4, 88, 105-6). There is evidence that a Norman exchequer roll for the year 1136 still existed in the eighteenth century (*ibid.*, p. 105).

The functions of the 'barons of the exchequer' in England at this time are well illustrated in *The Pipe Roll of 31 Henry I*, pp. 96, 140. The few documents from which their identity might be deduced (in England, *Regesta*, ii. nos. 1000, 1211, cf. Richardson and Sayles, *Governance*, p. 249; in Normandy, Haskins, *N.I.*, pp. 88-90) show that the same kind of men – holders of household offices and other members of the court – acted in both countries; but the evidence is not sufficient to enable us to say definitely whether it was usual for individuals to serve in both countries. It seems likely that the audit sessions were already being held simultaneously in kingdom and duchy, at Easter and Michaelmas (Michaelmas certainly, Haskins, *N.I.*, pp. 107, 176-8; *Pipe Roll 31 Henry I*, pp. xv-xx), which would make it impossible for one man to attend the corresponding sessions in the two countries; though there seems to be no compelling reason why he should not attend sometimes in one country and sometimes in the other.

[42] As, for example, in the duchies of Brittany and Burgundy in the thirteenth century still : Michael Jones, *Ducal Brittany, 1364-1399* (1970), pp. 23-5.

[43] This is asserted for England by D. M. Stenton in *English Justice between the Norman Conquest and the Great Charter* (1965), p. 58. Richardson and Sayles (*Governance*, p. 173) say that it is 'not impossible' though they know of no evidence for it. Douglas (*William the Conqueror*, p. 309) thinks that the Conqueror's practice after 1066 was 'substantially an innovation in England'. But see Jolliffe, *Constitutional History*, pp. 135-6. The development of royal justice as he describes it (*ibid.*, pp. 107 ff.) would seem to make some such action necessary from time to time. For Normandy, where it is certain, see e.g. *R.A.D.N.*, no. 209.

[44] England, e.g. F. M. Stenton, *Anglo-Saxon England* (1947), pp. 640-3; Normandy, Haskins, *N.I.*, p. 57.

if not very clearly defined body of men, drawn from the officers of the household, the bishops and the barons, came to form an established tribunal which was constantly in session in each country whether the king was available or not.[45] The king-dukes were also experimenting with local justices, men appointed to administer their justice in a shire or group of shires in England, in a *vicomté* or other local unit in Normandy, as well as with itinerant justices working in defined circuits.[46] In both countries, therefore, a judicial organization which was based on royal-ducal authority and which worked continuously, wherever the king-duke might be, was being created.

These developments in financial and judicial administration, although they are in principle identical in the two countries, raise a question of quite fundamental importance. Should we speak of an English administration and a Norman administration in the early twelfth century, or of a unitary organization which administered the two countries – with local adjustments no greater as between the two countries than might be found within either of them? It is a question which has not often been asked explicitly,[47] and it is one to which it may not be possible to give a clear and definite answer, though there are one or two points that may usefully be made.

First, it should be repeated that so long as one king-duke ruled both countries and the household was his household, and the *curia regis* in its various forms was taking an ever-increasing share in the administration of justice generally, government and administration were to that extent unitary and were common to the two countries. Moreover, although the financial and judicial developments of which I have been speaking seem to represent the beginnings of government departments, they were the beginnings only. The term 'barons of the exchequer' could refer to men acting as judges or to men acting as auditors; and since the object of the audit was to decide judicially on problems arising in the course of the accounting rather than to achieve arithmetical accuracy in the accounts,[48] it would still be hard to draw a clear line between the

---

[45] England, e.g. F. Pollock and F. W. Maitland, *History of English Law* (1898), i. 109-10; Richardson and Sayles, *Governance,* pp. 174-6; Stenton, *English Justice,* pp. 58-61 : Normandy, Haskins, *N.I..,* pp. 88-105 etc.

[46] England, H. A. Cronne, 'The Office of Local Justiciar in England under the Norman Kings', *Univ. Birmingham Hist. Journ.,* vi. (1957-8), 18-38; Stenton, *English Justice,* pp. 60-8 : Normandy, Haskins, *N.I.,* pp. 99-104.

[47] It is indeed put by Haskins (*N.I.,* pp. 112 ff.) and by de Bouard (*Histoire des Institutions françaises au moyen âge,* edd. F. Lot and R. Fawtier, i. *Institutions seigneuriales,* pp. 25-8), but neither pursues it to any conclusion, however tentative.

[48] This is what Richard fitzNeal says of Henry II's time – 'Assident inquam ad discernenda iura et dubia determinanda que frequenter ex incidentibus questionibus oriuntur. Non enim in ratiociniis sed in multiplicibus iudiciis excellens scaccarii scientia consistit' (*Dialogus,* ed. Johnson, p. 15) – and that this was also the case under Henry I is shown, e.g., by an entry in the *Pipe Roll, 31 Henry I,* p. 96. Cf. Liebermann's statement quoted above (note 41).

judicial and the financial administration in either country. Nor would it
be easy to draw a firm distinction between the itinerant parts of the
government and those which were beginning to settle down, or so it
seems, in each country; for there is every reason to suppose that each
delegated form of the *curia regis* proceeded from and was reabsorbed
into the undifferentiated 'court', and there were certainly men holding
household offices among those who served in the more 'localized' bodies.[49]
The difficulties that surround the origins of the office of justiciar reflect
the ambiguity or inadequacy of so much of the evidence; and this in turn
suggests that practice was only just beginning to form institutions.

It is much the same if we try to distinguish clearly between the
corresponding 'proto-institutions' on either side of the Channel, for
their interrelations both in personnel and in function seem to be at least
as important as their points of differention.

In terms of personnel, while it is true that some of Henry's principal
ministers seem to act officially only in one country (Roger of Salisbury,
Aubrey de Vere, Ralph and Richard Basset, William Mauduit in England; or John of Lisieux, Robert de Courcy, Henry de la Pommeraye in
Normandy), others, men like Geoffrey de Clinton, Robert Mauduit,
William de Pont de l'Arche and perhaps Robert de la Haye are found
acting in both. However, all those who, on the evidence, can only be
said to have acted in one country had important interests in the other.
Aubrey de Vere, for example, gave his priory of Hatfield Broadoak in
Essex to the abbey of Saint Melaine at Rennes and he probably still
had lands in the Cotentin; the Bassets, though they acted as justices only
in England so far as we know, maintained the family property in
Normandy and improved it with the money they had made in England;
Henry de la Pommeraye, conversely, though he appears as a 'baron of
the exchequer' only in Normandy, must have served as constable in
England and had extensive interests in the West Country as well as in
the Bessin. In the de Courcy family there were brothers or cousins
acting one in England and one in Normandy, but each branch of the
family had interests in both countries. All these men, without exception,
can be found at one time or another, and in some cases frequently, in
attendance on the king-duke in the country with which they were not
primarily associated. They were all of Norman origin; more than that,
even though offices were not perhaps strictly hereditary in Henry's time,
there was an important 'family element' in his government (the families,

---

[49] Most of those who, as there is some reason to suppose, were 'barons of the
exchequer' in Normandy held household offices (Haskins, *N.I.*, pp. 88-99); in
England, of the 16 men whom Richardson and Sayles accept as barons of the exchequer under Henry I, four certainly (the chancellor, William de Courcy *dapifer*,
William d'Anesy larderer and Herbert the Chamberlan) held household offices;
and a fifth ('Turstin the Chaplain') should probably be counted among them
(*Governance*, p. 249; cf. *Regesta*, ii. nos. 1000, 1211 etc.).

for instance, of Roger of Salisbury or of John of Lisieux, the Bassets, the de Courcys, the Tancarvilles and others); and since all these men must have been personally acquainted with one another, if only through their attendance at the itinerant court, it is difficult to suppose that they thought of themselves as staffing two separate and distinct adminis- trations. In any case the evidence is so fragmentary (one solitary refer- ence to the men who were 'barons of the exchequer' in Normandy, hardly more for England), that if one man is found acting officially only in England or only in Normandy this may well be due to no more than the accidents that attend the loss or survival of documents. It is more significant that the evidence, such as it is, shows some of these men acting for the king in both countries.[50]

With personal connections of this kind, it is not surprising to find functional connections as well. Although it had been found necessary to establish fixed treasuries and to detach men from the chamber to staff them, it was still possible for money that was owed to the king to be paid directly into the chamber, and to be spent by it, without ever going into one of the treasuries or passing through the exchequer audit.[51] The treasuries themselves had to work together, for money and treasure were conveyed from one country to the other and, no doubt, from place to place within each country, as required by the itinerant court. Money due to the king-duke in England could be paid into a Norman treasury and the account cleared in the English exchequer;[52] and though there was apparently one minister who presided over the English exchequer and another who presided over the Norman exchequer, there was still, according to the better opinion, but one chief treasurer at the head of a treasury organization that embraced the two countries.[53] There are thus good reasons, quite apart from the fact that it existed to serve the one king-duke rather than 'England' or 'Normandy', to think that Henry's financial administration was still fundamentally unitary.

The same is true, though not perhaps so clearly, of the administration of the king-duke's justice. Most of the litigation that came before the *curia regis* in its various forms, at least so far as surviving records go, concerned the landed possessions of the greater churches and the barons, and these were characteristically distributed over both countries. The kind of business that came before the *curia regis* was therefore much the

---

[50] On this paragraph, see Appendix.

[51] Tout, *Chapters*, i. 83 ff. For the incompleteness of the English pipe rolls and the Norman exchequer rolls as statements of royal-ducal revenue and expenditure, see, respectively, Richardson and Sayles, *Governance*, pp. 216-7; B. Lyon and A. Verhulst, *Medieval Finance* (1967), p. 45, quoting Delisle's 'Revenus publics en Normandie'.

[52] E.g. Haskins, *N.I.*, pp. 107-8, 113-14.

[53] Above, note 38.

same wherever and in whatever form it sat.[54] There were many reasons why a case should be heard as near as possible to the lands in question, among them the fact that their location might well determine the custom to be applied; but it could happen that a case relating to English lands in dispute between an Angevin and a Norman monastery could be heard in Normandy;[55] and so long as this was so and personal connections were as close as they seem to have been, it may come nearer to reality so far as we can know it if we speak of one judicial system rather than two.[56]

Yet, however great an importance we may attach to these characteristics of the king-duke's government that tended towards the integration of Normandy and England, this government had to work under conditions that differed from one side of the Channel to the other. This is clearly true of local institutions; for however forcefully it may now be argued that the Carolingian *pagi* had survived as local units in Normandy, they had not survived in a way that offered the same opportunities to the king-duke's government as the shires and hundreds did in England.[57] Though financial administration in England and in Normandy was, at least from Henry's time, closely interrelated and certainly organized on the same principles in the two countries, there were differences in detail between the sources of the royal and the ducal revenues, notably the absence of anything like the geld in Normandy, between the territorial units from which those revenues were collected as also between the officers who collected them; and these differences

---

[54] There is every reason to suppose that the business transacted in meetings of the *Curia Regis* was much the same whether it met in Normandy (Haskins, *N.I.*, pp. 86 ff.) or in England (as described, for example, in F. M. Stenton, *First Century of English Feudalism*, 1932, pp. 31-6). For William the Conqueror's reign, see Douglas, *William the Conqueror*, pp. 286-7.

[55] *Regesta*, i. no. 423 (Appendix, no. lxxiv). Douglas quotes an instance where Duke William, when he was at Domfront, heard a case between the abbeys of Marmoutier and Saint-Pierre-de-la-Couture at Le Mans concerning land at Laval (*William the Conqueror*, p. 151). This was before 1066, but after the annexation of the Passais and the conquest of Maine.

[56] Of the men whose names are listed in Haskins *N.I.*, pp. 88-99 and in *Regesta*, ii. p. xviii, only that of Geoffrey de Clinton appears in both (see Appendix). In the eleventh century, however, Geoffrey, bishop of Coutances, had acted as a justice both in Normandy and in England (*Regesta*, i. nos. 92, 132, 153-6, 184, 221, 230, 276 and Haskins, *N.I.*, p. 57). So had a Richard de Courcy (Appendix).

[57] The argument for the survival of the Carolingian *pagi* as local units in Normandy and its significance has been most fully set out by J. Yver in his magisterial study of 'Les premières institutions du duché de Normandie', *I Normanni e la loro espansione in Europa nell'alto medioevo* (Centro Italiano di studi sull'alto medioevo, Spoleto, 1969), pp. 309-12, 323-32; but as one example of the different possibilities offered to the royal-ducal government by the shires and hundreds on the one hand and the *pagi* on the other, Yver points out (in the article cited below, note 63) that in England the verdict of a sworn inquest was characteristically obtained *per comitatum* or *per homines hundredi* whereas in Normandy it was given by a much vaguer entity such as the *homines de visneto*.

must have made themselves felt and may partly account for those divergences in the procedure of the two exchequers, somewhat exaggerated in the *Dialogus,* that can be seen late in the century when the surviving Norman exchequer rolls can be compared with the English pipe rolls.[58]

Likewise, while it is true that much of the law in England and in Normandy was still local custom in the eleventh century,[59] so that we can hardly compare 'English law' and 'Norman law' as distinct and consistent legal systems at that time, yet men already spoke of 'the laws of King Edward', the author of *Leges Henrici* said that 'there is a threefold division of English law' (he meant a division by regions, but he said 'of English law'),[60] and in 1091 William Rufus and Robert Curthose, as they were setting up their 'condominium', could agree on 'the customs and rights of justice' which their father had had in Normandy,[61] implying that they recognized differences between his prerogatives as duke in Normandy and those which he might exercise as king in England. The men of the eleventh century, therefore, thought of 'English law' and 'Norman law' as differing from one another; and this could not but affect the working of the *curia regis,* however accustomed it may have been to meeting and taking account of customs that varied from place to place even within the kingdom or the duchy.

By the end of the twelfth century, however, when it is almost too late for this purpose, the treatise that goes by the name of Glanvill and the much slighter and less sophisticated tract that forms the first part of the 'Très Ancien Coutumier'[62] make something like a comparison between the law of England and the law of Normandy as they were at that time possible; but to make this comparison in any significant detail would be a technical matter that is far beyond my competence. Yet even

---

[58] Enumerated in Haskins, *N.I.,* pp. 176-8.

[59] For England, e.g. Pollock and Maitland, *History of English Law,* i. 26-7, 43, 105-7. In Normandy the *coutume* is thought to have 'crystallized' into a more or less consistent system towards the end of the eleventh century (J. Yver, 'Les caractères originaux du groupe de coutumes de l'ouest de la France', *Rev. hist de droit français et étranger,* 4e série, xxx, 1952, 22); but 'crystallization' is to some extent a matter of degree, for local customs persisted for a very long time.

[60] 'Legis etiam Anglicae trina est partitio . . . alia enim Westsexia, alia Mircena, alia Denelaga est' : Leges Henrici, 6, 2 (F. Liebermann, *Die Gesetze der Angelsachsen,* i, 1903, 552; Stubbs, *Select Charters,* 1929, p. 123).

[61] 'Hee sunt consuetudines et iusticie quas habet dux Normannie in eadem provincia . . . Hec est iusticia quam rex Guillelmus qui regnum Anglie adquisivit habuit in Normannia'; Haskins, *N.I.,* p. 281.

[62] *The Treatise on the Laws and Customs of the realm of England commonly called Glanvill,* ed. G. D. H. Hall (1965); *Coutumiers de Normandie,* i. Première partie, *Le Très Ancien Coutumier de Normandie,* Texte latin, ed. E.-J.Tardif (1881), pp. liii-lvii, lxv ff., xc-xciii, 1-57. Cf. R. Besnier, *La Coutume de Normandie, Histoire externe* (1935), pp. 50-5. It is accepted that the Latin rather than the French text of the T.A.C. is the original and that this tract was composed between 1199 and 1204.

a superficial reading of these texts shows that by 1200 there was in being a law of England and a 'coutume de Normandie'; that both had been formed very largely by the *curia regis* in its various manifestations; that there had been enormous and parallel developments in each during the preceding half-century; that they were therefore very closely related though differing in detail at very many points and in some important matters as well.[63] This suggests a number of questions which, if I could answer them, might affect my argument very considerably. At the time of the Norman Conquest assimilation between the customs of England and the customs of Normandy was possible, for some assimilation did undoubtedly take place.[64] Do the elements which they have in common at the end of the twelfth century represent the results of a process of assimilation still continuing but not yet complete? Or are the differences more significant, representing a process of differentiation already begun (and which would contribute, perhaps, to the débâcle of 1204), or indicating more fundamental divergences that would resist the assimilative effects of any common administration? Finally, and most important for this discussion, what was the position in 1135? Was that still a time of progressive assimilation?

In considering the extent to which the government of Normandy and the government of England formed one single organization in the time of the Norman kings, I may well have overstressed their unity; for historians seem to me to have limited their studies of Norman government to one side of the Channel or the other far too much, and a great deal more study may be needed before we are ready to strike a balance. Yet, even if the conditions making for separate administrations were more important than I have represented them to be, it is at least clear that differences of custom and of traditional institutions need be no bar to eventual political unification, given other conditions making for unity,

---

[63] The nearest thing to a sustained and technical comparison between the development of English and Norman law in the twelfth century seems to be J. Yver's important article 'Le bref anglo-normand', *Revue d'histoire du droit*, xxix (1961), 313-30. This is an article-review of R. C. van Caenegem, *Royal Writs in England from the Conquest to Glanvill* (Selden Soc., lxxvii, 1959) and is concerned to point out similarities and differences as van Caenegem deliberately confined himself to England. I have relied upon this article as a check upon my own inexpert impressions.

[64] E.g. Pollock and Maitland, *History of English Law,* i. 74-5. 107-8. However we may suppose it to have come about, there was certainly more in common between the feudalism of England and Normandy in the middle years of the twelfth century than there had been between the socio-political structure of the two countries before 1066 (*cf.* Douglas, *William the Conqueror*, pp. 283-4), with all that this implied in the formation of law; and since the writ was so important an element in the legal development of the two countries during the twelfth century, it is worth recalling that this was an English instrument, taken over by the Norman kings after the Conquest and used by them in Normandy as well as in England (for an early example, T. A. M. Bishop and P. Chaplais, *Facsimiles of English Royal Writs*, 1957, plate xii).

as the history of the kingdom of France – and indeed of the kingdom of England[65] – abundantly shows.

III

So far I have discussed this relationship between Normandy and England in simple bilateral terms; but this is not the whole story by any means. The conquest of England was not the only achievement of its kind in north-western Europe that the Normans could claim or plan or dream of, though it may have been their greatest; and the relationship between the two countries which it initiated has to be put into the context of the whole of their expansion in this part of the continent. If I were able to do this as I would like to do it, I think we should find that it adds considerably to our understanding of the Anglo-Norman relationship itself; but this is something that will have to wait for another occasion. I can do no more now than suggest the line which the argument would take.

Already, before 1066, the very process by which the original Norman settlement in the lower Seine Valley was growing into a powerful feudal principality had extended Norman interests far beyond the boundaries into which the duchy eventually settled;[66] and to William and his more energetic followers the conquest of England was but a step, if a long step, to yet greater things. Henry, in the last ten years of his life, was king of England and duke of Normandy, overlord in some way or other of the duke of Brittany, the count of Maine, the lord of the Bellême lands which stretched from the marches of Normandy far into 'France', the counts of Ponthieu, of Boulogne and of Flanders, the king of Scots

---

[65] The differences between the customs of Wessex, Mercia and the Danelaw which, as Maitland argues, were by no means negligible even in the late eleventh or early twelfth century (Pollock and Maitland, *History of English Law,* i. 106), seem to have presented no serious obstacle to the unification of England; though the process by which such provincial differences were overcome was very different from that by which the same result was eventually achieved in France.

[66] It seems that the Norman military aristocracy which joined Duke William in his great adventure of 1066 had been largely created by him and his immediate predecessors; and in their search for bold and trustworthy vassals (in the general sense of the term) they had looked far beyond the bounds of their duchy (Le Patourel, 'Norman Colonization', pp. 431-4 and references there given). This gave them an interest in neighbouring principalities and a reason, among others, for trying to subdue them. Thus William had direct relations with a number of Breton barons (L. Musset, in *Histoire de la Normandie,* ed. M. de Bouard, 1970, pp. 128-9), and there were precedents if no more for treating the 'duke' of Brittany himself as a vassal (Lemarignier, *Hommage en marche,* pp. 115-20). Similar developments may be seen in most of the principalities adjacent to Normandy; while William would no doubt have regarded it as the principal achievement of his 'conquest' of Maine that it should give him the direct allegiance of the barons of that county (*cf.* Orderic, ii. 103-4).

and the surviving native princes as well as the marcher lords in Wales.[67] Nor is there any reason to think that he or his family was satisfied with all this. His father may have contemplated a conquest of Ireland;[68] it is said that his brother William Rufus planned to take over Aquitaine by the same means as he had recovered Normandy and even to have aspired to the throne of France;[69] his uncle, Bishop Odo, to have plotted for the papacy;[70] and even the crusade of Robert Curthose had no doubt an element of knight errantry about it. As for Henry himself, from his point of view the marriage of his daughter and heiress to the heir of the count of Anjou should result in the absorption of all the lands and interests of the counts of Anjou into the great Norman complex – and at their level the Norman barons were making their fortunes in much the same way.[71] The ambition of these men seems beyond all measuring.

There is much to support the idea that the whole of this Norman complex of lands and overlordships was the effective political unit of its day, rather than Normandy or England or any other constituent part of it. This may be seen in the measures taken for its defence – the king-dukes were every bit as concerned to protect their continental lands and overlordships as they were to defend England. It can also be seen in the military forces which they had at their command. Men from England were frequently employed on the Continent,[72] and men from continental lands were used on this side of the Channel as well as in France;[73] there was a Scottish contingent, led by King Alexander, as

---

[67] As it stands, this sentence may perhaps be accepted without elaborate documentation; but it is important to define the precise degree of overlordship that Henry could exercise over principalities beyond England and Normandy, a matter that varied from one to another and from time to time. This is something which, though essential to any consideration of the expansion of Norman interests and dominion in north-western Europe, requires a lengthier treatment than can be given to it here.

[68] A.S.C., s.a. 1087; cf. R. W. Southern, *Saint Anselm and his Biographer* (1963), pp. 133-5.

[69] Orderic, iv. 79-80; Suger, *Vita Ludovici Grossi Regis*, ed. H. Waquet (1929), pp. 10-13.

[70] Orderic, iii. 188-9.

[71] Some examples are given in Le Patourel, *Norman Barons* Historical Association, 1971, pp. 7-8, 11-12, 15-16, 20 and *passim*). See above VI.

[72] E.g. in 1073, 1081, at Gerberoi in 1079-80, in 1106 at Tinchebrai and in Henry's French campaigns of 1116-1120: Douglas, *William the Conqueror*, pp. 242, 279; David, *Robert Curthose*, p. 174-5 and Appendix F; Henry of Huntingdon, *Historia Anglorum*, ed. T. Arnold (R.S. 1879), p. 240; but cf. C. Warren Hollister, *The Military Organization of Norman England* (1965), pp. 123-4.

[73] E.g., in 1085 William brought over 'a larger force of mounted men and infantry from France and Brittany than had ever come to this country' (A.S.C., s.a. 1085), and Florence adds 'with some from Normandy' (Florence of Worcester, *Chronicon*, ed. B. Thorpe, 1848-9, ii. 18). According to Orderic, Rufus had men from France, Burgundy, Flanders, Brittany and Normandy with him when he recovered Maine in 1098 (Orderic, iv. 44-5); while Henry had men from Normandy, Maine and Brittany as well as from England at Tinchebrai (David, *ubi supra*).

well as Welsh, English and Norman troops in the army which Henry led into North Wales in 1114, and the king of Powys, who presumably did not go unattended, accompanied him to France in the same year.[74] Although it is very unlikely that the king-dukes ever attempted to bring together in one concentration all the forces that they could call upon, the fact that they had so many sources on which they could draw, and that they could summon men from whichever of their lands or overlordships might be most convenient or appropriate in any situation, added greatly to their military potential; and it was this potential which any body of rebels, or the king of France or the count of Anjou or any other opponent, had to reckon with.

Yet, however much the peripheral overlordships may have contributed in men and occasional tribute, or simply by their allegiance, it seems likely that the king-dukes drew the bulk of their strength and their man-power from Normandy and England; and since, as it is coming to be appreciated, the mercenary element in their armies was far greater than we had supposed,[75] military strength was already as much a matter of the availability of money as of |men. Normandy, it seems, was a relatively wealthy country already in 1066, and the dukes had been able to mobilize its wealth for their purposes; but it is now suggested that England was wealthier still.[76] Certainly the circumstances of the Conquest, and the system of taxation they inherited from their Saxon predecessors, enabled the Norman kings to exploit the wealth of England even more fully,[77] and there are many indications that England did indeed contribute a good deal more than her share of the money needed to defend what they had won and to extend their lands and their

---

[74] A. A. M. Duncan, 'The Earliest Scottish Charters', *Scottish Historical Review,* xxxvii (1958), 134; J. E. Lloyd, *History of Wales* (1939), ii. 421-2, 463-4; Hollister, *Military Organization,* pp. 124, 229.

[75] J. O. Prestwich, 'War and Finance in the Anglo-Norman State', *T.R.H.S.,* 5, iv (1954), 19-43; Hollister, *Military Organization,* ch. vi.

[76] For Normandy, L. Musset, 'Les conditions financières d'une réussite architecturale . . .', *Mélanges offerts à Réné Crozet,* edd. P. Gallais and Y.-J. Riou (1966), pp. 312-13, earlier papers by the same writer there cited and *Histoire de la Normandie,* pp. 107-8, 126; Douglas, *William the Conqueror,* pp. 133-6. To demonstrate the duke's power to mobilize these resources it is unnecessary, perhaps, to do more than suggest that the invasion of England in 1066 could hardly have been mounted on promises and voluntary contributions alone. For England, P. H. Sawyer, 'The Wealth of England in the Eleventh Century', *T.R.H.S.,* 5, xv. (1965), 145-164 and e.g., Guillaume de Poitiers, *Gesta Guillelmi,* ed. R. Foreville (1952), pp. 252-5.

[77] William could double the Confessor's demesne, itself very considerable, continue to levy the geld and take over the profits of the coinage; while he and his successors could also, in effect, tax the grants of land and offices they made to their vassals and ministers by exacting huge reliefs, selling preferment and demanding payment for favours and facilities of all kinds : Le Patourel, 'Norman Colonization', pp. 435-6, and references there given.

overlordships and their interests still further.[78] Moreover, English land could be used directly for this purpose, as well as her gold and silver. Just as homage and military service could be obtained from the counts of Flanders in return for a pension that must have been raised in England,[79] so a grant of land in England helped considerably to fasten Norman overlordship upon the rulers, for example, of Boulogne, of Brittany and of Scotland.[80] Such overlordship, whatever it may have been to begin with, could be intensified, given favourable circumstances, into something very much more real. A distinction might be drawn, it is true, between obligations to the king-duke arising out of lands or rights in England or Normandy and obligations to another suzerain arising out

[78] There is a suggestive correlation between the entries in the Anglo-Saxon Chronicle that report royal expeditions overseas and those which complain of the imposition of 'severe taxes' in England : *A.S.C.* s.a. 1090, (1094), 1095-6, 1097, 1098, 1104, 1105, (1110), 1116, 1117 (cf. Huntingdon, *Historia Anglorum,* p. 240), 1118, 1124, (1125). In general, Prestwich, 'War and Finance', *passim;* Hollister, *Military Organization,* p. 185. As they were able to superimpose feudal or quasi-feudal methods of raising a revenue upon those they had inherited from their Anglo-Danish predecessors, the Norman kings certainly had the means to exact more from England than from their other lands; but in the nature of the case we have to be content with suggestions and indications that they actually did so.

[79] At least until after 1106. There were two treaties, one in 1101, the other in 1110 : *Regesta,* ii. nos. 515, 941; F. Vercauteren, *Actes des Comtes de Flandre, 1071-1128* (1938), nos. 30, 41 (dated 1103 and 1110); Rymer, *Foedera* (Rec. Comm.), I, i. pp. 6-7 (where they are printed in reverse order and dated 1103 and 1101).

[80] For the great 'honour' held by the counts of Boulogne in England, and the additions which Henry made to it, see Round, *Studies in Peerage and Family History,* pp. 147 ff. Henry arranged the marriage of his sister-in-law, Mary, to Count Eustace III and of their daughter and heiress, Matilda, to Stephen of Blois who was already his protégé and his vassal for extensive estates in Normandy and England (Florence of Worcester, *Chronicon,* ii. 51; William of Malmesbury, *Historia Novella,* ed. K. R. Potter, 1955, p. 57). He was thus at least exercising a very direct influence on the succession to the county. Among the Bretons who acquired fiefs in England after the Conquest, members of the Penthièvre branch of the 'ducal' family received what came to be known as the 'Honour of Richmond'; though the full effect of this was not seen until Conan IV (1156-71), already accepted by Henry II as earl of Richmond, made himself 'duke' of Brittany (C. T. Clay *The Honour of Richmond,* Part i; *E.Y.C.,* iv, 1935 pp. 84-93). On the degree of overlordship exercised by the Norman kings over Brittany, e.g. Lemarignier, *Hommage en marche,* pp. 120-1. There can be little doubt that David I's possession of the earldom of Huntingdon-Northampton, both for some time before his accession and as long as Henry lived, strengthened the suzerainty which the Norman kings had exercised over the kings of Scots since the homage of Malcolm III to William the Conqueror in 1072 (e.g. Duncan, 'The Earliest Scottish Charters', pp. 125-35; *C.P.,* vi 641-2; ix. 663-4; *D.N.B.,* 'David I'.). One climax to this development came when King William the Lion did liege homage to Henry II for his kingdom. A similar process of building up or intensifying suzerainty can be observed elsewhere; and lands or rents in England or Normandy generally seem to be involved in it. It is a matter which, though essential to any consideration of the expansion of Norman interests and dominion in this part of Europe, would require far more space than can be given to it here.

of other lands or lordships; but it is not clear that such distinctions could be effective in practice or that they were as yet generally made, for homage was not at this time necessarily tied to the grant of a fief.[81] When two incompatible or potentially incompatible relationships had been created only time could show which would prove the stronger; but all had the possibility of development.

We can take this argument a step further still, for the Normans not only exploited England to fulfill their wider ambitions, they exploited England for the direct enrichment of Normandy itself. It is difficult, for example, to disassociate Bishop Odo's building at Bayeux and his patronage of art and learning there from the wealth he had acquired in England;[82] and indeed many of the great building enterprises in Normandy at this time must have depended a good deal upon English money, as Musset has shown in the case of the two great abbeys at Caen.[83] It was perhaps natural that the king-dukes and their barons should include English lands and churches in the endowments they provided for religious houses in France: but these gifts, which in their totality were very considerable, were still being made long after William the Conqueror's time and were made in principle for ever; and for all that the monasteries and cathedrals of Normandy obtained in this way, it is hard to find an example, conversely, of an English foundation receiving lands in Normandy.[84] This suggests that Normandy was still the homeland, a suggestion that is supported by the amount of time and attention that the king-dukes gave to Normandy and its affairs[85] and by the tenacity with which so many families clung to a Norman estate that was often quite small in comparison with their lands across the Channel[86] – when to

[81] E.g. Lemarignier, *Hommage en marche,* pp. 80-92. A case in point where a distinction was clearly made between obligations to different seigneurs is to be found in the agreements between Henry and the count of Flanders (above, note 79)

[82] D. Nicholl, *Thurstan, Archbishop of York* (1964), pp. 3-7; S. E. Gleason, *An Ecclesiastical Barony of the Middle Ages* (1936), pp. 13-15; D. C. Douglas, 'The Norman Episcopate before the Norman Conquest', *Cambridge Historical Journal,* xiii (1957), 105, 112; J. Vallery-Radot, *La Cathédrale de Bayeux* ('Petites Monographies des grands édifices de la France', 1928?), pp. 10-11.

[83] 'Les conditions financières . . .', pp. 309-10.

[84] Above, note 16. Professor Knowles tells me that he cannot recall a single instance of an English foundation obtaining lands in Normandy.

[85] For William the Conqueror, see Stenton, *Anglo-Saxon England,* p. 601, and Douglas, *William the Conqueror,* pp. 211-12. On a rough calculation from the dates given in *British Chronology,* p. 31, Rufus spent 28 months in Normandy, or on continental campaigns based on Normandy and in the interests of Normandy, out of the 47 between September 1096 and August 1100; and Henry, likewise, about 210 out of 350 between September 1106 and December 1135. It is also clear that Rufus between 1088 and 1096 and Henry between 1100 and 1106 were determined to have Normandy.

[86] E.g. Clinton, Basset (Appendix) and Lacy (W. E. Wightman, *The Lacy Family in England and in Normandy, 1066-1194* (1966) ch. vii).

us it would seem that there was so much to be gained by concentrating and rationalizing their property. Northern France was on its way to become the land which 'took the lead and set the fashion', and no doubt the Normans and their neighbours who were bringing so much wealth into the country were helping to make it so. We may even begin to identify the dominant and exploiting group amongst these people. In William the Conqueror's time, the king-duke and no more than a dozen great barons, most of whom claimed kinship with him, held almost half the land of England between them in addition to their generally very large possessions on the Continent;[87] and it has been estimated that, in Henry's day, there were never more than about twenty men 'at the top', doing his work and enjoying the profits.[88] Quite a number of this 'top twenty' seem to have come from those parts of Normandy which Henry had held before he became king and to have joined him then.[89] When he secured the throne that they had helped him to win they entered into their promised land.

[87] 'Half the land', that is by value not by area. For these figures, Le Patourel, 'Norman Colonization', pp. 420-1 and and references there given.

[88] Southern, *Medieval Humanism*, p. 225. The writer seems to be thinking primarily of those who served Henry in England; but there are no 'Englishmen' among those he names.

[89] Round first suggested this possibility in his essay on 'The Origin of the Stewarts' (*Studies in Peerage and Family History*, pp. 124-5). He instanced fitzAlan (ancestor of the Stewarts, from the region of Dol in Brittany), Redvers (from Reviers in the Bessin, north-west of Caen), de la Haye (La Haye-du-Puits in the Cotentin), the d'Aubignys (later earls of Arundel, from Aubigny in the Cotentin), St John (Saint-Jean-le-Thomas near Avranches), Paynel (Les Moutiers-Hubert south of Lisieux, and Hambye in the Cotentin) as families which enjoyed Henry's favour and which came from those parts of Normandy or the marches of Brittany with which he had been associated between 1088 and 1100. Round later added Clinton to his list (from Semilly, near Saint-Lô, on the borders of the Cotentin and the Bessin) and the list could certainly be lengthened considerably. For the families of Vere, Pomeroy, Basset and de Courcy, and also Henry's two principal clerical ministers Roger of Salisbury and John of Lisieux, see Appendix.

Henry apparently got possession of the Cotentin and the Avranchin, with Mont-Saint-Michel, in 1088 (David, *Robert Curthose*, pp. 48-9). Some, perhaps all, of this was taken from him in 1091 by William Rufus and Robert Curthose acting together. During the struggle, Henry was raising troops in Brittany (*ibid.*, pp. 61-5). In 1092, however, the inhabitants of Domfront, exasperated with Robert de Bellême, invited Henry to be their lord. From that centre he set about to re-establish himself in south-west Normandy and may well have recovered a large part of his original lands in the Cotentin peninsula with the aid of Hugh of Chester and Avranches, Richard de Reviers, Roger de Mandeville (Magneville in the Cotentin – for these identifications, L. C. Loyd, *Origins of Some Anglo-Norman Families*, 1951) and others (David, *ubi supra*, pp. 78-80, 87). After 1096, Henry was on good terms with William Rufus who gave him the Cotentin and the Bessin (except for the towns of Bayeux and Caen), or confirmed him in the possession of them, and entrusted to him the construction and the keeping of his new castle at Gisors at the opposite extremity of the duchy (Guillaume de Jumièges, *Gesta Normannorum Ducum*, p. 275 – additions of Robert de Torigny).

The conclusion is plain. The Normans were Normans through all these years. Normandy was their home country, England their greatest source of the men, the money and the land they needed to hold the territories and the lordships and the wealth they had won and to extend all this far as it could be extended. Their empire and their ambitions were thus founded upon the continuing union of the two countries, which constituted one further and very powerful force to hold them together.

My whole argument may be summed up in one last question. In so far as men act rationally they must act with some idea of a future to which their acts are leading; and we as historians can only understand the actions of men in the past if we can form some idea of the future as it appeared to them. How would the future of the Norman lands have appeared to King Henry's barons and ministers? Did it seem likely to them that the association of Normandy and England must prove ephemeral, giving way naturally and inevitably to an insular kingdom of England and a Normandy absorbed into a kingdom of France? Or would they have thought that the association would continue, as it was very much in their interest that it should continue, developing into a more integral union still and even into a permanent kingdom that would turn the English Channel into a Norman Sea?

APPENDIX

Biographical Notes on Some of Henry's Ministers

The following biographical notes are notes only, intended to do no more than offer some support to general statements in the lecture. They may suggest, however, that more could be done in this way; and that the compilation of a *curriculum vitae* for rather more of Henry's ministers, together with some of his barons, might add greatly to our knowledge of his government and the way it worked. Such a compilation could only be based on the assumption that when a man's name appears among the witnesses to a charter or writ it means that he was in fact present at that time and place.

AUBREY DE VERE (II) was the son and heir of Aubrey de Vere (I), one of William the Conqueror's chamberlains.[1] The family came from Ver in the Cotentin (some 10 miles south of Coutances), and seems to have retained interests there.[2] It also had connections with Brittany (for when Aubrey II founded his priory of Hatfield Broadoak in Essex he gave it to Saint Melaine at Rennes)[3] and vast lands in England. There is no clear evidence that Aubrey was a royal chamberlain before 1133; though this is suggested by the fact that his father had held the office and by other indications.[4] In that year, however, he was granted by charter the office of 'magistram camerariam (regis) totius Anglie'.[5] He acted as sheriff or joint-sheriff of several English counties, as a local justice in Norfolk,[6] and was described by his son as 'justitiarius totius Anglie'.[7] Although he is known to have been with the king in Normandy, probably on at least two occasions,[8] there is no specific evidence of his acting in any official capacity in the duchy.

GEOFFREY DE CLINTON,[9] first in Orderic's list of the men whom Henry 'raised from the dust',[10] was described as 'thesaurarius meus et camerarius

[1] In general, *C.P.,* x. 193-9 and Appendix F; *D.N.B.,* 'Vere, Aubrey de'.
[2] L. C. Loyd, *Anglo-Norman Families,* p. 110.
[3] F. Joüon des Longrais, 'Les moines de l'abbaye Saint-Melaine de Rennes en Angleterre', *Recueil . . . Clovis Brunel* (1955), pp. 31-54.
[4] *Regesta,* ii. nos. 929, 975, 996.
[5] Above, note 25.
[6] *Pipe Roll, 31 Henry I, passim; Regesta,* ii. *passim.*
[7] Richardson and Sayles, *Governance,* pp. 174-6.
[8] *Regesta,* ii. nos. 1443, 1444, 1913-15, 1960.
[9] In general, *D.N.B.,* 'Clinton, Geoffrey de'; R. W. Southern, *Medieval Humanism,* pp. 214-18.
[10] Orderic, iv. 164-7.

meus' in the licence which the king gave him to found Kenilworth Priory.[11] White argues that he was one of the chamberlains of the treasury.[12] He was prominent in Henry's judicial and financial administration in England, where he acquired great wealth,[13] and also in Normandy where he was a treasurer and a justice – perhaps a 'baron of the exchequer'.[14] He attested Henry's acts in both countries.[15] Though his name is taken from Glympton in Oxfordshire, his hereditary estates were in Normandy, a castle at Semilly (Saint-Pierre-de-Semilly and La-Barre-de-Semilly, 7 km. east of Saint-Lô)[16] with other lands apparently in the Cotentin.[17] He, or his son, married a daughter of the earl of Warwick,[18] who also had interests in Normandy.

GEOFFREY RIDEL[19] was one of those whom Henry of Huntingdon describes as 'justitiarius totius Anglie',[20] was almost certainly a 'baron of the exchequer'[21] and a prominent minister in England during the earlier part of Henry's reign.[22] Nothing seems to be known of his origin. He married a daughter of Earl Hugh of Chester (who was also hereditary vicomte of Avranches) and his own daughter married Richard Basset (q.v.).[23] The Empress and Duke Henry restored to his grandson all his inheritance 'both in England and in Normandy';[24] but there is no evidence of his acting in any official capacity in the duchy and the only occasion when he is known to have been there with the king was just before the wreck of the White Ship in which he was drowned.[25]

HENRY DE LA POMMERAYE was one of the 'barons of the exchequer' in Normandy c. 1129.[26] He is named as a constable in the 'Constitutio',[27] though the office is not given with his name when he witnesses chart-

[11] *Regesta,* ii. 1428; but *cf.* White, *'Financial Administration',* p. 68.

[12] *Ibid.,* pp. 60-64; *cf. Regesta,* ii. p. xiii.

[13] Southern, *ubi supra;* Stenton, *English Justice,* pp. 63-4.

[14] *Pipe Roll, 31 Henry I,* p. 37; Haskins, *N.I.,* pp. 89-90, 113.

[15] *Regesta,* ii. *passim.*

[16] J. H. Round, 'A Great Marriage Settlement', *The Ancestor,* no. 11 (1904), pp. 153-7.

[17] Orderic, iii. 404, note.

[18] Round, *ubi supra;* Southern, *Medieval Humanism,* p. 218, note 1.

[19] *D.N.B.,* 'Ridel, Geoffrey'.

[20] *Historia Anglorum,* p.318.

[21] *Regesta,* ii. no. 1000; *cf.* Richardson and Sayles, *Governance,* p. 249.

[22] *Regesta,* ii. nos. 755, 796, 969, 975, 985, 1166, 1168.

[23] Stenton, *First Century,* pp. 33-5.

[24] *Regesta,* iii. nos. 43, 44.

[25] Orderic, iv. 418-19.

[26] Haskins, *N.I.,* pp. 88-9; *Regesta,* ii. no. 1584.

[27] *Dialogus de Scaccario,* ed. Johnson, p. 134.

ers.[28] He has been spoken of as 'a constable of Normandy';[29] but of the acts of Henry I that he is known to have attested[30] six are dated in England, and one certainly implies that he was with the court on its travels c. 1131.[31] The family came from La Pommeraye about 12 miles west of Falaise[32] and, as well as its lands in the Bessin, held an extensive estate in the West Country centred on Berry Pomeroy, Devon.[33]

JOHN, bishop of Lisieux, according to Orderic, was the son of Norman the Dean – dean of Séez, presumably – and was brought up from childhood among the clerks of that church. He was already known to the king when he came to England as a refugee in 1103, and may therefore have made Henry's acquaintance before his accession, possibly while he was lord of Domfront. Between 1103 and 1107 he was one of Henry's chaplains and principal advisers as well as archdeacon of Séez;[34] and, since at that time he must have been in contact with Roger of Salisbury, it has been suggested that some of the ideas from which the exchequer as an institution ultimately developed were worked out between them then.[35] From 1107, when he was given the bishopric of Lisieux, he came to occupy a position in the administration of Normandy similar to that held by Roger of Salisbury in England.[36] He seems never to have acted in an official capacity in England, though he must have been in the country with the king on a number of occasions.[37] He was one of the two bishops of Norman sees who did not attend Stephen's Easter court of 1136 (detained in Normandy, it may be, by his official duties); but he accepted Stephen's rule and attested his and his queen's acts while they were in Normandy in 1137.[38] He died soon after he had been forced to surrender his cathedral city to Geoffrey Plantegenêt in 1141.[39]

He had two nephews who were brothers; both in their time archdeacons of Séez, and both subsequently bishops, John of Séez and Arnulf of Lisieux. Both, while still archdeacons, acted in a judicial capacity in England;[40] John, after he had become bishop of Séez, attested Henry's

[28] White, 'The Household of the Norman Kings', p. 151.

[29] *Regesta*, ii. p. xvii, note 1.

[30] *Regesta*, ii. nos., 1292, 1339, 1464, 1465, 1468, 1584, 1693, 1764.

[31] *Ibid*, no. 1693.

[32] Loyd, *Anglo-Norman Families*, pp. 78-9.

[33] E. B. Powley, *The House of de la Pomeraye* (1944), pp. 12-17.

[34] Orderic, iv. 273-5.

[35] Round, 'Bernard the King's Scribe', pp. 427-8; R. L. Poole, *The Exchequer in the Twelfth Century* (1912), pp. 58-9.

[36] Haskins, *N.I.*, pp. 88-99.

[37] *Regesta*, ii. nos., 832, 1091, 1099, 1100, 1106, 1132, 1338, 1466.

[38] For the Easter court, Round, *Geoffrey de Mandeville*, pp. 262-6; i.e. *Regesta*, iii. nos. 944, 46, 271; and for his attestations, *ibid.*, 298, 327, 608, 843.

[39] Orderic, v. 132; Robert of Torigni, *Chronica*, ed. R. Howlett, 'Chronicles of the reigns of Stephen, Henry II and Richard I', iv (R.S. 1889), 142.

[40] *Regesta*, ii. no. 1364; iii. no. 506.

acts both in Normandy and in England[41] and Arnulf, while bishop of Lisieux, briefly attained to something like his uncle's position in the administration of Normandy early in the reign of Henry II as king.[42]

RALPH BASSET and RICHARD BASSET his son[43] were both described as 'justitiarius totius Anglie' by Henry of Huntingdon and both were certainly very prominent justices in England.[44] The family came, apparently, from Montreuil-au-Houlme (dépt. Orne, arr. Argentan, cant. Briouze), near enough to Domfront for Ralph to have joined Henry while he was lord of that town in the 1090's. He was certainly in the king's service soon after his accession (he comes second in Orderic's list of those whom Henry 'raised from the dust').[45] There is no evidence that either he or Richard ever acted in an official capacity in Normandy; but Ralph was with the king at Rouen, probably in 1129,[46] and they retained possession of the family lands at Montreuil until after Henry's death in 1135; indeed Orderic suggests that part of the enormous wealth that Richard acquired in England was invested in the building of a stone castle there.[47]

ROBERT DE COURCY was a justice and a 'baron of the exchequer' in Normandy, one of Henry's ministers in the duchy next in importance, probably, to Robert de la Haye (q.v.).[48] He attested Henry's acts as 'dapifer' in England as well as in Normandy;[49] and it was probably he who acted as a justice for Stephen in England,[50] attested the Empress's charters as 'dapifer' in England[51] and without title in Normandy,[52] served Geoffrey as 'dapifer' and justice[53] and finally Duke Henry as 'dapifer'.[54] The difficulty is to be sure that the attestations on which these identifications are based were all made by the same man, for the complex genealogy of the de Courcy family includes perhaps three possible Roberts at this point. Their common ancestor was Richard I de Courcy, whose father,

[41] *Regesta,* ii. nos. 1428, 1441-2, 1548, 1572, 1581, 1687-90, 1693, 1700, 1702, 1740-41, 1764, 1902, 1908.

[42] Haskins, *N.I.,* pp. 164-8; F. Barlow (ed.), *The Letters of Arnulf of Lisieux,* Camden Third Series, lxi (1939), pp. xi-xiv, xxvii-xxxii etc.

[43] *D.N.B.,* 'Basset, Ralph'; 'Basset, Richard'.

[44] *Historia Anglorum,* p. 318; cf. Richardson and Sayles, *Governance,* pp. 174-80; Stenton, *English Justice,* pp. 60-2; Southern, *Medieval Humanism,* pp. 218-19, 222.

[45] Orderic. iv. 164-5.

[46] *Regesta,* ii. no. 1576.

[47] Loyd, *Anglo-Norman Families,* p. 12; Orderic, v. 68-9; *Regesta,* ii. *passim.*

[48] Haskins, *N.I.,* pp. 88-99.

[49] Specifically as 'dapifer', *Regesta,* ii. nos. 1584 (=Haskins, *N.I.,* p. 88), 1742.

[50] *Regesta,* iii. p. xxii, no. 506.

[51] *Ibid.,* nos. 275, 634, 651.

[52] *Ibid.,* nos. 461, 805.

[53] *Ibid.,* nos. 55, 56, 57.

[54] *Ibid.,* no. 180.

Robert I, had acquired Courcy-sur-Dives (about 14 miles north-east of Falaise). By 1086 Richard, who inherited this, had also obtained a small estate in Oxfordshire. His younger son, William I de Courcy, added an extensive estate in the West Country to these Oxfordshire lands; his elder son, Robert II de Courcy, inherited the Norman estates. One of Robert II's sons was another Robert, Robert III de Courcy; while William I had three sons, William II, Richard II and Robert IV. It seems likely that the 'dapifer' and 'baron of the exchequer' was Robert III (of the Norman branch); but 'Richard de Courcy' (probably Richard I) had acted as a justice both in England and in Normandy,[55] and William I was also a 'dapifer' although, in surviving royal charters, he attests only in England.[56] While it is not possible to be entirely confident of some of these identifications, for those who have studied the family have held differing opinions, it seems that each branch had property interests in the country with which it was not primarily identified, and one can at least say that the family as a whole, in Henry's time, had a tradition of service both in England and in Normandy.[57]

ROBERT DE LA HAYE appears as a justice, a 'baron of the exchequer'[58] and 'dapifer'[59] in documents issued in Normandy during Henry's reign. Haskins regarded him as 'the chief lay officer of the Norman administration' and thought that he died about 1135.[60] A Robert de la Haye (La Haye-du-Puits in the Cotentin) was the son of Ranulf, seneschal of Robert count of Mortain, and grandson of Turstin (Richard) Haldup, lord of La Haye-du-Puits who with his son (evidently elder son) 'Eudes-au-Capel', Robert's uncle, founded Lessay Abbey. This Robert de la Haye married Muriel, daughter and ultimately heiress of Colswein of Lincoln, and through her became one of the greater barons of Lincolnshire and probably constable of Lincoln Castle. He also acquired the honour of Halnaker in Sussex, where he founded Boxgrove Priory, and gave both the priory and some of his properties in Lincolnshire and

---

[55] *Regesta,* ii. p. 390; *Regesta,* i. no. 207.

[56] As 'dapifer', *Regesta,* ii. nos. 544, 699; without title, *ibid., passim.*

[57] On the family and its lands, W. Farrer, *Honors and Knights Fees* (1923-5), i. 103 ff.; Sir Henry Maxwell-Lyte, 'Curci', *Proc. Somerset Arch. and Nat. Hist. Soc.,* lxvi (1921), 98-126; *Stogursey Charters,* edd. T. D. Tremlett and N. Blakiston, *Somerset Record Soc.,* lxi (1949), pp. xviii, xxiv.

[58] *Regesta,* ii. nos. 1352, 1584, 1593; cf. Haskins, *N.I.,* pp. 88-89.

[59] *Regesta,* ii. nos. 1688, 1693, 1698.

[60] Haskins, *N.I.,* pp. 88-99, 146.

Sussex to Lessay.[61] It has been generally accepted that these Roberts were one and the same man; but if we may trust the wording of a summary in the *Inventaire Sommaire* of the lost archives of Lessay[62] it is possible that they were cousins. Even if this were so, the family, if not the individual, had official as well as landed interests in Normandy and England.

ROGER, bishop of Salisbury,[63] described at the time of his election in 1103 as (a) 'priest of the church of Avranches',[64] served in Henry's household before 1100, most likely as seneschal,[65] and perhaps as chaplain.[66] He was Henry's chancellor from 1101 to 1102 (or 1103) and subsequently bishop of Salisbury. His position in Henry's government has been much discussed;[67] but while it had many of the characteristics of the late twelfth-century justiciarship, it is perhaps best described, without trying to give too much precision, as that of Henry's 'first minister in England'; and he continued to hold this position under Stephen until 1139. He seems to have exercised no official functions in Normandy, though he was there with Henry in 1129 or 1130.

His nephew NIGEL[68] was a treasurer in Normandy[69] and witnessed Henry's acts in both countries.[70] He became bishop of Ely in 1133; and early in Henry II's reign he purchased the office of treasurer for his son Richard, the author of the *Dialogus*.

Another nephew, ALEXANDER,[71] seems to have held no office in the royal administration before he was given the bishopric of Lincoln in 1123; but as such he probably acted as a local justice in Lincolnshire.[72] He was with Henry in Normandy on two occasions,[73] and with Stephen there in 1137.[74]

---

[61] J. H. Round, *Calendar of Documents . . . France* (1899), pp. xlviii-xlix, nos. 919, 921-3, 927; *Gallia Christiana*, instrumenta, cols., 224-9. On the family, Farrer, *Honors and Knights Fees*, iii. 56; J. W. F. Hill, *Medieval Lincoln* (1948), pp. 87-8; Loyd, *Anglo-Norman Families*, p. 51.

[62] Département de la Manche. *Inventaire Sommaire des Archives antérieures à 1790*. Archives ecclésiastiques, Série H, iii (1912). No. H. 4622 seems to show that 'Eudes-au-Capel' also had a son Robert.

[63] *D.N.B.*, 'Roger of Salisbury'.

[64] Neil Ker, *English Manuscripts in the Century after the Norman Conquest* (1960), plate 9a; cf. Richardson and Sayles, *Governance*, p. 158.

[65] William of Malmesbury, *Historia Novella*, pp. 37-8.

[66] *Regesta*, ii. p. ix.

[67] Most recently by Richardson and Sayles (*Governance*, pp. 157 ff.), Lady Stenton (*English Justice*, pp. 59-60) and F. J. West (*Justiciarship in England*, pp. 15-23).

[68] *D.N.B.*, 'Nigel'.

[69] *Regesta*, ii. no. 1691; *Pipe Roll, 31 Henry I*, pp. 54, 63; White, 'Financial Administration', pp. 68-70.

[70] *Regesta*, ii. *passim*.

[71] *D.N.B.*, 'Alexander'.

[72] *Regesta*, iii. p. xxiii etc.

[73] *Regesta*, ii. nos. 1426, 1895.

[74] Haskins, *N.I.*, pp. 124-5.

ATHELHELM, treasurer in 1137, was perhaps yet another nephew.[75] ROGER LE POER,[76] who was Stephen's chancellor from the beginning of the reign until 1139[77] and, as such, accompanied the king to Normandy in 1137,[78] was his son.[79]

THE MAUDUIT FAMILY.[80] William Mauduit I (died c. 1102) was probably a chamberlain connected with the Winchester treasury, for he was said to have held a 'camerariam thesauri' in a charter issued some 50 years after his death,[81] and he held lands in Hampshire (including Portchester) and in Winchester itself.[82] He also held lands in Normandy.[83] His elder son, Robert Mauduit (died c. 1129) was a 'chamberlain of the treasury'[84] who had some function in a Norman treasury;[85] his younger son, William Mauduit II recovered his mother's dower in England and his father's lands in Normandy,[86] served as chamberlain in the 'camera curie'[87] and attested King Henry's acts both in Normandy and in England.[88] He also attested Stephen's early acts in both countries,[89] but deserted to Matilda who described him as 'her chamberlain'.[90] In 1153, Duke Henry granted to him the chamberlainship (in the 'camera curia') with the lands pertaining to that chamberlainship in England and in Normandy (Portchester and other English lands specified) as he had held all this in 1135 and, in addition, a chamberlainship in the treasury ('camerariam mei thesauri') with the lands pertaining to that chamberlainship, whether in England or in Normandy, as his brother Robert had held it on the day of his death.[91]

WILLIAM DE PONT DE L'ARCHE.[92] There seems to be no information con-

---

[75] *Regesta,* iii. pp. ix, xix; Richardson and Sayles, *Governance,* pp. 220-1.

[76] *D.N.B.,* 'Roger Pauper'.

[77] *Regesta,* iii. p. x.

[78] *Ibid.,* no. 67 etc.

[79] Orderic, v. 119-21.

[80] White, 'Financial Administration', pp. 60-4, 72-8; Richardson and Sayles, *Governance,* pp. 429-37; *Regesta,* ii. p. xiv etc. Richardson and Sayles, the editors of *Regesta* ii and others have confused Robert Mauduit with Robert Mauconduit who was drowned in the wreck of the White Ship (White, *ibid.,* p. 61; Orderic, iv. 419).

[81] *Regesta,* iii. no. 582.

[82] *Regesta,* ii. no. 729 and p. 311; Domesday Book, i. f. 47 b.1.

[83] *Pipe Roll, 31 Henry I,* p. 38.

[84] *Regesta,* iii. no. 582.

[85] *Pipe Roll, 31 Henry I,* p. 37.

[86] *Ibid.,* p. 38.

[87] *Ibid.,* p. 134; *Regesta,* ii. nos. 1698, 1719.

[88] *Regesta,* ii. nos. 1507-8, 1689-90, 1695, 1698, 1710, 1760, 1781.

[89] *Regesta,* iii. nos. 255, 667, 727, 749.

[90] *Ibid.,* no. 581.

[91] *Ibid.,* no. 582.

[92] White, 'Financial Administration', *passim;* Tout, *Chapters,* i. 77-92.

cerning his parentage or his early life, though a Norman origin is implied by his name. He was sheriff of Hampshire for most of Henry's reign, and of Wiltshire, Berkshire and perhaps Sussex for shorter periods.[93] He was with the king in Normandy c. 1123 and in 1127-29,[94] whence he was sent to take possession of the bishopric of Durham for the king on the death of Ranulf Flambard.[95] He purchased Robert Mauduit's daughter, and with her the chamberlainship of the treasury that Robert had held, in 1129 or 1130,[96] and also a chamberlainship in the 'camera curie', the last possibly on behalf of his brother Osbert.[97] Osbert already had some position in a Norman treasury, where he received money that had been collected in England.[98] White has argued that William was the chief treasurer during Henry's later years;[99] he was certainly in charge of the treasury at Winchester at the time of Stephen's accession,[100] and continued to be styled 'chamberlain' under Stephen though he deserted temporarily to Matilda.[101] He had land in several southern counties,[102] a stone house in London[103] and a son called Robert who does not appear to have held any office.[104] He died c. 1145.

WILLIAM DE TANCARVILLE (d. 1129) and RABEL his son (d. 1140) were chamberlains.[105] William, whose father had been chamberlain to William the Conqueror while he was duke as well as while he was king, attested a charter as William fitzRalph, chamberlain, in 1082. From 1087 he served Duke Robert as chamberlain; but after Tinchebrai he held the same office under Henry, being succeeded therein by his son Rabel. There is no evidence that either William or Rabel was ever styled 'master chamberlain' or chamberlain 'in' or 'of' Normandy in any formal contemporary document. William attested a great many of the surviving acts of King Henry, and of these twice as many are dated in England as in Normandy.[106] Rabel attested very few; but one of them is dated in London, the remainder in Normandy or France.[107] Both had property

[93] *Pipe Roll, 31 Henry I*, pp. 36, 122; *Regesta*, ii. nos 948 (Hants), 948, 1185, 1517 (Wilts), 1780, 1833 (Sussex), and index, s.v. Hants, Sussex, Wilts.

[94] *Ibid.*, nos. 1418, 1499-1501, 1550, 1552, 1574, 1576, 1586.

[95] *Pipe Roll, 31 Henry I*, p. 131.

[96] *Ibid.*, p. 37; cf. *Regesta*, ii. no. 1746.

[97] *Pipe Roll, 31 Henry I*, p. 37; cf. White, *ubi supra*, pp. 73-4.

[98] *Pipe Roll, 31 Henry I*, p. 63; cf. Haskins, *N.I.*, pp. 108, 113-14.

[99] White, *ubi supra*, pp. 64-72.

[100] *Gesta Stephani*, ed. K. R. Potter (1955), p. 5; William of Malmesbury, *Historia Novella*, p. 15.

[101] *Regesta*, iii. p. xix etc.

[102] *Pipe Roll, 31 Henry I*, passim.

[103] *Regesta*, iii. no. 829.

[104] Richardson and Sayles, *Governance*, p. 427.

[105] G. H. White in *C.P.*, x. Appendix F.

[106] *Regesta*, ii. *passim*.

[107] *Ibid.*, nos. 1582, 1587, 1687, 1688, 1693, 1698, 1719 (London).

in England as well as in Normandy.[108] The family seat was at Tancar-ville in the Seine estuary. When the 'Annales de Saint-Wandrille' call William 'Camerarius Anglie et Normannie', they are presumably des-cribing his field of activity, not giving him an official title.[109]

[108] *Ibid., nos.* 1012 (*cf.* pp. 324-6), 1722.
[109] *Histoire Littéraire de la France,* xxxii (1898), p. 204.

VIII

THE PLANTAGENET DOMINIONS

THE TITLE of this lecture[1] has been a matter of some difficulty, and it might be well to begin by saying what is meant by it. I am using the term 'Plantagenet' as a conventional name for the family of the counts of Anjou. There is not much contemporary justification for this. 'Plantegenêt' was only one of the soubriquets given to Geoffrey, the father of King Henry II, and it was not treated as an hereditary surname until the fifteenth century.[2] From that time, however, it has been wished on to the family retrospectively; historians have used it in this sense and it is convenient. The word 'dominion' is used in the general sense in which it appeared until lately in the royal style,[3] that is, signifying political units, distinct in law and administration, ruled together by one monarch. In the twelfth century the word 'land' would generally have been used in this context; but 'dominium' was also used, certainly in the fourteenth century. It would have been possible to call this lecture simply 'The Angevin Empire'; and I shall often have occasion to use the word 'empire' in the general sense of an assemblage of 'lands' or 'dominions' under one ruler. But 'The Angevin Empire' as a title could have been misleading; though it is part of the present argument that the term has a much wider significance than is generally given to it.

The subject of this lecture, then, is the government of all those lands which in one way or another, and at one time or another, came into the possession or in some way under the authority of this family—Anjou, Touraine, Maine; Normandy, Aquitaine, England; Brittany, Ponthieu, Calais; the Celtic countries of the British Isles. The government of these countries in the Middle Ages has been the subject of an enormous volume of historical writing; but that they formed a governmental unit, or a unit of any kind over a considerable length of time, has not often been suggested. The argument that follows may be a little clearer if I say briefly how I arrived at it. The starting point was a study of the medieval

---

[1] Delivered at the Fifty-Ninth Annual Conference of the Historical Association held at Leeds, 31 December 1964. It is here printed as delivered, apart from verbal alterations and corrections, deliberately left in lecture-form as more appropriate to the content. The annotation is only intended to give a general idea of the evidence, as I hope to set it out more fully later on. Professor Cheney has kindly read the typescript; and though there are things in it still with which he would disagree, I am grateful to him for making me think over much of the argument again.

[2] J. Chartrou, *L'Anjou de 1109 à 1151* (1928), pp. 83–5; *Dict. Nat. Biog.*, art. 'Plantagenet, Family of'.

[3] As in 'George V, by the Grace of God of Great Britain, Ireland and the British Dominions beyond the Seas, King . . .'; not in the special sense used in the Statute of Westminster of 1931.

administration of the Channel Islands, a useful starting point since the history of the Islands, local history by the usual criteria, has to be seen against a background of the history not only of England but of France as well. In attempting to define this background, the 'whole' of which the history of the Islands must form a part, the notion of some sort of a 'Medieval British Empire' emerged, in which Normandy and Aquitaine and the rest appeared as dependencies of England. This is, after all, how they appear in most of our histories, at least by implication; sometimes explicitly, as in a well-known title, *Gascony under English Rule*. But as soon as it is seen that the relationship between England and Aquitaine, for example, as it was in the thirteenth and fourteenth centuries, grew naturally and continuously out of their relationship in the twelfth century, and that England was not at the centre of the Plantagenet dominions in the time of Henry II or Richard I, any such notion collapses; and so indeed does any conception of the matter that puts England at the centre all the time. In its place, the idea of a 'greater Angevin empire', of a complex of 'Plantagenet dominions', retaining its identity through periods of growth, transformation and decline, has been forming; and that is the idea that is set out here.

There is one final point of definition. I shall argue incidentally that the Plantagenets and their empire were French, at least for much of their history. It has been pointed out that while it is reasonable to say that they were not 'English', to call them 'French' only introduces a new confusion; for the adjective 'French' has as many nationalistic and other anachronistic overtones as 'English'. There is a real difficulty of language here. In this lecture, when referring to the Middle Ages, the term 'French' is used in the sense that Normandy, Anjou and the rest were 'French' at that time.

The beginnings of the subject do not lie in England. They lie in the feudal empires that were built up on the ruins of Carolingian government in West Francia, and, in particular, in the feudal empire that was built up from the Carolingian county of Anjou, *pagus Andecavorum*.

The family that established itself in possession of this county during the course of the tenth century descended from a half-legendary Enjeuger.[4] It seems that he had been entrusted with the eastern half of the county on the understanding that he would drive the Bretons out of the western half. By the time of Hugh Capet's accession in 987, Enjeuger and his successors had not only done this, but they had made themselves the hereditary counts of Anjou, seized the remaining royal properties and prerogatives there, and had already acquired important properties in the neighbouring county of Touraine to the south-east and

[4] For the early history of Anjou, see L. Halphen, *Le Comté d'Anjou au XIe siècle* (1906); J. Chartrou, *L'Anjou de 1109 à 1151* (1928); for the suzerainty of the counts of Anjou over Maine and its eventual incorporation into the family possessions, R. Latouche, *Histoire du comté du Maine* (1910); and for early relations with Normandy, D. C. Douglas, *William the Conqueror* (1964).

in the Pays des Mauges to the south-west. They found themselves surrounded by families which were doing much the same thing, the counts of Blois-Chartres, of Poitou, of Rennes, of Nantes and of Maine. To maintain their local pre-eminence, based ultimately upon wealth, they had to attract men to their service and vassalage, and continually invest their property in service; thus they had to be extending their possessions all the time. Under the two great counts of the eleventh century, Fulk Nerra and Geoffrey Martel, they conquered the Touraine, acquired a large interest in Aquitaine (not only the castles of Loudun and Mirebeau pointing towards Poitiers, but Saintes and neighbouring castles, perhaps the whole of Saintonge), and made themselves suzerains of the small county of Vendôme and the vast county of Maine. By 1060 the first Angevin empire was already in being.

For a while, after 1060, this empire went through a time of troubles during which some of the outlying possessions were lost. Yet the counts were strong enough still to maintain their hold on Maine, even though this brought them into direct confrontation with the dukes of Normandy. Fulk 'le Réchin' married his heir to the heiress of Maine; and thus Geoffrey Plantagenet, Fulk's grandson, inherited both Maine and Anjou and so absorbed Maine into the possessions of his family.

The really phenomenal expansion of Anjou, however, took place after 1128, the year in which Geoffrey Plantagenet married Matilda, daughter and heiress of Henry I, king of England and duke of Normandy. This expansion took a familiar form, the acquisition of rights by marriage, inheritance or in other ways, and their enforcement by war. Principalities at that time were treated as property by princely families. The marriage of Geoffrey and Matilda is generally considered from an Anglo-Norman point of view, in terms of Henry I's desperate search for an heir who would continue to rule England and Normandy together. But if it is looked at from the Angevin point of view, it appears as the culminating point of a century of warfare between Anjou and Normandy, when the heir of Anjou married the heiress of Normandy, and so brought Normandy, and England with it, into the family. Henry I was somewhat furtive over this marriage; in Angers it was a triumph. As it turned out, Geoffrey and Matilda had to fight for Henry's inheritance. Geoffrey had won Normandy by 1144; but he never made any attempt, personally, to secure England, and Matilda failed. It was not until their son Henry was a more powerful man, potentially at any rate, than his father had ever been, that he was able to make a satisfactory agreement with Stephen regarding the succession to England, and this after a good deal more than a show of force. For Henry had taken over the government of Normandy early in 1150,[5] had succeeded to Geoffrey in Anjou and its annexes in 1151,[6] and, in the next year, he

[5] Or, perhaps, at the end of 1149; Z. N. and C. N. L. Brooke, 'Henry II, Duke of Normandy and Aquitaine', *Eng. Hist. Rev.*, lxi (1946), pp. 81–4.
[6] J. Boussard, *Le Comté d'Anjou sous Henri Plantegenêt et ses fils* (1938), pp. 67 ff.

married Eleanor, the divorced wife of King Louis VII of France and heiress to the duchy of Aquitaine. Though Henry did not take the ducal title at once, and though it might be some time before he could enjoy such wealth as Aquitaine might bring, he could not but be regarded, after his marriage, as the greatest baron in France. And it was this prestige which, together with Stephen's recent misfortunes, at last gave force to his claims in England. From the end of the year 1154, he was 'King of the English, Duke of the Normans and Aquitanians, Count of the Angevins'.

During this phase of the accumulation of lands into what it is customary to call the 'Angevin Empire', Henry had taken over two other feudal empires. The duchy of Aquitaine, the first of these, was in its formation not unlike greater Anjou.[7] In spite of memories of a Roman province and a Carolingian kingdom, Aquitaine in the twelfth century was simply the 'empire' of the counts of Poitou, built up in much the same way as the empire of the counts of Anjou. Between 850 and 950 three lines of counts had in turn established a hegemony in what was then understood as Aquitaine, and had called themselves 'duke', sometimes 'duke of Aquitaine', as a decorative title to mark this hegemony. First it was the counts of Auvergne, then the counts of Poitou, then briefly the count of Toulouse, finally, and permanently, the counts of Poitou. From 987 the title 'duke of Aquitaine' was official in the sense that it was used by the chancery of the king of France; but this 'duchy' simply consisted of Poitou together with other counties which the family of the counts of Poitou had inherited or acquired (e.g. Limousin and Auvergne), together with others over which they had established their suzerainty (e.g. Périgord and Angoulême); and the alternative title 'count of Poitou' persisted through to Richard I's time and even into the thirteenth century.[8] In the middle of the eleventh century, the dukes of Aquitaine acquired the duchy of the Gascons in ways that are obscure but which seem to have involved inheritance, purchase and warfare. It is difficult to say what Gascony could have meant to them, for the Gascon counts and *vicomtes* who were nominally the duke's vassals were in practice independent, and there seems to have been very little ducal domain left. At all events, the dukes of Aquitaine saw no reason to move their chief residence south from Poitiers. When Henry married Eleanor, therefore, he put himself in the way of annexing the empire of the counts of Poitiers to the empire of the counts of Anjou. Aquitaine was not so large or so monolithic as it appears in most

---

[7] For the early history of the duchy of Aquitaine, I have found the following particularly valuable: A. Richard, *Histoire des comtes de Poitou*, I (1903); J. Dhondt, *Études sur la naissance des principautés territoriales en France* (1948), chs. i, iv; Ch. Higounet, *Bordeaux pendant le haut moyen âge* (1963); and, though with reserves, Y. Renouard, 'Les institutions du duché d'Aquitaine (Des origines à 1453)', *Histoire des Institutions françaises au moyen âge*, ed. Lot and Fawtier, I, *Institutions seigneuriales* (1957), pp. 156 ff.

[8] Richard of Cornwall was given the title 'Count of Poitou' in 1225 (N. Denholm-Young, *Richard of Cornwall*, 1947, pp. 4–6) and it is clear that his authority extended throughout the territories then in the obedience of the 'duke of Aquitaine' (*cf. Pat. Rolls, 1225–1232*, pp. 149–50, 186; *Cal. Pat. Rolls, 1232–1247*, p. 143).

historical atlases; but it represented an immense accession of prestige, if no more.

Two-and-a-half years after his marriage, when he was crowned king of England, Henry completed his acquisition of another feudal empire, the empire of the dukes of Normandy.[9] This Norman empire, apart from its first seventy years or so when it was little more than a Viking state living on plunder, had likewise been built up in the way which must now be familiar. By the usual methods of aggression, marriage and exploiting any opportunity to impose feudal suzerainty, the counts of Rouen, as the dukes were originally styled, not only acquired the lands that made up the historic duchy, but prepared the way to take possession of, or at least to acquire a considerable interest in Brittany, Maine, the Vexin, Ponthieu, perhaps Flanders—and England. At the same time, Normans were fighting in Spain and carving out principalities for themselves in South Italy. The feudal empire that William built up (though it was by no means all his own work) was basically of the same character as the feudal empires we have already considered. Even the fact that it had crossed the Channel and extended beyond the bounds of the kingdom of France was in no way exceptional. The counts of Flanders, and many other seigneurs down the eastern frontier, had similarly extended their possessions beyond the kingdom.

In one respect, however, this Norman empire was indeed exceptional. The conquest of England had been accompanied by a colonization of the country by the nobility, clergy and merchants of Northern France, Normandy in particular. The families that took estates in England mostly continued in possession of their lands in France, giving to England and Normandy one single aristocratic society, a French aristocracy which was a powerful force, with the interests of the royal-ducal family itself, for the maintenance of a union between the two countries. There seems to be no parallel to this elsewhere in the Plantagenet dominions,[10] save in the Celtic countries of British Isles, where the same men continued the work of colonization they had begun in England. It may also be argued that the conquest of England differed from other acquisitions in that it made William a king; and it is certainly true that he was very conscious of his new dignity and enhanced status. But England still did not take the place of his patrimony. He continued to give as much time and attention to his interests on the Continent as to those of his kingdom,[11] and he had to recognize that Normandy should descend to his eldest son. England's chief value to him and to his French

[9] Most of the vast literature on this subject is detailed in D. C. Douglas, *William the Conqueror*.

[10] Boussard has recently shown that Count Geoffrey Martel evicted a number of the count of Blois' tenants when he conquered the Touraine in 1044 (*Le Moyen Age*, LXIX (1963), pp. 141–9); but there seem to have been few confiscations when Geoffrey Plantagenet conquered Normandy a hundred years later, or when Henry took over the government of Brittany in 1166. The whole subject could well be investigated further.

[11] For the time William spent in England and Normandy respectively, see F. M. Stenton, *Anglo-Saxon England* (1947), p. 601, and F. M. Powicke and E. B. Fryde, *Handbook of British Chronology* (1961), p. 31. Anything like an exact calculation is, however, impossible.

followers was not the status she conferred, but her wealth in money[12] as well as in land.

Thus in the years from 1150 to 1154 the empire of the counts of Anjou had absorbed two other similar empires, the empire of the counts of Poitou and the empire of the dukes of Normandy. But the momentum of its expansion was not yet exhausted. Henry successfully asserted his feudal suzerainty over the king of Scots (King William the Lion, indeed, became his liege man for Scotland), and a similar, if less strictly feudal authority over the Welsh princes. Having planned a conquest of Ireland in 1155, he took charge of the conquest begun there in 1169 by the Norman marcher lords of South Wales, securing a share of the land for his own domain, the homage of the conquerors and the submission of the surviving Irish kings. As duke of Normandy he had long-standing claims to suzerainty over Brittany which were made the basis of what amounted to a conquest in 1166. As duke of Aquitaine, he strove un-successfully to recover what his predecessors had lost in Berry and Auvergne; and although his attempt to conquer the huge county of Toulouse was a failure, the count nevertheless did homage in 1173. Henry even made a marriage treaty with the count of Maurienne which, if the marriage had taken place, might have led him into Italy.

At this point, about the year 1180, the Plantagenet dominions stood at their widest extent. A very great deal has been written about them, from one point of view and another; and the latest work to offer a general description, during Henry's reign only, is a book of nearly 700 pages.[13] What follows are some of the considerations necessary to the present argument, and those alone.

We tend to use abstract expressions like 'the expansion of Anjou'. These are, it goes without saying, no more than a convenient short-hand. To describe the process with any approach to realism would take a long time; but such 'expansion' was clearly the work of men, of ambitious, greedy and forceful men, the most successful and the most ruthless among other ambitious, greedy and forceful men. William of Normandy did not undertake the conquest of England nor Geoffrey Plantagenet the conquest of Normandy for the greater good of England, or Normandy or Anjou, but to increase their own wealth and power and glory, to gain control over more lands and more men; and those who joined them did so out of loyalty, in part, but also for what they could gain for themselves. Apply these considerations to the history of the formation of the Angevin Empire and the obvious point must appear—obvious, but its implications are often overlooked—that this empire was made by the family of the counts of Anjou, partly directly and

[12] Cf. P. H. Sawyer, 'The Wealth of England in the Eleventh Century', *Trans. Royal Hist. Soc.*, 5th ser., XV (1965).
[13] J. Boussard, *Le gouvernement d'Henri II Plantegenêt* (1956). The author's summary, 'Les institutions de l'Empire Plantegenêt', *Institutions Seigneuriales*, pp. 35–69, is of great interest, but the point of view is wholly French.

partly by taking over the feudal empires already made by the counts of Poitou and the dukes of Normandy. The point may be demonstrated visually by a glance at the genealogical table. The succession was continuous in the male line, father to eldest surviving son, from Fulk 'le Réchin' to Richard 'Cœur-de-Lion'.

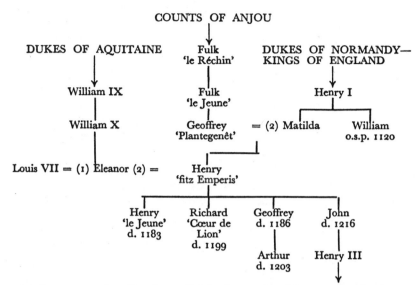

An important implication of this for us in this country is that the Angevin Empire was 'made in France'. In the sense in which the term is used in this lecture, Henry and his immediate descendants were Frenchmen, as French, certainly, as the Geoffreys and the Fulks and the Williams in their ancestry. Though Henry might be campaigning in Wales or in Ireland, the centre of his interests and ambitions lay in France. He was born at Le Mans, he died at Chinon and he is buried at Fontevrault. Even after he became king of England, he spent much more time in France than in England, more in Normandy alone.[14] England had in fact been gathered into a French feudal empire. It would be interesting to know how strong the suggestive power of our historical atlases has been. Just as Britain and the British Empire of modern times are coloured in red, so are the Plantagenet dominions in the British Isles and in France.[15] The suggestion, intended or not, is that England was at the centre of an empire in medieval as in modern times; and the preconception that underlies it has led to the incautious use of phrases like 'Gascony under English Rule', or 'la domination anglaise' when referring to Angevin rule in Aquitaine or Brittany. This

[14] *Cambridge Medieval History*, V, p. 554. But not all the time spent south of the Channel was spent in Normandy. A very rough calculation from R. W. Eyton, *Court, Household and Itinerary of King Henry II* (1878), gives Normandy 176 months, the French lands other than Normandy 84 months, England, Wales and Ireland 154 months; but these figures should only be taken as an indication of proportion.

[15] E.g. *Muir's Historical Atlas, Medieval and Modern*, ed. G. Goodall (1947), plates 22, 92, 96 etc. Plate 17 in the ninth edition hardly meets this criticism.

is quite wrong. England was then a conquered country. It had been colonized by Frenchmen and it was exploited by its Norman and Angevin rulers for their continental ambitions. The Angevin Empire was a French empire.

But this empire, this vast accumulation of property and authority over men, had to be governed and administered if its wealth and the power that its possession could give were to be enjoyed by its lords. Here there was a problem. Each of the major units of the empire, England, Normandy, Anjou, Brittany and (with some reservations) Aquitaine, were already, at the moment of their acquisition, principalities with their own systems of law and their own traditions of government, and in each of them government was still essentially the personal rule of count, duke or king. Yet no ruler could be everywhere at once. This problem was not peculiar to the Angevin Empire, and it was not new within the empire in 1154. It had faced William of Normandy after 1066 and Henry I after his conquest of Normandy in 1106; it faced Louis VII when, as duke of Aquitaine, he succeeded to the throne of France in 1137, and Geoffrey Plantagenet after he had conquered Normandy in 1144.

To some extent the problem was met by itineration. Rulers of this time were accustomed to move constantly about their lands, taking their 'household' with them and holding their court at convenient places. The acquisition of a new land simply extended the itinerary. The possibility of governing their lands from a fixed centre, impracticable in any case, did not arise. Thus William the Conqueror and Henry I circulated about England and Normandy, and Geoffrey Plantagenet spent some part of every year in Normandy between 1144 and his death in 1151.[16] In part they had to do this from military necessity and the need for what we might call police action, but not entirely; it was also a means of government. But by itself it was not sufficient. Any but the most primitive financial system, for example, required that the accounts of local officers should be rendered at regular intervals and if possible at a fixed place; judicial affairs could not always await the king-duke-count's next visit or attend him on his wanderings; and in any case, if he could not be present in person some substitute for his presence had to be found in each of his dominions or his authority would diminish.

There had been many experimental solutions of this part of the problem. William had appointed *ad hoc* regents to represent him during his absences from either England or Normandy; and this practice continued, beside others, for a long time.[17] On the other hand, Henry I developed the rôle of the officer who came to be known as the justiciar and made him almost a standing viceroy. In his time there was a justiciar of England and a justiciar of Normandy, in substance if not

[16] C. H. Haskins, *Norman Institutions* (1918), p. 143.
[17] *Handbook of British Chronology*, pp. 31–3; H. G. Richardson and G. O. Sayles, *The Governance of Medieval England* (1963), pp. 152–5.

very certainly in name.[18] Louis VII, when he became king, converted the personal, domestic seneschal of the dukes of Aquitaine into a territorial officer, virtually his viceroy in Aquitaine, quite distinct from the seneschal of the royal household.[19] Geoffrey Plantagenet did much the same in Anjou after 1144. At that point the 'count's seneschal' became the 'seneschal of Anjou';[20] and Geoffrey had a 'seneschal of Normandy' as well.[21] Seneschal or justiciar,[22] these officers were developing into standing representatives of the king-duke-count in each land. There was a third possibility. The counts of Anjou had, for some generations, associated their successor with them in the work of government during their declining years,[23] much as the kings of France did. In 1150 Geoffrey Plantagenet adapted this idea by making his son Henry duke of Normandy while he himself remained count of Anjou; and it seems most probable that this is what Henry in turn was doing when he made the Young Henry king of England and duke of Normandy, Richard duke of Aquitaine and Geoffrey duke of Brittany. The troubles which followed were those most naturally to be expected in such a situation.

All these means of supplying the king-duke's presence were employed, and it would take a great deal of working-out to define their relative importance at any one time; but by the end of the twelfth century it was the vice-regal justiciar or seneschal on whom the king-duke chiefly relied. In each country this officer was at the head of the administration, working with an exchequer in England, Ireland and Normandy, and

[18] Richardson and Sayles, *op. cit.*, pp. 159 ff. (though Henry probably did not create the office *ex nihilo* as here suggested); Haskins, *Norman Institutions*, pp. 87–99.

[19] William III de Mauzé, seneschal of Duke William X, was styled *dapifer comitis*, like all his predecessors who can be traced, in a charter of 1136 (G. Musset, *L'Abbaye de la Grace Dieu*, Arch. hist. de la Saintonge et de l'Aunis, XXVII, 1898, pp. 134–7). He continued as seneschal after Louis' accession to the throne, but is styled *Pictaviensis dapifer* in a royal charter of 1140 (T. Grailier, *Cartulaires inédits de la Saintonge*, II, 1871, pp. 50–1). The territorial title is the rule thereafter. Some indications of the seneschal's powers and functions at this time are contained in two documents, one printed in *Rec. Hist. France*, XV, p. 486, and the other in Grasilier, *op. cit.*, pp. 80–1.

[20] For the development of the office of seneschal in Anjou, see Halphen, *Le comté d'Anjou au XIe siècle*, pp. 102, 192; Chartrou, *L'Anjou de 1109 à 1151*, pp. 122–6; Boussard, *Le comté d'Anjou sous Henri Plantegenêt et ses fils*, pp. 113–28. The earliest instance of the territorial title comes in 1147 (Chartrou, *op. cit.*, p. 125); earlier seneschals were *senescallus* (or *dapifer*) *comitis* or simply *senescallus*.

[21] In the record of a case before the court at Rouen, Renaud de Saint-Valéry witnessed as *dapifer Normannie* (L. Valin, *Le duc de Normandie et sa cour*, 1910, pp. 265–7); but in other documents, it must be said, there is little to distinguish him from other justices (Haskins, *Norman Institutions*, pp. 146–9; Chartrou, *L'Anjou de 1109 à 1151*, pp. 126–30).

[22] It is a little puzzling that there should be justiciars in England, at first in Normandy and later in Ireland, and seneschals in the other Plantagenet dominions. At present it can only be suggested that in 1066, or even in 1106, the seneschals and stewards of Normandy and England were relatively undeveloped household officers (L. W. Vernon Harcourt, *His Grace the Steward*, 1907, pp. 3–29), not the obvious choice for vice-regal functions. On the other hand, both the king of England and the duke of Normandy had strong judicial powers: therefore in those countries it was an officer whose primary duty it was to administer the king-duke's justice that eventually became the 'viceroy'. In France, however, early in the twelfth century, the king's seneschal came to assume a very great importance (A. Luchaire, *Histoire des Institutions monarchiques*, I, 1885, pp. 177–85), and the seneschals of the counts of Anjou and of the dukes of Aquitaine may have profited by his example; so that, when a 'viceroy' was needed, they were the officers most likely to fill the bill.

[23] E.g. Chartrou, *L'Anjou de 1109 à 1151*, p. 23 note 3: Halphen, *Le comté d'Anjou au XIe siècle*, pp. 173–4.

with far less developed but still discernible institutions in the other continental dominions.[24]

The government of the Plantagenet dominions, by the end of the twelfth century, thus appears as a three-tiered structure. At the top, the king-duke-count, with his chamber,[25] chancery[26] and other household offices, itinerating ceaselessly over the length and breadth of his dominions, repressing disorder, defending the rights of churches, holding court and delivering justice, accessible to those who must bring their cases to the king and to the king alone. In the middle, the localized administrations organized and directed by justiciar or seneschal according to the laws and governmental traditions of each land; dealing with routine financial and judicial and sometimes military business on their own (delegated) authority and, on the king's order, with anything at all. At the bottom, the local administration of sheriff, reeve, *bailli*, *vicomte*, *prévôt* and so on, entirely the product of regional circumstances and history. It seems to make a rational system, and to give to the Angevin Empire that degree of coherence that makes it reasonable to argue that it was this empire, though still fundamentally the family estate of the Plantagenets, that constituted the political reality of the day, rather than any part of it. And it follows from this that the government of England was not a complete and autonomous system in the twelfth century, but part of a larger whole. Local institutions, the administration of justiciar, exchequer and the justices were specific to England; but the itinerant part of the government, king and household, were shared with the other Plantagenet dominions, and England's share was not disproportionately large.

Although few say it in so many words, the implication of most historical writers on the subject is that the Angevin Empire came to an end in John's reign. Certainly there were great changes at that time. As the result of John's condemnation in 1202, the king of France attacked and quickly overran Normandy and Poitou. The king of Castile saw his opportunity and invaded Gascony.[27] The defections were equally

---

[24] A great deal of work needs to be done on this point, though the outline seems clear. For the justiciars of England see, e.g., *Memoranda Roll, 1 John*, ed. H. G. Richardson (Pipe Roll Soc., N.S. XXI, 1943), pp. xi–xvi, lxvi–lxxvij etc.; the justiciar in Ireland, H. G. Richardson and G. O. Sayles, *The Administration of Ireland, 1172–1377* (1963), pp. 8–10, 29–30, 42–4, 73–5 etc.; the seneschal of Normandy, Haskins, *Norman Institutions*, pp. 174–85, and F. M. Powicke, *The Loss of Normandy* (1961), pp. 51–67; the seneschal of Anjou, Boussard, *Le comté d'Anjou sous Henri Plantegenêt et ses fils*, pp. 113–28; the seneschal of Brittany, B.-A. Pocquet du Haut-Jussé, 'Les Plantagenets et la Bretagne', *Annales de Bretagne*, LIII (1946), p. 22. In Aquitaine there was normally, at the turn of the twelfth and thirteenth centuries, a seneschal of Poitou and a seneschal of Gascony. Their powers and duties can be deduced from numerous entries in *Rotuli Chartarum* (Rec. Comm. 1837) and *Rotuli Litterarum Patentium* (Rec. Comm. 1835)—e.g. the men of Gascony were ordered to render military service and procurations due to the king-duke to Robert of Thornham, seneschal of Poitou and Gascony, 'loco nostro . . . tanquam persone nostre . . . si presentes ibi essemus' (*Rot. Litt. Pat.*, 3b).

[25] Richardson and Sayles, *Governance of Medieval England*, pp. 229–39.

[26] L. Delisle, *Recueil des actes de Henri II*, Introduction (1909); S. B. Chrimes, *Introduction to the Administrative History of Medieval England* (1952), pp. 67–9, 74–8.

[27] E. Berger, *Histoire de Blanche de Castile . . .* (1895), pp. 12–13.

serious. The count of Toulouse withdrew his allegiance immediately after the sentence;[28] the barons of Brittany and greater Anjou rebelled in 1203;[29] many of the more important barons in Aquitaine, like the vicomte of Limoges and the count of Périgord,[30] changed sides several times, but eventually adhered to the king of France. But all this, though in the end it seriously reduced the territorial extent of the Plantagenet dominions and deprived them of their original nucleus, did not amount to dissolution. The French, accepting the unity of the Angevin Empire, pursued their aim of destroying Plantagenet power by invading England, but they were soon driven out and the lands and lordships in the British Isles were territorially unaffected; John quickly recovered his position in Gascony and Poitou; the duke of Brittany, anxious to recover Richmond, was soon negotiating with John and actually did homage for his duchy to King Henry III;[31] the vicomte of Béarn did homage to Henry in 1242, and this was the first time in a hundred years that he had recognized the suzerainty of a duke of Aquitaine;[32] there were loyalists in Normandy for many years,[33] and no real need to despair of what had been lost until the 1240's. King Henry III continued to use the titles 'duke of Normandy' and 'count of Anjou' until 1259. There was no breach of continuity.

Yet in the end there was a great transformation, but a slow transformation going on throughout the thirteenth century. These are some of the changes that were brought about in the course of this transformation:

First: although allegiances and territorial holdings in France fluctuated during the century, yet by the Treaty of Paris of 1259 Henry had to renounce his title to Normandy, Anjou and Poitou;[34] and although this in itself involved no break in the government of the Plantagenet dominions as a whole, it did change the whole territorial balance. In Henry II's time these dominions formed a French feudal empire, the political centre of gravity of which was in France; but with the loss of much of the French lands, including the ancestral county of Anjou, England soon became by far the most important part of what was left. The political centre of gravity was shifting from France to England.

Second: in the time of Henry, Richard and John the Plantagenet dominions were governed by an itinerant monarch, who divided his time between his various lands as interest and policy directed. But in the thirteenth century, when departments of government generally

[28] Powicke, *Loss of Normandy*, p. 159; F. Lot, *Fidèles ou Vassaux?* (1904), pp. 129–323.
[29] Powicke, *Loss of Normandy*, pp. 153 ff.
[30] Ch. Petit-Dutaillis, *Étude sur la vie et le règne de Louis VIII* (1894), pp. 226–7, 278.
[31] S. Painter, *The Scourge of the Clergy, Peter of Dreux, Duke of Brittany* (1937), pp. 10–17, 32–48, 55–65.
[32] P. Tucoo-Chala, *La vicomté de Béarn et le problème de sa souveraineté* (1961), pp. 58–60.
[33] F. M. Powicke, *King Henry III and the Lord Edward* (1947), I, pp. 179–80, and references there given.
[34] Rymer, *Foedera* (Rec. Comm. ed.), I, 383–4; M. Gavrilovitch, *Étude sur le traité de Paris de 1259* (1899), p. 24 etc.

were beginning to settle down, the ruler of the Plantagenet dominions, after he had lost the greater part of his lands in France, would naturally choose England for his normal residence. Significantly, the justiciar-ship of England was abolished, for practical purposes, in 1234. Even so, government by itineration did not come to an end all at once. King John was in Aquitaine in 1206 and 1214 and in Ireland in 1210; Henry III was in Aquitaine in 1230, 1242–3 and 1253–4; Edward I as king-duke in 1273–4 and 1286–9. And these were not the purely military expeditions they have often been made out to be. A good deal of normal governmental business was transacted on each occasion. For the time, the king-duke was 'in residence', available for whatever had to be done, taking homages, settling disputes, calling assemblies, surveying the administration, refreshing loyalty.[35] Moreover the fuller records of the thirteenth century enable us to see something, on these occasions, of the practical relationship between the itinerant and the localized parts of Plantagenet government.[36] But these visits were growing more infrequent; and after 1289 there were none. It was one thing to cross the Narrow Seas and progress through Normandy, Anjou and Poitou to Bordeaux; it was quite another proposition to fit out an expedition which would take the king and his court and his army to Bordeaux by sea. Consequently the form of government in the remaining continental lands had to be adapted to deal with the king-duke's lengthening and ultimately permanent absence, just as in England it had to be adjusted to his more or less permanent presence.[37]

Third: not all the major changes affecting the Plantagenet dominions were taking place within their borders. Before about 1150 the counts of Anjou and dukes of Normandy were indeed vassals of the king of France, but in a personal sense and in a way that did not affect their government of their lands. If this had not been so, the formation

[35] For example, the military part of Henry III's visit to Aquitaine in 1242–3 seems to have been finished when the king reached Bordeaux in August 1242; but he stayed on in the city until the middle of September 1243. During that time he appears to have taken homages and fealties in a comprehensive operation comparable with Edward I's better-known cam-paign in 1273–4 (*Close Rolls, 1242–1247*, pp. 57, 59; *Cal. Pat. Rolls, 1232–1247*, pp. 352, 401, 376); there is good evidence of his judicial activity (e.g. *Close Rolls, 1242–1247*, pp. 57, 62–3, 64; *Cal. Pat. Rolls, 1232–1247*, pp. 368, 399) and two general assemblies were called (*Close Rolls, 1242–1247*, pp. 57–60, 70).

[36] In 1242–3, the king took his household, including the wardrobe and chancery and the 'great' seal, with him to Aquitaine, leaving the Archbishop of York as regent, with the ex-chequer and the English judicial organization, so far as it was separable from the king, in England. Some elements of the chancery had also to be left in England to issue writs for the exchequer and the courts. Consequently, two sets of chancery enrolments were kept, one of letters tested by the king in Aquitaine, the other of letters tested by the archbishop in England; but whereas the archbishop's set concerns routine business in England only, the king's set concerns the affairs of all his lands. For the time being his 'empire' was governed from Bordeaux. The summary, enrolled version of Peter Chaceporc's wardrobe account covering these years, has survived (Pipe Roll, 28 Henry III, m. 14); and this, with the entries in the Chancery rolls, shows that the relation of the wardrobe to the financial organiza-tion in Gascony, while the king was there, was very much the same as its relation to the exchequer when he was in England. Tout's account of these arrangements (*Chapters in Medieval Administrative History*, I (1920), pp. 268–70, 290–4) takes no account of the Gascon side of the matter. The whole subject needs a great deal more study.

[37] Cf. Lady Stenton, 'King John and the Courts of Justice', *Proc. British Academy*, XLIV (1958), pp. 105–8.

of the Angevin and Norman empires would have been impossible. After about 1150 the king of France began slowly to revive the idea of his sovereignty and to acquire the means to make it effective. The great vassals began to do their homage for specified lands, and then to describe it as liege;[38] and the king was able, in course of time, to deduce from the relationship so created a right to require service, to legislate generally, to hear appeals, to levy taxation and so forth. Technically, King John's condemnation in 1202 was based on an appeal from certain vassals to the court of his lord, the king of France. When the duchy of Aquitaine was reconstituted by the treaty of 1259, it was reconstituted on the basis of liege homage, and the acknowledgement of sovereignty in its mid-thirteenth-century sense which that had come to imply.[39] In this respect Edward I's or Edward II's position as duke of Aquitaine was very different from that of Henry II.

Fourth: the Plantagenet dominions of the twelfth century, though they were beginning to acquire some of the elements of a unitary political structure, could still be treated as a family assemblage. They had been accumulated for the benefit of a family, and they might be distributed in the interests of the members of that family. Geoffrey Plantagenet may have willed the division of his lands between two of his sons;[40] in 1155 Henry contemplated the conquest of Ireland to make provision for his youngest brother William;[41] the association of his sons Henry, Richard and Geoffrey in the government of England-cum-Normandy, Aquitaine and Brittany respectively implied a divided inheritance; and in fact, when Richard died in 1199, the empire did indeed fall apart momentarily—Aquitaine rallying to the Queen-Mother Eleanor, Brittany and Anjou to Arthur, Geoffrey's son, and England and Normandy to John. This happened because the rule of succession was still not defined in the circumstances of such an occasion; different solutions might find acceptance in the different dominions; and there was as yet no law to hold them together.[42]

When, however, Henry III constituted an appanage for his eldest son, the Lord Edward, he gave him Ireland, the Channel Islands, Oléron and Gascony, among other possessions, 'in such manner that the said lands ... may never be separated from the crown and that no one, by reason of this grant made to the said Edward, may have any claim to the said lands ..., but that they should remain to the kings

---

[38] J.-F. Lemarignier, *Recherches sur l'hommage en marche et les frontières féodales* (1945), pp. 92–100. The duke of Burgundy was first described specifically as the liege man of the king c. 1164 (Lot, *Fidèles ou Vassaux?*, pp. 45–6), the count of Flanders a little later (*ibid.*, pp. 19–20). The duke of Normandy is recorded as doing homage, apparently for the first time, in 1151 (Lemarignier, *op. cit.*, p. 94).

[39] Gavrilovitch, *Étude sur le Traité de Paris de 1259*, pp. 84 ff.; P. Chaplais, 'La souveraineté du roi de France et le pouvoir législatif en Guyenne au début du XIVe siècle', *Le Moyen Age*, LXIX (1963), pp. 449–69.

[40] William of Newburgh, *Historia*, ed. Howlett (R.S., Chronicles of the reigns of Stephen, Henry II and Richard I), I, pp. 112–13.

[41] J. H. Ramsay, *The Angevin Empire* (1903), p. 6.

[42] Powicke, *Loss of Normandy*, pp. 127–31.

of England in their entirety for ever'.[43] This was in 1254; and by this act the Plantagenet dominions were in effect given a constitution. Henceforth, whoever was the lawful king of England was, by that fact alone, the lawful duke of Aquitaine, lord of Ireland, and lord of the Channel Islands, at least in the eyes of English lawyers.

Taken together, these changes represent a great transformation. In the twelfth century, the Plantagenet dominions had been a family assemblage, governed by an itinerant 'central' government and localized administrations in each dominion under a justiciar or seneschal, and with the ruler's centre of interest in France. In the thirteenth century the monarchy was settling in England, and was coming to govern the other dominions more and more from England (a late symptom and landmark was the order of 1293 that the accounts of Ireland and Aquitaine should in future be audited at the English exchequer instead of by local commissions).[44] Yet in all this change there was continuity. This is so in the forms of government in England and Ireland; it is equally so in the forms of government in Aquitaine and the Channel Islands, though these had to be built up extensively to take account of the new political conditions and their phenomenal economic development; and it was so in the Plantagenet dominions as a whole.[45] Although English and French interpretations of the treaty of 1259 might differ and the changes it brought about were in any case very important, Edward I could claim to be duke of Aquitaine and lord of the Channel Islands just as much by right and inheritance as he was king of England.

In the English Chancery rolls of the fourteenth century the term *dominia transmarina* is occasionally used to denote the king's lands other than England. The use of the word *overseas* is significant; the Plantagenet dominions, in their transformed shape, were centred on England. The change-over was now complete from the Angevin Empire of the twelfth century, centred on France, to a political complex which could be described as England and 'the king's dominions overseas', centred on England. This phase may be dated, approximately, from the middle of the thirteenth to the middle of the fourteenth century. The territories now concerned were England, Wales, part of Ireland and, though

---

[43] Rymer, *Foedera*, I, 297. This was the last and the effective instrument. The formula must have been the result of careful consideration; *cf. Cal. Charter Rolls*, I, pp. 345, 389. It will have to be put into relation with the developing ideas of the impersonal 'Crown' and 'inalienability' (e.g. E. H. Kantorowicz, 'Inalienability', *Speculum*, XXIX (1954), pp. 488–502) and the French practice of annexing fiefs etc. to the crown (A. Luchaire, *Hist. des Instit. monarchiques*, II (1891), pp. 200–2; P. Viollet, *Hist. des Instit. pol. et admin.*, II (1898), pp. 163 ff.).

[44] *Rotuli Parliamentorum*, I, 98a. For earlier procedure in Ireland see Richardson and Sayles, *Administration of Medieval Ireland*, pp. 53–57; in Gascony, e.g. *Rôles Gascons*, ed. C. Bémont, II (1900), nos. 98, 97, 68, 764, etc.

[45] By good fortune, the surviving Chancery enrolments begin in 1199, when the Angevin empire was still fully in its twelfth-century form. The continuity of law and administration in the parts remaining to the Angevin rulers and their successors, though it is continuity in change, is apparent throughout.

briefly, Scotland, in the British Isles; and, in France, the duchy of Aquitaine reconstructed in accordance with the Treaty of Paris of 1259, the county of Ponthieu inherited by Queen Eleanor in 1279,[46] the Channel Islands (a relic of the duchy of Normandy) and what may be described, perhaps, as a 'special relationship' with the duchy of Brittany[47]—this last a very valuable asset.

During this phase the king-duke was no longer itinerant as he had been in the twelfth century. He never went to Ireland; his visits to Wales and Scotland were essentially military; Edward I, it is true, spent some time in Aquitaine, but his successors never went there. In 1286, Edward still took the Great Seal with him to Gascony, and the wardrobe; but the chancery staff was divided,[48] and more and more the household offices would be identified with England, as the seal, originally used by the king-duke in all his dominions, eventually became the Great Seal of England. The king, and what had been the itinerant part of Angevin government, that is to say, was coming more and more to be identified with England, and thus the administration of Gascony was being subordinated to what were primarily English institutions. The accounts of Aquitaine and Ireland were, as we have seen, ordered to be audited in the English exchequer; Gascon petitions were brought before the parliament of England. It can be little more than a suggestion at present, but what seems to be developing is a sedentary, 'metropolitan' government at Westminster, or at any rate one identified with England, with corresponding delegated, dependent governments in Aquitaine, Ponthieu, the Channel Islands, Ireland, and in any other lands that might come under the rule of the king-duke, capable of functioning in a situation in which his absence was normal.

In Aquitaine, so far as can be seen at present, the building-up of ducal government to meet this situation was very largely the work of Edward I,[49] though the process was a gradual one as the situation developed. First, the administration was unified. At the end of the twelfth century there were normally two seneschals, a seneschal of Poitou and a seneschal of Gascony;[50] and in the thirteenth, as lands came into the hands of the king-duke, a seneschal was appointed for each

---

[46] Hilda Johnstone, 'The County of Ponthieu', *Eng. Hist. Rev.*, XXIX (1914), pp. 435–52.

[47] The Richmond-Brittany relationship has not received the attention it deserves. For an indication of its importance, see Le Patourel, 'Edward III and the Kingdom of France', *History*, XLIII (1958), p. 186. The bare facts of dynastic relationships are given in G.E.C., *Complete Peerage*, art. 'Richmond'.

[48] Tout, *Chapters*, II, pp. 62–6, 115–18; but the account of the activities of the wardrobe in Gascony needs to be modified.

[49] For the almost contemporary reorganization of the administration in Ireland, see Richardson and Sayles, *The Administration of Ireland*, pp. 34–8, 54–7 etc. In Edward's time an administration was devised for the principality of Wales (W. H. Waters, *The Edwardian Settlement of North Wales*, 1935) and, though it was quickly destroyed, for the kingdom of Scotland (e.g. G. W. S. Barrow, *Robert Bruce*, 1965, pp. 189–92).

[50] For Richard's reign the best sources are L. Landon, *The Itinerary of King Richard I* (Pipe Roll Soc., N.S. XIII, 1935) and Richard, *Histoire des comtes de Poitou*, II. An important group of documents is printed by T. Grasilier in *Cartulaires inédits de la Saintonge*, I (1871), pp. 99–107. *Cf.* above, note 24.

of them, in John's reign for Périgord,[51] the Limousin[52] and the Angoumois,[53] and, after 1259, for the 'Three Dioceses',[54] Saintonge[55] and the Agenais.[56] But, from 1280, there was one chief seneschal, often styled the 'seneschal of Aquitaine',[57] and the others were made subordinate to him. Then, since the duties of the chief seneschal, originally embracing almost everything, were growing beyond the capacity of one man, his office was departmentalized, giving finance (the organization of which had been centralized at the same time) to the constable of Bordeaux and the controller, much of the seneschal's judicial responsibilities to professional judges, and some of his military and judicial duties to a lieutenant who ranked above him.[58] Finally he was given a professional council.[59] Such an administration, under the direction of the king and his council in England, and the Exchequer later on, could cope with anything short of an emergency. In the Channel Islands the office of warden (similar in function to that of the seneschal of Gascony) was likewise departmentalized—justice to the bailiffs of Jersey and Guernsey, finance to the receivers, and some military responsibilities to the constables of the royal castles.[60] What needs to be emphasized is that in the French lands these developments were characteristically French in form. The connection with England gave urgency to governmental developments in Aquitaine on account of the king-duke's absence, just as his commitments in France and consequent financial needs hastened institutional and constitutional developments in England; but it was the same sort of development, though speeded up, as would have taken place if the king-duke had been a normally resident ruler. The law remained purely native, and analogies in financial organization and

---

[51] *Rot. Litt. Pat.*, 115b.　　　[52] *Ibid.*, 112b.

[53] *Ibid.*, 116b.

[54] *Cal. Pat. Rolls, 1258–1266*, p. 109.

[55] *Rôles Gascons*, II, nos. 37, 94 etc.

[56] *Le Livre d'Agenais*, ed. G. P. Cuttino (1956), pp. xi, xx, xxi, 8, 9.

[57] *Rôles Gascons*, II, nos. 415, 416, 422, 423, 427, 737–42 etc.

[58] The process of transferring financial responsibility from seneschal to constable was a long one. It began when the first 'financial officer' was appointed for Gascony, to assist the seneschal, in 1243 (*Cal. Pat. Rolls, 1232–47*, p. 406; *Rôles Gascons*, I, no. 1232). The first constable of Bordeaux with financial duties, so far as is known, was appointed probably in 1254 (*Rôles Gascons*, I, nos. 3506, 4399, 4401 etc.); and gradually, from 1254, his financial responsibility grew until, with the ordinances of 1289, it was complete. The earliest known reference to the controller is of 1280 (*Rôles Gascons*, II, no. 428). A court of appeal, to relieve the seneschal, was created in 1255 (P. Chaplais, 'Le sceau de la cour de Gascogne . . .', *Annales du Midi*, LXVII (1955), pp. 19–20), but if this ever functioned it does not seem to have lasted long. In the following years, however, the seneschal made increasing use of deputies in the courts, some of whom were styled 'judges' (e.g. *Rôles Gascons*, II, 12, 127, 267, 270, 319, 741; *Recogniciones Feudorum in Aquitania*, ed. C. Bémont, 1914, nos. 23, 30–2, 366, 478 etc.). Lieutenants were appointed as occasion demanded, rather than in a regular succession, though from 1289 (*Rôles Gascons*, II, no. 1718) there were fairly regular appointments for 15 years or so. Most of these institutional developments were codified, as it were, in the great ordinance that Edward issued as he was leaving Gascony in 1289 (Cotton MS., Julius E.1, fos. 155–9).

[59] The earliest reference to a council so far known occurs in 1245 (*Close Rolls, 1242–47*, p. 361), but there are very few indications of its existence between that date and 1289. From 1289, however, it is clear that an official, salaried council, the king's council in Gascony, was in being (*Rôles Gascons*, II, no. 1028; III, nos. 1945, 1956, 4617 and p. xxxii, note).

[60] Le Patourel, *The Medieval Administration of the Channel Islands* (1937), pp. 40–52, 63–4, 71–3, 86–9 etc.

judicial administration were with contemporary Brittany, Burgundy or Toulouse, for example, not with England;[61] just as in the Channel Islands the law remained Norman and continued to develop on Norman lines for centuries after their political separation from the Norman mainland.[62]

This is partly because, though Gascony and the Channel Islands were in English law annexed to the crown of England, in French law the duke of Aquitaine, the count of Ponthieu and the lord of the Channel Islands was the liege vassal of the king and a peer of France, his lands in France an integral part of the kingdom. Therefore, like any other French baron, he owed homage on the usual occasions, military service and attendance at the king's court on summons, and loyalty—loyalty above all. He must submit to the fact that his courts in Aquitaine and Ponthieu were not sovereign, that his subjects there could appeal from them to the Court of France, the *Parlement de Paris*, and that French legislation might apply to his lands and even French royal taxation be levied in them.[63] Thus a large part of the king-duke's administration of his French lands was made up of the professional council which he, like other French barons, maintained in Paris to watch his interests in the Court of France;[64] and one reason why the seneschal of Aquitaine had to delegate so many of his duties was the amount of time he had to spend in French courts defending appeals against the decisions of courts held by him or in his name. Yet, although he had to watch his interests very carefully, there is nothing to show that Edward I regarded this situation as anything but the natural order of things during the first twenty years of his reign. But the war of 1294 changed much; and from 1300 at any rate the king-duke was endeavouring, as a matter of both doctrine and practice, to oppose a concept of ducal sovereignty to royal sovereignty in his French lands.[65] In this he was only a few decades and a few degrees ahead of his peers in the higher French baronage—the dukes of Brittany, for example.[66] One quite possible interpretation of the fourteenth-century phase of the Hundred Years War is that it was a revolt of the greater French barons against royal centralization, a revolt led by the greatest of their number, one who had immense resources outside the kingdom, that is, the duke of Aquitaine. This heavy commitment in France, indeed the extent to which they were 'Frenchmen' still, does much to explain the continental activities of Edward I and Edward III

[61] This needs to be worked out in detail. For a preliminary indication, see Le Patourel, 'The King and the Princes in Fourteenth-century France', in *Europe in the Late Middle Ages*, ed. Hale, Highfield and Smalley (1965). See below XV.

[62] Le Patourel, 'The Origins of the Channel Islands Legal System', *Solicitor Quarterly*, I (1962), pp. 198–210. See above II.

[63] P. Chaplais, 'Le duché-pairie de Guyenne', *Annales du Midi*, LXIX (1957), pp. 5–38, LXX (1958), pp. 135–60; 'La souveraineté du roi de France et le pouvoir législatif en Guyenne . . .', *Le Moyen Age*, LXIX (1963), pp. 449–69.

[64] E.g. G. P. Cuttino, *English Diplomatic Administration* (1940), pp. 96–9.

[65] P. Chaplais, 'English Arguments concerning the Feudal Status of Aquitaine . . .', *Bulletin of the Institute of Historical Research*, XXI (1948), pp. 203–13

[66] Le Patourel, 'The King and the Princes . . .' (above, note 61)..

(much of which had little relevance to purely English interests) and the failure of Edward II.

Another reason why the institutional development of Aquitaine and the Channel Islands was French (Ponthieu remained purely French) rather than English was simply that the kings of England were dukes of Aquitaine and lords of the Channel Islands by inheritance and tradition as ancient and well-established as that which gave them their kingdom. They were the lawful descendants of earlier native rulers; in a sense they were native rulers themselves. Though their kingdom conferred a higher status, their French lands provided resources and prestige that were not to be despised;[67] and there was no reason why Edward I, for example, should not still feel himself to be as much a French baron as an English king. It was one of the traditions of the Angevin empire that customs were not transported from one dominion to another,[68] that the government of each dominion should proceed according to its own laws and customs; and this tradition still held in the French lands and in England. But the policy of the Angevin rulers towards the Celtic countries was in complete contrast. There, their rule was based upon conquest rather than upon inheritance; and thus the institutions of government in Ireland, after the 'Anglo-Norman' conquest, were a reproduction of institutions in England, and there was at least a partial introduction of the law then obtaining in England. In Wales and in Scotland, after a long period during which the Norman and Angevin rulers of England had been satisfied with a recognition of suzerainty and the colonizing of the 'Anglo-Norman' nobility, Edward I was driven to attempt conquest and the introduction of some laws and institutions from England. In Wales he was reasonably successful; in Scotland he and his successors failed.

There is an epilogue which can only be touched upon briefly. In 1337 the king of France, in his court and in accordance with the law and procedure of the time, declared the lands of 'the king of England, duke of Aquitaine, peer of France, count of Ponthieu' in France to be confiscate.[69] Since Edward III resisted, and advanced counter-claims of his own, this precipitated what we call the Hundred Years War. Two-and-a-half years later, for reasons which we can only deduce but which, in great part, must have been implicit in all the long history of the Plantagenet dominions, Edward assumed the title 'king of France'. Together, these two events mark a break with the past; for they ended the feudal relationship which had hitherto existed, in its varying forms, between the ruler of the Angevin lands in France and the Capetian or Valois king of France. Yet in many respects there was continuity still.

---

[67] *Le Livre d'Agenais*, ed. G. P. Cuttino, pp. xiii–xiv.
[68] As a general rule, this holds; but there are exceptions, e.g. 'L'Assise au comte Geffroy', introducing the Norman rule of primogeniture for military tenures into Brittany (*La très ancienne Coutume de Bretagne*, ed. M. Planiol (1896), pp. 321–5).
[69] Froissart, *Chroniques*, ed. Kervyn de Lettenhove, XVIII (1874), pp. 33–7.

The lands in France which Edward III occupied or received by treaty during the course of the war, in Brittany,[70] Normandy,[71] the county of Guînes and Calais[72] (for some time even in Calais town, from which most of the French property-owners had been expelled), and in the lands ceded by the treaty of 1360, were governed for him as though he had been the lawful heir or representative of the native ruler; and in Normandy he actually assumed the ducal title for a few years. Local law and institutions were respected, and military exactions apart, the revenues collected were customary. Care was taken that Edward's assumption of the French royal title should do nothing to prejudice the laws and customs of Aquitaine;[73] and though its effect on the constitutional position of the Channel Islands is obscure, it is hard to see that it had any influence on their laws and institutions though prolonged war conditions naturally did influence them.[74] In short, Edward III, heir to all the traditions of the Plantagenet dominions, was still very much a French prince; the Angevin Empire, transformed and still in course of transformation, had not yet completely lost its identity.

The conclusion I should like to be able to draw is that what I have called 'the Plantagenet Dominions' or (though in a wider sense than is customary) 'the Angevin Empire' was a continuous political phenomenon, a historical entity, and sufficiently coherent to make it, rather than any of the units of which it was composed, the political reality of its day. As far as continuity in time goes, the case is perhaps made in dynastic terms (and it was men and families, more than impersonal forces, more even than ideas, that made states in the Middle Ages); the case may even have been made, to some extent at any rate, in territorial terms, for if the territorial content changed over the centuries, the Plantagenet dominions were by no means unique in that respect; but although I have suggested that in its political organization, and in the face that it presented to the rest of the western world, it was an effective unity, there is still much to be done on that score.

Supposing, however, that the case were fully made, there is one big implication which must be apparent but which still needs to be emphasized. As historians we tend to project the present into the past. We give courses of lectures and write books and series of books on 'English history from the earliest times to the present day', as though there was a kind of history that was 'English', as opposed to a French kind of history or a German kind of history, as though there had always been something

[70] Le Patourel, 'L'Administration ducale dans la Bretagne montfortiste (1345–1362)', *Revue historique de droit français et étranger*, 4e série, XXXII (1954), pp. 144–7.
[71] Le Patourel, 'Edouard III, "roi de France et duc de Normandie", 1356–1360', *ibid.*, XXXI (1953), pp. 317–18.
[72] Le Patourel, 'L'Occupation anglaise de Calais au XIVe siècle', *Revue du Nord*, XXXIII (1951), pp. 228–41. See below XIV.
[73] Rymer, *Foedera*, II, ii, 1127.
[74] Le Patourel, 'Origins of the Channel Islands Legal System', *Solicitor Quarterly*, I, pp. 201–2; *Medieval Administration of the Channel Islands*, pp. 31–2, 61–7. See above II.

fundamentally identical with the England of today, and as though all the 'history of England' were leading naturally and inevitably to the England we know. The French do the same with the history of France; and so 'English history' and 'French history' tend to be two separate and distinct subjects *at all times*.[75] The implication of the argument in this lecture, on the other hand, is that the effective political units from 1066 until some time in the fourteenth century were not England and France as we ordinarily think of them, but a Norman empire and an Angevin empire and a kingdom of France (the 'Capetian empire'), overlapping and interpenetrating; and there are many economic, cultural and social considerations that would support this idea. Only gradually, and certainly not by 1340, did England and France crystallize out as truly independent kingdoms. Before that happened, the French possessions of the men who were kings of England cannot be treated as appendages to England or as parts of France under alien rule, to be brought to mind only when their affairs happen to impinge upon the conventional narrative of national history; they must be regarded, with England, as part of the matrix from which England and France were eventually shaped. 'English History' in the twelfth and thirteenth centuries, as it is commonly understood, is provincial history.

[75] *Cf.* Tout, *France and England* (1922), p. 162: 'English and French medieval history are one subject.' See below XVIII.

IX

ANGEVIN SUCCESSIONS AND THE
ANGEVIN EMPIRE

I understand this to be the first seminar in a series on the general theme of 'Lordship, Seisin and Inheritance'. I hope that what I am going to talk about can be regarded as coming within this pretty broad field; because my concern is basically with the formation and the stability of what is usually called the 'Angevin Empire', that is for these purposes the dominions as a whole of Henry II, Richard and John. I have collected a certain amount of evidence to indicate that, in the practical business of rule and exploitation, there was a distinct tendency towards integration and a unitary form of government in these lands as a whole; and I have been tempted to go further and to say that this 'Angevin Empire' was at least as much of an integral and stable political unit as, for example, the contemporary kingdom of France. It is not to the point to develop that idea now; what I want to do is to see if there is any way of overcoming the first and most obvious objection to it. The received opinion seems to be that this empire was an accident, never planned or envisaged by anybody, certainly transient, and this opinion has been based chiefly on three points: (1) that Henry I of England married his daughter Matilda to Geoffrey Plantagenet (as I shall call him) of Anjou for immediate tactical reasons, and that he could have had no vision of an 'Angevin Empire' such as resulted indirectly from the marriage; (2) that Geoffrey Plantagenet himself willed a partition of the lands he held at the time of his death, his wife's inheritance of England and Normandy to his eldest son Henry (Henry II), and his own inheritance the counties of Anjou-Maine-Touraine to his second son another Geoffrey — so Geoffrey Plantagenet also had no notion of an 'Angevin Empire'; and (3) Henry II in turn planned a partition, England, Normandy and Anjou to his eldest surviving son, Aquitaine to the second, Brittany to the third and Ireland to the fourth — so neither did he have any idea that his empire could continue beyond his own lifetime.

If these interpretations are correct, there is no point in pursuing tendencies to integration. The sovereign kingdoms of France and

England were predestined from the beginning of time, and the 'Angevin Empire' was no more than an incident. The idea has been developed particularly by Prof. Hollister and Mr. Keefe in America,[1] and consecrated, with other arguments for the fragility of the 'empire', by Prof. Holt in his splendid Raleigh Lecture.[2] I myself was guilty of using an ill-judged phrase about the 'Empire', back in 1966, when I described it as a 'family assemblage',[3] a phrase that was given immortality, though quite non-committaly, in that lecture. Professor Warren over here,[4] and Prof. Bachrach in America,[5] have suggested modifications; though the first, anyway, does not seem to have won acceptance. I am going to argue now that other interpretations are possible, leading to a conclusion, not necessarily that the Angevin Empire was consciously formed by continuous policy, but that more than rules of inheritance were involved, and that the rulers concerned took every opportunity to add to their possessions, to hold on to what they had, and to pass it all on, substantially intact, to their successors. Integration was therefore possible. Clearly notions of inheritance and lordship are involved in all this; but I shall be concerned with the incidents themselves, the evidence for them and our interpretation of them; leaving the business of fitting them into general theories on such things to others more competent to do this than I am. In so far as I am reacting to Professor Holt's interpretation of a transitory Angevin Empire as expressed in the Raleigh Lecture, I do so with the greatest respect and diffidence − after all, he's got all the charters. I shall probably retire with my tail between my legs.

I shall proceed chronologically and consider first *the Angevin Marriage* of 1128. The circumstances of this event hardly need rehearsing. Henry I had but two legitimate children. He lost his son William in 1120, just after William had been recognized as his heir to England and Normandy; and Henry's second marriage did not produce further children. When his daughter Matilda, who had been married to the Emperor Henry V, was widowed in 1125, he brought her back to England and secured an oath from his barons to accept her as his heir in England and Normandy, and some versions extend this to her heirs. This oath was taken on 1 January 1127. Henry then set about finding a

1   'The making of the Angevin Empire', *Journal of British Studies,* xii (1973), 1-25. Cf. C. W. Hollister, 'The Anglo-Norman Succession Debate of 1126: Prelude to Stephen's Anarchy', *Journal of Medieval History,* (1975), 19-41.

2   'The End of the Anglo-Norman Realm', *Proceedings of the British Academy,* lxi (1975/6), 223-65.

3   *History,* L (1965), 301. See above VIII.

4   *Henry II* (1973), pp. 45-7.

5   B. S. Bachrach, 'The Idea of the Angevin Empire', *Albion,* x (1978), 293-9.

new husband for her, presumably to apply such force as might be necessary to secure the succession to her and her heirs when it came to the point. Negotiations for her marriage to Geoffrey Plantagenet, then heir to the county of Anjou, began in the spring, and formal betrothal took place towards the end of that year 1127. Matilda and Geoffrey were married in Le Mans Cathedral (lucky people!) in June 1128. Geoffrey was associated with his father, Count Fulk V, in the government of Anjou-Maine-Touraine within a month of his marriage; and he took over completely when Fulk departed for Jerusalem, probably in May 1129.

There can be no doubt that the initiative in negotiating the marriage was Henry's; and Hollister and Keefe are almost certainly right in claiming that Henry's *immediate* reason for picking on Geoffrey rather than anyone else was the political situation of the moment. For according to contemporary notions of rank he was hardly a worthy husband for an empress; he was not yet 14 and she was 25 at the time of the negotiations. Now at that time Henry's nephew, William Clito, the son of his imprisoned brother Robert Curthose, seemed really dangerous. Possibly as an immediate reaction to Henry's designation of Matilda as his heir to Normandy and England, King Louis of France had taken up the Clito's cause once again; had married a half-sister of his queen to him and had invested him with the Vexin Français. Clito advanced to the frontier and made a formal claim to Normandy – and it seems that he could count on some support in the duchy. Then, when Count Charles the Good of Flanders was murdered on 2 March 1127, King Louis forced Clito on the Flemings in his place. As count of Flanders, and with help from the French king, and some support in the duchy he could do a lot of damage in Normandy; and there was no reason to doubt that Count Fulk of Anjou would join in, as he had done before, for at that moment he was particularly unfriendly towards Henry, and he had his county of Maine to protect from Henry's designs. So Henry's policy was to detach him from the hostile alliance – hence the immediate marriage negotiations. As it turned out, the Clito's cause was visibly failing in Flanders well before the marriage took place, but he did not receive his fatal wound until after it. However, there is good evidence that Henry proceeded with the marriage, in the words of the Anglo-Saxon Chronicle, 'to have peace with the count of Anjou and to have help against his nephew William'. As far as all *that* goes, it was no more than a diplomatic move.[6]

6 Besides Hollister and Keefe, J. H. Round, *Geoffrey de Mandeville* (1892), pp. 29-32; J. Chartrou, *L'Anjou de 1109 à 1151* (1928), pp. 17-25; *English Historical Documents*, vol. II, *1042-1189*, ed. D. C. Douglas and G. W. Greenaway (1953), p. 193.

(Dukes of Aquitaine)　　　GEOFFREY PLANTAGENÊT = Matilda
　　　　　　　　　　　　　C. Anjou, Maine, Touraine　　(Empress)
　　　　　　　　　　　　　1129-51. D. Normandy 1144-50

　　　　Eleanor　=　HENRY (II) (b. 1133)　　　Geoffrey　　William
　　　　　　　　　　D. Normandy, 1150-89　　b. 1134　　b. 1136
　　　　　　　　　　C. Anjou, Maine, Touraine　d. 1158　　d. 1164
　　　　　　　　　　1151-89
　　　　　　　　　　D. Aquitaine, 1152/3/4-1189
　　　　　　　　　　K. England, 1154-89

William　　YOUNG HENRY　　RICHARD　　　　GEOFFREY　　　JOHN
d. 1156　　(K. England　　(D. Aquitaine 1169-)　(D. Brittany, d. 1186)　(Lord of Ireland
　　　　　　D. Normandy　　K. England, D.　　　　　　　　　　1185-)
　　　　　　C. Anjou etc.　Normandy and Aquitaine　　　　　　K. England,
　　　　　　1170-83)　　　C. Anjou 1189-99　　　　　　　　D. Normandy and
　　　　　　　　　　　　　　　　　　　　　　　　　　　　Aquitaine
　　　　　　　　　　　　　　　　　　　　　　　　　　　　C. Anjou
　　　　　　　　　　　　　　　　　　　　　　　　　　　　L. Ireland
　　　　　　　　　　　　　　　　　　　　　　　　　　　　1199-1216

HENRY III
K. England, L. Ireland, D. Normandy
and Aquitaine, C. Anjou, 1216-1259
K. England, L. Ireland, D. Aquitaine
　　　1259-72

EDWARD I
K. England, L. Ireland, D. Aquitaine
　　　1272-1307

EDWARD II
K. England, L. Ireland, D. Aquitaine
　　　1307-1327

EDWARD III
K. England, L. Ireland, D. Aquitaine
　　　1327-1340
K. England and France, L. Ireland
　　　1340-60, 1369-77

(1485)

But there could well be a good deal more to it. Between January 1127 and June 1128 Henry had plenty of time to consider the deeper implications of what he was doing. He would have remembered that the county of Maine, lying between Normandy and Anjou, had been a bone of contention between the two principalities for the best part of a century, that he himself had made considerable efforts to secure control of it and control of it was vital to the security of each of them. The marriage would certainly settle that one, improve Henry's position in Brittany and — remove all dangers to Normandy from the south and west. The consequent union of Normandy and Anjou must have occurred to him as at least a possibility; and even if Henry did think of Geoffrey as no more than a prince consort,[7] he must have known the ways of his world well enough to understand that if Matilda became queen of England Geoffrey was likely to be king. Henry could hardly hope to live long enough to ensure the direct succession of a grandson. The problem is Henry's attitudes and acts between 1128 and 1135. There is evidence that the oath to Matilda was renewed in 1131, and that it was extended to her son Henry in 1133. This evidence is not as good as one could wish. It did not convince Round, though it does convince Hollister.[8] On the other hand, beyond oaths, Henry did nothing to ensure the succession of Matilda or his grandson Henry. Geoffrey complained that he had not been given the castles that had been promised to him. He was clearly on bad terms with his father-in-law, who in the end quarrelled violently with Matilda as well. We need not discuss the possibility of a death-bed switch to Stephen: Geoffrey and Matilda were in the worst possible posture when Henry died in 1135.

But however one weighs up *those* points, it takes two to make a marriage. Count Fulk of Anjou would have looked at it entirely from his own point of view. His *son* was to marry the *daughter* of the king of England and duke of Normandy. And Prof. Bachrach is surely right to suggest that the power and the consequence of the counts of Anjou in the twelfth century had been built to no small extent on fortunate marriage, lots of them. If you accept Dr. Werner's arguments, the dynasty's fortunes had been founded originally on the marriages of Enjuger and Fulk le Roux back at the turn of the ninth and tenth centuries;[9] and, without cataloguing them, a series of marriages gave Count Geoffrey Martel I a temporary control of Aquitaine and

7   As argued by Hollister and Keefe, pp. 17-19.

8   *Ibid.*

9   K. F. Werner, 'Untersuchungen zur Frühzeit des französischen Furstentums (9.-10. Jahrhundert)', *Die Welt als Geschichte*, xviii (1958), 256-89; xix (1959), 146-93.

Vendôme[10] that could well have been made permanent and anticipated Henry's marriage to Eleanor by a century. Count Fulk himself who negotiated the marriage of Matilda and Geoffrey Plantagenet had secured the final union of the county of Maine to Anjou by his first marriage, and had won a kingly crown, albeit outre-mer, by his second. With that experience and the memories of his ancestors, the idea of uniting Normandy, possibly even England to Anjou by marriage cannot have seemed entirely fanciful to him. A vision of the Angevin Empire of the later twelfth century may or may not have appeared to King Henry I; to Count Fulk of Anjou it must have been clear and almost tangible. My genealogy shows the continuity in dynastic terms.

I come now to the second point for argument, Geoffrey Plantagenet's testament. The notion that he willed a partition of his lands and rights – to Normandy and England to his eldest son Henry, Anjou-Maine-Touraine to his second son Geoffrey (nothing, incidentally, to the third son William), depends entirely on William of Newburgh, who wrote a chapter in his History to explain why Henry was faced, very soon after his coronation, by a rebellion of his younger brother Geoffrey.

This is his story.[11] He begins by saying that the whole inheritance, derived from his father as well as from his mother, belonged by right to Henry, the eldest; but that Geoffrey Plantagenet, his father, fearing that Henry would not treat his brothers too generously, bequeathed 'the county of Anjou' to his younger son Geoffrey. However, since Henry was not yet in possession of England (this was in September 1151), he decided that Henry should not convey Anjou to Geoffrey until he had secured his mother's inheritance in full. Meanwhile, as security presumably, Geoffrey should have the three castles of Chinon, Loudun and Mirebeau. It so happened that Henry was not present at his father's deathbed, and Geoffrey Plantagenet caused the bishops and nobles at his side to swear that his body should not be buried until they had secured an oath from Henry to observe his father's wishes. Henry duly turned up for the funeral; and when this was put to him he hesitated long, but eventually and most unwillingly he took the oath. After the funeral, and when he was in full possession of the inheritance, he got papal absolution on the ground that he had been constrained to take

10 Bachrach, *loc. cit*.,; and in more detail, O. Guillot, *Le comte d'Anjou et son entourage* (1972) and L. Halphen, *Le comté d'Anjou au XIe siècle* (1906).

11 William of Newburgh, *Historia Rerum Anglicanum*, printed in *Chronicles of the Reigns of Stephen, Henry II and Richard I*, ed. R. Howlett (Rolls Series), 4 vols. 1884-9, i.11-408, ii.416-583, at i. 112-4. Unless otherwise stated all English chroniclers have been cited from the editions of their works in the Rolls Series and they are cited by name and volume number only.

12 Warren, *ubi supra*.

the oath without knowing what he was swearing to. He refused to hand over Anjou to his brother. Newburgh then goes on to describe Henry's expulsion of young Geoffrey from his castles and from everything he held in the county much as the Angevin chronicles do.

This story has been widely accepted as it stands; and when Prof. Warren recently cast doubts on it,[12] Mr. Keefe in America returned to the charge and stoutly defended it.[13] There are three points about it that I should like to make.

Firstly, I find it incredible in itself. Newburgh puts Geoffrey's rebellion which was in 1156 *after* the Welsh campaign of 1157 — but anybody could make a chronological mistake of that sort fifty years after the event. He begins by saying that Henry had a *right* to the whole inheritance, paternal as well as maternal, and then goes on to show how Geoffrey Plantagenet tried to subvert law and custom, as Newburgh understood it. As he tells it, the story is that Geoffrey conveyed his wishes to the bishops and nobles present. How does he expect us to believe that no one would spill the beans when Henry turned up and that Henry could persuade the papal court that he had been constrained to take an oath blind, to observe secret instructions of which he had no knowledge? And finally, how could Newburgh, having himself lived all through Henry's reign in England, expect anybody to believe that Count Geoffrey would think such a plan at all feasible, that Henry, the eldest, in possession and with right on his side, would give up his patrimonial inheritance to a younger brother?

Newburgh was writing in the north of England, nearly fifty years after the event, and there are several more nearly contemporary accounts of what happened. I put Robert de Torigni first, as nearest in time and place. He says that Geoffrey Plantagenet, before his death, granted the county of *Anjou* to his eldest son, Henry duke of Normandy; and to Geoffrey his second son he gave four castles.[14] Well, we know that Torigni was a partisan of Henry's, and if Henry had in fact denied his younger brother what had been bequeathed to him, Torigni could be expected to have disguised it as well as he could. But this is a perfectly direct and unambiguous statement, probably written within a year or so of Geoffrey's death, while Torigni was still prior of Le Bec — only a little over a hundred miles from Château-du-Loir where Geoffrey died. Likewise, Henry of Huntingdon says that Count Geoffrey handed over (*contradidit*) Anjou and Normandy to his

13 T. Keefe, 'Geoffrey Plantagenet's Will and the Angevin Succession', *Albion*, vi (1974), 266-74.

14 Robert of Torigni, in *Chrons. Stephen, Henry II and Richard I*, iv. 163 (cf. 161). Delisle in his edition (*Chronique de Robert de Torigni*, Soc. de l'hist. de Normandie, 2 vols. 1872-3) notes that Newburgh names *three* castles, but does not comment on the discrepancy in the numbers or the differing versions of Geoffrey's intentions.

first-born son Henry, and granted to him the hereditary right to England which he had acquired but failed to make good.[15] That can't have been written long after the event either; and though I don't know where Huntingdon got his information from, he and Torigni seem to be independent on this point. Gervase of Canterbury and John of Hexham, for what they may be worth, say much the same.[16] Other chronicles written in England simply note the succession without indicating Geoffrey Plantagenet's wishes in the matter.[17]

The local Angevin and Tourangeau chronicles, though not so direct, say or imply the same thing. The Great Chronicle of Tours, which has often been quoted in this connection though it was written in the next century, says that after Geoffrey Plantagenet's death his son Henry succeeded to him. Then, after his brother Geoffrey had failed to intercept Eleanor on her way from Beaugency to Poitiers after the divorce, and after Henry had married her, there was a war between Henry and King Louis; and young Geoffrey, who had Chinon, Loudun and Mirebeau *as his part of the inheritance* (*in partem hereditariam*), was attacked by Henry and driven out of those castles.[18] The Annals of Saint-Aubin (Angers) and the Chronicle of Vendôme imply a unitary succession.[19] The most interesting implication, however, comes in a passage of Jean de Marmoutier's life of Geoffrey Plantagenet, a passage so often quoted in another connection that it is surprising that this implication has apparently been missed. As Geoffrey lay dying, he says, he advised Henry, *his heir*, not to transfer customs from England or Normandy into the land of his countship (*in consulatus sui terram*) and conversely. Now 'his countship' could only be Anjou; and if Jean de Marmoutier did not get this straight from the horse's mouth, it could be one of the anecdotes which he picked up, as he says, among Geoffrey's associates — or possibly Henry's.[20]

There are finally two puzzles — that I know of. One is a statement in a Fragment of a history of the counts of Anjou. It was originally printed by Marchegay and Salmon without any indication of provenance; and re-printed tel quel by Halphen and Poupardin, who say that they have failed to find a MS. Nothing, therefore, can be said of date, authorship or probable authority. What it says is this: (omitting

15 Henry of Huntingdon, p. 283.
16 Gervase of Canterbury, i. 147 (probably derived entirely from Henry of Huntingdon); John of Hexham, in Symeon of Durham, ii. 326.
17 E.g. Roger of Howden, i. 213 (after Chron. Melrose); Ralph Diceto, i. 293.
18 *Recueil de Chroniques de Touraine*, ed. A. Salmon (Soc. arch. de Touraine, 1854), pp. 135-6.
19 *Recueil d'annales angevines et vendômoises*, ed. L. Halphen (1903), pp. 12-14, 70-1.
20 *Ibid.*, pp. 223-4.

irrevelancies) Henry duke of Normandy, son of Geoffrey Plantagenet by Matilda etc., was made (*creatus est*) count of Anjou in 1151 after his father's death. In the next year he married Eleanor... wherefore the counties of Anjou, Maine and the Touraine came to him..., and this was the origin of many wars.... Geoffrey, Henry's brother, was made count of Anjou (*creatus est* again); and as he would not accept what Henry offered him, he retreated into Anjou whither Henry pursued him.[21] That's one story. The other is equally dubious. It is printed in Bouquet as a fragment of a chronicle of the counts of Poitou, apparently (says the editor) by a monk of Saint-Maixent. Again no date, no provenance. This describes Eleanor's divorce, Henry's marriage and accession to England, and then goes on 'Henry, King of England, duke of Normandy and Aquitaine, count of Poitou, Anjou and Maine, appointed (*instituit*) his brother Geoffrey count of Anjou and Maine'.[22]

Well, whatever you make of those last two stories, I don't think that they can be put seriously into the scales against the rest of the evidence. But they could be related in a confused way to the entry in the Annals of Saint-Serge (Angers) which records that in the winter of 1155-6 Henry crossed the sea from England to deal with his brother Geoffrey *who was usurping his land of Anjou.*[23] If in fact Young Geoffrey did try to seize Anjou, with or without justification, it would explain quite a lot. It gives some support to Professor Warren's idea that Newburgh's story was based on a canard put out by Young Geoffrey to justify his attempt and to attract adherents, though the evidence for it remains purely circumstantial.[24] Such an attempt would, however, be precisely paralleled in the previous generation; for Geoffrey Plantagenet's younger brother Hélie had claimed the county of Maine and rebelled — some time after Geoffrey had established himself in the three counties and without any hereditary or testamentary justification at all so far as can be seen.[25] It would finally show what an incompetent Young Geoffrey was; for any idea that he would be

21 *Ibid.*, p. 251 and note.

22 *Recueil des Historiens de France (R. H. F.)*, ed. M. Bouquet *et al.*, 24 vols., 1738-1904, xii. 410.

23 *Recueil*, ed. Halphen, p. 102 (cf. 100).

24 This will have to be developed a little, quoting Warren's argument specifically. I am inclined to stress his point that Newburgh's story does not fit the fact that Young Geoffrey had already opposed Henry in 1152, in alliance with King Louis and Eustace, when England was far from having been won. Cf. the letter from John of Salisbury to the bishop of Norwich also quoted by Warren (*The Letters of John of Salisbury*, I. *The Early Letters (1153-1161)*, ed. W. J. Millor, H. E. Butler and C. N. L. Brooke (1955), pp. 21-2). There is also the point that Matilda, the heiress to England and Normandy and no negligible personality, does not figure at all in the discussions.

25 Chartrou, *L'Anjou*, pp. 29, 32-3.

allowed to have Anjou when Henry was in control of Aquitaine on the one side and England and Normandy on the other is just absurd.

For my part, I think that Geoffrey Plantagenet acted as his predecessors, counts of Anjou had acted. The family was very conscious of its history — Geoffrey's grandfather, Fulk le Réchin, seems to have composed a chronicle himself — and there can have been no lack of information on ancestral matters in the count's entourage. Geoffrey left his land, authority and claims, so far as they were his to leave, intact to his eldest son Henry. He provided three important castles in Anjou for his second son, under his elder brother's suzerainty, enough, and just enough, to keep him in the style to which he had been accustomed. Nothing to the youngest. The tradition goes back almost to the ninth century. It is most clearly shown, perhaps, in the arrangements made by Count Geoffrey Martel I in 1060, giving to the younger of two brothers the peripheral châtellenie of Vihiers, with the detached and distant lands in Saintonge, under the suzerainty of his elder brother, otherwise the whole inheritance, including the Touraine which he had conquered, to the elder.[26] In a sense, the periphery was expendable if it came to that; but the homage should keep it all together. The stability and steady expansion of Anjou would have been impossible if there had been a tradition of partition — expansion from half a Carolingian county to the whole of it, adding the Pays des Mauges and a large penetration into Poitou with small acquisitions all round; the conquest of the Touraine; penetration and union by marriage of Maine; marriage and conquest of Normandy — and so on. Count Fulk V may have had visions of a greater Anjou during the negotiations of 1127, 'wider still and wider'. Geoffrey Plantagenet, his son, did not betray those visions.

It may not seem so easy to explain away King Henry II's plans for the succession, as they are generally understood to have been; yet further consideration may well show that they did not diverge very much from Angevin tradition. We always have to remind ourselves that Henry II was an Angevin. Certainly he was king of England and all that; but he was born and brought up in greater Anjou, heir to Fulk Nerra and Geoffrey Martel, to Fulk le Réchin and Fulk 'of Jerusalem', to Geoffrey Plantagenet who *conquered* Normandy and left him to conquer England.

It should be observed first, perhaps, that there is no expression of his will relating to the succession that can be attributed directly to Henry himself. His testament properly so called, made in 1182, is entirely concerned with charitable bequests and its implications for the

26 Guillot, *Comte d'Anjou*, i. 102-5; Halphen, *Comté*, pp. 133-7.

succession are indirect.[27] According to Howden, in the *Gesta*, however, when Henry fell ill at La Motte de Ger near Domfront, in the summer of 1170, so that his life was despaired of, he divided his *regnum* and his lands among his sons, granting to Henry, the eldest, the kingdom of England, the duchy of Normandy and the counties of Anjou and Maine, and putting him in charge of his youngest son John. And he granted to Richard his (i.e. Henry's) duchy of Aquitaine, with its appurtenances, to hold of the king of France, and to Geoffrey the county of Brittany with the daughter of Count Conan, also to hold of the king of France.[28] Howden is the only chronicler to mention this so far as I know; he puts it a little differently in his Chronicle,[29] and the statement that Geoffrey should hold Brittany of the king of France seems wrong. Torigni mentions the illness, but not the partition;[30] and one may very well wonder whether Henry's unexpected recovery restored the status quo, whatever that was. There is, however, a charter of Henry's to be dated at some point in the 1170's, which speaks of Richard as Lord of Poitou, *dominus Pictavie* and Henry's heir, *heres meus Pictavie*;[31] and there may well be others with similar expressions relating to Henry's other sons; but Henry's idea of the succession has generally been deduced, and may perhaps be best deduced, from the position he gave to his sons during his lifetime, and from the events of his last few years when the succession, clearly, was very much in everybody's mind.

There can be little doubt, to begin with, that Henry intended his sons to have rule over the lands he assigned to them — in some sense. The question is, in what sense? The Young Henry, his eldest surviving son, was made to do homage to the king of France for Normandy in 1160. This was at the time of his marriage when he was five years old.[32] Two years later he received the homage of the barons of England[33] and in 1169 he did homage to the king of France for Anjou and Brittany.[34] Richard, then aged 12, did homage to the king of France for Aquitaine in 1169.[35] Geoffrey's marriage to Constance of

27 *Recueil des actes de Henri II, roi d'Angleterre et duc de Normandie*, ed. L. Delisle & E. Berger, 4 vols., 1909-27, ii. 219-21. It should perhaps be noted that religious institutions in Aquitaine, Brittany and Ireland scarcely figure at all although, in other contexts, Henry treated these countries as his own.

28 *Gesta*, i. 6-7.

29 *Chronica*, ii. 5-6.

30 Torigni, 246-8.

31 *Recueil*, ed. Delisle & Berger, ii. 82-3.

32 Torigni, 208.

33 *Ibid*., 216; Diceto, i. 306.

34 Torigni, 240; Gervase, i. 207-8.

35 Torigni, ibid.

Brittany was arranged in 1166, when he was 8;[36] and he did homage for Brittany to his brother, the young Henry as duke of Normandy in 1169.[37] The Young Henry was crowned in England in 1170,[38] with a second crowning ceremony in 1172;[39] about then Richard apparently went through ceremonies of installation as duke of Aquitaine in Poitiers and Limoges;[40] Geoffrey was solemnly received in Rennes Cathedral and took homages in Brittany.[41] From this time the princes were accorded the appropriate titles; though Richard seems to have borne the title 'count of Poitiers' more usually than 'duke of Aquitaine', and Geoffrey 'count' rather than 'duke' of Brittany. Henry, of course, continued to employ the style 'King of the English, Duke of the Normans and Aquitanians, count of the Angevins.'

However, these acts of homage, ceremonies of installation and titles gave the princes no authority in their respective countries that was independent of Henry. There can be no question but that the government and administration of *England* and *Normandy* continued to be carried on in Henry's name, and for him; and the incident of 1187, if nothing else (i.e. when Richard raided the treasury at Chinon)[42] shows that this was equally true of Anjou. The terms of Richard's commission, when he was sent to Aquitaine in 1175, at least as reported by Howden, make it quite clear that he went as a military commander, and that the ordinary administration continued to be carried on in Henry's name.[43] Torigni shows that Geoffrey's position in Brittany, at that time, was the same.[44] Certainly the Young Henry acted as regent in England and Normandy in the same way as William Aetheling had acted for Henry I;[45] Eleanor likewise in England, the northern French lands and in Aquitaine;[46] and it is likely that Richard came to be regarded as more of a regent than a mere military commander in Aquitaine, and Geoffrey in Brittany after his marriage in 1181. A regent exercises delegated authority.[47] Henry's sons were

36 *Ibid.*, 228.
37 *Ibid.*, 241.
38 Anne Heslin, 'The Coronation of the Young King in 1170', *Studies in Church History*, ii (1968), 165-78.
39 *Gesta*, i. 31 (cf. Warren, *Henry II*, p. 111).
40 *Gesta*, i. 81.
41 Torigni, 241-2.
42 *Gesta*, ii. 9.
43 Howden, ii. 72; *Gesta*, i. 81.
44 Torigni, 267.
45 F. J. West, *The Justiciarship in England, 1066-1232* (1966), p. 15.
46 Warren, *Henry II*, pp. 99, 101, 260.
47 Some materials for the study of their careers have been brought together in R. J. Smith, The Royal Family in the Reign of Henry II, Nottingham M. A. thesis 1961. For Geoffrey see also below X.

given no lands in the counties assigned to them such as might have served as the basis of an independent authority. This is made clear, not only by the Young Henry's repeated demand for an appanage, but by the terms of the treaty between Henry and his sons that brought the great rebellion of 1173-4 to an end — and here we have a formal state document rather than the chroniclers' reports. The princes were to return to a feudal as well as a familial relationship with their father; all barons who had taken part in the rebellion were to return to *his* allegiance; all castles were to be restored to *him*. The Young Henry could have two castles in Normandy, chosen by his father, and £15,000 angevin a year (*librae*, not *libratae*, and the currency specified suggests that it would be drawn on a Norman or Angevin treasury). Richard was to have two residences, such that they would not cause any harm to his father, and half the revenues of Poitou *in denariis*; Geoffrey half the maritagium, *in denariis*, of his future wife in Brittany. The key words here are '*in denariis*', in cash.[48] No land was involved; no basis for an authority that was not delegated by Henry.

It is clear that whatever de facto power the princes may have had at any time in the lands assigned to them — I am thinking particularly of Richard in Aquitaine — the real power and authority remained with Henry until, at any rate, the last year of his life. He could always recall his sons to his side; he could always resume his castles; he could command Richard to surrender Aquitaine to Eleanor in 1185, and be obeyed, however formal the act may have been. The Christmas courts, with all or most of the family present, continued almost to the end.

I do not claim to have got to the bottom of the problem of the princes' position in the countries assigned to them. It is likely that this will not be possible until Professor Holt's charters are available, but I am inclined to suggest that it was an adaptation to the circumstances of Henry's family and his far more extensive dominions of the traditional Angevin practice of association,[49] combined with the precedent of Henry I's use of his queen and his son as regents.[50] The point of fusion between the two practices comes, as it seems to me, when Geoffrey Plantagenet 'gave' (the word used is *reddere* or *tradere*) Normandy to Henry in 1150.[51] This act of Geoffrey's, at the earliest possible moment in Henry's career, is often quoted as showing that he had

48 *Gesta*, i. 77-8; *Recueil*, ed. Delisle & Berger, ii. 19-21.

49 Chartrou, *L'Anjou*, p. 23; Halphen, *Le comté d'Anjou*, pp. 173-4.

50 West, *Justiciarship*, pp. 14-16.

51 For the terms used see Torigni, 161; Ann. Saint-Evroul (Orderici Vitalis, *Ecclesiasticae Historiae*, ed. A. Le Prevost, 5 vols., 1837-55, v. 162); Ann. Saint-Etienne, Caen (*R. H. F.*,

conquered Normandy, not for himself, but for his son, regarding himself simply as trustee for his son in the duchy.[52] But occasional joint acts of father and son before 1150,[53] the fact that Geoffrey continued to act in Normandy after that date[54] — and I am not yet convinced that Geoffrey did give up the ducal title in the last 18 months of his life[55] — all suggest association, but association in one part of his lands, almost like a regent; and which was unusual, association with possession. If in fact Geoffrey had regarded himself simply as trustee of so much of his wife's inheritance as he had been able to win for her and their son, it is odd that she should appear to have had no part at all in the conveyance, though she was in Normandy

xii. 780); Ann. Saint-Aubin, Cont. Ann. Vendôme, Ann. Saint-Serge, in *Recueil*, ed. Halphen, pp. 12, 70, 100; Diceto, i. 291; Howden, i. 211. For the date and other points cf. Z. N. and C. N. L. Brooke, 'Henry II, duke of Normandy and Aquitaine', *E. H. R.*, lxi (1946), 81-6.

52 From C. H. Haskins, *Norman Institutions* (1918), pp. 130-2.

53 Few, in any case, are known. E.g. *Regesta Regum Anglo-Normannorum*, iii, nos. 9 (?), 17(?), 79, 304, 780. Geoffrey's father and predecessor, Fulk-le-Jeune, associated members of his family in his acts very freely and in varying combinations (Chartrou, *L'Anjou*, pp. 254-81 *passim*). The Empress Matilda participated in two of Geoffrey's non-Norman acts, and one such was addressed to his son Henry (Chartrou, nos. 113, 123, 153).

54 E.g. the third charter quoted in the following note and the military assistance he brought to Henry in Normandy during 1151 (Torigni, 161-2).

55 I know of three charters with dates later than January 1150 in which Geoffrey is given a comital title only. One of these, dated 28 October 1150 (Haskins, *Norman Institutions*, pp. 130-1 note 26; *Recueil*, ed. Delisle & Berger, Introduction, p. 138; Chartrou, no. 227; *Reg. Regum Anglo-Normannorum*, iii, no. 440) is in the Le Mans cartulary (*Liber Albus Cenomanensis*, no. 6) and, as Delisle observed, must have been drawn up elsewhere than in Geoffrey's chancery; the second, dated 10 June 1151, in which Geoffrey's sons participate, was for Saint-Aubin d'Angers (Chartrou, no. 233 from *Cart. Saint-Aubin*, ii. no. 864). Both are for non-Norman beneficiaries. The third was indeed addressed to the Archbishop and Chapter of Rouen, for a Norman beneficiary, and is an original (*Reg. Regum Anglo-Normannorum*, iii. no. 806; c.f. Haskins, *Norman Institutions*, p. 131 note 26, p. 147 note 90). It is dated 'Apud Mosterolium'. It could have been given at the siege of Montreuil-Bellay but, unlike the first, it does not say so; and although Ann. Saint-Aubin puts the beginning of the siege in 1150 and after the grant of Normandy to Henry (*Recueil*, ed. Halphen, p. 12), it seems that it could have begun in the previous autumn (*Hist. Gaufredi Ducis*, ed. Halphen and Poupardin, p. 216; Chartrou, p. 70). It is perhaps worth noting that the bishop of Le Mans, in a letter referring to the same transaction, gives Geoffrey the ducal as well as the comital title (Haskins, *Norman Institutions*, p. 148 note 90). It may indeed be that Geoffrey did not make use of the ducal title in the few months that elapsed between his handing over of Normandy to Henry (c. January 1150) and his death (7 September 1151); but given the small number of texts that can be cited in support of the statement that this is so, and the irregularity of Geoffrey's titles in the charters issued in his name for his non-Norman lands, it can hardly be said to be proved — and it might not have very much significance if it could. It may also be noted that Henry subscribed a charter of Geoffrey as *Hainrici ducis Normannorum et comitis Andecavorum*, giving himself two titles, while Geoffrey simply uses the Angevin one (*Recueil*, ed. Delisle and Berger, i. no. xviii, 11 June x September 1151).

or Anjou at the time. In the case of Henry's sons, the anticipatory homages to the king of France (like those of William Aetheling in 1120, and Eustace in 1137 and 1140, they did not give possession of the territory concerned), the coronations, the investitures and the titles, even the absence of any grant of land, all suggest association or, if you like, territorially limited association, like regencies, and association suggests a determined right of succession. Indeed, both in Capetian France and in Anjou, the device had been employed to ensure succession. Diceto (i. 291) says that Louis took Henry's homage for Normandy *and Anjou* sub anno *1150*, but after 'grant' of Normandy to Henry.

And yet, Henry's denial of a landed base to his sons in their principalities makes one wonder whether all this was quite a straightforward provision for the inheritance, whether, in fact, he was trying to reserve for himself the power to switch his sons round as the situation developed. He must have known that it was precisely this lack of a power-base in Normandy and England that had prevented his father and mother from gathering up his grandfather's inheritance in 1135. His sons, even if they did not have this experience particularly in mind, acted as though they did. The Young Henry, having failed to get an appanage in England or Normandy, began to intrigue with the barons of Aquitaine — and he had a way with him. Richard had had some spectacular military successes there; and though he duly handed over the ducal castles to Henry's men when required, I'd like to know more of what he did with captured baronial castles. At all events, though he did not fail to create considerable opposition to himself in Aquitaine, it is clear that he established, *de facto*, a very considerable foothold in the duchy. And that, no doubt, is why he would not do homage to the Young Henry, whom he might already hope to supplant, and why, after the Young Henry's death in 1183, he would not surrender Aquitaine to John, even for homage and an understanding that he would move into the Young Henry's place in the succession. He did not need to: with his firm base in Aquitaine and his mercenaries he would succeed to that in any case.[56]

From 1182 at the latest, the brothers were each trying to get a foothold in each other's territory; and from then on their confusing activities are only explicable in terms of their urge to get as much as they could, the lot if possible, each for himself. And Henry must have known all this. He knew what he had done to his younger brother — pushed him out of even the smallest share of his father's inheritance —;

56 For the events of Henry's last years and the manoeuvres of his sons see Warren, *Henry II*, pp. 559 ff.

he must have known what his father had done to his younger brother and what his maternal grandfather, Henry I, had done in 1106. He cannot have thought that any arrangements that he made for the succession would be observed after his death if they got in the way of somebody's ambition, or unless he provided that right should be combined with power. Thus a great deal more was involved in the succession to Henry's lands than any intentions of his. More even than the ambition and the violence of his sons. A long tradition of unity preserved against the claims of younger or elder brothers had maintained the integrity of Anjou and made its expansion possible.

And in fact, Henry's intentions relating to the succession, if they were constant, and if they were indeed what they appear to be, were not at variance with the traditions of his predecessors. He was not proposing a partition in the Carolingian manner. England, Normandy, Anjou-Maine-Touraine, suzerainty over Brittany, and the overlordships that went with all this, were to go to the eldest son. Only recently acquired and peripheral lands to younger sons, and then under the suzerainty of the eldest[57] — and a great deal of importance was attached to the feudal relationship at that time. It was the same in principle as Count Geoffrey Martel's provisions in 1160, or Geoffrey Plantagenet's in 1151 as I understand them, though on a vaster scale. Professor Holt will no doubt be thinking of the *Leges Henrici Primi* [58] and the Norman custom of *héritage* and *acquêts*;[59] but I still wonder whether it was not rather an attempt to preserve the essential unity of an 'empire' while providing for younger sons according to their rank;[60] how far, indeed, the customs of inheritance to ordinary property, themselves but half formed in the twelfth century, should be applied to kingdoms and principalities; and on the practical level, even if Aquitaine and Ireland might eventually detach themselves under such an arrangement, England and Normandy, with all that went with them, were enough to digest in one generation.

It was therefore not entirely a matter of chance that Henry's dominions descended intact to Richard, as the lands of every Angevin ruler as they were at the time of his death had done in the past —

---

57 Henry, if he had felt that he needed to tie it all up before he died, left the homages until it was too late — when Richard was already entrenched in Aquitaine and suspicious.

58 *Leges Henrici Primi*, ed. F. Downer (1972), pp. 224-5, c. 70, 21.

59 R. Génestal, 'Le formation du droit d'ainesse dans la Coutume de Normandie', *Normannia*, i (1928), 157-79.

60 As Count Geoffrey Martel I had done in 1060 (above), and as Duke Richard II of Normandy had done in 1026 (J. Le Patourel 'The Norman Succession, 996-1135', *E. H. R.*, lxxxvi (1971), 235-6). It should perhaps be remarked that in both these instances the younger brother supplanted the elder.

intact, because there is just enough evidence, I think, to show that Richard and his government regarded John as his vassal for Ireland as well as his other lands.[61] Intact again to John[62] — and John's treatment of Arthur was characteristic not only of himself but of his whole family (from the devil they came indeed). When what was left of those dominions, and the potential for recovery, descended together yet again to Henry III, his annexation of Aquitaine and the Channel Islands to the crown of England[63] simply provided a formal legal basis for what had become a unit of inheritance, and a unit in many other respects as well.

As I said to begin with, I am not trying to set up a new orthodoxy on rules of inheritance or testamentary dispositions in the twelfth century. I have been concerned to establish — to my own satisfaction if you do not puncture it now — that neither rules of inheritance nor the dispositions of the rulers themselves made the 'Angevin Empire' necessarily unstable or transitory. So I can go on happily looking for signs that, but for the inevitable though limited hostility of the kings of France and King John's loss of nerve, it might have developed a unitary form of government with no more provincial autonomies and separatisms than in the contemporary kingdom of France.

61 A. J. Otway-Ruthven, *History of Medieval Ireland*, (1968), p. 73; H. G. Richardson and G. O. Sayles, *Administration of Medieval Ireland 1172-1377* (1963), p. 74 and the evidence cited there.

62 The very difficulties that attended John's succession seem to show the unitary principle triumphing over tendencies to division (e.g. F. M. Powicke, *Loss of Normandy* (2nd edn. 1961), pp. 127-38). The famous conversation between the Marshal and the Archbishop of Canterbury is an interesting example of aristocratic interest in the succession and its effect on the countries involved. It seems that the word 'reignes' used in line 11871 of the *Histoire de Guillaume le Maréchal*, ed. P. Meyer, 3 vols. 1891-1901, ii. 63 and translated 'kingdom', should be understood in the same sense as Howden uses the word *regnum* in relation to Henry's reported disposition of his lands in 1170 (above and *Gesta*, i. 6-7). It will also be noted that the word 'terre' (1.11892) is used in the singular to denote the whole of Henry's and Richard's dominions.

63 *Foedera*, I, i. 296-7. Cf. J. Le Patourel, 'The Plantagenet Dominions', *History*, L (1965), 301-2, above no. VIII. The same formula of annexation was also used in relation to Ireland, Chester and other lands in England and Wales that formed part of the Lord Edward's appanage. It will be understood that the present paper is intended to modify the implications of the term 'family assemblage' as used in this earlier article.

X

HENRI II PLANTAGENÊT
ET LA BRETAGNE

En 1949, M. Pocquet du Haut-Jussé consacra un article aux *Annales de Bretagne* sous le titre « Les Plantagenets et la Bretagne » (1). C'est un article important, qui rectifie le nationalisme anachronique d'Arthur de la Borderie (est-il toujours nécessaire d'insister sur le fait que les Plantegenêt n'étaient pas des Anglais ?), et qui démontra la grande contribution du roi Henri à la formation de la principauté bretonne du bas moyen âge. Pocquet décrit le manque d'unité parmi les Bretons, surtout dans leur attitude ambiguë envers la politique envahissante d'Henri, mais aussi dans la structure politique de la Bretagne à cette époque. Selon lui, Henri dota la Bretagne d'une unité gouvernementale et administrative qu'elle n'avait pas connue depuis les invasions scandinaves, si ce fut jamais le cas ; et il y jeta les fondements d'un gouvernement vraiment ducal. En général, cette représentation de ses activités, en fin de compte salutaire malgré toute la violence et les destructions, est toujours valable. Je ne veux maintenant qu'offrir quelques notes supplémentaires, et peut-être une ou deux modifications légères, principalement à la lumière des informations de provenance anglaise.

En premier lieu, ce ne fut pas seulement la faiblesse exceptionnelle du pouvoir ducal pendant les années 1150 — le désaveu par le duc Conan III de son fils Hoël, la régence d'Eudon de Porhoët, la jeunesse de Conan IV « le Petit », le séparatisme de Nantes — qui donna au roi Henri l'occasion d'intervenir en Bretagne, que son agressivité et son ambition ne pouvaient pas négliger. Son intervention s'explique plutôt par des considérations plus profondes. Traditionnellement, le duc de Bretagne était le vassal du duc de Normandie (2). Pour Henri, c'était là un élément

---

(1) *Annales de Bretagne*, LIII (1946), 1-27.

(2) P. Jeulin, « L'hommage de la Bretagne en droit et dans les faits », *Annales de Bretagne*, XLI (1934), 411-8 ; J.-F. Lemarignier, *Recherches sur l'hommage en marche...* (1945), 115-22.

de son héritage, à rétablir et à garder. En plus, le manque d'unité de la Bretagne faisait de ce pays un voisin dangereux à la Normandie, un refuge et un lieu de recrutement pour des barons dissidents (3). Guillaume le Conquérant essaya de parer ce danger en prenant quelques grandes familles frontalières dans sa vassalité — les seigneurs de Fougères, par exemple (4) — et, plus tard et plus important, en cédant de vastes terres en Angleterre aux Bretons qui l'avaient aidé à conquérir ce pays (5).

L'intervention d'Henri de Bretagne se justifia plus particulièrement — à ses yeux du moins — parce que Conan IV était déjà son vassal en tant que seigneur de l'énorme « honneur » de Richmond en Angleterre, hérité de son père Alain de Penthièvre, le premier « earl » de Richmond en titre (6). Henri eut donc un double intérêt à soutenir son vassal. L'expédition de 1156, par laquelle Conan s'empara de la plus grande partie de la Bretagne et du titre ducal, avait dû être préparée en Angleterre avec la bienveillance, à tout le moins, du roi Henri (7). Ainsi, à la mort en 1158 de Geoffroi, le propre frère d'Henri et qui s'était fait comte de Nantes, Henri fut à même d'exiger la succession, non seulement en se prétendant l'héritier de son frère et en concentrant

---

(3) E.g., Henri Beauclerc en 1091 : Ordericus Vitalis, *Historia ecclesiastica* (éd. M. Chibnall, 1969-80), IV, 250, 256 ; (éd. A. Le Prévost, 1833-55), III, 377-9, 384.

(4) L. Musset, « Aux origines de la féodalité normande : l'installation par les ducs de leurs vassaux normands et bretons dans le comté d'Avranches (XIᵉ siècle) », *Revue historique de droit français et étranger*, XXIX (1951), 150 ; M. Fauroux, *Recueil des actes des ducs de Normandie (911-1066)*, (Mémoires de la Société des Antiquaires de Normandie, XXXVI, 1961), pages 348-52. Sans doute aussi les seigneurs de Dol-Combourg (*ibid.*, page 347).

(5) E.g., J. Le Patourel, *The Norman Empire* (1976), 15-16, 73-6, 215-6.

(6) C.T. Clay, *The Honour of Richmond*, I (*Early Yorkshire Charters*, IV ; Yorkshire Archaeological Society, Record Series, Extra Series, I, 1935, pages 84, 89-93). Cf. W. Farrer, *Early Yorkshire Charters*, I (Edinburgh, 1914), page 155 ; Robert de Torigni, *Chronica* (éd. L. Delisle, Société de l'histoire de Normandie, 1872-3 ; éd. R. Howlett, Rolls Series — « Collection du Maître des Rôles » — 1889), *sub anno* 1156 — « Conanus, comes de Richemont, veniens de Anglia in minorem Brittanniam... ». L'étendue de l'honneur de Richmond est indiquée par P. Jeulin, « Aperçus sur le « comté » de Richmond en Angleterre », *Annales de Bretagne*, XLII (1935), 265-302.

(7) Pendant l'année 1156, Henri se trouva en Normandie, Anjou et Poitou, pas loin de la Bretagne au cas où il aurait fallu intervenir. Raoul de Fougères, qui collabora activement avec Conan, eut, lui aussi, des possessions en Angleterre (*infra*, note 81).

ses forces militaires à Avranches, mais en menaçant de commise le comté de Richmond (8). Conan dut céder immédiatement, sans doute parce que le comté de Richmond valait presqu'autant pour lui que le duché de Bretagne (9). Il me semble que les historiens bretons n'ont pas donné assez de poids à cette considération. Il faut avouer, d'ailleurs, que les campagnes militaires en Bretagne, dirigées par Henri en 1164, 1166, 1167, 1168, donnent l'impression aussi bien de l'aide qu'un seigneur devait à son vassal contre ceux qui s'opposaient à ce dernier que d'étapes successives dans sa propre mainmise sur le duché (10).

En fait, de 1156 à 1166 et peut-être jusqu'à 1171, Conan semble avoir partagé son temps entre son « earldom » anglais et son duché breton. Il s'intitulait *Dux* (ou *Comes*) *Britannie et Comes Richemondie* (11). Il assista parmi les « earls » anglais au concile, où les célèbres « Constitutions of Clarendon » furent promulguées, avec le titre *Comes Britanniae* (12) ; quelques chartes survivantes, données en son nom, sont datées de Richmond ou se réfèrent à ses possessions anglaises (13) ; il est presque certain que la grosse tour du château, qui domine toujours la petite ville de Richmond dans le Yorkshire, fut érigée sur ses ordres (14) ; et il n'eut pas la possibilité d'épouser Marguerite d'Ecosse sans le consentement du roi Henri. Il se peut bien, donc, que ce ne fut pas seulement la puissance supérieure du roi, mais aussi les obligations d'un vassal à son seigneur, qui amena Conan, en 1166, à fiancer sa fille et héritière Constance à Geoffroi, le troisième fils survivant d'Henri,

---

(8) Torigni, *Chronica, sub anno* 1158 ; William of Newburgh, *Historia rerum Anglicarum* (éd. R. Howlett, Rolls Series, 1884-5), I, 114 ; *Great Rolls of the Pipe for the Second, Third and Fourth Years of... King Henry the Second* (ed. J. Hunter, 1844, 166) ; *Victoria County History, Cambridgeshire*, I, 374 ; VI, 6.

(9) Entre 1171 et 1183, pendant que le comté de Richmond était dans la main du roi, les comptes de ses revenus se trouvent sur les Pipe Rolls, 17-29 Henry II (Pipe Roll Society, Londres, XVI-XXXII, 1893-1911). Cf. Clay, *Honour of Richmond*, I, pages 108-112.

(10) Torigni, *Chronica, sub annis*.

(11) Le sceau du duc Conan est décrit par Clay, *Honour of Richmond*, I, pages 95-7 ; voir aussi planches VII, VIII, IX, X.

(12) *Materials for the History of Thomas Becket* (ed. J.C. Robertson, Rolls Series, 1875-85), V, 72.

(13) Clay, *Honour of Richmond*, I, pages 30-73.

(14) R.A. Brown, H.M. Colvin, A.J. Taylor, *History of the King's Works*, II (1963), 806.

dans l'intention évidente que Geoffroi succéderait dans le duché de Bretagne quand les temps seraient révolus (15).

Bien que Henri prît possession de la Bretagne peu à peu, sa mainmise fut en définitive totale : comte de Nantes, en effet, depuis la mort de son frère Geoffroi en 1158 ; pénétration de la Bretagne du nord-est par ses officiers, même avant 1166 (16) ; et, en cette année, fiançailles de Geoffroi et Constance, cession par Conan de la plus grande partie du duché et hommages de barons bretons à Henri (17) ; en 1169, prestation d'hommage par son fils aîné, Henri le Jeune, en tant que duc de Normandie, au roi de France pour la Bretagne et à cet Henri par Geoffroi, réception solennelle de Geoffroi dans la cathédrale de Rennes et prestation d'hommage par les Bretons à ce dernier et au roi Henri (18). Après cette année 1169, Geoffroi porta le titre *Dux* (ou *Comes*) *Britannie et Comes Richemondie,* bien que Conan fût encore en vie et portât les mêmes titres encore, paraît-il (19). Quand ce malheureux Conan

---

(15) En 1166, Conan n'avait qu'à peu près vingt-six ans (A. de la Borderie, *Histoire de Bretagne,* III, 1899, 269 ; G.E.C., *The Complete Peerage,* 1910-59, X, 791) ; sa femme vingt environ (*ibid.,* 793, note (e)). On ne peut que supposer qu'il y avait quelque condition physique bien connue des contemporains, mais non pas à nous, qui leur ôtait l'espoir d'un fils.

(16) Un sénéchal de Nantes, nommé par le roi Henri, était en fonctions dès l'année 1166 au plus tard (*infra,* note 24) ; il y avait un « justicia regis » à Combourg déjà en 1166 (Dom H. Morice, *Mémoires pour servir de preuves à l'histoire... de Bretagne,* 1742-46 (1968), I, 642) ; Henri prit possession de Rennes, et sans doute de Dol et de Combourg aussi, en cette même année (Torigni, *Chronica, sub anno*) ; la seigneurie de Dol-Combourg fut administrée à son compte en 1167 (Morice, *Preuves,* I, 658-9) ; et, l'année suivante, Etienne de Fougères, un des clercs de sa chancellerie, fut nommé évêque de Rennes (T.A.M. Bishop, *Scriptores Regis,* 1961, planche XXXI (b) ; L. Delisle et E. Berger, *Recueil des actes de Henri II* (1909-27), *Introduction,* 96-8, 458-9).

(17) Torigni, *Chronica, sub anno.*

(18) Torigni, *Chronica, sub annis* 1169, 1170 ; *Gesta regis Henrici* (ed. W. Stubbs, Rolls Series, 1867), I, 1.

(19) Geoffroi est intitulé par Torigni « filius regis » jusqu'à son installation à Rennes en 1169 ; après cet événement, « comes » ou « dux » (*Chronica, passim*). Cf. *Gesta regis Henrici,* I, pages XLIV-XLV, 3, 7, 42 et *passim ;* Clay, *Honour of Richmond,* I, pages 74-6 ; Morice, *Preuves,* I, 679-710 ; A. de la Borderie, *Recueil d'actes inédits des ducs et princes de Bretagne,* 1888, pages 116-9. Quelques chartes de Conan avec le titre ducal, et données, paraît-il, entre 1166 et 1171, sont indiquées par Clay, *op. cit.,* pages 70 (nᵒˢ 74, 75), 72 (nᵒ 78). Puisqu'il est bien probable que Conan continua d'exercer des droits et un certain pouvoir en Bretagne jusqu'à sa mort (e.g. sa guerre contre le vicomte de Léon en 1170), et il est certain

décéda en 1171, le roi Henri prit la totalité de la Bretagne et le comté de Richmond « dans son domaine » (20). Nous savons exactement ce que cela signifia en ce qui concerne Richmond, car les comptes des revenus de ce grand fief se trouvent dans les rôles de l'échiquier anglais (les « Pipe Rolls ») entre 1171 et 1183 (21). Quant à la Bretagne, ce fut en 1174, à la fin de la grande révolte, qu'Henri offrit à son fils Geoffroi la moitié de la dot de sa future femme Constance « en deniers » (22). Donc, ce fut lui, Henri, qui fut en pleine possession du duché. Bien qu'il eût maintenu une certaine distinction entre le comté de Nantes et le duché, semble-t-il, même après 1171 (23), il se trouva alors en mesure de réunir ce comté au reste de la Bretagne, d'éteindre à jamais la vieille rivalité entre Nantes et Rennes, et de donner à la Bretagne le gouvernement unifié qu'il lui avait manqué depuis le IXe siècle. Cette unité fut marquée d'abord par le fait que Guillaume, fils d'Hamon, qui se qualifia « sénéchal de Nantes » en 1166 et encore vers 1169, devint « sénéchal de Bretagne » précisément en cette année 1171, le premier à porter ce titre (24) ; et puis par la certitude que les droits exercés en Bretagne par Geoffroi et Constance après leur mariage en 1181, quels qu'ils fussent, s'étendirent au duché tout entier, y compris le comté de Nantes (25).

Cette unité fournit l'occasion de créer un gouvernement vraiment ducal. Entre la mort de Conan en 1171 et le mariage

---

qu'il continua en possession du comté de Richmond, les raisons alléguées contre l'authenticité de cette dernière charte (n° 78) ne sont pas convaincantes (cf. *Complete Peerage*, x, 793, note (d)).

(20) « Tota Brittannia et comitatus de Gippewis et honor Richemundiae... in dominio regis Henrici transierunt », Torigni, *Chronica, sub anno* 1171. Cf. « Chroniques annaux », Morice, *Preuves,* I, 104, *sub anno* 1171 ; « Henrico rege Angliae principante in Britannia » (1172), *ibid.,* 667-8, etc... Pour Richmond et le « comitatus de Gippewis » (= Ipswich), voir Clay, *Honour of Richmond,* I, pages 92, 108-10, 112.

(21) *Supra,* note 9.

(22) Delisle-Berger, *Recueil,* II, pages 19-21.

(23) Selon un autre acte se référant au traité de 1174, Henri donnerait à Geoffroi « medietatem reddituum Britannie, excepta Media » (*ibid.,* page 21, n° CCCCLXIX).

(24) Delisle-Berger, *Recueil,* I, pages 405-6 (n° CCLIX) ; P. de la Bigne-Villeneuve, *Cartulaire de l'abbaye de Saint-Georges de Rennes* (1876), pages 181-2 ; Torigni, *Chronica, sub anno* 1172 (1171). On n'a pas trouvé un officier avec le titre de « sénéchal de Bretagne » avant cette date.

(25) Morice, *Preuves,* I, 707 ; de la Borderie, *Recueil d'actes inédits,* pages 117-8 (n° LIX).

de Geoffroi et Constance en 1181, Henri gouverna la Bretagne
directement au moyen de ses officiers ; entre ce mariage et la mort
de Geoffroi en 1186, Henri intervint constamment et on ne peut
pas douter que l'administration était encore responsable envers lui.
Après 1186, la duchesse Constance, en tant que régente d'Arthur,
le fils posthume de Geoffroi — mais aussi comme héritière
légitime du duc Conan — gouverna le duché sous la suzeraineté
pesante des rois Henri et Richard (26). Elle ne changea pas le
régime, ni même le personnel administratif (27).

On peut supposer qu'Henri eut l'intention de se servir de son
fils Geoffroi pour gouverner la Bretagne ; mais de quelle façon
précise ? Il est très difficile de la définir. Avant son mariage, le
rôle de Geoffroi en Bretagne ne fut que purement nominal. Il ne
se trouva dans le duché que pendant les campagnes militaires de
1175, 1177 et 1179 (28). Après le mariage, Geoffroi fut, bien
entendu, le mari de l'héritière du duc Conan. En tant que tel, il
était en possession du domaine ducal en Bretagne et de l'honneur
et de l'*earldom* de Richmond en Angleterre (29) ; il prétendait à
l'autorité ducale (30) ; il pouvait tenir une cour ducale (31) ; il

---

(26) Constance tenait le comté de Richmond, en partie du moins, sous
la suzeraineté du roi jusqu'à 1199 (Clay, *Honour of Richmond,* I, pages 112-
3) ; elle fut remariée à Ranulf, earl of Chester « per donationem regis
Henrici » (*Gesta regis Henrici,* II, 29) ; en 1196, elle obéit au mandat du
roi Richard de se rendre auprès de lui en Normandie (Roger de Houedene,
(Howden), *Chronica,* ed. W. Stubbs, Rolls Series, 1868-71, IV, 7).

(27) *Infra.*

(28) Torigni, *Chronica, sub annis ; Gesta regis Henrici,* I, 81, 83, 190,
239 ; Houedene, *Chronica,* II, 72.

(29) *Bretagne :* « Constancia, uxor mea, Britannie comitissa, ad quam
comitatus Britannie jure hereditario pertinebat et per eam ad me interveniente
matrimonio devenerat », Morice, *Preuves,* I, 688 ; cf. les chartes données
au nom de Geoffroi, *ibid.,* 679 ; de la Borderie, *Recueil d'actes inédits,*
pages 117-8 (n° LIX). *Richmond :* Geoffroi fut mis en possession du manoir
de Cheshunt (Hertfordshire), parcelle de l'honneur de Richmond, dès l'an
1177 ; de Richmond dans son ensemble pas avant 1183 ; mais le roi gardait
toujours, paraît-il, les châteaux (Clay, *Honour of Richmond,* I, pages 111-2).

(30) *Supra,* note 25 (Morice, *Preuves,* I, 688).

(31) « Hujusmodi compositionem seu permutationem ad me delatam et
in curia mea publice recitatam, ego Gaufridus ratam habui », Morice,
Preuves, I, 688 ; cf. 694-5 ; « in curia mea coram me, terminatum fuisse
quod... ». Bertrand de Broussillon, *La maison de Laval (1020-1605),*
1895-1903, I, 123-4.

communiquait avec *ses* officiers en Bretagne (32). Mais il partagea son autorité avec sa femme, la duchesse Constance (33) ; et au-dessus des deux était l'autorité dominante de son père, le roi Henri, lequel avait toujours les moyens de reprendre les châteaux, de nommer les officiers et de diriger l'administration directement (34). Et, de fait, Geoffroi ne résida personnellement dans la Bretagne que de temps en temps (35).

Le chef de l'administration exerçant ses fonctions au nom du roi Henri dans le duché était un officier bien caractéristique du gouvernement angevin, le sénéchal. C'est en 1171 que le sénéchal du roi dans le comté de Nantes, Guillaume, fils d'Hamon, devint le « sénéchal de Bretagne » (36) ; mais il ne remplit ses nouveaux devoirs que bien peu de temps, car il mourut en 1172, probable-

---

(32) « Gaufridus, Henrici regis Angliae filius, dux Britanniae et comes Richemondiae, dilectis et fidelibus suis Rainaudo Boterelli senescallo suo et omnibus senescallis, praepositis, et viariis et baillivis suis per Britanniam constitutis... », Morice, *Preuves,* I, 689 ; cf. *ibid.,* 679, 707 ; de la Borderie, *Recueil d'actes inédits,* pages 117-8.

(33) E.g., Morice, *Preuves,* I, 688, 698 ; de la Borderie, *Recueil d'actes inédits,* pages 117-9 ; J.H. Round, *Calendar of Documents preserved in France* (1899), nᵒˢ 39, 40 ; « Assise au comte Geffroy », dans M. Planiol, *La très ancienne coutume de Bretagne* (1896), pages 321-3.

(34) Morice, *Preuves,* I, 687, 688-9. En 1183, « dominus rex disseisiavit eum (*Gaufridum*) de omnibus castellis suis et munitionibus suis Britanniae in misericordia sua » (*Gesta regis Henrici,* I, 304). En 1187, après la mort de Geoffroi (19 août), Guiomar et Hervé de Léon prirent les châteaux de Morlaix et de Châteauneuf sur les châtelains « quibus Radulfus de Fulgeriis ea tradidit per mandatum regis » (*ibid.,* 357). Le roi Henri reprit Morlaix l'année suivante (Houedene, *Chronica,* II, 318). Si Raoul de Fougères (sénéchal de Bretagne) confia aux châtelains les châteaux avant la mort de Geoffroi, cela veut dire que le roi était à même de donner ses ordres directement au sénéchal du vivant de Geoffroi ; si après, c'est une indication que le roi Henri avait repris les châteaux bretons à la mort de son fils, ou peut-être les avait tenu depuis 1183, avant de les rendre à la duchesse Constance, tout comme il avait fait des châteaux du comté de Richmond (Clay, *Honour of Richmond,* I, pages 112-3). Dans l'une ou l'autre hypothèse, sa souveraineté est démontrée.

(35) Il brûla une partie de la ville de Rennes et le château de Bécherel en 1182 ou 1183 (Torigni, *Chronica, sub anno* 1182) ; en 1183, il leva des troupes en Bretagne pour guerroyer en Poitou (*Gesta regis Henrici,* I, 292-3) ; il fut à Rennes en 1185 (Morice, *Preuves,* I, 703-4, 707) et à Nantes en 1186 (*ibid.,* 707). Autrement, il s'occupait des affaires de la famille royale partout dans les terres de son père ; et on ne sait rien de la durée de ses visites à son duché.

(36) *Supra,* note 24.

ment au mois de novembre (37). Il est possible que la Bretagne échappât à l'autorité du roi Henri pendant la grande révolte de 1173-1174 ; mais quand il envoya son fils Geoffroi en Bretagne, en 1175, pour y récupérer ses châteaux, il lui « assigna » Rolland de Dinan comme régisseur (*procurator*) du duché (38). Je n'ai pas trouvé mention de ce Rolland avec le titre de sénéchal, mais il exerça ses fonctions comme tel et un chroniqueur anglais l'intitula « justicier de Bretagne », et le « justicier d'Angleterre » fut l'équivalent des sénéchaux de Normandie, d'Anjou, etc... (39). Rolland fut suivi, en 1182 ou 1183, par Raoul de Fougères, lequel continua ses fonctions, semble-t-il, après la mort de Geoffroi. Avec le titre de « sénéchal de Bretagne », il figure comme témoin dans une charte du duc Geoffroi, dans deux de la duchesse Constance et, d'après Roger of Howden, il exécuta les mandats directs du roi (40). Après lui, Maurice de Craon et Alain de Dinan furent sénéchaux de Bretagne entre 1187 et 1201 ; mais on ne sait pas lequel précéda l'autre.

Guillaume, fils d'Hamon, et Rolland de Dinan furent nommés par le roi certainement, Raoul de Fougères très probablement. Tous les trois furent responsables, jusqu'à 1186 au moins, directement devant lui (42). Bien que nous n'ayons pas de preuves suffisantes pour définir avec précision les fonctions de ces « sénéchaux de Bretagne », ces fonctions étaient à la fois de

---

(37) Torigni, *Chronica*, éd. Delisle, II, 134, note 1 ; Pipe Roll, 19 Henry II (Pipe Roll Society, XIX, 1895), page 87. Cf. les trois rôles suivants.

(38) « Rex misit ... Gaufridum, filium suum, comitem Britannie, in Britanniam, assignans ei Rollandum de Dinam, ut esset procurator terrae suae », Torigni, *Chronica, sub anno* 1175. Dans l'interprétation stricte, « terrae suae » doit être « la terre d'Henri », et non pas celle de Geoffroi.

(39) « Justitia Britanniae », *Gesta regis Henrici*, I, 179 ; « justitiarius Britanniae », Houedene, *Chronica*, II, 136.

(40) Morice, *Preuves*, I, 704 (1185 ; mais cf. *ibid.*, 699-700, 703-4 ; ce fut en 1182 ou 1183 que Geoffroi brûla le château de Rolland de Dinan à Bécherel, Torigni, *Chronica, sub anno* 1182) ; de la Borderie, *Recueil d'actes inédits*, 134-5 (n° LXX) ; A. Oheix, *Essai sur les sénéchaux de Bretagne* (1913), page 17, note 4 ; et *supra* note 34.

(41) Morice, *Preuves*, I, 710.

(42) *Supra* notes 34, 38.

nature militaire (43), judiciaire (44), administrative (45) et sans doute financière (46). Bref, ils étaient les agents exécutifs du roi, hommes à tout faire (47).

Il y avait aussi en Bretagne, sous les Plantegenêt, des sénéchaux régionaux qu'il ne faut pas confondre avec les sénéchaux seigneuriaux. On ne peut pas dire que la division de la Bretagne en huit baillies, chacune administrée par un sénéchal, ainsi qu'il apparaît à la fin du XIII° siècle, fut créée en entier par le roi Henri ; mais cette organisation était déjà ébauchée. Guillaume de Lanvallay fut sénéchal de Rennes vers 1171 (48) et il eut pour successeur, paraît-il, Robert de Lanvallay (49) et, après lui, Renaud Boterel vers 1181 (50), Guillaume Ragot vers 1187 (51) et puis un Guillaume ou des Guillaume (52). Les sénéchaux de Nantes, pendant ces années, furent Guillaume, fils d'Hamon (1166-1171) (53), Pierre, fils de Gui (1181-1183), et peut-être Robert de

---

(43) En 1175, Geoffroi, envoyé en Bretagne pour récupérer les châteaux, n'avait que dix-sept ans. On peut bien supposer que Rolland de Dinan, assigné par le roi pour l'accompagner, fut en grande partie responsable du succès de la mission (cf. *Gesta regis Henrici*, I, 83, 101 ; Torigni, *Chronica*, *sub anno*).

(44) « Veniens itaque idem Haimo ante comitem Gaufridum... et ante Rollandum de Dinam, in eorum presentia recognovit... » (1182, Morice, *Preuves*, I, 694).

(45) « Volo eciam et precipio quod si predicti canonici habeant... cum hermitagio prenotato terram de mea foresta ad unam carrucham sicut Radulfus Filgeriis tunc temporis Britannie senescallus et servientes mei dividerunt... ». Oheix, *Sénéchaux*, page 17, note 4.

(46) On ne sait presque rien de la gestion des finances du duché pendant ces années, sauf que les revenus appartenaient au roi Henri. Par analogie avec les sénéchaux contemporains de Normandie et d'Anjou, le sénéchal de Bretagne a dû avoir de grandes responsabilités en cette matière.

(47) Voir, par exemple, l'histoire des reliques de saint Petrock (*Gesta regis Henrici*, I, 178-80 ; Houedene, *Chronica*, II, 136.

(48) Morice, *Preuves*, I, 659, 672.

(49) *Ibid.*, 716 ; Delisle-Berger, *Recueil, Introduction*, page 350.

(50) Morice, *Preuves*, I, 687, 689.

(51) *Ibid.*, 713.

(52) De la Borderie, *Recueil d'actes inédits*, pages 123-4 ; *Cart. de Saint-Georges de Rennes*, pages 187-8, 196-7.

(53) *Supra* note 24.

Doniol (54), Eudes, fils d'Erneis (1185) (55), et Maurice de Liré (1185) (56). On n'a que les noms de Merian, fils de Guihon, bailli de Tréguier vers 1199 (57), ou de Henri, fils de Henri, « bailli » de Cornouaille vers 1184 (58). Une lettre de la duchesse Constance (1190 ou 1196) mentionne « son sénéchal de Broërec », sans lui donner un nom (59). C'est peut-être un certain « Rodaudus filius Deriani », sénéchal de Broërec entre 1192 et 1201, ou peut-être ce Rodaudus fût-il son successeur (60). Sans doute, des recherches ultérieures étendront le catalogue.

A ce qu'il semble, les ressorts de ces sénéchaux régionaux étaient les comtés bretons, lesquels, au XII° siècle, étaient presque tous dans les mains de ceux qui s'intitulaient ducs de Bretagne. S'il en est ainsi, il est bien probable qu'ils furent les successeurs des sénéchaux des anciens comtes, d'abord domestiques puis territoriaux, avec le cumul des comtés par les ducs. Et, en fait, nous trouvons un « sénéchal de Rennes nommé Mainfinit » sous le comte de Rennes, Geoffroi Grenonat (61), et ce fut sans doute le même personnage que le « Mainfinit, sénéchal du comte de Bretagne, Alain » (Fergent) (62) ; un « Guillaume mon sénéchal de Rennes » (c'est-à-dire du duc Conan III), qui fut certainement le même que le « Guillaume sénéchal de Rennes » (63) et proba-

----

(54) Delisle-Berger, *Recueil, Introduction,* page 413 ; Oheix, *Sénéchaux,* 33, 193-5 ; *vide infra,* note 68.

(55) Delisle-Berger, *Recueil, Introduction,* 367.

(56) Morice, *Preuves,* I, 707.

(57) *Ibid.,* 773.

(58) Oheix, *Sénéchaux,* 186 ; P. Le Duc (publ. par R.-F. Le Men), *Histoire de l'abbaye de Sainte-Croix de Quimperlé,* page 602.

(59) Oheix, *Sénéchaux,* 34, 182 ; L. Rosenzweig, *Cartulaire du Morbihan* (1893-5), n° 231. La date est indiquée par la référence à Pierre Bertin, sénéchal de Poitou.

(60) Oheix, *Sénéchaux,* 34, 182. Une charte d'un Hamon de l'Epine (1182) mentionne Etienne Goiun, alors sénéchal du Poulet (Morice, *Preuves,* I, 694-5), mais ce fut vraisemblablement un sénéchal seigneurial, car le Poulet ne figure pas parmi les baillies du XIII° siècle, à moins qu'elle ne fût une « proto-baillie » qui n'a pas durée.

(61) « Siniscaldo Redonensi nomine Mainfinito », Morice, *Preuves,* I, 428 ; Oheix, *Sénéchaux,* 6, 10. Cf. « Agaat, Mainfeni filius dapiferi Redonensis », Morice, *Preuves,* I, 566 ; Oheix, *Sénéchaux,* 8 (note 3), 10.

(62) « Mainfinitus senescallus comitis Britanniae Alani », Morice, *Preuves,* I, 484 ; Oheix, *Sénéchaux,* 8.

(63) « Willelmus dapifer meus Redonensis ... prescriptus Willelmus Redonensis dapifer », Morice, *Preuves,* I, 574-5.

blement que le « Guillaume sénéchal du comte » (Alain Fergent)
(64), le « Guillaume sénéchal de Rennes » dans une charte de
Conan III (65) et le « Guillaume sénéchal » qui se trouve dans
les chartes des ducs Alain Fergent et Conan III (66). « Gui
sénéchal de Rennes » fut peut-être le successeur de ce Guillaume
sous le duc Conan IV (67) ; mais ce qui est important, c'est qu'il
fut témoin, comme tel, d'un document émis par « Guillaume de
Lanvallay, sénéchal de Rennes » (68). On a interprété ce document
comme preuve qu'il pouvait y avoir deux sénéchaux à la fois dans
une seule sénéchaussée. Il est plus probable, peut-être, que
Guillaume de Lanvallay, fonctionnant au nom du roi Henri, fut le
successeur de Gui, le sénéchal de Rennes pour Conan IV, et qu'il
s'est produit une succession sans violence et que Gui garda son
titre « en courtoisie ». Cette évolution, s'il en fut ainsi, de sénéchal
domestique à sénéchal territorial, officier permanent du duc dans
une circonscription traditionnelle, peut être mis en comparaison
avec ce qui arriva en Anjou quand le comte Geoffroi Plantegenêt
maîtrisa la Normandie en 1144, et le sénéchal du comte d'Anjou
devint le sénéchal d'Anjou à côté du sénéchal ou justicier de
Normandie ; ou ce qui s'est arrivé un peu plus tôt quand le duc
Louis d'Aquitaine monta sur le trône de France sous le nom
de Louis VII et que le « sénéchal du comte » en Aquitaine devint
le sénéchal d'Aquitaine à côté du sénéchal du royaume (69). De

(64) « Willelmus siniscallus comitis », Morice, *Preuves*, I, 470 ; Oheix,
Sénéchaux, 9 (note 3), 11 (note 2).

(65) Oheix, *Sénéchaux*, 11 (note 1).

(66) Morice, *Preuves*, I, 507 ; de la Borderie, *Recueil d'actes inédits*,
pages 90-91 (n° XXXI bis). Son contemporain, « Hugo Redonensis dapifer »,
cité par Oheix (*Sénéchaux*, 11, note 2 ; Morice, *Preuves*, I, 525, ne reproduit
le document qu'en partie), fut assurément le sénéchal de l'évêque de Rennes
(Morice, *Preuves*, I, 524, 438).

(67) « Guidone dapifero de Redon », Morice, *Preuves*, I, 662 (cf. Clay,
Honour of Richmond, I, page 51, n° 51) ; sans doute le même que « Guido
senescallus » ou « dapifer » (Morice, *Preuves*, I, 584, 617, 632 ; Clay,
op. cit., pages 45-6, n° 44).

(68) « Guillelmus de Lanvallei, senescallus Redoniae, notum facit quod
... Testibus ... et Guidone senescallo de Redonis » (Morice, *Preuves*, I, 659).
Il est plus difficile d'interpréter ainsi la charte citée par Delisle : « Petrus
filius Guidonis et Robertus de Doniol, senescalli domini Regis Angl' tunc
Nannet' » (Delisle-Berger, *Recueil, Introduction*, 413) ; mais ce n'est pas
tout à fait impossible. Furent-ils sénéchaux du roi « à Nantes » ou « de
Nantes » ? En tout cas, ce fut Pierre, fils de Gui, qui mit son sceau à la
charte. Cf. Oheix, *Sénéchaux*, 33 (note 1).

(69) Provisoirement, voir J. Le Patourel, « The Plantagenet Dominions »,
History, tome 50 (1965), page 297. Voir *supra* VIII.

plus, on peut en déduire que le système Plantegenêt de sénéchaux régionaux en Bretagne fut une adaptation et un développement d'une institution pré-existante plus qu'une innovation, et qu'il n'y fut pas imposé brutalement. C'est tout à fait caractéristique de leur politique partout.

Ces sénéchaux régionaux fonctionnaient sous l'autorité directe du roi, paraît-il, au moins pendant la décennie 1171-1181. Leurs charges furent à la fois judiciaires et exécutives. Guillaume de Lanvallay et Robert de Lanvallay présidèrent successivement « la cour du roi à Rennes » (70). Le sénéchal sans nom de Broërec fut président d'une cour de la duchesse Constance (71). Le duc Geoffroi commanda à Renaud Boterel, son sénéchal, et à tous ses sénéchaux, prévôts, voyers et baillis en Bretagne, de rétablir le monastère de Lehon dans toutes ses possessions (72). Malheureusement, on n'a trouvé aucune indication, à cette époque, des relations entre ces sénéchaux régionaux et le sénéchal de Bretagne.

Il se peut, d'ailleurs, que les Plantegenêt aient étendu et développé l'usage de l'enquête judiciaire, inauguré une législation ducale, remplacé le droit de bris par l'institution des « brefs de Bretagne » (73). Mais ce qui importe, c'est que la Bretagne fut incorporée dans le gouvernement de l'empire angevin pendant trente ans (74) ; peu de temps, il est vrai, mais assez pour révéler des possibilités de développement des institutions et du gouvernement, un développement nécessité surtout par la pluralité même des principautés qui se trouvaient sous la gouvernance des rois angevins.

Cette incorporation se voit dans l'unification définitive du duché ; dans la position du duc Geoffroi, comparable à celle de

---

(70) « Guillelmus de Lanvallei, senescallus Redoniae notum facit quod ... in curia domini regis Redoniae ... » (Morice, *Preuves*, I, 659) ; « Clamantibus... monachis ad curiam domini regis apud Redones, facta est coram nobis (sc. Robertus de Lanvalai senescallus Redonensis) in curia domini regis inter praedictas partes hujusmodi concordia » (*ibid.*, 716).

(71) *Supra* note 59.

(72) Morice, *Preuves*, I, 689.

(73) Pocquet du Haut-Jussé, « Les Plantagenets et la Bretagne », *Annales de Bretagne*, LIII (1946), 21-2, 23-5.

(74) C'est-à-dire depuis 1171 jusqu'à la mort de la duchesse Constance **en** 1201 ; car à plusieurs égards, on peut considérer le règne de Constance comme un prolongement de celui du duc Geoffroi.

ses frères dans leurs principautés, mais pour nous assez difficile
à catégoriser ; dans l'institution d'un sénéchal de Bretagne, dont
nous savons assez pour nous convaincre qu'il fut l'analogue
exact du grand justicier d'Angleterre et des sénéchaux contemporains de Normandie, d'Anjou et d'Aquitaine, et par le caractère
de son office et par ses fonctions. Les sénéchaux régionaux furent
aussi caractéristiques du gouvernement angevin par leur évolution,
par leur ressemblance avec les baillis de Normandie et parce
qu'ils représentaient une réforme de l'administration telle que les
souverains angevins l'ont pratiquée un peu partout dans leurs
terres, la réforme des sheriffs en Angleterre, l'institution des baillis
en Normandie, la pluralité des sénéchaux en Aquitaine.

Mais que la Bretagne fut, pour le temps, incorporée dans le
gouvernement de l'empire angevin dans son ensemble, se voit
surtout par le caractère des hommes employés par le roi Henri
et son fils dans l'administration du duché. Ils furent de deux
sortes : d'une part, des seigneurs importants, tels Raoul de
Fougères, Rolland de Dinan, Maurice de Craon, Alain de Dinan,
comparables à Richard, earl of Leicester, ou Geoffroi, fils de
Pierre, earl of Essex, justiciers d'Angleterre ; Robert du Neubourg,
sénéchal de Normandie ; Raoul de Faye, sénéchal d'Aquitaine ;
d'autre part, des hommes de rang plus modeste, tels Guillaume,
fils d'Hamon, et les sénéchaux régionaux, membres d'une classe
ou groupe administratif et presque professionnel, que le roi pouvait
employer n'importe où dans son vaste empire, comme par exemple
Guillaume, fils de Raoul, sénéchal de Normandie, ou Gautier de
Coutances, archevêque de Rouen et justicier d'Angleterre, anglais
d'origine tous les deux et au service du roi des deux côtés de la
Manche (75).

Prenons d'abord les grands seigneurs. Rolland de Dinan et
Raoul (II) de Fougères furent, tous les deux, des barons bretons
importants, seigneurs de vastes fiefs près de la frontière normande,
mais qui avaient aussi des intérêts considérables en Normandie et
en Angleterre. Les terres principales de Rolland de Dinan se
trouvaient dans la région de Saint-Malo - Dinan - Bécherel où il
possédait des châteaux qui pouvaient résister au roi Henri lui-même
en 1168 (76) ; mais il avait aussi des terres en Angleterre et des

---

(75) Delisle-Berger, *Recueil, Introduction,* 106-13, 467, 481-3.

(76) *Ibid.,* 453-4 ; de la Borderie, *Histoire de Bretagne,* III (1899), 64-5.

intérêts en Normandie (77). Il accepta Conan comme duc en 1156, paraît-il, mais s'opposa à Henri entre 1160 et 1168 (78). Réconcilié avec le roi en 1169 (79), loyal pendant la grande révolte de 1173-1174, il put être nommé « procureur » ou « justicier » de Bretagne en 1175. Raoul de Fougères était un grand seigneur trans-frontalier encore plus que Raoul de Dinan. Depuis longtemps, sa famille avait eu des possessions dans l'Avranchin (elle fournissait des fondateurs et des bienfaiteurs à l'abbaye normande de Savigny) (80) et son grand-père (Raoul I de Fougères) avait profité de la conquête normande de l'Angleterre pour gagner des terres au-delà de la Manche (81). Son père Henri s'était marié à Olive, fille d'Etienne de Penthièvre ; et en conséquence de ce mariage, Raoul II était cousin du duc Conan IV, parent de la famille de Saint-Jean dans l'Avranchin et possesseur d'un intérêt dans le « manor » de Long Benington dans le Lincolnshire (82). Naturellement, il aida Conan à gagner la Bretagne en 1156 (83) ; mais après la mort de Jean, seigneur de Dol-Combourg, en 1162, en laissant la tutelle de sa fille et sa seigneurie dans les mains de notre Raoul, des démêlés survinrent entre lui et le roi, d'où la mainmise d'Henri sur la tour de Dol (1162) et les châteaux de Combourg (1164) et de Fougères même (1166) (84), et la position de Raoul à la tête des rebelles

---

(77) Pour l'Angleterre, voir les « Pipe Rolls » du règne de Henri II, *passim* (Pipe Roll Society, I-XXXVIII, 1884-1925). D'après eux, il mourut vers 1189. Pour la Normandie, *Magni Rotuli Scaccarii Normanniae*, ed. T. Stapleton (1840-44), II, pages XLVI-XLVII.

(78) Morice, *Preuves*, I, 634 ; Clay, *Honour of Richmond*, I, pages 45, 47, 48, 49 ; Torigni, *Chronica, sub anno* 1168 ; Pipe Rolls, 7, 14-16 Henry II (Pipe Roll Society, IV, XII, XIII, XV, 1885, 1890-92).

(79) Torigni, *Chronica, sub anno* 1173 ; Pipe Rolls, *ut supra* note 78.

(80) *Infra* note 82.

(81) Il se trouve parmi les « tenants-in-chief » dans le Domesday Book (H. Ellis, *General Introduction to Domesday Book* (1833, ré-imp. 1971), I, 418 ; II, 316, s.v. FELGERES, FELGERIS, Rad. de). Quelques-unes de ses propriétés, en 1086, peuvent être identifiées avec celles de son petit-fils pendant le règne de Henri II.

(82) De la Borderie, *Histoire de Bretagne*, III, 57 ; Delisle-Berger, *Recueil, Introduction*, 416-7 ; L. Delisle, « Digest of Two Letters illustrative of the family of Clémence, Countess of Chester », *Journal of the British Archaeological Association*, VII (1851-2), 123-31 ; *supra* note 4 ; Torigni, *Chronica*, éd. Delisle, II, 298 ; Clay, *Honour of Richmond*, pages 69, 89.

(83) Torigni, *Chronica, sub anno* 1156. Cf. Morice, *Preuves*, I, 631.

(84) Torigni, *Chronica, sub annis*.

bretons en 1173 (85). Ses terres anglaises furent prises « dans la main du roi » pendant la révolte et il lui fallut, paraît-il, conclure un traité particulier avec le roi pour rentrer en grâce (86). Ils avaient donc, Rolland de Dinan et Raoul de Fougères, tous les deux, tant de puissance et d'influence en Bretagne que le roi dut les manœuvrer, même les employer dans son gouvernement ; mais leurs intérêts hors du duché, surtout en Angleterre, lui donnaient un moyen de les discipliner, s'il en était besoin.

Guillaume, fils de Hamon, et Guillaume de Lanvallay sont les exemples de la deuxième catégorie d'officiers royaux en Bretagne que nous connaissons le mieux. Le premier était un chevalier, normand d'origine, paraît-il, avec des terres dans le Cotentin et à Jersey suffisamment étendues pour qu'il soit réputé le fondateur, « avec le conseil et avec l'aide du seigneur roi », de l'abbaye de Saint-Hélier. Il avait aussi des terres en Angleterre et en Écosse même (87). Il s'associa avec Henri en 1149 au plus tard, et ses attestations aux chartes ducales et royales jusqu'à 1166 donnent l'impression qu'il suivit la cour dans ses déplacements presque sans interruption et dans tous les pays de l'empire angevin (88). Entre 1166 et sa mort en 1172 (89), il n'est témoin que dans deux ou trois chartes royales ; on peut donc supposer qu'il s'occupait à ses devoirs comme sénéchal de Nantes et puis de Bretagne. Guillaume de Lanvallay, s'il tirait son nom de Lanvallay près de Dinan, était Breton au moins d'origine. Il figure comme témoin dans les chartes du roi Henri entre 1155 et 1180 en Angleterre, en Normandie et en Anjou (90) ; il avait des terres en Angleterre

---

(85) *Ibid.*, 1173 ; *Gesta regis Henrici,* I, 47, 56-8.

(86) Pipe Rolls, 19-21 Henry II (Pipe Roll Society, XIX-XXII, 1895-7) ; Delisle-Berger, *Recueil,* II, pages 20, 181.

(87) *Supra* notes 24, 37 ; Torigni, *Chronica, sub anno* 1185 (cf. ed. Delisle, II, 31, note 3, 134, note 1) ; *Cartulaire des Iles Normandes* (La Société Jersiaise, Jersey, 1924), pages 307-25 ; Clay, *Honour of Richmond,* I, page 80 ; Pipe Rolls, 2-23 Henry II (Pipe Rolls, 2, 3, 4, Henry II, éd. J. Hunter ; Pipe Roll Society, I-XXVI, 1884-1908).

(88) *Regesta Regum Anglo-Normannorum,* III (edd. H.A. Cronne et R.H.C. Davis, 1968), n° 703 et *passim ;* Delisle-Berger, *Recueil,* I, *passim ; Introduction,* 479.

(89) *Supra* note 37.

(90) Delisle-Berger, *Recueil, passim ; Introduction,* 486-7 ; R.W. Eyton, *Court, Household, and Itinerary of King Henry II* (1878), *passim* (index, s.v. « Lanval »).

et y fut au service du roi comme gardien du très important château de Winchester où se trouvait le trésor principal de l'Angleterre (1172-1175), et comme juge itinérant avec Thomas Basset en quatorze comtés (1175) (91). Robert de Lanvallay, son successeur présumé comme sénéchal de Rennes, fut peut-être son frère (un fils s'appela Guillaume) (92), mais je n'ai trouvé aucun renseignement sur lui.

Pierre, fils de Gui, et Eudes, fils d'Erneis, sénéchaux successifs de Nantes, sont moins connus. Le premier fut un sénéchal de l'hôtel du roi Henri et peut-être de son fils, Henri le Jeune (93). Il se trouve parmi les témoins des chartes pour la plupart données en Normandie et Anjou (94), dans une (« vers 1161 ») en qualité de « gardien de la Tour du Mans » — associé, soit dit en passant, avec Guillaume, fils d'Hamon, et Guillaume de Lanvallay (95). Guillaume, fils d'Erneis, un baron de la Haute-Normandie, avait des terres et des intérêts en Angleterre qu'il ne perdit que momentanément pendant la révolte de 1173-1174 (97). Renaud Boterel est un peu à part. Breton d'origine, avec ses possessions majeures en Bretagne, il était membre d'une famille établie depuis 1139 parmi les tenanciers de l'honneur de Richmond en Angleterre (98). Puisqu'il ne figure pas comme témoin dans les chartes du roi Henri, semble-t-il, mais au contraire se trouve parmi les témoins de quatre chartes du duc Conan et une de la duchesse Berthe, dont quatre concernent Richmond (99), il est possible qu'il

---

(91) I.J. Sanders, *English Baronies* (1960), 92 ; *Pleas before the King or his Justices,* ed. D.M. Stenton, III (Selden Society, London, LXXXIII, 1967), pages LII, LVI ; Pipe Rolls, 18-21 Henry II (Pipe Roll Society, XVIII-XXII, 1894-7) et *passim.*

(92) Pipe Rolls (e.g. 34 Henry II, Pipe Roll Society, XXXVIII, 1925, page 156) ; Delisle-Berger, *Recueil, Introduction,* pages 350, 442, 487.

(93) Delisle-Berger, *Recueil,* II, page 33 ; *Introduction,* 259-61.

(94) Delisle-Berger, *Recueil, passim.*

(95) *Ibid.,* I, page 334 ; *Introduction,* 413.

(96) *Ibid., Introduction,* 367.

(97) Delisle-Berger, *Recueil,* II, page 21 ; *Introduction,* 367 ; *Gesta regis Henrici,* I, 46 ; Pipe Rolls, 14, 23, 29, 33, 34 Henry II, 2-6 Ric. I (Pipe Roll Society, XII, XXVI, XXXII, XXXVII, XXXVIII ; N.S., I-IV ; 1890, 1905, 1911-28). Il est mort vers 1193.

(98) Clay, *Honour of Richmond,* I, pages 51-3.

(99) *Ibid.,* pages 34-5, 55, 58, 71.

ait été employé dans l'administration de l'honneur ou dans l'hôtel de Conan, avant son apparition, une fois seulement, comme sénéchal de Rennes sous le duc Geoffroi (1181-1182) (100).

Ce qui est d'une importance capitale, d'ailleurs, c'est qu'il ne se produisit pas de rupture administrative à la mort de Geoffroi en 1186. La duchesse Constance ne remplaça pas Raoul de Fougères immédiatement comme sénéchal de Bretagne (101) ; et ses successeurs, qu'ils aient été nommés par la duchesse Constance ou par le roi, furent Maurice de Craon et Alain de Dinan. Maurice était le chef d'une grande famille baroniale d'Anjou, apparentée à la famille de Craon en Angleterre (102). Il était un loyal serviteur des rois Henri et Richard jusqu'à sa mort en 1196, surtout pendant la révolte de 1173-1174. Alain de Vitré fut l'héritier de Rolland de Dinan, duquel il prit et le nom « de Dinan » et les intérêts en Normandie et en Angleterre (103). Tous les deux furent dans la tradition d'administration angevine ; et si Maurice de Craon fût vraiment nommé par Constance, il est assez remarquable qu'elle ait choisi un homme si complètement identifié avec la royauté angevine. On sait que le système de sénéchaux régionaux, chacun régissant ce qui devenait une « baillie », fut continué et développé par les ducs bretons du XIII⁰ siècle (104). Il est vrai que l'office de sénéchal de Bretagne s'éteignit vers les années 1240 (105) ; mais, à cette époque, il y

---

(100) Morice, *Preuves*, ɪ, 687 ; cf. 689, 713.

(101) De la Borderie, *Recueil d'actes inédits,* pages 134-5 ; Oheix, *Sénéchaux,* 17, note 4.

(102) L.C. Loyd, *The Origins of some Anglo-Norman Families* (Harleian Society, ᴄɪɪɪ, Leeds, 1951), page 34 ; *Sir Christopher Hatton's Book of Seals* (edd. L.C. Loyd et D.M. Stenton, 1950), 223-4 ; Ralph « de Diceto », « Ymagines Historiarum », *Opera Historica,* ed. W. Stubbs (Rolls Series, 1876), ɪ, 380 ; « Annales de Saint-Aubin », *Recueil d'Annales angevines et vendômoises,* publ. L. Halphen (1903), 38. Il y avait deux « Maurice de Craon » contemporains, l'un de la branche anglaise de la famille de Craon, l'autre la branche angevine. En raison de la confusion qu'il en résulte, il est impossible de savoir si le Maurice de Craon, sénéchal de Bretagne, qui fut presque certainement de la branche angevine (Bertrand de Broussillon, *La maison de Craon, 1050-1480* (1893) ; J. Boussard, *Le comté d'Anjou sous Henri Plantegenêt et ses fils* (1938)), avait des intérêts directs en Angleterre.

(103) Torigni, *Chronica,* ed. Delisle, ɪɪ, 46 ; Pipe Roll, 33 Henry II (Pipe Roll Society, xxxvɪɪ, 1915), page 189.

(104) Oheix, *Sénéchaux,* 22-88.

(105) *Ibid.,* 20-22.

avait un duc de Bretagne en résidence, donc un sénéchal « vice-duc » n'était plus indispensable. Car le trait essentiel des grands sénéchaux angevins du XII° siècle, c'est qu'ils furent des vice-rois, des lieutenants d'un prince qui fut à la fois duc de Normandie, duc d'Aquitaine, comte d'Anjou, en substance duc de Bretagne, aussi bien que roi d'Angleterre, qu'un de ses fils fût en nom roi, duc ou comte au même temps ou non, et qui n'avait pas la possibilité de se trouver dans toutes ses terres simultanément. Ces conditions ne s'appliquaient plus à la Bretagne pendant le XIII° siècle ; mais l'essentiel de l'œuvre d'Henri II Plantegenêt y subsista.

GUILLAUME FILS HAMON,
PREMIER SÉNÉCHAL DE BRETAGNE

Guillaume fils Hamon appartenait à cette catégorie de seigneurs de moyenne importance dans laquelle Henri II Plantagenêt avait trouvé un grand nombre de ses ministres. Ses terres dans le Cotentin et dans l'ile de Jersey étaient probablement de son patrimoine. Il possédait des terres en Angleterre (acquisitions ou héritages, on ne sait pas); peut-être avait-il des intérêts en Bretagne et même en Ecosse. Ce n'était pas là une grosse fortune; mais les éléments en furent distribués géographiquement d'une façon tout à fait caractéristique de l'empire Plantagenêt et elle lui donna la possibilité de fonder l'abbaye de Saint-Hélier à Jersey «avec le conseil et avec l'aide du seigneur roi». Son nom se trouve régulièrement parmi les témoins dans les chartes d'Henri II depuis 1149 jusqu'à sa mort, survenue presque certainement en novembre 1172. Ses fonctions à la cour du roi ne se précisent qu'en 1166 et 1169, quand il se qualifie «sénéchal de Nantes», tandis qu'Henri était en possession du comté de Nantes mais exerçait seulement les droits d'un suzerain impérieux ailleurs dans le duché; et il est désigné comme «sénéchal de Bretagne» en 1171-1172 aussitôt après la mort du duc Conan IV («le Petit») et dès que Henri s'est emparé du duché tout entier.

Henri avait pu préparer cette mainmise sur la Bretagne parce que Conan était son vassal en tant que comte de Richmond et seigneur de l'immense «honneur» de Richmond en Angleterre qu'il avait hérité de son père, le comte Alain, premier mari de sa mère la duchesse Berthe. Cette vassalité de Conan avait donné à Henri les moyens de revivifier et renforcer les vielles prétentions des ducs de Normandie à l'hommage des ducs de Bretagne, prétentions reconnues formellement, aux dires du chroniqueur Orderic Vital, par le roi de France en 1113. Il est possible que Guillaume fils Hamon ait été accrédité à la cour du duc Conan pendant les années 1160 pour y représenter le roi Henri et pour veiller à ses intérêts en Bretagne. Mais son avancement de l'office de sénéchal de Nantes à celui de sénéchal de Bretagne, en synchronisation exacte avec l'élargissement de la domination d'Henri II en Bretagne, du comté de Nantes à la totalité du duché, marque et en quelque sorte symbolise deux événements très importants en l'histoire de Bretagne. 1) En tant que sénéchal de Bretagne, il était évidemment de pair avec les sénéchaux d'Anjou et d'Aquitaine, les sénéchaux ou justiciers de Normandie et les grands justiciers d'Angleterre. La Bretagne fut ainsi intégrée dans la structure du gouvernement de l'empire Plantagenêt — au moins jusqu'à la mort du quatrième fils d'Henri, Geoffroi, en 1186, celui auquel le roi avait donné le titre de duc de Bretagne avec l'héritage de sa femme, Constance, fille et héritière unique de Conan. 2) Plus important, il ne pouvait y avoir qu'un sénéchal de Bretagne; donc le gouvernement de la Bretagne reçut une unité dont il n'avait pas joui depuis le temps d'Alain le Grand, mort en 907. C'était là l'inauguration de la grande principauté que fut la Bretagne aux XIIIᵉ–XIVᵉ siècles.

GUILLAUME FILS RAOUL,
SÉNÉCHAL DE NORMANDIE, 1178-1200

Guillaume Fils Raoul fut nommé sénéchal de Normandie en 1178, et il resta en fonctions jusqu'en 1200. Ces 22 ans d'activité continue, et aussi sans doute sa personnalité, établirent l'office dans sa forme classique. D'après les documents qui concernent Guillaume expressément, le sénéchal remplaça le roi chaque fois que ce dernier fut absent du duché et inaccessible, ou presque, comme le fut Richard Coeur-de-Lion durant sa croisade et sa captivité en Allemagne. Quand le roi fut absent du duché mais accessible (en Angleterre par example ou Aquitaine), le sénéchal mit en exécution les ordres qu'il reçut de lui; mais le sénéchal put lui-même exercer presque tous les pouvoirs royaux de sa propre autorité. Même quand le roi et sa cour furent présents dans le duché, le sénéchal était toujours le chef de l'administration ducale. Sauf peut-être en cas d'urgence extrême, il commandait les forces militaires du roi dans le duché, et y contrôlait ses châteaux et ses garnisons. Il présidait l'échiquier des comptes et des plaids, aussi bien que les assises qui se tinrent en divers lieux à travers le duché. En matière de finance, en plus de ses responsabilités quand les barons de l'échiquier siégeaient pour vérifier les comptes, il contrôlait le mouvement des fonds d'un trésor royal à un autre, retirait de l'argent en grosses sommes pour ses besoins administratifs ou militaires et présentait son compte à l'échiquier, et, presque certainement, autorisait lui-même, en l'absence du roi, des versements. En matière judiciaire, l'auteur de la première partie du Très Ancien Coutumier le représente comme un juge autoritaire, qui put modifier la coutume et la procédure à son gré.[1] Pour être à même de remplir tous ces devoirs multiples, le sénéchal disposait d'un nombre de clercs, détachés, tout comme les clercs du grand justicier anglais, du personnel de la chancellerie royale itinérante. Ces clercs rédigèrent les brefs administratifs et judiciaires émis par le sénéchal, quelquefois au nom du roi, quelquefois à son propre nom[2]; et on ne peut pas douter qu'il pût dicter, dans une certaine mesure du moins, les formules de ces brefs — d'où, sans doute, les différences de détail entre les brefs judiciaires anglais et normands tels qu'ils se présentent dans le *Tractatus* de Glanville et le Très Ancien Coutumier.

Etant donné la part personnelle de Guillaume Fils Raoul dans l'évolution de l'administration normande et aussi de la Coutume, il est intéressant de constater qu'il appartenait à une famille baroniale d'importance mineure établie en Angleterre, dans le Derbyshire et probablement dès la Conquête, et que toute sa formation professionelle eut lieu en Angleterre. Il fut sheriff de Nottinghamshire et de Derbyshire entre 1170 and 1180, ce que lui donna connaissance des pratiques de l'échiquier anglais; il se trouva parmi les justiciers itinérants et ceux de la *Curia Regis* à partir de 1172; il tint une enquête sur la condition des domaines du roi en Angleterre et il fut membre d'une Commission pour imposer une taille sur ces domaines — les mêmes activités qu'il reprit en Normandie après 1178. Mais cela ne veut pas dire qu'il fut l'instrument d'un transfert d'institutions royales de l'Angleterre en Normandie. Bien plutôt, il fut membre d'un groupe de ministres, d'origine en général assez modeste, mais souvent ayant des intérêts dans plus d'un pays de l'empire Plantagenêt, que le roi employait également dans plus d'une de ses terres (un autre exemple est Guillaume Fils Hamon[3]); et bien qu'ils dussent respecter les coutumes originales de chaque pays, une assimilation dans la pratique était certainement à attendre. Ainsi pour une meilleure compréhension de l'évolution et du gouvernement de l'empire Plantagenêt, ce qu'il nous faut d'urgence, c'est une «prosopographie» de la classe administrative de cet empire; ce que l'on pourrait rédiger sans beaucoup de difficulté, mais pas en un jour.

---

1   *T.A.C.* (éd. Tardif), texte latin, chap. LX, LXI, LXII, LXIV, LXV..

2   *Ibid.*, chap. XXV. Cf. H.G. Richardson, *Memoranda Roll, 1 John*, (Pipe Roll Soc., 1943), Introduction, pp. lxxv-lxvii.

3   See above pp. 117-18.

THE ORIGINS OF
THE HUNDRED YEARS WAR

THE series of conflicts between the kings of France and of England that historians have agreed to call the 'Hundred Years War' was of such importance in the history of the two countries that a good deal has naturally been written on the causes of so prodigious a conflict. Dr Templeman[1] in England, Professor Wolff[2] in France and Professor Cuttino in the United States[3] have each, in recent years, published papers which survey the literature on the origins of the war and make it unnecessary to attempt any such survey here. All three, and other recent writers also,[4] are broadly in agreement that the root cause of the trouble lay in the position of King Edward III, sovereign[5] in his kingdom of England, a vassal of the king of France in his duchy of Aquitaine.[6] There are different nuances in their interpretations, as one would expect; Professor Wolff in particular addresses himself specifically to the problem presented by the fact that a relationship which appeared natural and reasonable in the time of St Louis and King Henry III proved impossible in the time of King Edward III and King Philip VI, a matter which certainly needs to be explained. Historians also seem to be mostly agreed that Edward III's claim to the throne of France was secondary, and was, indeed, little more than a tactical device for pursuing other aims. But there are really two quite distinct questions in this old problem of the origins of the Hundred Years War: What were the origins of the war that started in 1337? and, why was that war a 'Hundred Years' war? These two questions should be tackled separately.

I

By an order dated 24 May 1337, King Philip VI commanded his seneschal of Périgord and his bailli of Amiens, respectively, to take the duchy of Aquitaine and the county of Ponthieu into his hand.[7] The order stated that there had been long and serious discussion in the Council before the decision to do this had been reached; and while it implied that there were several reasons for the decision, the only reason stated explicitly was that the 'king of England, duke of Aquitaine, peer of France, count of Ponthieu' (i.e. King Edward III), who was the liegeman of the king of France by reason of the duchy, peerage and county, had received and given aid to Robert of Artois, who was the 'capital enemy' of the king of France and who had been banished from the kingdom 'for many crimes'. To harbour such a man was contrary to Edward's obligations as a liege vassal by universal feudal custom; and it entailed the penalty of 'commise', that is, the confiscation of his fiefs. Since the sanction, in this case, involved taking possession of territories like Aquitaine and Ponthieu, and such action would certainly be resisted, it meant war; and as French troops immediately overran Ponthieu, attacked (and for a while occupied) the Channel Islands and invaded Edward's lands in Aquitaine in execution of the king's order, these operations do indeed mark the beginning of the Hundred Years War. It is true that both sides had been fearing an outbreak for some time; that tension between them had been rising to the point where an explosion seemed very likely and that each side had been making preparations that could be considered provocative by the other; it is even possible that Edward III might have invaded France at some point even if Gascony had not been attacked; nevertheless the spark which did in fact light the fuse was the action of the king of France when he put into execution the sentence of confiscation. This was a feudal procedure, initiated for feudal reasons; it was based upon the feudal relationship between the two kings that existed because Edward III held his duchy of Aquitaine and his county of Ponthieu as a liege vassal of the king of France and as a peer of France.

In the form which it took in 1337, this feudal relationship had been created by the treaty of Paris of 1259.[8] That treaty had been intended to bring to an end the state of war that had existed more or less continuously since the accession of King Philip Augustus in 1180, and, in a positive sense, to create conditions of peace and justice for the future. As such treaties go, it was not unsuccessful. It did in fact keep the peace for thirty-five years and established a relationship which at least two successive kings of England and three successive kings of France thought was workable. By this treaty King Louis IX gave to King Henry III the rights which he had, as king of France, in the three dioceses of Limoges, Cahors and Périgueux, together with similar rights in the Agenais, southern Quercy (i.e. the part of the diocese of Cahors then held by the king's brother Alphonse de Poitiers) and the part of Saintonge to the south of the river Charente if certain conditions were fulfilled in the future. He also recognised King Henry's right to those parts of the kingdom of France of which he was at that moment in effective possession, that is, some fragments of the duchy of Aquitaine and certain off-shore islands (in practice, Oléron and the Channel Islands). In return, King Henry abandoned his rights in Normandy, in Anjou, Maine and Touraine and in Poitou,[9] and agreed to hold not only what he had acquired by the treaty, but what he had possessed in the kingdom of France at the time when the treaty was being negotiated, by liege homage and as a peer of France.

Whatever the relationship between the two kings had been before the wars which this treaty brought to an end (a matter which will be discussed later), their relationship from this point onward was quite clearly defined. King Henry had been given an opportunity to reconstruct the ancient duchy of Aquitaine for himself, and to hold securely the Channel Islands and Oléron which, if small in extent, were of very great importance to his communications with Bordeaux, now quite clearly the capital and economic centre of his duchy of Aquitaine. But these lands were specifically declared, in the treaty, to be part of the kingdom of France, and they could therefore only be held by King Henry and his successors under the overriding sovereignty, as it was then understood, of the king of France. This applied to the Channel Islands and to the county of Ponthieu (when King Edward I acquired it in 1279) as well as to the duchy of Aquitaine. Moreover, the liege homage which the king of England owed for these lands, was the most binding and comprehensive form of homage. Originally, there had been but one kind of homage, and it created an exclusive relationship between a vassal and his lord; but in course of time, as men placed more emphasis on the land for which a vassal did homage than upon the personal relationship which homage created, vassals began to hold land of several lords; and when that happened, naturally, the relationship between vassal and lord could no longer be exclusive. Liege homage had then been devised as a kind of 'priority' homage, the obligations of which took precedence over any other such obligations that the vassal might have; and this was the relationship that King Henry III entered into by the treaty of 1259.[10] The peerage simply reinforced this. Whatever the origins of the peers of France may have been, they were regarded in the thirteenth century as an inner ring of nobles whose relationship to the king was particularly intimate,[11] and the king took advantage of this to bind them more closely to his allegiance and service. Thus, when King Philip IV created a peerage for the duke of Brittany in 1297, he did so to flatter a great noble and to divert him from notions of autonomy; and a similar intention undoubtedly underlay the creation of a peerage for King Henry III, as duke of Aquitaine, in 1259.

King Louis IX was blamed by his contemporaries, and both he and King Henry III have been blamed by historians for accepting the terms of this treaty and for failing to foresee what their consequences were likely to be; but such criticism is quite beside the point. Neither the kings nor their advisers could see into the future any more than we can; the implications of the relationship they had created were in fact only worked out in detail in the following thirty years or so; and it could be said that it was quite a normal way of organising the relationships between kingdoms and principalities at the time. It was the way in which the kings of England had long tried to regulate their relations with the kings of the Scots.

If they did not show themselves at once, however, the implications of the relationship created by the treaty were very important when they did appear. The first was that, by feudal custom, a vassal had to do homage to his lord when he succeeded to the fief and when his lord succeeded to his lordship; and it was also the custom that the vassal should perform this act at his lord's principal residence. In this case the king of France insisted that the king-duke should do his homage in person, because, according to the ideas of the time, the relationship was not fully established until the vassal had done homage and had been received as vassal by his lord. Now, although the kings of England might have no overwhelming objection in principle to doing this homage (his lands in France were of considerable value to him), there were almost always difficulties to be settled about the precise extent of the lands and rights which formed the subject of the homage; it meant a journey to France at times that might not always be convenient to the king-duke; however fine a display he might make on the journey and at the ceremony, there was no getting away from the fact that at the central point of the ritual he appeared as the feudal inferior of a brother king; and this may have been made a little worse by the fact that the king of France, for his part, had established the doctrine that, even when he acquired lands for which homage was due, he personally did homage to no one. It was certainly made worse by the fact that, early in the fourteenth century, there was a series of short reigns in France (Louis X, 1314–16; Philip V, 1316–22; Charles IV, 1322–8), so that one act of homage had hardly been organised and performed before the demand came again.

A vassal owed loyalty and service to his lord. In the strictest interpretation there should be no conflict or interest between lord and vassal. This could have very important implications in the relationship between the king-duke and the king of France. For example: it had been the policy of the thirteenth-century kings of France to bring the county of Flanders more fully into their obedience than it had been in the eleventh and twelfth centuries, as it was their policy in other parts of the kingdom. The count's resistance led, in the 1290s, to war. Now the king of England also had a strong interest in Flanders, partly traditional, partly commercial; and it was not to his advantage that the king of France should establish a close control of the county. As early as 1292, Edward I was in secret negotiation with Count Guy; but he could not intervene openly until he had himself broken with King Philip in 1294, for to do so would have been as disloyal as Edward III was in his reception of Robert of Artois in the 1330s.[12] In effect, then, though it might be possible to distinguish in theory between the king of England and the duke of Aquitaine, in practice the fact that the king of England was a vassal of the king of France for his duchy of Aquitaine gave to the king of France a very large control over what we should now call 'English foreign policy' in western Europe, wherever, indeed, the king of France had any interest. When King Louis IX was defending the concessions he had made to Henry III in 1259, he said: 'It seems to me that I have made good use of what I have given him, for he was not my man and now he has entered into my homage.'[13] It is not impossible that Louis had such implications of 'loyalty' in mind at the time; whether he did or not, the territories and the promises of territory that he gave to Henry were a very sound political investment indeed.

A vassal also owed service to his lord and, at this level of the feudal hierarchy, service meant military service. The king of France, that is to say, could not only threaten to confiscate the duchy of Aquitaine and the county of Ponthieu if the king-duke supported his enemies, he could demand military service from him against them; and the king of France did in fact make such demands upon Edward I.[14] This clearly could put severe limitations upon the freedom of action of a ruler like King Edward I, who had a great many interests on the Continent in addition to those within the kingdom of France.

The most troublesome implication of the vassalage of the king of England in his capacity as duke of Aquitaine lay, however, in the developing ideas of royal sovereignty in France. Partly through the revived study of Roman law, partly by making more effective the powers which a feudal structure gave to a suzerain, as the king of France grew materially stronger during the course of the thirteenth century the idea grew, and was lovingly tended by his lawyers, that the

king was 'emperor in his kingdom'. This made the king not only independent of any other lay power, but made him the source of legislation
applicable to the whole of his kingdom, even within the great counties
and duchies, and made his court the ultimate court of appeal for all who
were in feudal relationship with him, together with their vassals and
sub-tenants; and it implied that the great counts and dukes should hold
their counties and duchies on conditions prescribed by the king and his
court, so that the government of those duchies and counties should be
ancillary to the royal administration, should concern itself, in fact, only
with those affairs which the royal administration was not yet prepared
to take over. Towards the end of the thirteenth century, and more in the
fourteenth, the king extended his legislation to Gascony;[15] and all that
the king-duke could do, in the last resort, was to legislate in the same
sense and argue that his courts in the duchy were applying his own laws
rather than those of the king of France, or come to some arrangement
by negotiation. The question of appeals[16] was more explosive because, if
the claims of the French lawyers were pressed, they could bring the
administration of the duchy to a standstill and discredit the ducal courts
there. When an appeal was made, the appellant was at once put under
the protection of the king of France, whose men could enter the duchy
to make that protection effective. If, for example, a man who had been
entrusted with the collection of some part of the ducal revenues failed
to render his account when it was due, and, having been brought before
the ducal courts, made an appeal, this meant that, even if he lost the
appeal in the end there would be considerable delay before he could be
brought to book and the ducal finances would suffer; but if he succeeded in his appeal, a most difficult situation would arise.[17] The
difficulties were there even if the French king's officers acted reasonably
and moderately; but they did not always do so. From time to time the
king-duke obtained, as a personal concession, that what were coming
to be regarded as the rights of the king of France in this respect would
not be pressed in Aquitaine; but such concessions did not remain
effective for very long. The king of England, therefore, though he was
as sovereign in his kingdom as the king of France was in his, could not
be sovereign in his French lands; and this was more than a matter of
legal theory, it might make the difference between being able to govern
his duchy and to realise the full value which it might have for him and
not being able to do so.

There were other causes of difficulty. When, for example, King
Louis IX ceded to King Henry III, by the treaty of 1259, 'what he

held' in the three dioceses of Limoges, Cahors and Périgueux, he meant that and no more. It soon became apparent that he had possessed very little there, and that many of the great seigneurs were 'privileged', that is, they had been given the privilege that their allegiance could not be transferred to another lord against their will. 'What the king held' in the three dioceses, other than his sovereignty of which he did not divest himself in 1259, was no more than a complex and varying bundle of rights and jurisdictions, often barely effective, a fruitful source of disputes and appeals – to such an extent that it has been said that the appellate jurisdiction of the king's court, the Parlement of Paris, was developed very largely on the appeals from the three dioceses in the years after 1259.[18] In the sense that ducal and royal rights and jurisdictions were often inextricably entangled, similar difficulties obtained over most of the lands held by Edward I in France. The king-duke would have a piece of land here, rights of jurisdiction there, the right to take or levy a custom somewhere else; in many places his jurisdiction was simply one point in a hierarchy of courts at the head of which was the king's court, the Parlement of Paris. No one, in the fourteenth century, could have put a board by a roadside, with the inscription on one side 'You are entering the territory of the king-duke', and on the other 'You are entering the territory of the king of France', for both might have rights over the same territory. The duchy of Aquitaine was not bounded by anything remotely like a modern frontier.

However, the full force of all these problems was not revealed until near the end of the thirteenth century. As far as can be seen, Edward I honestly tried to make the system work, unpromising as it may seem to us, for it did no violence to the ideas of the time; and since it had been established, there was much to be gained by taking the advantages which it offered. It was only as those who advised the kings of France developed the idea of his sovereignty and applied it more confidently and aggressively that the situation deteriorated. In 1293, King Philip IV claimed jurisdiction over certain acts of violence committed at sea and on the coasts of the Bay of Biscay, and summoned Edward I, as duke of Aquitaine, to attend his court and to answer for the conduct of his men, as any lord might require of his vassal. Edward sent his brother, Edmund of Lancaster, to negotiate; but King Philip, by what seems very like sharp practice, confiscated and took possession of Gascony. This led to the war of 1294.[19] It was concluded by the peace of 1303 which, so far as territory was concerned, restored the *status quo ante* completely. There are many things which are hard to understand in this war; but what was perhaps more important for the future than the fighting or the diplomatic manœuvres were the arguments which the English lawyers developed in the course of the protracted negotiations between the truce of 1297 and the peace; for they then produced a theory of English sovereignty in Aquitaine to counter the sovereignty which the French lawyers attributed to their king throughout his kingdom.[20] Henceforward it was, in a sense, one sovereignty against another in Aquitaine, and the king of England made less effort to accommodate himself to the relationship created by the treaty of 1259.

There was a second war between the years 1324 and 1327,[21] arising out of local resistance to the building of a French bastide at Saint-Sardos in the Agenais, when again Gascony and Ponthieu were in French hands for a while; but on this occasion only a part of the duchy was restored at the peace. The treaty was made only a few months after the accession of Edward III, when Isabella and Mortimer, who were then in control of England, had to liquidate all foreign commitments as quickly as they could. If personal feelings counted for anything, Edward might well have felt that a considerable part of his Aquitainian inheritance had been given up when he was powerless to prevent it; but the 'War of Saint-Sardos', as it is called, raised no new question of principle.

There were several attempts, between the years 1303 and 1337, to settle the problems to which this feudal relationship between the two kings gave rise by talking rather than fighting.[22] There was a meeting known as the 'Process of Montreuil' in 1306;[23] another, known as the 'Process of Périgueux' beginning in 1311,[24] and a 'Process of Agen' from 1332 to 1334.[25] In these meetings, naturally, each side put its claims at their highest; and for this reason alone these meetings probably did more harm than good (as in a modern international conference when positions are taken up more for their propaganda value than as serious points for negotiation), quite apart from the fact that these processes failed to produce any very useful result. For there was a fundamental misunderstanding. The English, as they approached these 'processes', envisaged a conference between equals; but the French always fell back on the sovereignty which their king claimed over all his kingdom and its adjacent waters, and tended to make the occasion more and more like an action in his court (a 'process') in which he was judge. This clearly made negotiation impossible.

Since the conditions under which the king-duke held his lands in France put so many restrictions not only upon his government of those lands but also upon his interests elsewhere, and since, in the complexities and intermingling of jurisdiction and administration both kings could so easily become involved in the miscalculations and even the sheer violence of those acting in their name, it is easy to see how a sailors' row, giving rise to a dispute over jurisdiction, could lead to the war of 1294, and how the refusal of Edward's seneschal of Aquitaine to attend the court of the French seneschal of Périgord to answer for the violent action of a lord of Montpezat could lead to the war of 1324, particularly in an atmosphere of tension when the king of France clearly thought Edward II was trying to avoid the homage he had been summoned to do; and again, how Edward III's 'disloyalty' in harbouring Robert of Artois, also in an atmosphere of tension when there were other causes of dispute (in Scotland and in Flanders), could lead to the war of 1337. But after the first war the whole of Ponthieu and Aquitaine, and after the second the whole of Ponthieu and at least part of Aquitaine, had been restored to the king-duke. The hold which the king of France had over him through his position as duke of Aquitaine, peer of France and count of Ponthieu was then of greater value than the absorption of Gascony into the royal demesne or its transfer to a French noble with no interests outside the kingdom could have been; and the king-duke, on his side, quite apart from the consideration that his honour demanded that he should defend his heritage, possessed in Aquitaine an asset of enormous value to him – a steady and reliable revenue from the wine customs levied in Bordeaux which,[26] since they could easily be assigned to pay off the loans which any active king desperately needed from time to time,[27] were worth far more to him even than the figures for their annual yield might suggest. Thus the 'feudal theory', 'the problem of Gascony' can explain why there was a war in 1337, but it does not explain why that war was different from the two earlier wars, why in fact it was a 'Hundred Years War'.

II

Even on the surface of things the war of 1337 looks as though it involved more than the feudal issue. In the wars of 1294 and 1324, even though Edward I did launch a belated campaign in Flanders during the year 1297, the fighting was essentially for the defence or the recovery of Gascony. In 1337 and in the years that followed, there was certainly fighting in Gascony as local forces in the allegiance of the king-duke strove, in the end successfully, to hold the invading French armies at bay, but many of the important campaigns, and all those in which King

Edward III was personally involved, took place in the north, far from Gascony, and apparently with other objectives. This at once suggests that other issues were in question beside Gascony. Of these issues, some go even deeper than the ramifications of the feudal relationship between the king-duke and the king of France; others were, in a sense, accidental.

The deeper issues involve the whole political development of the kingdom of France on the one hand and of the dominions of the rulers who were, among other things, kings of England, on the other. The Hundred Years War was not a conflict between two nations, France and England. National autonomy, though it was achieved to some extent in the two countries as the result of the war, certainly did not exist at the beginning of it; though one might say that the kings of France and England were brought into conflict as they groped their way towards some notion of national autonomy.

The treaty of 1259 had deprived the king-duke of more than it might appear to have done at first sight. King Henry had renounced all the rights which he had or had ever had in Normandy, in Anjou, Maine and Touraine, and in Poitou. Because he was not in possession of these lands at the time when the treaty was being negotiated, and had not been in possession of them (other than parts of Poitou) for over fifty years, historians have tended to treat his renunciation as a concession of relatively little importance; but the legal (as distinct from the military) basis on which King Louis could demand this renunciation was still the sentence of confiscation pronounced in the court of King Philip Augustus in 1202, and some people had doubted the legality of that sentence in general and, in particular, had doubted whether a punitive sentence directed against King John ought to go on being enforced against his innocent son. Henry III had found some support in Normandy in 1230, when he was making one of his attempts to recover his father's and his grandfather's lands in France;[28] his support among the barons of Poitou had flowed now one way and now the other; he was building up a very promising relationship with Brittany,[29] and even in the years immediately before the treaty a change in personalities and politics in France or in England might still have made it possible for a militarily competent king of England to recover the position that King John had held in 1200. Until 1259 Henry still used, formally, the titles 'Duke of Normandy and Aquitaine, Count of Anjou'. Thus the rights which he renounced in 1259 were not unsubstantial; and as we look further into them they appear quite fundamental, for Henry's ancestors in the male line had been dukes of Normandy, counts of Anjou and even dukes of Aquitaine before they had been kings of England, and their continental inheritance was quite as important to them, perhaps more important, than their insular kingdom.

Those who say that the Hundred Years War really began in 1066 are right in the sense that it was the Norman conquest of England, ultimately, which created the conditions which the treaty of 1259 was intended to bring up to date but which, in fact, largely survived it. Both the battle of Hastings and the less famous campaigns of Henry fitz-Empress in 1153 brought a French nobleman to the throne of England; but they did a great deal more than that. Though William the Conqueror might endeavour to rule England as an English king and Henry set about to restore the 'customs of his grandfather' in the country, both conquests not only brought about great changes there but also created a political relationship between England and parts of France. It is this relationship that must be analysed, and its development studied, if the Hundred Years War is to be understood.

William the Conqueror did not cease to be duke of Normandy after he had made himself king of England; and neither he nor his sons intended that England and Normandy should ever be separated. To them, England and Normandy, together with all the rights and superiorities which a king of England could exercise beyond his kingdom and a duke of Normandy beyond his duchy, constituted an indivisible inheritance,[30] as the kingdom of France had come to be for the kings of France. This in itself was a long step towards political integration. It is true that England and Normandy were separated by the Channel, though the sea could be as much of a highway as a barrier, and that they were separated not only by differences of language but also by differences in custom and tradition; but even these differences need not have proved more of a hindrance to political union in the long run than the differences of language and custom that were to be found within the kingdom of England itself; while unity was vastly strengthened by the fact that the higher ranks of the baronage, and not only they, characteristically possessed lands and interests on both sides of the Channel to the extent that one could not speak of a Norman baronage and an English baronage, but only of one single Normano-English baronial society. Except in so far as the provinces of Rouen, Canterbury and York were separate units of ecclesiastical government, the same was true of the higher ranks of the clergy. The union of England and Normandy was thus far more than a temporary union in the person of the ruler, as is shown, almost paradoxically, by the manner in which

Stephen of Blois obtained the kingdom and the duchy;[31] and there were beginnings, though only the beginnings, of institutions to cope with the problems of government which this union created.

When Henry fitzEmpress made himself King Henry II of England, he was already count of Anjou (and descended directly, in the male line, from the counts of Anjou), duke of Normandy and, since his marriage to Eleanor, duchess of Aquitaine in her own right, was beginning to style himself 'duke of the Aquitainians'.[32] Later he found the means to take over the government of Brittany, to establish his suzerainty over Scotland, over the still-independent princes of Wales, over the great county of Toulouse and other lands; and as a result of baronial enterprise in Ireland, he extended his rule over the colonists there and his suzerainty over the still-independent Irish kings, as over the Welsh princes. But the construction of this vast feudal empire was not accompanied by any fresh immigration from France into England, or at least none of any importance; though the relationship between Normandy and England created by the Norman king-dukes was revived and maintained. Such unity as Henry's empire came to achieve was brought about by other means.

The problem of governing this huge assemblage of territories stemmed from the fact that Henry claimed to be count of Anjou by hereditary right, and to be king of England and duke of Normandy also by hereditary right even though this right had had to be realised by force. He was thus bound to rule England as a Normano-English king, Normandy as a duke of Normandy, Anjou, with Touraine and Maine, in accordance with the customs and practices built up by his Angevin ancestors; while the circumstances of his acquisition of the duchy of Aquitaine meant that he could not do otherwise than act in a similar manner there. All demanded, to a greater or less degree, personal rule; but Henry could not be everywhere at once. Some means had to be found to overcome this difficulty if Henry was to continue to hold, and perhaps to extend, the accumulation of lands and authority he had acquired; and honour as well as the logic of the situation required that he should do this, since it seems to be a characteristic of such empires that they begin to disintegrate as soon as they cease to expand.

The constitutional history of the Angevin 'empire' has yet to be written, and historians have not, perhaps, recognised that there was any such thing; yet the Hundred Years War results from the converging and ultimately clashing development of the government of this empire, or what was left of it by 1337, and the development of royal government in the kingdom of France. It was more than the feudal relationship between king and king-duke; it was the overlapping and ultimately the conflict of two growing structures of government.

On the Angevin or Plantagenet side the scheme of government, which was to be the chief means of holding the various elements of the 'empire' together, grew out of the older traditions of each country included within it. To some extent, the king-duke could hold his lands together by itineration, visiting each of them whenever he was needed there and trying not to leave any one country too long without his presence. The king-dukes of England and Normandy had done the same; but something more was needed. To the businesslike minds of these kings, the accounts of their finances in England or Normandy could not wait for their next visit to the country; nor could a great many judicial matters; and there were other affairs which could be dealt with adequately by delegated authority and so prevented from piling up and defeating the king when he did come. During the course of the twelfth century a system of administration which met these difficulties and which went some way towards providing the empire with a unitary government, was gradually evolved.

The king-duke-count and his household, which included the organisation of the king's own finances (the Chamber) and the secretariat of his government (the Chancery) formed the common centre of government for all his lands, moving constantly from one to another and capable of issuing orders for any one of them from any point on the itinerary; and wherever the king might be, attended by his servants and courtiers and the magnates of the land in which he found himself, with others who had business there, he held his court, accessible to suitors from all parts. In those lands over which he exercised no more than suzerainty, Scotland and large parts of the periphery of the duchy of Aquitaine for example, the native ruler carried on his government with little interference in his internal affairs; but in those lands where the king was himself the 'native' ruler by inheritance or conquest, some form of continuous administration was needed. In these there was gradually evolved a responsible official, called a justiciar in England and in Ireland, a justiciar or seneschal in Normandy, a seneschal in Brittany, in Anjou and in Aquitaine (sometimes there were separate seneschals for Gascony and for Poitou and even for other parts of Aquitaine), and this official acted as head of the administration when the king-duke-count was present in the country and as something like a viceroy when he was elsewhere. This official directed a body of justices in England and

Normandy and the auditors who examined the accounts of the sheriffs in England and of the *vicomtes*, *prévôts* and *baillis* in Normandy. The two groups overlapped considerably, and made up what was called the 'Exchequer' in England, in Normandy and in Ireland. In Anjou, Aquitaine and Brittany the seneschals do not seem to have possessed so highly organised an administration to help them; but they did have a number of deputies, clerks and castellans under their orders, and a local organisation for the collection and administration of the duke-count's revenues and to keep the peace, with at least the beginnings of a judicial organisation. Local administration, the shires in England, the *bailliages*, *vicomtés*, *prévôtés* and other units in the continental lands, though they might be influenced by the fact that the government of the king-duke-count was concerned with many lands, largely retained their traditional forms and functions; and, indeed, the most important feature of the whole structure was that the administration of each land grew naturally out of the institutions that were beginning to form when its king, duke or count was that and nothing more. The process in the twelfth century was one of bringing them together and making them function in the service of one king-duke-count, not of imposing a common pattern.

In so far as this government had developed towards a logical system by the end of the century, it had a considerable unifying effect, tending more and more to make the Angevin empire an integrated political unit. The only ambiguous factor was the succession. Henry II's designation of his son Henry as king of England and duke of Normandy, Richard as duke of Aquitaine, Geoffrey as duke of Brittany and John as lord of Ireland, if this was indeed his plan for the succession, seems to imply partition, however he might try to insist that the younger brothers should do homage to the elder; though as it turned out all his lands descended substantially intact first to Richard and then to John.

The disasters of the early thirteenth century, when the king of France conquered Normandy and ultimately Poitou, and when Brittany and Anjou-Maine-Touraine went over to him, though they altered the whole territorial balance of the Plantagenet lands so that the centre of interest and the normal residence of the king-duke were now in England rather than in his continental lands, influenced but did not determine the constitutional development of the lands that remained to him. The fact that he still had important interests on the Continent, lands to be recovered and lands to be defended, as well as interests in Wales, Scotland and Ireland to be safeguarded and if possible extended, put enormous pressure upon England to provide the men and the money for enterprises beyond the kingdom. This pressure does much to explain the changes in military organisation and the development of Parliament during the thirteenth century, though these developments grew naturally out of English institutions and traditions. On the other side of the Channel, the fact that the king-duke could no longer visit the distant duchy of Aquitaine so frequently as he had done[33] meant that the hitherto somewhat rudimentary administration there would have to be vastly developed so that it could function effectively with the king-duke normally absent rather than frequently, if intermittently, present. Though there were some beginnings under Henry III, this was substantially the work of Edward I. The seneschal was relieved of his financial responsibilities by the creation of new offices, those of the constable of Bordeaux and the controller; some of his judicial responsibilities were taken off him by the appointment of judges at different levels; at the end of the century an officer with the title of lieutenant (i.e. lieutenant of the king-duke) was appointed to take over abnormal military responsibilities and some of the king-duke's appellate jurisdiction; and the seneschal was provided with an official council and with under-seneschals in various parts of the duchy. On their much smaller scale, similar developments took place in the Channel Islands. Finally, any doubt there may have been about the unity of the succession was cleared up in 1254 when Gascony, the Channel Islands and Ireland were formally declared to be annexed to the Crown of England, so that whoever in future was the lawful king of England was, by that fact alone, the lawful duke of Aquitaine and lord of Ireland and of the Channel Islands, at least in English law.

Though the superficial effect of these developments might seem to be to make each unit of the Plantagenet lands better able to stand on its own if need be, the more profound effect was to provide the necessary conditions for linking them in an integral political union. Thus even in the fourteenth century, his continental lands and his continental interests were as fully a part of the king-duke's dominions and responsibilities as his kingdom of England, not distant dependencies expendable in times of difficulty. Moreover, and this was perhaps even more important, King Edward I and his successors continued, in the government of their dominions as a whole, the tradition of Henry II's time. The considerable developments in the administration of Aquitaine and the Channel Islands did not follow an English model; they were, essentially, the developments that could have been brought about by a 'French' duke of Aquitaine or duke of Normandy if he had been that and nothing else;

they were entirely, that is to say, in the native tradition – and they were so notwithstanding the fact that something like a higher civil service was growing up whose members could serve in any of the king-duke's dominions, as the biographies of some leading officers clearly show.[34] This growing integration of the Plantagenet lands through political and administrative development, and the fact that the king-duke was not only a French prince by descent but was governing his French lands as a French prince of the time would have done, make it reasonable to suggest that when the English lawyers in 1297 and the following years claimed that Gascony was not a part of the kingdom of France according to the French idea of the kingdom, they were not simply making a slick answer to the French lawyers' assertion that their king was 'emperor in his kingdom'; there was a great deal of patient and inventive political construction behind their arguments. Other French dukes would soon be saying much the same thing about their duchies.[35]

However, on the French side, the king's claim to sovereignty over all his kingdom was equally the expression of at least two centuries of political construction and consolidation. At the time of the Norman Conquest, the great dukes and counts, such as the dukes of Normandy or the counts of Anjou, were the king's vassals certainly, but only in a personal sense, and the relationship influenced their actions very little. The dukes of Normandy did homage, when they did do it, 'on the march', that is on the frontier, implying an element of equality between duke and king. But the Capetian kings, having achieved the stability of their dynasty and the indivisibility of their inheritance so that their small achievements (as they were at first) could be cumulated from one generation to another, were gradually able to intensify this relationship until it became one of the chief principles on which their growing authority in their kingdom was built. This can well be seen in the history of the homages which the Norman and Angevin rulers did as dukes of Normandy. First it came to be specified that the homage was indeed for Normandy, i.e. Normandy was a fief held of the king by homage and fealty (this first appears in 1120); then, by the middle of the twelfth century, the homage is described as 'liege'.[36] Finally, when King John settled with King Philip Augustus, at Le Goulet in January 1200, the terms on which he should succeed to the lands of his brother and his father, it was made quite clear in the treaty that they were to be held as fiefs of the king of France in the fullest sense of the term.[37] The terms of the treaty of Paris of 1259 were, therefore, only the next step in a process of definition which had been going on since the beginning of the twelfth century or before, and in which the relationship created by homage was being intensified in the interest of the king of France and of the integration of his kingdom.

There were, naturally, other elements in this process whereby the king of France was bringing the whole of his kingdom more and more under his authority – the influence of Roman law, and the development, as elsewhere, of the actual machinery of administration. What the 'English' regarded as 'French' interference in Gascony was often the normal pressure of zealous officials and competent administrators carrying out their duties as they understood them; but it was the more galling to the king-duke's officers there precisely because they were willing and had the means to do all that the French officials were claiming to do. The difficulties in Aquitaine, therefore, were more than a conflict of two largely theoretical sovereignties occasionally applied; it was also the clash of the two state-building enterprises operating in the same territory. The 'Angevin empire' and the 'Norman empire' had been formed under the conditions of the eleventh and twelfth centuries, when the king of France was weak and his nobles could build principalities that included lands both within and beyond the kingdom. Those days were passing; but as they passed both the kingdom of France and the 'feudal empire' of the Plantagenets were developing with the times into ever-more complex and sophisticated political structures; and in the geographical regions and in the spheres of government where they overlapped it could not be supposed that such structures, patiently built up over the centuries, would be abandoned after a battle won or lost. And it may perhaps further be suggested that the political edifice which the Plantagenet king-dukes were constructing was as valid for its day as the Capetians' kingdom; and no one could then have said whether the future lay with the one or the other.

This is perhaps the chief reason why the war of 1337 developed into something more than a feudal dispute. It was also a large part of the force behind Edward III's claim to the throne of France.[38] There was nothing preposterous about this claim; one could almost say that it was to be expected sooner or later, for the kings of England were of French origin, they had retained very important interests in France and, as dukes of Aquitaine and peers of France, they were a part of the fabric of government in France. Edward III's mother was a French princess and the royal families of England and France had long been closely related. If there were at any time any serious doubt about the succession to the throne of France, it was in the highest degree likely that a claimant would be found in the royal family of England; and Edward in 1328 could rightly say that he was the nearest living relative of King Charles IV. In the crisis of that year his claim was rejected not entirely by law and reason, but very largely on the practical consideration that he was then a boy of fifteen and under the control of the hated Isabella and her lover Mortimer; Philip of Valois was in almost every way a more suitable candidate and he was on the spot. But Edward's claim was reasonable in itself and it always had some support in France; if he really believed in it, as he could well have done, it was his duty to prosecute it.

Even his claim had quite a long history to it. The idea that the king of England might have a claim to the kingdom of France or part of it first appeared explicitly in 1317; but it had been in a sense implicit in the claim to sovereignty in Aquitaine, for if that claim was not conceded, as it would not be, the only way to realise it would be to seize the kingdom itself. The suggestion that Edward should take the title was made in 1328, and the claim was formally made in that year. Though he was in no position to press it then, echoes of it sound in English official documents for the next two or three years. Edward actually assumed the French title in letters patent that were prepared in 1337, though probably never used; and when he took the title formally in January 1340, this can only have been as the result of long and careful deliberation. The claim had not been made lightly and it would not be abandoned lightly.

Behind the immediate issues of the 1330s, then, behind all the conflicts of jurisdiction and the administrative tangles in Gascony at that time and the failure to find any solution for them, there lay two political structures, both growing in complexity and effectiveness, both developing in part over the same ground, and both seeing in the war issues at stake that were vital to them. But, however deep-seated the cause of conflict, it could not have lasted so long if the two sides had not been fairly evenly matched, taking all things into consideration. At first the English armies were perhaps the better organised and the French were certainly unprepared for the tactics they employed. Once they had found success and all that went with it in booty and ransoms, many an Englishman looked upon France as a land where fortunes could easily and quickly be made; while many Gascons and Bretons and other 'Frenchmen' who gave their allegiance to Edward also found in the war a way to riches. In so far as Edward III, in his capacity as duke of Aquitaine, was resisting royal centralisation, he was leading a movement which others were prepared to join, the duke of Brittany, the cities of Flanders, even the duke of Burgundy; and Edward, by campaigns designed to win local acknowledgement of his right to the throne of France and by offering himself as an alternative king to all who were discontented with Valois rule, looked at one point as though he might almost win the kingdom of France by instalments.[39] In one sense the Hundred Years War could be described as a civil war in France, in which the two principles of royal centralisation and princely independence were disputed. But in the end, the reserves of men and wealth in France and the sheer size of the country were too much for Edward and his successors; though the combination of a good cause (in their own eyes) and the memory of early successes, quite apart from the deep traditions that this chapter has attempted to analyse, would not allow them to give up; while the French, for their part, either could not find the means to throw them out completely, or, very much more likely, took a long time to see that that was the only solution to their problem; for they also stood to benefit from the fact that the king of England was also the duke of Aquitaine – if only he would play their game.

The war of 1337 began in a way very similar to those of 1294 and 1324 and for very similar reasons. But the earlier wars were incidents in a feudal relationship when the confiscation of the fief was intended more to bring a disobedient vassal to heel than to deprive him permanently of his lands and so to break the relationship for ever. The argument over sovereignty, however, and the political developments centred on the kings of France and the king-dukes of the Plantagenet dominions were brought to a head by Edward III's claim to the throne of France; and a feudal dispute was converted into a long conflict in which the old feudal overlapping and interlocking gave way to the autonomous and self-contained national kingdoms of France and England; and   Frenchmen   and Englishmen began to hate one another as Englishmen and Frenchmen – perhaps not a very great advance after all.

BIBLIOGRAPHICAL NOTE

Standard accounts of the Hundred Years War and its origins will be found in
E. Perroy, *The Hundred Years War* (English trans. W. B. Wells, 1951) – though
the circumstances in which this book was written should be noted – in M.
McKisack, *The Fourteenth Century* (*The Oxford History of England*, iv, Oxford,
1959), and most recently, with new ideas and a full bibliography, in K. Fowler,
The Age of Plantagenet and Valois (1967). M. Gavrilovitch, *Étude sur le traité de
Paris de 1259* (Bibliothèque de l'École des Hautes Études, fasc. 125, Paris, 1899)
is fundamental. There are more detailed studies of the beginning of the war in
E. Déprez, *Les préliminaires de la guerre de Cent ans: La Papauté, la France et
l'Angleterre, 1328–1342* (Paris, 1902) and in H. S. Lucas, *The Low Countries
and the Hundred Years War, 1326–1347* (Ann Arbor, 1929); but the most significant of recent work on the general political conditions (though to us they may
well seem more legal than political) which led to the war is contained in a
number of articles by P. Chaplais, most of which are cited in the notes. To these
should be added his collection of documents on *The War of Saint-Sardos,
1323–1325* (Camden Third Series, lxxxvii, 1954). Some economic and social
conditions are brought out in R. Boutruche, *La crise d'une société: seigneurs et
paysans du Bordelais pendant la guerre de Cent ans* (Paris, 1947) and in Y.
Renouard (ed.), 'Bordeaux sous les rois d'Angleterre' in *Histoire de Bordeaux*,
ed. C. Higounet, iii (Bordeaux, 1965); while the structure of politics in France
itself, of considerable relevance if the first phase of the Hundred Years War is
regarded as having some of the characteristics of a French civil war, has been
made much clearer by R. Cazelles, *La Société politique et la crise de la royauté
sous Philippe de Valois* (Paris, 1958) and P. S. Lewis, *Later Medieval France, the
Polity* (1968).

The fundamental collection of official documents is contained in *Rymer's
Foedera*, Record Commission edition, ed. A. Clarke, J. Bayley, F. Holbrooke
and J. W. Clarke (1816–69); supplemented on the English side by the *Calendars
of Patent Rolls, Close Rolls*, etc. published by H.M. Stationery Office and, more
particularly, by the *Treaty Rolls* (vol. i, *1234–1325*, 1955) when later volumes
of this and connected series are published; and on the French side by *Comptes
Royaux*, ed. R. Fawtier and F. Maillard [*Recueil des historiens de France, Documents financiers*, iii, *1285–1314* (Paris, 1953–6), iv, *1314–1328* (Paris, 1961)] and
Registres du trésor des chartes, ed. R. Fawtier (*Archives nationales, Inventaires et
Documents*, Paris, 1958, 1966) as these two publications progress. A useful
indication of the scope of the registers of the Parlement is given by P.-C. Timbal,
La guerre de Cent ans vue à travers les registres du parlement, 1337–1369 (Paris,
1961). The two most important French chronicles on the origins and the early
phases of the war are those of Jean le Bel and Jean Froissart. The standard
edition of the first is *Chroniques de Jean le Bel*, ed. J. Viard and E. Déprez
(Société de l'histoire de France, Paris, 1904–5) and of the second, *Chroniques de
Jean Froissart*, ed. S. Luce, G. Raynaud, L. and A. Mirot (14 vols, Société de
l'histoire de France, Paris, 1869–1966), but there are a number of useful documents and tables published in an earlier edition of Froissart – *Oeuvres de
Froissart*, ed. Kervyn de Lettenhove: *Chroniques* (Brussels, 1867–77) especially
in vol. xviii. There are a number of translations of his chronicle into English.
Although *The Chronicle of Jean de Venette* (ed. R. A. Newhall, New York, 1953)
does not begin until 1340, it should be read as a corrective to the aristocratic
attitudes of Jean le Bel and Froissart and for the editor's valuable bibliography

(note in particular the articles of J. Viard). Perhaps the most relevant English chronicles are the *Continuatio Chronicarum* of Adam Murimuth and *De Gestis Mirabilibus Regis Edwardi Tertii* by Robert of Avesbury. These are edited together in one volume by E. M. Thompson (Rolls Series, 1889).

NOTES

1. G. Templeman, 'Edward III and the Beginnings of the Hundred Years War', *TRHS* 5th ser., ii (1952), 69–88.

2. Ph. Wolff, 'Un Problème d'origines: La Guerre de Cent Ans', in *Éventail de l'histoire vivante: Hommage à Lucien Febvre*, ii (1953), 141–8.

3. G. P. Cuttino, 'Historical Revision: the Causes of the Hundred Years War', *Speculum*, xxxi (1956), 463–77.

4. e.g. E. Perroy, *The Hundred Years War*, p. 69; M. McKisack, *The Fourteenth Century*, ch. iv. There is a full bibliography in K. Fowler, *The Age of Plantagenet and Valois*, pp. 204 ff.

5. The terms 'sovereign' and 'sovereignty' are used here in their medieval sense. For medieval theories of sovereignty, see W. Ullmann, 'The Development of the Medieval Idea of Sovereignty', in *EHR* lxiv (1949), 1–33; and for their application in this particular case, P. Chaplais, 'La Souveraineté du roi de France et le pouvoir législatif en Guyenne au début du XIVᵉ siècle', *Le Moyen Age*, lxix (1963), 449–69.

6. The terms 'Aquitaine', 'Guyenne' and 'Gascony' have often given rise to confusion. The king-duke's title was *Dux Aquitanie*, as it had been since Henry fitzEmpress (Henry II) married Eleanor of Aquitaine and subsequently made himself king of England. The duchy, which he then held in right of his wife, had been formed about a century before by the union of an earlier 'duchy of Aquitaine', centred on Poitou, with the duchy of the Gascons. When King John and King Henry III had lost Poitou in the thirteenth century, and with it most of the earlier duchy of Aquitaine, it was perhaps natural to speak of what remained as 'Gascony', even officially (e.g. 'Rotuli Vasconie' for the rolls of letters relating to the king-duke's interests in south-west France); and this continued even when Henry II's duchy of Aquitaine had been reconstructed to some extent in accordance with the provisions of the treaty of Paris of 1259. In this paper some attempt has been made to use the term 'Gascony' when it seemed geographically appropriate and 'Aquitaine' when referring to the duchy as a political unit whatever its effective geographical limits at the time; though it is difficult to make the distinction consistently. 'Guyenne' is simply a variant French form of 'Aquitaine'.

7. *Oeuvres de Froissart*, ed. Kervyn de Lettenhove, xviii, 33–7.

8. On the treaty and the conditions that it created see M. Gavrilovitch, *Étude sur le traité de Paris de 1259* (Paris, 1899), and P. Chaplais, 'The Making of the Treaty of Paris (1259) and the Royal Style', *EHR* lxvii (1952), 235–53. Chaplais has also studied the practical working out of these conditions in 'Le Duché-pairie de Guyenne', *Annales du Midi*, lxix (1957), 5–38, and ibid., lxx (1958), 135–60.

9. In this context 'Poitou' means primarily the historic county of Poitou; but as the title 'count of Poitou' remained as an alternative to 'duke of Aquitaine' almost to this date, it probably implied also 'all non-Gascon Aquitaine'.

10. On liege homage, e.g. F. L. Ganshof, *Feudalism* (trans. Grierson, 1952), pp. 93–5.

11. The origin of the peers is one of the mysteries of French history (M. Sautel-Boulet, 'Le rôle juridictionnelle la Cour des Pairs au xiiie et xive siècles', in *Recueil de Travaux offert à M. Clovis Brunel* (Paris, 1955), ii, 507–20). Unless the grant of the peerage to Henry III in 1259 be regarded as the revival of an earlier peerage held by the dukes of Aquitaine, the policy behind it seems to be an approach to that of the fourteenth century, on which see R. Cazelles, *La Société politique et le crise de la royauté sous Philippe de Valois* (Paris, 1958), pp. 379–82, and C. T. Wood, *The French Apanages and the Capetian Monarchy, 1224–1238* (Cambridge, Mass., 1966), pp. 33–5.

12. On Edward's relations with Flanders, H. Pirenne, *Histoire de Belgique*, i (5th ed., Brussels, 1929), 376–409; F. M. Powicke, *The Thirteenth Century*, pp. 622–3, 648, 659, 664–5, 667–9, etc.; P. Chaplais, 'Le Duché-pairie . . .', loc. cit., p. 28; and for Edward's similar embarrassments in the Spanish kingdoms, ibid., pp. 18–23.

13. 'Et me semble que ce que je li doing emploie-je bien, pour ce que il n'estoit pas mes hom, si en entre en mon hommaige.' *Histoire de Saint Louis par Jean, Sire de Joinville*, ed. Natalis de Wailly (Société de l'histoire de France, Paris, 1868), p. 245.

14. e.g. Chaplais, 'Le Duché-pairie . . .', loc. cit., pp. 19–20, 21–2.

15. P. Chaplais, 'La Souveraineté du roi de France . . .', loc. cit., pp. 449–69.

16. Gavrilovitch, op. cit., pp. 84–94; P. Chaplais, 'Gascon Appeals to England, 1259–1453' (London Ph.D. thesis, 1950).

17. e.g. an entry in the account of Adam Limber, constable of Bordeaux, for year 1322–3 (PRO, Pipe Roll, 12 Edward III, rot. 58); 'He [the constable] renders account of £1600 5s 3½d of new bordelais from the issues of the péage of Saint-Macaire which Amanieu d'Albret held of the king's grant for life, and which had been taken into the king's hand because Amanieu, refusing to render his account, had appealed to the Court of France. . . .' In this case the toll had been taken into the king-duke's hand; but it might not always be easy to do this.

18. Gavrilovitch, op. cit., pp. 68–71; cf. *EHR* lxxix (1964), 789–92.

19. e.g. R. Fawtier, *L'Europe occidentale de 1270 à 1328* (*Histoire générale: Histoire du Moyen Age*, ed. G. Glotz, vi, 1, Paris, 1940), pp. 314–25; P. Chaplais, 'Le Duché-pairie . . .', loc. cit., pp. 26–38.

20. P. Chaplais, 'English Arguments concerning the Feudal Status of Aquitaine in the Fourteenth Century', *BIHR* xxi (1948), 203–13.

21. P. Chaplais, 'Le Duché-pairie . . .', loc. cit., pp. 154–7.

22. P. Chaplais, 'Règlement des conflits internationaux franco-anglais au xive siècle (1293–1377)', *Le Moyen Age*, lvii (1951), 269–302.

23. G. P. Cuttino, *English Diplomatic Administration* (Oxford, 1940), ch. iii.

24. Gavrilovitch, op. cit., pp. 96–101, 124–44.

25. G. P. Cuttino, 'The Process of Agen', *Speculum*, xix (1944), 161–78.

26. For an estimate of the value of the revenues of the duchy at the beginning of the fourteenth century, G. P. Cuttino, *Le Livre d'Agenais* (1956), pp. xiii–xiv.

27. For Edward II's assignments of the revenues of Aquitaine to meet his debts, T. F. Tout, *The Place of Edward II in English History* (2nd ed., 1936), pp. 194–9; and Edward I's similar use of the revenues of Ponthieu, Hilda Johnstone, 'The County of Ponthieu, 1279–1307', in *EHR* xxix (1914), 448–9.

28. F. M. Powicke, *The Loss of Normandy* (Manchester, 1961), pp. 268–71; cf. the same writer's *King Henry III and the Lord Edward* (Oxford, 1947), i, 179–81.

29. Relations between the king of England and the duke of Brittany during the thirteenth century are summarised in *The Complete Peerage*, ed. G. E. Cokayne, new ed. V. Gibbs, x (1945), 800–14 (art. 'Richmond'): cf. S. Painter,

The Scourge of the Clergy, Peter of Dreux, Duke of Brittany (1937).

30. The writer hopes to argue this point in detail in a forthcoming article. Meanwhile, some of the points concerning the Norman colonisation of England and its consequences are suggested in Le Patourel, 'The Norman Colonization of Britain', in *I Normanni e la loro espansione in Europa nell'alto medio evo* (Spoleto, Centro Italiano di Studi sull'alto medioevo, 1969), pp. 409–38.

31. e.g. Ordericus Vitalis, *Historia Ecclesiastica*, ed. A. Le Prevost and L. Delisle (Société de l'histoire de France, Paris, 1838–55), v, 54–6.

32. For much of what follows, see Le Patourel, 'The Plantagenet Dominions', *History*, l (1965), 289–308, and 'The King and the Princes in Fourteenth-Century France', in *Europe in the Late Middle Ages*, ed. J. R. Hale, J. R. L. Highfield and B. Smalley (1965), and the evidence cited in these two articles.

33. It was one thing to cross the Channel from Southampton or Portsmouth to Barfleur, raise an army if necessary in Normandy and Anjou, and progress thus to Aquitaine; it was quite another thing to fit out a naval expedition on a comparable scale in England and to go to Bordeaux by sea.

34. Men like Henry Turberville (*DNB*, s.v. 'Turberville, Henry de') and Nicholas de Meules (references in Le Patourel, *Medieval Administration of the Channel Islands*, 1937, p. 122) in the thirteenth century, Otto de Grandison (C. L. Kingsford, 'Sir Otho de Grandison' in *TRHS* 3rd ser., iii, 125–95) and John Havering (C. Bémont, *Rôles Gascons*, iii, 1906, lii–lxi) at the turn of the century, or Oliver Ingham (*The Complete Peerage*, ed. G. E. Cokayne, new ed. V. Gibbs, vii, 58–60) and Adam Limber (T. F. Tout, op. cit., p. 351 and H. G. Richardson and G. O. Sayles, *Administration of Ireland*, 1963, p. 94) in the fourteenth century.

35. e.g. Brittany (B.-A. Pocquet du Haut-Jussé, *Les Papes et les ducs de Bretagne*, Paris, 1928, i, 420), Normandy (E. G. Léonard, *Histoire de Normandie*, Paris, 1944, p. 69).

36. J.-F. Lemarignier, *Recherches sur l'hommage en marche et les frontières féodales* (Lille, 1945), pp. 73–113.

37. 'Praeterea nobis dedit Rex Angliae viginti millia marcarum sterlingorum . . . propter rechatum nostrum. . . . Item Rex Angliae, sicut rectus heres, tenebit de nobis omnia feoda sicut pater ejus & frater ejus Rex Ricardus ea tenuerunt a nobis, & sicut feoda debent . . .', *Foedera*, i, 84; cf. Powicke, *Loss of Normandy*, pp. 134–8.

38. On Edward's claim, Le Patourel, 'Edward III and the Kingdom of France', *History*, xliii (1958), 173–89. See below XII.

39. Le Patourel, ibid., and 'The Treaty of Brétigny' in *TRHS* 5th ser., x (1960), esp. p. 25. See below XIII.

XII

EDWARD III
AND THE KINGDOM OF FRANCE

WHILE THE CAUSES of the Hundred Years War have given rise to a great deal of discussion, the war aims of the kings of England and France have generally been taken for granted rather than discussed.[2] It has been too easily assumed that the deeper causes of the conflict, whatever they were, determined the objectives of the contestants; and, since it now seems to be agreed that the problems of Aquitaine in some way lay at the root of the trouble,[3] it is argued that Edward's aim was no more than the defence of his duchy, if necessary by enlarging it or at least recovering its ancient limits, and that his claim to the throne of France was rather a tactical device, never taken really seriously, and easily thrown over for territorial concessions.[4] In this paper it will be argued, first, that Edward's claim to the throne of France was meant more seriously and deserves to be taken more seriously than it has been by historians during the present century, both as to its merits and as to its place in his war aims; and second, that his chances—and indeed his achievement—up to the winter of 1359–60 were a great deal better than they are generally reckoned to have been.

I

In any discussion of the French succession problems of the early fourteenth century, the fundamental consideration is that the situations of 1316 and 1328 were without precedent.[5] A monarchy which had been

---

[1] This paper represents, not a mature statement of conclusions, but an airing of ideas, substantially as they were presented at a Director's Conference in the Institute of Historical Research (November 1957). I am indebted to my audience on that occasion for the discussion that followed, and to Dr. Pierre Chaplais who has read and criticized the typescript.

[2] For a convenient discussion of the origins of the war, see G. Templeman, 'Edward III and the Beginnings of the Hundred Years War', *Transactions of the Royal Historical Society*, 5th series, II (1952), pp. 69–88; *cf*. Ph. Wolff, 'Un problème d'origines: La Guerre de Cent Ans', *Eventail de l'histoire vivante: homage à Lucien Febvre*, II (1953), pp. 141–8.

[3] E. Déprez, *Les Préliminaires de la guerre de Cent Ans*, 1902. *Cf*. E. Perroy, *The Hundred Years War* (trans. W. B. Wells, 1951), p. 69, and the same writer's valuable article 'Franco-English Relations, 1350-1400', *History*, XXI (1936–7), pp. 148–54.

[4] Perroy, *op. cit.*, pp. 69, 116, 129, 139; Templeman, p. 87.

[5] P. Viollet, 'Comment les femmes ont été exclues en France de la succession à la couronne', *Mémoires de l'Institut, Académie des Inscriptions et Belles Lettres*, XXXIV (1895), ii, pp. 125-78,

more elective than hereditary in the tenth century had become unquestionably hereditary in the fourteenth; but it had become so not
by enactment or by a series of disputes leading to clear decisions, but by
the fact of a continuous succession from father to son, uninterrupted
through three centuries. There was therefore no rule to which appeal
could be made when, as in 1316, the king's only son was a posthumous
infant who died within a few days of his birth or, as in 1328, when the
king left no son to succeed him. Every question was wide open. Had the
royal succession a rule of its own, or could analogies be adduced from
neighbouring kingdoms, from royal appanages in France, from the
great fiefs, from manors in the Ile de France?[6] Could females succeed in
default of males, or, if they could not succeed in person, could they
transmit their rights to their own heirs? All these points were argued
over and again; and perhaps all that can be said on the question of
absolute right is that no word was breathed in 1328 of a Salic Law and
that analogy, for what it might be worth, on the whole told in favour
of female rights in the succession. Indeed, as recently as 1314, when the
future Philip V had applied to his brother King Louis X for a ruling
on the succession to his appanage of Poitou, the king had said, 'Reason
and natural law instruct us that in default of male heirs females should
inherit and have succession to the goods and possessions of the fathers
of whom they are procreated and descended in legal marriage, in the
same way as males.'[7]

   The issue of 1316 was decided, not by discussion, but by the ambition
and ruthlessness of the man who became Philip V; and the opposition
he had to face, interested though it may have been, is testimony to the
strength of the feeling that women had a place in the succession, just as
the many bargains which he struck implicitly recognized their rights.
No serious objection seems to have been raised, in 1322, when his
brother Charles thrust aside Philip's daughters; but in 1328, the fact
that Philip VI allowed Jeanne, daughter of Louis X, to succeed to
Navarre, and made generous compensation for Champagne, shows that
the possibility of a queen regnant cannot have been entirely ignored.

   Now it is certainly true that, in a general sense, 'le fait crée le droit';
but in 1328 there were only two precedents for the exclusion of women,
they were recent and they did not entirely meet the case. In view of the
general feeling in favour of women's rights to succeed (to property
certainly, though not necessarily to the functions of monarchy) there

for the most part reproduced in the same writer's *Histoire des Institutions politiques et administratives de la France*, II (1898), pp. 52–86. Cf. Déprez, *Préliminaires*, chs. II, VI; J. Viard, 'Philippe
VI de Valois, la succession au trône', *Moyen Age*, XXXII (1921), pp. 218–22; J. M. Potter,
'The Development and Significance of the Salic Law of the French', *English Historical Review*,
LII (1937), pp. 235–53.
   [6] The general uncertainty is well shown by the judgements given in the king's court on
succession problems in the great fiefs during the fourteenth century: see the editor's notes in
The Chronicle of Jean de Venette, ed. R. A. Newhall (1953), pp. 151–3, 160–1, and authorities
there cited.
   [7] Quoted by Potter, *op. cit.*, p. 237; Viollet, p. 58.

was still room for argument, particularly on Edward's thesis that, even though his mother might not be able to succeed, she could transmit her rights to him and that, through her, he was in fact the nearest male heir to the late King Charles IV. What we know of the discussion in the great assembly which met in Paris during the spring of 1328 shows that there was some substance in this argument. Edward, as duke of Aquitaine and peer of France, was rightly represented there, and well represented it would seem, for, according to one manuscript of the *Grandes Chroniques*, his proctors convinced some of the doctors of civil and canon law of the validity of his argument.[8] If this is so, then Edward already had some support in France.

There is no need to bring in considerations of national feeling, which may or may not have existed at the time, in order to explain the final decision. It is true that the chronicler known as the First Continuator of Nangis states that some French barons said openly that they could not contemplate subjection to English rule with equanimity;[9] but before building too much on that remark, we must remember that it applies to the year 1328, when a decision in favour of Edward would have meant the rule of Isabella and Mortimer in France, a prospect which it might well have been difficult for the French to face with equanimity. Edward, after all, was no alien in France. His ancestry was as 'French' as Philip's; he was duke of Aquitaine, count of Ponthieu and a peer of France; he spoke French; and the case of Navarre provided a good and recent precedent for the rule of two kingdoms by one king. More revealing, perhaps, is the remark preserved in the *Chronographia*,[10] that Philip of Valois was preferred to Philip of Evreux (another possible candidate) because he was of more mature age. Philip of Valois was in fact 35 at the time, and Philip of Evreux 23; but Edward was still only 15 and in no sense his own master. There were thus good and practical reasons for preferring Philip of Valois to Edward, in 1328; and Philip was regent, well thought of and presumably in command of the situation. But while such considerations may explain what actually happened, they do nothing to weaken the merits of Edward's claim.

It was, indeed, opposed not by a rule of law but by a *fait accompli* or, perhaps one should say, by a short series of *faits accomplis*—unless it be argued, in face of the evidence, that the throne of France could be regarded as elective in the fourteenth century. Since, in the abstract, there was much to be said for it, there was no reason why Edward should not believe in his cause; and if the circumstances of the first ten years of his reign in England made it impossible for him to do much more than state his claim at that time[11] (and circumstances, indeed, had forced him to do homage for Aquitaine, an act which was taken to imply, and

---

[8] *Grandes Chroniques* (ed. J. Viard), IX (1937), pp. 72–3, note 2. *Cf. Chronique latine de Guillaume de Nangis . . . avec les continuations* (ed. H. Géraud), II (1843), pp. 82–4.

[9] *Ibid.*, p. 83.   [10] *Chronographia regum francorum* (ed. H. Moranvillé), I (1891), p. 292.

[11] But the claim was formally made in 1328, and some attempt to apply military pressure: Déprez, *Préliminaires*, pp. 35–6; *Fœdera* (Rec. Comm.), II, pp. 736–7, 743, 744, 749, 750–1.

was intended by the French to imply, a renunciation of his claim to the throne of France, though he was still under age and in no position to resist the demand for homage), it was not unnatural that he should take it up again when circumstances were more favourable. Indeed, if the claim meant anything to him he had no choice, for an inherited right implied a duty. Authority came from God. Edward made this point very clear in his manifestos of 1340:

> Whereas the kingdom of France has fallen to us by most clear right, by divine disposition and through the death of Charles of famous memory, late king of France, . . . and the lord Philip of Valois . . . intruded himself into the said kingdom by violence while we were still of tender years and occupies it in defiance of God and of justice; we, lest we should seem to neglect our right and the gift of celestial grace, or appear unwilling to put our will into conformity with divine pleasure, have put forward our claim to the said kingdom in due form and, trusting in the support of the heavenly kingdom, have undertaken the government of it, *as we ought to do*.[12]

This is too easily dismissed as common form or fine phrases. It rings true.

Considerations of this sort tend to establish Edward's good faith in his claim to the throne of France; they do not, by themselves, establish the point that the throne was his real war aim. This, perhaps, can best be argued from his military and political strategy, and from the whole manner in which he fought his war; but first it is necessary to consider the opposing thesis—that the claim and his assumption of the French royal title were simply a manœuvre and that his real objective was a secure and sovereign Aquitaine.

On the face of it, the war, up to 1360, does not look like a war in defence of Aquitaine. The campaigning started in the north-east of France and then moved to Brittany; only after six years or so was there any military activity of any consequence in the south. Although such a thing is difficult to measure quantitatively, it is perhaps reasonable to say that the greater part of Edward's military activity, until 1369, was in the north; and he himself led no campaign beyond the Loire. If all this activity in the north was a diversion, it was a very big diversion—too big to believe in, for it seems far-fetched to speak of defending Aquitaine on the moors of Brittany or the plain of Flanders.

More specifically, however, it is argued that Edward's real objective could not have been the throne of France because he showed himself ready, on more than one occasion, to abandon his claim in return for territorial concessions—in fact, for a sovereign Aquitaine. This argument needs closer examination. The incidents quoted in support of it are the discussions at Avignon in 1344, the negotiations leading to and

---

[12] *Fœdera*, II, pp. 1108-9; quoted by Avesbury (*De gestis mirabilibus*, ed. E. Maunde Thompson, R.S., 1889), pp. 309-10.

developing out of the draft treaty of Guines in 1354, and the ratification of the treaty of Brétigny in 1360.[13]

The discussions at Avignon during the autumn of 1344 are known to us in some detail owing to the survival of letters sent back by the English envoys and a journal written by one of them.[14] From these documents it is clear that they began by stating Edward's claim to the throne of France without qualification, that they returned to it again and again, and that although they could be persuaded to put it aside, as it were, in order to discuss other proposals that might tend towards a peace, they never retreated from their position that their king's demand was for the kingdom of France, as his right. It was the French delegates who insisted that the origins of the war lay in Aquitaine, and that the way to a settlement lay through a discussion of disputes arising in the duchy.

The treaty of Guines was drawn up in the spring of 1354.[15] According to the text printed by Bock, it would have given Aquitaine, the Loire provinces, Ponthieu and Calais to Edward, all in full sovereignty, in return for his renunciation of the throne of France. There is no mention of Brittany where Edward's forces and those of his Breton allies were well established. Final renunciations and ratifications were to be made at Avignon. A meeting duly took place there in the autumn, but no treaty was made. There is no direct evidence to show which side was responsible for this breakdown; most English chroniclers blame the French, but Knighton, whose information may ultimately have come from Henry of Lancaster, the leader of the English delegation, says that Lancaster refused specifically to give up Edward's claim and title to the kingdom of France.[16] Such a stand would have wrecked the treaty at once; and if he was at the same time negotiating with Charles of Navarre for a joint conquest and partition of France,[17] as he seems to have been, it may be that he came to Avignon with no intention of ratifying.[18]

However, the treaty of Brétigny does seem at first sight to destroy the argument, for here is a treaty in which Edward unquestionably renounced the throne of France in return for territory—an enlarged Aquitaine, Ponthieu, Calais and the county of Guines, all in full sovereignty. But, to divine Edward's intentions, the treaty must be

[13] Perroy, *Hundred Years War*, pp. 116, 129, 139.

[14] Froissart, *Chroniques*, ed. Kervyn de Lettenhove, XVIII (1874), pp. 202–56; E. Déprez, 'La Conférence d'Avignon (1344)', *Essays in Medieval History presented to Thomas Frederick Tout* (ed. A. G. Little and F. M. Powicke), 1925, pp. 301–320.

[15] G. Mollat, 'Innocent VI et les tentatives de paix entre la France et l'Angleterre (1353–55)', *Revue d'histoire ecclésiastique*, X (1909), pp. 729–43; F. Bock, 'Some new Documents illustrating the early years of the Hundred Years War (1353–1356)', *Bulletin of the John Rylands Library*, XV (1931), pp. 60–99.

[16] *Chronicon Henrici Knighton* (ed. J. R. Lumby, R.S.), II (1895), p. 78. But this part of the chronicle may have been written many years after the event, see V. H. Galbraith, 'The Chronicle of Henry Knighton', *Fritz Saxl, 1890–1948, A Volume of Memorial Essays* . . . (1957), pp. 136–48.

[17] R. Delachenal, 'Premières négociations de Charles le Mauvais avec les Anglais (1354–1355)', *Bibliothèque de l'Ecole des Chartes*, LXI (1900), pp. 253–82.

[18] But see the secret instruction printed by Bock, *Bulletin of the John Rylands Library*, XV, pp. 94–6.

considered in relation to the earlier drafts of 1358 and 1359 and the ratification at Calais in October 1360. The text of the first draft, which Delachenal discovered and which he called the 'First Treaty of London', would have given to Edward all that the treaty of 1360 gave him, together with suzerainty over Brittany.[19] Neither he nor other commentators seem to have noticed, however, that it demanded nothing whatever from Edward in return. The French territorial concessions would have been part of the price to be paid for King John's conditional release; nothing more. The second draft, produced rather more than a year later, in March 1359 ('the Second Treaty of London'),[20] demanded far greater territorial concessions from France, the whole of the old Angevin Empire, together with the counties of Ponthieu, Boulogne and Guines, and the town of Calais, all in full sovereignty and completely detached from the kingdom of France; but this time Edward promised to renounce his claim. However, if the seemingly casual way in which this promise is made is compared with the elaborate securities demanded of the king of France for the performance of his part in the treaty, and if one tries to visualize what France would have been like (shorn of all her western and northern provinces) if the treaty had been carried into effect, it is difficult to believe that it represents a sincere proposal for peace on Edward's part or, if it does, then his price for a promise to renounce the claim—a promise unsupported by any security—was the kingdom virtually delivered into his hands. This is how it must have seemed to the French Estates when, with superb courage, they rejected the treaty as 'ni passable ni faisable'.

If, a year later, Edward was prepared to give up his claim and his title for considerably less territory,[21] this was due to the overwhelming defeat he had suffered in the winter of 1359–60. The great campaign which was to have brought him to a coronation in Reims Cathedral petered out in the suburbs of Paris. Even so, the renunciation that he undertook to make was never actually made. French historians have seen in the detachment of the renunciation clauses from the ratification of the treaty at Calais, and their embodiment in a separate document to be put into force at a later date, a great victory for French diplomacy.[22] It may have been so. But the evidence which Dr. Chaplais has now put together suggests that it was Edward, not King John of France, who defaulted on the renunciations;[23] and if that is so, we may ask

[19] R. Delachenal, *Histoire de Charles V*, II (1927), pp. 59–77, 402–11.

[20] Text in E. Cosneau, *Les grands traités de la Guerre de Cent Ans* (1889), pp. 1–32. *Cf.* Delachenal, *op. cit.*, pp. 77–88.

[21] Texts of the treaties of Brétigny and Calais with subsidiary documents are printed in *Fœdera*, III, pp. 485–547. They are most conveniently studied in Cosneau, *op. cit.*, pp. 33–68, 173–4.

[22] Petit-Dutaillis and Collier, 'La diplomatie française et le traité de Brétigni', *Moyen Age*, X (1897), pp. 1–35; E. Perroy, 'Charles V et le traité de Brétigny', *ibid.*, XXXVIII (1928), pp. 255–81.

[23] P. Chaplais, 'Some Documents regarding the Fulfilment and Interpretation of the Treaty of Brétigny, 1361–1369', *Camden Miscellany*, XIX (1952), p. 7.

whether, having brought his army safely home in the summer, he no longer felt that the military situation was quite so desperate in October 1360 as it had appeared to those negotiating on his behalf in May. Had he given away more than he had any need to do?

It is difficult to be sure that Edward would never have renounced the title, short of military necessity, for a 'good peace'; but in fact no peace ever was good enough. Though he gave up the use of the French title for nine years, he never actually renounced the claim. The burden of proof still lies with those who maintain that Edward's aim was anything less than the throne of France.

II

Edward III was no fool. If he had really made the throne of France his war-aim, he must have felt that he had some chance of success. It is possible that recent historians have played down the dynastic issue, which a French writer has dismissed as 'preposterous',[24] because it seemed to them that Edward had no chance whatever of making himself effectively king of France, and therefore his real aim must have been something different. Now that the evidence can be seen to support the seriousness of Edward's claim, his chances must be re-examined.

In part, clearly, this is a matter of military organization. A good deal is now known about the organization of the English armies at this time,[25] but it is still difficult to compare it in detail with the French.[26] In part, similarly, it is a matter of personalities. England was favoured in the 'forties and the 'fifties with a rare constellation of military leaders, from the king himself, the Black Prince, and great nobles like Lancaster and Northampton, to men of much humbler origin such as Thomas Dagworth, Walter Mauny and Walter Bentley. No one can say, as yet, whether the presence of so much ability was a lucky chance, or whether there was something in the system that enabled the talent available to be used to the best advantage; and it would be good to know, more specifically than we do at present, how military and political policy was worked out and who was responsible. These questions become all the more interesting when it begins to appear that Edward's campaigns were not simply a matter of sending an army to France to look for a battle. There appears to be a pattern in these campaigns—perhaps it would be too much to call it a 'higher strategy'—a pattern that was closely related to political conditions.

The starting-point in this discussion must be Edward's assumption of the title 'King of France' at Ghent, on 26 January 1340. This was no

---

[24] Perroy, 'Franco-English Relations, 1350–1400', *History*, XXI (1936–7), p. 154.

[25] A. E. Prince, 'The Army and the Navy', in *The English Government at Work, 1327–1337*, ed. J. F. Willard and W. A. Morris, I (1940), pp. 332–76, and works cited there; N. B. Lewis, 'The Organisation of Indentured Retinues in Fourteenth-Century England', *Transactions of the Royal Historical Society*, 4th Series, XXVII (1945), pp. 29–39 etc.

[26] *Cf.* F. Lot and R. Fawtier, *Histoire des Institutions françaises au Moyen Age*, II, *Institutions royales* (1958), pp. 511–35.

impulsive and ill-considered act. The idea that Edward should assume the title is known to have been suggested by a deputation from Bruges as far back as 1328.[27] He actually used it in letters patent dated 7 October 1337;[28] and although its use on this occasion seems to have been for one particular purpose only,[29] it implies an intention to assume the title definitively at some suitable moment. The assumption of the French title had been under discussion between Edward and his allies for some months at least before January 1340,[30] and the decision must have been taken well before the date of the ceremony, for the new seal was used on that day.[31] Was it merely a coincidence that the ceremony took place so near to the anniversary of Edward's accession to the throne of England that his regnal years could be dated from the same day in both countries?[32] Moreover, as Jean le Bel pointed out,[33] Edward must have expected a great deal from this act if he was prepared to face the ridicule that would fall upon a ruler who called himself king of a country that he did not possess. It is quite possible that Edward's need for an alliance with Flanders provided the occasion; but the assumption of the French title could solve so many problems[34] that it is hard to believe that no considerations other than those directly affecting the Flemings were taken into account.

That much wider possibilities were in fact taken into consideration is shown by Edward's letters of reassurance to the people of Gascony[35] and the people of England,[36] and still more by the manifesto which he addressed to the people of France.[37] This last is a most important document which has not received the attention it deserves. It begins by stating the basis of Edward's claim and accuses Philip VI of usurping the kingdom of France while Edward was under age 'against God and against justice'. After long and mature deliberation, Edward had undertaken the government of the kingdom and had assumed the title, as he was in duty bound to do. It was not his intention to deprive the people of France of their rights; on the contrary, he was resolved to do justice to all 'and to re-establish the good laws and customs that were in force in the time of his progenitor St. Louis'. Nor was it his intention to seek his own gain at their expense, by variations in the currency or by un-

---

[27] H. Pirenne, *Histoire de Belgique*, II (4th ed. 1947), pp. 94–5.

[28] *Fœdera*, II, pp. 1000, 1001.

[29] Letters were issued on the same day without the French title (P.R.O., Treaty Roll 11, m. 2).

[30] H. S. Lucas, *The Low Countries and the Hundred Years' War, 1326–1347*, pp. 358 ff.

[31] *Fœdera*, II, p. 1107; letter dated 'apud Gandavum, xxvi die Januarii, anno regni nostri Franciae primo, Angliae vero quartodecimo'. This formula would not have been compatible with the old seal.

[32] A matter of considerable convenience: compare the complexities in the regnal years of Philip and Mary.

[33] *Chronique de Jean le Bel* (ed. J. Viard and E. Déprez), I (1904), pp. 167–8.

[34] *Cf.* the letter of summons addressed to the archbishop of Canterbury, 21 February 1340 (*Fœdera*, II, p. 1115): 'Non mirantes ex hoc quod stilum nostrum consuetum mutavimus, & Regem Franciae nos facimus nominari; nam diversae subsunt causae, per quas hoc facere necessario nos oportet.'

[35] *Fœdera*, II, p. 1127.   [36] Froissart, ed. Kervyn de Lettenhove, XVIII, pp. 129–30.

[37] *Fœdera*, II, pp. 1108–9, 1111.

lawful exactions and maltolts because, he thanked God, he had enough to support his estate and his honour; indeed, he hoped to ease their burdens and to maintain the liberties and privileges of everyone, especially those of Holy Church. In all matters affecting the kingdom of France he would seek the counsel of peers, prelates, nobles and other *sapientes* who were faithful to him; and he would never act capriciously or arbitrarily. All men of the kingdom of France who should recognize him as their lord and king before Easter following (as the people of Flanders had already rightly done) would be received into his especial peace and protection and would continue to enjoy their property undisturbed. The manifesto was ordered to be affixed to church doors so that all might take notice.

No doubt historians have taken little notice of this document because it seems, at first sight, so commonplace, the sort of appeal that any invader might put out. But in fact it is very carefully drafted. Whoever composed it knew a great deal about the history of France during the previous fifty years or so, for point by point it meets the grievances of the politically effective (or at any rate politically articulate) French against their government, as these were expressed, for example, in the provincial charters of 1314–15—taxation which was held to exceed the bounds of legality and which was regarded as an attack upon the rights, property and privileges of churches, nobility and townsmen: debasement of the currency: arbitrary acts of kings and their officials.[38] Edward does not merely denounce these evils; he offers himself as a 'constitutional' king, prepared to act always with the counsel of magnates and learned men; above all he undertakes (this is a direct echo of nearly all the provincial charters) to return to the customs 'of the time of the good St. Louis', that is, to the time when, as it was generally thought, these objectionable practices were as yet not prevalent.

What this really amounted to is that Edward might represent what we should call 'an alternative government', with a readily comprehensible political programme which was all the more telling because, though there had been opposition to royal centralization in France since the beginning of the century, it had so far failed to find effective political expression. Henceforward, however, any Frenchman who might find it convenient or profitable to change his allegiance, or who might be driven to it; anyone who might come to feel, as the result of defeats or disasters, that the Valois succession had not been blessed by God; all who were alienated by those arbitrary acts of cruelty and violence to which the early Valois kings were occasionally prone (such as the execution of the Breton seigneurs in 1343, of the count of Eu and Guines in 1350 and of the friends of Charles of Navarre in 1356)—all such could look for protection and comfort to one who was already acknowledged as the rightful king of France in Flanders (and presumably in Aquitaine)

[38] On the provincial charters, see A. Artonne, *Le mouvement de 1314 et les chartes provinciales de 1315* (1912).

and who had solemnly taken the title and assumed the responsibility of government; and they were provided with a legal pretext for so doing.

That there must have been some such calculation in the minds of Edward and his advisers, however vaguely, is shown by what followed. The leagues of 1314–15, and the provincial charters they produced, were the work of the nobility of the second order, not the dukes of Brittany or Burgundy or their peers, but nobility of provincial importance. This was shown clearly in Artois where the leaguers were as much concerned with the oppressions of the officers of the Countess as with the aggressions of the king's officers; and the really significant thing about these leagues is the most immediately obvious. In contrast to baronial movements in England during the thirteenth and fourteenth centuries, they were organized on a provincial basis and their aim was a charter of provincial liberties. This by itself shows that national consciousness, if indeed it existed in early fourteenth-century France, was still a very tender plant; and Edward, if he were prepared to conduct the conquest of France province by province, while not neglecting more traditional methods altogether, was provided with a fine opportunity which, as duke of Aquitaine, he should know how to exploit. His action in Normandy, during the years 1356–1360, offers a very good example.

The duchy, though incorporated into the royal domain after 1204, had preserved much of its individuality.[39] Its administration, staffed though it was by royal officers from Paris, remained distinct; nobles and prelates still attended the exchequer of pleas which, though no longer sovereign, continued to administer the custom of Normandy. This distinct legal system, so often described simply as 'the laws and customs of the country'—in practice, the liberties and privileges of individual churches, barons and communities quite as much as details of legal precepts and procedure—gave to the Normans the basis of their 'provincial consciousness'. To the Norman seigneurs and churchmen, the vast development in the activity of royal government during the thirteenth century appeared as a threat to their 'laws and customs', otherwise their properties and liberties. They objected to the practice of encouraging appeals from the exchequer to the parliament, because that endangered the custom; they objected to the methods and indeed to the fact of royal taxation as an assault upon their liberties and property; they objected to the activities of the royal *baillis* who strove continually to exalt royal jurisdiction against private rights of justice. They stood out for traditional feudal decentralization against royal centralization.

These grievances were given an opportunity to express themselves, and thereby to grow and be organized, in the assemblies which the king summoned from time to time to consent to his demands for taxation, particularly since such meetings were often called as assemblies of the duchy. One result was the 'Charte aux Normands' of 1315 which,

[39] A. Coville, *Les États de Normandie* (1894); J. R. Strayer, *The Administration of Normandy under St. Louis* (1932); R. Besnier, *La Coutume de Normandie, Histoire externe* (1935), pp. 70 ff.

because of its background, was a more effective document than any of the other provincial charters of the time. Among other things it restored its sovereignty to the Norman exchequer, thus safeguarding and, as it were, sealing the custom; and it offered some protection against taxation without consent, making it more difficult for the king to raise taxes in Normandy without calling a provincial assembly. The important implication of these concessions is that they made Normandy a distinct, privileged and quasi-political entity. But this did not end the Norman grievances, for the movement of 1314-15, as a whole, hardly affected the development of royal policy; though now, and for some time, the Normans were able to make consent to taxation conditional upon a confirmation of their privileges, and on one occasion the king had to associate himself with an extraordinary scheme for a new 'Norman Conquest of England' to divert their indignation away from himself.[40]

Edward's opportunity to turn all this to his own account came in 1356, when King John surprised a dinner-party that was being held by his son, the duke of Normandy, in Rouen Castle, took Charles of Navarre prisoner and executed four of his associates out of hand.[41] One of these was John, count of Harcourt, who, with his uncle Godfrey of Harcourt and Charles of Navarre himself, was among the leaders of the Norman opposition. Now although there may well have been an element of personal feud in this incident, there can be little doubt that the Norman grievances were at the bottom of it. Already, in 1354, Charles of Navarre had assured Edward that the Norman nobility was behind him to a man;[42] and now Philip of Navarre, Charles's brother, having failed to obtain satisfaction from King John, sent in his *défi* and opened negotiations with Edward. Godfrey of Harcourt did likewise; and both did homage to him as 'King of France and duke of Normandy',[43] for that was the condition which Edward imposed before he would give them assistance. It is easy to see that the simple title 'King of France' would not raise much enthusiasm in Normandy, for the Norman quarrel was with the king of France, his violence and his centralizing policy; but Edward could offer himself to the Normans as their duke, pledged to act in all things 'selon les lois, coutumes et usages du pays'. In the Cotentin, where the barony of St. Sauveur-le-Vicomte was bequeathed to him by Godfrey of Harcourt, he was able to put this principle into practice by appointing officers to the traditional posts of local government with such authority as pertained to their offices 'according to the custom of our duchy of Normandy'.[44]

---

[40] Coville, *op cit.*, pp. 47-50. A copy of the agreement was found, presumably in the archives of the town, during the sack of Caen in 1346. It was sent back to England and read at Paul's Cross—a superb gift to Edward's war propaganda (Avesbury, *De gestis mirabilibus*, pp. 363-7; *cf.* Murimuth, *Continuatio Chronicarum, ibid.*, pp. 205-12, 257-63).

[41] On this incident, see Delachenal, *Histoire de Charles V*, I, pp. 134-56.

[42] Froissart, ed. Kervyn de Lettenhove, XVIII, pp. 354-6.   [43] *Fœdera*, III, pp. 332, 340.

[44] L. Delisle, *Histoire du château et des sires de Saint-Sauveur-le-Vicomte* (1867). Le Patourel, 'Edouard III "roi de France et duc de Normandie", 1356-1360', *Revue historique de droit français et étranger*, 4e sér., XXXI (1953), pp. 317-18.

It is difficult to measure the degree of support that was given to Edward's cause in Normandy; but after Lancaster's brilliant campaign in the summer of 1356, the co-operation of his forces with those of Philip of Navarre brought English troops to the gates of Paris and even into the city, and established a number of English garrisons in Norman strongholds. Politically, Edward's action gave him recognition as king of France by a group of Norman seigneurs and their followers, which, whether large or small, was important simply because it existed. Edward had a foothold, perhaps more than a foothold, in the strategically vital duchy of Normandy.

Behind the opposition of this provincial nobility, however, there lurked, already in 1340, the beginnings of a still more dangerous reaction to royal centralization in France. The nobles of the front rank, the counts of Flanders, the dukes of Brittany and Burgundy—and the duke of Aquitaine—had been building up the structure of government in their duchies and counties just as the king had been building up the government of his kingdom, sometimes in advance of the king, as in Normandy and Flanders during the twelfth century, sometimes in imitation, as in Brittany and Burgundy during the thirteenth century when both were ruled by dynasties of Capetian origin. Each 'principality' had a *curia* in a more or less advanced state of specialization into *conseil, parlement* and *chambre des comptes* (though the names varied from one to another), and each had an organized system of local government. In Flanders the count's *baillis* can be seen pursuing precisely the same policy of disintegrating seigneurial autonomies as the king's *baillis* were pursuing in the kingdom at large; and each of these princes was building up a system of judicial appeals within their territories on the same principles as the king in his kingdom.[45]

Sooner or later the royal and princely governments were bound to clash for both were moving towards the same end. No doubt the princes felt the effects of royal centralization in their pride and in their pockets as much as the nobility of the second rank; but they also resented it as interference in their governments, as a threat to their authority, as a menace that might at any time throw their administration completely out of gear or bring it to a standstill. It is likely that this was felt as strongly by his officials as by duke or count himself—before the end of the century the lawyers were saying, both in Normandy and Brittany, that 'le duché n'est pas du royaume'.[46] Besides, most of the principalities had strong interests in countries outside the kingdom, Flanders in the Empire and in England, Brittany in England, Aquitaine in England and in Spain; and liege homage as it was being interpreted in the fourteenth century made it difficult or impossible

[45] F. Lot and R. Fawtier (ed.), *Histoire des Institutions françaises au Moyen Age*, I, *Institutions seigneuriales* (1957). This volume gives much of the information, but it is not the comparative constitutional history of the great French fiefs which is so much needed.
[46] E. G. Léonard, *Histoire de la Normandie* (1944), p. 69; B. A. Pocquet du Haut-Jussé, *Les papes et les ducs de Bretagne*, I (1928), p. 420.

for the princes to pursue the 'foreign policies' that their interests demanded.

The beginnings of a princely reaction can already be seen before 1340. It can be seen most clearly in Aquitaine, where Edward I had done all that careful organization could do to restrain or prevent appeals in Paris, to anticipate royal legislation and evade royal taxation, to build up a complete provincial government[47] and ultimately to set up a theory of English sovereignty in Gascony over against the French king's sovereignty in his kingdom.[48] The possibility of ducal sovereignty was hardly envisaged as yet in Brittany, where the duke was, in general, a very loyal vassal like his brother of Burgundy at this time; but he too could get it established that there should be no appeals to Paris from his duchy until all the resources of his own hierarchy of courts had been exhausted, and secure acknowledgement that he performed military service of his own free will and not as an obligation.[49] In Flanders the position was vastly complicated by the precocious economic and social —as well as political—development of the county, so that King Philip IV's demands led to what was in effect a war of independence in which England had been involved as far back as the 1290s.

Thus Edward's difficulties in Aquitaine, whatever their place may be in the origins of the war, were by no means peculiar to him. However loyal the princes might be personally, these same difficulties were present in all their duchies and counties to a greater or less degree. If one were to say that the first phase of the Hundred Years War was a civil war, a rebellion of the princes against royal centralization which threatened to reduce them before very long to mere landlords—a rebellion led by the duke of Aquitaine because of his great resources outside the kingdom—it would be an exaggeration of one aspect of the matter, but there would be a good deal of truth in it. There can be no doubt, at least, that the war greatly assisted the process which was raising these duchies and counties into real principalities that were independent *de facto* and all but sovereign *de jure* in the fifteenth century.[50]

However this may be, the situation offered great possibilities to a prince who, having a claim to the throne of France, might think of pursuing it province by province, adjusting his methods to the individual circumstances of each. The traditional alternative of a single decisive

[47] Unpublished theses, P. Chaplais, 'Gascon Appeals to England, 1259–1453' (University of London), and J. P. Trabut-Cussac, 'L'Administration anglaise en Gascogne sous Henri III et Edouard Ier' (École des Chartes); *cf.* Sir Maurice Powicke, *The Thirteenth Century, 1216–1307* (1953), ch. VII.

[48] P. Chaplais, 'English Arguments concerning the Feudal Status of Aquitaine in the Fourteenth Century', *Bulletin of the Institute of Historical Research*, XXI (1948), pp. 203–13.

[49] B. Pocquet du Haut-Jussé, 'Le grand fief breton', in *Histoire des Institutions françaises au Moyen Age*, ed. Lot and Fawtier, I, *Institutions seigneuriales* p. 277; E. Durtelle de Saint-Sauveur, *Histoire de Bretagne*, I (3rd ed. 1946), pp. 214–5.

[50] E. Perroy, 'Feudalism or Principalities in Fifteenth-century France', *Bulletin of the Institute of Historical Research*, XX (1947), pp. 181–5. B. Pocquet du Haut-Jussé, *Deux féodaux Bourgogne & Bretagne (1363–1491)*, 1935. It would be interesting to know how much the Breton principality of the fifteenth century owed to Edward's administration in the duchy from 1342 until 1362 and Duke John IV's upbringing in the English court.

engagement failed, as it was bound to do, for there was no reason why the king of France should risk all on such a judgement by battle. Edward tried it in 1339–40,[51] and even sent his personal challenge to Philip; but though his actions in the Low Countries and north-eastern France did not give him his battle and failed to win over the count of Flanders, it did give him some recognition and support in the great Flemish cities. That was so much gained; and it might have suggested a 'provincial strategy', for the essence of the agreement he made with those who would support him in Flanders was that he should give them those things which they could not obtain from King Philip—not economic facilities only, but release from ecclesiastical penalties imposed at the instance of King Philip, the restoration of the 'western provinces' lost in the wars of the past 150 years, a common currency for Flanders, Brabant and France, and protection in their persons and their property particularly from impositions and exactions laid upon them by the king of France[52]—and the campaign of 1340 was fought ostensibly to redeem his promise. Whatever his ultimate aim, the immediate objective then was of provincial significance.

This 'provincial strategy' is well seen in Edward's handling of the succession dispute in Brittany which arose on the death of Duke John III in April 1341.[53] In a sense Edward was following a policy which may perhaps be traced ultimately to the ambitions of the dukes of Normandy in the tenth and eleventh centuries, certainly to the time when the sea route from London and Southampton to Bordeaux and Bayonne came to have some importance for the kings of England. Their need to maintain a friendly Brittany is well shown in the use which John, Henry III and Edward I made of the earldom of Richmond, traditionally a possession of the ducal house of Brittany.[54] During Edward II's reign it seemed as though Richmond and Brittany might go to different branches of the family; but when John of Brittany died in 1334, Edward III restored Richmond to Duke John III, and followed this up with marks of signal favour.[55] Not only were Breton possessions in England specifically exempted from the general seizure of French property at the beginning of the war,[56] but the earldom of Richmond was left in Duke John's hands to the day of his death, notwithstanding the fact that he had taken part, on the French side, in the campaigns of 1339 and 1340.

It had long been known that his death would lead to a succession

---

[51] And again in 1355?—Delachenal, *Histoire de Charles V*, I, p. 108.

[52] *Calendar of Patent Rolls, 1338–1340*, pp. 511–16; H. S. Lucas, *The Low Countries and the Hundred Years' War*, pp. 362–3.

[53] The best account of the Breton war of succession, though it stands in need of considerable amendment both in detail and in general interpretation, is still A. Le Moyne de la Borderie, *Histoire de Bretagne*, III (1899). *Cf.* Durtelle de Saint-Sauveur, *Histoire de Bretagne*, I, pp. 237–52; E. Déprez, 'La "Querelle de Bretagne" . . .', *Mém. de la Soc. d'histoire et d'archéologie de Bretagne*, VII (1926), pp. 25–60.

[54] S. Painter, *The Scourge of the Clergy: Peter of Dreux, Duke of Brittany* (1937); G. E. C., *Complete Peerage*, art. 'Richmond'; *Victoria County History, York, North Riding*, pp. 1–9.

[55] E.g. *Cal. Close Rolls, 1339–1341*, p. 450—and note the date, 18 February 1340.

[56] *Fœdera*, II, p. 982. *Cf.* e.g. *Cal. Patent Rolls, 1340–43*, p. 73 etc.

dispute, and that, of the two candidates, the king of France favoured Charles of Blois. His rival, John of Montfort, was likely therefore to turn to Edward on general grounds, and also because the earldom of Richmond, if he could persuade Edward to grant it to him, would make a welcome addition to his meagre resources. Nevertheless, in the negotiations of the spring and summer of 1341, it was Edward who took the initiative, or so it seems.[57] These negotiations resulted in an alliance, a conditional grant of Richmond to John of Montfort and the promise of military assistance.[58]

Before the end of the year, John of Montfort was a prisoner, and his cause might well have foundered then and there but for the energy and determination of his 'lion-hearted' duchess. Fresh negotiations, conducted in her name, produced two agreements, one in the spring and the other in the summer of 1342; and this time, in return for military help, Edward was given recognition as king of France and suzerain of Brittany, the right to collect such ducal revenues as could still be levied and the use of such castles, towns and ports as he might require for his troops.[59] After John of Montfort's death in 1345, Edward acted as guardian of his heir and namesake (who was brought up in England), and governed the duchy, or such of it as he controlled, both as suzerain and as guardian. The civil administration which he set up there was as near normal as, in the circumstances, it could be. He set up courts and appointed officials according to the laws and customs of the country, and was able to maintain some degree of continuity in the forms and institutions of government.[60] He never attempted to occupy the duchy as a whole, though opportunities were presented to him in 1346 and 1352. His objective was to maintain a strong military foothold there, sufficient to give confidence and security to the supporters of John of Montfort who recognized him as king of France and suzerain of Brittany, to encourage their loyalty and to win new adherents by grants

[57] This point can hardly be said to be established, but it is strongly suggested by Edward's policy up to the time of John III's death and by the time-table of events, so far as we know them, in the weeks immediately following. John III died on 30 April, 1341. A letter patent dated 10 May refers to him as though he were still living (*Cal. Patent Rolls, 1340–43*, p. 185), though his lands were committed to custody by an order dated 16 May (*Cal. Fine Rolls, 1337–47*, p. 225). This suggests that the news reached the English court at some time between those dates. Now Richard Swaffham and Gavin Corder, who were sent on an important mission to John of Montfort 'super aliquibus eidem Duci ex parte Regis exponendis & ad audiendum & recipiendum & reportandum Regi super hiis deliberacionem & voluntatem dicti ducis', left London on 6 June (Swaffham's expenses account, Pipe Roll, 16 Edw. III m. 48r). The terms of their commission, as paraphrased in this account, suggests that it was Edward who was making proposals; and, seeing that the Council had to decide its policy and the English envoys had to prepare for their journey, this time-table hardly allows for the reception of a Breton mission before Swaffham's departure. This same account makes it quite clear that John of Montfort did not visit England during the summer of 1341.

[58] *Fœdera*, II, p. 1176. Great preparations were made for an expedition in the autumn of 1341, but Murimuth was probably right when he said 'Super quo fuit diu deliberatum, sed nihil factum hoc anno': *Continuatio Chronicarum*, p. 121.

[59] The text of these agreements does not appear to have survived; but their substance is preserved in the commissions given to Sir Walter Mauny and the earl of Northampton. Some of these commissions are printed in *Fœdera*, II, pp. 1189, 1205.

[60] Le Patourel, 'L'Administration ducale dans la Bretagne montfortiste, 1345–1362', *Revue historique de droit français et étranger*, 4ᵉ série, XXXII (1954), pp. 144–7.

of castles, lands and revenues seized from those who refused their allegiance. The objectives of Lancaster and the Black Prince in Aquitaine were fundamentally the same.

The Breton episode has been treated as something of a sideshow in the wider conflict of the fourteenth century; but when it is seen that Edward was doing in Brittany just what he was doing in Flanders, Normandy, Aquitaine, and elsewhere—gradually extending the 'area of recognition', bidding for the allegiance of seigneurs and towns—it assumes as much importance as any part of Edward's war. Indeed, it is beginning to appear that this competition for provincial allegiances, with its often sordid trade in 'confiscations', represents the way in which the war was being waged quite as much as the campaigns and the battles, and that many of the campaigns were designed as much to impress provincial opinion and provide 'confiscations' for distribution as anything else. The Valois throne was indeed at stake.

The purely military side of the war becomes more comprehensible when these provincial considerations are borne in mind. The campaigns in Brittany in 1342–3 seem to have been intended to do no more than establish a foothold in the duchy, though Edward was no doubt ready to take any opportunity that might present itself. Likewise, when it is suggested that he had nothing to show for the Crécy campaign and the exhausting siege of Calais but 'one battle and one town',[61] it is forgotten that, at the same time, Northampton and Dagworth had not only strengthened and extended his hold on Brittany so that it would have needed a tremendous effort on the part of the French to drive out his garrisons there, but they had also secured the person of Charles of Blois. Moreover there can be little doubt that these Breton campaigns were planned as a combined operation[62] with Lancaster's campaigns in Aquitaine, which completely restored the English position and prestige there. The king's invasion of Normandy may, indeed, have been secondary, designed to divert French forces from their counter-attacks in Aquitaine. The notion of simultaneous and related campaigns in several provinces had produced excellent results; and Neville's Cross was thrown in for good measure.

The outcome, when the similarly related campaigns of Lancaster in Normandy and the Black Prince in Aquitaine[63] had culminated in the battle of Poitiers, was impressive. Consider the situation early in 1359, irrespective of the internal dissensions which had been tearing France apart. Edward was recognized as king of France in his own duchy of

[61] Perroy, 'Franco-English Relations, 1350–1400', *History*, XXI, p. 149.

[62] This seems to follow from the terms of the commissions, *Fœdera*, III, 34–5, 37. Northampton was to operate in Brittany and France, Lancaster in Aquitaine and (as documents issued by him and enrolled on the Gascon rolls show) Languedoc. *Cf. Cal. Patent Rolls, 1348–50*, p. 541.

[63] H. J. Hewitt (*The Black Prince's Expedition of 1355–1357* (1958), pp. 101, 105–7) is doubtful if there was co-ordination between them; but if there was not, Lancaster's march to the Loire is hard to explain. *Cf.* Delachenal, *Histoire de Charles V*, I, pp. 129, 203, 266, and the indenture calendared in *The Black Prince's Register*, part IV (1933), pp. 143–5.

Aquitaine, secured and enlarged by the successes of Lancaster and the Black Prince; in a large part of Brittany, where allegiance was supported and maintained by English garrisons and by the later campaigns of Bentley and Lancaster; in Normandy likewise, thanks to the alliance with Philip of Navarre and the establishment of English garrisons there; in Calais and the surrounding country; and in large parts of Flanders.[64] Add to that one unlooked-for result of the indenture system and the static garrison warfare in Normandy and Brittany—the formation of what were in effect free companies that were now spreading almost unchecked far into the Loire provinces, into Picardy, Champagne and even into Burgundy[65]—and it will appear that Edward had some reason to think that the time had come for a 'coronation in force'. What the effect of such a coronation might have been is shown by a clause in the treaty of Guillon by which the duke of Burgundy agreed to accept Edward as king of France if he were duly crowned in Reims Cathedral.[66]

This methodical provincial strategy, this striving for local recognition, tend to confirm the evidence quoted earlier in favour of the thesis that Edward's objective was the crown of France and nothing less; and the situation of 1359, which explains and in a sense justifies the terms of the 'Second Treaty of London' (since nearly all that he demanded in that treaty was in some sense his already), suggests that he had come a great deal nearer to this objective than has commonly been thought.

The spring of 1359 saw the climax in his fortunes. Thereafter things soon began to go wrong. He ignored Charles of Navarre in his plans for the final campaign, with the result that that slippery prince remained neutral and non-participant when he might have been useful—or did Edward think that the time had come to throw him over since he, too, had claims to the throne of France? In addition, Edward's security was very bad in 1359. It was known so well in advance that he would make for Reims that the citizens had time to complete and strengthen the new defences of their city.[67] On this occasion it was the future Charles V who directed the defence of his country; and his strategy of avoiding an engagement at all costs, whatever the invading armies might be doing, won its first great victory. The treaty of Brétigny-Calais registers Edward's defeat; for although he might repent of his concessions and shirk the fulfilment of its terms, he had shot his bolt.

[64] By the Treaty of Brétigny, Edward undertook to renounce 'homagio, superioritati & dominio ducatuum Normannie & Turonie, comitatuum Andegavie & de Mayne; et superioritati & homagio ducatus Britannie; superioritati & homagio comitatus & patrie Flandrie...', *Fœdera*, III, 489.

[65] Delachenal, *Histoire de Charles V*, II, pp. 21–45; S. Luce, *Histoire de Bertrand du Guesclin ... La jeunesse de Bertrand* (1876), pp. 458–509; H. Denifle, *La Guerre de Cent Ans et la désolation des églises ...*, I, i (1899), pp. 217–316.

[66] *Fœdera*, III, p. 473; *cf.* Delachenal, *Histoire de Charles V*, II, p. 170.

[67] Delachenal, *Histoire de Charles V*, II, pp. 154–7.

XIII

THE TREATY OF BRÉTIGNY, 1360

THE course of events, military and diplomatic, which led from the battle of Poitiers (19 September 1356) to the ratification of the treaty of Brétigny (24 October 1360) was fully worked out, half a century ago, by Delachenal, in his great *Histoire de Charles V*.[1] His narrative, and his treatment of the policies and ambitions underlying the events, have won general acceptance.[2] He had studied the French evidence apparently exhaustively and showed himself to be well acquainted with the English documents. It was he who first suggested that a document bound up into Cotton MS. Caligula D.III was a draft of the terms agreed upon in May 1358, and this, among other things, enabled him to give a connected and intelligible account of the diplomacy of these years, which is poorly documented even by medieval standards.

The story he tells may be summarized somewhat as follows. Negotiations were opened, at the instance of the papacy, while the Black Prince and his royal captive were still at Bordeaux. These resulted in a truce (23 March 1357),[3] which was to last until 9 April 1359, and in a preliminary, secret agreement on the terms of peace, of which nothing is known. When the Black Prince had brought King John to London, negotiations were reopened in England; and in course of time these produced an agreement which Delachenal called 'the first treaty of London' (May 1358). The terms of this agreement, so far as they can be reconstructed (for no formal document is known to survive), he regarded as

---

[1] R. Delachenal, *Histoire de Charles V*, ii (Paris, 1909, repr. 1927), chapters II–VI. I am very much indebted to Dr Chaplais, Professor W. Croft Dickinson and Professor J. G. Edwards for reading this paper in draft and for their help and criticism; but I must take responsibility for the opinions expressed herein.

[2] T. F. Tout, *Chapters*, iii (1928), pp. 221–30; E. Perroy, *The Hundred Years War* (London, 1951), pp. 136–40.

[3] Rymer, *Foedera* (Rec. Comm. ed.), III. i, 348–51.

reasonable and moderate, and as anticipating, in a remarkable way, the terms later accepted at Brétigny. The treaty was not implemented, however, for a number of reasons, of which one was, in all probability, the failure of the French to raise the first instalment of King John's ransom by the appointed day. Negotiations were resumed early in 1359, when the end of the truce was already in sight; and these resulted in an extension of the truce to 24 June and in a new draft treaty, Delachenal's 'second treaty of London' (March 1359). The terms, since they demanded the surrender of quite half the kingdom of France, were clearly impossible and were summarily rejected by the French Estates assembled in Paris. Edward therefore proceeded with the great campaign which he had been preparing and which was launched in November. It met with so little success that when the French made contact, late in April 1360, Edward was prepared to negotiate once more. The agreement, known as the treaty of Brétigny (more properly the articles of a treaty, for it was drawn up in the names of the two princes and required ratification by the two kings), was produced in three or four days, an achievement which was only possible, Delachenal thought, because it represented, for all practical purposes, a return to the terms of 1358.

This treaty, which gave to Edward an enlarged and sovereign Aquitaine in return for his renunciation of the French throne, has always been considered as a great triumph for him, since it gave him what he had been fighting for. His claim to the French throne and his assumption of the title had been but tactical devices, readily expendable for solid advantages; his real objective had been an Aquitaine freed from the restrictions upon the king-duke's authority there which had been imposed by the treaty of Paris (1259) and subsequent French policy, restrictions which were rapidly reducing that authority to nullity. All this he had achieved with territorial extensions thrown in. When, however, the treaty was ratified at Calais in October 1360, the provisions relating to King John's formal renunciation of his rights and sovereignty in those territories which the treaty assigned to Edward, with Edward's renunciation of the French throne and all that he was giving up by the treaty, were taken out of the main document and embodied in a separate agreement (*Littere cum clausula c'est assavoir*), which also laid down the procedure by which these renunciations were to be made and the date, about a year later, when the final exchange of documents should take place. In the event, these renunciations were never made; and this fact enabled King Charles V to argue, later on, that since the sovereignty of the king of France over Aquitaine had never been formally surrendered he was legally entitled to accept the appeals which precipitated a renewal of the war. In the fighting which followed, the French recovered much more than they had lost during the years from 1340 to 1360. To Petit-Dutaillis and Collier,[1] writing some years before Delachenal, this possibility had been foreseen by the Regent Charles, as he then was, at the time of the ratification; and it was he and his advisers (it could not have been King John, who had shown himself to be interested in little but his personal freedom) who were responsible for this postponement of the renunciations, thus putting off the evil day, as it turned out, for ever. To Delachenal, as to others, such diplomatic prescience was scarcely credible; but he, on the assumption that the French had most to lose by the full implementation of the treaty (for John was abandoning all rights over extensive parts of his kingdom while Edward gave up no more than 'prétentions chimériques et surannées, qu'il était impuissant à soutenir'[2]), regarded the separation of the renunciation clauses from the main treaty, and their postponement,[3] as a diplomatic victory for the French, since it made the whole treaty conditional upon the carrying out of the renunciations in due form and on the prescribed date. If this condition was not fulfilled, 'il n'y avait plus de traité de Brétigny'.[4] Edward, that is to say, who had harvested his military victories at Brétigny, was defeated by French subtlety[5] at Calais, a notion which has appealed to historians on both sides of the Channel.

There is much that is arguable in this thesis, but to argue it fully would demand a lengthy treatise. A systematic re-examination of all the evidence, both in England and in France, might well be very rewarding, but this is not being attempted here. Delachenal based his narrative upon a very extensive body of evidence, and the argument of this paper is founded, essentially, upon that same body of evidence, with all the limitations which

---

[1] Ch. Petit-Dutaillis and P. Collier, 'La Diplomatie française et le Traité de Brétigny', *Moyen Age*, x (1897), pp. 1–35.

[2] Delachenal, *op. cit.*, ii, p. 243.

[3] *Ibid.*, p. 244.   [4] *Ibid.*, p. 248.

[5] *Ibid.*, pp. 248 and 250, n. 1.

that may imply. Its object is to re-open questions rather than to try to settle them.

Little is known of the course of the negotiations[1] leading to the agreement of 1358, Delachenal's 'first treaty of London'. The comings and goings of envoys can be chronicled from the record of safe-conducts issued to them,[2] but there is nothing to tell us what they did or what they said. Knighton, however, has a story which is worth remembering, though it is not directly supported by any other evidence. He says that the papal envoys, who were then in England, opened the proceedings early in July 1357 by offering Edward 'all the lands of his ancestors' as a basis for negotiation. To this Edward replied shortly that if some of these lands were temporarily out of his possession, he would recover them when God willed, 'and he said to them that they should speak of the crown of France, which he claimed'. The envoys answered that their commission did not extend to such difficult matters, and the discussions were adjourned for a while.[3]

Negotiations were resumed in the autumn, and the agreement that was eventually reached must have been dated 8 May 1358.[4] No formal instrument embodying its terms is known to survive, but evidence of its nature is not lacking. Delachenal thought that a document, now bound up with others in Cotton MS. Caligula D.III,[5] might be an early draft, representing perhaps the report which the French envoys presented to the dauphin and his council on 27 January 1358.[6] This document bears no note of identifica-

---

[1] Delachenal, *op. cit.*, ii, pp. 47–67.

[2] Treaty Rolls 35 and 36 (Rotuli Franciae, 31 and 32 Edward III). Delachenal's narrative could be usefully supplemented here.

[3] Knighton, *Chronicon*, ed. J. R. Lumby (R[olls] S[eries], 1889–95), ii, pp. 94–95.

[4] *Chronica Johannis de Reading et Anonymi Cantuariensis*, ed. J. Tait (1914), p. 208; *Chronique des règnes de Jean II et de Charles V*, ed. R. Delachenal (Soc. de l'hist. de France, 1910–20), i, p. 176. Walsingham (*Historia Anglicana*, ed. H. T. Riley, R. S. (1863–64), i, p. 284) gives the date as 2 May.

[5] British Museum, Cotton MS. Caligula D. III, 84–88, printed in Delachenal, *op. cit.*, ii, pp. 402–11. The printed text could be improved considerably.

[6] *Chronique ... de Jean II et de Charles V*, i, pp. 143–44: 'Le Samedy xxviie jour du mois de janvier, les messages du roy qui estoient venus d'Angleterre ... firent leur rapport au duc de Normandie, en la presence de pluseurs de son Conseil ... sur le traictié de l'accort fait en Angleterre ...'

tion or date; for the most part it is written in the language of an agreement but ends with a note of two matters which were 'also discussed'. This and the title—'Le Trattie et la parlaunce de la paix parentre nostre seignur le Roi et la partie de France'—both suggest that it is the report of a formal conversation between the two kings; a study of its provisions and its terminology leave no doubt that it belongs to the negotiations of 1357–58. It is written in an English hand with many corrections in the text, some of which may be significant. The king of England, for instance, is referred to as 'nostre seigneur le Roi' or 'le roi d'Angleterre', and in nearly every case these words have been written over an erasure.[1] Perhaps there had been some difficulty over Edward's titles: perhaps the non-committal style had been adopted to make the report acceptable to the French. We can only guess; but, whatever its precise nature, there can be little doubt that this document records the points agreed upon at some stage in these negotiations. Another document from Cotton MS. Caligula D.III, also used by Delachenal,[2] briefly reports a conversation between the two kings at Windsor, evidently at the time of the festivities of St George there in April 1358. This report refers to the agreement as already concluded in principle and states that the final details were to be worked out by the two commissions sitting in London with the cardinals. In addition, Delachenal quotes several official documents concerned with the collection of King John's ransom[3] as fixed by the agreement; and there is a very precise reference both to the terms and the date in the chronicle of the Anonymous of Canterbury,[4] published after Delachenal's book.

[1] The ultra-violet lamp has so far failed to reveal the words erased.

[2] Cotton MS. Caligula D.III, 129; Delachenal, *op. cit.*, ii, pp. 66–67. This text could be improved also.

[3] Delachenal, *op. cit.*, ii, p. 63, n. 2, and pp. 70–73.

[4] *Chronica Johannis de Reading et Anonymi Cantuariensis*, p. 208. Other English chroniclers were not very clear about the agreement: Knighton, ii, p. 99 (ransom one million marks, 14 hostages); John of Reading, *Chronicon*, p. 128 (ransom 600,000 florins before release, to be paid by 11 November plus hostages); Walsingham, *Hist. Ang.*, i, p. 284 (ransom 600,000 florins by 11 November and hostages); Sir Thomas Gray connects the agreement with Anglo-papal affairs, *Scalachronica* (ed. J. Stevenson, 1836), p. 177. The French give no details: *Chronique normande*, ed. A. and E. Molinier (Soc. de l'hist. de France, 1882), p. 123; Jean le Bel, *Chronique*, ed. J. Viard and E. Déprez (Soc. de l'hist. de France, 1904–1905), ii, p. 240; *Chroniques . . . de Jean II et de Charles V*, i, pp. 176–77.

The territorial provisions, as given in the first Cotton document, are that Edward should have—in addition to what he already held in Guienne, Gascony and the Channel Islands—Saintonge, Angoumois, Poitou, Limousin, Quercy, Périgord, Bigorre, Gaure and the Agenais, with Ponthieu, Calais and its neighbourhood and the county of Guines, all in full sovereignty. This is supported by the statement of the Anonymous of Canterbury that Edward should have 'all Gascony and Aquitaine, with the Agenais and the town of La Rochelle, without doing homage or service or paying tribute to anyone', together with Calais, Guines and certain other places.[1] The Cotton document puts the ransom at 4 million 'florins d'or à l'écu', with a first instalment of 600,000 florins to be paid before release.[2] The French documents quoted by Delachenal confirm the figure for the first instalment, and add that it was due by 1 November[3] (the Anonymous of Canterbury doubles the figure for the whole ransom and says nothing about the instalments).[4] Other points of importance in the Cotton document—the detailed provisions for hostages and for the settlement of the Breton dispute (with the stipulation that, whatever the outcome, the sovereignty of Brittany should remain with the king of England), and the demand that the king of France should break his alliance with the Scots and make an alliance with England—are not specifically confirmed by other evidence, but a comparison with the corresponding provisions in the other documents of the series suggests no reason for doubt. The text of the Anonymous of Canterbury is defective at the point where he seems to be saying that the king of France should secure the pope's confirmation of the agreement and oaths from the magnates of his realm;[5] and the report of the kings' conversation at Windsor adds what may have been the vital point—that the terms of the agreement must be fulfilled to the letter and to the day or the whole would be void.[6]

This is the agreement which Delachenal regarded as moderate and reasonable, as foreshadowing the treaty made at Brétigny; and certainly this is the impression it must give at first sight, particularly if compared with the articles of 1359. But it does not

---

[1] Delachenal, *op. cit.*, ii, pp. 402–405; *Chronicon*, p. 208.
[2] Delachenal, *op. cit.*, ii, p. 407.
[3] *Ibid.*, p. 63, n. 2.   [4] *Chronicon*, p. 208.
[5] *Ibid.*   [6] Delachenal, *op. cit.*, ii, pp. 67, 69.

seem to have been noticed that there is nothing in the surviving documents, so far as they go, to suggest that Edward made any concessions whatever. The documents speak only of the conditions to be fulfilled by King John in order to obtain his release. If this were in fact the nature of the agreement, it would have left Edward with the title 'king of France', a title which had already won recognition in many parts of France, and, in favourable circumstances, might be accepted in many more; and, moreover, in addition to the territories and rights which would have been surrendered to him, it would have left him free to maintain his military hold on Brittany, his military foothold in Normandy, his hold on Calais and its protective ring of fortresses and the castles which were being seized and held in his name (at least nominally) in almost every part of France save the Midi, and his alliance with Charles and Philip of Navarre and with the Flemings.[1] Such an agreement does not look like an attempt to make a general settlement. It seems to be concerned simply with the ransom which King John must pay and the conditions he must fulfill in order to secure his release, leaving the dynastic question and many other issues of the war undecided, and, since the ransom was calculated to wreck his finances, to put King John in a position of helpless dependence upon Edward, who, should he ever decide to renew the war on one pretext or another, would do so in more favourable circumstances than ever before.

These observations, since they might put such a different complexion upon the negotiations of 1357–58 and Edward's presumed objectives therein, are bound to provoke a number of questions. Is it possible, for instance, since we have no text of the final agreement, that Edward's concessions have been mislaid? Or, if in fact he did offer no concessions, is it conceivable that the French would have accepted an agreement which, in its ultimate implications, was every bit as severe as the treaty of 1359 which they rejected?

On the first question there is the positive point that the English chroniclers speak of this agreement, so far as they distinguish it clearly, as though it were concerned simply with King John's ransom,[2] something that we might call, for convenience, a 'ransom treaty'; and this evidence is somewhat strengthened by the

[1] Le Patourel, 'Edward III and the Kingdom of France', *History*, xliii (1958), pp. 179–89. See above XII.   [2] Above, p. 23, n. 4.

fact that Edward had just negotiated two other treaties of precisely the same character. These were the treaty of Westminster (August 1356),[1] the agreement by which Charles of Blois, duke of Brittany, was released from prison, and the treaty of Berwick, dated 3 October 1357 (concluded, that is, while the negotiations with the French were in progress), which laid down the conditions on which David II of Scotland was allowed to return to his country.[2] In each case the captive bound himself to pay a sum proportionately so great that neither ransom was ever paid in full; in each case the captive was released on parole until the ransom should be fully paid, and must give himself up if payments failed;[3] in each case Edward made no concessions whatever in respect of his claims and possessions in Brittany or Scotland. Subsequent events in both countries make it clear that these were regarded simply as 'ransom treaties', independent of any general settlement that might be concluded later on. It is also worth noting that, in the agreement which Edward made with Charles of Navarre in August 1358, the crown of France was specifically reserved to Edward;[4] and it is at this point that Knighton's story of Edward's insistence on the primacy of his claim to the throne of France may appropriately be brought to mind. Ransoms were a military convention of the time, and they could be made to serve military and political purposes. The difficulties to which King David's ransom gave rise in Scotland, and those caused later by King John's ransom in France, are significant. It is likely that such ransoms were regarded as a continuation of the war 'by other means'. Why should not Edward apply to King John the technique that he was applying to other rulers who had fallen into his hands?

---

[1] *Foedera*, III. i, 336–37; cf. E. Déprez, 'La Querelle de Bretagne', *Mém. Soc. d'hist. et d'arch. de Bretagne*, vii (1926), pp. 25–60; F. Bock, 'Some new documents . . .', *Bull. John Rylands Library*, xv (1931), pp. 60–99.

[2] *Foedera*, III. i, 372–74; cf. E. W. M. Balfour-Melville, *Edward III and David II* (Historical Assoc. Leaflet, 1954); G. Burnett, *Exchequer Rolls of Scotland*, ii (1878), pp. xxxvii ff. The history of the earlier treaty of Berwick, 1354 (*Foedera*, III. i, 281, 291, 293), and the obvious relation it bears to the course of the negotiations with the French in 1354–55, show that events on the French and Scottish fronts were intimately connected at this time.

[3] This provision is not found in the documents we have for the 1358 agreement with the French, but it appears in 1359 (§ 39), and King John's return to England in 1363 is well known.

[4] *Foedera*, III. i, 228; Delachenal, *op. cit.*, ii, pp. 1–7.

But was it likely that the French would accept such a 'ransom treaty'? Those in France who, Delachenal thought, were un-enthusiastic for King John's return might well have been those who saw the implications most clearly, and the rejection of the treaty of 1359 shows that the French did not lack courage. But things were really desperate in 1357–58. Apart from the turbulent Estates, the Jacquerie, Charles of Navarre, his brother Philip and the ambiguous position of the dauphin until he assumed the authority of regent in March 1358, there was the stranglehold of the companies, still believed to be operating in Edward's name and under his control. Delachenal seems to have been misled by a passage in the *Grandes Chroniques*, which, he thought, implied that the dauphin and his council were pleased with the terms. What the chronicle says, however, is this: 'The said treaty greatly pleased the said duke and his councillors, *so they said.*' [1] The *Chronique normande* complains that nothing could be found out about it in Paris.[2] The regent and his council may well have felt, at that time, that King John's acceptance of the treaty could hardly be ignored and that, disastrous as its terms might be, they were not likely to do much better. If so, it would be wise for them to put a bold face on it and keep the documents on the secret list as long as possible. But the treaty must have been accepted in principle, for the first instalment of the ransom was being collected during the summer.

It is difficult to say precisely when or why the treaty of 1358 failed. The Anonymous of Canterbury suggests that the French put off ratification from date to date through the summer;[3] Walsingham states that they refused to produce the hostages;[4] Anglo-papal differences may have had something to do with it.[5] In any case the first instalment had not been paid by November 1;[6] and if Edward had insisted that the whole treaty was dependent upon punctual and precise performance, he could take this as

---

[1] *Chroniques . . . de Jean II et de Charles V*, i, p. 144: 'Le quel traictié plot moult aus diz duc et conseilliers, si comme ilz disoient.'

[2] *Chronique normande*, p. 123: 'De ces lectres ne peurent riens savoir ceulz des III estaz par le regent ne par son conseil . . .'

[3] *Chronicon*, p. 208.

[4] *Hist. Angl.*, i, p. 284.

[5] Tout, *Chapters*, iii, p. 221; Delachenal, *op. cit.*, ii, pp. 73–77

[6] *Ibid.*, pp. 72–73.

justifying a breach. John of Reading says that he told the French to prepare for war on 20 November[1] (the papal envoys had already left the country two months earlier, by 22 September);[2] the earliest order for the mobilization of a fleet is dated 6 December.[3] By January 1359, preparations for what was intended to be the decisive campaign in France were well under way, and the agreement of 1358 was quite dead.

There is no evidence relating directly to the negotiations which led to a prolongation of the truce from 9 April to 24 June 1359 and to the agreement dated 24 March, Delachenal's 'second treaty of London'. But in this case we have the full text (no 'original', but several copies, and they would be worth re-editing), so that there can be no doubt of its provisions.[4] The form of the document is that of an indenture recording 'the points and articles discussed and negotiated at London', to the English part of which the king of England put his privy seal. It is, however, only the articles of a treaty, and leaves several matters over for further discussion.

This has always been regarded as a very tough treaty, as marking the point at which Edward overplayed his hand. The ransom remained at the same figure as in 1358, but Edward's territorial demands were much heavier, including Touraine, Anjou, Normandy and the county of Boulogne in addition to all that had been asked in the earlier agreement; and, as before, all were to be conveyed in full sovereignty, so that they should be completely and effectively severed from what was left of the kingdom of France.

[1] *Chronicon*, p. 128. This story is repeated by Walsingham.

[2] Exch[equer] K. R., Acc[ounts] Var[ious], 508/27.

[3] *Foedera*, III. i, 412–13.

[4] Printed (indifferently) in Froissart, *Chroniques*, ed. Kervyn de Lettenhove, xviii (1874), pp. 413–33, and E. Cosneau, *Les grands traités de la Guerre de Cent Ans* (1889), pp. 3–32. Delachenal (ii, p. 81, n. 1) lists three copies (two of the fourteenth century); there is a fourth in the John Rylands Library (F. Bock, 'An Unknown Register of the Reign of Edward III', *Eng. Hist. Rev.*, xlv (1930), p. 370). Although the date is given, in the text, as 'le xxiiiie jour de mars, l'an de la Nativité Nostre Seigneur, l'an mil trois cens cinquante et neuf', the year can be none other than the historical year 1359; *cf.* the account of Denys de Collors, printed in *Notes et documents relatifs à Jean de France et à sa captivité en Angleterre*, ed. Henry d'Orléans, duc d'Aumâle (Philobiblon Soc., 1854), pp. 87, 113, 125, 138; nor can there be any doubt that this was the very treaty which was rejected by the French Estates on 25 May 1359 (*Chroniques . . . de Jean II et de Charles V*, i, pp. 232–36).

Other provisions, such as those relating to the delivery of hostages, the restoration of their lands and possessions to those banished or disinherited by either side, and the detailed mechanism of the transfer of territories and sovereignty, amount to much the same as in the Cotton document of 1357–58, but, as we should expect, are set out more fully and with greater definition. In particular it is stipulated that the French king should remain the 'loyal prisoner' of the king of England and his heirs until the terms of the treaty were fully and completely carried out, and that if he failed in any respect he would give himself up again. This time, however, Edward promised that when the king of France had carried out all the territorial provisions of the treaty, he would renounce 'the name, crown and kingdom of France . . . and all that he ought to renounce', for himself and his heirs, without prejudice to their rights in the territories to be ceded to them.[1] Questions concerning the restoration to the king of France of castles occupied by English forces but situated on lands which were to remain to him, the manner of his return to his own country, the Anglo-Flemish and the Franco-Scottish alliances, were reserved for further discussion.

At first sight it appears that the significance of this treaty might be that Edward had been persuaded to give up his claim to the kingdom of France in return for additional French territories; but when the territorial concessions demanded of the king of France are put on a map, doubts must arise. For what was being asked was half the kingdom, including some of the richest provinces and including the whole coastline from Calais to Bayonne, and all this was to be wholly and eternally detached from 'the kingdom of France'. Did anyone seriously suppose that these territorial provisions could be carried out, or, if they were, that the rump of the kingdom of France could have survived as an independent state? Did Edward promise to renounce the throne of France knowing that the conditions precedent to his renunciation could not be fulfilled? The casual way in which his promise appears in this indenture, when compared with the elaborate undertakings and securities demanded of the king of France for all that he had to do, certainly suggest that Edward's promise was lightly made. Similar doubts arise over the terms of the ransom. The total figure remained the same as in 1358; but whereas the French had then

[1] Cosneau, *op. cit.*, p. 17.

been given six months in which to raise a first instalment of
600,000 florins, they were now given but four months in which
to raise 3 million.[1] This was so patently impossible that it is hard
to believe that King Edward and his council, perhaps even King
John, did not know it.

How did this preposterous treaty come to be drawn up? No
trace has been found, so far, of any French delegation coming
to England in the early months of 1359; and as the indenture was
taken to Paris by a group of French prisoners released on parole
for the purpose,[2] it is likely that none came. If so, it suggests
that the treaty was negotiated by King John himself, with such
familiares as were with him at the time. During February and
March mobilization for Edward's great campaign was in full
swing and the truce of Bordeaux was due to expire on April 9.
There was no mystery about Edward's intentions. This was to be
the final blow, delivered by all his armies acting together as one
huge force and culminating in Edward's coronation as king of
France in Reims Cathedral. There can be little doubt that King
John negotiated this treaty as a desperate man, as one who would
agree to almost anything—not for his personal liberty, as French
historians have so uncharitably suggested—but to delay, if possible to avert, the invasion that might well destroy his country.

It is not so easy to see why Edward should have agreed to
negotiate. His preparations were going slowly—in the event he
was not ready to move until late in the autumn—and he certainly
had nothing to lose by the grim farce of proposing terms which
could not be carried out. But was there anything to be gained by
it? Did he think that a French refusal or failure to implement
would help him to raise enthusiasm for the campaign he had certainly decided upon? What actually happened is well known.
When, by a tremendous effort, the Regent Charles had brought
the Estates together, they rejected the treaty as neither acceptable
nor practicable.[3] For all the difficulties which remained, the situa-

---

[1] By the agreement of 8 May 1358 the first instalment of the ransom was
due by 1 November following: by this agreement of 24 March 1359 the first
instalment was due by 1 August following.

[2] Delachenal, *op. cit.*, ii, p. 84; *Foedera*, III. i, 423, 425.

[3] 'Et après ce que ilz orent eu deliberacion, ilz respondirent au dit regent
que le dit traictié n'estoit passable, ne faisable. Et pour ce ordenerent à faire
bonne guerre au dit Anglois'—*Chroniques . . . de Jean II et de Charles V*,
i, p. 236.

tion in France was a good deal less menacing than it had been a year earlier.

When Edward was persuaded to negotiate again, at the end of April 1360, agreement was reached in a few days. To Delachenal this seemed possible only because the treaty of Brétigny,[1] dated 8 May, was, in effect, a revival of the agreement of 1358, which only needed to be modified in detail.[2] No doubt the negotiators were not starting, as it were, from the beginning; the ground had been worked over many times in the past three years; but the total effect of this treaty was very different from either of its predecessors.

For on almost every major point Edward had to give way. The territorial concessions demanded of the French seem very similar to those of 1358, if much less than those of 1359; but although Aquitaine is defined rather more generously,[3] this would not compensate for the loss of the sovereignty of Brittany, which he had exercised *de facto* for the past eighteen years. King John's promise to renounce his sovereignty over the lands assigned to Edward in 1358 was balanced then by no comparable renunciation on Edward's part, so far as we know. But now in 1360 he undertook to renounce, after the king of France had made his renunciation, 'the style, right and crown of the kingdom of France', the 'homage, sovereignty and domain of the duchy of Normandy, Touraine, and the counties of Anjou and Maine', 'the sovereignty and homage of Brittany' and 'the sovereignty and homage of the county of Flanders'. Moreover, these renunciations would not be empty words, the abandonment of 'prétentions chimériques'. In some sense he had possessed all these things; he had even gone a long way towards establishing his claim to the throne of France; and if his possession had never been more than partial, the king of France, on his side, had not been able to exercise his sovereignty over Aquitaine since the war began and it had been constantly opposed for half a century before that.[4]

---

[1] *Foedera*, III. i, 487–94; Cosneau, *Les grands traités*, pp. 33–68, 173–74.

[2] Delachenal, *op. cit.*, ii, pp. 196–201.

[3] Rouergue was added in 1360 and Poitou defined more precisely.

[4] P. Chaplais, 'English Arguments concerning the feudal status of Aquitaine in the Fourteenth Century', *Bull. Inst. Hist. Research*, xxi (1948), 203–13; 'Le duché-pairie de Guyenne', *Annales du Midi*, lxix (1957), pp. 5–38.

King John's ransom was reduced from four to three million florins, of which 600,000 was to be paid before his release (or within 7 months) and the remainder in annual instalments of 400,000, a somewhat more realistic schedule. Edward must give up his alliance with the Flemings in return for John's abandonment of the Scots, and the castles which the English had occupied in territories which were to remain French must be evacuated.

Now, however these concessions of Edward's may be reckoned individually, together they represent a very big change, and above all a change of principle. Hitherto Edward had been insisting upon a 'ransom treaty' (for the treaty of 1359, so far as it is to be taken seriously, was little more than that), and he no doubt regarded such a treaty as an incident in the long-term pursuit of his objectives. But in 1360 there was give and take; and what emerged was a treaty that might form the basis of a general settlement.

Such a radical change can only be understood if we admit that Edward had suffered a real defeat in the winter campaign of 1359–60. It was not that he had been beaten in the field, for the French had wisely refused to meet him; it was not that his army was demoralized by the storm on Black Monday; it was the fact that King Edward, the Black Prince, the duke of Lancaster and all those commanders who had been so successful on their own, could now take over to France one of the largest armies ever seen there and achieve nothing.[1] The walls of Reims had held and there was no coronation in the cathedral; whatever Edward was trying to do in the suburbs of Paris produced no result; he was in full retreat when the French made contact and induced him to negotiate.[2] Only the fear of imminent disaster, and the realization that his vast effort had not advanced his cause one inch, can have persuaded him to negotiate in such a situation; and the differences between the treaty of Brétigny and the two preceding attempts to

[1] Save, if it can be regarded as an achievement, the ransoming of Burgundy (Delachenal, *op. cit.*, ii, pp. 161–72). For the army, see A. E. Prince, 'The Strength of the English Armies in the Reign of Edward III', *Eng. Hist. Rev.*, xlvi (1931), pp. 367–68.

[2] *Cf.* the words attributed to Lancaster by Froissart (*Chroniques*, ed. S. Luce, vi, p. 4), 'Si vous conseille que, entrues que vous en poés issir à vostre honneur, vous en issiés et prendés les offres que on vous presente; car, monsigneur, nous poons plus perdre sus un jour que nous n'avons conquis dedens vingt ans.'

reach agreement are the measure of his fear, his disillusion,[1] and the growing strength of the French government.

It was the French, then, who were victorious at Brétigny, and their victory had been won by keeping their heads in a desperate crisis. They had forced Edward to compromise, to agree to give up his claims and much of his possessions in France. But this agreement at Brétigny was provisional. It still had to be ratified by the two kings at Calais; several matters—mostly concerned with the practical application of principles agreed at Brétigny—were left for discussion when the two kings should meet; and, most important, the French had to find the first instalment of the ransom and do several other things.

The matters specifically referred to the meeting of the kings at Calais were these: they were to discuss and decide how and when the renunciations should take place; when and in what manner the hostages should be released; and the two parties to the Breton dispute were to state their case before the kings who were to do their best to bring about a settlement: it is implied, though not directly stated, that this last should take place at Calais. Evidently something in the nature of a conference was envisaged, for at any moment the discussion of such matters might throw up questions of principle, and the two kings would not wish to make decisions until every point had been fully investigated and discussed.

That such a conference took place is well known, but its nature has been misunderstood. Delachenal thought that there was little for it to do, apart from the question of the renunciations,[2] and Tout described it as a 'fortnight of frenzied negotiation',[3] for both thought that the business was transacted between Edward's arrival on 9 October and the ceremony of ratification on the 24th. The sheer number of formal documents produced at Calais[4] alone

---

[1] Edward himself seems to have had no part in the negotiations at Brétigny, but he accepted the terms a month or so later.

[2] Delachenal, *op. cit.*, ii, p. 241.   [3] *Chapters*, iii, p. 229.

[4] *Foedera*, III. i, 514–47. Some reality is given to this mountain of clerical labour by notes of payments to certain clerks 'pro labore suo ac scriptura diuersorum litterarum instrumentorum et aliorum munimentorum tractatum pacis inter nos et carissimum fratrem nostrum Francie apud Cales' nuper habitum tangencium', to John Bras 'pro officio spigurnelli ibidem facto', to William Winterton 'pro irrotulamento litterarum instrumentorum et aliorum munimentorum predictorum ac pro labore et expensis suis eundo

makes this improbable. But Chaplais has shown that it was a much longer,[1] and a consideration of the time-table will show it to have been a far more elaborate affair. It is exasperating that the only records of its proceedings known to survive are the formal documents and the expense accounts of some of the English envoys.

According to the time-table prescribed at Brétigny, King John was to be brought to Calais by 15 July. Within three weeks of his arrival there both kings must have sought and obtained papal approval of the terms and all the dispensations and absolutions that might be required. The first instalment of the ransom must be paid within four months of John's arrival in Calais; when this had been done, and when certain of the hostages (specified by name) had surrendered themselves (some had been prisoners since Poitiers), and when the town and fortresses of La Rochelle and the county of Guines had been handed over, all within the same four months, the king of France would be released. The precise point at which the treaty would be ratified was not prescribed; Edward, no doubt, would have to be satisfied that these stipulations were being carried out; but letters of confirmation were to be exchanged within one month of the release of the king of France, when he was at last a free agent. The provision that he should be maintained free of charge during his first month at Calais, but should pay 10,000 royals for his upkeep in each subsequent month that he stayed there 'par deffaut de lui ou de ses gens', was presumably intended to discourage delay. Finally the surrender of all rights and sovereignty in the territories which the king of France was giving up by the treaty was to be completed by Michaelmas 1361 at the latest.

Edward returned to England ahead of his army, reaching Westminster on 19 May. King John published his acceptance of the treaty in letters dated 22 May; but Edward made no move until the kings exchanged promises of ratification on 14 June. Delachenal was puzzled by this delay;[2] but it is easy to understand that Edward would wish his experts to study the terms agreed upon so

de Castro de Farnham vsque Ciuitatem nostram London' pro certis transcriptis quarumdam litterarum obligatoriarum dictum tractatum tangencium scribendis . . .' Warrants for Issue, file 41 (13 March).

[1] P. Chaplais, 'Some Documents regarding the fulfilment and interpretation of the treaty of Brétigny', *Camden Miscellany*, xix (1952), pp. 6–7.

[2] Delachenal, *op. cit.*, ii, pp. 211–12, 216–18.

hastily in his name at Brétigny before he committed himself personally to them. Arrangements were soon put in hand for transferring King John to Calais, where he landed on 8 July after a leisurely journey.[1] There was much to be done on both sides. The chief problem facing the French was to raise the first instalment of the ransom. The Regent had set about this as soon as the agreement at Brétigny was concluded;[2] a commission was appointed on 22 July to receive the cash at Saint-Omer,[3] and the Regent himself arrived there, to supervise the collection, in August.[4] Preparations also had to be made for the surrender of La Rochelle and Guines and the assembling of the hostages.[5] Edward, who might still feel that he had been caught at a disadvantage and rushed into this treaty, had to decide on a policy and select the men who were to conduct the effective negotiations before he himself went to Calais for the final formalities. The evidence suggests that a complete plan and time-table had been drawn up by the end of July at the latest.

The plan envisaged preliminary contacts at clerical level, followed by an imposing delegation of 'magnates of the council', under whose supervision the effective negotiations would be carried on before the king arrived. John Brancaster was sent to Calais from 29 July to 5 August on a mission later described as 'secret business with which we charged him before we sent the magnates of our council there';[6] Walter 'de Roka' was there from 10 August until 9 September, apparently negotiating for the transfer of Guines;[7] Miles Stapleton from 13 August to 7 December[8]—and no doubt other traces of this first stage could be found. In France, the Regent moved from Saint-Omer to Boulogne on 23 August:[9] on the following day the English 'magnates of the council', headed by the Black Prince and the duke of Lancaster, left their respective castles and palaces for Calais, and remained there until early in November.[10] They had drawn a prest on their

---

[1] Delachenal, *op. cit.*, ii, pp. 218–19.   [2] *Ibid.*, pp. 221 ff.
[3] *Ibid.*, pp. 226–27.   [4] *Ibid.*, p. 241, note 2.   [5] *Ibid.*, p. 220.
[6] Pipe Roll, 33 Edw. III, m. 36; Warrants for Issue, file 41 (19 April): 'du temps q' nous lui enuoiasmes ore tard' de Londres tanq' a nostre ville de Caleys pur aucunes secrees busoignes dont nous lui auions chargez; deuant ce q' nous y enuoiasmes illeoqes les grantz de nostre conseil'.
[7] Pipe Roll, 35 Edw. III, m. 43.
[8] Warrants for Issue, file 40, no. 73.   [9] Delachenal, *op. cit.*, ii, p. 241.
[10] Exch. K. R., Acc. Var. 314/1–12, 620/12; Pipe Roll, 35 Edw. III, m. 51.

wages at the treasury on 6 August,[1] and as these were then stated
to be payable as from 24 August the timing of the embassy had
been settled at least three weeks in advance. Edward seems to
have thought that a fortnight or so would suffice for their work;
for the preparations for his own journey can be traced back to
6 August and he was standing by with his ships in Sheppey as
early as 6 September, waiting for the news that all was ready at
Calais.[2] Walter 'de Roka' reported to the council at Dover on
9 September,[3] but the news he brought cannot have been encouraging. Sir William Burton, who had been in Calais 'super
tractatu pacis' since 1 September, came to the king at Sandwich
a month later, on 6 October, and returned to Calais on the same
day 'super tractatu predicto'.[4] It must have been he who finally
gave Edward the signal, for the king arrived in Calais on the 9th.[5]

All this gives the impression of negotiations carefully planned
and controlled at least until early in September. The difficulties
which then arose were unexpected; for when Brancaster was again
sent to Calais on 31 August, the king had told him that he did not
think that the business should last very long.[6] But during September some very strenuous negotiating must have been carried on,
and these are not the conditions in which one side could hoodwink
the other very easily.

It is against this background that the treatment of the renunciations at Calais—their separation from the main treaty—should
be considered. The two kings were to 'discuss and decide where
and when the said renunciations should be made'. No specific

---

[1] Exch. K. R., Acc. Var. 314/2–5, 7, 12; Issue Roll, no. 401 (34 Edw. III),
mm. 26–28.
[2] Enrolled Accounts (W. and H.), 4, m. 5; Chaplais, 'Some Documents
. . .', *Camden Miscellany*, xix, pp. 6–7.
[3] Pipe Roll, 35 Edw. III, m. 43.   [4] Exch. K. R., Acc. Var. 314/11.
[5] *Chronique . . . de Jean II et de Charles V*, i, p. 320.
[6] Pipe Roll, 33 Edw. III, m. 36—'in quo breui inter cetera continetur
quod Rex nuper intendens tractatum pacis inter ipsum et Regem Francie facte
paruo tempore esse duraturum assignauit prefatum magistrum Johannem
ad transfretandum vsque Cales' et ibidem morandum super tractatu predicto'.
Later Brancaster was rewarded 'ob fructuosa obsequia nobis per ipsum in
partibus tam transmarinis quam cismarinis non absque laboribus solicitis
et indefessis laudabiliter impensa' (Warrants for Issue, file 39, no. 48).
Apparently it is his initials that appear on one copy of the treaty of 1359
(Delachenal, *op. cit.*, ii, p. 81, n. 1). On Brancaster himself, see Tout,
Chapters, index *s.v.* 'Brancaster'.

connexion is made, in the agreement at Brétigny, between the transfer of rights and sovereignty and their formal renunciation; but the clause relating to the renunciations follows that which defines the rights to be conveyed, and common sense suggests that formal renunciation should follow transfer. Since this agreement gave 29 September 1361 as the latest date for transfer, it is reasonable to suppose that the date then envisaged for the renunciations would be some time after that; so that if the treaty was to be ratified within four months of King John's arrival at Calais, it must have been clear to everyone that the renunciations would have to be taken out of it and legislated for separately.

And this is what happened. The *littere cum clausula c'est assavoir*,[1] which embody the agreement as to the occasion and the procedure of the renunciations, lay down that the king of France should transfer the lands and rights in question by 24 June 1361, if possible, and that letters recording that the renunciations had been duly made should be sent, by each side, to Bruges, and exchanged there by 15 August; or, if this were not possible, the dates should be 1 and 30 November respectively. There is no *postponement* here; on the contrary, it looks as though an attempt had been made to advance the date of the renunciations. The idea of postponement comes, it seems, from the phrase in the *littere cum clausula c'est assavoir* which introduces these arrangements. After rehearsing the territorial clauses of the treaty, they say: 'on these matters, after many altercations concerning them and, in particular, because the renunciations are not being made at present, we have finally reached agreement in the manner following, that is to say (*c'est assavoir*)'. This has been read as though it meant 'because there were altercations, therefore the renunciations are not being made at present'. But that is not what the documents say. Certainly they say that the renunciations were not being made 'at present', but who, before the conference at Calais, expected that they would be? On the other hand, if an attempt had been made, at Calais, to secure the French king's renunciations before 29 September 1361, or even on the spot, in advance of the transfer of territory, it would be easy to understand why it was necessary to state that the renunciations were not being made 'at present', why alternative dates were prescribed and why there were 'altercations'. Had this been Edward's policy?

[1] *Foedera*, III. i, 522–25.

There is certainly some evidence that he was in a hurry. He had brought King John to Calais a week earlier than was necessary, and he was ready to go there himself early in September even though, six weeks later, when the treaty was ratified, not more than two-thirds of the first instalment of the ransom was in sight,[1] there had been trouble over the hostages,[2] nothing had been done about the transfer of Guines[3] and La Rochelle was openly resisting.[4] A matter which had not been specifically referred to the meeting at Calais, but which was certainly discussed there, was the evacuation of castles held by the English in territories which were to remain French, in return for the delivery of the counties of Ponthieu, Montfort (to Jean de Montfort, duke of Brittany), Angoumois and Saintonge. The dates fixed at Calais were 2 February 1361 for the evacuation of the castles and 2 March for the delivery of the counties.[5] Surely the military men at Calais, if not the clerks, must have seen that this was quite impossible.[6]

Was Edward really hoping to secure the territories assigned to him soon or at once, with, or even without, the French king's renunciations, and then to find reasons why he should not make his own renunciations? It is a grave charge and the intention cannot be proved; but it is strongly suggested by what he actually did in the years following[7] and by this drive to speed things up at Calais. It is also suggested by the fact that whereas in most English official documents the purpose of the Calais conference is described as 'tractatus pacis', in a few instances it is 'liberacio regis Francie',[8] as though it were still primarily concerned with a ransom, and by the careful way in which Edward safeguarded

---

[1] Delachenal, *op. cit.*, ii, pp. 220–31, 252.

[2] *Ibid.*, p. 240.

[3] *Ibid.*, p. 332. Edward had been enquiring about the transfer of Guines, perhaps in August and September (Pipe Roll, 35 Edw. III, m. 43).

[4] Delachenal, *op. cit.*, ii, pp. 240, 332.

[5] *Foedera*, III. i, 535–36.

[6] Edward even secured letters from John undertaking that he would not hold up the execution of the treaty because 'one or two' fortresses had not been evacuated within the stipulated time (*Foedera*, III. i, 536–37).

[7] Delachenal, *op. cit.*, ii, pp. 331–45; Chaplais, 'Some Documents...', *Camden Miscellany*, xix, pp. 7–8; E. Perroy, 'Charles V et le traité de Brétigny', *Moyen Age*, xxxviii (1928), pp. 255–81.

[8] Exch. K.R., Acc. Var. 314/4: 'ad tractandum super deliberacione Regis Francie'; Pipe Roll, 33 Edw. III, m. 36 (Brancaster's account): 'pro tractatu ... super liberacione Regis Francie'.

his right to the titles 'king of France' and 'duke of Normandy',[1] notwithstanding any words used in the treaty itself or in the subsidiary agreements. Was he reconciled, even now, to the abandonment of his dynastic claims?

The conclusions to which this argument is leading, though tentative indeed, are very different from those advanced by Delachenal. They are that the agreement of 1358 was a 'ransom treaty', similar to those which Edward had just imposed upon King David of Scotland and Charles of Blois; for it was concerned with nothing but the conditions of King John's release from prison, and, if put into effect, would have left Edward's ambitions and all that he had won in France intact (this may well seem to be a more likely interpretation than Delachenal's idea of a moderate treaty on quite general grounds, for why should Edward offer easy terms in 1358 when his victories were still fresh and France was in chaos?):[2] that the draft treaty of 1359, though very puzzling, was still essentially a 'ransom treaty': and that the articles of Brétigny were, for the first time, a matter of give and take, in which each side surrendered something that it had hitherto held to be vital, the sovereignty of the king of France over the whole of his kingdom, Edward's right to the throne of France.[3] Yet to bring Edward to this point of compromise had been a great French achievement; for since the agreement followed the disaster of Edward's winter campaign, it cannot be argued that his claim to the throne of France had never been serious because it was given up in his name at Brétigny. As for the diplomacy at Calais, the French did not achieve the postponement of the renunciations by subtlety, for the renunciations were not postponed and their separation from the treaty as ratified was natural and inevitable. It is more likely that Edward was trying to recover what he had lost at Brétigny; and if, later on, the French were able to turn his bad faith to their advantage, that is another story.

[1] *Foedera*, III. i, 532; *cf. ibid.*, 550-51 (1 November).

[2] This general consideration is a further argument for thinking that the evidence we have for the 1358 treaty is complete in all essentials.

[3] *Cf.* the negotiations at Avignon in 1344, Froissart, *Chroniques*, ed. Kervyn de Lettenhove, xviii, pp. 235-56; E. Déprez, 'La Conférence d'Avignon (1344)', *Essays . . . presented to Thomas Frederick Tout*, ed. A. G. Little and F. M. Powicke (1925), pp. 301-20; *History*, xliii, p. 177.

L'OCCUPATION ANGLAISE DE CALAIS
AU XIVe SIÈCLE

Dans leur volume *La France et l'Angleterre en conflit*, MM. Calmette et Déprez, relatant les négociations qui aboutirent à la paix de 1396, et citant entre autres les demandes présentées pour un retour de Calais à la France, ajoutent le commentaire suivant : « Base d'opérations navale et militaire, entrepôt commercial, forteresse, colonie de peuplement, ce serait la dernière ville que l'Angleterre abandonnerait ». Et encore : « Cette ville, conquise en août 1347, peuplée d'Anglais, dotée d'un personnel administratif nombreux, n'était pas une possession française des rois d'Angleterre, mais un petit morceau d'Angleterre *overseas*[2] ». Description qui peut ou non convenir au Calais des xve et xvie siècles. Mais s'applique-t-elle vraiment à la situation telle qu'elle se présentait dans la seconde moitié du xive siècle, encore qu'elle traduise assez bien l'opinion courante des historiens, celle-là même que je partageais quand j'ai entrepris cette enquête ?

Nul ne contestera, certes, que Calais ait été une base militaire et navale. Personne à ma connaissance n'a encore examiné en détail le rôle joué par Calais dans les campagnes que les Anglais lancèrent dans la France du Nord pendant la seconde moitié du xive siècle. Il n'est que de lire les manuels, cependant, pour se convaincre que la ville n'a cessé d'être un point de concentration, un port de débarquement, une base de ravitaillement. Pendant quelques années même, après 1347, elle fut aussi la base d'une « patrouille de la mer ». Au même moment, on s'efforce également de concentrer tout le trafic régional de la traversée de la Manche sur la ligne Douvres-Calais. Il serait intéressant d'explorer les possibilités navales de Calais, et l'on peut se demander si un plan de stratégie navale n'est pas impliqué dans la possession d'une ligne de forteresses maritimes occupées par les Anglais à cette époque : Calais, Cherbourg, Château-Cornet et Brest.

Il est également exact de décrire Calais comme une « forteresse ». La ville même était très forte, avec murailles et lignes d'eau. Sa garnison était distincte de celle du château de Calais, à l'ouest de la ville, et du fort Rysbank qui gardait l'entrée du port. Elle se trouvait au centre de ce qui devait être, eu égard à sa superficie, l'une des régions les plus

1. Note du traducteur. Le présent article a fait l'objet d'une communication à la conférence historique anglo-américaine tenue à Londres en juillet 1950. M. Le Patourel, professeur à l'Université de Leeds, y a précisé les résultats d'une enquête préliminaire sur la politique d'Édouard III à l'égard de Calais. Bien qu'il se propose de poursuivre ses recherches, qui pourront l'amener finalement à corriger quelques-unes de ses conclusions, nous avons pensé qu'il était intéressant de présenter dès à présent à nos lecteurs les résultats provisoires de ses investigations, et nous le remercions d'avoir consenti, sur nos pressantes instances, à laisser publier sa remarquable étude (E. P.).

2. Paris, 1937 (t. VII, Ire partie de l'*Histoire du Moyen Age*, de l'*Histoire Générale*, publ. sous la dir. de G. Glotz), p. 255.

fortifiées de l'Europe d'alors. On dépensait des sommes énormes pour les réparations et l'extension de ces forteresses, la solde des garnisons, leur approvisionnement en nourriture et munitions, dont presque tout devait être importé d'Angleterre. Avec ses châteaux satellites, on estimait généralement Calais imprenable. Tant qu'ils tiendraient la ville, les Anglais pourraient croire toujours possible la reprise des provinces perdues en France.

Au début, on ne considéra le développement commercial de Calais que comme un corollaire de sa sécurité militaire. Marchands et colons furent invités à s'établir dans la ville afin de pouvoir garder ses murs et pour que le roi d'Angleterre n'eût pas à se reposer sur la seule fidélité de ses sujets français. Mais quand l'étape des laines y fut établie en 1363, Calais devint ce qu'avaient été Bruges et Anvers, le principal centre des marchands anglais sur le continent, le marché obligatoire des laines et le siège de la Compagnie de l'Étape. C'était certainement « un entrepôt commercial » de première importance.

A première vue, il semble également exact de la décrire comme une « colonie de peuplement », « un fragment d'Angleterre outre-mer ». On ne peut douter qu'il y ait eu, en 1347, un mouvement considérable d'émigration de la population française de Calais. Une telle ville n'avait pas supporté sans pertes humaines un siège de onze mois, sans parler de l'expulsion des « bouches inutiles ». Les chroniqueurs du temps, bien que leurs chiffres varient, sont unanimes pour affirmer qu'une poignée seulement d'habitants reçut permission de demeurer dans la ville après qu'Édouard III en eut pris possession. Le fait est corroboré, du côté français, par l'établissement des réfugiés à Saint-Omer et dans des villes plus éloignées, jusqu'à Carcassonne même, par la concession de tenures que le roi accorda aux Calaisiens dépossédés, par leur nomination à des offices vacants. Cette dernière indication pourtant suppose que les réfugiés appartenaient à une classe assez élevée, encore que je ne veuille pas, pour l'instant, insister sur ce point. Les preuves d'une immigration anglaise semblent à première vue tout aussi fortes. Quelques jours après son entrée dans la ville, Édouard lança une proclamation dans les comtés du Nord et de l'Est de l'Angleterre, faisant appel à des colons et leur promettant libertés et privilèges commerciaux. Ce qui nous montre que son appel ne fut pas sans réponse, c'est que l'on trouve environ 190 concessions de tenures enregistrées en bloc dans les « Patent Rolls [3] » de 1347, que suivirent des concessions analogues égrenées dans les « French Rolls [4] » ; on a même la preuve que quelques concessions au moins s'y ajoutèrent, accordées par simple ordre oral. De plus, en 1349, pouvoir fut donné aux bailli et capitaine de Calais d'accorder des tenures sous le sceau que le roi leur avait donné à cette fin. Les produits, modestes mais réguliers, des émoluments du sceau, que mentionnent

---

3. *Calendar of Patent Rolls*, 1345-1348, pp. 561-8.
4. Public Record Office, Chancery, Treaty Rolls (qui comprennent les « French Rolls », les « Almain Rolls », etc.)

les comptes du trésorier, montrent que ce pouvoir fut effectivement exercé. Et l'on peut admettre que la majeure partie de ces concessions fut accordée à des Anglais.

Il n'est nullement certain, toutefois, que tous ces textes fournissent la preuve irréfutable d'un changement complet de population, malgré les apparences. Bien plus, une « colonie de peuplement », un « fragment d'Angleterre outre-mer », dont on peut concevoir à la rigueur l'établissement sur une côte d'outre-Atlantique, en un pays de faible peuplement, n'aurait pu se créer, dans le Nord de la France au XIVe siècle, sans une politique consciente et rigoureuse, menée avec ténacité par le gouvernement anglais. Le plan impliquait, au demeurant, dans une large mesure, le transport des lois et coutumes et des formes administratives de la mère-patrie, non moins que celui des habitants. Si cette politique s'était manifestée, elle aurait affecté non seulement la ville de Calais, mais les territoires avec lesquels elle était liée au point de vue stratégique, politique et administratif. Nous devrions nous attendre à voir disparaître les institutions indigènes, remplacées par des formes anglaises de gouvernement, la loi anglaise substituée à celle du pays, les propriétaires fonciers relayés par des émigrants anglais. Dans quelle mesure cela se passa-t-il au XIVe siècle [5] ?

Examinons d'abord les quelque douze années qui s'étendent entre la prise de Calais (août 1347) et les traités de Brétigny-Calais (1360). L'occupation anglaise de Calais et des territoires voisins n'était alors réglée par aucun traité ; la trêve de septembre 1347 qui, bien que mal gardée, devait se prolonger annuellement jusqu'en 1355, n'en reconnaissait que la possession de fait. Or, une trêve, évidemment, n'établit aucun droit. Celle de 1347, cependant, indiquait les territoires que les Anglais avaient l'intention d'occuper, puisqu'elle était déclarée valable pour « la ville de Calais, la seigneurie de Marck et d'Oye et leurs territoires ». Les rédacteurs de la trêve employaient là des termes politico-géographiques dont le sens était des plus clairs. Ils désignaient deux bailliages administratifs du comté d'Artois, celui de Calais et celui de Marck qui englobait la seigneurie d'Oye. Mais cette organisation en bailliages n'avait probablement pas plus de cent-cinquante ans d'âge et s'était superposée à de plus anciennes unités, dont il faut rappeler brièvement le développement si l'on veut comprendre ce qui se passa en 1347.

Dans les premiers siècles de notre ère, le site de Calais et d'une partie

---

5. Pour l'histoire de Calais au quatorzième siècle, voir surtout G. DAUMET, *Calais sous la domination anglaise* (Arras, 1902) ; F. LENNEL, *Histoire de Calais* (3 vol., Calais, 1908-13) ; *Dictionnaire historique et archéologique du département du Pas-de-Calais* (Commission départementale des monuments historiques du Pas-de-Calais, 15 vol., Arras, 1873-85) ; A. DE MENCHE DE LOISNE, *Dictionnaire topographique du département du Pas-de-Calais* (Coll. des documents inédits, Paris, 1907) ; J. LESTOCQUOY, *Histoire des territoires ayant formé le département du Pas-de-Calais* (Arras, 1946). Bibliographie et catalogue de documents inédits dans LENNEL, *op. cit.* Je ne prétends pas avoir consulté même la plupart des documents imprimés ou inédits. Mon étude est fondée sur les « French Rolls » — imprimés en partie, mais en partie seulement, dans RYMER, *Foedera...* (Record Commission, 1816-69) —, les « Exchequer Accounts » et les « Pipe » et les « Foreign Account Rolls » au Public Record Office, Londres.

importante de son arrière-pays était ennoyé sous la mer. L'une des premières terres qui émergea fut sans doute une langue parallèle à la côte moderne, entre l'estuaire de l'Aa et celui du Nieulay. Elle s'élargit à mesure que les marécages s'asséchèrent et devint la terre de Marck, laquelle au xive siècle en était arrivée à inclure les villages d'Oye, Marck, Les Attaques, Guemps, Nouvelle-Église, Offerque, Vieille-Église et Coulogne, et, auparavant, avait compris Calais. Ce territoire, primitivement isolé par les marais et les wateringues, constituait une communauté administrée par un collège d'échevins qui, depuis la fin du xiie siècle, se trouvait présidé par un représentant comtal, le bailli. Cette communauté avait ses lois et ses coutumes propres, plus tard reconnues par une charte, et un gouvernement en partie autonome. Elle était tombée, à une date inconnue, peut-être vers 1000, en la possession des comtes de Boulogne, qui, cependant, en faisaient hommage au comte de Flandre, même après que le comté de Boulogne fut lui-même passé sous la vassalité directe de la couronne. Ce territoire était séparé du comté proprement dit par la partie du comté de Guines qui atteignait la mer vers Sangatte. Il passa ensuite dans l'héritage des comtes d'Artois (milieu du xiiie siècle) et advint ainsi aux ducs de Bourgogne en 1330.

Au cours du xiie siècle, sur le territoire de Marck, était apparu un village de pêcheurs appelé Calais. Cette excroissance de l'établissement plus ancien de Pétresse ou Saint-Pierre se trouvait sur la rive sud de la vaste lagune formée par l'estuaire du Nieulay, ce qui lui donnait un magnifique port naturel, en attendant que survînt son ensablement. Le commerce et la guerre firent la fortune de Calais. Là se déchargèrent les vins du Midi que consommaient les hôtels seigneuriaux et les villes industrielles de la région, la laine anglaise pour les métiers de Saint-Omer. Là débarquèrent les troupes de Richard Cœur-de-Lion en route pour la croisade. Là, le prince Louis concentra ses transports et s'embarqua pour l'Angleterre en 1216-1217. Avec le temps, Calais supplanta Wissant et même Boulogne en tant que terminus méridional de la navigation du Détroit. Et quand les affaires étaient mauvaises, les Calaisiens s'adonnaient volontiers à la piraterie. Ne nous abusons pas pourtant : quoique l'importance de Calais eût grandi au cours des xiiie et xive siècles, c'était encore un port secondaire quand Édouard III y mit le siège en 1346.

Cette communauté urbaine avait grandi au milieu de la communauté rurale de Marck, et son statut urbain avait été reconnu des 1160, bien que la plus ancienne charte conservée ne remonte qu'à 1181. Même si Calais ne pouvait rivaliser avec les grandes communes flamandes, on trouva utile de séparer la ville du territoire de Marck où elle était née. Au début du xiiie siècle apparaît donc un nouveau territoire découpé dans celui de Marck : il comprend la ville de Calais et une importante banlieue ; il est doté d'un bailli, d'un corps d'échevins, d'un corps parallèle de coremans ; il a ses libertés et ses coutumes propres, encore

qu'en souvenir de la filiation on ait conservé le droit d'appel à l'échevinage de Marck dans les cas où la coutume était douteuse.

Quand donc les négociateurs de 1347 parlaient d'appliquer la trêve à
« la ville de Calais, la seigneurie de Marck et d'Oye et leurs territoires »,
ils pensaient certainement à ces bailliages qui constituaient aussi des
communautés civiles douées d'une longue tradition d'administration
locale, d'une individualité consciente et d'une autonomie judiciaire.
Il nous reste à voir ce qu'Édouard III fit de ces coutumes.

La documentation pour Marck n'est pas aussi claire qu'on le dési-
rerait. Les châteaux de Marck et d'Oye furent occupés par une garnison
anglaise au début de 1348, sinon plus tôt, et les pêcheries proches des
châteaux furent affermées peu après. Mais j'ai l'impression, qu'il m'est
encore impossible de transformer en certitude, que le territoire proprement dit de Marck ne fut pas occupé entre 1347 et 1360 et que l'administration locale y continua sans changements, dans la mesure où elle
pouvait fonctionner.

A Calais, au contraire, c'est-à-dire dans la ville et sa *banlieue* ou
territoire, la situation était naturellement tout autre. Non seulement on y
vit l'arrivée massive des soldats mais, puisque le roi Édouard comprit,
dès le premier jour, qu'à moins d'attirer de nombreux résidents anglais,
en d'autres termes de faire de la ville la résidence des marchands anglais,
elle resterait indéfendable en dernière analyse, il encouragea également
l'immigration des civils. Un problème de gouvernement se posait donc :
pour le moins, il fallait régler les relations entre indigènes, immigrants
et soldats, et établir un embryon d'administration anglaise.

Par bonheur, nous avons conservé le texte de quatre documents
qui donnent, dans l'ensemble, une idée claire des mesures prises et
des principes qui les dictèrent [6]. Tous quatre sont recopiés dans les
« French Rolls » pour la 21e année du règne, et bien que trois d'entre
eux soient dépourvus de date, il est vraisemblable que tous furent rédigés
quelques mois au plus après la prise de Calais en août 1347. Le premier
s'intitule : « Certains articles à observer dans la ville de Calais ». C'est
en fait une série de réglements d'urgence pour la nouvelle conquête.
On parle d'un capitaine et d'un maréchal dotés du commandement
militaire et responsables, en dernier ressort, de la défense ; d'un sénéchal,
déjà fonctionnaire civil et qui, nous le savons, allait vite troquer son
titre pour celui, plus traditionnel, de bailli ; de la nécessité de former
un corps d'échevins, d'abord en partie à la nomination des officiers
royaux, puis plus tard d'après les règles de l'ancienne coutume ; enfin
du corps des bourgeois. On ordonne l'expulsion de tous les Calaisiens,
sauf de ceux qui ont obtenu du roi la permission de rester, et l'on définit
les relations entre la garnison et la population civile. Mais en tête du
document on inscrit la règle suivante, qui domine clairement tout le

---

6. RYMER, *Foedera*, III, i, pp. 139, 142-4 ; LENNEL, *Histoire de Calais*, I, 281-6 ; G. ESPINAS,
*Recueil de documents relatifs à l'histoire du droit municipal en France, des origines à la Révolution,
Artois* (Paris, 1934-43), II, pp. 335-338, 357-362.

reste : « C'est la volonté du roi que les anciennes coutumes et franchises qui existaient dans la ville de Calais avant sa prise y soient à l'avenir, gardées et préservées dans tous leurs points ».

Les trois autres documents renforcent cette doctrine. L'un est la copie, intitulée «Chest la ley de Caleys», de la charte accordée à Calais, en 1317, par la comtesse Mahaut d'Artois, et selon les termes de laquelle la ville avait été administrée entre 1317 et 1347. Le second reproduit la même charte, mais y ajoute des clauses de vidimus et de confirmation : « Nous, acceptant et approuvant les dites lois et usages, accordons et confirmons'lesdites lois et usages à nos bons et loyaux sujets résidant dans notre ville de Calais, au nom de nous et de nos héritiers, à avoir et à en jouir dans notre dite ville dans la forme susdite. » Le dernier, peut-être le plus intéressant, est resté ignoré des historiens anglais, n'ayant pas été imprimé dans le *Foedera* de Rymer avec les autres. Il commence ainsi : « La ville et le château de Calais appartenaient au duc de Bourgogne, comte d'Artois, en raison de son comté ; et il y avait haute justice, moyenne et basse, et nul autre sinon lui ; et il y avait un grand bailli qui le représentait » etc. Ce long document contient une déclaration détaillée des droits respectifs, en matière judiciaire, administrative et financière, du seigneur et des bourgeois de Calais, des droits et devoirs des officiers et des corps municipaux, des coutumes à lever, et ainsi de suite. Il n'est pas daté, mais les éléments qui permettent d'en fixer la date importent au plus haut point pour notre propos. Puisqu'il cite le duc de Bourgogne comme ancien seigneur de Calais, ce qu'il ne fut pas avant 1330, puisqu'il est tout entier écrit au passé, et qu'enfin il fut recopié dans les « French Rolls » pour l'année 1347 avec les autres textes relatifs aux lois et coutumes de Calais, on ne peut douter qu'il représente les conclusions d'une enquête minutieuse sur le gouvernement et les revenus de Calais, faite au nom du roi Édouard, aussitôt que la ville fut tombée entre ses mains.

Évidemment la politique du roi anglais était conservatrice à l'égard de Calais. Dans la mesure où les préoccupations militaires et le progrès commercial le rendaient possible, les lois et les coutumes calaisiennes devaient continuer comme auparavant. Mais dans quelle mesure cela était-il possible ?

L'administration militaire, notons-le, englobait, dès l'origine, un ensemble plus complexe que la ville et le château de Calais. Il y eut une garnison dans la ville, une autre, sous un commandement séparé, dans le château, d'autres encore dans les châteaux de Marck et d'Oye. Peu à peu, au cours d'hostilités intermittentes qui se déroulèrent autour de Calais, malgré les trêves, les Anglais s'emparèrent d'un certain nombre de châteaux voisins : Coulogne et Sangatte (1350), Guines et Fréthun (1352), Hammes et Poyle ultérieurement. Au début, il semble qu'il y ait eu autant d'unités séparées ; mais au début de 1349, le capitaine de Calais reçut le pouvoir de casser et nommer les capitaines des autres châteaux, et il est certain qu'il exerça ce pouvoir. En 1353, il fut nommément institué capitaine de tous les châtelains ses subordonnés ; en 1356-1358, il s'intitule « gardien de la ville et marche de Calais ». On le tenait pour l'agent responsable du gouvernement royal à Calais et dans les environs ; il possédait de larges pouvoirs judiciaires, se voyait à l'occasion réprimandé pour avoir laissé d'indésirables étrangers passer de Calais en Angleterre. L'administration était entre les mains d'un trésorier et d'un « victuailler », dont les activités s'exerçaient sur toute l'étendue de la domination anglaise en Artois. Le trésorier, avant tout, payait la garnison, tâche difficile qui l'amena vite à exercer un contrôle sur toutes les affaires financières des possessions royales dans la région, y compris la Monnaie de Calais. Le victuailler, qui recevait et distribuait toutes sortes de munitions, avait son importance aussi, puisque, du moins dans les premiers temps, tout devait être importé d'Angleterre.

Pourtant cette administration, encore essentiellement militaire à cette période, étendait sa tâche bien au-delà de Calais, et ne pouvait pas, par sa nature, exercer les fonctions d'une administration civile dans les limites du bailliage de Calais ; elle pouvait même n'intervenir que rarement dans l'administration civile. Il n'est pas inutile de noter que, même sous les comtes d'Artois, le bailli de Calais, du moins en tant que bailli, n'avait aucune fonction militaire. Quand et aussi longtemps que la nécessité s'en faisait sentir, un capitaine militaire était placé au-dessus de lui [1]. Rien donc n'incitait l'administration militaire à modifier profondément la politique gouvernementale qui tendait à préserver les anciennes lois et coutumes de Calais.

L'expansion commerciale présentait, semble-t-il, un obstacle plus sérieux, car elle impliquait l'établissement de bourgeois anglais en nombre certainement considérable. J'ai déjà cité les textes qu'on allègue généralement en faveur de cette immigration. Ce qu'il faudrait savoir, mais qu'on ne pourra probablement préciser qu'au prix de longues et laborieuses recherches, c'est ce que les bénéficiaires anglais firent des tenures calaisiennes qu'on leur distribua si généreusement en l'automne 1347 et plus tard : ce transfert massif de propriétés amena-t-il un mouvement parallèle de population ? Je ne puis apporter encore que quelques indications : la reine Philippa reçut un bloc de tenures qu'elle aliéna en 1357 en faveur du comte de March. Ni ces personnages, ni les autres princes et nobles qui reçurent des propriétés n'y élirent résidence, encore qu'ils pussent trouver commode de posséder un hôtel à Calais quand l'armée opérait dans le nord de la France. Des financiers comme Thomas Swanland et Gilbert Wendlingborough pouvaient avoir avantage à posséder bureaux et magasins à Calais, mais ils n'y résidaient point, nous en avons la quasi-certitude. Qu'advint-il des 200 ou 300 citoyens ou marchands de Londres ou d'ailleurs ? Nous ne possédons encore que des preuves négatives. Ces bourgeois n'ont pas abandonné

---

7. J.-M. RICHARD, « Les baillis de l'Artois au commencement du xiv⁰ siècle », Archives du Pas-de-Calais, *Inventaire Sommaire, Série A*, t. II.

leurs propriétés anglaises, que le roi prit sous sa protection en leur accordant certains privilèges fiscaux. De plus on a l'impression que, sous le règne d'Édouard III, il fut souvent difficile de maintenir les effectifs d'immigrants. Les bourgeois de Calais se plaignaient constamment que le nombre trop grand des tenures vacantes rendît le guet et la garde trop lourds pour les habitants. Et pourtant, en sa constitution de 1363, Édouard III dut préciser qu'aucun marchand ne serait contraint de résider plus de trois ans à Calais. Puisque nous savons qu'au moins un petit nombre d'habitants français reçut permission royale d'y rester, il semble logique d'en conclure que Calais ne devint pas immédiatement ni complètement une ville anglaise, même en tenant compte de l'apport nécessairement important des immigrants anglais.

Aucun obstacle insurmontable, donc, dû à l'organisation militaire ou au développement économique. Il n'en est que plus naturel de constater dans quelle mesure le gouvernement anglais réalisa son intention de conserver les lois et l'administration anciennes de Calais. L'ancien bailliage, comprenant la ville et sa banlieue, fut maintenu comme unité administrative. Le sénéchal, cité dans les articles de 1347, changea vite son nom pour reprendre celui, plus traditionnel, de bailli. Les lettres de nomination à cet office, peu après 1350, l'assimilaient explicitement au « grand bailli » des comtes d'Artois. En gros, ces baillis exerçaient les fonctions de leurs prédécesseurs français ; ils présidaient le corps des échevins, élus, après 1347, selon la coutume ancienne, et qui disaient la coutume du territoire et prononçaient des jugements, comme l'avaient fait leurs prédécesseurs français. Ces échevins étaient maintenant presque certainement anglais, ce qui ne manque pas d'intérêt. On voit aussi les baillis percevoir les rentes des tenures, des boutiques, des étaux de marché, tandis que les « anciennes coutumes » du port de Calais continuaient à être levées. Il y eut donc continuité de la loi et des coutumes. Bref, dans les formes extérieures du moins, le gouvernement anglais, pendant ces premières années, a effectivement conservé les lois et les rouages anciens. Le seul changement important, à part la disparition assez mystérieuse du corps des coremans, consiste en ce que, au lieu de compter avec le receveur d'Artois, le bailli rend maintenant ses comptes au trésorier de Calais. Dans les limites du bailliage de Calais, le roi d'Angleterre s'est substitué au comte d'Artois. Telle n'est pas la solution qu'on s'attendrait à trouver dans un colonie de peuplement. Mais cela rappelle étrangement la politique du roi d'Angleterre dans toutes ses possessions françaises.

Les traités conclus en 1360 transformèrent complètement la situation de Calais. Juridiquement, l'occupation de fait fut consolidée en une suzeraineté de droit. Politiquement, le territoire gouverné par les Anglais s'agrandit considérablement. Jusqu'en 1360, à part des châteaux isolés, il semble que seul le territoire de Calais ait été occupé et administré. A ce territoire s'ajouta maintenant le comté de Guines, tel que l'avait tenu son dernier comte, le territoire de Marck et (bien que les Anglais n'en aient jamais pris possession) le pays de Langle. Dans le texte du traité, cet ensemble de territoires était divisé en trois zones concentriques. La zone interne comprenait la ville de Calais, apparemment à l'intérieur des murs ; tout ce territoire passait dans le domaine royal, où il était entré en fait depuis la prise de la ville. La zone médiane, qu'on peut difficilement délimiter sur la carte, englobait la banlieue de Calais, le territoire de Marck, les parties les plus proches du comté de Guines, et aurait dû comprendre aussi le Pays de Langle. Dans cette zone, le roi annexait à son domaine tous les fiefs et propriétés d'une valeur supérieure à 100 livres, de la monnaie du pays : mesure de sécurité qui, nous le savons, fut mise à exécution ; les propriétés plus petites ne furent pas touchées. La zone externe, c'est-à-dire le reste du comté de Guines, devait être tenu comme l'avait tenu le dernier comte de Guines : ce que le comte avait en domaine, le roi le tiendrait en domaine, mais les seigneurs et communautés conserveraient leurs fiefs, châteaux et libertés comme par le passé.

De même que la trêve de 1347, les traités de Brétigny et de Calais furent évidemment rédigés par des légistes et des diplomates, non par des soldats. Sauf pour la délimitation de ce que j'ai appelé la « zone médiane », frontière intérieure qui n'eut pas d'importance durable, les limites étaient celles des unités politiques et administratives déjà existantes, et non des lignes stratégiques. Le résultat fut d'ajouter le comté de Guines et le territoire de Marck à celui de Calais. Dans les textes de 1360 et des années suivantes, l'ensemble est généralement désigné comme « le comté de Guines avec les seigneuries de Calais et de Marck », ce qui, sans aucun doute, représente correctement la réalité.

Nous avons déjà précisé les limites de Marck et de Calais. Quelques mots sont nécessaires sur le comté de Guines [8]. Formé au Xe siècle, en grande partie aux dépens du comté de Boulogne, il avait connu une période de grande splendeur à la fin du XIIe siècle et au début du XIIIe jusqu'au moment où le comte se laissa entraîner dans les intrigues qui provoquèrent la bataille de Bouvines et en sortit ruiné. Dans la suite le comté périclita ; après 1350, date où Raoul de Brienne, connétable de France et comte de Guines, fut exécuté pour trahison, le roi Jean le Bon avait tenu le comté à sa main. Le gouvernement du pays était caractéristique de la région. La cour du comte prenait deux formes : cour plénière, composée des pairs et barons du comté ; plaid général, auquel assistaient les hommes libres. Pour l'administration locale, il était divisé en quatre châtellenies : Guines, Ardres, Audruicq et Tournehem ; cette dernière avait été aliénée à la fin du XIIIe siècle et par conséquent ne

---

8. Pour le comté de Guines, voir TAILLIAR et COURTOIS, *Le livre des Usaiges et anciennes coustumes de la Conté de Guysnes* (Soc. des Antiquaires de la Morinie, St-Omer, 1856) ; COURTOIS, « Topographie du comté de Guines », dans Godefroy MÉNILGLAISE, *Chronique de Guines et d'Ardres par Lambert* (Paris, 1855), pp. 505-516 ; *Dictionnaire historique et topographique du département du Pas-de-Calais, Boulogne*, t. III (Haigneré) ; DE LOISNE, *Dictionnaire topographique du département du Pas-de-Calais* ; M. CHANTEUX-VASSEUR, « Étude géographique et historique sur le comté de Guines des origines à 1283 », *École des Chartes, Position de thèses*, 1935, thèse qui reste malheureusement inédite, mais que j'ai eu le privilège de consulter grâce à l'obligeance extrême de Madame Chanteux.

fut pas comprise dans le transfert de 1360. C'est ce qu'implique, dans le traité, l'expression : « le comté de Guines comme le dernier comte l'avait tenu. » Dans chaque châtellenie, le comte était représenté par un bailli qui, semble-t-il, exerçait des pouvoirs analogues à ceux des baillis d'Artois. Des trois châtellenies cédées à Édouard III, celle d'Audruicq s'étendait sur la totalité du pays de Bredenard, un de ces groupes de villages formant communauté, administré par un corps d'échevins, comme Marck et le pays de Langle. Ardres, au contraire, semble avoir d'abord été un fief séparé, uni ultérieurement à Guines, tandis que la châtellenie de Guines était évidemment le noyau primitif du comté.

Entre 1347 et 1360, le problème du gouvernement de Calais s'était restreint à savoir comment administrer un territoire exigu et presque entièrement urbain, avec quelques châteaux satellites dispersés dans un pays qui, bien que contrôlé militairement par des forces anglaises, n'était pas administré par des fonctionnaires anglais. Après 1360, le problème se modifia, puisqu'au territoire de Calais on avait ajouté celui de Marck et les trois quarts du comté de Guines. Une constellation de forteresses s'était transformée en une seigneurie territoriale considérable. Pour faire face à cette situation nouvelle, on ne modifia guère les cadres de l'administration anglaise, mais les fonctions de chaque officier s'en trouvèrent proportionnellement accrues. Ainsi le titre de capitaine se mua en celui de gouverneur ; outre des attributions militaires étendues, il reçut le pouvoir suprême, *merum et mixtum imperium*, avec justice haute et basse en tous procès civils et criminels. Ces larges pouvoirs, tout comme celui de siéger comme juge d'appel, constituent peut-être une délégation de l'autorité du roi en tant que « comte de Guines ». De même le trésorier devint « trésorier du comté de Guines et des seigneuries de Marck et de Calais » et ses fonctions s'élargirent d'autant : il devint le chef d'un Échiquier local, comptable lui-même devant le roi à Westminster. Le victuailler dut maintenant approvisionner de nouveaux châteaux ; plus tard pourtant, surtout pendant le règne de Richard II, on estima plus commode de confondre les deux offices.

Dans l'administration du comté, il semble que le droit et les institutions indigènes se maintinrent dans l'ensemble. Aucun changement délibéré n'apparaît dans les lois et les coutumes. En novembre 1360, les barons, pairs et hommes libres du comté — sauf ceux de la châtellenie de Tournehem, et quelques autres dont les fiefs étaient proches de la frontière du Boulonnais — avec les échevins d'Ardres, de la ville d'Audruicq et du pays de Bredenard, comparurent devant les représentants du roi à Calais et reçurent confirmation de leurs coutumes et libertés. Les chartes de confirmation pour le territoire de Marck, les « pairs de la châtellenie d'Ardres », la ville d'Audruicq et le Pays de Bredenard étaient toutes enregistrées sur les « French Rolls » [9], de même que l'ordre donné aux officiers anglais de Calais et des environs d'obéir

---

9. Espinas, *Recueil de documents relatifs à l'histoire du droit municipal*, Artois, I, 202-3, 603-4; II, 266 ; III, 153-4.

à l'évêque de Thérouanne dans toutes les matières relevant de la juridiction épiscopale. Parallèlement, la commission du gouverneur lui enjoignit de faire justice à tous « selon la loi et la coutume de ces parties».

Dans le domaine administratif, je n'ai pu encore savoir si le gouverneur excerça ses pouvoirs de haute juridiction en une cour analogue aux anciennes cours centrales du comté de Guines. Mais les signes d'une continuité dans le gouvernement local ne font pas défaut. Les comptes du trésorier énumèrent ces unités locales : « la ville et châtellenie de Guines », « la ville et châtellenie d'Ardres » et « la ville d'Audruicq avec la seigneurie de Bredenard ». Dans chacune, un bailli présidait une ou plusieurs cours d'échevins ; à côté de lui, bien que les offices pussent être réunis, un receveur percevait l'ensemble des revenus traditionnels. Dans les premiers comptes, ces officiers semblent porter des noms locaux, encore que la chose, avouons-le, ne se continua pas longtemps. En tous cas, l'ensemble paraît correspondre à l'ancienne administration locale. On y trouve, en plus, deux châtellenies dont aucune trace ne s'est conservée avant 1360, celles de Sangatte et Colville ; mais une note ajoute que le bailli y était *ex nova constitutione*. L'explication la plus plausible est que les administrateurs anglais trouvèrent expédient de partager entre de nouveaux districts l'une des anciennes châtellenies, probablement celle de Guines. Enfin, hors du comté proprement dit, le territoire de Marck maintenait son autonomie sous le nom de « ville et seigneurie de Marck et Oye », avec sa cour *coram baillivo et scabinis* ; de même Calais qui, pour l'instant, conservait son ancienne constitution, avec bailli et échevins, et dont les lois et coutumes restaient intactes.

Certaines conclusions, qu'il s'agira ensuite de nuancer, s'imposent à l'esprit. Tout d'abord, pour le gouvernement anglais du XIVe siècle, « Calais » signifie bien plus que la ville seule, si importante qu'elle apparaisse. Sous le titre, donné en 1360, de « comte de Guines avec les seigneuries de Calais et de Marck », cela signifiait un territoire d'une superficie analogue à celle du comté médiéval de Middlesex, formé au surplus de complexes unités. Du point de vue militaire, Calais et les territoires ruraux qui l'entouraient constituaient un tout, placé sous un commandement unique. Quant à l'administration, il y avait une organisation d'ensemble pour le territoire entier. Pour le gouvernement ce complexe représentait une unité. Or, jusqu'à la mort d'Édouard III je n'ai trouvé aucune preuve de l'acquisition, par des Anglais, de propriétés hors des murs de Calais. Au contraire, le cas n'est pas rare de propriétaires indigènes confirmés dans leurs possessions. Le droit et l'administration indigènes ayant été en grande partie conservés, et quelque importance qu'ait eu Calais dans cet ensemble, il est manifestement exagéré de parler d'une « colonie de peuplement ». Des forces anglaises exerçaient le contrôle militaire ; les intérêts mercantiles anglais cherchaient à obtenir le contrôle de la ville et du port de Calais ; mais en ce qui concerne le droit et l'administration, le gouvernement anglais semble avoir été aussi traditionaliste qu'en Ponthieu, dans les îles anglo-normandes ou ailleurs en France. Calais, dans son sens large, ne forma pas une exception aussi nette qu'on l'a parfois soutenu dans l'ensemble des possessions anglaises en France.

Trois événements, avant la fin même du xive siècle, ont provoqué à la longue d'importantes modifications à cet état de choses : l'établissement de l'étape à Calais en 1363, la reprise de la guerre en 1369, l'éclosion du Grand Schisme en 1378.

L'établissement de l'étape en 1363 eut pour conséquence de donner le bailliage de Calais, ville et banlieue, à une corporation de marchands, gouvernée par vingt-quatre *aldermen* et deux maires. Le gouvernement municipal, les revenus, les douanes et même la défense de la ville avec toutes ses machines de siège, furent placés entre leurs mains, pour une ferme annuelle de 500 marcs. Pour des raisons diverses, notamment la réaction très vive de l'ensemble des marchands, accusant maires et *aldermen* de trop gouverner l'étape et la ville à leur profit personnel et exclusif, ce régime fut aboli moins d'un an plus tard. A sa place fut établi un système plus normal, analogue à celui qu'on avait vu fonctionner dans l'étape anglaise depuis 1353 ; deux organisations distinctes, l'étape avec son maire et ses deux connétables, la ville et sa banlieue sous un maire et douze *aldermen*. Dans ce nouveau régime, le roi reprenait tous les revenus de la ville à sa main et payait le maire et les *aldermen* ; mais, passé 1376, maires, connétables et *aldermen* furent élus par leurs administrés respectifs.

L'établissement de l'étape fit de Calais une ville d'importance européenne. Mais ce fut aussi un pas dans l'anglicisation de la ville. Cependant toute trace de l'ancien Calais n'en fut pas effacée d'un coup. Pendant la courte période où la ville fut gouvernée par la Compagnie de l'Étape, bailli et échevins continuèrent à siéger. L'Étape, en quelque sorte, se superposa tout simplement à l'organisation plus ancienne. Quant au maire et aux *aldermen* qui succédèrent à l'étape dans le gouvernement de la ville, ils semblent l'avoir également hérité du bailli et des échevins. Pendant tout le règne de Richard II, on continua de nommer des baillis de Calais, dont il est difficile de dire ce qu'ils faisaient, mais il n'y a plus trace d'échevins. En revanche, le ressort du maire et des *aldermen* coïncidait avec l'ancien bailliage (ou « ville et échevinage », comme on commençait à l'appeler maintenant qu'il n'y avait plus d'échevins) ; les *aldermen* étaient juges autant que conseillers ; et le droit qu'ils appliquaient restait l'ancien droit de Calais, sauf dans les actions possessoires, jugées selon la loi anglaise. Au vrai, même en tenant compte de ce que l'étape constituait maintenant une « liberté » à l'intérieur de la ville, avec juridiction sur toutes les affaires commerciales, la substitution au bailli et aux échevins du maire et des *aldermen* ressemble plus à un changement de titulaires qu'à un système entièrement nouveau.

Tout cela, cependant, n'affectait que la ville de Calais. La reprise de la guerre, en 1369, de son côté, toucha profondément l'administration générale de la région. Aussitôt, le gouverneur vit son titre restreint à celui de Capitaine de Calais, appellation qui devint usuelle, sinon invariable, pendant tout le reste du siècle, car son rôle se réduisait maintenant à celui d'un simple châtelain. Les pouvoirs suprêmes en matière judiciaire et militaire furent donnée à un grand seigneur avec le titre de « Lieutenant en Picardie » ou plus souvent de « Lieutenant dans le royaume de France ». Savoir comment cette lieutenance s'agençait avec les pouvoirs locaux, c'est chose qui mérite une enquête. Mais le résultat fut de transférer la plupart des fonctions du gouverneur à une autorité supérieure ; le comté de Guines, avec Calais et Marck, en perdit de sa cohérence politique et de son individualité. Seul le trésorier continua de s'intituler « trésorier du comté de Guines avec la seigneurie de Marck et de Calais ».

Plus catastrophique encore fut l'invasion française de 1377, qui s'enfonça presque jusqu'à Calais et reprit définitivement aux Anglais les châtellenies d'Audruicq et d'Ardres. Le roi de France tenait maintenant trois des quatre châtellenies dont se composait le comté de Guines ; tout naturellement, elles formèrent un comté français ou, comme nous dirions, un comté « libéré » de Guines. Le résultat sur la domination anglaise en fut évidemment de détruire l'équilibre entre Calais et les seigneuries rurales qui l'entouraient. Il était exact, en 1361, de parler du « comté de Guines avec les seigneuries de Calais et de Marck », car c'était mettre les choses dans leur ordre réel et dans leur perspective vraie. Désormais, il sembla préférable de parler de « Calais et les Marches » appellation plus familière de ce qui, avec ses frontières réduites, devait durer jusqu'en 1558.

Pour finir, Calais, et les territoires voisins sous domination anglaise furent transférés, par ordre du Pape, en 1379, du diocèse de Thérouanne à celui de Canterbury [10]. Conséquence immédiate du Grand Schisme, où l'Angleterre et la France avaient rallié des obédiences rivales ; ainsi le clergé et les fidèles des territoires anglais ne pouvaient plus trouver audience auprès de leur évêque, d'où le transfert imaginé. Pour la même raison, les îles anglo-normandes furent temporairement transférées du diocèse de Coutances à celui de Nantes, et Cherbourg, peut-être, mais pour peu de temps, à celui de Winchester. Dans le cas de Calais et des Marches, et sauf pendant la période 1420-40, le transfert dura autant que la domination anglaise. Résultat important pour notre propos : des clercs anglais, en nombre sans cesse croissant, accaparèrent les bénéfices, hâtant ainsi le processus d'anglicisation.

Et pourtant — je ne parle toujours que du XIVe siècle — l'effet de ces événements ne se fit sentir pleinement que beaucoup plus tard. Même à la fin du siècle, aucun changement catastrophique n'avait été apporté aux principes de l'administration de Calais, de Marck et de ce qui restait du comté de Guines. En fait, dans le domaine du droit et de la coutume, la meilleure preuve de la survivance des anciennes

10. E. PERROY, *L'Angleterre et le Grand Schisme d'Occident* (Paris, 1933), pp. 103-110 ; I. J. CHURCHILL, *Canterbury Administration* (London, 1933), I, pp. 510-519.

lois et coutumes est fournie par le fait que le texte auquel nous devons presque tout ce que nous savons du droit médiéval et de l'administration du comté de Guines, le « Livre des usaiges et anciennes coustumes de la conté de Guysnes », fut apparemment compilé pendant l'occupation anglaise et contient un document issu de la chancellerie anglaise.

J'ai surtout, dans les pages que l'on vient de lire, tenté de définir une politique. J'en ai tiré la conclusion que Calais, dans le sens où j'ai défini ce mot, connut pendant tout le xive siècle un régime beaucoup plus normal que celui qu'on lui prête, et non celui d'une « colonie de peuplement » — un régime, au contraire, très voisin de celui des autres possessions anglaises en France. Mais dire que Calais possédait un régime normal suppose l'existence d'une règle, et cette règle n'a pas été définie. Une telle règle existait-elle, correspondant à ce que nous pourrions appeler une politique coloniale dans les siècles ultérieurs, pour diriger l'administration des territoires français possédés par l'Angleterre pendant la guerre de Cent Ans ?

11.[5] TAILLIAR et COURTOIS, *Le livre des Usaiges... de la Conté de Guysnes* ; réédité par G. ESPINAS, *Les Origines du Capitalisme*, IV, *Le droit économique et social d'une petite ville artésienne à la fin du moyen âge*, Guines (Lille, 1949).

Note

In the same issue of *Revue du Nord*, xxxiii (1951), 218-27, Edouard Perroy discussed 'L'administration de Calais en 1371-1372' (reprinted in *Etudes d'histoire médiéval*, Paris 1979, pp. 319-28) and he later edited the 'Compte de William Gunthorp, trésorier de Calais 1371-1372', *Mémoires de la commission départementale des monuments historiques du Pas-de-Calais*, x (1959). But the only other major contribution to the study of English-held Calais in this period since John Le Patourel wrote has been S. J. Burley, 'The Victualling of Calais, 1347-1365', *Bulletin of the Institute of Historical Research*, xxxi (1958), 49-57, though under Professor Le Patourel's supervision S. B. Storey-Challenger produced a valuable study of *L'administration anglaise du Ponthieu après le traité de Brétigny, 1361-1413*, (Abbeville 1975) and French counter-measures on the northern frontier against the English garrisons of the Pale were discussed by M. Rey, *Les finances royales sous Charles VI. Les causes du déficit, 1388-1413*, Paris 1965, pp. 372-8.

XV

THE KING AND THE PRINCES
IN FOURTEENTH-CENTURY FRANCE

The history of medieval France is often presented as though the process by which power and authority was centralized in the king's hand and ultimately made effective thoughout the kingdom was the only matter of consequence in the political development of the country. The monarchy is indeed important for, historically, it represents the principle of French unity, and unity triumphed in the end. But there were other possibilities. Monsieur Pocquet du Haut-Jussé has shown how two French dukes, the dukes of Burgundy and Brittany, behaved like independent princes in the fifteenth century,[1] and suggested that they should not be treated necessarily as traitors and rebels when they opposed the king, but as builders of subordinate states, very similar to the kingdom in their organization, sometimes in advance of it, more often modelled upon it. France, like Germany and Italy, passed through an 'age of principalities';[2] and, though her experience was shorter than theirs, unity under the king was not the only possible outcome. It is in any case a commonplace that the monarchy eventually took over the princely governments as the basis of its provincial organization.

The more sinister side of this phase was brought out in a short paper by Monsieur Perroy,[3] wherein he showed how the

---

[1] B.-A. Pocquet du Haut-Jussé, *Deux Féodaux, Bourgogne et Bretagne* (1935).

[2] B.-A. Pocquet du Haut-Jussé, *Les Papes et les ducs de Bretagne*, 2 vols. (1928), xi–xiii.

[3] E. Perroy, 'Feudalism or Principalities in Fifteenth-century France', *Bulletin of the Institute of Historical Research*, xx (1947), 181–5.

princes and magnates of the fifteenth century, not content with establishing their independence in fact, plundered and pillaged the monarchy, so that the civil wars of the fifteenth century in France, as in England, were struggles for the royal patronage, the royal revenues, ultimately for the monarchy itself. As Perroy observed, however, the process by which these counts and dukes (whom it is convenient to call 'princes') had established their high degree of independence has not been studied as a general phenomenon. It is not that local and regional monographs are lacking; they abound; and many of them represent historical writing on as high a plane, by any standards, as works on a national or wider scale. But they have, in general, treated each duchy, county or seigneurie by itself;[1] whereas the growth of regional autonomies, organized internally as kingdoms in miniature and approaching independence in their relations with the king, with one another and with external powers, seems to be characteristic of late-medieval France as a whole. The object of this paper is to show some of these fifteenth-century principalities in the making, and to suggest that, at the stage they had reached already in the fourteenth century, their progress towards autonomy has to be taken into account in any consideration of the politics of that time.

By the early part of that century the king's authority and his government had advanced a long way from the primitive feudal kingship of the eleventh and twelfth centuries.[2] Partly by good fortune, partly by successful warfare, partly by the growth of a higher ideal of kingship, the king had been able to insist, in the later part of the twelfth and the early part of the thirteenth century, on a much clearer definition of the relationship between the great lords and himself, whether based technically on liege homage or not, as with the duke of Burgundy in 1186, the Plantagenet lands in 1200, with Brittany in 1213, with the reconstituted Aquitaine in 1259; and, largely as a result of King Philip Augustus' successful war with King John, the king of

---

[1] At first sight *Histoire. des Institutions françaises au Moyen Age*, ed. F. Lot and R. Fawtier, i, *Institutions seigneuriales* (1957) (hereinafter cited as *Inst. seign.*) seems to be the general work that is required; but it is in fact a collection of unrelated monographs which is not concerned with establishing general tendencies or comparative constitutional development.

[2] Convenient summary, with essential references in R. Fawtier, *L'Europe Occidentale de 1270 à 1328* (Histoire générale: Histoire du Moyen Age, ed. G. Glotz, vi, i, 1940).

France had raised himself in wealth and prestige clear above any of the lords, however independent they might seem to be. In his later life, and certainly in retrospect, King Louis IX had made the monarchy almost sacred. In secular matters, the king had come to claim sovereignty both within his kingdom and in his relations with external powers: *rex in regno suo est imperator*. Not only did he insist on the normal feudal services, service in the field and in his court, the right to *aides*, but he was claiming to legislate for the whole kingdom, to take action, judicial or other, in any part of the kingdom in the interests of peace and justice, claims which were based upon a higher notion of kingship than feudalism offered, upon the idea of descent from the great Charlemagne, the king's consecration, the miraculous power of healing and the tradition of Saint Louis. These claims, it is true, were not all accepted all the time; it was sometimes necessary, particularly in matters of military service and taxation, to accept compromises, though this could be done without surrendering the principle. But whatever compromises might have to be made, the claims were being asserted ever more frequently and confidently.

To translate these claims into practice, the king had already built up a governmental structure of some maturity; but though it was rapidly acquiring a professional, bureaucratic complexion, the king was still effectively in command. The chief central institutions, *conseil*, *parlement* (high court) and *chambre des comptes* (accounting department), were being formed by groups of professionals within the old *curia regis*, and were only just beginning to have a separate identity as autonomous departments. They were beginning also to work permanently, with their accumulating bulk of records, in the king's palace in Paris, making it necessary for the king to have what amounted to a duplicate organization (*chambre aux deniers, maîtres des requêtes de l'Hotel*, etc.) in his household, to follow him in his itineration. In moments of crisis the king would call great assemblies which, in some sort, represented the people of his kingdom; but it is not at all clear how these were related to the normal conduct of affairs. Local government was in the hands of officers called *baillis* in some parts of the kingdom (mostly in the north) and *sénéchaux* elsewhere. Originally members of the king's court sent out to supervise the older *prévôts, vicomtes* and castellans, they had settled down into more or less stable

territorial units with almost every function of local government
on their hands. Naturally they soon needed assistants, notaries,
who drew up private acts and sealed them with a royal seal of
contracts, judges, and receivers who took over their financial
duties, both collecting and accounting.

In principle this organization was concerned with the royal
domain, now very considerable, and the king's relations with
his direct vassals; but already, owing to the development of the
idea of kingship, the king's increasing need of money and the
enthusiasm of his officers, it was reaching out much further.
From the middle of the thirteenth century the king's court
(later, specifically, the *parlement*) was developing the doctrine
that, if a seignorial court failed to do justice or gave a false
judgment, an appeal might be made; and the grounds of appeal
were constantly being widened. Potentially this brought everyone in the kingdom, whoever his lord might be, within the
purview of the king's court; while the protection which might
have to be given to appellants, and the inquiries which might be
necessary for the hearing of the appeal, were bringing the king's
officers into every great fief. Monasteries and towns might seek
the king's protection or the privilege that their litigation should
come only before the king's court; landowners might seek to put
themselves directly into the king's homage; enclaves of royal
domain and ecclesiastical lands might likewise bring the king's
officers into the great fiefs on the king's business. In the early
fourteenth century the indications were, indeed, in spite of the
reaction which these developments produced in 1314–15, that
principles already enunciated, and governmental machinery
that was being rapidly perfected, would soon make the unity of
the kingdom under the king's rule a reality. Yet within a hundred years France was beginning to look more like a loose
confederation of principalities under a king whose authority was
virtually excluded from them.

Some general reasons for this failure are obvious; military
defeat; the inability to mobilize the king's resources in men and
money to full effect. But while, if attention is fixed upon the king
and his government, it seems that by the beginning of the
fourteenth century they must be well on their way to breaking
down the autonomy of the great lords, these great lords, for their
part, had been building governments of their own within their
seigneuries; and as the king's officers were concerned to magnify

the king's authority and to make it effective throughout the kingdom, so the seignorial officers, who also had careers to make, were concerned to establish their lord's exclusive authority within his lordship, and to make it effective and even sovereign.

The duchy of Aquitaine,[1] as it existed towards the end of the thirteenth century, consisted of most of the ancient duchy of Gascony, the Bordelais, the Agenais, Saintonge south of the River Charente and certain lands in the 'Three Dioceses' of Limoges, Cahors and Périgueux, a large discrete principality with boundaries (legal as well as territorial) which were in constant dispute. It was unlike most of the other principalities of France in that its duke, being also the king of England, was usually an absentee ruler; but the habit which English historical atlases have of colouring the king-duke's lands red, as though they were part of some medieval British Empire, gives a very wrong impression. Edward I, king of England and duke of Aquitaine, owed his duchy to legitimate and continuous inheritance, ultimately from Duke William X and his predecessors; his great-grandfather, Henry II, had been duke of Aquitaine before he was king of England. Aquitaine was as much a part of the kingdom of France as Brittany or Burgundy; Henry III had done liege homage for the duchy in 1259.

In the twelfth century Aquitaine had been an enormous, loosely constructed, feudal principality, formed by the union of the earlier duchies of Aquitaine and Gascony, and centred on Poitiers. Much of it was held by semi-independent barons who might respond to inspiring leadership or pensions, but could hardly be disciplined. When, after 1154, the duke was also duke of Normandy, count of Anjou, king of England and, later, effective overlord of Brittany, Aquitaine could only be governed by frequent visits or by partial delegation (to Queen Eleanor or to Richard, for example); but at all times, it seems, the

[1] Y. Renouard in *Inst. seign.*, 157–83 and references there; P. Chaplais, 'Le Duché-pairie de Guyenne', *Annales du Midi*, lxix (1957), 5–38, lxx (1958), 135–60 and 'Gascon Appeals to England (1259–1453)', unpublished London Ph.D. thesis (1951). Only the 'positions' of J.-P. Trabut-Cussac's thesis on 'L'Administration anglaise en Gascogne sous Henri III et Edouard Ier de 1252 à 1307' have been published, though many of his conclusions are embodied in F. M. Powicke, *The Thirteenth Century* (1953), ch. vii. But there is still no general account of the development of government in the duchy during the thirteenth and fourteenth centuries. What follows is based chiefly upon the published rolls of the English chancery.

administration was directed by one or more seneschals holding 'vice-regal' powers, who, though they did not have the institutions that the justiciars of England and Normandy had at their command, nevertheless held equivalent status and functions.

The constitutional history of Aquitaine in the thirteenth century is a function of two developments: the progressive infrequence of the king-duke's visits, hitherto an essential element in the government of the duchy, and the definition and departmentalization of the seneschal's office. King John was in Aquitaine at some time during each of the first four years of his reign, in 1206 and in 1214; Henry III very briefly in 1230, for longer periods, when serious business could be done, in 1242–3 and 1253–4; Edward I for ten months in 1273–4 and for more than two years in 1286–9; Edward II and his successors not at all. It was necessary, therefore, to build up an administration that would function competently in the king-duke's lengthening and ultimately permanent absence; though it must have been some time before it was generally understood that his absence would be permanent.

For some time the duchy was not treated as an administrative unit. There were seneschals of Gascony, of Poitou, of La Marche, of the Three Dioceses (Limoges, Cahors and Périgueux), or two of these might be combined; it was not until the transfer of the Agenais in 1279 raised the whole question that the seneschal of Gascony was made seneschal 'of Aquitaine', and the seneschals of the Three Dioceses, the Agenais, Saintonge and Gascony 'outre Landes' subordinated to him. In this way a coherent administration was at last achieved. But this territorial extension, added to the economic development of the duchy (of which the growth of the wine trade and the proliferation of bastides are the most conspicuous evidence), relations with neighbouring principalities and judicial innovations which often required the seneschal's presence in Paris, so increased his responsibilities, that there was no longer any possibility that they could be discharged by one man. During King Henry's visit in 1242–3, a financial officer was appointed to assist the seneschal, hitherto responsible for collection, expenditure and accounting; during his visit of 1253–4 the earliest recorded financial officer with the title 'constable of Bordeaux', was appointed. During the next thirty years the constable took over more and more of the financial administration until, in the ordinances of 1289, he was given full responsibility. Likewise the seneschal could no longer personally attend to all the courts that were coming to be held in the name of the king-duke. More and more of these were being held by men who described themselves as 'lieutenants of the seneschal' and who were, in increasing proportion, professional lawyers. By 1290 a complete governmental structure had been created. The king-duke had just spent some while in the duchy, and it was no doubt expected that he would return from time to time. He had appointed a lieutenant, who represented his authority in a more immediate sense than the seneschal could now do; and with seneschal, an official council, sub-seneschals, constable, receivers and judges, a clear chain of command and a workable distribution of duties, the ducal government seemed competent to deal with anything short of an overwhelming emergency. What is important, however, is that this administration had been built upon native tradition. The law was the law of the country, whether *droit coutumier* or *droit écrit*; the courts were of the kind to be found in southern France; the internal financial administration seems to be similar to that of contemporary Brittany or Burgundy; the seal of the court of Gascony seems, in origin, very like the seal of the court of Burgundy. The king-duke governed the duchy as duke of Aquitaine, not as king of England, and there was certainly no transplantation of English institutions to Aquitaine as there was, for example, from England to Ireland. Aquitaine was the king-duke's inheritance, Ireland his conquest.

From 1202 until 1259, the relation between the duke of Aquitaine and the king of France was one of war or, at best, of truce; but as part of the treaty of 1259 King Henry did liege homage both for what he still held *de facto* and for what was then given him by the treaty, and he accepted a peerage of France as duke of Aquitaine. This meant that as the appeal jurisdiction of the courts of the king of France developed, appeals would be made from the duke's courts in Aquitaine, and the duchy thus laid open to the centralizing activities of the French royal officers. These caused more trouble in Aquitaine than in most of the other great fiefs; partly, no doubt, because the duke was also a king, but much more because there were few clear-cut boundaries. In the Three Dioceses, especially, fiefs owing direct allegiance to the king of France were interspersed with those of the duke of Aquitaine, and conflicts of jurisdiction could hardly be avoided. Appeals were indeed so frequent, and often so important politically, that the king-duke soon found it advisable to be permanently represented in Paris by a body of lawyers, who formed themselves into a 'council', to watch over his interests. Naturally he did what he could to provide a complete judicial service for his Aquitanian subjects. He could hear cases in England or send out commissions of oyer and terminer; he could see to it that a case was not taken to Paris before all the 'grades' of appeal in Aquitaine had been exhausted; he could anticipate royal legislation.[1] But before the war of 1294 he did not affront the system; he might himself initiate litigation in the court of the king of France; it was part of the natural order of things.

Much was changed by the war of 1294 in Aquitaine, as in the almost contemporary war in Flanders. A dispute over jurisdiction led to the seizure of Aquitaine by the king of France and war. It was in the lengthy negotiations that followed the truce of 1297 that the English lawyers began to argue that Gascony (they do not seem to have distinguished between Gascony and Aquitaine in their argument) was an 'allod', had always been an 'allod', and that nothing in the treaty of 1259, as it had been carried out, had altered its status.[2] Whether there was any legal or historical foundation for this argument is a matter for discussion; what is important is that the duke's officers were finding it difficult to secure their lord's rights through protest and the ordinary process of law; they were being driven to attack French sovereignty as it was developing and to assert the independence of the duchy.

By the treaty of 1303 the *status quo ante*, in name at least, was restored; but all the old difficulties remained, and it has long been held that they were among the causes not only of the war of 1324–7, but of the greater war which broke out in 1337, for both started with a confiscation of the duchy for alleged failure, on the part of the king-duke, to act as a loyal vassal. Whatever motives King Edward III may have had for assuming the title

---

[1] P. Chaplais, 'La souveraineté du rois de France et le pouvoir législatif en Guyenne au début du XIVe siècle', *Moyen Age*, Livre Jubilaire, 1963, 449–469.

[2] P. Chaplais, 'English Arguments concerning the feudal status of Aquitaine in the fourteenth century', *Bulletin of the Institute of Historical Research*, xxi (1948), 203–13; 'Le Traité de Paris de 1259 et l'inféodation de la Gascogne allodiale', *Le Moyen Age*, lxi (1955), 121–37.

'king of France' in 1340, that claim, and the state of war or truce which made up Anglo-French relations for the next hundred years and more, meant that Aquitaine was *de facto* independent of the kingdom of France until its final conquest in 1453; and in all the negotiations of those years, whatever military extremity they might be in, the English insisted on nothing less. A principality, independent of the Valois king of France, yet within the kingdom as traditionally understood, had been formed.

In the early years of the fourteenth century, Brittany[1] was a well-found feudal principality.[2] The ruling dynasty had been established when King Philip Augustus married Peter of Dreux, a member of a junior branch of the royal family which had no connection with Brittany, to Alice, daughter of Constance of Brittany by Guy of Thouars. Peter ruled first on behalf of his wife (1213–21), then for his son during his minority (1221–37). John I ruled on his own account from 1237 until 1286, and his son and successor, John II, from 1286 until 1305. As these were able and constructive men, their long lives gave Brittany a period of stability which it badly needed; for the duchy they had taken over was little more than a duchy in name, disunited and weak.

In Carolingian times Brittany had been a kingdom, but it had disintegrated into a number of counties and they into smaller *seigneuries*. The ducal title survived only as a decoration for the counts of Rennes, who were, however, gathering the other counties into their hands. Some measure of unity had been achieved under King Henry II after 1166, and under his son Geoffrey, who was duke from 1181 to 1186, but this unity had not survived the troubled years from 1186 to 1213. Peter of Dreux found a remote and isolated country, in which the ducal

---

[1] Dukes: Peter I, 1213–37; John I, 1237–86; John II, 1286–1305; Arthur II, 1305–12; John III, 1312–41; (Charles of Blois, 1341–64; John of Montfort, 1341–5); John IV, (1345–64) 1364–99.

[2] B.-A. Pocquet du Haut-Jussé, 'Le Grand Fief breton', *Inst. seign.*, 267–88, and references there given; with two important articles by the same writer, 'Les Faux Etats de Bretagne et les premiers états de Bretagne', *Bibliothèque de l'Ecole des Chartes*, lxxxvi (1925), 388–406, and 'La Genèse du législatif dans le duché de Bretagne', *Revue historique de Droit français et étranger*, 4ᵉ series, xl (1962), 350–72. Add (for Peter I), Sidney Painter, *The Scourge of the Clergy, Peter of Dreux, Duke of Brittany* (1937), and (for John IV), J. Calmette and E. Déprez, *La France et l'Angleterre en conflit* (Histoire générale, Histoire du Moyen Age, ed. G. Glotz, vii, i, 1937), 197–230.

domain was small; almost the whole of the north and west was under the lordship of the Penthièvre family and the vicomtes of Léon who scarcely admitted the suzerainty of the duke; the duke had little control over his barons and almost none over his bishops. To set up a firm ducal government was a work of some moment. Peter of Dreux made war inside and outside the duchy; John I was more peaceful and patient; together they enlarged the ducal domain out of all recognition, defeated and largely dispossessed the lords of Penthièvre and the vicomtes of Léon, established the rule that baronial fortifications required a ducal licence, and built several ducal castles at strategic points. They struggled to establish the rights of wardship and relief over their barons, partly for revenue, more perhaps, as a symbol of suzerainty; and they eventually compromised with the *droit de rachat* which preserved the principle and was probably more profitable in practice. With the Church they were less successful; but at least they had proclaimed the principle that the bishops should hold their temporalities of the duke and that he should have some say in their appointment.

In all this the dukes were assisted by two factors peculiar to Brittany, by the traditional connection with the earldom of Richmond in England and by the Breton coast-line. As long as the kings of England were dukes of Aquitaine, they had a direct and practical interest in the country which lay across their communications; and as long as they hoped to recover something of the position in northern France which they had lost in 1204, they looked to the duke of Brittany as a valuable ally. During the twelfth century the great earldom of Richmond had come to be held by the dukes of Brittany; and during the thirteenth, though Peter of Dreux had but the slenderest possible claim to the earldom, he and his successors were allowed to possess it whenever relations between the kings of England and France made it possible or the duke of Brittany was prepared to face the difficulties of a double allegiance. It may well be that the kings of England did not merely permit this connection, but used it as an instrument of policy; to the duke of Brittany, Richmond was at least a very considerable if somewhat uncertain source of revenue.[1] The coast-line of

---

[1] P. Jeulin, 'Un grand "Honneur" anglais: Aperçus sur le comté de Richmond', *Annales de Bretagne*, xlii (1935), 265–302, does not exhaust the subject by any means. There is no satisfactory study of the Brittany-Richmond relationship as a whole. See G. E. C. *Complete Peerage*, s.v. 'Richmond' (779–824) for chronology.

Brittany provided revenue through the right of wreck. In the twelfth century this had been exercised by any seigneur who could lay claim to a stretch of the sea-shore; but during the thirteenth the duke, by various means, made it a ducal prerogative and then (or possibly earlier) converted it into something rather different. Instead of claiming the wrecked ship and all its contents, a barbarous custom which it might not always be easy to exercise effectively in practice, the duke devised a form of sealed document which guaranteed the holder, on any one voyage, from seizure in case of misadventure on the Breton coast. These *sceaux* or *brefs*, as they were called, were sold to masters of ships not only in the Breton ports, but in Bordeaux and La Rochelle as well. Since this was virtually a toll on all shipping passing the coast, it became a regular, increasing and very profitable source of revenue.[1]

In the course of the thirteenth century, therefore, the duke had acquired sufficient wealth and sufficient control of his duchy to stand out as one of the great barons of France. He had married his daughters into French baronial families; he had taken part in crusades and royal expeditions; John II was brother-in-law to King Edward I; moreover, in addition to the connection with Richmond, the two marriages of Arthur II brought the county of Montfort and the *vicomté* of Limoges into the ducal family. For administrative purposes the duchy was divided into eight *bailliages*, each administered by an officer generally called a seneschal. These seneschals held courts, partly of first instance for men of knightly rank, partly for appeals from inferior ducal or seignorial courts; from the seneschals' courts (save that of Nantes), appeals could be made to the court of the seneschal of Rennes, and from Rennes and Nantes to the ducal *curia*. Revenue was collected partly by the seneschals, partly by *ad hoc* farmers of towns, forests and the like; most expenditure was by assignment upon these local collectors, and accounts were presented, probably quite irregularly, at the ducal court. When this court sat for judicial business, it was coming to be called the duke's *parlement*; and though there was as yet little trace of a *chambre des comptes*,

---

[1] H. Touchard, 'Les brefs de Bretagne', *Revue d'Histoire économique et sociale*, xxxiv (1956), 116–40, argues for a thirteenth-century origin; B.-A. Pocquet du Haut-Jussé, 'L'Origine des brefs de sauveté', *Annales de Bretagne*, lxv (1958), 255–62, for a twelfth-century origin.

surviving fragments[1] of accounts and the preparation of *brefs* for distribution to the ports both imply the rudiments of a financial organization within the ducal *curia*.

But the duke was the liege man of the king of France. In 1297, indeed, the king had formally recognized Brittany as a duchy and had created a peerage for the duke, partly as a compliment, more, one must think, to bind him more firmly to the monarchy. The king could, and did, demand military service and levy subsidies in Brittany; litigants could, and did, appeal from the duke's *parlement* to the king's *parlement*; and, as in Aquitaine, royal officers entered Brittanny to protect appellants, those who had obtained royal *sauvegardes* and those who had contrived to put themselves under the king's direct vassalage. Nor were these officers always restrained from attracting litigants to the king's *parlement* or the assizes of the king's *baillis* of Tours and the Cotentin before all the judicial resources of the duchy had been exhausted. The duke, while not contesting the king's sovereignty in principle, protested against these extensions of its exercise; protested so frequently and obtained so many re-iterated promises that the immediate impression must be that protests and promises were ineffective. But since, in fact, very few Breton appeals seem to have reached the French courts,[2] it is more likely that the duke was holding his own by continuous vigilance; and there is evidence that his officers were building up a useful body of precedents for successful resistance.

The great crisis in the development of Brittany as an autonomous principality came in the 'War of Succession' of 1341–64. It began with an unequivocal recognition of royal sovereignty by both claimants, Charles of Blois and John of Montfort, when they submitted their offer of homage to the king, and judgment between them could only be made in the king's *parlement* 'garnished' with peers. But this dispute was quickly swept into the current of war between Edward III and Philip VI. Both kings had tried to pre-judge the issue; Edward III had as strong an interest in Brittany as any of his predecessors, strengthened indeed by his ambitions in France, while the king of France was obviously concerned to prevent the establishment of English forces in the duchy. In the event, Edward

---

[1] B.-A. Pocquet du Haut-Jussé, 'Le plus ancien rôle des comptes du duché. 1262', *Mémoires de la Société d'Histoire et d'Archéologie de Bretagne*, xxvi (1946), 49–68,
[2] B.-A. Pocquet du Haut-Jussé, *Les Papes et les ducs de Bretagne*, i, vii.

succeeded not only in putting down garrisons in Brittany and keeping an army of occupation in part of the duchy, but also in maintaining a body of native support for young John de Montfort (son of the claimant of 1341, who had died in 1345) and the elements of a civil administration in his name; while John was brought up in England. When he came of age, Edward turned all this over to him and gave him the military support which enabled him to defeat and kill Charles of Blois at Auray (1364), and to win his duchy by judgment of battle and in defiance of the king of France and his court.

When peace was made, the relationship of the duke of Brittany to the king of France was subtly changed. King Charles V demanded liege homage, but had to be satisfied with an ambiguous formula which, in the next century, was converted into an explicit denial that homage was liege. John IV, as he is styled, called himself duke of Brittany *Dei gracia*; his successor staged a ceremony in Rennes Cathedral that was closely modelled on the royal coronation. Already, in 1341, both Charles of Blois and John de Montfort, in the case they put to the *parlement*, recalled that Brittany had once been a kingdom 'and still has the dignity of a kingdom', adding significantly, 'and the said royal dignity has been in no way impaired by the peerage of France'.[1] Such phrases were commonplace under John IV. They were made the foundation for his claim to 'regalities such as coinage, rights over churches, wreck and other things included *in his quae sunt Regalia Regni*';[2] the king should be satisfied with his right of ultimate judicial appeal. In 1394 two Breton clerks surprised the papal court by declaring that the duchy of Brittany did not lie within the kingdom of France, nor was the duke subject to any secular prince.[3]

These claims were accompanied by a rapid development in the ducal institutions of government. The duke's *curia* still consisted chiefly of bishops and barons, though the professional element was growing. In its narrowest form, it was the duke's council; in fuller session, for judicial and political matters of importance, it was his *parlement*, with a *président* or *juge universel*,

---

[1] 'Et tient encore les Noblesses de Royaume, . . . et ladite Noblesse de Royaume n'a pas été ostée par la Pairie de France,' Dom Lobineau, *Histoire de Bretagne*, (1707), ii, col. 480.

[2] 'Choses Royalles, comme monnoyes, garde d'Eglises, bris de mer et autres choses continus *in his quae sunt Regalia Regni*'. Ibid., col. 646.

[3] B.-A. Pocquet du Haut-Jussé, *Les Papes et les ducs de Bretagne*, i, 420.

though the duke often presided in person 'assis en sa majesté'; in its fullest form, when it might include representatives of the towns, it was still officially styled *parlement*, though in the next century such meetings would be regarded as meetings of 'the estates'. The duke was beginning to levy his own taxation, insisting that only he could do so in Brittany, in the form of *fouages* and customs on goods entering and leaving the ports. These taxes required the consent of a reasonably full session of the *parlement*, as a matter of political prudence rather than of constitutional necessity, for representatives of those to be taxed were still not always included. The consequent increase in ducal revenues necessitated the appointment of a '*trésorier et receveur général*', responsible both for the older revenues (domain, justice, *brefs*, etc.) and the new forms of taxation, and also a much clearer definition of the *chambre des comptes* as a professional body of auditors under a president. In addition, there was a chancellor who, besides attending to the normal duties of chancellor, presided over the council and acted as the duke's chief adviser, a marshal who directed the duke's still somewhat undeveloped military resources, and an admiral who organized the convoying of merchantmen and the impressment of ships for naval expeditions and coastal defence.

In short, by the end of the fourteenth century, the duke of Brittany was contesting all but a residual sovereignty in the king of France and had built up the institutions of government in the duchy to a point at which they would support his sovereignty 'in practice'. Whether he desired a higher degree of independence, it is hard to say; his relations with England at the time were both an opportunity and an obstacle. Edward III had not given him his assistance during the 'war of succession' for nothing. Duke John IV found himself bound to his English father-in-law by debts, English garrisons and English 'military experts', not to mention his English upbringing and his two English wives. When the Anglo-French war broke out again in 1369, loyalty to the king of France and neutrality were probably equally impossible for him; and when he made his alliance with Edward in 1372 and Richmond was restored to him, a French punitive expedition soon drove him into exile. For five years King Charles V administered the duchy. When, however, the king decided to annex the duchy to the domain, the Breton nobility, even Charles of Blois' widow, protested, formed leagues, and invited Duke John to return. But when he came back and was seen to lean too heavily on English support in order to ward off the French armies, the same Bretons assembled at Rennes and appealed to King Charles for an accommodation. The moral is clear. The Bretons wanted a duke who would maintain the quasi-independence built up during the thirteenth and fourteenth centuries and neutrality in the Anglo-French war; to be tied not so closely to France that commerce with England and elsewhere was difficult, not so closely with England that peaceful relations with France were impossible. For a moment at the end of his life, temporarily improved relations between England and France enabled John IV to enjoy the earldom of Richmond and the duchy of Brittany together once more. His successors in the fifteenth century, though they continued to use the title, never possessed the earldom; but they won the independence in all but name which he never quite achieved.

The county of Flanders[1] was among the most precocious of the feudal principalities of France.[2] Its organization dated, in the main, from the great days of the eleventh and twelfth centuries when Flanders had enjoyed a real independence and its rulers took a not inconspicuous part in the affairs of Europe. The counts' strength in their county was based on the circumstances in which it had come into being. Descended from the Carolingian counts of the original county of Flanders, they had converted their official functions into a lordship and the royal lands to their own use; by warfare and by other means they had added county to county; they had acquired control over church lands and established their right to waste lands including the land that was being recovered from the sea. They were thus wealthy; they could build castles and establish their monopoly of military service within their territory; they co-operated in the enforcement of the Peace of God and converted it into the

---

[1] Counts: (with Hainault)—Baldwin VIII, 1191–5; Baldwin IX, 1195–1205; Jeanne, 1205–44 (married 1, Ferdinand of Portugal; 2, Thomas, Count of Maurienne); Margaret, 1244–78 (married 1, Bouchard of Avesnes; 2, William of Dampierre); (Flanders)—Guy of Dampierre, 1278–1305; Robert of Béthune, 1305–22; Louis of Nevers (II), 1322–46; Louis of Male, 1346–84.

[2] F. L. Ganshof, 'La Flandre', *Inst. seign.*, 343–426 and references there given: in particular, H. Pirenne, *Histoire de Belgique*, i (5th ed. 1929), ii (4th ed. 1947); R. Monier, *Les Institutions centrales du comté de Flandre* (1943), *Les Institutions financières du Comté de Flandre* (1948).

count's peace. They had, in fact, resisted the disintegrating tendencies of feudalism to a quite remarkable extent; the count had made himself *dominus terrae.*

In all this, the counts of Flanders were no doubt assisted by the fact that they had acquired lands in Germany as well as in France, by the situation of their lands at the extremity of either kingdom, and also by the enormous development of the towns in Flanders which they were able to assist, to their very great profit. In the contemporary sense they were vassals of the king of France for their French lands and of the king of Germany for those in Germany, and, when it was convenient, they performed their feudal duties; but neither king had any control over them. They were accustomed to conduct their 'foreign policy' among the principalities that were forming in the ancient Lotharingia, and even further afield. At least from the beginning of the twelfth century they were vassals of the king of England for a pension. From time to time the counts ruled other principalities as well: Philip of Alsace held the county of Vermandois in right of his wife; the count of Flanders was also the count of Hainault through much of the thirteenth century; Guy of Dampierre was also marquis of Namur. Such unions were personal and did not often endure; but they added wealth and prestige.

In the government of Flanders, local institutions, until the thirteenth century, were more remarkable than those at the centre. The basis of local government was the *châtellenie,* a district dependent upon a comital castle, administered by a *châtelain* to whom the count had delegated military, police and judicial functions. The courts he held were public courts, in which the judges were benches of *échevins.* For financial purposes the county was divided into *métiers* (*officia*), in which the count's revenues were collected and at least partly spent by 'notaries'. During the twelfth century *baillis* (very similar to the king's *baillis*) were superimposed. They were the count's agents, appointed, removed and paid by him; they took over the holding of the *échevinages,* both urban and rural, and the local feudal courts. At the centre was the count himself, itinerant with his household and court (so far as they can be distinguished). These were of the usual kind save that the office of chancellor (which was combined with that of general receiver of the revenues) had been given to the provost of Saint-Donatien at Bruges in 1089, to be held by him and his successors for ever. During the thirteenth century, however, with the growth of the revenue, the 'notaries' were replaced by local receivers, the chancellor's financial responsibilities taken over by the 'receiver of Flanders', and the local receivers' accounts were presented to a *Cour des Hauts Renneurs*—a very early example of professional audit.

This powerful, well-organized and idiosyncratic principality had been built up while the king was still remote and weak; during the thirteenth century it was subjected to a determined campaign to bring it under royal control and administration. The campaign was conducted in two phases. During the first, which extends from the beginning of the century to the time of Guy of Dampierre, the king was primarily concerned to secure fidelity. The participation of Ferdinand of Portugal, husband of the Countess Jeanne, in the Anglo-Imperial coalition that was smashed at Bouvines, enabled King Louis VIII to impose a peace by which he annexed the western part of the county (Artois) and imposed sanctions which would guarantee the loyalty of countess, count, their vassals and the towns (Treaty of Melun, 1226). When the Countess Margaret succeeded in 1244, a dispute broke out between the children of her two marriages, and this dispute was referred to King Louis IX. The king ruled that Flanders should go to Guy of Dampierre and Hainault to John of Avesnes. It was a measure of the king's authority that he not only settled the succession to Flanders (which his predecessor had been unable to do in 1127), but to Hainault as well, and Hainault was not within his kingdom. On the ground that he had no right to do this, John of Avesnes repudiated the agreement and, in alliance with other princes of the Low Countries who feared the extension of French influence, attacked Flanders. The Countess Margaret was very glad to accept French assistance, and Guy of Dampierre owed his county very largely to the king. He began his rule in 1278 as a faithful vassal.

Royal intervention in the internal affairs of the county, which marks the second phase, was occasioned by events in the towns. The enormous economic development of Flanders had expressed itself in the growth of a number of manufacturing towns whose size and wealth gave them greater political consequence in the county than either nobility or clergy. Their wealth may be measured by the fact that in 1305, Ypres, Bruges and Ghent alone were assessed at 38 per cent of a sum which had to be raised in the county. Such power had early manifested itself in political action. It was the resistance of the towns which prevented the king from imposing a count on the county in 1127–8. Later in the twelfth century the count found it advisable to consult representatives of the seven largest towns (Arras, Bruges, Douai, Ghent, Lille, Saint-Omer and Ypres—reduced to five after 1226 and to three after 1312 by French annexations) on matters of general concern. But internally, the towns were divided between the rich merchants who dominated the municipal governments and the craftsmen, many of whom were wage-earners in the modern sense.

In order to control the towns which, under weaker or more distant rule might have formed city-states like those of north Italy, Count Guy seemed to support the 'commons' in their often legitimate grievances against the patrician-dominated town governments; and this, when the king's *parlement* was ready to receive them, provoked appeals from the municipalities. The royal officers moved quickly. The *baillis* of Amiens and Vermandois took Flanders into their jurisdiction and royal *sergents* were sent in to protect the appellants. The count's resistance led eventually to a French invasion and the incorporation of the county into the royal domain, with the count and his sons prisoners in Paris (1300). Autonomous Flanders might have come to an end at this point, like Normandy in 1204, but for a revolt in Bruges and the defeat of the French punitive expedition at the astonishing battle of Courtrai (1302). To some extent this was a flash in the pan; the subsequent fighting was not all to the advantage of the Flemings, and the king of France imposed a ferocious peace (Athis-sur-Orge) in 1305, gradually modified in the course of the next fifteen years. As a result of this treaty, the *châtellenies* of Lille and Douai were annexed to the royal domain (1312) but there was no longer any question of annexing the whole of Flanders.

There was another element in the situation. For two centuries at least, the count of Flanders had been in close relation with England, partly because the Flemish towns grew ever more dependent upon England for the wool they made into cloth. Politically this relationship had not always been fortunate. The alliance of 1213–14 led to the disaster at Bouvines and the Treaty of Melun; Count Guy's alliance with Edward I (who as duke of Aquitaine was also faced by the problem of French administrative expansion) in 1297 was equally disastrous, for Edward's help came too late to save him from French invasion. But the economic relationship lost none of its urgency. When Edward III sought to draw Flanders into a coalition of princes in the Low Countries, as war with France was approaching, he met with a blank refusal from Count Louis of Nevers who, owing his county to the king's support at the time of the great revolt of 1323–8, would not be detached from his loyalty for any reason whatever. But when Edward applied the pressure of blockade there was such distress in Flanders that the Three Towns (that is, the three remaining 'good towns' which the count had been accustomed to consult, Ypres, Bruges and Ghent), led by James van Artevelde of Ghent, took matters into their own hands and negotiated treaties first of neutrality then of alliance with Edward. This extraordinary situation persisted for many years. The great towns, and all that part of the county which they controlled, recognized Edward as king of France and gave him more than token military support; while Count Louis remained faithful to King Philip and died fighting on his side at Crécy. From time to time there was a temporary accommodation, for only the count could give lawful authority to public acts in the county; but unless some way could be found to reconcile the economic interests of the towns, their social problems, the authority of the count and the sovereignty of the king, no stability was possible.

This seems to have been understood by Count Louis' successor, Louis of Male. The problem was thrust upon him at once, for as soon as he had done homage to King Philip, the towns put pressure on him to ally himself with King Edward. His solution was the ambiguous Treaty of Dunkirk (1348) which, given obedience to the count, allowed the agreements which the towns had made with Edward to remain in force. Such a settlement could only be made in time of truce; but it was Louis' achievement to maintain good relations with both England and France, rather than a negative neutrality, through most of his rule. By diplomatic skill and good fortune in war he was able to settle his relations with Brabant and the combined counties of Hainault, Holland and Zeeland very much to his advantage; and, secure on that side, he was able to make his own terms when he found the kings of France and England bidding against one another for the marriage of his daughter and heiress, Margaret. In the end, the king of France won. Louis' price was the restoration of the castellanies of Lille and Douai. Margaret was married to Philip the Bold, the king's brother and duke of Burgundy; and the ultimate consequence of this marriage was the fateful union of Flanders and Burgundy in 1384.

During the 1360s and '70s Count Louis had achieved a remarkable degree of independence diplomatically, and this was backed both by economic prosperity and by developments in government. Given reasonable dynastic good fortune, it is likely that Flanders would have been as independent as Brittany in the fifteenth century, even if there had been no union with Burgundy. Its government was being centralized and professionalized. The old comital *curia* had contracted, early in the century, into a more professional council, from which the nobility, as such, almost disappeared. This council could meet in a full session as the *Grand Conseil*, which might include representatives of the towns; it was developing a judicial 'department', the *Audience*, which was encouraging the appeal system within the county and coming to have some of the characteristics of a *parlement*, and a *chambre légale*, a diminishing survival of the old feudal jurisdiction of the *curia*. The men who staffed the council, in its various forms, were appointed, dismissed and salaried by the count; as in Brittany or Aquitaine they were professionals, jurists and doctors of law who had a definite interest in developing the authority of the count's courts. Financially, a transaction known as the 'transport de Flandre', by which the king of France had conveyed part of the indemnity exacted by the Treaty of Athis to the count in return for the definitive cession of Lille and Douai in 1312, had provided him with a regular and profitable source of revenue, for the count continued to raise the 'indemnity' for his own purposes; otherwise, and perhaps for that reason, taxation does not seem to have advanced far beyond individual bargains with the towns before the union with Burgundy. The *receveur de Flandre* was supplemented by a *souverain bailli*, a general supervisor of the administration; the functions, though not the title, of chancellor were taken from the provost of Saint Donatien and given to a *chancelier du comte*; and the auditing of all but the traditional domain revenues was given to an increasingly professional commission of the council soon to be known as the *chambre des comptes*. This centralizing policy, which was seen for what it was by the great towns jealous of their autonomy, was one cause of the revolt of 1379–85; but it was giving Flanders that practical independence which the other principalities in their several ways were achieving. King Charles V had to negotiate with Louis of Male on the marriage question almost as though he were a foreign prince; appeals to the *parlement* of Paris, though technically possible, were so rare that the comital courts were sovereign in practice,[1] and there was no longer any question of French administrative intervention within the county.

It was the dynastic union of the duchy of Burgundy[2] and of the county of Flanders in 1384 that formed the basis of the 'Burgundian state' of the fifteenth century.[3] The two principalities had this much in common that they were both situated on the frontier of the kingdom and both were able to profit by the opportunity to acquire lands in the empire; and after the union it was possible to standardize their administration to some extent. But their historical development had been very different.

The history of Flanders from the ninth to the end of the twelfth centuries had been one of almost continuous expansion from a central nucleus; and the count, preserving much of the Carolingian order and adding to it his enormous wealth as a landowner, was able to build up a compact and well-organized principality. The history of Burgundy, over the same period, was one of disintegration. Its origin lay in the relatively small part of the ancient kingdom of Burgundy that was left to West Francia in the partitions of the ninth century, and it was

[1] R. van Caeneghem, 'Les Appels flamands au parlement de Paris au moyen âge', *Etudes d'histoire du droit privé offertes à Pierre Petot* (1959), 61–8.

[2] Dukes: (Capetian)—Hugh III, 1162–92; Odo III, 1192–1218; Hugh IV, 1218–72; Robert II, 1272–1306; Hugh V, 1306–15; Odo IV, 1315–49; Philip of Rouvres (1349–60), 1360–1. (Valois)—(King John II, 1361–3); Philip the Bold, 1363–1404.

[3] J. Richard, 'Les Institutions ducales dans le duché de Bourgogne', *Inst. seign.*, 209–47 and references there given; in particular—J. Richard, *Les Ducs de Bourgogne et la formation du duché* (1954); H. Jassemin, 'Le contrôle financier en Bourgogne sous les derniers ducs capétiens', *Bibliothèque de l'Ecole des Chartes*, lxxix (1918), 102–41 (but cf. Richard, *Les Ducs de Bourgogne*, 441 ff.); *Registres des Parlements de Beaune et de Saint-Laurent-lès-Chalon*, ed. P. Petot (1927), intro.; and for the later fourteenth century, R. Vaughan, *Philip the Bold* (1962), with excellent bibliography.

organized then as a 'duchy', that is, a group of counties under a royal officer with special military powers. The office of duke was not strictly hereditary, though there was a strong hereditary tendency, until King Henry I established his brother Robert as duke in 1032. Robert founded the Capetian line of dukes which persisted until 1361; but the duchy which he ruled was much smaller than its Carolingian predecessor. The dukes lost control of the counties in which they were not themselves count, and even those they held disintegrated into ecclesiastical immunities and lay *seigneuries*, so that the Carolingian administrative framework had entirely disappeared before the end of the eleventh century. The duchy survived to form the basis of a feudal principality chiefly because the ducal family itself survived, and because the dukes, though there were no great figures among them, managed to retain some control of castle-building as a vestige of their original military authority.[1] They were therefore able to organize a number of *châtellenies* which provided the nucleus about which they were later able to rebuild their authority. But within the duchy of Burgundy, however defined, there were several prelates (the bishop of Langres for example) who held their lands independently of the duke, many royal enclaves, many allods. The duchy was simply a bundle of rights, not yet indivisible, and with very little territorial or political consistence.

When something like a 'war of independence' was being fought in Flanders during the thirteenth and the earlier part of the fourteenth centuries, the dukes of Burgundy were loyal and co-operative vassals of the king. Duke Hugh III, it is true, had acquired lands in the empire by his marriage with Beatrice of Albon, and seems to have thought, at one moment, of playing off emperor against king. But when the lord of Vergy, whom he had occasion to chastise, appealed to King Philip Augustus, the king intervened to great effect; after that there was no question but that the duke of Burgundy was the liege vassal of the king of France, as that was coming to be understood, and often closely connected with him by family ties. Very few obstacles were placed in the way of the development of French royal sovereignty over Burgundy or the entry into the duchy of French royal officials. This, no doubt, was largely because the conception of

[1] This is Richard's thesis.

Burgundy as a territorial entity was itself only just beginning to form. But as the duke gradually built up his domain by purchase and other usual means, and as he gradually defined and standardized his relations with his vassals, he was perpetually brought into contact with other authorities—the king, the greater churchmen, the counts of Champagne—who were doing the same thing and competing with one another for the homage of landowners converting their allods into fiefs. In the process, the dukes and their rivals defined their respective spheres of interest; the notion of a ducal *baronnie* was formed—a bundle of inalienable rights, a stretch of territory in which the duke was *dominus terrae*, an indivisible inheritance. Even at the end of the thirteenth century this was still rather more doctrine than fact, and it was not undisputed; so far as it was law it depended on judgments of the king's court.

In these circumstances it is not to be expected that the political institutions of the duchy would be very precocious. The ducal household and the ducal *curia* were of the usual kind save in one important particular. At the turn of the thirteenth and fourteenth centuries, it became the custom to delegate the hearing of appeals and other judicial work of the *curia* to *auditeurs des causes d'appeaux*. These were ducal councillors, professional lawyers, who formed themselves into a court which did much of the judicial work of the *curia* in the fourteenth century, though the *curia* still held *jours généraux* at Beaune from which the *parlement* of Burgundy grew as a formal institution later in the century. Local government shows the usual progression from the purely domanial agents of the twelfth to the *baillis* of the thirteenth and fourteenth centuries; but the evolution was slow and late. Until the end of the thirteenth century the accounts of local and other officers were still being heard, in principle and often in fact, by the duke himself whenever and wherever it was convenient; a ducal receiver to centralize receipts did not appear until then, and the beginnings of a *chambre des comptes*, in the sense of a small group of councillors detailed to hear accounts, but still unspecialized, cannot be put before the beginning of the fourteenth century.

A quickening of development can be detected under Duke Odo III; and it is significant that this came at a time when, as ruler of the counties of Burgundy and Artois, in right of his wife, he had other things to attend to besides the duchy. But the real organization of ducal government was the work of King John II and the French royal administration. When Odo III died in 1349, his heir Philip of Rouvres, was an infant. Philip's mother, Jeanne, took as her second husband the duke of Normandy who, in 1350, succeeded to the throne of France as King John II. Though he moved carefully, King John was in charge of the duchy, as guardian, by 1353, and this meant that the administration was taken over by French royal officers. Late in 1360, King John reluctantly delivered Burgundy to young Philip, who died of the plague within a year. The king then took possession of the duchy claiming to be the heir; but in 1363 he gave it as an appanage to his son Philip, known to history as Philip the Bold. This did not mean that the activity of French lawyers and administrators came to an end in Burgundy by any means; Philip the Bold was very much a French prince, spending a good deal of his time in Paris. In the great reorganization of his dominions carried out in 1386, after he had taken over the government of Flanders and other territories, French personnel and French administrative experience and practice were still very prominent.

The reconstruction of Burgundian institutions on the model of the French monarchy can be seen in almost every sphere of ducal government in the years between the death of Odo III and the reorganization of 1386. King John had introduced royal officers into the ducal council, making it, since he himself was necessarily absent from the duchy for most of the time of his wardship, a more definite and more professional body than it had hitherto been. Likewise the detailing of two or three of these councillors regularly to audit accounts, the provision of a *clerc des comptes* and of a place in which they could meet regularly, soon made the embryonic *chambre des comptes* at Dijon into a replica of its counterpart in Paris. For judicial purposes, the royal officers worked to make the occasional *jours généraux* of the ducal *curia* into a *parlement* on the Parisian model. They were not whole-hearted in this, perhaps, and they were not wholly successful; for there was already a court of appeal in Burgundy, the court of the *auditeurs des causes d'appeaux*, and though appeals therefrom to the Burgundian *parlement* were coming to be allowed, there was always the *parlement* of Paris ready to accept litigation and to get round any rules of restraint that it might be forced from time to time to make for itself. Besides, there were many seigneurs in Burgundy, chiefly ecclesiastical, from whose courts an appeal could lawfully be made directly to the *parlement* of Paris. By maintaining a number of proctors in Paris and at the courts of the royal *baillis* of Sens and Mâcon (as the duke of Aquitaine had to do at Paris and in the courts of the *baillis* of Toulouse and Périgord), the duke did what he could to preserve his rights as a peer; but he cannot be said to have been more than moderately successful. Like the duke of Aquitaine and the other great lords, he himself used the royal courts when it was convenient to do so. Successful resistance to French judicial sovereignty in Burgundy was not made until the fifteenth century. Finally, the first assembly recognized as the Estates of Burgundy was summoned by King John in 1352. Before then the dukes had occasionally asked for subsidies on a purely local basis, as the king did in France; but it was the desperate needs, first of the king and then of the duke, in the 1350s and 1360s, which established the institution.[1] The substitution of ducal for royal taxation, on a permanent basis, came a little later. Philip the Bold secured a grant of *aides* to be levied in Burgundy on the authority of the estates of the kingdom from King Charles V, and then continued to levy them for himself on the authority of the estates of Burgundy.

In so far, therefore, as Burgundy emerges as an autonomous principality before the union with Flanders, with characteristic institutions of government, these were, if not created, at least greatly hastened in their development by the king himself, his officers and his lawyers—naturally in imitation of royal institutions. It is a far cry from Flanders or Aquitaine.

This same tendency towards the growth of independent principalities in France can be seen in its earlier stages in the counties of Champagne or Toulouse,[2] both annexed to the Crown in the course of the thirteenth century; it can also be seen in small-scale affairs like the county of Forez (where a *chambre des comptes* developed very precociously in the early fourteenth century, in direct imitation, it seems, of the royal institution), the county of Beaujolais,[3] or the minuscule county of Guînes

[1] J. Billioud, *Les Etats de Bourgogne aux XIVe et XVe siècles* (1922).
[2] *Inst. seign.*, 71–99; 123–36.
[3] For Forez and Beaujolais, see E. Perroy, 'L'Etat bourbonnais' in *Inst. seign.* 289–317.

with its institutions of the Flemish type.[1] There are many others. At its most spectacular it can be seen in the Pyrenean *vicomté* of Béarn,[2] where the *vicomtes*, having been vassals, in the contemporary sense of the term, of the dukes of Gascony during the eleventh century, transferred their allegiance to the king of Aragon in the middle of the twelfth, and returned to do homage to Henry III of England and Aquitaine in 1242. Amid these changes the *vicomte's* vassalage cannot often have had much practical import; and Gaston Fébus took what might seem to be the final step when he specifically refused liege homage for Béarn to the Black Prince in 1364. Gaston, in the end, out of dislike for Matthew de Castelbon, his nephew and nearest surviving heir, bequeathed his dominions to the king of France (Treaty of Toulouse, 1390); but after his death the *cour majour* and the *cour des communautés*, hitherto separate institutions, met together spontaneously as the first assembly of the Estates of Béarn and assisted Matthew to negotiate the king's renunciation of the treaty, thus preserving the 'sovereignty' of Béarn to the extent that it had been achieved up to that point. As in Brittany influential men worked for independence when their lord seemed to fail them.

Perhaps the most striking example of the tendency is to be found in what may be described as the 'posthumous' history of the duchy of Normandy.[3] When the duchy was annexed to the royal domain in 1204 its individuality was not destroyed. Though the office of seneschal was abolished, and many offices filled by men taken from the royal administration, the duchy preserved its law and most of its institutions. The exchequer continued as the high court although, as the practice of appeals to the king's court developed in the thirteenth century, it had to allow appeals from its judgments; and it continued to act as the central financial institution of the duchy, though it accounted to the king's officers in Paris. But as the royal *baillis* attacked the judicial privileges of the seigneurs, in Normandy as elsewhere, as the king developed his claims to levy general taxation during the reign of Philip IV, and as appeals from the

---

[1] Le Patourel, 'L'Occupation anglaise de Calais au XIVe siècle', *Revue du Nord*, xxxiii (1951), 236–7 and references there given. See above XIV.

[2] P. Tucoo-Chala, 'Les Institutions de la vicomté de Béarn', *Inst. seign.*, 319–41; also *La Vicomté de Béarn et le problème de sa souveraineté* (1961).

[3] A. Coville, *Les Etats de Normandie* (1894); J. R. Strayer, *The Administration of Normandy under Saint Louis* (1932); R. Besnier, *La Coutume de Normandie: Histoire externe* (1935).

exchequer to the king's court seemed to endanger the autonomy of Norman law, the Normans joined in the movement of 1314 and 1315, and secured the one effective provincial charter that was given at that time, the famous 'charte aux Normands'. This provided that there should be no further appeals from the exchequer to the *parlement* of Paris, that there should be no taxation without consent, save in a defined emergency, and that Norman customs should be respected. The assemblies called from time to time in Normandy to consent to taxation enabled the Normans to make collective protests against anything they considered to be an infringement of their liberties, and to maintain their consciousness as a people distinct from others within the kingdom of France. By the end of the century it could be said in Normandy, as in Brittany, that 'le duché n'est pas du royaume'[1]—and this in a dukeless duchy whose only dukes in the fourteenth century, and those in name only, had been heirs to the throne.[2]

These brief sketches should show that the tendency towards the formation of autonomous principalities was general in the France of the fourteenth century, and that there was more to the political development of France in the thirteenth and fourteenth centuries than the progress of the monarchy. The means by which autonomy was achieved differed from principality to principality, and the whole process would be more comprehensible if a comparative constitutional history of the great French fiefs had been written. That would be a big undertaking; but already the outline is clear.

The great fiefs of the eleventh and twelfth centuries were, in a sense, as independent as those of the fifteenth century. The duke of Normandy or the count of Flanders might recognize the king as his suzerain and might occasionally attend his court; but they might also make war upon him and among themselves and establish independent relations with countries outside the kingdom. But towards the end of the twelfth century and in the thirteenth the king was in various ways able to insist on liege homage; and this carried with it a recognition of his judicial and legislative sovereignty—in practice, the submission of the great

---

[1] E. G. Léonard, *Histoire de la Normandie* (1944), 69.
[2] John, created duke in 1332 (succeeded to the throne in 1350), Charles in 1355 (succeeded in 1364).

lords to the jurisdiction of the king's court, acceptance of the appellate jurisdiction of this court and the administrative intervention of the king's officers in the great fiefs to protect appellants, to collect taxation and so forth. To some extent the development of princely independence can be represented as a reaction to this extension of the royal government, as a resistance leading to the formation of their own hierarchy of courts, their own financial administrations, their own bodies of professional administrators who imitated and rivalled the king's lawyers and administrators. The kingdom and the principalities were growing up together as rival organizations.

But this is not the whole story. Although professional councils, *chambres des comptes, parlements,* and estates were coming into being in all the principalities (sometimes with different nomenclature), and very similar conventions, say, in the use of seals, these institutions did not all originate or develop in the same way. One or two of the principalities (Flanders and Normandy were examples) were in advance of the monarchy in the twelfth century; others were more backward. Each had its own peculiar circumstances. In Flanders it was a position at the extremity of the kingdom, a Germanic population at the centre, the survival of Carolingian institutions, relations with external powers including England, and above all an exceptional economic development; in Burgundy a close relation between the ducal and the royal families; Brittany had her position on the sea routes, her relations with England and her Celtic nucleus; Aquitaine, a relationship first with the Angevin empire and later with England, and all the ramifications of the wine trade. Politics and personalities also played their part. The very fact that the history of each of the principalities has hitherto been studied separately is in itself significant, for they had many of the characteristics of states in miniature.

In the fourteenth century the monarchy was challenged as it had not been challenged since the turn of the eleventh and twelfth centuries. Organized resistance to royal centralization among the seigneurs of the second rank showed itself in the leagues of 1314 and 1315; the professionalization of council, judiciary and finance was appearing in the princely governments as in the royal government; the economic development of the twelfth and thirteenth centuries had begun to produce taxable wealth for princes as well as for the king; and the princes were coming to look upon their lands not as so many units of property but as political entities with interests which might not coincide with those of the kingdom as seen by the king. In many of them a critical point in their development was reached in the fourteenth century: Flanders in the 'war of independence' and the 'neutrality' of Louis of Male; Brittany in the 'war of succession'; Burgundy in the minority and premature death of Philip of Rouvres and the reconstruction of the ducal government by royal officers; Aquitaine (in relation to the Valois kings of France) in Edward III's assumption of the title 'king of France' in 1340; Béarn when Gaston Fébus refused homage in 1364. Edward III's attempts to make capital out of the resistance to royal centralization, and, in Flanders, Normandy, Brittany and elsewhere to identify his cause with local interests,[1] all suggest that the first phase of the Hundred Years War, while fundamentally a war of succession, also showed some of the characteristics of a French civil war in which the princes, led by the duke of Aquitaine who was also the king of England, fought against the efforts of the king of France to make the unity of his kingdom a reality. And they were so far successful that the issue between king and princes was in doubt for a century or so.

Note

The relationship of the King and the Princes in later Medieval France has given rise to a very large literature in recent years. Among important contributions since the appearance of this article there may be noted the valuable survey by A. Leguai, 'Les 'Etats' princiers en France à la fin du moyen âge', *Annali della Fondazione Italiana per la Storia amministrativa*, iv (1967), 133-57, together with his work on the Bourbonnais, largely summarised in *De la seigneurie à l'état. Le Bourbonnais pendant la Guerre de Cent Ans*, Moulins 1969; P. S. Lewis, *Later Medieval France: the Polity*, London 1968; Michael Jones, *Ducal Brittany 1364-1399*, Oxford 1970, and 'Mon Pais et ma nation: Breton Identity in the Fourteenth Century', in *War, Literature and Politics in the Late Middle Ages*, ed. C. T. Allmand, Liverpool 1976, pp. 144-168, and various contributions to *Les Principautés au Moyen Age (Actes des congrès de la société des historiens médiévistes de l'enseignement supérieur public, Bordeaux 1973)*, Bordeaux 1979.

---

[1] Cf. Le Patourel, 'Edward III and the Kingdom of France', *History*, xliii (1958), 173–89. See above XII.

XVI

THE MEDIEVAL BOROUGH OF LEEDS

THE FIRST STEP towards making Leeds a town, and ultimately
a great industrial city, was taken just about 750 years ago;
but Leeds as a human settlement is far older than that. Its
name, which was certainly pronounced as a two-syllable word
throughout the Middle Ages and perhaps later — *Leedis* — is
accepted as identical with the Celtic word *Loidis* which appears
as the name of a British region in the Pennines at the time of
the Anglo-Saxon settlement of Northumbria. It is a reasonable
assumption that this region was a political entity of some sort
before the coming of our English ancestors; and by some process, which it is not impossible to imagine, the regional name
Loidis has been perpetuated, in its uncompounded form, as
the name of one place, perhaps the chief place, within it; and,
however this may have come about, that place must surely
have been in existence while the region still retained some
significance. On this argument Leeds, as a place, is at least
1,500 years old; but of the character of this original British
Leeds we know nothing.

We know little more about its Anglo-Saxon, Anglo-Danish
or Anglo-Norse successors, though continuity of habitation is,
again, a very reasonable assumption. The chief evidence for
this lies in the carved stones now preserved in the parish
church and the museum. From these it can be argued that
there was an important church in Leeds at least from the end
of the eighth century, possibly a monastery, more probably
perhaps a minster, in the contemporary sense of that term —
that is, a church which in origin at least was a missionary
centre served by a group of priests. Evidence of a church,
even an important church, does not quite amount to evidence
of a civil settlement; but priests or monks have to be fed and
clothed and housed, and at least we can postulate a small
settlement of farmers and craftsmen.

Some time before the Norman Conquest, as Domesday Book
shows, Leeds had become a fair-sized village, if indeed it had

not always been so. In the time of King Edward seven thanes held the place 'for seven manors'; in 1086 there were 27 villeins, 4 sokemen and 4 bordars, that is, at the least, 35 families together with a priest. Leeds can have suffered little from King William's savage harrying of Yorkshire, for it had been worth £6 before the Conquest, while at the time of the survey its value has risen to £7. But there is nothing in all this to differentiate Leeds from her rural neighbours. There was a church and a mill; the manor was an important one held by an important Norman baron; but there is no suggestion as yet of urban development. Domesday Leeds was simply a large village, its inhabitants occupied in rural pursuits.

The beginnings of Leeds as a town, and it is fairly certain that this really was the beginning, is marked by the creation of a small borough within the manor by Maurice Paynel (or 'de Gant'), then lord of the manor. The document which records this act is the well-known charter, given in his name, which is printed in Whitaker's *Loidis and Elmete*. Besides this printed text, of unknown origin, there are two others still in manuscript; one, apparently of the seventeenth century in the Spencer-Stanhope Collection at the Cartwright Memorial Hall in Bradford, the other, slightly later, among the Stevens MSS. in the Leeds Reference Library. All three are bad copies, to the point of unintelligibility in many passages; and partly for this reason, no doubt, partly because no original or near-contemporary copy is known to exist, and partly also, perhaps principally, because the subsequent history of the borough which it created has been so little known, this charter has been looked upon somewhat doubtfully by historians. There is really no cause for such doubt. The relationship of the existing copies one to another and to the lost original from which all, directly or indirectly, must be derived, can only be described in outline; but since the Leeds charter is clearly founded upon, indeed copied from, Roger de Lacy's charter to Pontefract, in a manner that is perfectly normal in the twelfth and thirteenth centuries, there is no reason why the original text should not be re-established with some precision. There is, moreover, nothing suspicious about the charter; it belongs to a recognised category of borough charters (Manchester's medieval charter belongs to this same category); and its provisions are so completely in accord with what we can now know of the borough in the fourteenth and fifteenth centuries, that we could have inferred much of its content from the later extents and reeves' accounts of the manor even if no other trace of the charter itself had survived. In short, the evidence that can be brought in favour of the authenticity of this first municipal charter of Leeds is far stronger than anything that can be said against it; and the same is true of the date it bears — 1207.

It is a modest little charter, not worth anyone's forging. It gave the burgesses no political rights, no self-government, no mayor, no aldermen; it did not licence any gild-merchant nor any trade gilds; it did not give any widespread exemption from tolls or other such hindrances to commerce; it did not allow for the election by the burgesses even of their humble reeve, nor treat them as in any sense a community or association; it did not create a market in Leeds and its reference to a fair is of doubtful significance. Clearly Maurice Paynel's borough can have had little in common with boroughs like Bristol, Nottingham or Newcastle.

Let us see what, in general terms, the charter did give. It provided that the burgesses should be free; that they should hold their tenements freely, at a rent of 16d. a year for each full tenement or burgage; that these burgages might be bought and sold, as units or subdivided; and that the holder should be free to build what he pleased upon his burgage. It created a borough court, in which the procedure should be somewhat freer, more suited to a trading or industrial population, than that of the ordinary manorial court; and it provided that the burgesses need answer a charge in no other court save in pleas of the Crown. It gave the burgesses freedom from toll but only within the manor, for Maurice Paynel had no power to grant a more extensive exemption. Finally it reserved the lord's right to force his burgesses like other humble tenants on the manor, to bake their bread in his bakehouse, and to pay him a proportionate sum whenever the king imposed an aid upon his boroughs. All this may be summed up as personal freedom, free tenure and a borough court with a somewhat freer procedure. These are simply the lowest conditions precedent for urban development; and such modest privileges imply that there was little, more probably no such development in Leeds already. That is why it can be said that the charter marks the very beginning of Leeds as a town.

Indeed, the whole thing was something of a speculation on

the part of the lord of the manor. This was the great period of town development in Western Europe. In countries and regions where trade had begun to flow early, after the great stagnation of the Dark Ages, in North Italy, in North-Eastern France and the Low Countries, towns had grown quickly and had often had to fight for their freedom against their lords; where this movement had come more gradually, as in England, the towns, if not consistently encouraged, were at least tolerated and fitted into the political and social structure. But once it had been shown that towns might be profitable, for they could be taxed, military service could be demanded of their citizens, tolls levied on their trade and rents collected from shops and stalls in their markets, then enterprising lords, lords who could afford if necessary to take a chance, might try to establish towns from nothing or almost nothing, on their estates. It meant giving up revenue derived from the land as agricultural land in the hope of securing much greater revenue, and some prestige, from trade in the future. Some schemes were more ambitious than others; some had an eye to military as well as financial advantages; some succeeded and some did not. Maurice Paynel was doing in Leeds what hundreds of his contemporaries were doing up and down Europe; but his was one of the modest schemes partly because he was not, after all, one of the greatest lords of the land, and partly because he could not foresee the conditions of five hundred years later. There can have been very little but faith to encourage the founding of a town in Leeds in the reign of King John.

From the terms of the charter, from some of the later evidence and from legitimate analogy, Mr Woledge has been able to locate Maurice Paynel's little borough and describe its physical shape. It was not, as it used to be thought, co-extensive with the manor, but consisted of a group of tenements, and a relatively small group, within it. Maurice, it seems, first set out the line of a street, a wide street that might hold a market, the street we call Briggate. Along this street and on both sides of it, he marked out a number of building plots, of standard size, and offered these, on the terms set out in the charter, to his tenants and, presumably, to anyone who would come. With each plot went half an acre in Burmantofts. Acceptance of one of these tenements made a man a burgess, with all the liberties laid down in the charter. Such tenements were, it goes without saying, intended to attract those who were engaged or who proposed to engage in trade or some industrial activity; for, although there was nothing to prevent a burgess from acquiring other land on the manor, such tenements were far too small by themselves to provide a living for a family. The embryonic borough of Leeds, on the ground, was no more than the aggregate of these tenements, physically distinguished, if at all, from the rest of the manor only by their garden fences. In this it resembled many such foundations.

It was a modest charter and it was the first step. It did not create a town in Leeds, still less recognise the existence of one that had already developed spontaneously; it simply provided an opportunity. Men cannot engage in trade or industry if they are subject to the unfreedom of the ordinary manorial tenant: if they are personally bound to the manor: if they must work some days in each week on the lord's demesne: if they cannot buy or sell or divide the land on which their shops and workshops are built: if their trading disputes can only be submitted to the archaic procedure of the manorial court. Maurice Paynel gave his burgesses the primary, the essential liberties; but he could not create trade; and it was only the growth of trade and industry in Leeds that would determine whether his little borough would grow into a town.

Very little evidence has been discovered so far to show how the borough fared during the first century of its existence, save that some time between 1207 and 1258 the Monday market was established. Indeed it is not until the early years of Edward III's reign that we can take stock of the growth of Leeds as a town. For this period we have the keepers' accounts for the last five years of Edward II's reign, when the manor was in the king's hands following the forfeiture of Earl Thomas of Lancaster, the almost illegible extent of 1327, and the important extent of 1341 of which a half, but quite unaccountably only a half, has been printed in translation in vol. XXXIII of the Society's publications. At this time the lord's revenue from the whole of his manor of Leeds amounted to about £90 a year in the currency of the period; and in 1341 those items which can be classified broadly as industrial and commercial were leased for £41 a year, that is just under half the total. The most profitable of these items was Leeds mill, the double water-mill on the river, which was leased for £12 a year in the middle of the thirteenth century, and now in 1341 for £24 a year. Not strictly an urban institution, for any agricultural centre needed a corn mill; but Leeds mill always seems to have been something out of the ordinary and may well have contributed to the industrial beginnings of the town. Then there were the burgage rents, reckoned at £4. 5s. 10d. a year, and the profits of the seignorial bake-house, £1. 6s. 8d. There was the toll which the lord levied at the fairs held in Leeds on the feasts of St Peter and St Paul and of St Simon and St Jude (29 June and 28 October respectively), the toll he levied on goods brought by non-burgesses to the Monday market, and the rents he drew from the stalls erected there. All these, together with the profits of the borough court, were valued at £9. 6s. 8d. In addition to this, the accounts of the last years of Edward II's reign mention one fuller's mill in Leeds, a forge and a coal-mine at Carlton Cross.

In considering these figures, it should be borne in mind that they are only assessments made as a guide to the manorial officials when they were leasing these various items; what profit the lessee might be able to make in any particular year, over and above the sum he had to pay in, we have no means of knowing. They are only of significance relative to one another. Nevertheless, assuming that the value of money was constant over the interval, the revenue of the manor had more than doubled between 1258 and 1341; and though the evidence does not permit us to attribute the advance wholly to the growth of the town, this must have had something to do with it. And already the pattern of this growth is beginning to appear. In this first century there is no sign of any phenomenal development of trade in Leeds; one might even suggest that the terms of Maurice Paynel's charter showed that he hardly expected any such development, for trade demands far more advanced liberties. Clearly the Leeds fairs and the Leeds market were of local importance only. The one fuller's mill, the forge and the coal-mine were more significant. Leeds would be built on cloth, on iron and on coal.

For the remainder of the fourteenth century, four reeves' accounts of the manor are known, those for the years 1356-7, 1373-4, 1383-4 and 1399-1400. Originally the series must have been complete year by year, and there was at least one other extent made during the course of the century; but so far as is known these four accounts are the sole survivors of what must once have been a splendid series of records. Fortunately they are well spaced, and in themselves full and complete. From them, with subsidy rolls and other stray documents, it should be possible to get to know something at least of the more important and interesting inhabitants of fourteenth-century Leeds, such as Adam Gibbarne the reeve, the successive generations of the Passelew family, Ralph Poteman, a vicar of Leeds to whom we can now give a date, or John, the master of the schools, whose appearance in these records takes the history of education in Leeds back to 1343. From them, also, it should be possible eventually to describe the topography of medieval Leeds and generally, if the expression may be permitted, to provide the city with a 'medieval history'. So far as the growth of the town, as a town, is concerned, one's first impression on reading these accounts is of extraordinary stability, almost of stagnation. Seignorial revenue remained remarkably constant with, if anything, a tendency to decline at the end of the century. A closer examination suggests that urban or at least industrial progress is not necessarily proportional to the total revenue of the manor.

The evidence provided by these accounts for industrial development during the later part of the fourteenth century is fragmentary but suggestive. There was one fulling mill in 1322, and it was worth 10s. a year. In 1357 it was worth 24s., and there was a second fulling mill, a new one, worth 13s. 4d. a year; in 1374 the two mills were leased for 30s. and 17s. a year respectively, and in 1384 for 30s. and 26s. 8d. In 1357, for the first time so far as these accounts go, two empty plots were being leased for tenters, and their rents are thereafter a constant item. Cloth manufacture may have been developing very slowly in Leeds but it was developing. Our first real glimpse of Leeds market comes in 1374 when 4s. was collected from the rent of 12 shops there and Robert Passelew was renting an empty plot on which to re-erect his stall. Another hint is perhaps contained in the fact that Agnes Baxter was paying 2s. a year for licence to bake bread in her own house. Was the seignorial bakehouse no longer able to cope with the demand? The coal-mines, on the other hand, do not seem to have maintained the revenue they produced in 1321; but at least there were three of them in 1384 in place of the one in Edward II's reign.

It must be said, however, that these scraps of evidence, welcome as they may be, are scraps and no more. They do not tell the whole story, and they do not even tell the story that might be told. Perhaps one cannot expect that each small social or economic development will be reflected immediately and directly in an account of manorial revenues. And indeed we have proof that this is not so. When an inquiry was made, in 1399, into the activities of those who, throughout the county of York, were producing cloth contrary to the monopoly given by King Henry II to the weavers of York city, two were reported in Leeds, John Morley and Robert Webster, each of whom was said to have produced four cloths a year for the past 22 years contrary to the said monopoly. It is not that there is anything remarkable about this; more than two such weavers were found in many neighbouring villages; and quite possibly there were others who were not reported; the point is that this is evidence of industrial activity of which the manorial accounts tell us nothing. There may well be much else besides; but while we may hope that additional evidence may come to light, it is unlikely that we shall ever be able to measure, quantitatively, the industrial growth of Leeds during the Middle Ages.

The impression remains, however, and will remain unless something wholly unexpected turns up to modify it, that the development of Leeds as a town, to the end of the fourteenth century, was steady but slow. Yet even that is very different from saying, as Professor Hamilton Thompson said in 1926, that 'the medieval borough, thus created in 1207, has no further history'. He was led to make this statement, we may suppose, partly because he did not know of the fourteenth-century reeves' accounts, but partly also because he seems to have misunderstood the nature of Maurice Paynel's borough. In his essay on 'The Charters of Leeds' he writes as though the charter of 1207 was intended to transform the whole manor into a borough, and to create thereby something on the lines of Nottingham or Leicester. But Mr Woledge has shown, and evidence found since he wrote his essay has confirmed his conclusion, that the borough was a small foundation within the manor; and, as we have seen, the ambitions of its founder were very modest. It is perfectly true, as Hamilton Thompson observed, that in later manorial documents manorial affairs are more prominent than borough affairs; but that is not because the borough had lost its status and sunk back into the manorial organization, but because the manor always was much larger, both in area and value, than the borough. The borough, as such, was never anything but one element in the manor. It is likely also that he was technically correct in maintaining that there was a breach of continuity, of institutional continuity, between the borough created in 1207 and the borough created in 1626; but that was because the town had so completely outgrown the medieval borough that there was no point in resurrecting Maurice Paynel's charter in the reign of King Charles I. Leeds grew up, in the later Middle Ages, as an industrial rather than a commercial centre, and its industries did not need the spectacular liberties claimed by merchants and artisans in the great chartered boroughs. The thirteenth-century borough, since the liberties on which it was founded were largely personal and tenurial, gradually, over the centuries, ceased to differentiate itself from the manor, as the personal and tenurial condition of the manorial tenants at large was levelled up to that of the burgesses. This process, in the present state of our knowledge, is only a hypothesis, and the demonstration of it will not be possible until the long, continuous run of reeves' accounts belonging to the fifteenth and sixteenth centuries has been studied. But the evidence that we have been considering of the growth of industry and local trade during the fourteenth century does show the real significance of Maurice Paynel's charter in the history of Leeds. It was the first step: it provided the opportunity which a small island of freedom in a sea of manorialism might afford at a time when even such modest liberties as it gave could make a great deal of difference; and, if progress was slow, it was at least such that when the great drift of industry from the older urban centres into the countryside began in the fifteenth century, Leeds was ready to take its share in the inheritance of York, and much besides; and from that moment the future greatness of the town was assured.

BIBLIOGRAPHICAL NOTE

3. THE MEDIEVAL BOROUGH. The documents upon which the foregoing paper is based will be found in Le Patourel, *Documents relating to the Manor and Borough of Leeds, 1066-1400* (*Publications of the Thoresby Society*, XLV, 1957). Hamilton Thompson's essay on 'The Charters of Leeds', is contained in the *Handbook of the Old Leeds Exhibition* (1926), pp. 28 ff., and Mr Woledge's valuable paper, 'The Medieval Borough of Leeds', in *Publications of the Thoresby Society*, XXXVII (1945), pp. 288-309. I owe the reference to the enquiry of 1399 to the kindness of Professor Carus-Wilson.

XVII

IS NORTHERN HISTORY A SUBJECT?

MY TITLE IS SHORT and snappy but not very precise. So let me begin by trying to indicate what I have in mind. History is an infinity; hardly a subject, rather a particular way of finding out about ourselves and the world we live in. From time to time, therefore, we do have to consider, not what history is as a subject, but what are historical subjects, what are the units of our investigations. I take it that by 'Northern History' we mean 'the History of the North of England', and the question I am asking is this: does the 'History of the North of England' constitute a rational unit of historical study, is it a subject in that sense? Like those who launched the journal sponsored by the School of History here at Leeds, I fell for the eye-catching title; and as they had to explain what they meant in a sub-title, *A Review of the History of the North of England*, I have to begin in a similar way. The organizers of this colloquium, as you would expect, got it right first time.

When your invitation came, I had this sort of question very much in mind; for I was then trying to put into shape some earlier notions about the relationship between the history of my native Channel Islands and more general historical ideas, and this involved identifying what it is that should form the substance of their history, how that stands in relation to their environment, what that environment is and has been at different times and what are the general historical concepts to which they and their environment have to be related. This brought me up against just this problem of what is a historical subject, or rather, what is a historical subject when territory and people in varying degrees of association are involved, for obviously there are many other things that can be the subject of an historical enquiry. No doubt the Channel Islands are a very different kettle of fish from the North of England, though in the same category as a matter of territory and people; but they have been my starting-point in this as in many other ventures, and I mention them now only because I want to make it clear that I am looking at the history of the North of England from the outside. Thirty years of residence and working have made me feel quite at home here; but I have never done more than dabble in one or two very localized bits of northern history, and then chiefly because

*What follows formed the opening lecture in the Colloquium on the History of the North of England held in Leeds in September 1975. It is here printed as it was delivered. Although I have added a couple of sentences and altered a word here and there, I have not modified the colloquial style in any way. The views expressed are personal.

I can never keep my fingers out of the history of the place in which I happen to be living or working. I am very conscious of the fact that I am addressing people who know a great deal more about the subject than I do, that I may ask questions to which you all know the answers and make points that seem obvious and trite. I can only hope that there is something in the idea that you can see more of the shape of a thing from the outside than from the inside. I had to be away from the place for a good deal more than thirty years before I could see the sort of shape in Channel Island history that I have recently been trying to describe.

It is usual in this country to think of social and political groupings that are based on territories in terms of local history and national history. Local history seems generally to be thought of as concerned with units that are quite small, the village, the parish, the town, at most the county; national history as the history of the sovereign political unit. National is regarded as superior to local history; it often supplies the point and the framework for a synthesis of other kinds of history. To some extent this has always been so; but for the last hundred years or thereabouts, it has seemed almost unavoidable. This is partly because history emerged as an academic subject in the late nineteenth century as an offshoot of classical studies, and it had to justify itself as a proper vehicle for the education of those who were going to occupy positions of responsibility in church and state, or at least to be intelligent members of a community which thought of itself as a democracy. Hence the long dominance of political and constitutional history in university syllabuses; and as this was happening at a time when the nation-state was claiming the exclusive allegiance and if necessary the lives of all its citizens, as the highest form of political organization to which human beings could aspire, national history naturally became the prime unit, the standard. Local history, indeed other kinds of history (the history of art, science, economic and social organization, and so on) were contributory, ancillary, incomplete in themselves. The history of the parish was thought to bear somewhat the same relation to the history of the nation as the parish itself bore to the state.

But this dichotomy and hierarchy is breaking down. We are no longer so sure that the nation-state is the ideal, the ultimate form of political organization, or even that it is likely to endure; yet, since we generally face the future looking backwards, we shall seek the foundations of future forms of organization in the past. There have, indeed, long been studies of ideas and phenomena outside the national framework, such as feudalism, the Renaissance or renaissances, political and industrial revolutions, ecclesiastical and commercial organization; and although these have not always been so far removed from national history as they pretend to be (we speak of 'French' feudalism, the 'Italian' renaissance), such studies will no doubt attract increasing attention at the expense of the old-fashioned national histories. And there has always been the problem of what I may perhaps call the historical identity of the nation-state. Not only is the concept itself a relatively recent development, but the territorial and other elements of which present countries are composed have mostly been differently assorted in the past. The extent and the composition even of those states which show some sort of continuity have usually changed at some point in the past. This problem of identity seems most obvious when you consider, for example, the medieval history of Belgium or Holland; it is implicit in all the problems of continuity as between Gaul and Francia and France, or Roman Britain and Anglo-Saxon and post-Conquest England. We often conceal this fundamental problem from ourselves by talking of 'English History', 'French History', or 'German History', terms that can mean almost anything we want them to mean.

At first sight this question of historical identity, at least, is not so acute in local history. You can define a village, a parish or a county, and you may find that your definition holds through several centuries; but you cannot put a fence about its history. The essential characteristic of local history, as generally understood, is that it is the history of something which is part of something larger. The history of Weymouth, say, can only be understood in the context of the history of Dorset, of central southern England, of England itself and so on; but it will also have to be considered in relation to other places in the same or a similar category — English towns, the towns of Western Europe, with the sub-classes of English watering-places and south-coast ports. Why is Weymouth different from Scarborough? Why did it not develop like Southampton or Portsmouth or Plymouth? Moreover the larger unit or category or environment may itself change. The example I cherish is that of Stony Stratford in Buckinghamshire. The place gained its early prosperity from its position on the Roman and medieval Watling Street, as shown still by its two ancient and famous inns, the Cock and the Bull; it was by-passed first by the canal and then by the railway, brought back to the highway by the internal combustion engine until the number of cars and lorries on the A.5 multiplied beyond a certain point, and it had to be by-passed again by the M.1. The history of such a place can only be understood in relation to developments that were quite external to it. Or, finally, my Channel Islands, which started me off on this tack. They are islands, and as such are as easily and permanently definable as any places can be, and they still have and have long had a measure of autonomy which marks them off as distinct communities. Yet, at different times, they have formed part of the territory of a Gaulish tribe, a Roman Empire, a Breton kingdom, a Norman duchy, a Norman empire, an Angevin empire, a kingdom of France, the dominions of a king of England within the kingdom of France and so on. Changes in these larger structures and developments broader still are as much a part of their history as anything that happened in the Islands themselves; and an important part of their history is precisely the form which those changes took in the Islands and the insular reaction to them.

But when you begin thinking along these lines it soon becomes evident that there is really no significant distinction, in historiographical terms, between local history and national history. We are at one of those moments in our history when we are uncomfortably aware that what is going on beyond our shores may affect our future as much as anything we can do for ourselves. But it was always so. No community however local, no nation however defined, however situated geographically, has ever been able to isolate itself from things going on beyond its bounds — whether it is the movement of the herring shoals (if the early modernists still tell that story), the discovery of new sources of power and new technologies, the formation of dictatorships, or movements and fortunes of peoples at the far end of the world. National history enjoys no sovereignty; it is as much involved with wider concerns as local history; and there is certainly no hierarchy. Local history poses problems as intellectually demanding, potentially as important a part of our effort to understand ourselves and the world we live in, as national or international history. Your unit of historical investigation, therefore, cannot simply be a territory and all the people who have ever lived on it; or a people, however they may have moved around; or the simple projection of a present unit into the past, like 'English History'. The unit can only be the problem, or more usually, given human capability, a problem within a problem. Why is England the sort of political, social and economic entity it is, or may be tomorrow? What sort of an entity is it? Why does it differ from France or Ireland? How does it differ from these other countries? Why do places like Leeds, Otley and York differ so much from each other, though so near and sharing so much of their geographical environment? How do they differ? What sort of places are they? A moment's reflection will show that definition is not simply the beginning but the ultimate objective of historical investigation and that historical enquiry is indeed an essential part of identification and description. We are studying ourselves and the world we live in; and the enquiry, however local in origin, will extend further and further out like ripples on a pond, to be halted only by practical and human limitations. The unit of historical enquiry, the 'subject', can only be the problem and the extent to which it is feasible to investigate it. That is one reason why all history is relative, relative to historians, to their individual points of view (in the literal sense) and to the point in time at which they open and conclude their investigations. There are no eternal answers.

*　　*　　*

It is with these ideas in mind, with the notion that a historical subject can only be a historical problem, or rather the use of historical evidence and historical technique in the investigation of a problem, that I would approach my question 'Is Northern History a Subject?' — and you can see why I wish that I had not used the term 'Northern History' in my title. Does 'the North of England', since the phrase is certainly in current use, express a concept which corresponds to some reality beyond mere geographical location? And can we be helped to answer that question and then to define and so to understand that reality, if it exists, by studying what it may have been and showing how much of the past survives and conditions the present, unrecognized perhaps until brought out into the open by the historian?

At first sight the possibilities of this being a problem with any meaning do not seem at all promising. Certainly, the North of England does not seem to fall into the traditional categories of history — it could hardly be called local, it is certainly not national, and in this country we do not seem to have anything in between. In France, for instance, they can have provincial histories, histories of Normandy, of Brittany, Burgundy and so on, for they have an idea of provinces that has survived the Revolution, the passionate centralization of the French state and even the institution of the departments which were clearly intended to break up the older provinces. These French provinces may now be more a matter of sentiment than hard governmental fact, but sentiment can be very powerful. We have no provinces like that in England. Here the unit has been the county or shire, quite as ancient and even more persistent than the French province and with quite as large a part in the formation and character of the country as a whole, though quite different. The French provinces mostly began as more or less autonomous principalities, which came into existence independently of higher authority; and even when integrated into the kingdom preserved individualities in law, administration, way of life and so on; whereas the English county began as a unit of people, not so much a territory, certainly not independent; and if it may have begun with its own ideas of law and how to do things these were soon made obsolete or standardized. It was created by royal authority and given duties, with a mind of its own which would ultimately be expressed in Parliament.

There was nothing like that in France or in any of the European countries that produced representative institutions before the nineteenth century. We speak still of Normans, Bretons and Gascons (not even the French, with their fondness for such things, have been able to find a collective name for the inhabitants of Deux-Sèvres, Loir-et-Cher or Basses Alpes) and there is a roadside notice which we have often passed on our way back to the ferry: 'Ici commence la Normandie'. Who would introduce himself in London as a 'North-of-Englander'? A Yorkshireman, perhaps a lassie from Lancashire or a Geordie. But if the county is the natural and historical unit in England rather than the province, we are in a difficulty at once; for the North of England consists of a number of counties. I was never quite sure whether the number of counties to be included in 'The North' should be four or six (or even eight if you took the Trent as the line on which to put up your notices announcing 'The North of England'); and what the number is since April Fools Day 1974 is a matter that I should prefer to leave undecided at this point.

It is true that the term 'provinces' is not unknown in this country; but we speak of 'the provinces' as opposed to London, not of specific provinces; and Donald Read who makes this point in his book on *The English Provinces* also shows that the term came to supersede 'the country', or at least to be used alongside it, in the course of the Industrial Revolution. In so far as it was used of political movements and opinion outside London it referred to what was being said and done in the rising industrial cities rather than in broad provinces, so that, in his analysis, one could speak of the politics of Manchester or Leeds or Sheffield, but hardly of opinion in the North of England as a whole. Likewise, when Fawcett produced a geographer's study of the possibilities of political devolution in his book *Provinces of England* (not, you will notice, *The* Provinces of England) he divided the North into several provinces, and even changed his mind on what the number should be and where their boundaries should be drawn. And for no modern administrative purpose that I can think of does the North serve as a single unit. Town and Country, east and west of the Pennines, the Lakes, the Dales and the conurbations, traditional Yorkshire, Lancashire and Tyneside, seem perpetually to divide it.

And yet there can be no doubt that to most English people 'The North of England' does mean something — something, perhaps, rather more distinctive than 'The Midlands', the 'South-East' or the 'South-West'. The people of the North are generally supposed to have certain characteristics; and although there are many dialects in the North, in the popular idea of what a dialect is, it is not usually thought to be a nonsense to talk of 'northern speech', or, for that matter, of northern habits of mind and northern attitudes. The North is credited with certain qualities in modern literature; even the trade provides an assortment of wares that can be distinguished from those it provides for other parts of the country. But if present-day political and administrative arrangements give little substance to such an idea of the North, what is it based on? Is it pure sentiment or even illusion? Or is it something derived from earlier conditions which, rather like geological formations, give the country its character and its contours, though largely unseen, and which can only be discovered and identified by enquiry, by historical enquiry? And if it seems to be so derived, what is the nature of these earlier conditions, and in what form have they survived? Would they be strong enough still, at one extreme, to support the idea of a province or state 'twixt Humber and Tweed, Ribble and Solway, in some future United States of Great Britain; or are they merely vestigial, such that we can only watch them grow weaker and fainter before the standardizing forces of modern communications and media and the trend towards larger and larger units in everything?

That might be one way of stating the problem. As for a solution, the substance we can give to the idea of the North of England by studying its history, I can only offer one or two ideas and principles — partly because this is a lecture and not a treatise, partly because I am an outsider, and partly also because historical truth, even the statement of an historical problem, is rather like the horizon, something we can see, something we must move towards, but something that retreats as we approach — we make progress but we never get there.

One such principle would be that if we are to look for the substance of our notion of the North of England in its past we must not be too rigid in setting our territorial limits. There are two considerations involved here. One is that, in common with traditional local or national history, many of the events or developments that we should have to consider as possibly contributing to the individuality of the North have taken place beyond it on any definition, perhaps far away. More immediately, however, the territorial limits of its own internal characteristics have not always been the same by any means. I do not know, for example, precisely what was the territory occupied or controlled by the Brigantes. It did not apparently include the eastern part of historic Yorkshire, though in their territory for the first time, so far as we can see, there came into existence a unit which corresponded in general terms to the North of England of later times. Similarly, the Anglian kingdom of Northumbria might at one time include little more than the coast-lands from the Humber to the Lammermuirs, and at another most of England north of the Humber-Mersey line together with a good deal of modern Scotland south of the Forth, and perhaps a little beyond it; the Danish and Norse kingdoms which succeeded to it were different and the earldom which to a large degree perpetuated these successive kingdoms until after the Norman Conquest was different again. Yet each in its turn was an autonomous political and cultural unit corresponding generally to our *prima facie* notion of the North of England, though varying considerably in territorial extent.

Another principle might be that the North long had the character of a frontier region, and that from a very early date. Whatever they did elsewhere in the country that was to become England, the Romans never really Romanized the North. They treated it as a defensive zone, as the hinterland of a frontier; and this character persisted, whether the enemy without was Picts and Scots, or Scots in a later sense of the word, and it is worth retaining as a possible element in the individuality of the North. Professor Hay sees a considerable territory on either side of the Tweed–Solway line, throughout the Middle Ages and well into early modern times, as forming a homogeneous frontier region, with its own way of life — and of death — very like the frontier regions that were formed on either side of the Pyrenees and elsewhere. The North of England generally was the hinterland of this region on the English side and could be regarded as an extension of it, sharing many of its characteristics. In the fourteenth century the Scots were to be feared as far south as Leeds. In fact many of the conditions of the frontier, considered as a region rather than a line, were to be found throughout the North, which was a good deal further from the centres of English political and military power than it was from the Scottish border, and it often had to look after itself.

Whether there was or could be any continuity in people, customs or ideas between pre-Roman and Roman Brigantia on the one hand and the Anglian kingdom of Northumbria on the other, is a large question that I can hardly discuss now; though the fashion today is to say that the great conquests and colonizations — Anglo-Saxons, Franks, Danes, Normans and so on — did not destroy everything in their path but preserved and adapted a very great deal in the countries they dominated. We still have the city of York, whether it is a survival or a revival, and no doubt Professor G. R. J. Jones would say that we have a very great deal more. But conditions were different in the North, as elsewhere in Britain, when the Roman political organization was replaced by a multiplicity of German and Celtic tribes. For our purposes it is interesting that one of the earlier steps that were taken in the process of amalgamating these tribal units into substantial kingdoms was in fact taken in the North, and that the formation of the Anglian kingdom of Northumbria was accompanied by a cultural flowering that included some elements at least that were non-Germanic and possibly native, and some from Gaul and beyond. In the seventh and eighth centuries the 'North of England', alias this kingdom of Northumbria, not only formed an autonomous political and cultural unit but one which for a time was dominant in Britain.

This northern kingdom was overlaid, in the ninth and tenth centuries, by a Scandinavian immigration, from the west and north as well as from the east, the intensity of which is a matter which I shall leave to Professor Sawyer, but which resulted in new Scandinavian kingdoms in the North. These also achieved a political and cultural autonomy which, if it was precarious, was real enough while it lasted and was certainly built upon earlier foundations. Even when the last Norse king was disposed of and his kingdom drawn into the West Saxon empire out of which the kingdom of England was being fashioned, the North could long hold the rest of the country at arms length. The later West Saxon and Danish kings of England liked to have an earl of Northumbria and an archbishop of York who at least had some ties with the South; but they themselves rarely if ever came north on a peaceful errand, and not very often on a warlike one, and they left the country pretty much to itself. The great ecclesiastical reform of the tenth century, which had so much to do with the growth of kingly power and authority in England, did not touch the North at all. The position on the eve of the Norman Conquest was very well shown when the Northumbrian magnates forced out Earl Tostig and, though they acknowledged that only King Edward could formally appoint Morcar whom they had chosen in his place, they could insist that he appointed Morcar and no one else. The North of England, therefore, has known its times of independence, just like Normandy or Brittany, and this is something which has to be taken into account.

All that, of course, was a long time ago, and a great deal of water has flowed under Ouse Bridge, and London Bridge for that matter, since then. But what had happened between, say, A.D. 400 and 1066, had introduced elements which, though certainly not unique individually in England, were nevertheless combined into a specific blend in the North — Scandinavian, Anglian, Celtic and whatever underlies them all. Geographically the North has natural connexions with the lands across the North Sea, with Scotland and with Ireland, as the South has its more immediate connexions with Flanders and with France; and the peoples that came to the North during these centuries established these connexions on a human, almost a political level. For the Danes, presumably, came directly over the North Sea to settle among the Angles east of the Pennines; the Norse came immediately from the Western Isles and Ireland, already involved with the peoples of those lands and settling on the western seaboard and in the Pennine valleys leading to it where the Anglian element in the population must have been very much more dilute. This intensified the dividing function of the Pennines — not that they are a very great barrier in themselves though they do constitute a vast area which has never supported more than a sparse population, and they divide the westward-looking west from the eastward-looking east. For the country west of the Pennines belongs to what the archaeologists call the 'Irish Sea Province', a region in which communications have been very much easier by sea than by land and in which the sea has served to bind together the lands around its shores. To some extent the North Sea has functioned in the same way, as have the English Channel and the Mediterranean in other contexts. Thus it was easy for the immigrants to the North of England of the ninth and tenth centuries to maintain contact with their original homelands, as we know they did, the Hiberno-Norse with Ireland, the Danes with the Continent. If any notion of a North of England could survive this situation it could only be as the result of centuries of political union and independence. Hence the importance for our purpose of the Anglian kingdom of Northumbria and the Scandinavian kingdoms of York — but perhaps Dr Steele will be telling us, in effect, that the 'Irish Sea Province' is still a reality.

However, unity in diversity seems to be all that we can achieve, if we can achieve that, and few modern nations can show more. Some of the unity and autonomy which had been achieved in the North before the Norman Conquest did in fact survive that catastrophe, certainly the individuality; though the Conquest marks the point at which the integration of the North into the kingdom of England really began. In this connection it is interesting to speculate on what might have happened if the Battle of Hastings had gone the other way, and Harold Godwinson and his successors had been able to hold Normans and Scandinavians at bay; for what Harold had done earlier in the year 1066 was very like what Hugh Capet did in the kingdom of West Francia in 987. Hugh Capet's accession represented the capture of the monarchy by the ruler of one of the principalities into which the kingdom had disintegrated; and his fellow princes used the opportunity it gave to intensify their independence. Harold Godwinson's accession was the seizure of the English kingdom by the earl of Wessex; and although the English earldoms of the mid-eleventh century were not yet principalities on the continental model by any means, they seem to have been going that way, and the result in England might have been much the same. Harold's defeat and William's replacement of the remaining English earldoms with something quite different, though preserving the name, is probably the ultimate reason why we have no provinces in England as they have or have had in France.

But the North resisted the Normans longer than other parts of the country and very special measures had to be taken to deal with it. These included not only William's famous 'Harrying', which, with the contemporary invasions of the Scots, had many consequences, but the establishment of an unusually large number of compact estates centred on castles. These were used in the first instance as a means of conquest and colonization; but they retained considerable importance in a country where the shire organization was weak — weak because it had been devised for Wessex and the Midlands at a time when the North was inaccessible, and because invasion from over the Border was long to be feared. Hence the North might 'know no king but a Percy' until well into early modern times. I make the point on the basis of a few examples known to me and the impression that the social and political conditions which we commonly call 'feudal' lasted longer in the North than in many other parts of the country; but I should like to have the notion confirmed. Perhaps Mr Forster will show whether county organization was still significantly different in the North in the seventeenth century and Dr Marshall how far feudal or quasi-feudal conditions lingered on in the North-West. Matters of this sort may be another element in the background of any individuality we may eventually discover in the North of England.

It would indeed be hardly surprising if the North did feel somewhat apart for a long time after 1066. It was by far the largest part of England that is 200 miles or more from London — two or three days journey from the political centre of gravity before the railways came. Moreover, throughout the time when the king's physical presence was an important element in government, and the royal itineration the means by which it was made effective, the court was in the North relatively infrequently; and the more it tended to settle down the more firmly it was anchored in the South-East. For a couple of centuries after 1066 the king of England spent a great deal more time across the Channel than across the Humber. By reason partly of his family origins and connexions, his continental lands meant more to him in terms of prestige, and no doubt of wealth and power, a readier means to cut a figure in the larger affairs of Christendom, than the bleak moorlands of the North. It was not until the middle of the thirteenth century, when the royal government began to take a real interest in Scotland, that the North of England acquired thereby at least a strategic importance, and York could be the capital of England for short periods.

But if apart, the North was not isolated. When I had occasion some years ago to look at the personnel of the cathedral chapter at York in the twelfth century, I found it as cosmopolitan as any other cathedral body in England. The great cathedral at Durham stands as one of the grandest monuments of Romanesque architecture in Europe and, if individual in style, it is certainly not provincial in the art-historian's sense of the word. Many of the great estates that were created in the North soon after the Norman Conquest were, or became, parcels of great property complexes extending into many other parts of the country — Richmond, Pontefract, Lancaster, Wakefield, the Mowbray lands and so on. I would like to know how characteristic this was; how important, relatively, the great Anglo-Scottish families, Bruces, Balliols, were in the North of England; how far there was a nobility or gentry whose interests were centred in the North, whose customs and *mores* were specifically northern (Professor Sawyer will be telling us this, perhaps), and ultimately whether there would be any truth at all in the idea that all the North lacked was a prince to make it a principality like Brittany or Burgundy in the Middle Ages, and whether indeed it was the Norman Conquest that destroyed the possibility for ever.

For the problem is, as with all historical studies of communities and territories, the balance between characteristics which are specific to a particular unit, characteristics which are common to much wider regions, those which are shared with some neighbours but not all, and those which are modified locally but still recognizable as belonging to a general class. You will have seen the way the argument is going. We do not have provinces in England and we have not generally thought in terms of provincial history, but the North of England and its history may be the nearest we have — an original autonomy well in the past, its own particular ethnical blend, its own individual set of connexions with the outside world, its own diversities — just like Aquitaine or Brittany or Flanders.

From this point the problem becomes one of the persistence of these characteristics, how far they have survived all the pressures of national integration, how far they underlie the individuality that remains, how far they have been watered down to mere sentiment. Even a superficial view, which is all I can offer, suggests that there is at least a case to be made for some survival. The later Middle Ages drew an administrative line for some purposes along the River Trent (there was, for a time, an escheator *citra Trentam* for the South and an escheator *ultra Trentam* for the North, and it is easy to see in which part of the country that distinction was drawn); the creation of the Council in the North shows the persistence of some specific characteristics, particularly those of a frontier region, into the seventeenth century, and incidentally the re-emergence of York as a political capital; for long there were relatively few towns of any consequence in the North as compared with other parts of the country (a list of 25 leading towns in the early part of the sixteenth century could show as few as three north of the Trent), relatively less commerce, relatively fewer people. It could be summed up by saying that it is the largest area of England with the characteristics of Sir Cyril Fox's 'Highland Zone', large enough to amount to something.

The question then is whether the individuality that I am postulating was strong enough in the eighteenth century to influence or even determine the form which industrial revolution and political reform took in the North, to create a significant difference from the form these changes took, say, in the West Midlands or the South-East. Did, for example, the existence of a relatively free peasantry in the North throughout the Middle Ages, a characteristic shared with other parts of eastern England but not with the West Midlands, have any bearing on these changes or the great agricultural developments of the sixteenth and later centuries? The North could produce a Pilgrimage of Grace, but did it ever produce a Peasant's Revolt of any importance? Did the fact that the poeple who came to work in the coalmines and the factories, and to live in the great new cities, were drawn from a country where towns were few and rural communities often remote, life generally harder, and even the new work-places often no more than a stone's throw from the moors, have any distinctive influence on their character as an industrial society? Do such considerations, and others which you will easily think of, underlie the present problems of the North, in so far as these may differ from those of the country as a whole? To the extent that our historical enquiries are set to pursue such matters, directly or indirectly and however small the detail on which we may be specifically engaged, then, for me at any rate, 'the History of the North of England' is a perfectly good subject.

*   *   *

In our investigation of it there are one or two principles, arising out of what I said to begin with, which I should like to reiterate and emphasize in conclusion. Our enquiry will not be confined to events, conditions, or developments within whatever limits we assign to the North of England at any particular time. What may be going on beyond those limits may be as relevant as anything within them, provided they can be shown to be relevant; and indeed one important part of the enquiry will always be to identify the particular effect which some more general tendency or development may have had upon the North, and its reaction to it as compared with other parts of the country. Constant comparison and contrasting is essential if we are to perceive such individuality as the North of England

B

may have. There is indeed implicit comparison in everything we say about the past because we can only describe past conditions in present-day language, and the very words we use imply a comparison between present and past conditions and phenomena; but we can only identify and describe social or other conditions in the North at any particular time by comparing them explicitly with the conditions of other regions at that time and both with other times. The same applies to all the communities and economic or administrative units that make up the North — towns, villages, parishes, counties, development areas or what you will. Only so will the identity of the North be established.

And finally I shall take my courage in both my hands and say that all phenomena whatsoever that can be used as evidence of past conditions and events must be used for this purpose. When I was young I was taught that the history of this country began in 55 B.C., for that is the point at which it first appears in a written record. But this is not so. Its history begins now, and it goes back as far as we need to go or can go, and its investigation will not be confined to the evidence of written documents. Everything from which some judgement on the past can be made is relevant. No doubt the proper techniques are required for each category of evidence, and these have to be mastered. The archaeologists have their own way with certain material objects, and they no longer confine themselves to arte-facts; the philologists, the numismatists, the statisticians and, among those who are dealing with written documents in the ordinary sense, the charter specialists and those concerned with works that can be described as literary in some sense, all have their own mysteries; and likewise those who deal with the environment, the geologists, geographers and climatolo-gists. The title of Dr McCord's seminar would have been scarcely con-ceivable a generation ago.† The great historical revolution of our time is implicit in the way in which new techniques of securing information about the past are being introduced almost every day, techniques that were undreamed of when I began trying to be a historian — the application of sophisticated scientific tests to objects of all sorts, to documents as well as to artefacts in the ordinary sense and to natural objects; the use of equally sophisticated statistical methods by historians as well as archaeo-logists. But this constant discovery of new techniques, and their appli-cation to objects and documents many of which have not hitherto been regarded as of any relevance to archaeologist or historian, can only mean that the old categories are breaking down and that all our studies of the past, which we undertake in order the better to understand ourselves and

†The title was, 'The use of archaeological evidence in modern social history'.

the world we live in, are one discipline, whether you call it history, archaeology or what you will; and only by pressing every kind of evidence and every kind of technique into service shall we begin to learn what the North of England is and has been. Northern History is as comprehensive as that.

But if so comprehensive, am I really saying that it is no subject at all but an infinity? In a sense, yes. In the sense that we have to look further and further out for the great changes and events that have had as great a part in the making of the North of England as anything that has taken place within its bounds; in the sense that almost everything we perceive may be used as historical evidence if only we can find the right technique to interpret it; in the sense also that our successors will have new problems and new techniques — yes, it is an unattainable infinity like any other historical problem worth considering. But here theory has to come to terms with practical considerations, human curiosity and even human needs. We want to know and we need to know; and if we want to know what the North of England is we shall try to find out, among other things, what it has been; and we shall pursue this enquiry as far as it is humanly and practically possible to do so. We shall acknowledge the infinity, in ideas as well as in the physical universe, and do the best we can.

FRANCE AND ENGLAND IN THE MIDDLE AGES*

My text this evening is taken from a set of lectures on the history of France and England, published more than 50 years ago by the great Thomas Frederick Tout of Manchester. 'Whether we like it or not', he said, 'English and French medieval history are one subject'. I have given myself a very broad title and the 'medieval history' of Tout's remark is a comprehensive term; it would include all such matters as language, literature and art, law and institutions, in which we are accustomed to acknowledge a historical relationship between France and England. You would not expect me to discourse on language and literature, certainly not in this company; and rather than trying to be comprehensive I am going to discuss the *basis*, as I see it, of the relationship between the two countries during the middle ages, from which has evolved the love-hate relationship we still know. It was a political and social basis: it was a mutual involvement and interpenetration of the two countries so that it is impossible to draw a clear dividing line between them as political structures; and my argument is going to be that although the mutual involvement was initiated by the Norman Conquest of 1066, as everyone knows, its intensity and its consequences, cultural and other, were due quite as much to constant renewal over a period of three centuries as to the overwhelming effects of the Norman Conquest itself. In this sense, certainly, 'English and French medieval history are one subject'.

Nevertheless my starting-point must be that Conquest — not, I hasten to add, that there had been any lack of contact before 1066 between the people living in the land which was to become England and those who lived in the land which was to become France. Contact between them had indeed been close, and it goes back as far as the historical eye can see; but it was normal and neighbourly, as neighbourliness was then understood, and it did not involve the kind of interpenetration that took place after 1066. However, if we are to appreciate just what the Norman Conquest did towards bringing about that mutual involvement in the affairs of England and France, we have to be clear about the character of the two kingdoms as they were then. What we mark as 'France' on our historical maps of the eleventh century, was the result of a process of disintegration in the western part of the Carolingian empire of the ninth century, a

* The Seventh Clapton Memorial Lecture delivered on 10 March 1977 at the University of Leeds.

disintegration which had reached the point where the country was effectively divided into a number of autonomous duchies, counties and seignories. The ruler of one group of counties, centred on Paris, still had the title 'king of the Franks'; the others were by tradition his *fideles* or vassals, which gave him some nominal authority over them, an authority with potential for development, but no effective control at the time. England, by contrast, was a synthesis of what had been a large number of small units, the more successful of which had expanded by conquest, annexation and amalgamation. By 1066 the kings of Wessex had extended their authority over all the country south of the Thames; they had annexed the old kingdom of Mercia in the Midlands and conquered the Scandinavian settlements to the east and the north. Superficially, the 'kingdom of England' which they had thus created was a unity, though the old divisions still showed through, particularly in the North; on the other hand the king had established a lordship over the Welsh kings and the kings of Scots, and these overlordships were at least as effective as the authority of the king of Franks over the dukes and counts within his traditional kingdom, and had as great a potential for development.

The Norman Conquest, then, was the conquest by one northern French duchy of an imperfectly integrated kingdom which, in its widest sense, included the whole of the island of Britain. Most of the men who 'came over with the Conqueror', and took the land of this country, were from Normandy. There were some from Flanders and Brittany and other parts of France north of the Loire, very few indeed from further afield. Significantly, a contingent from Poitou that had joined William's army took their money and went home after Hastings. The effect of the Conquest was that Duke William of Normandy took over the 'kingdom of the English' as it had been under Edward the Confessor, with its varying degrees of authority in different parts of Britain, and with its lands and its wealth; a fairly small band of his relatives and followers took the land which William had not kept for himself or allowed the Church to possess; Norman churchmen took the English bishoprics and the greater abbeys, with their lands, and they and the barons gave English churches and lands to cathedrals and monasteries in Normandy and elsewhere in France; several English towns received a French settlement, sufficient in some cases to form a second town alongside the old one. The native landed aristocracy perished at Hastings, or in subsequent resistance to the invader, or were driven out; ecclesiastical posts, and some lay ones like the sheriffdoms, were filled with Normans as they fell vacant. It meant a complete change of the governing and property-owning class in this country.

Now, just as William did not give up his duchy and the other rights and claims he had in northern France when he took the kingdom, so his barons did not emigrate but added what they obtained in England to what they already possessed in Normandy; and the churchmen, if they could hardly hold important churches in plurality, did not cut their ties with the land in which they had grown up. Thus king and duke were normally one person; the barons of England and Normandy formed a single aristocratic community; the churchmen, though divided administratively among the ecclesiastical provinces of Rouen, Canterbury and York, were a homogeneous body. It was this colonization (for naturally the Normans behaved in England as they behaved at home) which produced a considerable assimilation as between England and northern France. The Normans by this time were completely French. Their spoken language was the French of the north, their written language Latin. Consequently most of what was written in England for some time to come was in Latin or French, not in Old English. The churchmen brought their ideas of the way in which a cathedral or a monastery should be organized, how the buildings should be designed, decorated and furnished, what church law should be and what courts should enforce it. At the time of the Conquest the social organization of the Norman aristocracy was approaching the form we call feudalism. They perfected it in England and carried the finishing touches back to Normandy. In neither country were law and custom uniform or stabilized in 1066; but in this matter the Norman kings did not so much assimilate as superimpose a law that was being developed in their own court; and as this court was fundamentally the same body whether it met in England or in Normandy they did this in the same way and on the same principles in both countries.

Such an overwhelming change could not take place all at once; but it was progressive and no one can say how far it might have gone if the dynasty had survived beyond Henry I. I must not overdo this. The English were not exterminated. They were needed to till the fields and create wealth for their new lords. In course of time, a fairly long time, they would rise again and absorb their conquerors. Their language survived, and, as it moved slowly up the social scale, was greatly enriched by its contact with French. Some of their institutions survived, including the all-important shire and shire-court, deftly adapted by the Normans to suit their ideas and purposes; and there was in the end a Common Law of England and a Coutume de Normandie, twins that were to follow very different careers.

None of this seriously modifies the conclusion that England was greatly Frenchified by the Normans. But how are we to describe this in

terms of a relationship between France and England? The nature of the
two kingdoms was such that we are clearly not dealing with sovereign
states or international relations in the modern sense. And the contacts
which had been made were contacts between the kingdom of the English,
as I have described it, and the northern parts of France only — a point of
great importance given the enormous difference that existed between the
lands to the north of the Loire and those to the south, then and for a long
time to come. The essential thing is the identity of the king of the English
and the duke of the Normans. Normally one and the same man, King
William or King Henry, he was not even thought of as acting in two
capacities, king and duke, at least not clearly and consistently. He ruled
Normandy, not perhaps as king of the Normans, but certainly as a king;
for he governed both countries directly, by moving constantly from one
to the other, and he could hardly leave his consecrated kingship in the
left-luggage office at Southampton, to rule as a mere duke in Normandy,
and pick it up again when he returned. Now the dukes of Normandy, up
to a decade or so before 1066, had been the *fideles* or vassals, in the
contemporary sense, of the king of France. This need not mean very
much, whatever it might become; but after he had made himself king,
William did not behave in the least like a vassal and Henry I directly
refused to do homage when it was demanded of him. Neither did Stephen
do homage after he had made himself king; though he and Henry before
him each made his eldest son, who was heir to England, Normandy and all
that went with them, do homage to the king of France for Normandy.
However we are to describe the political relationship so created, and it was
certainly ambiguous, it must involve England as well as Normandy. Given
the identity of king and duke, and the community of aristocracy and
hierarchy, with England in effect an extension of Normandy and
Normandy a part of the traditional kingdom of France, the affairs of the
two countries were thoroughly enmeshed. How could you draw a clear
line between them? The count of Flanders, for example, had entered into
a feudal contract with the Norman king, to provide troops in England or
Normandy, paid for with English money, and he could somehow square
this with his traditional relationship to the king of France; Henry I had
firmly established the old claims of the Norman dukes to lordship over the
dukes of Brittany, yet the Breton bishoprics were in the province of Tours
and still had direct links with the king of France; some of the greatest
Norman barons had lands and interests, not only in Normandy and
England and maybe in Wales or Scotland, but beyond Normandy into
'France' as well, which meant that they too must be in the allegiance of
the king of France as well as in that of the Norman king; and it was not

only Norman monasteries that obtained lands and churches in England, but others deep into France, like Marmoutier near Tours (which indirectly had Leeds Parish Church) and Cluny in Burgundy.

This Norman empire (the term is convenient and there is something to be said for it) fell apart under Stephen in the 1140's; and there was a period of 10 years and more when England and Normandy might well have gone their separate ways for ever. Whether anything like the England we know could have come into being if that had happened is exceedingly doubtful; for the strength of the medieval relationship between France and England (from which the 'Frenchness' in our make-up is derived) lay in its perpetuation; and that required a second conquest, and by another French principality, this time Anjou.

Most of the great duchies and counties in twelfth-century France had come into being by accretion. Normandy, for example, had started with a Viking settlement in the lower Seine Valley, had gradually dominated the whole of the later province and extended its lordship over a large part of northern France before it burst through the bounds of the traditional kingdom to conquer England and all that went with it. The counts of Anjou, for their part, starting in the early tenth century with a part of the old Carolingian county centred on Angers, annexed the Touraine and Maine to form a powerful principality in the Loire valley, which we may call Greater Anjou, with extensions into Vendôme, Poitou and even Brittany. In the 1140's Count Geoffrey (Plantegenêt) conquered Normandy from Stephen and gave the dukedom to his eldest son Henry (the future Henry II) in 1150. From that point expansion was explosive. Henry inherited Greater Anjou in 1151; married the duchess of Aquitaine in 1152; launched a campaign in England that forced Stephen to accept him as heir to the kingdom in 1153; and he was crowned in 1154. Not content with all that, he re-established the old Norman lordship over the king of Scots and the Welsh princes and took over a conquest of Ireland begun by Anglo-Norman adventurers. On the Continent he re-established the old Norman superiority over Ponthieu, Boulogne and Flanders and began to extend it among the princes of the Low Countries; he adjusted his frontier with the king of France in the Seine Valley to his advantage, converted the Norman overlordship in Brittany into something like direct rule and established the old claim of the dukes of Aquitaine to lordship over the counts of Toulouse.

Historians like continuity and they have been greatly influenced by Henry's own propaganda, for he grounded the legitimacy of his rule in England very explicitly on his descent from the Norman kings through his mother. Yet since family identity was already reckoned normally as continuing in the male line, we must recognize his accession as a change of dynasty in this country. Moreover his campaign of 1153, if it produced no battle like Hastings, was nevertheless a real conquest. Henry's vast empire, though he had reconstructed and gathered the old Norman empire into it, was a new and quite different structure. It had been formed by a different family; it was far more extensive; its nucleus and its political centre of gravity were different and it included a large part of the *south* of France. One French historian has seen this as the first effective political link between north and south in post-Carolingian France; it has even greater significance for us as the beginning of the connection between England and Aquitaine. There were other significant differences. The Norman empire had been founded on an aristocratic and ecclesiastical colonization of England, mainly from Normandy, where the colonists did not abandon their homeland but maintained their properties and interests in both countries. There was no new colonization of England after 1154 by men from the Loire Valley or from Aquitaine, or none of any consequence; though the Norman families that had possessed lands on both side of the Channel recovered what they had lost under Stephen and there was certainly no obstacle to the formation of more cross-Channel estates. To this extent, the Anglo-Norman involvement survived, though bishoprics, abbacies and offices in the royal government of England were no longer so exclusively occupied by men of Norman or French origin. Under the Angevin kings there was movement of this sort in both directions. You could have an English seneschal of Anjou or Poitou, and, for a year or two, the justiciar of England was also the archbishop of Rouen and the seneschal of Normandy was an Englishman by birth and training. The Normans had been assimilators; they had made their conquest at a time when law and custom were hardly territorialized, certainly malleable; but by the mid-twelfth century law and custom were far more stabilized into territorial units, and the Angevin kings ruled on the principle that law and custom were as much a part of a land as the fields and the trees. They ruled, in fact, as native dukes of the people of Aquitaine in Aquitaine, as dukes of the Normans in Normandy, as kings of the English in England. That is not to say that they never attempted general legislation for all their lands together, or extended administrative devices from one to another; they did, and what they did deserves more study than it has yet received. But that is not incompatible with respect for existing custom, for legislation is often needed to meet conditions which custom has not provided for. The Custom of Normandy is still the basis of the law in Guernsey; and that is why it was on my twentieth birthday, not my twenty-first or eighteenth, that my father said to me: 'The difference between you today and you yesterday is that you are now responsible for your debts'. But the *Coutume*, compiled in the thirteenth century, could have nothing to say about the regulation of traffic by air, or on the ground for that matter.

Henry's vast empire has not been given much credit for political coherence or credibility. It seems huge and unwieldy, impossible to hold together for any length of time. It even looks as though Henry himself thought of dividing his dominions among his sons — and the quarrrels, betrayals and sheer viciousness of those sons are well known. But you wouldn't expect any political structure to solve all its problems within a few years of its creation; and if instead of looking only at the reign of Henry II you take a rather longer period of time it looks somewhat different. The problem of securing an orderly and unitary succession was indeed solved; a bit late in the day perhaps, but it is after all one of the most fundamental and difficult of all political problems. The empire found an effective form of organization; again, not all at once, but with more drive and inventiveness than most. The organization was based upon the direct rule of all his lands by a constantly moving king, court and household. No country was left on its own for very long, and the king dealt with matters as they arose wherever he was and whichever country they might primarily concern. Thus English affairs could be dealt with when king and court were in Anjou, and conversely. But more than this was needed. Of necessity a great deal of the king's government had to be delegated, and routine administration must go on whether the king and court were near at hand or not. In England and Normandy the Angevin kings had the work of their Norman predecessors to build on, and in both countries a very sophisticated judicial and financial structure was erected with a vice-regal (but non-royal) justiciar at its head in England, and a corresponding officer, though called a seneschal, in Normandy. Ireland, Brittany, Anjou, Aquitaine were by no means so far advanced politically at the time of Henry's accession; but what seems to me so significant is that they were each being brought up to a similar level of administrative effectiveness — Ireland on the model of England, Brittany somewhat on the model of Normandy, Anjou and Aquitaine in their own native idiom. The result, in the early thirteenth century, was not a standardized system (you would not expect that in any medieval kingdom, not even within England), but a coherent organization, held together by the itinerant king.

Now England was an integral part of this vast Angevin empire which extended over more than half the kingdom of France, the more firmly integrated into it as the empire itself was progressively organized. The relationship of England to France was therefore completely bound up with that of the Angevin rulers to the king of France. Unlike the Norman kings, but in the tradition of their ancestors the counts of Anjou, Henry II and his sons made no bones about homage to the king of France. Even after they were anointed kings they performed liege homage, specifically for their lands within the traditional kingdom of France, Normandy, Brittany, Anjou, Aquitaine. It had long been possible for a man to hold lands of more than one lord, doing homage to each lord for the lands held of him. This might happen not only within a kingdom but across its frontiers, as with those Norman barons who held land in Normandy and in 'France'; and since what we would call politics and property were so bound up with one another in any feudal order, this in itself smudged the boundaries between kingdoms. Liege homage, however, was a priority homage, and no man could do liege homage to more than one lord. Naturally the king of France, as soon as he was able to do so, that is in the second half of the twelfth century, insisted on liege homage from all the great dukes and counts in his kingdom, including the duke of Normandy and Aquitaine; and it was by this means that he gradually secured the integrity of his kingdom. The implications of liege homage in the Angevin dominions were spelled out in the course of the thirteenth century, though they were there long before. The man doing liege homage, be he King Henry II himself, must be loyal to his lord, serve his interests, provide counsel and assistance when required, in money or in fighting men, and submit to a much greater degree of supervision in his lands than a Norman king would have tolerated — in particular to accept that his courts were not sovereign, that, as in the case of the Angevin rulers, a vassal from Anjou or Aquitaine could appeal from their courts to that of the king of France. Now, since these homages were real, that is, performed in respect of specified lands, and Britain and Ireland were not so specified, you could argue that they were at least implicitly excluded and not affected. After all, they had never formed a part of the kingdom of France by any definition or at any time. Yet England was involved, simply as a part of the Angevin empire. If the count of Anjou did homage, and did it in person the king of England knelt before the king of France and placed his hands in his, for count and king were the same person; if to maintain his loyalty, the duke of Aquitaine took action or refrained from taking action in Languedoc or Spain hereby because the king of France had interests there, the king of England was thereby restricted in what we might think of as his foreign policy. In an age of personal rule, distinctions of capacity could hardly be more than theoretical.

Much of this was largely implicit still in the time of King Henry II; but in 1202 some of King John's vassals brought it out into the open by appealing against him in the court of the king of France. Since, as king, John refused to appear before that court, as he should have done in his capacity as duke of Aquitaine, all the lands which he held by homage in France were adjudged to be forfeited; and, now that the king of France was richer and stronger he could put that judgment into execution by invading John's lands in France. But the judgment also sparked off a widespread movement of protest that had been building up against Angevin rule. This movement has generally been treated as two distinct affairs, the war in France that resulted in the loss of most of the Angevin dominions in that country, and the civil war in England that produced Magna Carta; but really these are all one and demonstrate nicely the interpenetration of French and English affairs at this time. John's continental barons did not have to resort to difficult and dubious constitutional experiments; by generally recognized feudal custom they could renounce their homage and transfer their allegiance to a lord they judged to be more satisfactory, in this case the king of France. That is what the counts of Toulouse and of Périgord and many others did, what the barons of Anjou and Brittany did; and in effect it was what the barons of Poitou and those whose chief interests were in Normandy did by offering minimal resistance to the French king's armies. Naturally an overlord would normally resume possession of the lands of a vassal who acted in this way (if he could); but while it is true that John seems to have lost his nerve at a critical time, it is also very likely that effective action on his part was impracticable, for though the continental barons defected individually they did so more or less simultaneously.

The barons of Normandy, however, were still to a very large extent the barons of England as well, and the French military conquest of the duchy split their community right down the middle. It was King John, so Professor Holt now tells us, who decided that they must choose: that they could not offer allegiance to the king of France in respect of the lands they held in Normandy and to King John for the lands they held in England, as they might well expect to do and as many had done in the past. Those who chose to stand by their possessions in England, and lost their lands in Normandy, found their political interests concentrated in this country, and they still had King John and Angevin methods of government to cope with. Thus, when their difficulties showed no sign of finding a solution (the financial implications of John's efforts to recover lands and allegiance in France were among the greater difficulties) the simple solution of transferring allegiance without losing their lands was no longer so easy. It was this that drove a number of barons of England, as they now were, not only to renounce their allegiance in the traditional manner, but to make war on John, who fought back with troops from the French lands. Magna Carta of 1215 was an attempt at a peace treaty which should also embody certain general principles of reform. When it failed, those barons could see no alternative to following the example of their continental peers a few years before. They offered their allegiance to the heir to the throne of France. The result was a French invasion of England in 1216 which might well have succeeded. The judgment against John in 1202, on the basis of his homage specifically for his dominions in France, came perilously close to driving him and the Angevin dynasty out of England as well.

But you would have thought that the way was then clear for a complete disentangling of the two kingdoms — when John's son was safely on the throne and the French invaders had been got rid of, when the king of England had lost control, as he did in the end, of very nearly all his French lands; when the dynasty had lost the land of its origin in Anjou; when all legal relationships with the kingdom of France had been broken, for after the judgment against John in 1202 a state of war, broken only by truces, lasted for 50 years. During that war neither John nor Henry III could be the vassal of the king of France, and the ever-diminishing territory that they managed to retain in the kingdom was held by force of arms only, and must have seemed very precarious. Yet, however familiar we may be with the idea that nationalism as we know it has no place in medieval affairs, it still comes as something of a shock to find that when peace was made in 1259 the old feudal relationship was re-established, with its implications clearer than ever.

The Treaty of Paris of 1259 is of some historical importance, partly because it is one of the earliest such treaties of which we can follow the diplomatic preliminaries in some detail, but much more for the nature of its terms. Briefly, King Henry III of England renounced all right to mainland Normandy, to Greater Anjou and to Poitou, and to anything within the kingdom of France which he did not hold at that moment. In consequence he dropped the titles 'duke of Normandy' and 'count of Anjou' from his royal style. On the French side, King Louis IX (Saint Louis), legalized, as he would think of it, Henry's possession of what he then held *de facto* in France (Bordeaux, Bayonne, and, as I am more especially bound to add, the Channel Islands); he also conceded his rights, such as they were, in the three dioceses of Limoges, Cahors and Périgueux, and undertook to transfer the Agenais, Lower Saintonge and part of Quercy also, if certain conditions were fulfilled. But, King Henry was to hold all this as duke of Aquitaine and a peer of France, and must do liege homage before the treaty could come into operation. Henry accepted all these provisions and duly performed the homage.

In territorial terms this meant that although the king of England must abandon the Angevin dominions in the north of France, including the ancestral lands in Anjou, he was given the possibility of reconstructing a duchy of Aquitaine — a possibility that he largely realized. The special relation he had built up with the duke of Brittany who, as earl of Richmond, held vast estates in England from Yorkshire to Sussex, was tacitly acknowledged. Nevertheless, the political centre of growth of the Angevin dominions had moved decisively from France to England. The interests of the king of England in France were now in the south of the country, not the north; they could not begin to over-balance his interests in the British Isles; and these new conditions would tend to make Angevin government less itinerant, so that his lands in France would eventually, though not yet, come to look like appendages to his kingdom of England — in short, a complete reversal of the situation under Henry II.

But far more important than the territorial provisions of the treaty was the re-establishment, in even more explicit form, of the relationship based on liege homage. Both as peer of France and as duke of Aquitaine, the king of England was now a part of the political structure of the kingdom of France, a structure based upon the liege homage of all the great nobles and influenced by the revived study of Roman law. In particular, the system of appeals from the courts of the dukes and counts to the king's court was being greatly developed, and the king was beginning to enforce his legislation and even to collect taxation within their territories. It meant that while the king of England might be sovereign in his own kingdom, his duchy was being absorbed into the French system, his courts there were becoming simply one grade in a judicial hierarchy, he was ever more closely supervised from above and often frustrated in his efforts to provide a competent government for his Aquitainian people. Among other things, he had to maintain a 'council' of lawyers in the court at Paris to watch his interests there, as the other great dukes and counts were doing.

What seems so astonishing to us is that all this appeared to be quite natural and normal to King Henry III, though he may not have been able to foresee in 1259 quite how it would develop; and it was accepted equally by his successor Edward I, at least until the end of the century. Henry had performed his liege homage; Edward did so twice. Moreover, Edward did on occasion fulfill his feudal duty by providing military service for a French campaign, and he accepted restrictions on his policy towards Flanders which would have served English interests; and while he did everything possible to neutralize French legislation in Aquitaine by legislating himself in the same sense, and to deflect appeals from the duchy to the Court of France by providing better courts and an appeal organization of his own working in or from England, he did not directly challenge the system before the war of 1294.

What I think that we, as English students of history, have to accept is that King Edward I of England did not see anything incongruous in his rôle as a French prince. Aquitaine was as much his heritage as England was, it was even of material value to him, and he had many interests in other parts of France. He was of French origin himself, closely related to the French royal family; he spoke French; and France was then the most prestigious kingdom in Christendom, the home of chivalry and of the great clerical civilization of the north. The situation was one that he had inherited; it could be paralleled all over Europe at that time; he was himself treating the king of Scots as the king of France was treating him; and if his relationship with France involved his kingdom of England, as it did, so that the two kingdoms were still mutually involved and interpenetrating, that was still 'the system'.

But facts and circumstances change, and the political systems we erect on them must eventually change too. The war of 1294 showed that the system would no longer work, that the operation of the various manifestations of French sovereignty in Aquitaine would soon reduce the authority of the duke in his duchy to a shadow, diminish his revenues and change it from an asset into a liability. In the protracted negotiations for peace at the turn of the century, therefore, Edward's lawyers tried to put over the argument that the part of Aquitaine which the king of England held had not been a fief of the kingdom of France before 1259, and, since the treaty had not been fully carried out on the French side, that treaty had not made it one. They were trying, in effect, to substitute an English sovereignty for a French sovereignty in Aquitaine, to detach the duchy completely from the kingdom of France as they were in process of detaching the Channel Islands; and this was supported by the massive development of institutions and administration in the duchy during the previous half-century, a development which was producing new and clearly defined links with the government in England and a lively interchange of administrative personnel between Bordeaux and Westminster. Naturally the French would have none of it; the treaty which eventually concluded the war simply restored the *status quo ante bellum*; and in all the conferences and confrontations that preceded what we call the Hundred Years War 35 years later the French would not concede their sovereignty over any part of the traditional kingdom of France for any concessions or considerations whatsoever.

And it is easy to see why. The history of the feudal kingdom of France, as well as that of England, showed the power of the overlord constantly growing at the expense of the autonomy of the vassal, as the resources of the king grew and he could draw out the implications of the feudal relationship in his favour. That is how the kingdom was being made. So long as sovereignty, as the word was used in France at that time, was preserved, however vestigial it might be in practice, the integrity of the kingdom was secure. More than that, it was a positive advantage to the king of France to have the king of England as his vassal, well worth the inconveniences which English involvement in the affairs of France might cause, as St. Louis fully understood in 1259. It gave him a hold over a potentially troublesome neighbour, who must be 'loyal' if he was to keep his French duchy, its revenues and its prestige. It was easy to discipline him, for it was a far simpler matter for the king of France to send an army into Aquitaine than it was for the king of England to send a relieving force by sea to Bordeaux; but he must not be pushed right out, for that would break the relationship. And it was not until well into the fifteenth century that the French fully understood that that, nevertheless, was what they must do.

On the English side, if the French would not allow the king of England full control over what he regarded as his heritage in France, or at least put some restraint on the exercise of their sovereignty in it, the only solution, ultimately, was to make the king of England king of France as well, so that he could exercise sovereignty in Aquitaine as king of France. With the very close dynastic relationship between the two royal families, Edward III had a claim that was not negligible in law nor was it simply trumped up for an occasion; and he was so far successful, up to the 1360's, in making his French title a reality, with a plan of conquest based ultimately on the interests and principles of the old Angevin empire, a plan that can be made to seem viable even now, that his successors did not finally renounce this will-o-the-wisp until 1801. But when Edward III added the title 'king of France' to his royal style, he made it clear that the government of his kingdom of France, including Aquitaine, would be completely separate from that of the kingdom of England. With the French insisting upon the legal integrity of their kingdom and now making no serious claims to territory across the Channel, this marks the end of my theme of involvement and interpenetration, for both sides could now see the two kingdoms as separate and distinct. That was in the 1340's; but it took another hundred years, indeed a Hundred Years War with all the passions it generated, to produce a clean separation and a national monarchy in each country, with exclusive allegiance, that would lay the foundations of the national states that we know. Yet the political involvement of these four hundred years had established cultural and sentimental relationships which even the following five hundred years and all the rest of the wars could not destroy.

INDEX